# PROBLEMS OF ETHICS

# PROBLEMS

edited by

# ROBERT E. DEWEY

*University of Nebraska*

# FRANCIS W. GRAMLICH

*Dartmouth College*

# DONALD LOFTSGORDON

*Occidental College*

# OF ETHICS A BOOK OF READINGS

*The Macmillan Company*

Seventh Printing, 1970

Library of Congress catalog card number: 61-5086

The Macmillan Company
Collier-Macmillan Canada, Ltd., Toronto, Ontario

Printed in the United States of America

# Preface

With this book we have sought to make available for a college course in ethics a set of readings organized topically rather than chronologically, presenting selections from representatives of the major traditions in moral philosophy and also from their critics.

Wherever practicable, it seems to us better for students of philosophy to read original writings of philosophers rather than secondary texts commenting upon and summarizing these materials. Since writing in ethics tends in many cases to be less technical than in other branches of philosophy, a course in ethics particularly lends itself to study from source materials. Accordingly, in this book the moral philosophers state their own views; we have held our introductions to a minimum.

This book is intended for use in a problems-type course in ethics. We believe such a course is often more valuable than one which is historically-oriented; a problems-type approach centers attention not merely upon the viewpoints of a series of moral philosophers, but stresses the questions with which they wrestle; we hope that students may thus be stimulated to do their own thinking about these fundamental questions. Topical organization may, however, become too confining; we have therefore endeavored to make the over-all structure of this book flexible enough to permit substantial re-arrangement to suit the purposes of individual instructors.

Books of readings in philosophy are frequently prone to present a succession of positive statements of viewpoint, with too little attention to objections which might be lodged against the positions. But it seems more fruitful for students to read philosophy in the light of explicit critical comment; accordingly, except for the concluding sub-section on the "Good Reasons" Approach, each positive ethical doctrine treated in this book is accompanied by a selection embodying criticism of the view.

With respect to the particular readings, we have intended that selections should satisfy two criteria: (1) that they be representative of important traditional and contemporary ethical viewpoints, or of important criticisms of these viewpoints; and (2) that each be readable as a unit, not unduly technical or discursive, and not requiring prior knowledge of the author's general philosophic position. The large majority of our selections have been taken from the standard works of moral philosophy; in some instances, however, we have included less well-known selections because they seemed to satisfy our requirements better than passages which are more widely known. Thus we have chosen to include a selection from Francis Wayland (rather than from Joseph Butler) as representative of the conscience theory in ethics; and we have chosen to include passages from Henry W. Wright to represent the self-realization theory of idealism.

In selecting our material we have been helped by the valuable comments and criticisms of Professor John Ladd of Brown University. We are indebted to him especially for his suggestions concerning Section III of this book. We also wish to acknowledge the cooperation given us by the staff of Love Library of the University of Nebraska; and we wish to thank all those at The Macmillan Company who have given us help.

R.E.D.
F.W.G.
D.L.

# Table of Contents

# PROBLEMS OF ETHICS

# Introduction

MEN ARE by nature decision-makers. Unable to do all they would like to do, they constantly find it necessary to choose among alternatives available to them. It follows that men come to mark some kinds of conduct as preferable to others and to distinguish between things which they deem worth pursuing and those which they would seek to avoid. Thus all men are moral, at least in the sense that they do make judgments concerning what is desirable and undesirable, good and bad, right and wrong.

To note that all men make moral distinctions does not imply, however, that they are able to formulate and defend the principles they more or less consciously use in making decisions; nor does it imply that all men adopt the same principles of evaluation. Indeed, most men make moral decisions without critical examination of the principles upon which they rest; their rules of conduct tend simply to be drawn from whatever specific moral training they have received since earliest childhood and from whatever customary patterns of behavior prevail in the culture in which they live.

Since moral beliefs are derived from so many different sources, it is inevitable that men should find themselves in disagreement about what is right and wrong; and it is not surprising that the principles which underlie their divergent judgments should appear to be as various as the differing environmental influences to which they have been subject. Given these diversities, it is natural that men should seek to state more clearly the moral principles they employ and to discover the grounds which render some moral principles more reasonable than others.

When men begin to reflect upon their moral experience, they engage in that inquiry called "ethics." Ethics consists in the systematic and critical study of man's moral beliefs: it is the *theory* of morals, the attempt to make our moral beliefs clear, self-consistent, and consistent with the facts we know about man and the world.

Ethical inquiry is focused upon questions which concern what men *ought* to do in contrast to the study of what men *in fact* do. The fundamental concepts of ethics (such as "good" and "bad," "right" and "wrong," "virtue" and "vice") are employed when men intend not only to *describe* human behavior and character but to *evaluate* them by reference to ideals and norms. Consequently, ethics is frequently characterized as a "normative" study and is in this way distinguished from the factual inquiries of "descriptive" sciences such as anthropology, psychology, and sociology.

1

Although the distinction between normative and descriptive studies has much to recommend it, factual matters are not totally irrelevant to ethics. Rather, there are some fundamental questions of fact which appropriately may be considered before beginning normative inquiry proper. In what follows, these questions will receive our first examination.

# I. Preliminary Problems

THE FUNDAMENTAL concern of ethics is with normative questions, but there are at least three questions of fact—questions asking what *is* the case—which raise preliminary problems crucial for ethics. The questions are:

(1) Do all the actions of men proceed from the sole motive of self-love?
(2) Are all the moral judgments of men completely derived from the customs of the society in which they live?
(3) Are all human choices and actions wholly determined by past causes?

These questions are of importance to ethics because answers to them have implications which bear upon many of the traditional ethical problems and theories. Thus, if we conclude in answer to the first question that all men do act solely from the motive of self-love (the view of *psychological egoism*), we then have reason to reject any moral theory which presupposes man's capacity to act selflessly. If we answer the second question by maintaining that morality is completely derived from what is customary in a given society (the view of *cultural relativism*), we may then be led to reject ethical theories which assert that standards of right and wrong ought to be the same for all men everywhere. As to the third question, if we hold that all human choices and actions are wholly determined by past causes (the view of *determinism*), then we may well doubt whether *any* ethical discussion is meaningful; it is commonly supposed that it would make no sense to discuss what men *ought* to do, if *in fact* all their actions have been determined by influences from their past.

3

# A. PSYCHOLOGICAL EGOISM

Psychological egoism is the doctrine which gives an affirmative answer to the first of the questions mentioned above: Do all the actions of men proceed from the sole motive of self-love? The psychological egoist does not deny that there are actions which appear at first sight to be efforts by men to promote the welfare of others; nor does he deny that some individuals appear to act in selfless devotion to their ideals. He would contend, however, that when one probes below the surface appearance of these actions, one discovers in every case that the acts have really been performed only to serve the particular interests of the individual in question.

Psychological egoism is a theory about human motivation; it is not a theory about what men *ought* to do, but is concerned with what they *in fact* do. Such a doctrine should therefore be distinguished from the views held by *normative* egoists who maintain that men *ought* always to seek their own good, even if in fact they do not always do so.

The first selection on psychological egoism is from PLATO'S *Republic*. In the passage presented, the speaker, Glaucon, suggests that men would never observe rules of justice if they could benefit themselves by unjust action and yet escape all penalties. In the second selection, HELVÉTIUS argues a similar thesis and also maintains that all of man's pretended love of justice is a mere mask to hide his desire for power, prestige, and self-aggrandizement. In the final selection, SHARP submits such contentions to critical examination and rejects them.

# PLATO

PLATO (427/8–347/8 B.C.), one of the great Greek philosophers, has exerted more influence upon the development of Western philosophy than any other writer with the possible exception of his student, Aristotle. He established the Academy in Athens, the first of the major schools of ancient Greece. His works, written in dialogue form and featuring his teacher Socrates as the principal figure, have continued to be widely read not only for their intellectual content but also for their literary merit. Among his writings of interest to the student of ethics are: *Euthyphro, Apology, Crito, Phaedo, The Republic, Protagoras, Gorgias,* and *Philebus.*

## The Story of Gyges*

[Glaucon speaking to Socrates.] I . . . shall begin by speaking . . . of the nature and origin of justice.

They say that to do injustice is, by nature, good; to suffer injustice, evil; but that the evil is greater than the good. And so when men have both done and suffered injustice and have had experience of both, not being able to avoid the one and obtain the other, they think that they had better agree among themselves to have neither; hence there arise laws and mutual covenants; and that which is ordained by law is termed by them lawful and just. This they affirm to be the origin and nature of justice;—it is a mean or compromise, between the best of all, which is to do injustice and not be punished, and the worst of all, which is to suffer injustice without the power of retaliation; and justice, being at a middle point between the two, is tolerated not as a good, but as the lesser evil, and honoured by reason of the inability of men to do injustice. For no man who is worthy to be called a man would ever submit to such an agreement if he were able to resist; he would be mad if he did. Such is the received account, Socrates, of the nature and origin of justice.

Now that those who practice justice do so involuntarily and because they have not the power to be unjust will best appear if we imagine something of this kind: having given both to the just and the unjust power to do what they will, let us watch and see whither desire will lead them; then we shall discover in the very act the just and unjust man to be proceeding along the same road, following their interest, which all natures deem to be their good,

* From *The Republic* of Plato, Book II, 358 ff. Translated by Benjamin Jowett (1892).

and are only diverted into the path of justice by the force of law. The liberty which we are supposing may be most completely given to them in the form of such a power as is said to have been possessed by Gyges, the ancestor of Croesus the Lydian. According to the tradition, Gyges was a shepherd in the service of the king of Lydia; there was a great storm, and an earthquake made an opening in the earth at the place where he was feeding his flock. Amazed at the sight, he descended into the opening, where, among other marvels, he beheld a hollow brazen horse, having doors, at which he stooping and looking in saw a dead body of stature, as appeared to him, more than human, and having nothing on but a gold ring; this he took from the finger of the dead and reascended. Now the shepherds met together, according to custom, that they might send their monthly report about the flocks to the king; into their assembly he came having the ring on his finger, and as he was sitting among them he chanced to turn the collet of the ring inside his hand, when instantly he became invisible to the rest of the company and they began to speak of him as if he were no longer present. He was astonished at this, and again touching the ring he turned the collet outwards and reappeared; he made several trials of the ring, and always with the same result—when he turned the collet inwards he became invisible, when outwards he reappeared. Whereupon he contrived to be chosen one of the messengers who were sent to the court; where as soon as he arrived he seduced the queen, and with her help conspired against the king and slew him, and took the kingdom. Suppose now that there were two such magic rings, and the just put on one of them and the unjust the other; no man can be imagined to be of such an iron nature that he would stand fast in justice. No man would keep his hands off what was not his own when he could safely take what he liked out of the market, or go into houses and lie with any one at his pleasure, or kill or release from prison whom he would, and in all respects be like a God among men. Then the actions of the just would be as the actions of the unjust; they would both come at last to the same point. And this we may truly affirm to be a great proof that a man is just, not willingly or because he thinks that justice is any good to him individually, but of necessity, for wherever any one thinks that he can safely be unjust, there he is unjust. For all men believe in their hearts that injustice is far more profitable to the individual than justice, and he who argues as I have been supposing, will say that they are right. If you could imagine any one obtaining this power of becoming invisible, and never doing any wrong or touching what was another's, he would be thought by the lookers-on to be a most wretched idiot, although they would praise him to one another's faces, and keep up appearances with one another from a fear that they too might suffer injustice.

# CLAUDE ADRIEN HELVÉTIUS

CLAUDE ADRIEN HELVÉTIUS (1715–71) was a leading French philosopher of the Enlightenment. His major works include: *Essays on the Mind* (1758) and *A Treatise on Man* (1772).

## A Treatise on Man*

### Of Justice

Justice is the conservator of the life and liberty of the citizens. Each one desires to enjoy his several properties; each one therefore loves justice in others, and would have them behave justly toward him. But who is solicitous to be just toward others? Do men love justice for the sake of justice, or for the consideration it procures? This is the object of my inquiry.

Man is so often ignorant of himself: we perceive so much contradiction between his conduct and his discourse,[1] that to know him we must study his actions and his nature itself. . . .

What is the love man has for justice? To determine this question, we must place him above all hope and fear: make him an oriental monarch.

When seated on his throne, he can levy on his people taxes without limits. Ought he to do it? No. The measure of all taxes is the wants of the state. Every tax, when pushed beyond those wants, is a robbery, an injustice. No truth more evident than this. Yet, notwithstanding man's pretended love for equity, there is no Asiatic monarch who does not commit this injustice, and commit it without remorse. What can we infer from this fact? That man's love for justice is founded either on a fear of the evil attendants on iniquity, or from the hope of the good consequences of esteem, consideration, and, in short, from the power attached to the practice of justice.

---

* From *A Treatise on Man*, by C. A. Helvétius, Vol. I, Section 4. Translated by William Hooper (1777).

[1] In morality, as in religion, there are a few sincere, and a great many hypocrites. A thousand men adorn themselves with sentiments not their own, and that they cannot have. When we compare their conduct with their discourse, we find none but knaves that would make dupes. We ought in general to mistrust the probity of those who pretend to extraordinary probity, and set themselves up for ancient Romans. There are those who appear really virtuous at the moment the curtain is drawn up, and they are going to perform a great part on the theatre of the world. But behind the scenes how many are there who preserve the same character of equity, and are always just? . . .

The necessity we are under to form virtuous men, to reward and punish, to institute wise laws, and to establish a regular form of government, are so many evident proofs of this truth. . . .

If a difference arise between two men nearly equal in power, each of them, restrained by a reciprocal fear, has recourse to justice; each of them submits to its decision; that he may interest the public in his favour, and by that means acquire a certain superiority over his adversary.

But let one of these two men be greatly superior in power to the other, so that he can rob him with impunity; and then, deaf to the voice of justice, he does not litigate, but command. It is not equity, nor even the appearance of equity, that determines between the weak and the powerful; but force, crime, and tyranny. . . .

Let what I have said of man be applied to nations. Two nations are neighbors; they are, in certain respects, in a reciprocal dependence: they are consequently forced to make conventions between them, and to form the law of nations. Do they regard it? Yes, so long as they reciprocally fear each other, so long as a certain balance of power subsists between them. When this balance is destroyed, the strongest nation violates their conventions without concern. It becomes unjust, because it can be so with impunity.

The so much boasted respect in man for justice is never anything more than a respect for power. . . .

## Of Virtue

The word Virtue, equally applicable to prudence, courage, and charity, has . . . only a vague signification. However it constantly recalls to the mind the confused idea of some quality useful to society.

When qualities of this sort are common to the greatest part of the citizens a nation is happy within itself, formidable without, and worthy of imitation by posterity. Virtue, always useful to man, and consequently always respectable, ought, at least in certain countries, to reflect power and consideration on its possessors. Now it is the love of consideration that man takes to be in him the love of virtue. Each one pretends to love it for itself. This phrase is in every one's mouth, but in no one's heart. What motive makes the monk fast, wear a hair cloth, and flog himself? The hope of eternal happiness: the fear of hell, and the desire of heaven.

Pleasure and pain, those productive principles of monastic virtue, are the principles of the patriotic virtues also. The hope of rewards makes them flourish. Whatever disinterested love we may affect to have, *without interest to love virtue there is no virtue*. To know man, in this respect, we must study him; not by his conversation, but his actions. When I speak I put on a mask;

when I act I am forced to take it off. It is not, therefore, by what I say, but what I do, that men are to judge me; and they will judge me rightly. . . .

To know the real esteem in which virtue is held, let us suppose it banished to the dominion of a monarch where it can expect no grace or favour. What respect will be paid at his court to virtue? None. Nothing can be there respected but baseness, intrigue, and cruelty, disguised under the names of decency, wisdom, and firmness. . . .

### Of Self-Love

Man is sensible of bodily pleasure and pain, consequently he flies from the one, and pursues the other; and it is to this constant pursuit and flight that is given the name of self-love.

This sentiment, the immediate effect of corporeal sensibility, and consequently common to all, is inseparable from man. As a proof I offer its permanence, impossibility of destruction, or even alteration. Of all our sentiments it is the only one that has these properties: it is to this we owe all our desires, and all our passions; which are nothing more in us than the application of self-love to particular objects.

It is therefore to this sentiment, diversely modified according to the education we receive, the government under which we live, and the different situations in which we are placed, that we are to attribute the amazing difference in the passions and characters of men.

Self-love makes us totally what we are. Why are we so covetous of honours and dignities? Because we love ourselves, and desire our own happiness, and consequently the power of procuring it. The love of power, and the means of procuring it, is therefore necessarily connected in man with the love of himself. Every one would command, because every one would increase his felicity, and engage all his fellow-citizens to promote it. Now among all the methods to engage them, the most certain is power or force. The love of power, founded on that of happiness, is therefore the common object of all our desires. Thus riches, honour, glory, envy, importance, justice, virtue, intolerance, in a word, all the factitious passions[2] are in us nothing but the love of power, disguised under those different names.

Power is the only object of man's pursuit.

[2] All our passions are factitious, except corporeal wants, pains, and pleasures.

# FRANK C. SHARP

FRANK CHAPMAN SHARP (1866–1943) taught at the University of Wisconsin. Concerned primarily with problems in ethics, he was noted especially for his empirical studies of actual moral judgments. His major works include: A *Study of the Influence of Custom on the Moral Judgment* (1908), *Ethics* (1928), *Business Ethics* (with Philip G. Fox, 1937), and *Good Will and Ill Will* (1950).

## Egoism and Altruism*

### Definitions of Egoism and Altruism

Egoistic action can not be defined, as it sometimes has been, as the fulfilling of one's own desires, for every voluntary action is and can be nothing other than this. Whether I desire to go to the theater this evening or to send a friend who has little money and little opportunity for enjoyment, whether I desire education for myself, or, in another period of life, for my children, whether I desire to save myself or a child in the street from being run over by an automobile, whether I desire revenge, or the possession of power, or the glory or welfare of my country, the desire, in the very nature of the case, must be *mine*. Whose else could it be? The characteristic feature of egotistic action, as distinguished from altruistic, must be found, not in its source, but in its object. Again egoistic action can not be defined, as it also has been, as action which has self for its immediate object. It is a well-established fact of criminal psychology that the repentant sinner, in indignation against himself, some times deliberately seeks suffering and even death for himself, or refuses to attempt to avoid it when it is brought upon him by others. Egoism, as the word is commonly used, involves some kind of concern for one's own interests, and therefore can never include the wish to injure self solely for the sake of injury. To call such a phenomenon egoism would be as much a blurring of distinctions as to call the desire to humiliate or destroy your enemy altruism.

A third definition is open to us, and this, I believe, supplies us with an answer to our question. According to this an egoistic action is one which I perform with a view to the attainment of some good for myself. . . .

---

* From *Ethics*, by Frank Chapman Sharp, Chap. 5. Copyright, 1928, The Century Company. Used by permission of Appleton-Century-Crofts, Inc.

The desire for my good . . . is always the desire for my future good. When a man is raising a glass of water to his lips he is acting with the purpose of bringing into existence a state of himself not yet existing. But the act of preserving the *status quo*, as where he replenishes the fire in order to maintain the present temperature of the room, is also an act which looks to the future. Egoism, therefore, must be defined as the desire for a future state of myself which I believe to be good.

In defining egoism we have at the same time been paving the way for a definition of altruism. Like egoism it is the desire for good, in this case the good of some person, or persons, or group besides self. Like egoism it must, from the very nature of voluntary action, refer to the future, even though it be a future removed from the present by the tick of a watch. Altruism, then, is the desire for a future state of another or others which I believe will be a good state for them to be in. It should go without saying that a desire is altruistic only in so far as the good of the other is desired as an end in itself, not as a means to some good for myself.

From our definitions of egoism and altruism there follows a very important conclusion: Egoism and altruism are not separate and independent desires like curiosity and approbativeness; they are simply two different directions of the same force. The fundamental principle, of which each is a manifestation, may be formulated as follows: The thought of a good as such tends to arouse a desire for its realization or attainment. Since it is convenient to have a name for this spring of action I suggest that in psychological and ethical discussion we employ for this purpose the term *benevolence*, using it, of course, not in its common but in its etymological significance as the willing well to anyone. . . .

### The Existence of Altruism

As the existence of altruism has always been denied by some, we must now inquire whether there is really anything in human nature corresponding to the name. Certainly the burden of proof rests upon him who denies. For however great may be the total volume of egoistic actions, anyone who does not live in a Hell on earth has assuredly had the opportunity to see any number of actions in which altruistic desire was, to all appearance, at least a factor, even a leading factor, and far from infrequently the sole, or the sole decisive factor. Examples range from the parental or the fraternal devotion which denies itself luxuries and sometimes what are considered necessities, in order that a son or daughter, a brother or sister, may be given an education, to the man who, face to face with death, elects to die that others may live. And it shows itself, of course, not merely in positive service but also in numberless forbearances,—in the refusal to injure another for the sake of personal gain.

"There is always a supply of courage when needed," says a magazine article, apropos of the heroic death of a fireman. Our Civil War was fought largely by volunteers on both sides; while the English, the Canadian, and the Australian armies in the World War were either entirely or in large part composed of men who offered their lives to save the life of their country. The motives of those who made the great surrender were undoubtedly of more than one kind; the commonplace and the ignoble alike appearing, and sometimes mingling with the highest considerations in the same person. But what I wish to emphasize here is the fact that the altruistic motives are present also, equally with the love of adventure and the fear of public opinion.

But "peace hath her victories"—and her heroes—"no less renowned than war." Shortly after the close of the Spanish-American War the American commission appointed to investigate the cause of yellow fever called for volunteers among the enlisted men of the American army of occupation in Cuba to enable them to test their theories of the relation of yellow fever to the bite of the infected mosquito. There were more volunteers offering themselves for the service than were needed. All faced the certainty that some would undergo a serious and painful illness, with the possibility of death at the end. In addition, those who volunteered to test the view that the germs of yellow fever were carried by clothing, slept for three weeks in a closed cabin, in stifling heat, using bedclothes and night clothes which had covered those who had died of yellow fever and which were foul and filthy with its excreta to an unimaginable degree.

The germ of the capacity for such devotion is not even the property of a select few—the moral *élite*—but is spread broadcast, even though it may not be absolutely universal, in the race. For no one whole-heartedly admires a man for heroism unless he feels within himself at least some stirrings of the impulse to do likewise; unless, in other words, he wishes he had the will which would enable him to act in like manner under the same conditions. Otherwise he despises the man as a fool. Thus most persons on the whole feel contempt rather than admiration for Saint Simeon Stylites, who stood on the top of a pillar in the desert for the last half of his life as the most ingenious and effective method he could contrive for making himself thoroughly miserable. In the darkest days of our Civil War, Jay Gould, "Jim" Fiske, Daniel Drew, and a number of other financial cutthroats went to President Lincoln with a "proposition" which would net him "millions." He was to be let into one of their little deals, on condition, of course, of a suitable return of favors on his part. When he refused to have anything to do with their scheme, they felt no admiration for his patriotism. On the contrary they thought and said that he was "crazy" for being wrapped up in "saving the Union," when he might be making his fortune. He was simply a being beyond their powers of comprehension. If, then, you feel the attraction of the finer manifestations of character, even though you are too weak to imitate them in your own life, this means that there is something in the end for which the sacrifice was made that appeals to you. It points to the existence in you of a corresponding desire, however impotent it might prove to be in the face of serious temptation.

These potentialities for sacrifice show themselves as living forces in certain situations, even in men in whom they commonly fail to reveal their existence in the ordinary routine of everyday life. After the sinking of the *Titanic*, Mr. George Kennan, the celebrated traveler and authority on Russian affairs, wrote a letter to the *Outlook*, a part of which reads as follows:

The courage and unselfishness shown by an overwhelming majority of the passengers on the ill-fated steamship *Titanic* have recalled to my mind the remarkable exhibition of the same heroic and generous characteristics by the citizens of San Francisco during the great earthquake and fire of 1906. I did not myself reach the city until some weeks after the disaster, but the remembrance of the events of that period of strain and suffering was still fresh in the mind of every observer or participant, and I was greatly impressed by the enthusiasm and deep feeling shown by everybody in speaking of the behavior of the population. One friend of mine in Oakland—a man not at all inclined to be "gushing" or effusive in speech—said to me: "I am glad that I lived to see the things that happened in the first ten days after that great catastrophe. Those days were the best and most inspiriting part of my life. Religious people talk about the 'kingdom of heaven,' but few of them expect to live long enough to see it realized on earth. I saw something that very nearly approached it in San Francisco, Berkeley, and Oakland in the week that followed the fire. Cowardice, selfishness, greed, and all the baser emotions and impulses of human character practically disappeared in the tremendous strain of that experience, and courage, fortitude, sympathy, generosity, and unbounded self-sacrifice took their places. Men became, and for a short time continued to be, all that we may suppose their Creator intended them to be, and it was a splendid and inspiriting thing to witness. We imagine that we live in a selfish and materialistic age, and perhaps we do; but I know now of what human nature—humanity as a whole—is capable, and I can never again take a pessimistic view of the world's future."[1] . . .

### The Denials of the Existence of Altruism: (1) The Argument from the Effects of Praise and Blame

All of these things are open to the light of day. But many of them, especially if each is taken singly and considered by itself, can perhaps be explained away as the result of the hunger for praise or the fear of blame, and thus as done, after all, from a selfish motive. The whole mass of it, in its totality, however, can not be so explained. For praise and blame could never come

[1] *Outlook*, Vol. 101, 1912, p. 84.

into existence in a world consisting solely of pure egoists. To be sure, since there is probably no such thing as a completely selfish man we can not tell precisely what this kind of a being would do. But those who represent the closest approach to this state do not blame others who, in the pursuit of their personal interests, injure them; any more than they admire those who sacrifice themselves for their benefit. . . .

In a society . . . consisting exclusively of complete egoists praise and blame would not exist. If they did, who would sacrifice pleasure or undergo pain in order to obtain them? Would not everyone know from self-observation that they were simply a device employed to squeeze out of him, for the benefit of another, actions which otherwise he would have no sufficient motive for performing? You can pass a counterfeit coin where there are only a few such coins in circulation. But how can you conceive of a coinage consisting of nothing but counterfeits?

### The Denial of the Existence of Altruism: (2) The Argument from the Nature of Desire

If one attack fails perhaps another may have better luck. The man we call altruistic commonly derives a certain satisfaction from helping others, and feels uneasy and dissatisfied when he injures them or leaves them in the lurch; what more obvious than the suggestion that it is the attainment of this satisfaction or the avoidance of this dissatisfaction which supplies the motive of his action?

Abraham Lincoln (in reality one of the most altruistic of men) once expressed this theory of the will in the course of a famous incident, one version of which reads as follows:

Mr. Lincoln once remarked to a fellow-passenger on an old-time mud-coach that all men were prompted by selfishness in doing good. His fellow-passenger was antagonizing this position when they were passing over a corduroy bridge that spanned a slough. As they crossed this bridge they espied an old razor-backed sow on the bank making a terrible noise because her pigs had got into the slough and were in danger of drowning. As the old coach began to climb the hill, Mr. Lincoln called out, "Driver, can't you stop just a moment?" Then Mr. Lincoln jumped out, ran back, and lifted the little pigs out of the mud and water and placed them on the bank. When he returned, his companion remarked: "Now, Abe, where does selfishness come in on this little episode?" "Why, bless your soul, Ed, that was the very essence of selfishness. I should have had no peace of mind all day had I gone on and left that suffering old sow worrying over those pigs. I did it to get peace of mind, don't you see?"[2]

The fallacy of this explanation, however, is very easy to expose. The attainment of every desire, of whatever sort, tends to arouse a feeling of satisfaction.

[2] Quoted from the Springfield (Ill.) *Monitor* in the *Outlook*, Vol. 56, p. 1059.

There is, for example, the desire to know certain facts, whether these refer to the size of the great star Betelgeuze in the constellation of Orion, or the status of the young man who calls so assiduously on the girl next door. When the knowledge comes, satisfaction is normally felt. But the rise into consciousness of this satisfaction is due to the existence of the desire; and the object of the desire, therefore, was not the satisfaction, but the satisfaction was rather the consequence of the preëxisting desire. This statement of course holds equally for dissatisfaction, from its weakest form as a vague feeling of uneasiness to its most massive and intense manifestations as sorrow or grief. Each is the sign of an aversion from a state of things which now is, or which is expected to come into existence. If there had been no such aversion there would have been no feeling.

All this applies to altruism. As with all other desires, attainment brings, or tends to bring satisfaction or joy; failure normally brings dissatisfaction, and in extreme cases sorrow. But the satisfaction could never have been obtained, dissatisfaction would never have come, if the desire for the realization of the other person's welfare had not been there in the first place. Therefore when a man's peace of mind is interfered with by the sufferings of another he must have at least some amount, whether great or small, of direct desire for their good and aversion from their harm. . . .

### Why is There More Egoism Than Altruism?

. . . Why, it may be asked, is there so much more egoistic action in the world than altruistic?

The answer turns on the cumulative effects of a number of well-known psychological forces. Of these the first in importance is the imagination. Of the many spurs to benevolence this is undoubtedly the most powerful, always excepting the influence of love upon altruism. The effect of any imagined state upon the will tends . . . to be in direct ratio to the concreteness and completeness (within certain limits) with which it is pictured. Now I can usually imagine my own future more effectively than the present or future state of another, simply because there are more data at the disposal of the imagination in one case than in the other. Suppose, for example, I am considering the purchase of a hundred-dollar rug. I am, of course, well aware that I might spend that money in helping to feed the starving in the war-ravaged districts of China. But I know precisely how my room looks now with that horrible bare space in the floor; I can easily imagine precisely how it will look covered with a handsome rug, especially if I have seen the rug in a shop window; whereas the sufferings of the Chinese—well, I have never starved to death.

It follows from the preceding that altruism requires, on the average, a broader range of experience and a more highly developed power of imagining than does egoism. Consequently the child is apt to be distinctly more egoistic than altruistic. Thereupon enters a second factor, that of habit. The child begins by thinking of his own interests, and the more they occupy the mind the more they tend to occupy it. Thoughtlessness makes a large part of our indifference to others; and thoughtlessness is nothing more nor less than the habit of thinking so much about our own interests that those of others are either completely pushed aside, or are presented only in a hasty, vague, sketchy fashion. In the grip of these habits almost every human being grows to maturity.

The conditions of social existence reinforce these influences. They involve a struggle for personal ends, and thus narrow still farther the range of facts with which the imagination may build, organize, and fortify its habits of thought. In this struggle altruistic interests often die of mere inanition; there is no time for the exercise that is necessary in order to keep them alive. Often again they perish through the direct attack of such emotions as resentment, envy, or disappointment, which the struggle of life so frequently engenders. . . .

### Altruism Not a Miracle

There has been a certain tendency even among those who believe in the existence of altruism to regard it as a kind of miracle. "Altruism," says von Ihering in Der Zweck im Recht, "is as wonderful as if water should run up hill." It may be remarked in passing that if water did not run up hill it would certainly not long continue to run down; while no one can seriously maintain that the laws of evaporation are more wonderful than those of gravitation. Von Ihering's argument seems to be somewhat as follows: Altruism is less primitive or less common than egoism. Therefore it is a "miracle." It seems hardly necessary to say that the conclusion does not follow from the premises. The instinct of walking follows that of winking by a number of months in the development of the child, but this does not constitute walking a miracle. Furthermore, the premises themselves are largely a fiction. Egoism, as we have defined it, is no more primitive in the child's mind than is altruism. It is true of him in his second and third years, as Spencer and Gillen say of the Australian savage, that he obeys literally the command of the gospel: "Take no thought for the morrow." His voluntary acts are determined chiefly by unreflective impulse and by desire for a good immediately in front of his eyes; and where this is not the case the range of his effective vision scarcely extends beyond the setting sun. Offer the average three-year-old child a choice between one piece of candy now and two pieces tomorrow, and see which he will take. Yet this same child may be willing to divide today's candy with his mother. A seven-year-old boy of my acquaintance could not be moved by any argument or other form of pressure to devote even the shortest portion of his precious time to earning money as such, though he understood perfectly the function of money as an instrument of future satisfaction. But for a couple of weeks in December he worked with exemplary assiduity to earn money with which to buy his mother a Christmas present. The concrete good of his mother appealed to him more strongly than the abstract good of self.

## PSYCHOLOGICAL EGOISM—SUGGESTED READINGS

Baylis, C. A., *Ethics*, New York, Holt, 1958, Chap. 7, pp. 144-64. (critic)

Broad, C. D., "Egoism as a Theory of Human Motives," *Hibbert Journal*, XLVIII (1949-50), pp. 105-14. (critic)

Butler, J., *Fifteen Sermons Preached at the Rolls Chapel*, 2nd ed., 1729, Preface, Sermons I and XI. (critic)

Hobbes, T., *Leviathan*, 1651, esp. Chaps. 6, 11, and 13-15. (proponent)

Holt, E. B., "The Whimsical Condition of Social Psychology, and of Mankind," in *American Philosophy Today and Tomorrow*, ed., H. M. Kallen and S. Hook, New York, Lee Furman, 1935. (proponent)

Mandeville, B., *The Fable of the Bees: or, Private Vices, Publick Benefits*, Oxford, Clarendon Press, 1924, Vols. I and II. (proponent)

# B. CULTURAL RELATIVISM

Cultural relativists hold that all the moral judgments of men are completely derived from the customs of the society in which they live; that whenever we use moral terms such as "right" and "wrong" or "good" and "bad," for example, we mean nothing other than that which is approved and disapproved by our particular society. Cultural relativists observe that there is a wide variability in the moral standards accepted by men in different societies and at different times; they cite sociological and anthropological evidence to show that there are many cases in which the same type of action is considered right in one culture and wrong in another. It is argued that there is no universal right and wrong which is binding upon all men; that where two cultures disagree, there is no basis for any claim that one of the two cultures is morally superior.

In the selections which follow, SUMNER presents the case for cultural relativism. He observes that, as men seek to satisfy their needs, ways of acting become habitual which are accepted by all the members of a given group. Although these "folkways" differ widely from society to society, men naturally make their own group the center from which they judge all others; they believe that their own ways of acting are the only right ways. Against the view of the cultural relativist, STACE asserts that we are not entitled to conclude that there is no true morality simply because men have different opinions about what is moral. He argues that cultural relativism cannot be reconciled with the moral feelings most men possess.

case the rule of obligation and duty is set by the mores. The interest comes under vanity. The sanction of the caste rules is in a boycott by all members of the caste. The rules are often very harmful. "The authority of caste rests partly on written laws, partly on legendary fables or narratives, partly on the injunctions of instructors and priests, partly on custom and usage, and partly on the caprice and convenience of its votaries." The harm of caste rules is so great that of late they have been broken in some cases, especially in regard to travel over sea, which is a great advantage to Hindoos. The Hindoo folkways in regard to widows and child marriages must also be recognized as socially harmful.

*30. How "true" and "right" are found.* If a savage puts his hand too near the fire, he suffers pain and draws it back. He knows nothing of the laws of the radiation of heat, but his instinctive action conforms to that law as if he did know it. If he wants to catch an animal for food, he must study its habits and prepare a device adjusted to those habits. If it fails, he must try again, until his observation is "true" and his device is "right." All the practical and direct element in the folkways seems to be due to common sense, natural reason, intuition, or some other original mental endowment. It seems rational (or rationalistic) and utilitarian. Often in the mythologies this ultimate rational element was ascribed to the teaching of a god or a culture hero. In modern mythology it is accounted for as "natural."

Although the ways adopted must always be really "true" and "right" in relation to facts, for otherwise they could not answer their purpose, such is not the primitive notion of true and right.

*31. The folkways are "right." Rights. Morals.* The folkways are the "right" ways to satisfy all interests, because they are traditional, and exist in fact. They extend over the whole of life. There is a right way to catch game, to win a wife, to make one's self appear, to cure disease, to honor ghosts, to treat comrades or strangers, to behave when a child is born, on the warpath, in council, and so on in all cases which can arise. The ways are defined on the negative side, that is, by taboos. The "right" way is the way which the ancestors used and which has been handed down. The tradition is its own warrant. It is not held subject to verification by experience. The notion of right is in the folkways. It is not outside of them, of independent origin, and brought to them to test them. In the folkways, whatever is, is right. This is because they are traditional, and therefore contain in themselves the authority of the ancestral ghosts. When we come to the folkways we are at the end of our analysis. The notion of right and ought is the same in regard to all the folkways, but the degree of it varies with the importance of the interest at stake. The obligation of conformable and coöperative action is far greater under ghost fear and war than in other matters, and the social sanctions are severer, because group interests are supposed to be at stake. Some usages contain only a slight element of right and ought. It may well be believed that notions of right and duty, and of social welfare, were first developed in connection with ghost fear and other-worldliness, and therefore that, in that field also, folkways were first raised to mores. "Rights" are the rules of mutual give and take in the competition of life which are imposed on comrades in the in-group, in order that the peace may prevail there which is essential to the group strength. Therefore rights can never be "natural" or "God-given," or absolute in any sense. The morality of a group at a time is the sum of the taboos and prescriptions in the folkways by which right conduct is defined. Therefore morals can never be intuitive. They are historical, institutional, and empirical.

World philosophy, life policy, right, rights, and morality are all products of the folkways. They are reflections on, and generalizations from, the experience of pleasure and pain which is won in efforts to carry on the struggle for existence under actual life conditions. The generalizations are very crude and vague in their germinal forms. They are all embodied in folklore, and all our philosophy and science have been developed out of them.

15. *Ethnocentrism* is the technical name for this view of things in which one's own group is the center of everything, and all others are scaled and rated with reference to it. Folkways correspond to it to cover both the inner and the outer relation. Each group nourishes its own pride and vanity, boasts itself superior, exalts its own divinities, and looks with contempt on outsiders. Each group thinks its own folkways the only right ones, and if it observes that other groups have other folkways, these excite its scorn. Opprobrious epithets are derived from these differences. "Pig-eater," "cow-eater," "uncircumcised," "jabberers," are epithets of contempt and abomination. The Tupis called the Portuguese by a derisive epithet descriptive of birds which have feathers around their feet, on account of trousers. For our present purpose the most important fact is that ethnocentrism leads a people to exaggerate and intensify everything in their own folkways which is peculiar and which differentiates them from others. It therefore strengthens the folkways.

16. *Illustrations of ethnocentrism.* The Papuans on New Guinea are broken up into village units which are kept separate by hostility, cannibalism, head hunting, and divergences of language and religion. Each village is integrated by its own language, religion, and interests. A group of villages is sometimes united into a limited unity by connubium. A wife taken inside of this group unit has full status; one taken outside of it has not. The petty group units are peace groups within and are hostile to all outsiders. The Mbayas of South America believed that their deity had bidden them live by

making war on others, taking their wives and property, and killing their men.

17. When Caribs were asked whence they came, they answered, "We alone are people." The meaning of the name Kiowa is "real or principal people." The Lapps call themselves "men," or "human beings." The Greenland Eskimo think that Europeans have been sent to Greenland to learn virtue and good manners from the Greenlanders. Their highest form of praise for a European is that he is, or soon will be, as good as a Greenlander. The Tunguses call themselves "men." As a rule it is found that nature peoples call themselves "men." Others are something else—perhaps not defined—but not real men. In myths the origin of their own tribe is that of the real human race. They do not account for the others. The Ainos derive their name from that of the first man, whom they worship as a god. Evidently the name of the god is derived from the tribe name. When the tribal name has another sense, it is always boastful or proud. The Ovambo name is a corruption of the name of the tribe for themselves, which means "the wealthy." Amongst the most re-markable people in the world for ethnocentrism are the Seri of Lower California. They observe an attitude of suspicion and hostility to all outsiders, and strictly forbid marriage with outsiders.

18. The Jews divided all mankind into themselves and Gentiles. They were the "chosen people." The Greeks and Romans called all outsiders "bar-barians." In Euripides' tragedy of *Iphigenia in Aulis* Iphigenia says that it is fitting that Greeks should rule over barbarians, but not contrariwise, because Greeks are free, and barbarians are slaves. The Arabs regarded themselves as the noblest nation and all others as more or less barbarous. In 1896, the Chinese minister of education and his counselors edited a manual in which this statement occurs: "How grand and glorious is the Empire of China, the middle kingdom! She is the largest and richest in the world. The grandest men in the world have all come from the middle empire." In all the literature of all the states equivalent statements occur, although they are not so naïvely expressed. In Russian books and newspapers the civilizing mission of Russia is talked about, just as, in the books and journals of France, Germany, and the United States, the civilizing mission of those countries is assumed and referred to as well understood. Each state now regards itself as the leader of civilization, the best, the freest, and the wisest, and all others as inferior. Within a few years our own man-on-the-curbstone has learned to class all foreigners of the Latin peoples as "dagos," and "dago" has become an epithet of contempt. These are all cases of ethnocentrism.

34. *Definition of the mores.* When the elements of truth and right are developed into doctrines of welfare, the folkways are raised to another plane. They then become capable of producing inferences, developing into new

forms, and extending their constructive influence over men and society. Then we call them the mores. The mores are the folkways, including the philosophical and ethical generalizations as to societal welfare which are suggested by them, and inherent in them, as they grow.

42. *Purpose of the present work.* "Ethology" would be a convenient term for the study of manners, customs, usages, and mores, including the study of the way in which they are formed, how they grow or decay, and how they affect the interests which it is their purpose to serve. The Greeks applied the term "ethos" to the sum of the characteristic usages, ideas, standards, and codes by which a group was differentiated and individualized in character from other groups. "Ethics" were things which pertained to the ethos and therefore the things which were the standard of right. The Romans used "mores" for customs in the broadest and richest sense of the word, including the notion that customs served welfare, and had traditional and mystic sanction, so that they were properly authoritative and sacred. It is a very surprising fact that modern nations should have lost these words and the significant suggestions which inhere in them. The English language has no derivative noun from "mores," and no equivalent for it. The French *mœurs* is trivial compared with "mores." The German *Sitte* renders "mores" but very imperfectly. The modern peoples have made morals and morality a separate domain, by the side of religion, philosophy, and politics. In that sense, morals is an impossible and unreal category. It has no existence, and can have none. The word "moral" means what belongs or appertains to the mores. Therefore the category of morals can never be defined without reference to something outside of itself. Ethics, having lost connection with the ethos of a people, is an attempt to systematize the current notions of right and wrong upon some basic principle, generally with the purpose of establishing morals on an absolute doctrine, so that it shall be universal, absolute, and everlasting. In a general way also, whenever a thing can be called moral, or connected with some ethical generality, it is thought to be "raised," and disputants whose method is to employ ethical generalities assume especial authority for themselves and their views. These methods of discussion are most employed in treating of social topics, and they are disastrous to sound study of facts. They help to hold the social sciences under the dominion of metaphysics. The abuse has been most developed in connection with political economy, which has been almost robbed of the character of a serious discipline by converting its discussions into ethical disquisitions.

43. *Why use the word mores.* "Ethica," in the Greek sense, or "ethology," as above defined, would be good names for our present work. We aim to study the ethos of groups, in order to see how it arises, its power and influence, the modes of its operation on members of the group, and the various attri-

butes of it (ethica). "Ethology" is a very unfamiliar word. It has been used for the mode of setting forth manners, customs, and mores in satirical comedy. The Latin word "mores" seems to be, on the whole, more practically convenient and available than any other for our purpose, as a name for the folkways with the connotations of right and truth in respect to welfare, embodied in them. The analysis and definition above given show that in the mores we must recognize a dominating force in history, constituting a condition as to what can be done, and as to the methods which can be employed.

44. *Mores are a directive force.* Of course the view which has been stated is antagonistic to the view that philosophy and ethics furnish creative and determining forces in society and history. That view comes down to us from the Greek philosophy and it has now prevailed so long that all current discussion conforms to it. Philosophy and ethics are pursued as independent disciplines, and the results are brought to the science of society and to statesmanship and legislation as authoritative dicta. We also have *Völkerpsychologie, Sozialpolitik,* and other intermediate forms which show the struggle of metaphysics to retain control of the science of society. The "historic sense," the *Zeitgeist,* and other terms of similar import are partial recognitions of the mores and their importance in the science of society. It can be seen also that philosophy and ethics are products of the folkways. They are taken out of the mores, but are never original and creative; they are secondary and derived. They often interfere in the second stage of the sequence—act, thought, act. Then they produce harm, but some ground is furnished for the claim that they are creative or at least regulative. In fact, the real process in great bodies of men is not one of deduction from any great principle of philosophy or ethics. It is one of minute efforts to live well under existing conditions, which efforts are repeated indefinitely by great numbers, getting strength from habit and from the fellowship of united action. The resultant folkways become coercive. All are forced to conform, and the folkways dominate the societal life. Then they seem true and right, and arise into mores as the norm of welfare. Thence are produced faiths, ideas, doctrines, religions, and philosophies, according to the stage of civilization and the fashions of reflection and generalization.

61. *The mores and institutions.* Institutions and laws are produced out of mores. An institution consists of a concept (idea, notion, doctrine, interest) and a structure. The structure is a framework, or apparatus, or perhaps only a number of functionaries set to coöperate in prescribed ways at a certain conjuncture. The structure holds the concept and furnishes instrumentalities for bringing it into the world of facts and action in a way to serve the interests of men in society. Institutions are either crescive or enacted. They are crescive when they take shape in the mores, growing by the instinctive efforts

by which the mores are produced. Then the efforts, through long use, become definite and specific. Property, marriage, and religion are the most primary institutions. They began in folkways. They became customs. They developed into mores by the addition of some philosophy of welfare, however crude. Then they were made more definite and specific as regards the rules, the prescribed acts, and the apparatus to be employed. This produced a structure and the institution was complete. Enacted institutions are products of rational invention and intention. They belong to high civilization. Banks are institutions of credit founded on usages which can be traced back to barbarism. There came a time when, guided by rational reflection on experience, men systematized and regulated the usages which had become current, and thus created positive institutions of credit, defined by law and sanctioned by the force of the state. Pure enacted institutions which are strong and prosperous are hard to find. It is too difficult to invent and create an institution, for a purpose, out of nothing. The electoral college in the constitution of the United States is an example. In that case the democratic mores of the people have seized upon the device and made of it something quite different from what the inventors planned. All institutions have come out of mores, although the rational element in them is sometimes so large that their origin in the mores is not to be ascertained except by an historical investigation (legislatures, courts, juries, joint stock companies, the stock exchange). Property, marriage, and religion are still almost entirely in the mores. Amongst nature men any man might capture and hold a woman at any time, if he could. He did it by superior force which was its own supreme justification. But his act brought his group and her group into war, and produced harm to his comrades. They forbade capture, or set conditions for it. Beyond the limits, the individual might still use force, but his comrades were no longer responsible. The glory to him, if he succeeded, might be all the greater. His control over his captive was absolute. Within the prescribed conditions, "capture" became technical and institutional, and rights grew out of it. The woman had a status which was defined by custom, and was very different from the status of a real captive. Marriage was the institutional relation, in the society and under its sanction, of a woman to a man, where the woman had been obtained in the prescribed way. She was then a "wife." What her rights and duties were was defined by the mores, as they are to-day in all civilized society.

62. *Laws.* Acts of legislation come out of the mores. In low civilization all societal regulations are customs and taboos, the origin of which is unknown. Positive laws are impossible until the stage of verification, reflection, and criticism is reached. Until that point is reached there is only customary law, or common law. The customary law may be codified and systematized with

respect to some philosophical principles, and yet remain customary. The codes of Manu and Justinian are examples. Enactment is not possible until reverence for ancestors has been so much weakened that it is no longer thought wrong to interfere with traditional customs by positive enactment. Even then there is reluctance to make enactments, and there is a stage of transition during which traditional customs are extended by interpretation to cover new cases and to prevent evils. Legislation, however, has to seek standing ground on the existing mores, and it soon becomes apparent that legislation, to be strong, must be consistent with the mores. Things which have been in the mores are put under police regulation and later under positive law. It is sometimes said that "public opinion" must ratify and approve police regulations, but this statement rests on an imperfect analysis. The regulations must conform to the mores, so that the public will not think them too lax or too strict. The mores of our urban and rural populations are not the same; consequently legislation about intoxicants which is made by one of these sections of the population does not succeed when applied to the other. The regulation of drinking places, gambling places, and disorderly houses has passed through the above-mentioned stages. It is always a question of expediency whether to leave a subject under the mores, or to make a police regulation for it, or to put it into the criminal law. Betting, horse racing, dangerous sports, electric cars, and vehicles are cases now of things which seem to be passing under positive enactment and out of the unformulated control of the mores. When an enactment is made there is a sacrifice of the elasticity and automatic self-adaptation of custom, but an enactment is specific and is provided with sanctions. Enactments come into use when conscious purposes are formed, and it is believed that specific devices can be framed by which to realize such purposes in the society. Then also prohibitions take the place of taboos, and punishments are planned to be deterrent rather than revengeful. The mores of different societies, or of different ages, are characterized by greater or less readiness and confidence in regard to the use of positive enactments for the realization of societal purposes.

63. *How laws and institutions differ from mores.* When folkways have become institutions or laws they have changed their character and are to be distinguished from the mores. The element of sentiment and faith inheres in the mores. Laws and institutions have a rational and practical character, and are more mechanical and utilitarian. The great difference is that institutions and laws have a positive character, while mores are unformulated and undefined. There is a philosophy implicit in the folkways; when it is made explicit it becomes technical philosophy. Objectively regarded, the mores are the customs which actually conduce to welfare under existing life

conditions. Acts under the laws and institutions are conscious and voluntary; under the folkways they are always unconscious and involuntary, so that they have the character of natural necessity. Educated reflection and skepticism can disturb this spontaneous relation. The laws, being positive prescriptions, supersede the mores so far as they are adopted. It follows that the mores come into operation where laws and tribunals fail. The mores cover the great field of common life where there are no laws or police regulations. They cover an immense and undefined domain, and they break the way in new domains, not yet controlled at all. The mores, therefore, build up new laws and police regulations in time.

83. *Inertia and rigidity of the mores.* We see that we must conceive of the mores as a vast system of usages, covering the whole of life, and serving all its interests; also containing in themselves their own justification by tradition and use and wont, and approved by mystic sanctions until, by rational reflection, they develop their own philosophical and ethical generalizations, which are elevated into "principles" of truth and right. They coerce and restrict the newborn generation. They do not stimulate to thought, but the contrary. The thinking is already done and is embodied in the mores. They never contain any provision for their own amendment. They are not questions, but answers, to the problem of life. They present themselves as final and unchangeable, because they present answers which are offered as "the truth." No world philosophy, until the modern scientific world philosophy, and that only within a generation or two, has ever presented itself as perhaps transitory, certainly incomplete, and liable to be set aside to-morrow by more knowledge. No popular world philosophy or life policy ever can present itself in that light. It would cost too great a mental strain. All the groups whose mores we consider far inferior to our own are quite as well satisfied with theirs as we are with ours. The goodness or badness of mores consists entirely in their adjustment to the life conditions and the interests of the time and place. . . . Therefore it is a sign of ease and welfare when no thought is given to the mores, but all coöperate in them instinctively. The nations of southeastern Asia show us the persistency of the mores, when the element of stability and rigidity in them becomes predominant. Ghost fear and ancestor worship tend to establish the persistency of the mores by dogmatic authority, strict taboo, and weighty sanctions. The mores then lose their naturalness and vitality. They are stereotyped. They lose all relation to expediency. They become an end in themselves. They are imposed by imperative authority without regard to interests or conditions (caste, child marriage, widows). When any society falls under the dominion of this disease in the mores it must disintegrate before it can live again. In that diseased state of the mores all learning consists in committing to memory

the words of the sages of the past who established the formulæ of the mores. Such words are "sacred writings," a sentence of which is a rule of conduct to be obeyed quite independently of present interests, or of any rational considerations.

232. *Mores and morals; social code.* For every one the mores give the notion of what ought to be. This includes the notion of what ought to be done, for all should coöperate to bring to pass, in the order of life, what ought to be. All notions of propriety, decency, chastity, politeness, order, duty, right, rights, discipline, respect, reverence, coöperation, and fellowship, especially all things in regard to which good and ill depend entirely on the point at which the line is drawn, are in the mores. The mores can make things seem right and good to one group or one age which to another seem antagonistic to every instinct of human nature. The thirteenth century bred in every heart such a sentiment in regard to heretics that inquisitors had no more misgivings in their proceedings than men would have now if they should attempt to exterminate rattlesnakes. The sixteenth century gave to all such notions about witches that witch persecutors thought they were waging war on enemies of God and man. Of course the inquisitors and witch persecutors constantly developed the notions of heretics and witches. They exaggerated the notions and then gave them back again to the mores, in their expanded form, to inflame the hearts of men with terror and hate and to become, in the next stage, so much more fantastic and ferocious motives. Such is the reaction between the mores and the acts of the living generation. The world philosophy of the age is never anything but the reflection on the mental horizon, which is formed out of the mores, of the ruling ideas which are in the mores themselves. It is from a failure to recognize the to and fro in this reaction that the current notion arises that mores are produced by doctrines. The "morals" of an age are never anything but the consonance between what is done and what the mores of the age require. The whole revolves on itself, in the relation of the specific to the general, within the horizon formed by the mores. Every attempt to win an outside standpoint from which to reduce the whole to an absolute philosophy of truth and right, based on an unalterable principle, is a delusion. New elements are brought in only by new conquests of nature through science and art. The new conquests change the conditions of life and the interests of the members of the society. Then the mores change by adaptation to new conditions and interests. The philosophy and ethics then follow to account for and justify the changes in the mores; often, also, to claim that they have caused the changes. They never do anything but draw new lines of bearing between the parts of the mores and the horizon of thought within which they are inclosed, and which is a deduction from the mores. The horizon is widened

by more knowledge, but for one age it is just as much a generalization from the mores as for another. It is always unreal. It is only a product of thought. The ethical philosophers select points on this horizon from which to take their bearings, and they think that they have won some authority for their systems when they travel back again from the generalization to the specific custom out of which it was deduced. The cases of the inquisitors and witch persecutors who toiled arduously and continually for their chosen ends, for little or no reward, show us the relation between mores on the one side and philosophy, ethics, and religion on the other.

494. *Honor, seemliness, common sense, conscience.* Honor, common sense, seemliness, and conscience seem to belong to the individual domain. They are reactions produced in the individual by the societal environment. Honor is the sentiment of what one owes to one's self. It is an individual prerogative, and an ultimate individual standard. Seemliness is conduct which befits one's character and standards. Common sense, in the current view, is a natural gift and universal outfit. As to honor and seemliness, the popular view seems to be that each one has a fountain of inspiration in himself to furnish him with guidance. Conscience might be added as another natural or supernatural "voice," intuition, and part of the original outfit of all human beings as such. If these notions could be verified, and if they proved true, no discussion of them would be in place here, but as to honor it is a well-known and undisputed fact that societies have set codes of honor and standards of it which were arbitrary, irrational, and both individually and socially inexpedient, as ample experiment has proved. These codes have been and are imperative, and they have been accepted and obeyed by great groups of men who, in their own judgment, did not believe them sound. Those codes came out of the folkways of the time and place. Then comes the question whether it is not always so. Is honor, in any case, anything but the code of one's duty to himself which he has accepted from the group in which he was educated? Family, class, religious sect, school, occupation, enter into the social environment. In every environment there is a standard of honor. When a man thinks that he is acting most independently, on his personal prerogative, he is at best only balancing against each other the different codes in which he has been educated, e.g., that of the trades union against that of the Sunday school, or of the school against that of the family. What we think "natural" and universal, and to which we attribute an objective reality, is the sum of traits whose origin is so remote, and which we share with so many, that we do not know when or how we took them up, and we can remember no rational selection by which we adopted them. The same is true of common sense. It is the stock of ways of looking at things which we acquired unconsciously by suggestion from the environ-

ment in which we grew up. Some have more common sense than others, because they are more docile to suggestion, or have been taught to make judgments by people who were strong and wise. Conscience also seems best explained as a sum of principles of action which have in one's character the most original, remote, undisputed, and authoritative position, and to which questions of doubt are habitually referred. If these views are accepted, we have in honor, common sense, and conscience other phenomena of the folkways, and the notions of eternal truths of philosophy or ethics, derived from somewhere outside of men and their struggles to live well under the conditions of earth, must be abandoned as myths.

*438. Specification of the subject.* The ethnographers write of a tribe that the "morality" in it, especially of the women, is low or high, etc. This is the technical use of morality—as a thing pertaining to the sex relation only or especially, and the ethnographers make their propositions by applying our standards of sex behavior, and our form of the sex taboo, to judge the folkways of all people. All that they can properly say is that they find a great range and variety of usages, ideas, standards, and ideals, which differ greatly from ours. Some of them are far stricter than ours. Those we do not consider nobler than ours. We do not feel that we ought to adopt any ways because they are more strict than our traditional ones. We consider many to be excessive, silly, and harmful. A Roman senator was censured for impropriety because he kissed his wife in the presence of his daughter.

*439. Meaning of "immoral."* When, therefore, the ethnographers apply condemnatory or depreciatory adjectives to the people whom they study, they beg the most important question which we want to investigate; that is, What are standards, codes, and ideas of chastity, decency, propriety, modesty, etc., and whence do they arise? The ethnographical facts contain the answer to this question. . . . "Immoral" never means anything but contrary to the mores of the time and place. Therefore the mores and the morality may move together, and there is no permanent or universal standard by which right and truth in regard to these matters can be established and different folkways compared and criticised.

# WALTER
# T. STACE

WALTER TERENCE STACE (1886–    ) was
born in London and educated at Edinburgh
and Trinity College, Dublin. He served in
the Ceylon Civil Service from 1910 to 1932
and then taught philosophy at Princeton
University from 1932 until his retirement in
1955. His major works include: *A Critical
History of Greek Philosophy* (1920), *The
Theory of Knowledge and Existence* (1932),
*The Concept of Morals* (1937), *The Destiny
of Western Man* (1942), *Time and Eternity*
(1952), and *Religion and the Modern Mind*
(1952).

## Ethical Relativity*

### I

There is an opinion widely current nowadays in philosophical circles
which passes under the name of "ethical relativity." Exactly what this phrase
means or implies is certainly far from clear. But unquestionably it stands as
a label for the opinions of a group of ethical philosophers whose position
is roughly on the extreme left wing among the moral theorizers of the day.
And perhaps one may best understand it by placing it in contrast with the
opposite kind of extreme view against which, undoubtedly, it has arisen as
a protest. For among moral philosophers one may clearly distinguish a left
and a right wing. Those of the left wing are the ethical relativists. They are
the revolutionaries, the clever young men, the up to date. Those of the right
wing we may call the ethical absolutists. They are the conservatives and the
old-fashioned.

According to the absolutists there is but one eternally true and valid moral
code. This moral code applies with rigid impartiality to all men. What is a
duty for me must likewise be a duty for you. And this will be true whether
you are an Englishman, a Chinaman, or a Hottentot. If cannibalism is an
abomination in England or America, it is an abomination in central Africa,
notwithstanding that the African may think otherwise. The fact that he sees
nothing wrong in his cannibal practices does not make them for him morally
right. They are as much contrary to morality for him as they are for us.

* From *The Concept of Morals*, by W. T. Stace, Chaps. 1 and 2. Copyright, 1937, The
Macmillan Company. Used by the kind permission of the author and The Macmillan
Company.

The only difference is that he is an ignorant savage who does not know this. There is not one law for one man or race of men, another for another. There is not one moral standard for Europeans, another for Indians, another for Chinese. There is but one law, one standard, one morality, for all men. And this standard, this law, is absolute and unvarying.

Moreover, as the one moral law extends its dominion over all the corners of the earth, so too it is not limited in its application by any considerations of time or period. That which is right now was right in the centuries of Greece and Rome, nay, in the very ages of the cave man. That which is evil now was evil then. If slavery is morally wicked today, it was morally wicked among the ancient Athenians, notwithstanding that their greatest men accepted it as a necessary condition of human society. Their opinion did not make slavery a moral good for them. It only showed that they were, in spite of their otherwise noble conceptions, ignorant of what is truly right and good in this matter.

The ethical absolutist recognizes as a fact that moral customs and moral ideas differ from country to country and from age to age. This indeed seems manifest and not to be disputed. We think slavery morally wrong, the Greeks thought it morally unobjectionable. The inhabitants of New Guinea certainly have very different moral ideas from ours. But the fact that the Greeks or the inhabitants of New Guinea think something right does not make it right, even for them. Nor does the fact that we think the same things wrong make them wrong. They are *in themselves* either right or wrong. What we have to do is to discover which they are. What anyone thinks makes no difference. It is here just as it is in matters of physical science. We believe the earth to be a globe. Our ancestors may have thought it flat. This does not show that it *was* flat, and is *now* a globe. What it shows is that men having in other ages been ignorant about the shape of the earth have now learned the truth. So if the Greeks thought slavery morally legitimate, this does not indicate that it was for them and in that age morally legitimate, but rather that they were ignorant of the truth of the matter.

The ethical absolutist is not indeed committed to the opinion that his own, or our own, moral code is the true one. Theoretically at least he might hold that slavery is ethically justifiable, that the Greeks knew better than we do about this, that ignorance of the true morality lies with us and not with them. All that he is actually committed to is the opinion that, whatever the true moral code may be, it is always the same for all men in all ages. His view is not at all inconsistent with the belief that humanity has still much to learn in moral matters. If anyone were to assert that in five hundred years the moral conceptions of the present day will appear as barbarous to the people of that age as the moral conceptions of the middle ages appear to us now, he need not deny it. If anyone were to assert that the ethics of Christianity are by no means final, and will be superseded in future ages by vastly nobler moral ideals, he need not deny this either. For it is of the essence of his creed to believe that morality is in some sense objective, not man-made, not produced by human opinion; that its principles are real truths about which men have to learn—just as they have to learn about the shape of the world—about which they may have been ignorant in the past, and about which therefore they may well be ignorant now.

Thus although absolutism is conservative in the sense that it is regarded by the more daring spirits as an out of date opinion, it is not necessarily conservative in the sense of being committed to the blind support of existing moral ideas and institutions. If ethical absolutists are sometimes conservative in this sense too, that is their personal affair. Such conservatism is accidental, not essential to the absolutist's creed. There is no logical reason, in the nature of the case, why an absolutist should not be a communist, an anarchist, a surrealist, or an upholder of free love. The fact that he is usually none of these things may be accounted for in various ways. But it has nothing to do with the sheer logic of his ethical position. The sole opinion to which he is committed is that whatever is morally right (or wrong)— be it free love or monogamy or slavery or cannibalism or vegetarianism—is morally right (or wrong) for all men at all times. . . .

This brief and rough sketch of ethical absolutism is intended merely to form a background against which we may the more clearly indicate, by way of contrast, the theory of ethical relativity. Up to the present, therefore, I have not given any of the reasons which the absolutist can urge in favour of his case. It is sufficient for my purpose at the moment to state *what* he believes, without going into the question of *why* he believes it. But before proceeding to our next step—the explanation of ethical relativity—I think it will be helpful to indicate some of the historical causes (as distinguished from logical reasons) which have helped in the past to render absolutism a plausible interpretation of morality as understood by European peoples.

Our civilization is a Christian civilization. It has grown up, during nearly two thousand years, upon the soil of Christian monotheism. In this soil our whole outlook upon life, and consequently all our moral ideas, have their roots. They have been moulded by this influence. The wave of religious scepticism which, during the last half century, has swept over us, has altered this fact scarcely at all. The moral ideas even of those who most violently reject the dogmas of Christianity with their intellects are still Christian ideas. This will probably remain true for many centuries even if Christian theology, as a set of intellectual beliefs, comes to be wholly rejected by every educated person. It will probably remain true so long as our civilization lasts.

A child cannot, by changing in later life his intellectual creed, strip himself of the early formative moral influences of his childhood, though he can no doubt modify their results in various minor ways. With the outlook on life which was instilled into him in his early days he, in large measure, lives and dies. So it is with a civilization. And our civilization, whatever religious or irreligious views it may come to hold or reject, can hardly escape within its lifetime the moulding influences of its Christian origin. Now ethical absolutism was, in its central ideas, the product of Christian theology.

The connection is not difficult to detect. For morality has been conceived, during the Christian dispensation, as issuing from the will of God. That indeed was its single and all-sufficient source. There would be no point, for the naïve believer in the faith, in the philosopher's questions regarding the foundations of morality and the basis of moral obligation. Even to ask such questions is a mark of incipient religious scepticism. For the true believer the author of the moral law is God. What pleases God, what God commands—that is the definition of right. What displeases God, what he forbids—that is the definition of wrong. Now there is, for the Christian monotheist, only one God ruling over the entire universe. And this God is rational, self-consistent. He does not act upon whims. Consequently his will and his commands must be the same everywhere. They will be unvarying for all peoples and in all ages. If the heathen have other moral ideas than ours —inferior ideas—that can only be because they live in ignorance of the true God. If they knew God and his commands, their ethical precepts would be the same as ours.

Polytheistic creeds may well tolerate a number of diverse moral codes. For the God of the western hemisphere might have different views from those entertained by the God of the eastern hemisphere. And the God of the north might issue to his worshippers commands at variance with the commands issued to other peoples by the God of the south. But a monotheistic religion implies a single universal and absolute morality.

This explains why ethical absolutism, until very recently, was not only believed by philosophers but *taken for granted without any argument*. The ideas of philosophers, like the ideas of everyone else, are largely moulded by the civilizations in which they live. Their philosophies are largely attempts to state in abstract terms and in self-consistent language the stock of ideas which they have breathed in from the atmosphere of their social environment. This accounts for the large number of so-called "unrecognized presuppositions" with which systems of philosophy always abound. These presuppositions are simply the ideas which the authors of the systems have breathed in with the intellectual atmospheres by which they happen to be surrounded—which they have taken over therefore as a matter of course, without argument, without criticism, without even a suspicion that they might be false. . . .

We can now turn to the consideration of ethical relativity which is the proper subject of this chapter. The revolt of the relativists against absolutism is, I believe, part and parcel of the general revolutionary tendency of our times. In particular it is a result of the decay of belief in the dogmas of orthodox religion. Belief in absolutism was supported, as we have seen, by belief in Christian monotheism. And now that, in an age of widespread religious scepticism, that support is withdrawn, absolutism tends to collapse. Revolutionary movements are as a rule, at any rate in their first onset, purely negative. They attack and destroy. And ethical relativity is, in its essence, a purely negative creed. It is simply a denial of ethical absolutism. That is why the best way of explaining it is to begin by explaining ethical absolutism. If we understand that what the latter asserts the former denies, then we understand ethical relativity.

Any ethical position which denies that there is a single moral standard which is equally applicable to all men at all times may fairly be called a species of ethical relativity. There is not, the relativist asserts, merely one moral law, one code, one standard. There are many moral laws, codes, standards. What morality ordains in one place or age may be quite different from what morality ordains in another place or age. The moral code of Chinamen is quite different from that of Europeans, that of African savages quite different from both. Any morality, therefore, is relative to the age, the place, and the circumstances in which it is found. It is in no sense absolute.

This does not mean merely—as one might at first sight be inclined to suppose—that the very same kind of action which is *thought* right in one country and period may be *thought* wrong in another. This would be a mere platitude, the truth of which everyone would have to admit. Even the absolutist would admit this—would even wish to emphasize it—since he is well aware that different peoples have different sets of moral ideas, and his whole point is that some of these sets of ideas are false. What the relativist means to assert is, not this platitude, but that the very same kind of action which *is* right in one country and period may *be* wrong in another. And this, far from being a platitude, is a very startling assertion.

It is very important to grasp thoroughly the difference between the two ideas. For there is reason to think that many minds tend to find ethical relativity attractive because they fail to keep them clearly apart. It is so very obvious that moral ideas differ from country to country and from age to age. And it is so very easy, if you are mentally lazy, to suppose that to say this means the same as to say that no universal moral standard exists,—or in other words that it implies ethical relativity. We fail to see that the word "standard" is used in two different senses. It is perfectly true that, in one sense, there are many variable moral standards. We speak of judging a man by the standard of his time. And this implies that different times have different standards. And this, of course, is quite true. But when the word "standard" is used in this sense it means simply the set of moral ideas current during the period in question. It means what people *think* right, whether as a matter of fact it *is* right or not. On the other hand when the absolutist asserts that there exists a single universal moral "standard," he is not using the word in this sense at all. He means by "standard" what *is* right as distinct from what people merely think right. His point is that although what people think right varies in different countries and periods, yet what actually is right is everywhere and always the same. And it follows that when the ethical relativist disputes the position of the absolutist and denies that any universal moral standard exists he too means by "standard" what actually is right. But it is exceedingly easy, if we are not careful, to slip loosely from using the word in the first sense to using it in the second sense; and to suppose that the variability of moral beliefs is the same thing as the variability of what really is moral. And unless we keep the two senses of the word "standard" distinct, we are likely to think the creed of ethical relativity much more plausible than it actually is.

The genuine relativist, then, does not merely mean that Chinamen may think right what Frenchmen think wrong. He means that what *is* wrong for the Frenchman may *be* right for the Chinaman. And if one enquires how, in those circumstances, one is to know what actually is right in China or in France, the answer comes quite glibly. What is right in China is the same as what people think right in China; and what is right in France is the same as what people think right in France. So that, if you want to know what is moral in any particular country or age all you have to do is to ascertain what are the moral ideas current in that age or country. Those ideas are, *for that age or country*, right. Thus what is morally right is identified with what is thought to be morally right, and the distinction which we made above between these two is simply denied. To put the same thing in another way, it is denied that there can be or ought to be any distinction between the two senses of the word "standard." There is only one kind of standard of right and wrong, namely, the moral ideas current in any particular age or country.

Moral right *means* what people think morally right. It has no other meaning. What Frenchmen think right is, therefore, right *for Frenchmen*. And evidently one must conclude—though I am not aware that relativists are anxious to draw one's attention to such unsavoury but yet absolutely necessary

conclusions from their creed—that cannibalism is right for people who believe in it, that human sacrifice is right for those races which practice it,
and that burning widows alive was right for Hindus until the British stepped
in and compelled the Hindus to behave immorally by allowing their widows
to remain alive.

When it is said that, according to the ethical relativist, what is thought
right in any social group is right for that group, one must be careful not to
misinterpret this. The relativist does not, of course, mean that there actually
is an objective moral standard in France and a different objective standard
in England, and that French and British opinions respectively give us correct
information about these different standards. His point is rather that there
are no objectively true moral standards at all. There is no single universal
objective standard. Nor are there a variety of local objective standards. All
standards are subjective. People's subjective feelings about morality are the
only standards which exist.

To sum up. The ethical relativist consistently denies, it would seem, whatever the ethical absolutist asserts. For the absolutist there is a single universal
moral standard. For the relativist there is no such standard. There are only
local, ephemeral, and variable standards. For the absolutist there are two
senses of the word "standard." Standards in the sense of sets of current
moral ideas are relative and changeable. But the standard in the sense of
what is actually morally right is absolute and unchanging. For the relativist
no such distinction can be made. There is only one meaning of the word
standard, namely, that which refers to local and variable sets of moral ideas.
Or if it is insisted that the word must be allowed two meanings, then the
relativist will say that there is at any rate no actual example of a standard
in the absolute sense, and that the word as thus used is an empty name to
which nothing in reality corresponds; so that the distinction between the two
meanings becomes empty and useless. Finally—though this is merely saying
the same thing in another way—the absolutist makes a distinction between
what actually is right and what is thought right. The relativist rejects this
distinction and identifies what is moral with what is thought moral by certain
human beings or groups of human beings. . . .

. . . It was easy enough to believe in a single absolute morality in older
times when there was no anthropology, when all humanity was divided clearly
into two groups, Christian peoples and the "heathen." Christian peoples
knew and possessed the one true morality. The rest were savages whose moral
ideas could be ignored. But all this is changed. Greater knowledge has
brought greater tolerance. We can no longer exalt our own morality as alone
true, while dismissing all other moralities as false or inferior. The investigations of anthropologists have shown that there exist side by side in the world

a bewildering variety of moral codes. On this topic endless volumes have been written, masses of evidence piled up. Anthropologists have ransacked the Melanesian Islands, the jungles of New Guinea, the steppes of Siberia, the deserts of Australia, the forests of central Africa, and have brought back with them countless examples of weird, extravagant, and fantastic "moral" customs with which to confound us. We learn that all kinds of horrible practices are, in this, that, or the other place, regarded as essential to virtue. We find that there is nothing, or next to nothing, which has always and everywhere been regarded as morally good by all men. Where then is our universal morality? Can we, in face of all this evidence, deny that it is nothing but an empty dream?

This argument, taken by itself, is a very weak one. It relies upon a single set of facts—the variable moral customs of the world. But this variability of moral ideas is admitted by both parties to the dispute, and is capable of ready explanation upon the hypothesis of either party. The relativist says that the facts are to be explained by the non-existence of any absolute moral standard. The absolutist says that they are to be explained by human ignorance of what the absolute moral standard is. And he can truly point out that men have differed widely in their opinions about all manner of topics including the subject-matters of the physical sciences—just as much as they differ about morals. And if the various different opinions which men have held about the shape of the earth do not prove that it has no one real shape, neither do the various opinions which they have held about morality prove that there is no one true morality.

Thus the facts can be explained equally plausibly on either hypothesis. There is nothing in the facts themselves which compels us to prefer the relativistic hypothesis to that of the absolutist. And therefore the argument fails to prove the relativist conclusion. If that conclusion is to be established, it must be by means of other considerations.

This is the essential point. But I will add some supplementary remarks. The work of the anthropolgists, upon which ethical relativists seem to rely so heavily, has as a matter of fact added absolutely nothing *in principle* to what has always been known about the variability of moral ideas. Educated people have known all along that the Greeks tolerated sodomy, which in modern times has been regarded in some countries as an abominable crime; that the Hindus thought it a sacred duty to burn their widows; that trickery, now thought despicable, was once believed to be a virtue; that terrible torture was thought by our own ancestors only a few centuries ago to be a justifiable weapon of justice; that it was only yesterday that western peoples came to believe that slavery is immoral. Even the ancients knew very well that moral customs and ideas vary—witness the writings of Herodotus. Thus the

principle of the variability of moral ideas was well understood long before
modern anthropology was ever heard of. Anthropology has added nothing
to the knowledge of this principle except a mass of new and extreme examples
of it drawn from very remote sources. But to multiply examples of a principle
already well known and universally admitted adds nothing to the argument
which is built upon that principle. The discoveries of the anthropologists have
no doubt been of the highest importance in their own sphere. But in my considered opinion they have thrown no new light upon the special problems of
the moral philosopher.

Although the multiplication of examples has no logical bearing on the
argument, it does have an immense *psychological* effect upon people's minds.
These masses of anthropological learning are impressive. They are pro-
pounded in the sacred name of "science." If they are quoted in support of
ethical relativity—as they often are—people *think* that they must prove
something important. They bewilder and over-awe the simple-minded, batter
down their resistance, make them ready to receive humbly the doctrine of
ethical relativity from those who have acquired a reputation by their immense
learning and their claims to be "scientific." Perhaps this is why so much ado
is made by ethical relativists regarding the anthropological evidence. But we
must refuse to be impressed. We must discount all this mass of evidence
about the extraordinary moral customs of remote peoples. Once we have
admitted—as everyone who is instructed must have admitted these last two
thousand years without any anthropology at all—the principle that moral
ideas vary, all this new evidence adds nothing to the argument. And the argument itself proves nothing for the reasons already given. . . .

## II

. . . The case against [ethical relativity] consists, to a very large extent, in
urging that, if taken seriously and pressed to its logical conclusion, ethical
relativity can only end in destroying the conception of morality altogether,
in undermining its practical efficacy, in rendering meaningless many almost
universally accepted truths about human affairs, in robbing human beings of
any incentive to strive for a better world, in taking the life-blood out of every
ideal and every aspiration which has ever ennobled the life of man. In short,
the charge against it is that it revolts and outrages man's moral *feelings*.

To all such arguments it is always possible to reply that they are merely
pragmatic, mere appeals to feeling which have no logical cogency and no
scientific value. I will not for the moment argue the question whether feelings
have any value at all in the search for truth, or whether they ought to be
utterly disregarded. . . . For the moment let us rather see what these arguments of the anti-relativist are. We will frankly recognise from the outset their

quasi-emotional character. If we do this, we shall perhaps be saved from disappointment and misunderstanding. The reader should not be either disappointed or surprised if in what follows I seem to him to be merely appealing to feelings and not to facts or logic. This in fact is what I shall be doing. And I shall be doing it because it is the only way in which the case of the anti-relativist can be communicated to the reader. . . . It cannot be wrong, it cannot be irrelevant for us, and for the relativist himself, to see what his doctrine actually implies in the way of practical consequences; to see how it tallies with the demands of the "moral consciousness." . . .

First of all, then, ethical relativity, in asserting that the moral standards of particular social groups are the only standards which exist, renders meaningless all propositions which attempt to compare these standards with one another in respect of their moral worth. And this is a very serious matter indeed. We are accustomed to think that the moral ideas of one nation or social group may be "higher" or "lower" than those of another. We believe, for example, that Christian ethical ideals are nobler than those of the savage races of central Africa. Probably most of us would think that the Chinese moral standards are higher than those of the inhabitants of New Guinea. In short we habitually compare one civilization with another and judge the sets of ethical ideas to be found in them to be some better, some worse. The fact that such judgments are very difficult to make with any justice, and that they are frequently made on very superficial and prejudiced grounds, has no bearing on the question now at issue. The question is whether such judgments have any *meaning*. We habitually assume that they have.

But on the basis of ethical relativity they can have none whatever. For the relativist must hold that there is no *common* standard which can be applied to the various civilizations judged. Any such comparison of moral standards implies the existence of some superior standard which is applicable to both. And the existence of any such standard is precisely what the relativist denies. According to him the Christian standard is applicable only to Christians, the Chinese standard only to Chinese, the New Guinea standard only to the inhabitants of New Guinea.

What is true of comparisons between the moral standards of different races will also be true of comparisons between those of different ages. It is not unusual to ask such questions as whether the standard of our own day is superior to that which existed among our ancestors five hundred years ago. And when we remember that our ancestors employed slaves, practiced barbaric physical tortures, and burnt people alive, we may be inclined to think that it is. At any rate we assume that the question is one which has meaning and is capable of rational discussion. But if the ethical relativist is right, whatever we assert on this subject must be totally meaningless. For here again there is no common standard which could form the basis of any such judg-ments.

This in its turn implies that the whole notion of moral *progress* is a sheer delusion. Progress means an advance from lower to higher, from worse to better. But on the basis of ethical relativity it has no meaning to say that the standards of this age are better (or worse) than those of a previous age. For there is no common standard by which both can be measured. Thus it is nonsense to say that the morality of the New Testament is higher than that of the Old. And Jesus Christ, if he imagined that he was introducing into the world a higher ethical standard than existed before his time, was merely deluded.

There is indeed one way in which the ethical relativist can give some sort of meaning to judgments of higher or lower as applied to the moral ideas of different races or ages. What he will have to say is that we assume *our* standards to be the best simply because they are ours. And we judge other standards by our own. If we say that Chinese moral codes are better than those of African cannibals, what we *mean* by this is that they are better *according to our standards*. We mean, that is to say, that Chinese standards are *more like our own* than African standards are. "Better" accordingly *means* "more like us." "Worse" means "less like us." It thus becomes clear that judgments of better and worse in such cases do not express anything that is really true at all. They merely give expression to our perfectly groundless satisfaction with our own ideas. In short, they give expression to nothing but our egotism and self-conceit. Our moral ideals are not really better than those of the savage. We are simply deluded by our egotism into thinking they are. The African savage has just as good a right to think his morality the best as we have to think ours the best. His opinion is just as well grounded as ours, or rather both opinions are equally groundless. And on this view Jesus Christ can only have been led to the quite absurd belief that his ethical precepts were better than those of Moses by his personal vanity. . . . The change which Jesus Christ actually brought about was merely a change from one set of moral ideas to another. And as the new set of ideas was in no way better than the set it displaced—to say that it was better would be meaningless for the reasons already given—the change was really a sheer waste of time. And of course it likewise follows that anyone who in the future tries to im-prove the moral ideas of humanity will also be wasting his time.

Thus the ethical relativist must treat all judgments comparing different moralities as either entirely meaningless; or, if this course appears too drastic, he has the alternative of declaring that they have for their meaning-content nothing except the vanity and egotism of those who pass them. We are asked to believe that the highest moral ideals of humanity are not really any better than those of an Australian bushman. But if this is so, why strive for higher ideals? Thus the heart is taken out of all effort, and the meaning out of all human ideals and aspirations.

The ethical relativist may perhaps say that he is being misjudged. It is not true that, on the basis of his doctrine, all effort for moral improvement is vain. For if we take such a civilization as our own, and if we assume that the standard of morals theoretically accepted by it is that of Christian ethics, then there is surely plenty of room for improvement and "progress" in the way of making our practice accord with our theory. Effort may legitimately be directed towards getting people to live up to whatever standards they profess to honour. Such effort will be, on the relativistic basis, perfectly meaningful; for it does not imply a comparison of standards by reference to a common standard, but only a comparison of actual achievements with an admitted and accepted standard within a social group.

Now I do not believe that even this plea can be accepted. For as soon as it comes to be effectively realized that our moral standard is no better than that of barbarians, why should anyone trouble to live up to it? It would be much easier to adopt some lower standard, to preach it assiduously until everyone believes it, when it would automatically become right. But even if we waive this point, and admit that the exhortation to practice what we preach may be meaningful, this does not touch the issue which was raised above. It will still be true that efforts to improve moral *beliefs*, as distinguished from moral *practice*, will be futile. It will still be true that Jesus Christ would have done better had he tried only to persuade humanity to live up to the old barbaric standards than he did in trying to propagate among them a new and more enlightened moral code. It will still be true that any reformer in the future who attempts to make men see even more noble ideals than those which we have inherited from the reformers of the past will be wasting his time.

I come now to a second point. Up to the present I have allowed it to be taken tacitly for granted that, though judgments comparing different races and ages in respect of the worth of their moral codes are impossible for the ethical relativist, yet judgments of comparison between individuals living within the same social group would be quite possible. For individuals living within the same social group would presumably be subject to the same moral code, that of their group, and this would therefore constitute, as between these individuals, a common standard by which they could both be measured. We have not here, as we had in the other case, the difficulty of the absence of any common standard of comparison. It should therefore be possible for the ethical relativist to say quite meaningfully that President Lincoln was a better man than some criminal or moral imbecile of his own time and country, or that Jesus was a better man than Judas Iscariot.

But is even this minimum of moral judgment really possible on relativist grounds? It seems to me that it is not. For when once the whole of humanity is abandoned as the area covered by a single moral standard, what smaller areas are to be adopted as the *loci* of different standards? Where are we to draw the lines of demarcation? We can split up humanity, perhaps,—though the procedure will be very arbitrary—into races, races into nations, nations into tribes, tribes into families, families into individuals. Where are we going to draw the *moral* boundaries? Does the *locus* of a particular moral standard reside in a race, a nation, a tribe, a family, or an individual? Perhaps the blessed phrase "social group" will be dragged in to save the situation. Each such group, we shall be told, has its own moral code which is, for it, right. But what *is* a "group"? Can anyone define it or give its boundaries? . . .

The difficulty is not, as might be thought, merely an academic difficulty of logical definition. If that were all, I should not press the point. But the ambiguity has practical consequences which are disastrous for morality. No one is likely to say that moral codes are confined within the arbitrary limits of the geographical divisions of countries. Nor are the notions of race, nation, or political state likely to help us. To bring out the essentially practical character of the difficulty let us put it in the form of concrete questions. Does the American nation constitute a "group" having a single moral standard? Or does the standard of what I ought to do change continuously as I cross the continent in a railway train? Do different States of the Union have different moral codes? Perhaps every town and village has its own peculiar standard. This may at first sight seem reasonable enough. "In Rome do as Rome does" may seem as good a rule in morals as it is in etiquette. But can we stop there? Within the village are numerous cliques each having its own set of ideas. Why should not each of these claim to be bound only by its own special and peculiar moral standards? And if it comes to that, why should not the gangsters of Chicago claim to constitute a group having its own morality, so that its murders and debaucheries must be viewed as "right" by the only standard which can legitimately be applied to it? And if it be answered that the nation will not tolerate this, that may be so. But this is to put the foundation of right simply in the superior force of the majority. In that case whoever is stronger will be right, however monstrous his ideas and actions. And if we cannot deny to any set of people the right to have its own morality, is it not clear that, in the end, we cannot even deny this right to the individual? Every individual man and woman can put up, on this view, an irrefutable claim to be judged by no standard except his or her own.

If these arguments are valid, the ethical relativist cannot really maintain that there is anywhere to be found a moral standard binding upon anybody against his will. And he cannot maintain that, even within the social group, there is a common standard as between individuals. And if that is so, then even judgments to the effect that one man is morally better than another become meaningless. All moral valuation thus vanishes. There is nothing to prevent each man from being a rule unto himself. The result will be moral chaos and the collapse of all effective standards. . . .

But even if we assume that the difficulty about defining moral groups has been surmounted, a further difficulty presents itself. Suppose that we have now definitely decided what are the exact boundaries of the social group within which a moral standard is to be operative. And we will assume—as is invariably done by relativists themselves—that this group is to be some actually existing social community such as a tribe or nation. How are we to know, even then, what actually *is* the moral standard within that group? How is anyone to know? How is even a member of the group to know? For there are certain to be within the group—at least this will be true among advanced peoples—wide differences of opinion as to what is right, what wrong. Whose opinion, then, is to be taken as representing *the* moral standard of the group? Either we must take the opinion of the majority within the group, or the opinion of some minority. If we rely upon the ideas of the majority, the results will be disastrous. Wherever there is found among a people a small band of select spirits, or perhaps one man, working for the establishment of higher and nobler ideals than those commonly accepted by the group, we shall be compelled to hold that, for that people at that time, the majority are right, and that the reformers are wrong and are preaching what it immoral. We shall have to maintain, for example, that Jesus was preaching immoral doctrines to the Jews. Moral goodness will have to be equated always with the mediocre and sometimes with the definitely base and ignoble. If on the other hand we say that the moral standard of the group is to be identified with the moral opinions of some minority, then what minority is this to be? We cannot answer that it is to be the minority composed of the best and most enlightened individuals of the group. This would involve us in a palpably vicious circle. For by what standard are these individuals to be judged the best and the most enlightened? There is no principle by which we could select the right minority. And therefore we should have to consider every minority as good as every other. And this means that we should have no logical right whatever to resist the claim of the gangsters of Chicago—if such a claim were made—that their practices represent the highest standards of American morality. It means in the end that every individual is to be bound by no standard save his own.

The ethical relativists are great empiricists. *What* is the actual moral standard of any group can only be discovered, they tell us, by an examination on the ground of the moral opinions and customs of that group. But will they tell us how they propose to decide, when they get to the ground, which of the many moral opinions they are sure to find there is *the* right one in that group? To some extent they will be able to do this for the Melanesian Islanders—from whom apparently all lessons in the nature of morality are in future to be taken. But it is certain that they cannot do it for advanced peoples whose members have learnt to think for themselves and to entertain among themselves a wide variety of opinions. They cannot do it unless they accept the calamitous view that the ethical opinion of the majority is always right. We are left therefore once more with the conclusion that, even within a particular social group, anybody's moral opinion is as good as anybody else's, and that every man is entitled to be judged by his own standards.

Finally, not only is ethical relativity disastrous in its consequences for moral theory. It cannot be doubted that it must tend to be equally disastrous in its impact upon practical conduct. If men come really to believe that one moral standard is as good as another, they will conclude that their own moral standard has nothing special to recommend it. They might as well then slip down to some lower and easier standard. It is true that, for a time, it may be possible to hold one view in theory and to act practically upon another. But ideas, even philosophical ideas, are not so ineffectual that they can remain for ever idle in the upper chambers of the intellect. In the end they seep down to the level of practice. They get themselves acted on. . . .

These, then, are the main arguments which the anti-relativist will urge against ethical relativity. And perhaps finally he will attempt a diagnosis of the social, intellectual, and psychological conditions of our time to which the emergence of ethical relativism is to be attributed. His diagnosis will be somewhat as follows.

We have abandoned, perhaps with good reason, the oracles of the past. Every age, of course, does this. But in our case it seems that none of us knows any more whither to turn. We do not know what to put in the place of that which has gone. What ought we, supposedly civilized peoples, to aim at? What are to be our ideals? What is right? What is wrong? What is beautiful? What is ugly? No man knows. We drift helplessly in this direction and that. We know not where we stand nor whither we are going.

There are, of course, thousands of voices frantically shouting directions. But they shout one another down, they contradict one another, and the upshot is mere uproar. And because of this confusion there creeps upon us an insidious scepticism and despair. Since no one knows what the truth is, we will deny that there is any truth. Since no one knows what right is, we will deny that there is any right. Since no one knows what the beautiful is, we will deny that there is any beauty. Or at least we will say—what comes to the same thing—that what people (the people of any particular age, region, society)—think to be true is true *for them*; that what people think morally right is morally right *for them*; that what people think beautiful is beautiful *for them*. There is no common and objective standard in any of these matters. Since all the voices contradict one another, they must be all equally right (or equally wrong, for it makes no difference which we say). It is from the practical confusion of our time that these doctrines issue. When all the despair and defeatism of our distracted age are expressed in abstract concepts, are erected into a philosophy, it is then called relativism—ethical relativism, esthetic relativism, relativity of truth. Ethical relativity is simply defeatism in morals.

And the diagnosis will proceed. Perhaps, it will say, the current pessimism as to our future is unjustified. But there is undoubtedly a wide spread feeling that our civilization is rushing downwards to the abyss. If this should be true, and if nothing should check the headlong descent, then perhaps some historian of the future will seek to disentangle the causes. The causes will, of course, be found to be multitudinous and enormously complicated. And one must not exaggerate the relative importance of any of them. But it can hardly be doubted that our future historian will include somewhere in his list the failure of the men of our generation to hold steadfastly before themselves the notion of an (even comparatively) unchanging moral idea. He will cite that feebleness of intellectual and moral grasp which has led them weakly to harbour the belief that no one moral aim is really any better than any other, that each is good and true for those who entertain it. This meant, he will surely say, that men had given up in despair the struggle to attain moral truth. Civilization lives in and through its upward struggle. Whoever despairs and gives up the struggle, whether it be an individual or a whole civilization, is already inwardly dead.

## CULTURAL RELATIVISM—SUGGESTED READINGS

Asch, S. E., *Social Psychology*, New York, Prentice-Hall, 1952, Chap. 13. (critic)

Benedict, R., *Patterns of Culture*, Boston, Houghton Mifflin, 1934. (proponent)

Duncker, K., "Ethical Relativity?" *Mind*, XLVIII (1939), pp. 39–57. (critic)

Ginsberg, M., *Essays in Sociology and Social Philosophy*, Vol. I, *On the Diversity of Morals*, New York, Macmillan, 1957, esp. Chap. 7. (critic)

Herskovits, M. J., *Man and His Works*, New York, Knopf, 1948, Chap. 5. (proponent)

Westermarck, E., *Ethical Relativity*, New York, Harcourt, Brace, 1932. (proponent)

# C. FREEDOM *VS.* DETERMINISM

Few problems in the history of moral philosophy have occasioned more dispute than the problem of freedom *versus* determinism. The question at issue is whether all human choices and actions are wholly determined by past causes. When we attempt to answer this question, significant areas of our experience seem to come into conflict.

For many reasons, we appear to be committed to a belief in human freedom. For instance, when we make decisions and act upon them, we seem to be directly aware of our freedom to choose and to pursue other alternatives than those we have selected. Furthermore, a belief in human freedom seems to be necessary if we are to justify many of our ordinary feelings and judgments, and much of our behavior. Thus, we feel obligations to perform various moral duties; we feel regret when we perform wrong actions; we hold other persons morally responsible for at least some of their actions; and we are willing at times to give praise and blame, or rewards and punishments, to those whose actions seem to merit such awards. In each of these cases, we seem to assume the presence of a capacity to choose freely among real alternatives.

On the other hand, the progress of the sciences in coming to understand human behavior suggests that there are definite causes for every human choice and action. It would appear that if we could learn all the scientific laws which govern human behavior, we would be able to predict in detail every future choice and action of any given individual. And, if this be so, we seem driven to the conclusion that freedom of choice and action are illusions.

In the following selections, HOLBACH presents the traditional case in favor of determinism. In contrast, PRICE and JAMES state their reasons for rejecting determinism and for continuing to believe in the reality of human freedom. Finally, STACE argues that the entire dispute is verbal. He suggests that when we clarify the key terms at issue, we shall see that it is possible to retain a belief in human freedom without rejecting a belief in the causation of human choice and behavior.

spurred him on to this folly. Madness is a state, that depends upon the heat of the blood, not upon the will. A fanatic or a hero, braves death as necessarily as a more phlegmatic man or a coward flies from it.[2] . . .

To be undeceived on the system of his free agency, man has simply to recur to the motive by which his will is determined; he will always find this motive is out of his own controul. It is said: that in consequence of an idea to which the mind gives birth, man acts freely if he encounters no obstacle. But the question is, what gives birth to this idea in his brain? was he the master either to prevent it from presenting itself, or from renewing itself in his brain? Does not this idea depend either upon objects that strike him exteriorly and in despite of himself, or upon causes, that without his knowledge, act within himself and modify his brain? Can he prevent his eyes, cast without design upon any object whatever, from giving him an idea of this object, and from moving his brain? He is not more master of the obstacles; they are the necessary effects of either interior or exterior causes, which always act according to their given properties. A man insults a coward, this necessarily irritates him against his insulter, but his will cannot vanquish the obstacle that cowardice places to the object of his desire, because his natural conformation, which does not depend upon himself, prevents his having courage. In this case, the coward is insulted in despite of himself; and against his will is obliged patiently to brook the insult he has received.

The partisans of the system of free agency appear ever to have confounded constraint with necessity. Man believes he acts as a free agent, every time he does not see any thing that places obstacles to his actions; he does not perceive that the motive which causes him to will, is always necessary and independent of himself. A prisoner loaded with chains is compelled to remain in prison; but he is not a free agent in the desire to emancipate himself; his chains prevent him from acting, but they do not prevent him from willing; he would save himself if they would loose his fetters; but he would not save himself as a free agent; fear or the idea of punishment would be sufficient motives for his action.

Man may, therefore, cease to be restained, without, for that reason, becoming a free agent: in whatever manner he acts, he will act necessarily, according to motives by which he shall be determined. He may be compared

----

[2] There is, in point of fact, no difference between the man that is cast out of the window by another, and the man who throws himself out of it, except that the impulse in the first instance comes immediately from without, whilst that which determines the fall in the second case, springs from within his own peculiar machine, having its more remote cause also exterior. When Mucius Scævola held his hand in the fire, he was as much acting under the influence of necessity (caused by interior motives) that urged him to this strange action, as if his arm had been held by strong men: pride, despair, the desire of braving his enemy, a wish to astonish him, an anxiety to intimidate him, etc., were the invisible chains that held his hand bound to the fire. . . .

to a heavy body that finds itself arrested in its descent by any obstacle whatever: take away this obstacle, it will gravitate or continue to fall; but who shall say this dense body is free to fall or not? Is not its descent the necessary effect of its own specific gravity? The virtuous Socrates submitted to the laws of his country, although they were unjust; and though the doors of his jail were left open to him, he would not save himself; but in this he did not act as a free agent: the invisible chains of opinion, the secret love of decorum, the inward respect for the laws, even when they were iniquitous, the fear of tarnishing his glory, kept him in his prison; they were motives sufficiently powerful with this enthusiast for virtue, to induce him to wait death with tranquillity; it was not in his power to save himself, because he could find no potential motive to bring him to depart, even for an instant, from those principles to which his mind was accustomed.

Man, it is said, frequently acts against his inclination, from whence it is falsely concluded he is a free agent; but when he appears to act contrary to his inclination, he is always determined to it by some motive sufficiently efficacious to vanquish this inclination. A sick man, with a view to his cure, arrives at conquering his repugnance to the most disgusting remedies: the fear of pain, or the dread of death, then becomes necessary motives; consequently this sick man cannot be said to act freely.

When it is said, that man is not a free agent, it is not pretended to compare him to a body moved by a simple impulsive cause: he contains within himself causes inherent to his existence; he is moved by an interior organ, which has its own peculiar laws, and is itself necessarily determined in consequence of ideas formed from perceptions resulting from sensations which it receives from exterior objects. As the mechanism of these sensations, of these perceptions, and the manner they engrave ideas on the brain of man, are not known to him; because he is unable to unravel all these motions; because he cannot perceive the chain of operations in his soul, or the motive principle that acts within him, he supposes himself a free agent; which, literally translated, signifies, that he moves himself by himself; that he determines himself without cause: when he rather ought to say, that he is ignorant how or for why he acts in the manner he does. It is true the soul enjoys an activity peculiar to itself: but it is equally certain that this activity would never be displayed, if some motive or some cause did not put it in a condition to exercise itself: at least it will not be pretended that the soul is able either to love or to hate without being moved, without knowing the objects, without having some idea of their qualities. Gunpowder has unquestionably a particular activity, but this activity will never display itself, unless fire be applied to it; this, however, immediately sets it in motion.

It is the great complication of motion in man, it is the variety of his action, it is the multiplicity of causes that move him, whether simultaneously or in continual succession, that persuades him he is a free agent: if all his motions were simple, if the causes that move him did not confound themselves with each other, if they were distinct, if his machine were less complicated, he would perceive that all his actions were necessary, because he would be enabled to recur instantly to the cause that made him act. A man who should be always obliged to go towards the west, would always go on that side; but he would feel that, in so going, he was not a free agent: if he had another sense, as his actions or his motion, augmented by a sixth, would be still more varied and much more complicated, he would believe himself still more a free agent than he does with his five senses.

It is, then, for want of recurring to the causes that move him; for want of being able to analyze, from not being competent to decompose the complicated motion of his machine, that man believes himself a free agent: it is only upon his own ignorance that he founds the profound yet deceitful notion he has of his free agency; that he builds those opinions which he brings forward as a striking proof of his pretended freedom of action. If, for a short time, each man was willing to examine his own peculiar actions, search out their true motives to discover their concatenation, he would remain convinced that the sentiment he has of his natural free agency, is a chimera that must speedily be destroyed by experience. . . .

Man either sees or believes he sees much more distinctly the necessary relation of effects with their causes in natural philosophy than in the human heart: at least he sees in the former sensible causes constantly produce sensible effects, ever the same, when the circumstances are alike. After this he hesitates not to look upon physical effects as necessary; whilst he refuses to acknowledge necessity in the acts of the human will: these he has, without any just foundation, attributed to a motive-power that acts independently by its own peculiar energy, which is capable of modifying itself without the concurrence of exterior causes, and which is distinguished from all material or physical beings. Agriculture is founded upon the assurance, afforded by experience, that the earth, cultivated and sown in a certain manner, when it has otherwise the requisite qualities, will furnish grain, fruit and flowers, either necessary for subsistence or pleasing to the senses. If things were considered without prejudice, it would be perceived, that in morals, education is nothing more than *the agriculture of the mind:* that, like the earth, by reason of its natural disposition, of the culture bestowed upon it, of the seeds with which it is sown, of the seasons, more or less favourable that conduct it to maturity, we may be assured that the soul will produce either virtue or vice—*moral fruit*, that will be either salubrious for man or baneful to society. *Morals* is the science of the relations that subsist between the minds, the wills, and the actions of men, in the same manner that geometry is the science of the relations that are found between bodies. Morals would be a chimera and would have no certain principles, if it was not founded upon the knowledge of the motives which must necessarily have an influence upon the human will, and which must necessarily determine the actions of human beings. . . .

In despite of the gratuitous ideas which man has formed to himself on his pretended free agency; in defiance of the illusions of this supposed intimate sense, which, maugre his experience, persuades him that he is master of his will; all his institutions are really founded upon necessity: on this, as on a variety of other occasions, practice throws aside speculation. Indeed, if it was not believed that certain motives embraced the power requisite to determine the will of man, to arrest the progress of his passions; to direct them towards an end, to modify him, of what use would be the faculty of speech? What benefit could arise from education, from legislation, from morals, even from religion itself? What does education achieve, save give the first impulse to the human will; make man contract habits; oblige him to persist in them; furnish him with motives, whether true or false, to act after a given manner? When the father either menaces his son with punishment, or promises him a reward, is he not convinced these things will act upon his will? What does legislation attempt except it be to present to the citizens of a state those motives which are supposed necessary to determine them to perform some actions that are considered worthy; to abstain from committing others that are looked upon as unworthy? What is the object of morals, if it be not to show man that his interest exacts he should suppress the momentary ebullition of his passions, with a view to promote a more certain happiness, a more lasting well-being, than can possibly result from the gratification of his transitory desires? Does not the religion of all countries suppose the human race, together with the entire of nature, submitted to the irresistible will of a necessary being who regulates their condition after the eternal laws of immutable wisdom? Is not this God, which man adores, the absolute master of their destiny? Is it not this divine being who chooses and who rejects? The anathemas fulminated by religion, the promises it holds forth, are they not founded upon the idea of the effects these chimeras will necessarily produce upon ignorant and timid people? Is not man brought into existence by this kind Divinity without his own knowledge? Is he not obliged to play a part against his will? Does not either his happiness or his misery depend on the part he plays?[3]

[3] Every religion is evidently founded upon fatalism. Among the Greeks they supposed men were punished for their *necessary* faults—as may be seen in Orestes, in Œdipus, etc., who only committed crimes predicted by the oracles. Christans have made vain efforts to justify God Almighty in throwing the faults of men on their *free will*, which is opposed to *Predestination,* another name for *fatalism.* However, their system of *Grace* will by no

Education, then, is only necessity shown to children: legislation, is necessity shown to the members of the body politic: morals, is the necessity of the relations subsisting between men, shown to reasonable beings: in short, man grants necessity in every thing for which he believes he has certain unerring experience: that of which he does not comprehend the necessary connexion of causes with their effects he styles probability: he would not act as he does, if he was not convinced, or, at least, if he did not presume that certain effects will necessarily follow his actions. . . .

From all that has been advanced in this chapter, it results, that in no one moment of his existence is man a free agent. He is not the architect of his own conformation, which he holds from nature; he has no controul over his own ideas, or over the modification of his brain; these are due to causes, that, in despite of him, and without his own knowledge, unceasingly act upon him; he is not the master of not loving or coveting that which he finds amiable or desirable; he is not capable of refusing to deliberate, when he is uncertain of the effects certain objects will produce upon him; he cannot avoid choosing that which he believes will be most advantageous to him; in the moment when his will is determined by his choice he is not competent to act otherwise than he does. In what instance, then, is he the master of his own actions? In what moment is he a free agent?[4]

That which a man is about to do, is always a consequence of that which he has been—of that which he is—of that which he has done up to the moment of the action: his total and actual existence, considered under all its possible circumstances, contains the sum of all the motives to the action

---

means obviate the difficulty, for God gives grace only to those whom he pleases. In all countries religion has no other foundation than the fatal decrees of an irresistible being who arbitrarily decides the fate of his creatures. All theological hypotheses turn upon this point; and yet those theologians who regard the system of fatalism as false or dangerous, do not see that the Fall of Angels, Original Sin, Predestination, the System of Grace, the small number of the Elect, etc., incontestably prove that religion is a true system of fatalism.

[4] The question of *Free Will* may be reduced to this:—Liberty, or Free Will, cannot be associated with any known functions of the soul; for the soul, at the moment in which it acts, deliberates, or wills, cannot act, deliberate, or will otherwise than it does, because a thing cannot exist and not exist at the same time. Now, it is my will, such as it is, that makes me deliberate; my deliberation, that makes me choose; my choice that makes me act; my determination that makes me execute that which my deliberation has made me choose, and I have only deliberated because I have had motives which rendered it impossible for me not to be willing to deliberate. Thus liberty is not found either in the will, in the deliberation, in the choice, or in the action. Theologians must not, therefore, connect liberty with these operations of the soul, otherwise there will be a contradiction of ideas. If the soul is not free when it wills, deliberates, chooses, or acts, will theologians tell us when it can exercise its liberty?

It is evident that the system of liberty, or free will, has been invented to exonerate God from the evil that is done in this world. But is it not from God man received this liberty? Is it not from God he received the faculty of choosing evil and rejecting the good? If so, God created him with a determination to sin, else liberty is essential to man and independent of God.

he is about to commit; this is a principle the truth of which no thinking being will be able to refuse accrediting: his life is a series of necessary moments; his conduct, whether good or bad, virtuous or vicious, useful or prejudicial, either to himself or to others, is a concatenation of action, as necessary as all the moments of his existence. *To live*, is to exist in a necessary mode during the points of that duration which succeed each other necessarily: *to will*, is to acquiesce or not in remaining such as he is: *to be free*, is to yield to the necessary motives he carries within himself.

If he understood the play of his organs, if he was able to recall to himself all the impulsions they have received, all the modifications they have undergone, all the effects they have produced, he would perceive that all his actions are submitted to that *fatality*, which regulates his own particular system, as it does the entire system of the universe: no one effect in him, any more than in nature, produces itself by *chance*; this . . . is a word void of sense. All that passes in him; all that is done by him; as well as all that happens in nature, or that is attributed to her, is derived from necessary causes, which act according to necessary laws, and which produce necessary effects from whence necessarily flow others.

*Fatality*, is the eternal, the immutable, the necessary order, established in nature; or the indispensable connexion of causes, that act, with the effects they operate. Conforming to this order, heavy bodies fall; light bodies rise; that which is analogous in matter reciprocally attracts; that which is heterogeneous mutually repels; man congregates himself in society, modifies each his fellow; becomes either virtuous or wicked; either contributes to his mutual happiness, or reciprocates his misery; either loves his neighbour, or hates his companion necessarily, according to the manner in which the one acts upon the other. From whence it may be seen, that the same necessity which regulates the physical, also regulates the moral world, in which every thing is in consequence submitted to fatality. Man, in running over, frequently without his own knowledge, often in despite of himself, the route which nature has marked out for him, resembles a swimmer who is obliged to follow the current that carries him along: he believes himself a free agent, because he sometimes consents, sometimes does not consent, to glide with the stream, which, notwithstanding, always hurries him forward; he believes himself the master of his condition, because he is obliged to use his arms under the fear of sinking. . . .

The false ideas he has formed to himself upon free agency, are in general thus founded: there are certain events which he judges *necessary*; either because he sees that they are effects constantly and invariably linked to certain causes, which nothing seems to prevent; or because he believes he has discovered the chain of causes and effects that is put in play to produce those events: whilst he contemplates as *contingent* other events of whose causes he is ignorant, and with whose mode of acting he is unacquainted: but in nature, where every thing is connected by one common bond, there exists no effect without a cause. In the moral as well as in the physical world, every thing that happens is a necessary consequence of causes, either visible or concealed, which are of necessity obliged to act after their peculiar essences. *In man, free agency is nothing more than necessity contained within himself.*

# RICHARD PRICE

RICHARD PRICE (1723–91) was born in Wales. He served as an Unitarian minister in various English communities throughout his life and also wrote extensively upon scientific, political, and philosophical subjects. During his own day, he was most widely known for defending the causes of both the American and French revolutions. His major contribution to philosophy was *A Review of the Principal Questions in Morals* (1758).

## Practical Virtue Supposes Liberty*

*Practical* virtue supposes liberty. Whether all will acknowledge this or not, it cannot be omitted.

The *liberty* I here mean is the same with the power of *acting* and *determining:* And it is self-evident, that where such a power is wanting, there can be no moral capacities. As far as it is true of a being that he *acts*, so far he must *himself* be the cause of the action, and therefore not necessarily determined to act. Let any one try to put a sense on the expressions; *I will; I act;* which is consistent with supposing, that the volition or action does not proceed from myself. Virtue supposes determination, and determination supposes a determiner; and a determiner that determines not himself, is a palpable contradiction. Determination requires an efficient cause. If this cause is the being himself, I plead for no more. If not, then it is no longer *his* determination; that is, *he* is no longer the determiner, but the motive, or whatever else any one will say to be the cause of the determination. To ask, what effects *our* determinations, is the very same with asking who did an action, after being informed that such a one did it. In short; who must not *feel* the absurdity of

* From *A Review of the Principal Questions in Morals*, by Richard Price, Chap. 8 (1758).

saying, *my* volitions are produced by a *foreign* cause, that is, are not *mine*; I determine *voluntarily*, and yet *necessarily?*—We have, in truth, the same constant and necessary consciousness of liberty, that we have that we think, chuse, will, or even exist; and whatever to the contrary any persons may say, it is impossible for them in earnest to think they have no active, self-moving powers, and are not the causes of *their own* volitions, or not to ascribe to *themselves*, what they must be conscious *they* think and do.

But, not to enter much further into a question which has been strangely darkened by fallacious reasonings, and where there is so much danger of falling into a confusion of ideas, I would only observe, that it is hard to say what virtue and vice, commendation and blame, mean, if they do not suppose *agency*, free choice, and an absolute dominion over our resolutions.—It has always been the *general*, and it is evidently the *natural* sense of mankind, that they cannot be accountable for what they have no power to avoid. Nothing can be more glaringly absurd, than applauding or reproaching ourselves for what we were no more the causes of, than our own beings, and what it was no more possible for us to prevent, than the returns of the seasons, or the revolutions of the planets. The whole language of men, all their practical sentiments and schemes, and the whole frame and order of human affairs, are founded upon the notion of liberty, and are utterly inconsistent with the supposition, that nothing is made to depend on ourselves, or that our purposes and determinations are not subjected to our own command, but the result of physical laws, not possible to be resisted.

# WILLIAM JAMES

WILLIAM JAMES (1842–1910), one of America's foremost philosophers, taught at Harvard University. An important psychologist as well as a philosopher, he founded the first American experimental laboratory for psychology in 1876. In philosophy, he was one of the leading pragmatists and sought through his writings to show how the principles of this school might be applied in the solution of traditional philosophical problems. His major works include: *The Principles of Psychology* (1890), *The Will to Believe and Other Essays in Popular Philosophy* (1897), *The Varieties of Religious Experience* (1902), *Pragmatism* (1907), *A Pluralistic Universe* (1909), and *Essays in Radical Empiricism* (1912).

## The Dilemma of Determinism*

A common opinion prevails that the juice has ages ago been pressed out of the free-will controversy, and that no new champion can do more than warm up stale arguments which every one has heard. This is a radical mistake. I know of no subject less worn out, or in which inventive genius has a better chance of breaking open new ground—not, perhaps, of forcing a conclusion or of coercing assent, but of deepening our sense of what the issue between the two parties really is, of what the ideas of fate and of free will imply. . . . If I can make two of the necessarily implied corollaries of determinism clearer to you than they have been made before, I shall have made it possible for you to decide for or against that doctrine with a better understanding of what you are about. And if you prefer not to decide at all, but to remain doubters, you will at least see more plainly what the subject of your hesitation is. I thus disclaim openly on the threshold all pretension to prove to you that the freedom of the will is true. The most I hope is to induce some of you to follow my own example in assuming it true, and acting as if it were true. If it be true, it seems to me that this is involved in the strict logic of the case. Its truth ought not to be forced willy-nilly down our indifferent throats. It ought to be freely espoused by men who can equally well turn their backs upon it. In other words, our first act of freedom, if we are free, ought in all

* From "The Dilemma of Determinism," by William James, an address to the Harvard Divinity Students, published in *Unitarian Review*, September 1884.

inward propriety to be to affirm that we are free. This should exclude, it seems to me, from the free-will side of the question all hope of a coercive demonstration—a demonstration which I, for one, am perfectly contented to go without.

With thus much understood at the outset, we can advance. But not without one more point understood as well. The arguments I am about to urge all proceed on two suppositions: first, when we make theories about the world and discuss them with one another, we do so in order to attain a conception of things which shall give us subjective satisfaction; and, second, if there be two conceptions, and the one seems to us, on the whole, more rational than the other, we are entitled to suppose that the more rational one is the truer of the two. I hope that you are all willing to make these suppositions with me; for I am afraid that if there be any of you here who are not, they will find little edification in the rest of what I have to say. I cannot stop to argue the point; but I myself believe that all the magnificent achievements of mathematical and physical science—our doctrines of evolution, of uniformity of law, and the rest—proceed from our indomitable desire to cast the world into a more rational shape in our minds than the shape into which it is thrown there by the crude order of our experience. The world has shown itself, to a great extent, plastic to this demand of ours for rationality. How much farther it will show itself plastic no one can say. Our only means of finding out is to try; and I, for one, feel as free to try conceptions of moral as of mechanical or of logical rationality. If a certain formula for expressing the nature of the world violates my moral demand, I shall feel as free to throw it overboard, or at least to doubt it, as if it disappointed my demand for uniformity of sequence, for example; the one demand being, so far as I can see, quite as subjective and emotional as the other is. The principle of causality, for example—what is it but a postulate, an empty name covering simply a demand that the sequence of events shall some day manifest a deeper kind of belonging of one thing with another than the mere arbitrary juxtaposition which now phenomenally appears? It is as much an altar to an unknown god as the one that Saint Paul found at Athens. All our scientific and philosophic ideals are altars to unknown gods. Uniformity is as much so as is free will. If this be admitted, we can debate on even terms. But if any one pretends that while freedom and variety are, in the first instance, subjective demands, necessity and uniformity are something altogether different, I do not see how we can debate at all. . . .

What does determinism profess?

It professes that those parts of the universe already laid down absolutely appoint and decree what the other parts shall be. The future has no ambiguous possibilities hidden in its womb: the part we call the present is compatible with only one totality. Any other future complement than the one fixed from eternity is impossible. The whole is in each and every part, and welds it with the rest into an absolute unity, an iron block, in which there can be no equivocation or shadow of turning.

> With earth's first clay they did the last man knead,
> And there of the last harvest sowed the seed.
> And the first morning of creation wrote
> What the last dawn of reckoning shall read.

Indeterminism, on the contrary, says that the parts have a certain amount of loose play on one another, so that the laying down of one of them does not necessarily determine what the others shall be. It admits that possibilities may be in excess of actualities, and that things not yet revealed to our knowledge may really in themselves be ambiguous. Of two alternative futures which we conceive, both may now be really possible; and the one become impossible only at the very moment when the other excludes it by becoming real itself. Indeterminism thus denies the world to be one unbending unit of fact. It says there is a certain ultimate pluralism in it; and, so saying, it corroborates our ordinary unsophisticated view of things. To that view, actualities seem to float in a wider sea of possibilities from out of which they are chosen; and, *somewhere*, indeterminism says, such possibilities exist, and form a part of truth.

Determinism, on the contrary, says they exist *nowhere*, and that necessity on the one hand and impossibility on the other are the sole categories of the real. Possibilities that fail to get realized are, for determinism, pure illusions: they never were possibilities at all. There is nothing inchoate, it says, about this universe of ours, all that was or is or shall be actual in it having been from eternity virtually there. The cloud of alternatives our minds escort this mass of actuality withal is a cloud of sheer deceptions, to which "impossibilities" is the only name that rightfully belongs.

The issue, it will be seen, is a perfectly sharp one, which no eulogistic terminology can smear over or wipe out. The truth *must* lie with one side or the other, and its lying with one side makes the other false.

The question relates solely to the existence of possibilities, in the strict sense of the term, as things that may, but need not, be. Both sides admit that a volition, for instance, has occurred. The indeterminists say another volition might have occurred in its place: the determinists swear that nothing could possibly have occurred in its place. Now, can science be called in to tell us which of these two point-blank contradicters of each other is right? Science professes to draw no conclusions but such as are based on matters of fact, things that have actually happened; but how can any amount of assurance that something actually happened give us the least grain of information as to whether another thing might or might not have happened in its place? Only facts can be proved by other facts. With things that are possibilities and not facts, facts have no concern. If we have no other evidence than the evidence of existing facts, the possibility-question must remain a mystery never to be cleared up.

And the truth is that facts practically have hardly anything to do with making us either determinists or indeterminists. Sure enough, we make a flourish of quoting facts this way or that; and if we are determinists, we talk about the infallibility with which we can predict one another's conduct; while if we are indeterminists, we lay great stress on the fact that it is just because we cannot foretell one another's conduct, either in war or statecraft or in any of the great and small intrigues and businesses of men, that life is so intensely anxious and hazardous a game. But who does not see the wretched insufficiency of this so-called objective testimony on both sides? What fills up the gaps in our minds is something not objective, not external. What divides us into *possibility* men and *anti-possibility* men is different faiths or postulates—postulates of rationality. To this man the world seems more rational with possibilities in it—to that man more rational with possibilities excluded; and talk as we will about having to yield to evidence, what makes us monists or pluralists, determinists or indeterminists, is at bottom always some sentiment like this.

The stronghold of the deterministic sentiment is the antipathy to the idea of chance. As soon as we begin to talk indeterminism to our friends, we find a number of them shaking their heads. This notion of alternative possibility, they say, this admission that any one of several things may come to pass, is, after all, only a round about name for chance; and chance is something the notion of which no sane mind can for an instant tolerate in the world. What is it, they ask, but barefaced crazy unreason, the negation of intelligibility and law? And if the slightest particle of it exist anywhere, what is to prevent the whole fabric from falling together, the stars from going out, and chaos from recommencing her topsy-turvy reign? . . .

The sting of the word "chance" seems to lie in the assumption that it means something positive, and that if anything happens by chance, it must needs be something of an intrinsically irrational and preposterous sort. Now, chance means nothing of the kind. It is a purely negative and relative term, giving us no information about that of which it is predicated, except that it happens to be disconnected with something else—not controlled, secured, or necessitated by other things in advance of its own actual presence. At this point is the most subtile one of the whole lecture, and at the same time the point on which all the rest hinges, I beg you to pay particular attention to it. What I say is that it tells us nothing about what a thing may be in itself to call it "chance." It may be a bad thing, it may be a good thing. It may be lucidity, transparency, fitness incarnate, matching the whole system of other things, when it has once befallen, in an unimaginably perfect way. All you mean by calling it "chance" is that this is not guaranteed, that it may also fall out otherwise. For the system of other things has no positive hold on the chance-thing. Its origin is in a certain fashion negative: it escapes, and says, Hands off! coming, when it comes, as a free gift, or not at all.

This negativeness, however, and this opacity of the chance-thing when thus considered *ab extra*, or from the point of view of previous things or distant things, do not preclude its having any amount of positiveness and luminosity from within, and at its own place and moment. All that its chance-character asserts about it is that there is something in it really of its own, something that is not the unconditional property of the whole. If the whole wants this property, the whole must wait till it can get it, if it be a matter of chance. That the universe may actually be a sort of joint-stock society of this sort, in which the sharers have both limited liabilities and limited powers, is of course a simple and conceivable notion.

Nevertheless, many persons talk as if the minutest dose of disconnectedness of one part with another, the smallest modicum of independence, the faintest tremor of ambiguity about the future, for example, would ruin everything, and turn this goodly universe into a sort of insane sand-heap or nulliverse— no universe at all. Since future human volitions are as a matter of fact the only ambiguous things we are tempted to believe in, let us stop for a moment to make ourselves sure whether their independent and accidental character need be fraught with such direful consequences to the universe as these.

What is meant by saying that my choice of which way to walk home after the lecture is ambiguous and matter of chance as far as the present moment is concerned? It means that both Divinity Avenue and Oxford Street are called; but that only one, and that one *either* one, shall be chosen. Now, I ask you seriously to suppose that this ambiguity of my choice is real; and then to make the impossible hypothesis that the choice is made twice over, and each time falls on a different street. In other words, imagine that I first walk through Divinity Avenue, and then imagine that the powers governing the universe annihilate ten minutes of time with all that it contained, and set me back at the door of this hall just as I was before the choice was made. Imagine then that, everything else being the same, I now make a different choice and traverse Oxford Street. You, as passive spectators, look on and see the two alternative universes—one of them with me walking through Divinity Avenue in it, the other with the same me walking through Oxford Street. Now, if you are determinists you believe one of these universes to have been from eternity impossible: you believe it to have been impossible because of the intrinsic irrationality or accidentality somewhere involved in it. But looking outwardly at these universes, can you say which is the impossible and accidental one, and which the rational and necessary one? I doubt if the most iron-clad determinist among you could have the slightest glimmer of light on this point. In other words, either universe *after the fact* and once there would, to our means of observation and understanding, appear just as rational as the other. There would be absolutely no criterion by which we might judge one necessary and the other matter of chance. Suppose now we relieve the gods of their hypothetical task and assume my choice, once made, to be made forever. I go through Divinity Avenue for good and all. If, as good determinists, you now begin to affirm, what all good determinists punctually do affirm, that in the nature of things I *couldn't* have gone through Oxford Street—had I done so it would have been chance, irrationality, insanity, a horrid gap in nature—I simply call your attention to this, that your affirmation is what the Germans call a *Machtspruch,* a mere conception fulminated as a dogma and based on no insight into details. Before my choice, either street seemed as natural to you as to me. Had I happened to take Oxford Street, Divinity Avenue would have figured in your philosophy as the gap in nature; and you would have so proclaimed it with the best deterministic conscience in the world.

But what a hollow outcry, then, is this against a chance which, if it were present to us, we could by no character whatever distinguish from a rational necessity! I have taken the most trivial of examples, but no possible example could lead to any different result. For what are the alternatives which, in point of fact, offer themselves to human volition? What are those futures that now seem matters of chance? Are they not one and all like the Divinity Avenue and Oxford Street of our example? Are they not all of them *kinds* of things already here and based in the existing frame of nature? Is any one ever tempted to produce an *absolute* accident, something utterly irrelevant to the rest of the world? Do not all the motives that assail us, all the futures that offer themselves to our choice, spring equally from the soil of the past; and would not either one of them, whether realized through chance or through necessity, the moment it was realized, seem to us to fit that past, and in the completest and most continuous manner to interdigitate with the phenomena already there?

The more one thinks of the matter, the more one wonders that so empty and gratuitous a hubbub as this outcry against chance should have found so great an echo in the hearts of men. It is a word which tells us absolutely nothing about what chances, or about the *modus operandi* of the chancing; and the use of it as a warcry shows only a temper of intellectual absolutism, a demand that the world shall be a solid block, subject to one control—which temper, which demand, the world may not be bound to gratify at all. In every outwardly verifiable and practical respect, a world in which the alternatives that now actually distract *your* choice were decided by pure chance would be by *me* absolutely undistinguished from the world in which I now live. I am, therefore, entirely willing to call it, so far as your choices go, a world of chance for me. To *yourselves*, it is true, those very acts of choice, which to me are so blind, opaque, and external, are the opposites of this, for you are within them and effect them. To you they appear as decisions; and decisions, for him who makes them, are altogether peculiar psychic facts. Self-luminous and self-justifying at the living moment at which they occur, they appeal to no outside moment to put its stamp upon them or make them continuous with the rest of nature. Themselves it is rather who seem to make nature continuous; and in their strange and intense function of granting consent to one possibility and withholding it from another, to transform an equivocal and double future into an inalterable and simple past.

But with the psychology of the matter we have no concern this evening. The quarrel which determinism has with chance fortunately has nothing to do with this or that psychological detail. It is a quarrel altogether metaphysical. Determinism denies the ambiguity of future volitions, because it affirms that nothing future can be ambiguous. But we have said enough to meet the issue. Indeterminate future volitions *do* mean chance. Let us not fear to shout it from the house-tops if need be; for we now know that the idea of chance is, at bottom, exactly the same thing as the idea of gift— the one simply being a disparaging, and the other a eulogistic, name for anything on which we have no effective *claim*. And whether the world be the better or the worse for having either chances or gifts in it will depend altogether on *what* these uncertain and unclaimable things turn out to be.

And this at last brings us within sight of our subject. We have seen what determinism means: we have seen that indeterminism is rightly described as meaning chance; and we have seen that chance, the very name of which we are urged to shrink from as from a metaphysical pestilence, means only the negative fact that no part of the world, however big, can claim to control absolutely the destinies of the whole. But although, in discussing the word "chance," I may at moments have seemed to be arguing for its real existence, I have not meant to do so yet. We have not yet ascertained whether this be a world of chance or no; at most, we have agreed that it seems so. And I now repeat what I said at the outset, that, from any strict theoretical point of view, the question is insoluble. To deepen our theoretic sense of the *difference* between a world with chances in it and a deterministic world is the most I can hope to do; and this I may now at last begin upon, after all our tedious clearing of the way.

I wish first of all to show you just what the notion that this is a deterministic world implies. The implications I call your attention to are all bound up with the fact that it is a world in which we constantly have to make what I shall, with your permission, call judgments of regret. Hardly an hour passes in which we do not wish that something might be otherwise; and happy indeed are those of us whose hearts have never echoed the wish of Omar Khayam—

> That we might clasp, ere closed, the book of fate,
>     And make the writer on a fairer leaf
> Inscribe our names, or quite obliterate.
>
> Ah! Love, could you and I with fate conspire
> To mend this sorry scheme of things entire,
>     Would we not shatter it to bits, and then
> Remould it nearer to the heart's desire?

Now, it is undeniable that most of these regrets are foolish, and are quite on a par in point of philosophic value with the criticisms on the universe of that friend of our infancy, the hero of the fable "The Atheist and the Acorn"—

> Fool! had that bough a pumpkin bore,
> Thy whimsies would have worked no more, etc.

Even from the point of view of our own ends, we should probably make a botch of remodelling the universe. How much more than from the point of view of ends we cannot see! Wise men therefore regret as little as they can. But still some regrets are pretty obstinate and hard to stifle—regrets for acts of wanton cruelty or treachery, for example, whether performed by others or by ourselves. Hardly any one can remain *entirely* optimistic after reading the confession of the murderer at Brockton the other day: how, to get rid of the wife whose continued existence bored him, he inveigled her into a desert spot, shot her four times, and then, as she lay on the ground and said to him, "You didn't do it on purpose, did you, dear?" replied, "No, I didn't do it on purpose," as he raised a rock and smashed her skull. Such an occurrence, with the mild sentence and self-satisfaction of the prisoner, is a field for a crop of regrets, which one need not take up in detail. We feel that, although a perfect mechanical fit to the rest of the universe, it is a bad moral fit, and that something else would really have been better in its place.

But for the deterministic philosophy the murder, the sentence, and the prisoner's optimism were all necessary from eternity; and nothing else for a moment had a ghost of a chance of being put into their place. To admit such a chance, the determinists tell us, would be to make a suicide of reason; so we must steel our hearts against the thought. And here our plot thickens, for we see the first of those difficult implications of determinism and monism which it is my purpose to make you feel. If this Brockton murder was called for by the rest of the universe, if it had to come at its preappointed hour, and if nothing else would have been consistent with the sense of the whole, what are we to think of the universe? Are we stubbornly to stick to our judgment of regret, and say, though it *couldn't* be, yet it *would* have been a better universe with something different from this Brockton murder in it? That, of course, seems the natural and spontaneous thing for us to do; and yet it is nothing short of deliberately espousing a kind of pessimism. The judgment of regret calls the murder bad. Calling a thing bad means, if it mean anything at all, that the thing ought not to be, that something else ought to be in its stead. Determinism, in denying that anything else can be in its stead, virtually defines the universe as a place in which what ought to be is impossible—in other words, as an organism whose constitution is afflicted with an incurable taint, an irremediable flaw. . . . Regret for the murder must transform itself, if we are determinists and wise, into a larger regret. It is absurd to regret the murder alone. Other things being what they are, *it* could not be different. What we should regret is that whole frame of things of which the murder is one member. I see no escape whatever from this pessimistic conclusion if, being determinists, our judgment of regret is to be allowed to stand at all.

The only deterministic escape from pessimism is everywhere to abandon the judgment of regret. That this can be done, history shows to be not impossible. The devil, *quoad existentiam*, may be good. That is, although he be a *principle* of evil, yet the universe, with such a principle in it, may practically be a better universe than it could have been without. On every hand, in a small way, we find that a certain amount of evil is a condition by which a higher form of good is brought. There is nothing to prevent anybody from generalizing this view, and trusting that if we could but see things in the largest of all ways, even such matters as this Brockton murder would appear to be paid for by the uses that follow in their train. An optimism *quand même*, a systematic and infatuated optimism like that ridiculed by Voltaire in his *Candide*, is one of the possible ideal ways in which a man may train himself to look on life. Bereft of dogmatic hardness and lit up with the expression of a tender and pathetic hope, such an optimism has been the grace of some of the most religious characters that ever lived.

> Throb thine with Nature's throbbing breast,
> And all is clear from east to west.

Even cruelty and treachery may be among the absolutely blessed fruits of time, and to quarrel with any of their details may be blasphemy. The only real blasphemy, in short, may be that pessimistic temper of the soul which lets it give way to such things as regrets, remorse, and grief.

Thus, our deterministic pessimism may become a deterministic optimism at the price of extinguishing our judgments of regret.

But does not this immediately bring us into a curious logical predicament? Our determinism leads us to call our judgments of regret wrong, because they are pessimistic in implying that what is impossible yet ought to be. But how then about the judgments of regret themselves? If they are wrong, other judgments, judgments of approval presumably, ought to be in their place. But as they are necessitated, nothing else *can* be in their place; and the universe is just what it was before—namely, a place in which what ought to be appears impossible. We have got one foot out of the pessimistic bog, but the other one sinks all the deeper. We have rescued our actions from the bonds of evil, but our judgments are now held fast. When murders and treacheries cease to be sins, regrets are theoretic absurdities and errors. The theoretic and the active life thus play a kind of see-saw with each other on the ground of evil. The rise of either sends the other down. Murder and treachery cannot be good without regret being bad: regret cannot be good without treachery and murder being bad. Both, however, are supposed to have been foredoomed; so something must be fatally unreasonable, absurd, and wrong in the world. It must be a place of which either sin or error forms a necessary part. From this dilemma there seems at first sight no escape. . . .

The only consistent way of representing a pluralism and a world whose parts may affect one another through their conduct being either good or bad is the indeterministic way. What interest, zest, or excitement can there be in achieving the right way, unless we are enabled to feel that the wrong way is also a possible and a natural way—nay, more, a menacing and an imminent way? And what sense can there be in condemning ourselves for taking the wrong way, unless we need have done nothing of the sort, unless the right way was open to us as well? I cannot understand the willingness to act, no matter how we feel, without the belief that acts are really good and bad. I cannot understand the belief that an act is bad, without regret at its happening. I cannot understand regret without the admission of real, genuine possibilities in the world. Only *then* is it other than a mockery to feel, after we have failed to do our best, that an irreparable opportunity is gone from the universe, the loss of which it must forever after mourn. . . .

You will remember that I expressly repudiated awhile ago the pretension to offer any arguments which could be coercive in a so-called scientific fashion in this matter. And I consequently find myself, at the end of this long talk, obliged to state my conclusions in an altogether personal way. This personal method of appeal seems to be among the very conditions of the problem; and the most any one can do is to confess as candidly as he can the grounds for the faith that is in him, and leave his example to work on others as it may.

Let me, then, without circumlocution say just this. The world is enigmatical enough in all conscience, whatever theory we may take up toward it. The indeterminism I defend, the free-will theory of popular sense based on the judgment of regret, represents that world as vulnerable, and liable to be injured by certain of its parts if they act wrong. And it represents their acting wrong as a matter of possibility or accident, neither inevitable nor yet to be infallibly warded off. In all this, it is a theory devoid either of transparency or of stability. It gives us a pluralistic, restless universe, in which no single point of view can ever take in the whole scene; and to a mind possessed of the love of unity at any cost, it will, no doubt, remain forever inacceptable. A friend with such a mind once told me that the thought of my universe made him sick, like the sight of the horrible motion of a mass of maggots in their carrion bed.

But while I freely admit that the pluralism and the restlessness are repugnant and irrational in a certain way, I find that every alternative to them is irrational in a deeper way. The indeterminism with its maggots, if you please to speak so about it, offends only the native absolutism of my intellect —an absolutism which, after all, perhaps, deserves to be snubbed and kept in check. But the determinism with its necessary carrion, to continue the figure of speech, and with no possible maggots to eat the latter up, violates my sense of moral reality through and through. When, for example, I imagine such carrion as the Brockton murder, I cannot conceive it as an act by which the universe, as a whole, logically and necessarily expresses its nature without shrinking from complicity with such a whole. And I deliberately refuse to keep on terms of loyalty with the universe by saying blankly that the murder, since it does flow from the nature of the whole, is not carrion. There are *some* instinctive reactions which I, for one, will not tamper with. . . .

No! better a thousand times, than such systematic corruption of our moral sanity, the plainest pessimism, so that it be straight-forward; but better far than that the world of chance. Make as great an uproar about chance as you please, I know that chance means pluralism and nothing more. If some of the members of the pluralism are bad, the philosophy of pluralism, whatever broad views it may deny me, permits me, at least, to turn to the other members with a clean breast of affection and an unsophisticated moral sense. And if I still wish to think of the world as a totality, it lets me feel that a world with a *chance* in it of being altogether good, even if the chance never comes to pass, is better than a world with no such chance at all. That "chance"

whose very notion I am exhorted and conjured to banish from my view of
the future as the suicide of reason concerning it, that "chance" is—what?
Just this—the chance that in moral respects the future may be other and
better than the past has been. This is the only chance we have any motive
for supposing to exist. Shame, rather, on its repudiation and its denial! For its
presence is the vital air which lets the world live, the salt which keeps it
sweet.

# WALTER T. STACE

WALTER TERENCE STACE (1886–      ) was
born in London and educated at Edinburgh
and Trinity College, Dublin. He served in
the Ceylon Civil Service from 1910 to 1932
and then taught philosophy at Princeton
University from 1932 until his retirement in
1955. His major works include: A Critical
History of Greek Philosophy (1920), The
Theory of Knowledge and Existence (1932),
The Concept of Morals (1937), The Destiny
of Western Man (1942), Time and Eternity
(1952), and Religion and the Modern Mind
(1952).

## The Problem of Free Will*

It is certain that if there is no free will there can be no morality.
Morality is concerned with what men ought and ought not to do. But if a
man has no freedom to choose what he will do, if whatever he does is done
under compulsion, then it does not make sense to tell him that he ought not
to have done what he did and that he ought to do something different. All
moral precepts would in such case be meaningless. Also if he acts always
under compulsion, how can he be held morally responsible for his actions?
How can he, for example, be punished for what he could not help doing?

It is to be observed that those learned professors of philosophy or psychology who deny the existence of free will do so only in their professional moments and in their studies and lecture rooms. For when it comes to doing
anything practical, even of the most trivial kind, they invariably behave as if
they and others were free. They inquire from you at dinner whether you will
choose this dish or that dish. They will ask a child why he told a lie, and will

---

* From Religion and the Modern Mind, by W. T. Stace, Chap. 11. Copyright, 1952,
by W. T. Stace. Published by J. B. Lippincott Company. Used by permission.

punish him for not having chosen the way of truthfulness. All of which is inconsistent with a disbelief in free will. This should cause us to suspect that the problem is not a real one; and this, I believe, is the case. The dispute is merely verbal, and is due to nothing but a confusion about the meanings of words. It is what is now fashionably called a semantic problem.

How does a verbal dispute arise? Let us consider a case which, although it is absurd in the sense that no one would ever make the mistake which is involved in it, yet illustrates the principle which we shall have to use in the solution of the problem. Suppose that someone believed that the word "man" means a certain sort of five-legged animal; in short that "five-legged animal" is the correct *definition* of man. He might then look around the world, and rightly observing that there are no five-legged animals in it, he might proceed to deny the existence of men. This preposterous conclusion would have been reached because he was using an incorrect definition of "man." All you would have to do to show him his mistake would be to give him the correct definition; or at least to show him that his definition was wrong. Both the problem and its solution would, of course, be entirely verbal. The problem of free will, and its solution, I shall maintain, is verbal in exactly the same way. The problem has been created by the fact that learned men, especially philosophers, have assumed an incorrect definition of free will, and then finding that there is nothing in the world which answers to their definition, have denied its existence. As far as logic is concerned, their conclusion is just as absurd as that of the man who denies the existence of men. The only difference is that the mistake in the latter case is obvious and crude, while the mistake which the deniers of free will have made is rather subtle and difficult to detect.

Throughout the modern period, until quite recently, it was assumed, both by the philosophers who denied free will and by those who defended it, that *determinism is inconsistent with free will*. If a man's actions were wholly determined by chains of causes stretching back into the remote past, so that they could be predicted beforehand by a mind which knew all the causes, it was assumed that they could not in that case be free. This implies that a certain definition of actions done from free will was assumed, namely that they are actions *not* wholly determined by causes or predictable beforehand. Let us shorten this by saying that free will was defined as meaning indeterminism. This is the incorrect definition which has led to the denial of free will. As soon as we see what the true definition is we shall find that the question whether the world is deterministic, as Newtonian science implied, or in a measure indeterministic, as current physics teaches, is wholly irrelevant to the problem.

Of course there is a sense in which one can define a word arbitrarily in any way one pleases. But a definition may nevertheless be called correct or incorrect. It is correct if it accords with a *common usage* of the word defined. It is incorrect if it does not. And if you give an incorrect definition, absurd and untrue results are likely to follow. For instance, there is nothing to prevent you from arbitrarily defining a man as a five-legged animal, but this is incorrect in the sense that it does not accord with the ordinary meaning of the word. Also it has the absurd result of leading to a denial of the existence of men. This shows that *common usage is the criterion for deciding whether a definition is correct or not*. And this is the principle which I shall apply to free will. I shall show that indeterminism is not what is meant by the phrase "free will" *as it is commonly used*. And I shall attempt to discover the correct definition by inquiring how the phrase is used in ordinary conversation.

Here are a few samples of how the phrase might be used in ordinary conversation. It will be noticed that they include cases in which the question whether a man acted with free will is asked in order to determine whether he was morally and legally responsible for his acts.

*Jones*   I once went without food for a week.
*Smith*   Did you do that of your own free will?
*Jones*   No. I did it because I was lost in a desert and could find no food.

But suppose that the man who had fasted was Mahatma Gandhi. The conversation might then have gone:

*Gandhi*   I once fasted for a week.
*Smith*   Did you do that of your own free will?
*Gandhi*   Yes. I did it because I wanted to compel the British Government to give India its independence.

Take another case. Suppose that I had stolen some bread, but that I was as truthful as George Washington. Then, if I were charged with the crime in court, some exchange of the following sort might take place:

*Judge*   Did you steal the bread of your own free will?
*Stace*   Yes. I stole it because I was hungry.

Or in different circumstances the conversation might run:

*Judge*   Did you steal of your own free will?
*Stace*   No. I stole because my employer threatened to beat me if I did not.

At a recent murder trial in Trenton some of the accused had signed confessions, but afterwards asserted that they had done so under police duress. The following exchange might have occurred:

*Judge*   Did you sign this confession of your own free will?
*Prisoner*   No. I signed it because the police beat me up.

Now suppose that a philosopher had been a member of the jury. We could imagine this conversation taking place in the jury room.

*Foreman of the Jury*   The prisoner says he signed the confession because he was beaten, and not of his own free will.
*Philosopher*   This is quite irrelevant to the case. There is no such thing as free will.
*Foreman*   Do you mean to say that it makes no difference whether he signed because his conscience made him want to tell the truth or because he was beaten?
*Philosopher*   None at all. Whether he was caused to sign by a beating or by some desire of his own—the desire to tell the truth, for example—in either case his signing was causally determined, and therefore in neither case did he act of his own free will. Since there is no such thing as free will, the question whether he signed of his own free will ought not to be discussed by us.

The foreman and the rest of the jury would rightly conclude that the philosopher must be making some mistake. What sort of a mistake could it be? There is only one possible answer. The philosopher must be using the phrase "free will" in some peculiar way of his own which is not the way in which men usually use it when they wish to determine a question of moral responsibility. That is, he must be using an incorrect definition of it as implying action not determined by causes.

Suppose a man left his office at noon, and were questioned about it. Then we might hear this:

*Jones*   Did you go out of your own free will?
*Smith*   Yes. I went out to get my lunch.

But we might hear:

*Jones*   Did you leave your office of your own free will?
*Smith*   No. I was forcibly removed by the police.

We have now collected a number of cases of actions which, in the ordinary usage of the English language, would be called cases in which people have acted of their own free will. We should also say in all these cases that they *chose* to act as they did. We should also say that they could have acted otherwise, if they had chosen. For instance, Mahatma Gandhi was not compelled to fast; he chose to do so. He could have eaten if he had wanted to. When Smith went out to get his lunch, he chose to do so. He could have stayed and done some more work, if he had wanted to. We have also collected a number of cases of the opposite kind. They are cases in which men were not able to exercise their free will. They had no choice. They were compelled to do as they did. The man in the desert did not fast of his own free will. He had no choice in the matter. He was compelled to fast because there was nothing for him to eat. And so with the other cases. It ought to be quite easy, by an inspection of these cases, to tell what we ordinarily mean when we say that a man did or did not exercise free will. We ought therefore to be able to extract from them the proper definition of the term. Let us put the cases in a table:

| Free Acts | Unfree Acts |
| --- | --- |
| Gandhi fasting because he wanted to free India. | The man fasting in the desert because there was no food. |
| Stealing bread because one is hungry. | Stealing because one's employer threatened to beat one. |
| Signing a confession because one wanted to tell the truth. | Signing because the police beat one. |
| Leaving the office because one wanted one's lunch. | Leaving because forcibly removed. |

It is obvious that to find the correct definition of free acts we must discover what characteristic is common to all the acts in the left-hand column, and is, at the same time, absent from all the acts in the right-hand column. This characteristic which all free acts have, and which no unfree acts have, will be the defining characteristic of free will.

Is being uncaused, or not being determined by causes, the characteristic of which we are in search? It cannot be, because although it is true that all the acts in the right-hand column have causes, such as the beating by the police or the absence of food in the desert, so also do the acts in the left-hand column. Mr. Gandhi's fasting was caused by his desire to free India, the man leaving his office by his hunger, and so on. Moreover there is no reason to doubt that these causes of the free acts were in turn caused by prior conditions, and that these were again the results of causes, and so on back indefinitely into the past. Any physiologists can tell us the causes of hunger. What caused Mr. Gandhi's tremendously powerful desire to free India is no doubt more difficult to discover. But it must have had causes. Some of them may have lain in peculiarities of his glands or brain, others in his past experiences, others in his heredity, others in his education. Defenders of free will have usually tended to deny such facts. But to do so is plainly a case of special pleading, which is unsupported by any scrap of evidence. The only reasonable view is that all human actions, both those which are freely done and those which are not, are either wholly determined by causes, or at least as much determined as other events in nature. It may be true, as the physicists tell us, that nature is not as deterministic as was once thought. But whatever degree of determinism prevails in the world, human actions appear to be as much determined as anything else. And if this is so, it cannot be the case that what distinguishes actions freely chosen from those which are not free is that the latter are determined by causes while the former are not.

Therefore, being uncaused or being undetermined by causes, must be an incorrect definition of free will.

What, then, is the difference between acts which are freely done and those which are not? What is the characteristic which is present to all the acts in the left-hand column and absent from all those in the right-hand column? Is it not obvious that, although both sets of actions have causes, the causes of those in the left-hand column are *of a different kind* from the causes of those in the right-hand column? The free acts are all caused by desires, or motives, or by some sort of internal psychological states of the agent's mind. The unfree acts, on the other hand, are all caused by physical forces or physical conditions, outside the agent. Police arrest means physical force exerted from the outside; the absence of food in the desert is a physical condition of the outside world. We may therefore frame the following rough definitions. *Acts freely done are those whose immediate causes are psychological states in the agent. Acts not freely done are those whose immediate causes are states of affairs external to the agent.*

It is plain that if we define free will in this way, then free will certainly exists, and the philosopher's denial of its existence is seen to be what it is— nonsense. For it is obvious that all those actions of men which we should ordinarily attribute to the exercise of their free will, or of which we should say that they freely chose to do them, are in fact actions which have been caused by their own desires, wishes, thoughts, emotions, impulses, or other psychological states.

In applying our definition we shall find that it usually works well, but that there are some puzzling cases which it does not seem exactly to fit. These puzzles can always be solved by paying careful attention to the ways in which words are used, and remembering that they are not always used consistently. I have space for only one example. Suppose that a thug threatens to shoot you unless you give him your wallet, and suppose that you do so. Do you, in giving him your wallet, do so of your own free will or not? If we apply our definition, we find that you acted freely, since the immediate cause of the action was not an actual outside force but fear of death, which is a psychological cause. Most people, however, would say that you did not act of your own free will but under compulsion. Does this show that our definition is wrong? I do not think so. Aristotle, who gave a solution of the problem of free will substantially the same as ours (though he did not use the term "free will") admitted that there are what he called "mixed" or borderline cases in which it is difficult to know whether we ought to call the acts free or compelled. In the case under discussion, though no actual force was used, the gun at your forehead so nearly approximated to actual force that we tend to say the case was one of compulsion. It is a borderline case.

Here is what may seem like another kind of puzzle. According to our view an action may be free though it could have been predicted beforehand with certainty. But suppose you told a lie, and it was certain beforehand that you would tell it. How could one then say, "You could have told the truth"? The answer is that it is perfectly true that you could have told the truth *if* you had wanted to. In fact you would have done so, for in that case the causes producing your action, namely, your desires, would have been different, and would therefore have produced different effects. It is a delusion that predictability and free will are incompatible. This agrees with common sense. For if, knowing your character, I predict that you will act honorably, no one would say when you do act honorably, that this shows you did not do so of your own free will.

Since free will is a condition of moral responsibility, we must be sure that our theory of free will gives a sufficient basis for it. To be held morally responsible for one's actions means that one may be justly punished or rewarded, blamed or praised, for them. But it is not just to punish a man for what he cannot help doing. How can it be just to punish him for an action which it was certain beforehand that he would do? We have not attempted to decide whether, as a matter of fact, all events, including human actions, are completely determined. For that question is irrevelant to the problem of free will. But if we assume for the purposes of argument that complete determinism is true, but that we are nevertheless free, it may then be asked whether such a deterministic free will is compatible with moral responsibility. For it may seem unjust to punish a man for an action which it could have been predicted with certainty beforehand that he would do.

But that determinism is incompatible with moral responsibility is as much a delusion as that it is incompatible with free will. You do not excuse a man for doing a wrong act because, knowing his character, you felt certain beforehand that he would do it. Nor do you deprive a man of a reward or prize because, knowing his goodness or his capabilities, you felt certain beforehand that he would win it.

Volumes have been written on the justification of punishment. But so far as it affects the question of free will, the essential principles involved are quite simple. The punishment of a man for doing a wrong act is justified, either on the ground that it will correct his own character, or that it will deter other people from doing similar acts. The instrument of punishment has been in the past, and no doubt still is, often unwisely used; so that it may often have done more harm than good. But that is not relevant to our present problem. Punishment, if and when it is justified, is justified only on one or both of the grounds just mentioned. The question then is how, if we assume determinism, punishment can correct character or deter people from evil actions.

Suppose that your child develops a habit of telling lies. You give him a mild beating. Why? Because you believe that his personality is such that the usual motives for telling the truth do not cause him to do so. You therefore supply the missing cause, or motive, in the shape of pain and the fear of future pain if he repeats his untruthful behavior. And you hope that a few treatments of this kind will condition him to the habit of truth-telling, so that he will come to tell the truth without the infliction of pain. You assume that his actions are determined by causes, but that the usual causes of truth-telling do not in him produce their usual effects. You therefore supply him with an artificially injected motive, pain and fear, which you think will in the future cause him to speak truthfully.

The principle is exactly the same where you hope, by punishing one man, to deter others from wrong actions. You believe that the fear of punishment will cause those who might otherwise do evil to do well.

We act on the same principle with non-human, and even with inanimate, things, if they do not behave in the way we think they ought to behave. The rose bushes in the garden produce only small and poor blooms, whereas we want large and rich ones. We supply a cause which will produce large blooms, namely fertilizer. Our automobile does not go properly. We supply a cause which will make it go better, namely oil in the works. The punishment for the man, the fertilizer for the plant, and the oil for the car, are all justified by the same principle and in the same way. The only difference is that different kinds of things require different kinds of causes to make them do what they should. Pain may be the appropriate remedy to apply, in certain cases, to human beings, and oil to the machine. It is, of course, of no use to inject motor oil into the boy or to beat the machine.

Thus we see that moral responsibility is not only consistent with determinism, but requires it. The assumption on which punishment is based is that human behavior is causally determined. If pain could not be a cause of truth-telling there would be no justification at all for punishing lies. If human actions and volitions were uncaused, it would be useless either to punish or reward, or indeed to do anything else to correct people's bad behavior. For nothing that you could do would in any way influence them. Thus moral responsibility would entirely disappear. If there were no determinism of human beings at all, their actions would be completely unpredictable and capricious, and therefore irresponsible. And this is in itself a strong argument against the common view of philosophers that free will means being undetermined by causes.

# FREEDOM *VS.* DETERMINISM—SUGGESTED READINGS

Campbell, C. A., *In Defence of Free Will*, Glasgow, Jackson, Son, 1938. (a case for free will)

Hobart, R. E., "Free Will as involving Determination and inconceivable without it," *Mind*, XLIII (1934), pp. 1–27. (a case for reconciling free will and determinism)

Hook, S. (ed.), *Determinism and Freedom in the Age of Modern Science*, New York, New York University Press, 1958. (a collection of essays representing different points of view)

Nowell-Smith, P., "Freewill and Moral Responsibility," *Mind*, LVII (1948), pp. 45–61. (a case for reconciling free will and determinism)

Reid, T., *Essays on the Active Powers of Man*, 1788, Essay IV. (a case for free will)

Wood, L., "The Free-will Controversy," *Philosophy*, XVI (1941), pp. 386–97. (a case for determinism)

# II. The Search for a Moral Standard

ALL MEN make particular judgments about what is right and wrong, and it is their common experience that these judgments often do not agree with those made by other men. When particular moral judgments disagree, it is natural for each of the disputants to invoke some wider principle to justify the correctness of his moral judgment as against that of his opponent. Ideally, what each seeks is a universal moral standard—a standard for distinguishing right from wrong actions which will be valid for all men at all times and everywhere. The attempt to establish such a universal moral standard has provided the central theme of traditional ethical theory.

In their search for a universal moral standard, philosophers have proposed a wide variety of theories, each of which describes the standard in a significantly different way. It is possible, however, to classify all such proposals into one of two general types: the theories may be said to be either *deontological* or *teleological*.

The term "deontological" is derived from the Greek word *deon*, meaning "duty." Deontological ethical theories assert that men have a duty to perform certain actions whether or not they can foresee any good resulting from them. Some types of behavior are thus held to be intrinsically right or wrong. The deontologist further maintains that the rightness of an action may be discovered by an appeal to a purely *formal moral criterion*, i.e., by an appeal to a standard which determines the rightness of an action without consideration of its consequences. But what is the formal criterion of rightness? Upon this point, deontological theories differ among themselves. In the selections to follow, we shall consider proposals that this criterion of rightness lies (1) in the authority of God, (2) in conscience, and (3) in the principle which Immanuel Kant has called "the categorical imperative."

The term "teleological" is derived from the Greek word *telos*, meaning "end" or "purpose." The central emphasis of teleological ethics is upon the purposes achieved in action, upon the consequences of action. No behavior is held to be intrinsically right or wrong—an act is right only if it produces, or tends to produce, good results. The problem for teleological ethical theories is to determine what *is* good; on this matter, the theories offer different answers. In the selections to follow, we shall consider proposals that the good is (1) pleasure, (2) self-realization, (3) fulfillment of interest.

# A. AN ACT IS RIGHT IF IT CONFORMS TO A FORMAL MORAL CRITERION

## 1. THE AUTHORITY OF GOD

Some theologians have maintained that in the commands of the Deity we find the universal moral standard and the formal criterion of rightness. They would hold that an act is right only if it conforms to the will of God. But there are many and conflicting accounts as to what the will of God decrees. How, then, is the authentic will of God to be known? More particularly, in what form is the will of God expressed? As rules of law? Or as direct personal commands? These questions are of crucial importance for any ethics based upon divine authority.

BRUNNER maintains that an act is right only if it is done in obedience to the direct personal command of God. He argues that it is treason against religious faith to try to capture and express the will of God in any general propositions, formulae, or laws; according to Brunner, God issues specific commands in specific situations to individual men. What God wills can never be known ahead of time; we learn what God commands in the situation itself, if we enter into a direct, personal relationship with Him.

Cardinal MERCIER would reject, as would St. Thomas Aquinas, Brunner's view that the "free decree of the Divine Will" makes acts right or wrong. Mercier holds that the will of God is expressed in the immutable precepts of the natural law, that God has implanted the natural law in the faculty of human reason, and that this natural law provides us with general rules of conduct which *can* be known in advance. Mercier agrees with Brunner, however, that the ultimate source for the distinction between right and wrong, and the ultimate ground of moral obligation, lie in the authority of God.

EWING inquires whether an act is good *because* God wills it, or whether God wills it *because* it is good. If we maintain the latter proposition, says Ewing, then we must have some other way than by appeal to the will of God to decide whether an act is good. DENNES argues that reference to divine authority can give us no assistance in our search for an ethical standard. He contends that morality must of necessity be based upon the values and preferences of men.

# EMIL
# BRUNNER

HEINRICH EMIL BRUNNER (1889–    ) was
Professor of Theology at the University of
Zurich, Switzerland, from 1924 until his retirement in 1953. A leader in the Protestant
neo-orthodox movement, his major works
include: *The Philosophy of Religion from
the Standpoint of Protestant Theology*
(1926), *The Divine Imperative* (1932), *God
and Man* (1936), *Revelation and Reason*
(1941), *Justice and the Social Order* (1943),
and *Christianity and Civilization* (1948–49).

## *The Divine Imperative**

### Chapter IX

### The Definition of the Christian Ethic

1. There is no general conception of ethics which would also include the
Christian ethic. Such a general definition of ethics does not even exist for
rational thought. . . .

It is of course true that even the Christian ethic is concerned with the
definition of conduct, which as "right" conduct has to be distinguished from
conduct which is accidental or wrong; but this distinction or definition does
not take place by means of an ultimate principle, which, as such, would
be intelligible and valid. . . . The Christian conception of the Good differs
from every other conception of the Good at this very point: that it cannot
be defined in terms of principle at all.

Whatever can be defined in accordance with a principle—whether it be
the principle of pleasure or the principle of duty—is legalistic. This means
that it is possible—by the use of this principle—to pre-determine "the right"
down to the smallest detail of conduct. . . . This legalistic spirit corrupts the
true conception of the Good from its very roots. The Christian moralist
and the extreme individualist are at one in their emphatic rejection of
legalistic conduct; they join hands, as it were, in face of the whole host of
legalistic moralists; they are convinced that conduct which is regulated by
abstract principles can never be good. But equally sternly the Christian
moralist rejects the individualistic doctrine of freedom, according to which

* From *The Divine Imperative,* by Emil Brunner, Chaps. 9 and 11. Translated by Olive
Wyon. Copyright, 1947, by W. L. Jenkins, The Westminster Press. Used by permission
of the Westminster Press and Lutterworth Press.

there is no longer any difference between "right" and "wrong." Rather, in the Christian view, that alone is "good" which is free from all caprice, which takes place in unconditional obedience. There is no Good save obedient behaviour, save the obedient will. But this obedience is rendered not to a law or a principle which can be known beforehand, but only to the free, sovereign will of God. The Good consists in always doing what God wills at any particular moment.

This statement makes it clear that for us the will of God cannot be summed up under any principle, that it is not at our disposal, but that so far as we are concerned the will of God is absolutely free. The Christian is therefore "a free lord over all things," because he stands directly under the personal orders of the free Sovereign God. This is why genuine "Christian conduct"—if we may use this idea as an illustration—is so unaccountable, so unwelcome to the moral rigorist and to the hedonist alike. The moral rigorist regards the Christian as a hedonist, and the hedonist regards him as a rigorist. In reality, the Christian is neither, yet he is also something of both, since he is indeed absolutely *bound* and obedient, but, since he is bound to the *free* loving will of God, he is himself free from all transparent bondage to principles or to legalism. Above all it is important to recognize that even love is not a principle of this kind, neither the love which God Himself *has*, nor the love which He *requires*. Only God Himself defines love in His action. We, for our part, do not know what God is, nor do we know what *love* is, unless we learn to know God in His action, in faith. To be in this His Love, is the commandment. Every attempt to conceive love as a principle leads to this result: it becomes distorted, either in the rigoristic, legalistic sense, or in the hedonistic sense. Man only knows what the love of God is when he sees the way in which God acts, and he only knows how he himself ought to love by allowing himself to be drawn by faith into this activity of God.

2. "To know God in His action" is only possible in faith. The action of God, in which He manifests Himself—and this means His love—is His revelation. God reveals Himself in His Word—which is at the same time a deed—in an actual event—in Jesus Christ; and He reveals Himself operatively in His living Word, which is now taking place—in the Holy Spirit. Because only conduct which takes place on the basis of this faith (and indeed in this faith in God's Word) can be "good conduct," in the sense of the Christian ethic, therefore, the science of good conduct, of ethics, is only possible within that other science which speaks of the Divine act of revelation, that is, within dogmatics. Reflection on the good conduct of man is only one part of more comprehensive reflection on the action of God in general. For human conduct can only be considered "good" when, and in so far as,

God Himself acts in it, through the Holy Spirit. Hence just as this action is connected with the Divine action, so the Christian ethic is connected with dogmatics.

The attempt to make a clear-cut distinction between dogmatics and ethics from the point of view that the one is concerned with Divine and the other with human action spoils both dogmatics and ethics. The New Testament proclamation of the Word of God is characterized by the fact that it makes no distinction between the "dogmatic" and the "ethical" elements. The great Christological passages occur in the midst of practical exhortations, and moral instructions are always most closely connected with "dogmatic" ideas. As the indicative and the imperative suddenly alternate, as speech about the redeeming love of God flows directly into the claim for human love, so the whole New Testament is an indissoluble blend of "ethics" and "dogmatics." This is true also, more or less, of the great confessional works of the Reformation; this is also true of the greatest—and, indeed, the only genuinely reformatory—dogmatic work of the Reformation: Calvin's *Institutes*. Every theme of dogmatics is also inevitably a theme of ethics. Dogmatics does not exist independently, nor does ethics, but dogmatic knowledge as such always aims at existential, that is, ethical, thought, and ethical knowledge is rooted in knowledge of dogmatics.

We can only rightly represent the whole of ethics as a part of dogmatics, because it is concerned with God's action in and through man. Not only the commandments of God, not only the New Birth and conversion, but also man's sanctification—if it really *is* what it is called—is wholly the work of God, certainly with this distinction: it is that one of His works which is expressed in our own external conduct.

On the other hand, once we have recognized legalism as *the* evil, once we have seen that the Good, in the moral sense, is that which God does in us and through us, how could we possibly seriously consider severing ethics from dogmatics? The specific element in the Christian ethic . . . is precisely this: that the Good in human conduct only arises out of the fact that it is set within the action of God. All other forms of conduct are legalistic. This is what the authors of the Heidelberg Catechism meant when they summed up all ethics under the heading—which is certainly easy to misunderstand—of "gratitude." Good can only take place in grateful acknowledgment of the action of God. The separation of dogmatics from ethics would lay dogmatics open to the danger of speculative aberrations and ethics to the danger of moralistic distortions.

Really good Christian conduct—speaking from the point of view of principle—ought to have the whole of the Christian knowledge of God "behind" it. Luther, in his Shorter Catechism, has expressed this very well, since he begins the explanation of every commandment with the words: "we ought thus to fear and love God, in order that we . . ."

The God who is thus to be feared and loved, however, is the One who is manifested in His revelation, "the whole God." Every ethical consideration is thus connected with the whole Idea of God. . . .

4. . . . The scientific presentation of the Christian ethic can certainly never represent the Good as a general truth, easy to be perceived, and based on a universal principle. Were it to do this, it would be an act of treason towards the Christian Faith. The meaning of the Christian ethic is the exact opposite; its task is to work out scientifically the characteristic element in the Christian knowledge of the Good, namely, that the Good, as faith knows it, can never be legalistic, or a matter of abstract principle; thus that the Christian ethic can never count on general recognition in the sense of a truth of reason, but, explicitly, only on the recognition of those who believe. For one who does not believe cannot understand the Christian conception of the Good.

But this does not mean that the Christian ethic makes no claim to universal validity. Whatever God demands *can* only be universal, that is, valid for all men, even if those who do not hear this demand do not admit this validity and indeed do not even understand the claim to universal validity. The believer alone clearly perceives that the Good, as it is recognized in faith, is the sole Good, and that all that is otherwise called good cannot lay claim to this title, at least not in the ultimate sense of the word. It is precisely faith and faith alone which knows this: that alone is good which God does; and, indeed, faith really consists in the fact that man knows this— and that he knows it in such a way as it alone can be known, namely, in the recognition of faith. But once man does know this he also knows the unlimited unconditional validity of this conception and of the divine demand. . . .

5. But what is the function of a system of ethics in regard to the central ethical question: What ought we to do? Can ethics tell us what we are to do? If it could, it would mean that the Christian ethic also is an ethical system based on law and on abstract principles. For where ethics is regarded purely as a science, there general, and to some extent timeless, propositions are stated. If these were to define what we ought to do, then the Good would be defined in legalistic terms. Therefore no such claim can be made either by or for ethics. The service it renders cannot be that of relieving us of the necessity for making moral decisions, but that it prepares the way for such decisions. How this takes place can only be made clear in the explication of the part which is played by law within a morality which is not legalistic. The significance of the law is the same as the significance of ethics,

namely: that it prepares the way for a voluntary decision, or for the hearing of the divine command.

In this explicit rejection of the legalistic definition of the Good the truly Christian ethic is also distinguished from the Roman Catholic ethic. In accordance with its juridically defined conception of faith and of the Church its conception of the Good is also rigidly legalistic, and therefore its ethical system is fundamentally a system of casuistry. The lesser stipulations are logically derived from the universal law, and by means of a closely woven network of further minor regulations the whole realm of human life is legally defined, so that for every case, in actual practice, it is possible to look up the ethical code and find out what is commanded and what is forbidden. The relation of knowledge in general and application to the particular case is determined by the purely logical relation of subsumption of the particular under the universal. . . . This conception cannot be combined with the knowledge of justification by faith alone. Ethical "orthodoxy"—the legalistic view of the Good—is just as bad as dogmatic orthodoxy, that is, as a legalistic view of faith and of the Word of God. . . .


## Chapter XI

### The Divine Command as Gift and Demand

2. . . . *The Good consists simply and solely in the fact* that man receives and deliberately accepts his life as a gift from God, as life dependent on "grace," as the state of "being justified" because it has been granted as a gift, as "justification by faith." Only thus can we know the Will of God, that is, in this revelation of Himself in which He manifests Himself as disinterested, generous Love.

3. But this Divine giving is not accomplished in any magical way; it simply takes place in the fact that *God "apprehends" man;* God *claims* us for His love, for His generous giving. But this means that He claims our whole existence for Himself, for this love of His; He gives us His love. He gives us His love in such a way that He captures us completely by the power of His love. *To belong* to Him, to this love, and through His love, means that we are the *bondslaves* of this will. To believe means to become a captive, to become His property, or rather, to know that we are His property. The revelation which makes it plain that the will of God is lavish in giving *to* man, makes it equally clear that His will makes a demand *on* man. His will *for* us also means that He wants something *from* us. He claims us for His love. This is His Command. It is the *"new* commandment," because only now can man perceive that it is the command of One who gives before He

demands, and who only demands something from us in the act of giving Himself to us. . . .

4. He claims us for *His* love, not for an *idea* of love—and not for a conception of the divine love which can be gained from merely reading the Bible. He claims us for His present, living activity of love, which can only be, and must always remain, His work. Therefore we can never know beforehand what God will require. God's command can only be perceived at the actual moment of hearing it. It would denote a breaking away from obedience if we were to think of the Divine Command as one which had been enacted once for all, to be interpreted by us in particular instances. To take this line would mean reverting to the legalistic distortion of His love. Love would then have become a "principle." The *free* love of God requires us to remain *free*, that we may be freely at His disposal. *You* cannot say what it means to love here and now; *He* alone can tell you what this means for you at this moment.

The Good is simply what *God* wills that we should do, not that which we would do on the basis of a principle of love. God wills to do something quite definite and particular through us, here and now, something which no other person could do at any other time. Just as the commandment of love is absolutely universal so also it is absolutely individual. But just as it is absolutely individual so also it is absolutely devoid of all caprice. "I will guide thee with Mine eye." No one can experience this "moment" save I myself. The Divine Command is made known to us "in the secret place." Therefore it is impossible for us to know it beforehand; to wish to know it beforehand—legalism—is an infringement of the divine honour. The fact that the holiness of God must be remembered when we dwell on His love means that we cannot have His love at our disposal, that it cannot ever be perceived as a universal principle, but only in the act in which He speaks to us Himself; even in His love He remains our *Master* and Lord. But He is our "Lord" in the sense that He tells us Himself what it means to "love," here and now. . . .

7. It is *His* will that God wills to accomplish in the world; He is not the servant of some purpose outside Himself. God Himself is His own End. In His love, however, He sets up an End outside Himself—without ceasing to be His own End; this "end" is the communion of the creature with Himself, the Creator. This Divine will for "community" is God's Sovereign Will. Therefore salvation, beatitude, the fulfilment of the purpose of life, both for humanity as a whole, and for the individual, is included in God's royal purpose. The tables of prohibition in the Bible may be compared with the notices on power circuits: Do Not Touch! Because God wills to control our life, He commands and He forbids. This is the "eudaemonism" of the

Gospel, and at the same time its absolutely serious view of duty. God wills our true happiness; but *He* wills it, and He wills it in such a way that no one else knows what His will is. It remains outside our disposal, and indeed we do not know it. We never know what is right for us, nor what is best for the other person. We go astray when we think that we can deduce this from some principle or another, or from some experience, and we distort the thought of the divine love if we think that we know what He ought to do for us in accordance with His love. But of one thing we may be quite sure: His will is love, even when we do not understand it—when He commands as well as when He gives.

Therefore in His revelation God's will is expressed by His sanctions, by rewards and punishments. God alone gives life; to be with Him is life, to resist Him is ruin. It is impossible to exist apart from God; it is impossible to be neutral towards Him. He who is not for Him is against Him. God's Command means eternal life and God means nothing else than this. He is Love. But His will is utterly serious; it is the will of the Lord of Life and Death. Anyone who—finally—resists Him, will only dash himself to pieces against the rock of His Being. This is the holiness of the love of God. As the divine love cannot be separated from His gift of life, so the Holiness of God cannot be separated from His judicial wrath, the denial and destruction of life. To have a share in the will of God, in the sense of union with His will, means salvation; to resist Him spells utter disaster.

The abstract legalistic system of ethics, because ideas have no connexion with life, can only judge this connexion of the moral element with reward and punishment as heteronomy, as the perversion of the moral endeavour. "We ought to do the Good for the sake of the Good." It does not perceive that behind this phrase, "for the sake of the Good," there lies concealed, "for My sake." And it does not understand that the Good is done for the sake of the Good when it is done for the sake of God, in obedience to the Divine Command. We ought to obey God because He commands it, not because obedience means happiness and disobedience means unhappiness. Faith would not be faith, obedience would not be obedience, if things were otherwise. But obedience would not be obedience towards *God*, did we not know that His Command means life and His prohibition death. The primary concern is not that which refers to my Ego, to my life; no, the primary concern is this: that it is God's will, the will of Him to whom my life belongs. But that which refers to *me*, that which refers to *my* life, is the necessary second element for it concerns the will of Him who Himself is life—even *my* life. Obedience would be impure if this second element were made the first. But it would be unreal, and indeed impossible, if this second element, as the second, were not combined with the first. We cannot do anything good which has no significance for life, and we cannot avoid anything evil, unless at the same time we know it to be harmful. It is not the question whether all morality is not mingled with self-interest—without self-interest nothing would concern us at all—but the question is this: is this self-interest regarded as founded in God or in myself? To do the Good for the sake of the Good is only a pale reflection of the genuine Good; to do the Good for the sake of God means to do the Good not because my moral dignity requires it, but because it is that which is commanded by God.

# CARDINAL MERCIER

DÉSIRÉ FÉLICIEN FRANÇOIS JOSEPH CARDINAL MERCIER (1851–1926) was Professor of Thomist Philosophy at the University of Louvain, Belgium. He served as Archbishop of Malines and a member of the College of Cardinals of the Roman Catholic Church. A leader of the Neo-Scholastic movement, his major works include: *Psychology* (1892), *Logic* (1894), *Metaphysics* (1894), *The Origins of Contemporary Psychology* (1897), *Criteriology* (1899), and A *Manual of Modern Scholastic Philosophy* (1917).

## The Moral Order*

### I. Moral Good and Evil

30. *There is a Real, Intrinsic Distinction between Moral Good and Moral Evil.* 1. ARGUMENT DRAWN FROM CONSCIOUSNESS. Certain things come before our consciousness as good and right, other things as bad and wrong, and this distinction imposes itself upon us with irresistible evidence. Similarly there are certain judgments about good and evil, justice and injustice, virtue and vice, the truth of which it is impossible to contest with any sincerity.

2. INDUCTIVE ARGUMENT. Induction confirms the data of consciousness. The distinction between good and evil is always presented before us with such notes of necessity, universality and persistence—and this in spite of the contrary solicitations of passions and interests—that a sufficient reason for it can only be found in the objective manifestation of truth, or better, of com-

---

* From A *Manual of Modern Scholastic Philosophy*, by Cardinal Mercier, Vol. II, "Ethics," Part I, Chap. 3. Part I written by A. Arendt, based upon Cardinal Mercier's notes. Translated by T. L. and S. A. Parker. Copyright, 1917, Kegan Paul, Trench, Trubner and Company. Used by permission of Routledge and Kegan Paul, Ltd.

pelling truths which are anterior to every code of merely human origin and independent of all contingent circumstances. Hence, short of denying the natural capacity of human reason to know the truth, and of thus logically professing scepticism, we must admit that the distinction between moral good and evil is founded on the very nature of things.

No doubt the application of moral principles to particular facts allows of divergencies and variations more or less considerable; but the root ideas of good and evil, of just and unjust, of lawful and unlawful, are the same at all times and among all peoples.

3. DEDUCTIVE ARGUMENT. Another argument may be drawn from the study of human nature itself. The good or right is by definition that which leads to the end of man's rational nature; conversely, we call wrong whatever is in opposition to the end of human nature. Now there must be some objects suitable, others unsuitable to human nature. Therefore between moral good and evil there must be a distinction which is founded on the nature of things.

31. *The Distinction between the Goodness and Badness of Human Actions is not explained in its Ultimate Analysis by any Extrinsic or Positive Influence, whether Human or even Divine.* Many writers think that purely positive influences can account for this distinction, such as traditional prepossessions, social conventions or laws, or an absolutely free decree of God. Montaigne thought it enough to appeal to the prejudices created by education. Hobbes and Rousseau both made the civil law the foundation of morality. It would seem that Puffendorf, and before him Descartes, attributed to God's free will the power of creating the distinction made by us between moral good and evil.

In the first place, this distinction is not explained by any human influence. (*a*) The nature of good and evil, as presented to our consciousness and reproduced in the invincible convictions of the human race, has already shown that the distinction between the rightness and wrongness of certain actions is independent of all positive intervention or system of government. A cause that is local, particular and changing cannot explain an effect that is universal, general and constant. (*b*) It is useless to have recourse with Hobbes to the despotic commands of an absolute monarch, or with Rousseau to the exigencies of a social contract; such commands or contracts do not themselves possess, *ex hypothesi*, an intrinsic goodness and consequently cannot communicate it to the acts which it is their purpose to regulate.

In the second place, this distinction does not rest on a free decree of the Divine Will. The opinion that makes the distinction between good and evil depend on the free will of God leads to inadmissible consequences: (*a*) God might then make blasphemy, perjury, violation of contracts, and the like obligatory upon us. (*b*) Whatever is morally good would be obligatory, and even heroism would be a duty forced upon us. (*c*) If all moral law owed its origin to a free act of the sovereign will of God, a positive revelation would be necessary for us to discern the difference between good and evil. Such conclusions as these condemn the principle from which they logically follow.

## II. *The Foundation of the Distinction between Moral Good and Evil*

32. *The Distinction between Good and Evil is founded on the Natural Conformity or Non-conformity of our Acts with our Supreme End.* If the good is what answers to the natural tendency of a being, the moral good is what answers to the tendency of the rational nature of man and is that by which he perfects himself. Now the end of our rational nature is the knowledge and love of God together with the joy that results from this knowledge and love. Hence a morally good act is one which, whether directly or indirectly, helps us to know and love God, and in so doing contributes to the perfecting of our rational nature; similarly, a thing is morally good which is the object of a morally good act.

Moral evil, on the other hand, is what is in opposition to the end of our rational nature; it is the act which is prejudicial to the perfecting of our rational nature, or it is the object of this act; in its ultimate analysis it is whatever withdraws us from the perfect knowledge and love of the Supreme Being and from the happiness which these acts should bring us.

What, as a matter of fact, is the criterion by which we judge of the intrinsic morality of an action? Do we not always find it in the connexion of this action with the perfection of our nature or, what comes to the same, in its connexion with our supreme end? We condemn drunkenness and licentiousness, we look upon them as vices, because they degrade and disgrace us. We esteem temperance and chastity as true virtues, because they ennoble us and answer to the demands of our dignity as men.

33. *Corollary.* Every good act is, at least implicitly or virtually, an act which contributes to the glory of God, just as every bad act is an offence against the majesty of God. Hence, St. Thomas teaches that every morally bad act, inasmuch as it cannot be referred to God, the last end of creation, is blame-worthy in His sight.

## III. *The Moral Law*

40. *Man is Subject to a Natural Law, that is, to an Inclination which habitually disposes him to know and will the End of his Rational Nature and what conduces to it, as well as to discern and reject what is contrary to it.* 1. ARGUMENT FROM ANALOGY. Every being in this world has within it an inclination towards some end, and its law is to tend towards it. Man is no exception; he is likewise set towards his end. This end directs human

activity by influencing the reason and the will; and this influence exercised by the end upon the higher faculties of man is called the natural law. Therefore man is under a natural law.

2. ARGUMENT FROM CONSCIOUSNESS. Man is conscious that a higher attraction carries him on towards the good which his reason points out to him, and he yields to evil solicitation only by overcoming interior resistance and after self-reproach for his own weakness: hence the satisfaction that is given by the practice of virtue and the shame that follows an evil act.

3. ARGUMENT DRAWN FROM PROVIDENCE. Before creating the world by His free act, God must have set Himself some end in view and have chosen means adapted to its realization. Being infinitely wise, He could not be deceived with regard to the relation of proportion between a creature and its end; being infinitely holy, He approved and willed this necessary relation; being infinitely powerful, He was able to bring it into being according to the capacity of the respective natures of the agents He created. God has therefore given to created beings an impulse towards their ends, a principle which directs their activities in conformity with the eternal designs of His Providence; in a word, He must have implanted in each created agent the natural law. Now this natural law must be in harmony with the constitution of the subject under its sway. The natural law implanted in man's nature, which is rational and free, cannot be, then, a fatalistic law; on the contrary, it must consist in an intellectual tendency to form some principles of reason with certainty, and in an impulse which, without forcing or necessarily determining the will, inclines it towards the real good apprehended by the intellect.

43. *Foundation of Moral Obligation.* In the opinion of most Christian moralists since the time of Kant, moral duty admits of only one possible explanation, namely the authority of God, the supreme Legislator of the moral order as He is of the physical. If there is a difference of opinion it is only on the question whether it is His essence, His intellect, His will, or His intellect and will combined, which gives the obligatory character to the moral law.

What are the arguments on which this interpretation of moral duty is based?—There cannot be law, we are reminded, without a lawgiver, nor a command without a superior who has the power and right to issue commands to his subjects. Now God alone has the power and right to issue commands that have a universal and absolute value; in God alone then do we find the principle of moral obligation. And secondly, the theological interpretation of moral duty is the only one which separates us from the theories of "the autonomy of reason" and "independent morality" as put forward by the rationalistic schools.

However, it would seem to us, this necessity of choosing between the theological morality, as explained above, and autonomous morality is in no way forced upon us. Consequently we prefer to follow unreservedly the opinion of St. Thomas which makes the moral obligation rest on a double foundation—immediately, upon human nature; remotely, upon the intelligence of God who rules all things by His Providence.

45. *The Ultimate Reason of the Distinction between Good and Evil, and consequently of Moral Obligation and Law, is found in God; it is formally in the Practical Reason of Him who has destined Beings to a Necessary Last End or, more briefly, in the Practical Reason of Providence.* God knows His own essence. He knows Himself as a necessary good. He accordingly knows how the beings He has power to create are related to His Essential goodness, and sees that every created being must of necessity have for its end the Divine Being, who alone is the necessary and infinite good.

If God wills creatures to exist distinct from Himself, it is impossible that He should not perceive by His practical reason the necessary relations of subordination which must exist between these creatures and the essential goodness of the Divine Being. These relations as conceived by the Divine Mind are "the eternal law." Such is the ultimate foundation of the distinction between good and evil, and of the natural law and of moral obligation.

# A. C. EWING

ALFRED CYRIL EWING (1899–   ) teaches at Cambridge University. A leading representative of intuitionism in ethics, he has also written extensively upon problems in metaphysics and social philosophy. His major works include: *The Morality of Punishment* (1929), *Idealism: A Critical Survey* (1934), *The Individual, The State, and World Government* (1947), *The Definition of Good* (1947), *The Fundamental Questions of Philosophy* (1951), and *Ethics* (1953).

## Ethics and the Commands of God*

A theological definition of ethical terms is the commonest and most intelligible type of metaphysical definition, and the natural form it would assume would be that "A ought to be done" is to be analysed as "A is commanded by God." . . .

* From *The Definition of Good*, by A. C. Ewing, pp. 106–9. Copyright, 1947, The Macmillan Company. Used by permission.

To a theological definition of the fundamental ethical concepts there seem to me to be fatal objections. . . . In the first place, if "obligatory" just means "commanded by God," God cannot command an act because it is right, and there is no reason whatever for his commands, which therefore become purely arbitrary. It would follow that God might just as rationally will that our whole duty should consist in cheating, torturing, and killing people to the best of our ability, and that then it would be our duty to act in that fashion. . . .

Secondly, why obey God's commands? Because I ought to do so? Since "I ought to do A" is held to mean "God commands me to do A," this can only mean that I am commanded by God to obey God's commands, which supplies no further reason. Because I love God? But this involves the assumptions that I ought to obey the commands of God if I love him, and that I ought to love God. So it again presupposes ethical propositions which cannot without a vicious circle be validated by referring once more to God's commands. Because God is good? This could on the view under discussion only mean that God carries out his own commands. Because God will punish me if I do not obey? This might be a very good reason from the prudential point of view, but these considerations of self-interest cannot be an adequate basis for ethics. Even if there is some affinity between command and obligation, a mere command, however powerful the being who issues it, cannot of itself create obligation. Without a prior conception of God being good or his commands being right God would have no more claim on our obedience than Hitler except that he would have more power than even Hitler ever had to make things uncomfortable for those who disobeyed him. It is only because the notion of God (for Christians at least, not to mention other religions) already includes the notion of perfect goodness that we are inclined to think it self-evident that we ought to obey God. And even if it were self-evident, without presupposing this, that we ought to obey God's commands, the proposed analysis of "ought" still could not be accepted. It is plain that the sentence "We ought to obey God's commands" does not just mean "We are commanded by God to obey his commands." But in any case it is obvious that doing what one ought could not be equated with obeying the commands of any sort of God but only with obeying those of a good God. . . .

We can find no necessary relation between being commanded by God and being obligatory, unless we already assume the goodness of God, thus exposing ourselves to a vicious circle, for we should in that case have both defined God in terms of goodness and goodness in terms of God.

# WILLIAM
# R. DENNES

WILLIAM RAY DENNES (1898–      ) is Professor of Philosophy at the University of
California. A naturalist in orientation, he has
published a number of articles in recent
philosophical journals. He has also contributed to *Knowledge and Society* (1938),
*Naturalism and the Human Spirit* (1944),
and to many of the volumes in the *University
of California Publications in Philosophy*.

## *Preface to an Empiricist Philosophy of Religion*\*

God's laws, we are often told, are moral commandments, rather than descriptions or prescriptions of natural order (if such prescriptions are taken as anything but moral). Here we must face two related questions. The first: . . . Can the commands, or the will, of deity make anything right that would not be right irrespective of such commands? or add anything to the right-ness of what is right irrespective of them? The second is the question: How do we recognize moral commands as proceeding authentically from deity?

We cannot consider these questions without some explanation of what we shall mean by 'value' or 'good,' and by 'right.' I understand 'valuable' to mean that in which men (or plants or animals) are positively interested, that in which delight is taken. And 'right' I take to be the adjective that designates such actions as will probably yield (in their particular situations) the most valuable results, in the sense of 'valuable' just defined. . . .

But if interest or delight make their objects valuable, should we then have to say that the objects of God's interest or delight or love have at least as good (for the religious, incomparably better) claims to be called valuable as have any objects or acts or institutions in which men may delight? No. Not only are we not obliged to say this, but should we try to say it we should be making a verbal distinction which expressed no distinction of meaning. For *the only ground any of us could have for sincerely accepting certain revealed preferences as the preferences of gods and not of devils, is the ground that the preferences agree with our own.* Hence, we are unable to say that what we call divine preferences can institute, or can enhance, values so as to distinguish them in any way from the objects of human love. If divine

* From "Preface to an Empiricist Philosophy of Religion," by W. R. Dennes, *College of Pacific Publications in Philosophy*, III (1934). Used by the kind permission of the College of Pacific.

preferences differed from our own, we could not sincerely describe them as determining what we should call valuable. Of course, we may trust a friend's, or an expert's, or a prophet's judgment rather than our own. But in matters of value, such trust is reasonable only as expressing the hope and expectation that, if we had the wider experience of him whose judgment we trust, we should share his preference. We can have no grounds for such expectation except the knowledge that our preference and the expert's agree with respect to some (or all) of those objects with which we are both acquainted, plus the evidence that the expert is probably acquainted with a wider range of objects than we are. And nothing could verify our expectation or justify our trust except the discovery that, in the event, we do come actually to agree with the expert's preference as we become conversant with the situations about which he advised us when we were ignorant of them. The expert's, or the god's, preference, therefore, can never be recognized as binding upon us until it becomes our preference. And, once it becomes our own preference, it constitutes its objects valuable in the only sense in which we can significantly or honestly call anything valuable for us, quite independently of any expert or authoritative preference. The new values which, following upon expert advice, we may come to appreciate are, in their status as valuable, independent of whatever influences may have led us to discover them. . . .

If we reject the definitions of 'right' and 'valuable' which I have employed, and define 'the right' as simply 'what God commands,' how are we to determine which of the various commands, offered to us by diverse religions as having divine origin and authority, are actually what their sponsors say they are? . . . Unless we know what is right by some mark other than that a god (or even all the gods) commands it, we shall be unable to distinguish the commands of gods from the commands of impostors. For although a command is punctuated by thunderbolts, or miraculously written on stone tablets, or spoken insistently in the hearts of men, it does not follow that it would be right to obey the command—unless we mean by 'right' nothing more than obedience to the thunderer, or the carver of stone tablets, or the still small voice. If we have reason for obeying any of these, it can only be that its expressions have seemed to us true and righteous in terms of *our* norms of truth and right. And, if the expressions were thus, and upon such grounds, true and righteous, then they were (and are) true and righteous whether they are said to be the voice of God or the voice of conscience, or are given no such reference to anything beyond what they themselves convey or advise.

We seem to be driven to the conclusion . . . that religious experience and theological doctrine add nothing to the meaning or truth of any statement or to the validity of any rule of conduct—add nothing which is not finally traceable to, and which does not owe its meaning and its probability to, observations and loves and preferences which remain what they are, and mean all that they do, whether or not they are referred to, or taken as evidence of, deity. . . . The confused notion that reference to deity confers validity has sometimes fired men's hearts to great undertakings. Unfortunately we must judge many of those undertakings to have been intolerant, mean-spirited, full of a persecuting zeal the more hideous because it pretended to an assurance of impeccable righteousness. And of the undertakings, those we regard as noble and fine we so regard because they were aimed towards, or contributed to, the things we love—not because they were commanded by any sort of authority—terrestrial or celestial.

It remains true, of course, that some religious geniuses have been among the wisest and noblest of men. That from their sayings, and from the example of their lives, we have a great deal to learn. Indeed, about some aspects of the conduct of life, many of the most accomplished of our moralists seem as innocent babes when compared with some of the "saints." But if our analysis has been acceptable, there is very great danger in confusing the truth and the rightness of what any man says, with the alleged authority of the speaker or of the speaker's source or inspiration. The nub of the whole matter is that such confusion leaves us no way whatever to distinguish the better from the worse, or "false gods from true."

The great danger to values in our time—to the very values which the greatest religious geniuses have loved—is that we may far too insufficiently perceive those values (perceiving them requires much study, much discipline, much labor), far too little appreciate them, and serve them. If we think their whole validity rests upon a theological sanction, then the moment that sanction is thrown into doubt (as it is to-day upon all sides, and for cogent reasons), at that very moment our confidence in the values themselves is destroyed. But if we took seriously what is actually the case, viz., that "whatsoever things are true, whatsoever things are honest, whatsoever things are just, whatsoever things are pure, whatsoever things are lovely, whatsoever things are of good report," are lovely and good for those who delight in them, and will be for all persons who may be brought to know and delight in them, irrespective of reference to authority—then no doubts could assail us, except the very proper and fruitful doubt whether we are taking the likeliest means to spread among men for their happiness, an appreciation of the fair practices, the beautiful objects and interesting techniques, and the knowledge, which we may love and know to be good. I say this doubt is proper and fertile, for it should be the source of a constant scrutiny and overhauling of our institutions, our conduct, and our objectives in order to make sure that we are not failing (more than our limitations may "excuse"), in the one

*35970*

satisfactory vocation (or, better, the combination of all the satisfactory vocations) that is within our powers. That vocation is: to develop and extend values in human experience. It is the task of replacing misery by joy, and waste of human life and capacities by interesting and useful work. Some sorts of human anguish we may never find ways to remove. But much positive suffering, and much missing of joyful and interesting work, we already know enough to correct. It is time we set ourselves to that business in earnest. Our vocation, as philosophers and as lovers of the genuine spiritual excellences dear to the religious, is not to ground values in a trans-empirical authority. Such an authority could, as we have seen, add nothing to the security of values, since the choice and the very authoritativeness of authorities themselves derives, and can derive, from no other source than our loves and hopes. Our vocation as philosophers is to be clear about these matters. . . .

Religion has been a great and precious symbol for much that is dearest to us. Its scriptures, its liturgy, its poetry and building and music and painting, are among the finest achievements of man. It was once sincerely believed that, without reference to deity, all these achievements must lose their worth. It is a great and tragic irony that this very belief should now be a source of danger to the values it was supposed to establish. For thoughtful men are coming to see that, irrespective of questions as to their truth or probability, references to deity cannot have the meanings once supposed. Hence, so far as they should hold the belief that divine sanction is the ground of excellence, they are now likely to become, not only skeptical of, but even cynically indifferent to, the values that have been dear to the religious. They are like children brought up to think of a parent or a government as clothed with inherent authority who, once they discover their mistake, are likely to consider worthless all that the parent or the government in question supported. Once such a confusion is cleared away, we shall see that all that was, or could have been, precious in religious experience is as secure as it ever was—secure, not as authoritative, but as important, insight with respect to objects worthy of human attention and appreciation, objects the cultivation of which is likely to be fruitful of new insights and new loves which may further human happiness.

The various goods the religions have enshrined stand on their own feet in human experience. All that we must give up is the meaningless conviction that we had reached absolutes—absolute truths about the whole cosmos, absolute duties irrespective of their results in experience, absolute values "valid" irrespective of human preference. This conviction added nothing to the preciousness of anything. All too often it lulled men's efforts by a false sense of security, and blinded them to the pains that must be taken if what is valuable is to be defended against its enemies, and developed and extended in the lives of men.

## THE AUTHORITY OF GOD—SUGGESTED READINGS

Barth, K., *The Word of God and the Word of Man.* Boston. Pilgrim Press, 1928, esp. Chap. 5. (proponent)

Brandt, R. B., *Ethical Theory,* Englewood Cliffs, N.J., Prentice-Hall, 1959, Chap. 4. (critic)

Cohen, M. R., *The Faith of a Liberal,* New York, Holt, 1946, Chap. 41. (critic)

Paley, W., *The Principles of Moral and Political Philosophy,* 1785, Book II. (proponent)

Plato, *Euthyphro.* (critic)

Tolstoy, L., "Religion and Morality," in *On Life and Essays on Religion,* London, Oxford University Press, 1934. (proponent)

## 2. CONSCIENCE

According to a familiar type of deontological ethical theory, the formal criterion of rightness resides not in an external authority, but as a voice within men: an act is right only if it is done in obedience to the commands of conscience. Conscience is taken to be the ultimate moral faculty: it approves our right actions, and makes us uneasy when we act wrongly. But what is the origin of conscience? Is it given us by God? Or is it developed in us as the result of our particular moral training? And do the consciences of all men command them to do the same things? Or does the *content* of conscience differ from place to place and from time to time? These questions we must ask of any conscience theory.

In the selections to follow, WAYLAND contends that conscience is God-given, that it gives the same moral commands to all men, and that it is the ultimate arbiter between right and wrong. DRAKE argues that conscience is a cultural product of natural and not supernatural origin, that one man may feel conscience-bound to perform an act which another man's conscience would condemn, and that, accordingly, conscience cannot be taken to be the ultimate moral authority. FROMM seeks to bring the insights of modern psychoanalysis to bear upon what he calls the "Authoritarian Conscience." It is his view that obedience to an authoritarian conscience, far from being a requirement of morality, is often highly undesirable.

# FRANCIS WAYLAND

FRANCIS WAYLAND (1796–1865) was the fourth president of Brown University, a position he held from 1827 until 1855. Active also as a Baptist minister and a teacher of philosophy, he preached and wrote extensively upon ethical and religious subjects. His major works include: *The Elements of Moral Science* (1835), *The Elements of Political Economy* (1837), *The Limitations of Human Responsibility* (1838), and *The Elements of Intellectual Philosophy* (1854).

## Conscience, or the Moral Sense*

### Is There a Conscience?

By conscience, or the moral sense, is meant that faculty by which we discern the moral quality of actions, and by which we are capable of certain affections in respect to this quality.

By *faculty* is meant any particular part of our constitution by which we become affected by the various qualities and relations of beings around us. Thus, by taste, we are conscious of the existence of beauty and deformity; by perception, we acquire a knowledge of the existence and qualities of the material world. And, in general, if we discern any quality in the universe, or produce or suffer any change, it seems almost a truism to say that we have a faculty, or power, for so doing. A man who sees, must have eyes, or the faculty for seeing; and *if he have not eyes,* this is considered a sufficient reason why *he should not see.* And thus it is universally admitted that there may be a thousand qualities in nature of which we have no knowledge, for the simple reason that we have not been created with the faculties for discerning them. There is a world without us and a world within us, which exactly correspond to each other. Unless *both exist,* we can never be conscious of the existence of either.

Now, that we do actually observe a moral quality in the actions of men, must, I think, be admitted. Every human being is conscious that, from childhood, he has observed it. We do not say that all men discern this quality with equal accuracy, any more than that they all *see* with equal distinctness; but we say that all men perceive it in some actions, and that there is a multitude of cases in which their perceptions of it will be found universally to

* From *The Elements of Moral Science,* by Francis Wayland, Chap. 2 (1835).

agree. And, moreover, this quality, and the feeling which accompanies the perception of it, are unlike those derived from every other faculty.

The question would then seem reduced to this: Do we perceive this quality of actions by a single faculty, or by a combination of faculties? I think it must be evident, from what has already been stated, that this notion is, in its nature, simple and ultimate, and *distinct from every other notion*. Now, if this be the case, it seems self-evident that we must have a *distinct and separate faculty* to make us acquainted with the existence of this *distinct and separate quality*. This is the case in respect to all other distinct and original qualities: it is, surely, reasonable to suppose that it would be the case with this, unless some reason can be shown to the contrary.

But, after all, this question is, to the moral philosopher, of but compara- tively little importance. All that is necessary to his investigations is, that it be admitted that there is such a quality, and that men are so constituted as to perceive it, and to be susceptible of certain affections in consequence of that perception. Whether these facts are accounted for on the supposition of the existence of a single faculty, or a combination of faculties, will not affect the question of moral obligation. If it be granted that we do actually recognize moral distinctions, and feel the pressure of moral obligation, it matters little whether in thus acting we make use of one power of the mind or of several.

It may, however, be worth while to consider some of the objections which have been urged against the supposition of the existence of such a faculty.

*I.* It has been said, if such a faculty has been bestowed, it must have been bestowed universally: but it is not bestowed universally; for what some nations consider right, other nations consider wrong: as infanticide, parricide, duelling, etc.

1. To this it may be answered, first, the objection seems to admit the uni- versality of the existence of conscience, or the power of discerning in certain actions a moral quality. It admits that everywhere men make this distinction, but affirms that in different countries they refer the quality to different actions. Now, *how this difference is to be accounted for*, may be a question; but the *fact* as stated in the objection shows the universality of the power of observing such a quality in actions.

2. But, secondly, we have said that we discover the moral quality of actions in the *intention*. *Now it is not the fact* that this difference exists, as stated in the objection, if the *intention* of actions be considered. Where was it not considered right to *intend* the happiness of parents? Where was it not con- sidered wrong to *intend* their misery? Where was it ever considered right to intend to requite kindness by injury? and where was it ever considered wrong to intend to requite kindness with still greater kindness? In regard

to the *manner* in which these intentions *may be fulfilled,* there may be a difference; but as to the moral quality of these *intentions themselves,* as well as of many others, there is a very universal agreement among men.

3. And still more, it will be seen, on examination, that in these very cases in which wrong actions are practised, they are justified on the ground of a good *intention,* or of some view of the relations between the parties, which, if true, would render them innocent. Thus, if infanticide be justified, it is on the ground that this world is a place of misery, and that the infant is better off not to encounter its troubles; that is, that the parent wishes or intends well to the child: or else it is defended on the ground that the relation between the parent and child is such as to confer on the one the right of life and death over the other; and, therefore, that to take its life is as innocent as the slaying of a brute or the destruction of a vegetable. Thus also are parricide, and revenge, and various other wrong actions defended. Where can the race of men be found, be they ever so savage, who need to be told that ingratitude is wrong, that parents ought to love their children, or that men ought to be submissive and obedient to the Supreme Divinity?

4. And still more, I think one of the strongest exemplifications of the universality of moral distinctions is found in the character of many of the ancient heathen. They perceived these distinctions, and felt and obeyed the impulses of conscience, even though at variance with all the examples of the deities whom they worshipped. . . .

II. Again, the objection has been made in another form. It is said that savages violate, without *remorse* or *compunction,* the plainest principles of right. Such is the case when they are guilty of revenge and licentiousness.

This objection has been partly considered before. It may, however, be added,

*First.* No men, nor any class of men, violate *every* moral precept without compunction, without the feeling of guilt, and the consciousness of desert of punishment.

*Secondly.* Hence the objection will rather prove the existence of a *defective* or *imperfect conscience,* than that no such faculty exists. The same objection would prove us destitute of taste or of understanding; because these faculties exist only in an imperfect state among savages and uncultivated men.

III. It has been objected, again, that if we suppose this faculty to exist, it is, after all, useless; for if a man please to violate it, and to suffer the pain, then this is the end of the question, and, as Dr. Paley says, "the moral instinct man has nothing more to offer."

To this it may be answered:

The objection proceeds upon a mistake respecting the function of conscience. Its use is to teach us to discern our moral obligations, and to impel us towards the corresponding action. It is not pretended, by the believers in a moral sense, that man may not, after all, do as he chooses. All that they contend for is, that he is constituted with such a faculty, and that the possession of it is necessary to his moral accountability. It is in his power to obey it or to disobey it, just as he pleases. The fact that a man may obey or disobey conscience, no more proves that it does not exist, than the fact that he sometimes does and sometimes does not obey passion, proves that he is destitute of passion. . . .

### The Authority of Conscience

We have thus far endeavored to show that there is in man a faculty denominated conscience. . . .

The object of the present section is to show that this is *the most authoritative impulse of which we find ourselves susceptible.*

The supremacy of conscience may be illustrated in various ways.

*I.*   It is involved in the very conception which men form of this faculty.

The various impulses of which we find ourselves susceptible, can differ only in two respects, that of *strength* and that of *authority.*

When we believe them to differ in nothing but *strength*, we feel ourselves perfectly at liberty to obey the strongest. Thus, if different kinds of food be set before us, all equally healthful, we feel entirely at liberty to partake of that which we prefer; that is, of that to which we are most strongly impelled. If a man is to decide between making a journey by land, or by water, he considers it a sufficient motive for choice, that the one mode of travelling is more pleasant to him than the other. But when our impulses differ in *authority*, we feel obliged to neglect the difference *in strength* of impulse, and to obey that, be it ever so weak, which is of the higher *authority.* Thus, suppose our desire for any particular kind of food to be ever so strong, and we know that it would injure our health, self-love would admonish us to leave it alone. Now, self-love being a more authoritative impulse than passion, we feel an *obligation* to obey it, be its admonition ever so weak, and the impulse of appetite ever so vehement. If we yield to the impulse of appetite, be it ever so strong, in opposition to that of self-love, be it ever so weak, we feel a consciousness of self-degradation, and of acting unworthily of our nature; and if we see another person acting in this manner, we cannot avoid feeling towards him a sentiment of contempt. " 'Tis not in folly not to scorn a fool." And, in general, whenever we act in obedience to a lower, and in opposition to a higher sentiment, we feel this consciousness of degradation, which we do not feel when the impulses differ *only in degree.* And, conversely, whenever we feel this consciousness of degradation for acting in obedience to one instead of to another, we may know that we have violated that which is of the higher authority.

If, now, we reflect upon our feelings consequent upon any moral action, I think we shall find that we always are conscious of a sentiment of self-degradation whenever we disobey the monition of conscience, be that monition *ever so weak*, to gratify the impulse of appetite, or passion, or self-love, be that impulse *ever so strong*. Do we consider it any palliation of the guilt of murder, for the criminal to declare that his vindictive feelings impelled him much more strongly than his conscience? whereas, if we perceived in these impulses no other difference than that of *strength*, we should consider this not merely an excuse, but a justification. And that the impulse of conscience is of the highest authority is evident from the fact that we cannot conceive of any circumstances in which we should not feel guilty and degraded from acting in obedience to any impulse whatever in opposition to it. And thus, we cannot conceive of any more exalted character than that of him who, on all occasions, yields himself up implicitly to the impulses of conscience, all things else to the contrary notwithstanding. I think no higher evidence can be produced to show that we do really regard the impulse of conscience as of higher authority than any other of which we are conscious.

II. The same truth may, I think, be rendered evident by observing the feelings which arise within us when we compare the actions of men with those of beings of an inferior order.

Suppose a brute to act from appetite, and injure itself by gluttony; or from passion, and injure another brute from anger: we feel nothing like *moral* disapprobation. We pity it, and strive to put it out of its power to act thus in future. We never feel that a brute is disgraced or degraded by such an action. But suppose a man to act thus, and we cannot avoid a feeling of disapprobation and of disgust; a conviction that the man has done violence to his nature. Thus, to call a man a brute, a sensualist, a glutton, is to speak to him in the most insulting manner: it is to say, in the strongest terms, that he has acted unworthily of himself, and of the nature with which his Creator has endowed him.

Again. Let a brute act from deliberate selfishness; that is, with deliberate caution seek its own happiness upon the whole, unmindful of the impulsions of present appetite, but yet wholly regardless of the happiness of any other of its species. In no case do we feel disgust at such a course of action; and in many cases, we, on the contrary, rather regard it with favor. We thus speak of the cunning of animals in taking their prey, in escaping danger, and in securing for themselves all the amount of gratification that may be in their power.

We are sensible, in these cases, that the animal has acted from the highest impulses of which the Creator has made it susceptible. But let a man act thus. Let him, careful merely of his own happiness upon the whole, be careful for nothing else, and be perfectly willing to sacrifice the happiness of others, to any amount whatsoever, to promote his own, to the least amount soever. Such has been, frequently, the character of sensual and unfeeling tyrants. We are conscious, in such a case, of a sentiment of disgust and deep disapprobation. We feel that the man has not acted in obedience to the highest impulses of which he was susceptible; and poets and satirists and historians unite in holding him up to the world as an object of universal detestation and abhorrence.

Again. Let another man, disregarding the impulses of passion and appetite and self-love, act, under all circumstances, in obedience to the monitions of conscience, unmoved and unallured by pleasure, and unawed by power; and we instinctively feel that he has attained to the highest eminence to which our nature can aspire; and that he has acted from the highest impulse of which his nature is susceptible. We are conscious of a conviction of his superiority, which nothing can outweigh; of a feeling of veneration, allied to the reverence which is due to the Supreme Being. And with this homage to virtue all history is filled. The judge may condemn the innocent, but posterity will condemn the judge. The tyrant may murder the martyr, but after-ages will venerate the martyr, and execrate the tyrant. And if we will look over the names of those on whom all past time has united in conferring the tribute of praise-worthiness, we shall find them to be the names of those who, although they might differ in other respects, yet were similar in this, that they shone resplendent in the lustre of unsullied virtue.

Now, as our Creator has constituted us such as we are, and as by our very constitution we do thus consider conscience to be the most authoritative impulse of our nature, it must be the most authoritative, unless we believe that he has deceived us, or, which is the same thing, that he has so formed us as to give credit to a lie.

III. The supremacy of conscience may be also illustrated by showing the necessity of this supremacy to the accomplishment of the objects for which man was created.

When we consider any work of art, as a system composed of parts, and arranged for the accomplishment of a given object, there are three several views which we may have of it, and all of them necessary to a complete and perfect knowledge of the thing.

1. We must have a knowledge of the several *parts* of which it is composed. Thus, he who would understand a watch, must know the various wheels and springs which enter into the formation of the instrument. But

this alone, as, for instance, if they were spread separately before him upon a table, would give him a very imperfect conception of a watch.

2. He must, therefore, understand how these parts are put together. This will greatly increase his knowledge; but it will still be imperfect, for he may yet be ignorant of the *relations* which the parts sustain to each other. A man might look at a steam boat until he was familiarly acquainted with its whole machinery, and yet not know whether the paddles were designed to move the piston-rod, or the piston-rod to move the paddles.

3. It is necessary, therefore, that he should have a conception of the *relation* which the several parts sustain to each other; that is, of the effect which every part was designed to produce upon every other part. When he has arrived at this idea, and has combined it with the other ideas just mentioned, then, and not till then, is his knowledge of the instrument complete.

It is manifest that this last notion—that of the relations which the parts sustain to each other—is frequently of more importance than either of the others. He who has a conception of the cause of motion in a steam-engine, and of the manner in which the ends are accomplished, has a more valuable notion of the instrument than he who has ever so accurate a knowledge of the several parts, without a conception of the relation. Thus, in the history of astronomy we learn that the existence of the several parts of the solar system was known for ages, without being productive of any valuable result. The progress of astronomy is to be dated from the moment when the relation which the several parts hold to each other was discovered by Copernicus.

Suppose, now, we desire to ascertain what is the relation which the several parts of any system are designed, by its author, to sustain to each other. I know of no other way than to find out that series of relations in *obedience to which* the system will accomplish the object for which it was constructed. Thus, if we desire to ascertain the relation which the parts of a watch are designed to sustain to each other, we inquire what is that series of relations in obedience to which it will accomplish the purpose for which it was constructed; that is, to keep time. For instance, we should conduct the inquiry by trying each several part, and ascertaining by experiment whether, on the supposition that *it was the cause of motion*, the result, namely, the keeping of time, could be effected. After we had tried them all, and had found that under no other relation of the parts to each other than that which assumes the mainspring to be the source of motion, and the balance-wheel to be the regulator of the motion, the result could be produced; we should conclude with certainty that this was the relation of the parts to each other, intended to be established by the maker of the watch.

And, again, if an instrument were designed for several purposes, and if it was found that not only a single purpose could not be accomplished, but that no one of them could be accomplished under any other system of relations than that which had been at first discovered, we should arrive at the highest proof of which the case was susceptible, that such was the relation intended to be established between the parts by the inventor of the machine.

Now, man is a system composed of parts in the manner above stated. He has various powers, and faculties, and impulses; and he is manifestly designed to produce some result. As to the ultimate design for which man was created, there may be a difference of opinion. In one view, however, I presume there will be no difference. It will be allowed by all that he was designed for the production of his own happiness. Look at his senses, his intellect, his affections, and at the external objects with which these are brought into relation; and at the effects of the legitimate action of these powers upon their appropriate objects; and no one can for a moment doubt that this was *one* object for which man was created. Thus it is as clear that the eye was intended to be a source of pleasure as that it was intended to be the instrument of vision. It is as clear that the ear was intended to be a source of pleasure as to be the organ of hearing. And thus of the other faculties.

But when we consider man as an instrument for the production of happiness, it is manifest that we must take into the account, man as a society as well as man as an individual. The larger part of the happiness of the individual depends upon society; so that whatever would destroy the happiness of man as a society, would destroy the happiness of man as an individual. And such is the constitution under which we are placed, that no benefit or injury can be, in its nature, individual. Whoever truly promotes his own happiness, promotes the happiness of society; and whoever promotes the happiness of society, promotes his own happiness. In this view of the subject, it will then be proper to consider man as a society, as an instrument for producing the happiness of man as a society, as well as man as an individual, as an instrument for producing the happiness of man as an individual.

Let us now consider man as an instrument for the production of human happiness, in the sense here explained.

If we examine the impulsive and restraining faculties of man, we shall find that they may generally be comprehended under three classes:

1. *Passion or appetite.* The object of this class of our faculties is to impel us towards certain acts which produce immediate pleasure. Thus, the appetite for food impels us to seek gratification by eating. The love of power impels us to seek the gratification resulting from superiority; and so of all the rest.

If we consider the nature of these faculties, we shall find that they impel us to immediate gratification, without any respect to the consequences, either to ourselves or to others; and that they know of no limit to indulgence, until, by their own action, they paralyze the power of enjoyment. Thus, the love of food would impel us to eat, until eating ceased to be a source of pleasure. And where, from the nature of the case, no such limit exists, our passions are insatiable. Such is the case with the love of wealth, and the love of power. In these instances, there being in the constitution of man no limit to the power of gratification, the appetite grows by what it feeds on.

2. *Interest or self-love.* This faculty impels us to seek our own happiness, considered in reference either to a longer or shorter period, but always to one beyond the present moment. Thus, if appetite impelled me to eat, self-love would prompt me to eat such food, and in such quantity, as would produce for me the greatest amount of happiness upon the whole. If passion prompted me to revenge, self-love would prompt me to seek revenge in such a manner as would not involve me in greater distress than that which I now suffer; or to control the passion entirely, unless I could so gratify it as to promote my own happiness for the future, as well as for the present. In all cases, however, the promptings of self-love have respect solely to the production of our own happiness; they have nothing to do with the happiness of any other being.

3. *Conscience.* The office of conscience, considered in relation to these other impulsive faculties, is, to restrain our appetites within such limits that the gratification of them will injure neither ourselves nor others; and so to govern our self-love, that we shall act, not solely in obedience to the law of our own happiness, but in obedience to that law which restricts the pursuit of happiness within such limits as shall not interfere with the happiness of others. It is not here asserted that conscience always admonishes us to this effect, or that when it admonishes us it is always successful. We may, if we please, disobey its monitions; or, from reasons hereafter to be mentioned, its monitions may have ceased. What we would speak of here is the tendency and object of this faculty, and the result to which, if it were perfectly obeyed, it would manifestly lead. And that such is its tendency, I think that no one, who reflects upon the operations of his own mind, can for a moment doubt.

Suppose, now, man to be a system for the promotion of happiness, individual and social, and these various impelling powers to be parts of it. These powers being frequently, in their nature, contradictory—that is, being such that one frequently impels *to* and another repels *from* the same action—the question is, In what relation of these powers to each other can the happiness of man be most successfully promoted?

1. It cannot be asserted that when these impulsions are at variance it is a matter of indifference to which of them we yield; that is, that a man is just as happy, and renders society just as happy, by obeying the one as the other. For, as men always obey either the one or the other, this would be to assert

that all men are equally happy, and that every man promoted his own happiness just as much by one course of conduct as by another; than which nothing can be more directly at variance with the whole experience of all men in all ages. It would be to assert that the glutton who is racked with pain is as happy as the temperate and healthy man; and that Nero and Caligula were as great benefactors to mankind as Howard or Wilberforce.

2. If, then, it be not *indifferent* to our happiness to *which* of them we yield the supremacy, the question returns, Under what relation of each to the other can the happiness of man be most successfully promoted?

1. Can the happiness of man be promoted by subjecting his other impulses to his appetites and passions?

By referring to the nature of appetite and passion, as previously explained, it will be seen that the result to the individual of such a course would be sickness and death. It would be a life of unrestrained gratification of every desire, until the power of enjoyment was exhausted, without the least regard to the future; and of refusal to endure any present pain, no matter how great might be the subsequent advantage. Every one must see that, under the present constitution, such a course of life must produce nothing but individual misery.

The result upon society would be its utter destruction. It would render every man a ferocious beast, bent upon nothing but present gratification, utterly reckless of the consequences which gratification produced upon himself, either directly or through the instrumentality of others, and reckless of the havoc which he made of the happiness of his neighbor. Now, it is manifest that the result of subjecting man to such a principle would be not only the destruction of society, but also, in a few years, the entire destruction of the human race.

2. Can the happiness of man be best promoted by subjecting all his impulses to self-love?

It may be observed that our knowledge of the future, and of the results of the things around us, is manifestly insufficient to secure our own happiness, even by the most sagacious self-love. When we give up the present pleasure, or suffer the present pain, we must, from necessity, be wholly ignorant whether we shall ever reap the advantage we anticipate. The system, of which every individual forms a part, was not constructed to secure the happiness of any single individual; and he who devises his plans with sole reference to himself, must find them continually thwarted by that Omnipotent and Invisible Agency which is overruling all things upon principles directly at variance with those which he has adopted. Inasmuch, then, as we can never certainly *secure* to ourselves those results which self-love anticipates, it seems necessary that, in order to derive from our actions the happiness which they are capable of producing, they involve in themselves some element, irrespective of future result, which shall give us pleasure, let the result be what it may. . . .

Besides, a man acting from uncontrolled self-love knows of no other object than his *own* happiness. He would sacrifice the happiness of others to any amount, how great soever, to secure his own, in any amount, how small soever. Now, suppose every individual to act in obedience to this principle; it must produce universal war, and terminate in the subjection of all to the dominion of the strongest, and in sacrificing the happiness of all to that of one; that is, producing the *least amount* of happiness of which the system is susceptible. And still more, since men who have acted upon this principle have been proverbially unhappy, the result of such a course of conduct is to render *ourselves miserable* by the *misery of every one else*; that is, its tendency is to the *entire destruction of happiness*. It is manifest, then, that the highest happiness of man cannot be promoted by subjecting all his impulses to the government of self-love.

*Lastly.* Suppose, now, all the impulses of man to be subjected to *conscience*.

The tendency of this impulse, so far as this subject is concerned, is, to restrain the appetites and passions of man within those limits that shall conduce to his happiness on the whole, and so to control the impulse of self-love, that the individual, in the pursuit of his own happiness, shall never interfere with the rightful happiness of his neighbor. Each one, under such a system, and governed by such an impulse, would enjoy all the happiness which he could create by the use of the powers which God had given him. All men doing thus, the whole would enjoy all the happiness of which their constitution was susceptible. The happiness of man as an individual, and as a society, would thus be, in the best conceivable manner, provided for. And thus, under the relation which we have suggested—that is, conscience being supreme, and governing both self-love and passion; and self-love, where no higher principle intervened, governing passion—man individual and man universal, considered as an instrument for the production of happiness, would best accomplish the purpose for which he was created. This, then, is the relation between his powers, which was designed to be established by his Creator.

# DURANT
# DRAKE

DURANT DRAKE (1878–1933) taught at Vassar College. A person of broad interests, he wrote upon a wide variety of philosophical subjects. His major works include: *Problems of Conduct* (1914; rev. ed., 1921), *Problems of Religion* (1916), *Mind and Its Place in Nature* (1925), *The New Morality* (1928), and *Invitation to Philosophy* (1933).

## On Conscience*

### Out of What Has Conscience Developed?

The "conscience" of our moralizing and religious literature figures as a sharply defined and easily recognizable "faculty," like "will" or "reason." But this classification, though useful, is misleading by its simplicity. If we observe by introspection what goes on in our minds when we "will" or "reason" or "listen to conscience," we shall find all sorts of emotions, ideas, impulses, surging back and forth, altering from moment to moment, never twice the same. At another period of our lives, or in another man's mind, the psychological stuff pigeonholed under these names may be almost entirely different. A great many diverse mental elements have at one time or other taken the rôle of, or formed an ingredient in, the function we label "conscience." We will enumerate the more important:—

(1) Experience quickly teaches her pupils that certain acts to which they feel a strong impulse will lead to an aftermath of pain or weariness, or will stand in the way of other goods which they more lastingly desire or more deeply need. The memory of these consequences of acts remains as a guide for future conduct, not so often in the form of a clearly recognized memory as in a dim realization that the dangerous act must be avoided, a vague pressure against the pull of momentary inclination, or an uncomprehended feeling of impulsion toward the less inviting path. This residuum of the moral experience of the individual is one ingredient in what we call his conscience.

(2) But there is much more than this. The individual is a member of a group. The customs and expectations of this group not only bear upon him from without but find a reflection in his own motor-mechanism. He hears the voice of the community in his heart, an echo of the general condemna-

tion and approval. This acquired response, the reverberation of the group-judgment, may easily supplant his personal inclinations. Primitive man is sensitive to the judgments and emotional reactions of his fellows; the tribal point of view is unquestioned and authoritative over him. So important is this pressure in his mental life, though not understood or recognized for what it is, that conscience is defined by many moralists as the pressure of the judgment of the tribe in the mental life of its members, or in similar terms. Paulsen calls it "the existence of custom in the consciousness of the individual." This is to neglect unjustly the other sources of the sense of duty; but certainly the pulls and pushes arising from these two sources, which we may call the inner aspect of individual moral experience and of loyalty to the community-morals, reinforcing one another as they generally do, produce a very powerful form of conscience.

(3) A number of primitive emotions join forces with them. Sympathy is generally on their side, and the instinctive glow of patriotism or pride in the tribe's success. The shrinking from disapproval, the craving for esteem, the very early emotions of shame and vanity, help to pull away from the self-indulgent or selfish impulse. The spontaneous admiration of others for their virtues and anger at them for their sins is applied involuntarily by a man to himself; contempt for his own weakness and joy in his superiority according to the generally accepted code are powerful deterrents. The consciousness of the resentment that others will feel if he does evil, the instinctive application to himself of a trace of the resentment he would feel toward another who should act thus toward him or toward these fellow tribesmen of his—such complex states of mind complicate his mental processes and help check his primary instincts.

(4) To these ingredients we must early add the more or less conscious fear of the penalties of the tribal law, of the vengeance of chiefs or powerful members of the tribe, of the tribal gods and their jealous priests. These fears may be but dimly felt and not clearly discriminated; but however subconscious they may be in a given case of moral conflict, they play a large part. The peace of mind that accompanies a sense of conformity to the will of rulers or of gods, contrasted with the anxiety that follows infraction, gives a greatly increased weight to that growing pressure of counter-instincts which comes so largely to override a man's animal nature.

Most of the sources of conscience thus date far back beyond the dawn of history. But they can be pretty safely inferred from the earliest records, from a study of existing savage races, and from the study of childhood. The definite conception of "conscience" is very late, scarcely appearing until very modern times. And the fact that conscience itself, even in its rudimentary forms, was much later in growth than the underlying animal instincts which it developed to control and guide, is shown by its late development in the child—not, normally, until the beginning of the third year. The early life of the individual parallels the evolution of the race; and the later-developed faculties in the child are those which arose in the later stages of human progress. But the existence of our well-defined moral sense, with its significant rôle in modern life, needs no supernatural explanation. It has grown up and come to be what it is as naturally as have our language, our customs, and our physical organs. . . .

## Can We Base Morality Upon Conscience?

To the popular mind very often, the approval or disapproval of conscience is immediate, intuitive, and unerring. Its authority is absolute and not to be questioned. We have this faculty within us that tells us as surely what is right and what wrong as our color-sense tells us what is red and what green. Some people may, to be sure, be color-blind, or have defective consciences; but the great mass of unsophisticated people possess this innate guide and commandment, a quite sufficient warrant for all our distinctions of good and evil. Honest men do not really differ in their moral judgments. They may misunderstand one another's concepts and engage in verbal disputes; but at bottom their moral sense approves and disapproves the same acts. Our moral differences come mainly from the deluding effects of passion and the sophisti-cated ingenuities of the intellect. We should . . . listen to the inner voice. If we sincerely listen and obey we shall always do right.

We cannot but recognize a certain amount of practical truth in this picture. But it is over-simplified, and it is fundamentally unsatisfactory to the intellect. We shall now pass in review its most obvious inadequacies.

## Do the Deliverances of Different People's Consciences Agree?

Nothing is more notorious to an unbiased observer than the conscientious differences between men. Even among members of a single community, with closely similar inheritance and environment, we find marked divergence in moral judgment. And when we compare widely different times and places we are apt to wonder if there is any common ground. It is only a very smug provincialism that can attribute the alien standards of other races and na-tions to a disregard of the light. Mohammedans and Buddhists have believed as firmly in, and fought as passionately for, their moral convictions as Chris-tians have for theirs. When we survey the vast amount of material amassed by anthropologists, we find that, as has been often said, there is hardly a vice that has not somewhere been deemed a virtue, and hardly a virtue but has been branded as a vice. History is full of the pathos of havoc wrought by conscientious men, of foolish and ruinous acts which they have braced them-

selves to do for conscience' sake. One has but to think of the earnest and
prayerful inquisitors and persecutors in the mediæval Church, of the Puritans
destroying the stained-glass windows and paintings of the Madonna, of the
caliph who destroyed the great Alexandrian library, bereaving the world at
one blow of that priceless culture-inheritance. Written biography, fiction
which truly represents life, and individual memory are full of sad instances
where deadlocks of conscience have sundered those who truly loved and
wrought irremediable pain and loss. Lately the newspapers told us of the
heroic suicide of General Nogi and his wife, who felt it their duty not to
survive their emperor. To a Catholic Christian this imperious dictate of the
Japanese conscience would be a deadly sin. And so it goes. There is no need
to multiply instances of what can be observed on every hand. Conscience
reflects the traditions and influences amid which a man grows up.

But if the deliverances of different men's consciences conflict, how shall
we know which to trust? If any particular command of the inner voice may
be morally wrong, how can we trust it at all? There are obviously morbid and
perverted consciences; but if conscience itself is the ultimate authority, and
is not to be justified and criticized by some deeper test, what right have we
to call any of its manifestations morbid or perverted? Is it not a species of
egotism to hold one's own moral discernment as superior to another's; and if
so, do we not need some criterion by which to judge between them? Surely
the diversity of its judgments makes conscience an impossible foundation for
morality; we should have as many codes as consciences and fall into a hopeless confusion.

### If Conscience Everywhere Agreed in its Dictates, Could We Base Morality upon it?

Even, however, if conscience led us all in the same direction, would that
prove its authority? Perhaps we should all be following a will o' the wisp, and
foolishly sacrificing our desires to an idol of the tribe, a universal superstition.
Must it not show its credentials before it can legitimately command our
allegiance? It is but one specific type of impulse among many; why should it
be given the reins, the control over all? Do we say, because conscience makes
for our best welfare? The answer would, in general, be true; but we should
then be putting as our test and ultimate authority the attainment of our
welfare, which would be to abandon the point of view we are discussing. Conscience claims authority. But that might conceivably be mere impudence and
tyranny. Moreover, there are those who feel no call to follow conscience;
how could we prove to them that they ought? Is it not the height of irrationality to bow down before an unexplained and mysterious impulse and
allow it to sway our conduct without knowing why? If the "ought" is really

shot out of the blue at us, if there is no justification, no imperious demand for morality but the existence of this inner push, why might we not raise our heads, refuse to be dominated by it, and live the life of free men, following the happy breezes of our desires? . . .

A further realization of the inadequacy of the . . . theory comes when we observe that conscience is by no means always clear in its dictates. It often leaves us in the lurch. Developed in us as it has been by circumstance and suggestion, it helps us usually only in certain recognized types of situation. When new cases arise, it is hopelessly at sea. As a practical working principle, conscientiousness is not only apt to be a perverted and provincial guide, it is insufficient for the solving of fresh and difficult problems. . . . Morality must remain largely experimental, individual. Conscience will play a very useful rôle in spurring us to our recognized duty in the commoner situations, but for all the more delicate decisions we need a more ultimate touchstone. We must grasp the underlying principles of right conduct, and weigh the relative goods attainable by each possible act. A well-balanced and normal conscience will save us the recurrent reasoning out of typical perplexities, but it must be supplemented by an insight into the ends to be aimed for and kept rather strictly in its place. . . .

———

Our discussion, though rapid, should show that we cannot start with the "ought" of our conscience, or moral sense, and erect our moral theory upon that. Conscience itself needs to be explained. Its commands need to be justified by reference to some more ultimate criterion. It needs to be pruned of its fanaticism, developed where it is weak, and kept in line with our growing insight into what is best in conduct. Ruskin once summed the matter up by saying, "Obey thy conscience! But first be sure it is not the conscience of an ass!" Conscience may be a very dangerous guide. And even where it is normal and useful it must not be invested with any absolute and irrational authority.

# ERICH FROMM

ERICH FROMM (1900–    ) is a psycho-
analyst who has written widely upon problems in ethics, social philosophy, and religion.
His major works include: *Escape from Freedom* (1941), *Man for Himself* (1947),
*Psychoanalysis and Religion* (1950), *The
Sane Society* (1955), and *The Art of Loving*
(1956).

## Authoritarian Conscience*

The authoritarian conscience is the voice of an internalized external
authority, the parents, the state, or whoever the authorities in a culture
happen to be. As long as people's relationships to the authorities remain
external, without ethical sanction, we can hardly speak of conscience; such
conduct is merely expediential, regulated by fear of punishment and hope
for reward, always dependent on the presence of these authorities, on their
knowledge of what one is doing, and their alleged or real ability to punish
and to reward. Often an experience which people take to be a feeling of
guilt springing from their conscience is really nothing but their fear of such
authorities. Properly speaking, these people do not feel *guilty* but *afraid*. In
the formation of conscience, however, such authorities as the parents, the
church, the state, public opinion are either consciously or unconsciously
accepted as ethical and moral legislators whose laws and sanctions one adopts,
thus internalizing them. The laws and sanctions of external authority become part of oneself, as it were, and instead of feeling responsible to something outside oneself, one feels responsible to something inside, to one's
*conscience*. Conscience is a more effective regulator of conduct than fear of
external authorities; for, while one can run away from the latter, one can
not escape from oneself nor, therefore, from the internalized authority which
has become part of oneself. The authoritarian conscience is what Freud has
described as the Super-Ego. . . .

While authoritarian conscience is different from fear of punishment and
hope for reward, the relationship to the authority having become internalized,
it is not very different in other essential respects. The most important point
of similarity is the fact that the prescriptions of authoritarian conscience are

* From *Man for Himself*, by Erich Fromm, Chap. 4. Copyright, 1947, by Erich Fromm.
Used by permission of Holt, Rinehart and Winston, Inc.

not determined by one's own *value judgment* but exclusively by the fact that its commands and tabus are pronounced by authorities. If these norms happen to be good, conscience will guide man's action in the direction of the good. However, they have not become the norms of conscience *because* they are good, but because they are the norms given by authority. If they are bad, they are just as much part of conscience. A believer in Hitler, for instance, felt he was acting according to *his* conscience when he committed acts that were humanly revolting.

But even though the relationship to authority becomes internalized, this internalization must not be imagined to be so complete as to divorce conscience from the external authorities. Such complete divorcement, which we can study in cases of obsessional neurosis, is the exception rather than the rule; normally, the person whose conscience is authoritarian is bound to the external authorities *and* to their internalized echo. In fact, there is a constant interaction between the two. The presence of external authorities by whom a person is awed is the source which continuously nourishes the internalized authority, the conscience. If the authorities did not exist in reality, that is, if the person had no reason to be afraid of them, then the authoritarian conscience would weaken and lose power. Simultaneously, the conscience influences the image which a person has of the external authorities. For such conscience is always colored by man's need to admire, to have some ideal, to strive for some kind of perfection, and the image of perfection is projected upon the external authorities. The result is that the picture of these authorities is, in turn, colored by the "ideal" aspect of conscience. This is very important because the concept a person has of the qualities of the authorities differs from their real qualities; it becomes more and more idealized and, therefore, more apt to be re-internalized. Very often this interaction of internalization and projection results in an unshakable conviction in the ideal character of the authority, a conviction which is immune to all contradictory empirical evidence.

The contents of the authoritarian conscience are derived from the commands and tabus of the authority; its strength is rooted in the emotions of fear of, and admiration for, the authority. *Good conscience is consciousness of pleasing the (external and internalized) authority; guilty conscience is the consciousness of displeasing it.* The good (authoritarian) conscience produces a feeling of well-being and security, for it implies approval by, and greater closeness to, the authority; the guilty conscience produces fear and insecurity, because acting against the will of the authority implies the danger of being punished and—what is worse—of being deserted by the authority.

In order to understand the full impact of the last statement we must remember the character structure of the authoritarian person. He has found inner security by becoming, symbiotically, part of an authority felt to be greater and more powerful than himself. As long as he is part of that authority —at the expense of his own integrity—he feels that he is participating in the authority's strength. His feeling of certainty and identity depends on this symbiosis; to be rejected by the authority means to be thrown into a void, to face the horror of nothingness. Anything, to the authoritarian character, is better than this. To be sure, the love and approval of the authority give him the greatest satisfaction; but even punishment is better than rejection. The punishing authority is still with him, and if he has "sinned," the punishment is at least proof that the authority still cares. By his acceptance of the punishment his sin is wiped out and the security of belonging is restored.

The Biblical report of Cain's crime and punishment offers a classic illustration of the fact that what man is most afraid of is not punishment but rejection. God accepted Abel's offerings but did not accept Cain's. Without giving any reason, God did to Cain the worst thing that can be done to a man who can not live without being acceptable to an authority. He refused his offering and thus rejected *him*. The rejection was unbearable for Cain, so Cain killed the rival who had deprived him of the indispensable. What was Cain's punishment? He was not killed or even harmed; as a matter of fact, God forbade anyone to kill him (the mark of Cain was meant to protect him from being killed). His punishment was to be made an *outcast*; after God had rejected him, he was then separated from his fellow men. This punishment was indeed one of which Cain had to say: "My punishment is greater than I can bear."

So far I have dealt with the formal structure of the authoritarian conscience by showing that the good conscience is the consciousness of pleasing the (external and internalized) authorities; the guilty conscience, the consciousness of displeasing them. We turn now to the question of what the *contents* of good and of guilty authoritarian conscience are. While it is obvious that any transgression of positive norms postulated by the authority constitutes disobedience and, therefore, guilt (regardless of whether or not these norms in themselves are good or bad), there are offenses which are intrinsic to any authoritarian situation.

The prime offense in the authoritarian situation is rebellion against the authority's rule. Thus disobedience becomes the "cardinal sin"; obedience, the cardinal virtue. Obedience implies the recognition of the authority's superior power and wisdom; his right to command, to reward, and to punish according to his own fiats. The authority demands submission not only because of the fear of its power but out of the conviction of its moral superiority and right. The respect due the authority carries with it the tabu on questioning it. The authority may deign to give explanations for his commands and prohibitions, his rewards and punishments, or he may refrain from doing so; but never has the individual the *right* to question or to criticize. If there seem to be any reasons for criticizing the authority, it is the individual subject to the authority who must be at fault; and the mere fact that such an individual dares to criticize is *ipso facto* proof that he is guilty.

The duty of recognizing the authority's superiority results in several prohibitions. The most comprehensive of these is the tabu against feeling oneself to be, or ever able to become, *like* the authority, for this would contradict the latter's unqualified superiority and uniqueness. The real sin of Adam and Eve is . . . the attempt to become like God; and it is as punishment for this challenge and simultaneously as deterrence of a repetition of it that they are expelled from the Garden of Eden. In authoritarian systems the authority is made out to be fundamentally different from his subjects. He has powers not attainable by anyone else: magic, wisdom, strength which can never be matched by his subjects. Whatever the authority's prerogatives are, whether he is the master of the universe or a unique leader sent by fate, the fundamental inequality between him and man is the basic tenet of authoritarian conscience. One particularly important aspect of the uniqueness of the authority is the privilege of being the only one who does not follow another's will, but who himself wills; who is not a means but an end in himself; who creates and is not created. In the authoritarian orientation, the power of will and creation are the privilege of the authority. Those subject to him are means to his end and, consequently, his property and used by him for his own purposes. The supremacy of the authority is questioned by the attempt of the creature to cease being a *thing* and to become a creator.

But man has never yet ceased striving to produce and to create because productiveness is the source of strength, freedom, and happiness. However, to the extent to which he feels dependent on powers transcending him, his very productiveness, the assertion of his will, makes him feel guilty. The men of Babel were punished for trying by the efforts of a unified human race to build a city reaching to heaven. Prometheus was chained to the rock for having given man the secret of fire, symbolizing productiveness. Pride in the power and strength of man was denounced by Luther and Calvin as sinful pride; by political dictators, as criminal individualism. Man tried to appease the gods for the crime of productiveness by sacrifices, by giving them the best of the crop or of the herd. Circumcision is another attempt at such appeasement; part of the phallus, the symbol of male creativeness, is sacrificed to God so that man may retain the right to its use. In addition to sacrifices in which man pays tribute to the gods by acknowledging—if only symbolically—their monopoly on productiveness, man curbs his own powers by feelings of guilt, rooted in the authoritarian conviction that the exercise of his own will and creative power is a rebellion against the authority's prerogatives to be the sole creator and that the subjects' duty is to be his "things." This feeling of guilt, in turn, weakens man, reduces his power, and increases his submission in order to atone for his attempt to be his "own creator and builder."

Paradoxically, the authoritarian *guilty* conscience is a result of the feeling of strength, independence, productiveness, and pride, while the authoritarian *good* conscience springs from the feeling of obedience, dependence, powerlessness, and sinfulness. St. Paul, Augustine, Luther, and Calvin have described this good conscience in unmistakable terms. To be aware of one's powerlessness, to despise oneself, to be burdened by the feeling of one's own sinfulness and wickedness are the signs of goodness. The very fact of having a guilty conscience is in itself a sign of one's virtue because the guilty conscience is the symptom of one's "fear and trembling" before the authority. The paradoxical result is that the (authoritarian) *guilty conscience becomes the basis for a "good" conscience, while the good conscience,* if one should have it, *ought to create a feeling of guilt.*

The internalization of authority has two implications: one, which we have just discussed, where man submits to the authority; the other, where he takes over the role of the authority by treating himself with the same strictness and cruelty. Man thus becomes not only the obedient slave but also the strict taskmaster who treats himself as his own slave. This second implication is very important for the understanding of the psychological mechanism of authoritarian conscience. The authoritarian character, being more or less crippled in his productiveness, develops a certain amount of sadism and destructiveness. These destructive energies are discharged by taking over the role of the authority and dominating oneself as the servant. In the analysis of the Super-Ego, Freud has given a description of its destructive components which has been amply confirmed by clinical data collected by other observers. It does not matter whether one assumes, as Freud did in his earlier writings, that the root of aggression is to be found mainly in instinctual frustration or, as he assumed later, in the "death-instinct." What matters is the fact that the authoritarian conscience is fed by destructiveness against the person's own self so that destructive strivings are thus permitted to operate under the disguise of virtue. Psychoanalytic exploration, especially of the obsessional character, reveals the degree of cruelty and destructiveness conscience sometimes has, and how it enables one to act out the lingering hate by turning it against oneself. Freud has convincingly demonstrated the correctness of Nietzsche's thesis that the blockage of freedom turns man's instincts "backward against man himself. Enmity, cruelty, the delight in persecution, in surprises, change, destruction—the turning of all these instincts against their own possessors: this is the origin of the 'bad conscience.' "[1]

[1] F. Nietzsche, *The Genealogy of Morals*, II, 16.

## CONSCIENCE—SUGGESTED READINGS

Baylis, C. A., *Ethics*, New York, Holt, 1958, Chap. 4, pp. 80–94. (critic)

Bergler, E., *The Battle of the Conscience*, Washington, Washington Institute of Medicine, 1948. (a psychiatric study of conscience)

Butler, J., *Fifteen Sermons Preached at the Rolls Chapel*, 2nd ed., 1729, Preface, Sermons II and III. (proponent)

Martineau, J., *Types of Ethical Theory*, 3rd ed., Oxford, Clarendon Press, 1898, Part II, Book I, Chaps. 1, 5, and 6. (proponent)

Reid, T., *Essays on the Active Powers of Man*, 1788, Essay III, Part III, esp. Chaps. 6–8. (proponent)

Russell, B., *The Conquest of Happiness*, New York, Liveright, 1930, Chap. 7. (critic)

# 3. THE CATEGORICAL IMPERATIVE

Immanuel Kant, perhaps more strongly than any other moral philosopher, emphasizes the thesis of deontological ethics that man has a duty to perform actions regardless of their consequences. He asserts that "nothing can possibly be conceived in the world, or even out of it, which can be called good without qualification, except a *good will*." For him, a good will consists in the disposition to do one's duty simply for its own sake; actions performed by such a will are right not because they serve any human desire, but because they conform to the dictates of duty.

How then is man's duty established? According to Kant, the standard of morality may be discovered by reflection upon the nature of reason alone. The essence of rationality is consistency; to contradict one's self is the epitome of irrationality. Kant seeks to apply the notion of consistency to conduct; he maintains that if a man is to act rationally, and not contradict himself, he must act upon those moral principles which he is willing that others should employ as well. Accordingly, the ultimate principle of conduct is: "Act only on that maxim whereby thou canst at the same time will that it should become a universal law." This ultimate principle is termed "the categorical imperative," emphasizing both that the standard of morality is an imperative commanding us to perform actions and that the imperative does not permit men to attach conditions to their obedience. Men as moral beings cannot bargain with their duties by performing them only upon the condition that they wish to do so, or upon the condition that they can envision some gain for themselves. Rather, they are categorically commanded to do what is right simply because it is right.

Taken by itself, the categorical imperative describes the general nature of rational conduct. Nevertheless, this principle is not intended to be a mere abstraction which tells us nothing of the specific duties of men; according to Kant, the principle provides *the* test in the light of which one can determine whether a specific type of conduct is moral or immoral.

In the selections to follow, KANT states his ethical position. RASHDALL argues that Kant is mistaken in assuming that we can learn our duties merely by reasoning in the light of the categorical imperative. According to Rashdall, it is impossible for men to tell what they ought to do without turning to experience and learning thereby which lines of behavior promote the greatest good.

# IMMANUEL KANT

IMMANUEL KANT (1724–1804), one of the most original philosophers in the history of philosophy, taught at the University of Königsberg in East Prussia. His thesis that the human mind forms our knowledge of the world was a major influence in the development of idealism and his effort to reconcile the conclusions of science with man's moral and religious experience has proved to be a starting point for subsequent philosophers of many schools. His major works include: *Critique of Pure Reason* (1781; 2nd ed., 1787), *Fundamental Principles of the Metaphysic of Morals* (1785), *Critique of Practical Reason* (1788), *Critique of Judgment* (1790), *Religion Within the Limits of Bare Reason* (1793), and *Perpetual Peace* (1795).

# Fundamental Principles of the Metaphysic of Morals*

## First Section

## Transition from the Common Rational Knowledge of Morality to the Philosophical

Nothing can possibly be conceived in the world, or even out of it, which can be called good without qualification, except a *good will*. Intelligence, wit, judgment, and other *talents* of the mind, however they may be named, or courage, resolution, perseverance, as qualities of temperament, are undoubtedly good and desirable in many respects; but these gifts of nature may also become extremely bad and mischievous if the will which is to make use of them, and which, therefore, constitutes what is called *character*, is not good. It is the same with the *gifts of fortune*. Power, riches, honor, even health, and the general well-being and contentment with one's condition which is called *happiness*, inspire pride, and often presumption, if there is not a good will to correct the influence of these on the mind, and with this also to rectify the whole principle of acting, and adapt it to its end. The sight of a being who is not adorned with a single feature of a pure and good

* From *Fundamental Principles of the Metaphysic of Morals*, by Immanuel Kant, Sections 1 and 2. Translated by T. K. Abbott (1898).

will, enjoying unbroken prosperity, can never give pleasure to an impartial rational spectator. Thus a good will appears to constitute the indispensable condition even of being worthy of happiness.

There are even some qualities which are of service to this good will itself, and may facilitate its action, yet which have no intrinsic unconditional value, but always presuppose a good will, and this qualifies the esteem that we justly have for them, and does not permit us to regard them as absolutely good. Moderation in the affections and passions, self-control, and calm deliberation are not only good in many respects, but even seem to constitute part of the intrinsic worth of the person; but they are far from deserving to be called good without qualification, although they have been so unconditionally praised by the ancients. For without the principles of a good will, they may become extremely bad; and the coolness of a villain not only makes him far more dangerous, but also directly makes him more abominable in our eyes than he would have been without it.

A good will is good not because of what it performs or effects, not by its aptness for the attainment of some proposed end, but simply by virtue of the volition—that is, it is good in itself, and considered by itself is to be esteemed much higher than all that can be brought about by it in favor of any inclination, nay, even of the sum-total of all inclinations. Even if it should happen that, owing to special disfavor of fortune, or the niggardly provision of a step-motherly nature, this will should wholly lack power to accomplish its purpose, if with its greatest efforts it should yet achieve nothing, and there should remain only the good will (not, to be sure, a mere wish, but the summoning of all means in our power), then, like a jewel, it would still shine by its own light, as a thing which has its whole value in itself. Its usefulness or fruitlessness can neither add to nor take away anything from this value. It would be, as it were, only the setting to enable us to handle it the more conveniently in common commerce, or to attract to it the attention of those who are not yet connoisseurs, but not to recommend it to true connoisseurs, or to determine its value.

There is, however, something so strange in this idea of the absolute value of the mere will, in which no account is taken of its utility, that notwithstanding the thorough assent of even common reason to the idea, yet a suspicion must arise that it may perhaps really be the product of mere high-flown fancy, and that we may have misunderstood the purpose of nature in assigning reason as the governor of our will. Therefore we will examine this idea from this point of view.

In the physical constitution of an organized being, that is, a being adapted suitably to the purposes of life, we assume it as a fundamental principle that no organ for any purpose will be found but what is also the fittest and best adapted for that purpose. Now in a being which has reason and a will, if the proper object of nature were its *conservation*, its *welfare*, in a word, its *happiness*, then nature would have hit upon a very bad arrangement in selecting the reason of the creature to carry out this purpose. For all the actions which the creature has to perform with a view to this purpose, and the whole rule of its conduct, would be far more surely prescribed to it by instinct, and that end would have been attained thereby much more certainly than it ever can be by reason. Should reason have been communicated to this favored creature over and above, it must only have served it to contemplate the happy constitution of its nature, to admire it, to congratulate itself thereon, and to feel thankful for it to the beneficent cause, but not that it should subject its desires to that weak and delusive guidance, and meddle bunglingly with the purpose of nature. In a word, nature would have taken care that reason should not break forth into *practical exercise*, nor have the presumption, with its weak insight, to think out for itself the plan of happiness and of the means of attaining it. Nature would not only have taken on herself the choice of the ends but also of the means, and with wise foresight would have entrusted both to instinct.

And, in fact, we find that the more a cultivated reason applies itself with deliberate purpose to the enjoyment of life and happiness, so much the more does the man fail of true satisfaction. And from this circumstance there arises in many, if they are candid enough to confess it, a certain degree of *misology*, that is, hatred of reason, especially in the case of those who are most experienced in the use of it, because after calculating all the advantages they derive—I do not say from the invention of all the arts of common luxury, but even from the sciences (which seem to them to be after all only a luxury of the understanding)—they find that they have, in fact, only brought more trouble on their shoulders rather than gained in happiness; and they end by envying rather than despising the more common stamp of men who keep closer to the guidance of mere instinct, and do not allow their reason much influence on their conduct. And this we must admit, that the judgment of those who would very much lower the lofty eulogies of the advantages which reason gives us in regard to the happiness and satisfaction of life, or who would even reduce them below zero, is by no means morose or ungrateful to the goodness with which the world is governed, but that there lies at the root of these judgments the idea that our existence has a different and far nobler end, for which, and not for happiness, reason is properly intended, and which must, therefore, be regarded as the supreme condition to which the private ends of man must, for the most part, be postponed.

For as reason is not competent to guide the will with certainty in regard to its objects and the satisfaction of all our wants (which it to some extent even multiplies), this being an end to which an implanted instinct would have led with much greater certainty; and since, nevertheless, reason is imparted to us as a practical faculty, that is, as one which is to have influence on the *will*, therefore, admitting that nature generally in the distribution of her capacities has adapted the means to the end, its true destination must be to produce a *will*, not merely good as a *means* to something else, but *good in itself*, for which reason was absolutely necessary. This will then, though not indeed the sole and complete good, must be the supreme good and the condition of every other, even of the desire of happiness. Under these circumstances, there is nothing inconsistent with the wisdom of nature in the fact that the cultivation of the reason, which is requisite for the first and unconditional purpose, does in many ways interfere, at least in this life, with the attainment of the second, which is always conditional—namely, happiness. Nay, it may even reduce it to nothing, without nature thereby failing of her purpose. For reason recognizes the establishment of a good will as its highest practical destination, and in attaining this purpose is capable only of a satisfaction of its own proper kind, namely, that from the attainment of an end, which end again is determined by reason only, notwithstanding that this may involve many a disappointment to the ends of inclination.

We have then to develop the notion of a will which deserves to be highly esteemed for itself, and is good without a view to anything further, a notion which exists already in the sound natural understanding, requiring rather to be cleared up than to be taught, and which in estimating the value of our actions always takes the first place and constitutes the condition of all the rest. In order to do this, we will take the notion of duty, which includes that of a good will, although implying certain subjective restrictions and hindrances. These, however, far from concealing it or rendering it unrecognizable, rather bring it out by contrast and make it shine forth so much the brighter.

I omit here all actions which are already recognized as inconsistent with duty, although they may be useful for this or that purpose, for with these the question whether they are done *from duty* cannot arise at all, since they even conflict with it. I also set aside those actions which really conform to duty, but to which men have *no* direct *inclination*, performing them because they are impelled thereto by some other inclination. For in this case we can readily distinguish whether the action which agrees with duty is done *from duty* or from a selfish view. It is much harder to make this distinction when the action accords with duty, and the subject has besides a *direct* inclination to it. For example, it is always a matter of duty that a dealer should not overcharge an inexperienced purchaser; and wherever there is much commerce the prudent tradesman does not overcharge, but keeps a fixed price for everyone, so that a child buys of him as well as any other. Men are thus *honestly* served; but this is not enough to make us believe that the tradesman has so acted from duty and from principles of honesty; his own advantage required it; it is out of the question in this case to suppose that he might besides have a direct inclination in favor of the buyers, so that, as it were, from love he should give no advantage to one over another. Accordingly the action was done neither from duty nor from direct inclination, but merely with a selfish view.

On the other hand, it is a duty to maintain one's life; and, in addition, everyone has also a direct inclination to do so. But on this account the often anxious care which most men take for it has no intrinsic worth, and their maxim has no moral import. They preserve their life *as duty requires*, no doubt, but not *because duty requires*. On the other hand, if adversity and hopeless sorrow have completely taken away the relish for life, if the unfortunate one, strong in mind, indignant at his fate rather than desponding or dejected, wishes for death, and yet preserves his life without loving it— not from inclination or fear, but from duty—then his maxim has a moral worth.

To be beneficent when we can is a duty; and besides this, there are many minds so sympathetically constituted that, without any other motive of vanity or self-interest, they find a pleasure in spreading joy around them, and can take delight in the satisfaction of others so far as it is their own work. But I maintain that in such a case an action of this kind, however proper, however amiable it may be, has nevertheless no true moral worth, but is on a level with other inclinations, for example, the inclination to honor, which, if it is happily directed to that which is in fact of public utility and accordant with duty, and consequently honorable, deserves praise and encouragement, but not esteem. For the maxim lacks the moral import, namely, that such actions be done *from duty*, not from inclination. Put the case that the mind of that philanthropist was clouded by sorrow of his own, extinguishing all sympathy with the lot of others, and that while he still has the power to benefit others in distress, he is not touched by their trouble because he is absorbed with his own; and now suppose that he tears himself out of this dead insensibility and performs the action without any inclination to it, but simply from duty, then first has his action its genuine moral worth. Further still, if nature has put little sympathy in the heart of this or that man, if he, supposed to be an upright man, is by temperament cold and indifferent to the sufferings of others, perhaps because in respect of his own he is provided with the special gift of patience and fortitude, and supposes, or even requires, that others should have the same—and such a man would certainly not be the meanest product of nature—but if nature had not specially framed him for a philanthropist, would he not still find in himself a source from whence to give himself a far higher worth than that of a good-natured temperament could be? Unquestionably. It is just in this that the moral worth of the character is brought out which is incomparably the highest of all, namely, that he is beneficent, not from inclination, but from duty.

To secure one's own happiness is a duty, at least indirectly; for discontent with one's condition, under a pressure of many anxieties and amidst unsatisfied wants, might easily become a great *temptation to transgression of duty.* But here again, without looking to duty, all men have already the strongest and most intimate inclination to happiness, because it is just in this idea that all inclinations are combined in one total. But the precept of happiness is often of such a sort that it greatly interferes with some inclinations, and yet a man cannot form any definite and certain conception of the sum of satisfaction of all of them which is called happiness. It is not then to be wondered at that a single inclination, definite both as to what it promises and as to the time within which it can be gratified, is often able to overcome such a fluctuating idea, and that a gouty patient, for instance, can choose to enjoy what he likes, and to suffer what he may, since, according to his calculation, on this occasion at least, he has [only] not sacrificed the enjoyment of the present moment to a possibly mistaken expectation of a happiness which is supposed to be found in health. But even in this case, if the general desire for happiness did not influence his will, and supposing that in his particular case health was not a necessary element in this calculation, there yet remains in this, as in all other cases, this law—namely, that he should promote his happiness not from inclination but from duty, and by this would his conduct first acquire true moral worth.

It is in this manner, undoubtedly, that we are to understand those passages of Scripture also in which we are commanded to love our neighbor, even our enemy. For love, as an affection, cannot be commanded, but beneficence for duty's sake may, even though we are not impelled to it by any inclination—nay, are even repelled by a natural and unconquerable aversion. This is *practical* love, and not *pathological*—a love which is seated in the will, and not in the propensions of sense—in principles of action and not of tender sympathy; and it is this love alone which can be commanded.

The second* proposition is: That an action done from duty derives its moral worth, *not from the purpose* which is to be attained by it, but from the maxim by which it is determined, and therefore does not depend on the realization of the object of the action, but merely on the *principle of volition* by which the action has taken place, without regard to any object of desire.

* The first proposition was that to have moral worth an action must be done from duty. Translator's footnote.

It is clear from what precedes that the purposes which we may have in view in our actions, or their effects regarded as ends and springs of the will, cannot give to actions any unconditional or moral worth. In what, then, can their worth lie if it is not to consist in the will and in reference to its expected effect? It cannot lie anywhere but in the *principle of the will* without regard to the ends which can be attained by the action. For the will stands between its *a priori* principle, which is formal, and its *a posteriori* spring, which is material, as between two roads, and as it must be determined by something, it follows that it must be determined by the formal principle of volition when an action is done from duty, in which case every material principle has been withdrawn from it.

The third proposition, which is a consequence of the two preceding, I would express thus: *Duty is the necessity of acting from respect for the law.* I may have *inclination* for an object as the effect of my proposed action, but I cannot have *respect* for it just for this reason that it is an effect and not an energy of will. Similarly, I cannot have respect for inclination, whether my own or another's; I can at most, if my own, approve it; if another's, sometimes even love it, that is, look on it as favorable to my own interest. It is only what is connected with my will as a principle, by no means as an effect—what does not subserve my inclination, but overpowers it, or at least in case of choice excludes it from its calculation—in other words, simply the law of itself, which can be an object of respect, and hence a command. Now an action done from duty must wholly exclude the influence of inclination, and with it every object of the will, so that nothing remains which can determine the will except objectively the *law*, and subjectively *pure respect* for this practical law, and consequently the maxim that I should follow this law even to the thwarting of all my inclinations.

Thus the moral worth of an action does not lie in the effect expected from it, nor in any principle of action which requires to borrow its motive from this expected effect. For all these effects—agreeableness of one's condition, and even the promotion of the happiness of others—could have been also brought about by other causes, so that for this there would have been no need of the will of a rational being; whereas it is in this alone that the supreme and unconditional good can be found. The pre-eminent good which we call moral can therefore consist in nothing else than *the conception of law* in itself, *which certainly is only possible in a rational being*, in so far as this conception, and not the expected effect, determines the will. This is a good which is already present in the person who acts accordingly, and we have not to wait for it to appear first in the result.

But what sort of law can that be the conception of which must determine the will, even without paying any regard to the effect expected from it, in order that this will may be called good absolutely and without qualification? As I have deprived the will of every impulse which could arise to it from obedience to any law, there remains nothing but the universal conformity of its actions to law in general, which alone is to serve the will as a principle, that is, I am never to act otherwise than so *that I could also will that my maxim should become a universal law.* Here, now, it is the simple conformity to law in general, without assuming any particular law applicable to certain actions, that serves the will as its principle, and must so serve it if duty is not to be a vain delusion and a chimerical notion. The common reason of men in its practical judgments perfectly coincides with this, and always has in view the principle here suggested. Let the question be, for example: May I when in distress make a promise with the intention not to keep it? I readily distinguish here between the two significations which the question may have: whether it is prudent or whether it is right to make a false promise? The former may un- doubtedly often be the case. I see clearly indeed that it is not enough to extricate myself from a present difficulty by means of this subterfuge, but it must be well considered whether there may not hereafter spring from this lie much greater inconvenience than that from which I now free myself, and as, with all my supposed *cunning,* the consequences cannot be so easily fore- seen but that credit once lost may be much more injurious to me than any mischief which I seek to avoid at present, it should be considered whether it would not be more *prudent* to act herein according to a universal maxim, and to make it a habit to promise nothing except with the intention of keeping it. But it is soon clear to me that such a maxim will still only be based on the fear of consequences. Now it is a wholly different thing to be truthful from duty, and to be so from apprehension of injurious consequences. In the first case, the very notion of the action already implies a law for me; in the second case, I must first look about elsewhere to see what results may be combined with it which would affect myself. For to deviate from the principle of duty is beyond all doubt wicked; but to be unfaithful to my maxim of prudence may often be very advantageous to me, although to abide by it is certainly safer. The shortest way, however, and an unerring one, to discover the answer to this question whether a lying promise is consistent with duty, is to ask myself, Should I be content that my maxim (to extricate myself from difficulty by a false promise) should hold good as a universal law, for myself as well as for others; and should I be able to say to myself, "Every one may make a deceitful promise when he finds himself in a diffi- culty from which he cannot otherwise extricate himself"? Then I presently become aware that, while I can will the lie, I can by no means will that lying should be a universal law. For with such a law there would be no promises at all, since it would be in vain to allege my intention in regard to my future actions to those who would not believe this allegation, or if they over-hastily did so, would pay me back in my own coin. Hence my maxim, as soon as it should be made a universal law, would necessarily destroy itself.

I do not, therefore, need any far-reaching penetration to discern what I have to do in order that my will may be morally good. Inexperienced in the course of the world, incapable of being prepared for all its contingencies, I only ask myself: Canst thou also will that thy maxim should be a universal law? If not, then it must be rejected, and that not because of a disadvantage accruing from it to myself or even to others, but because it cannot enter as a principle into a possible universal legislation, and reason extorts from me immediate respect for such legislation. I do not indeed as yet *discern* on what this respect is based (this the philosopher may inquire), but at least I understand this—that it is an estimation of the worth which far outweighs all worth of what is recommended by inclination, and that the necessity of acting from *pure* respect for the practical law is what constitutes duty, to which every other motive must give place because it is the condition of a will being good *in itself*, and the worth of such a will is above everything. . . .

## Second Section

### Transition from Popular Moral Philosophy to the Metaphysic of Morals

. . . Everything in nature works according to laws. Rational beings alone have the faculty of acting according *to the conception* of laws—that is, according to principles, that is, have a *will*. Since the deduction of actions from principles requires *reason*, the will is nothing but practical reason. If reason infallibly determines the will, then the actions of such a being which are recognized as objectively necessary are subjectively necessary also, that is, the will is a faculty to choose *that only* which reason independent on inclination recognizes as practically necessary, that is, as good. But if reason of itself does not sufficiently determine the will, if the latter is subject also to subjective conditions (particular impulses) which do not always coincide with the objective conditions, in a word, if the will does not *in itself* completely accord with reason (which is actually the case with men), then the actions which objectively are recognized as necessary are subjectively contingent, and the determination of such a will according to objective laws is *obligation*, that is to say, the relation of the objective laws to a will that is not thoroughly good is conceived as the determination of the will of a rational being by principles of reason, but which the will from its nature does not of necessity follow.

The conception of an objective principle, in so far as it is obligatory for a will, is called a command (of reason), and the formula of the command is called an Imperative.

All imperatives are expressed by the word *ought* [*or shall*], and thereby indicate the relation of an objective law of reason to a will which from its subjective constitution is not necessarily determined by it (an obligation). They say that something would be good to do or to forbear, but they say it to a will which does not always do a thing because it is conceived to be good to do it. That is practically *good*, however, which determines the will by means of the conceptions of reason, and consequently not from subjective causes, but objectively, that is, on principles which are valid for every rational being as such. It is distinguished from the *pleasant* as that which influences the will only by means of sensation from merely subjective causes, valid only for the sense of this or that one, and not as a principle of reason which holds for every one.

A perfectly good will would therefore be equally subject to objective laws (viz., laws of good), but could not be conceived as *obliged* thereby to act lawfully, because of itself from its subjective constitution it can only be determined by the conception of good. Therefore no imperatives hold for the Divine will, or in general for a *holy* will; *ought* is here out of place because the volition is already of itself necessarily in unison with the law. Therefore imperatives are only formulae to express the relation of objective laws of all volition to the subjective imperfection of the will of this or that rational being, for example, the human will.

Now all *imperatives* command either *hypothetically* or *categorically*. The former represent the practical necessity of a possible action as means to something else that is willed (or at least which one might possibly will). The categorical imperative would be that which represented an action as necessary of itself without reference to another end, that is, as objectively necessary.

Since every practical law represents a possible action as good, and on this account, for a subject who is practically determinable by reason as necessary, all imperatives are formulae determining an action which is necessary according to the principle of a will good in some respects. If now the action is good only as a means *to something else*, then the imperative is *hypothetical*; if it is conceived as good *in itself* and consequently as being necessarily the principle of a will which of itself conforms to reason, then it is *categorical*.

Thus the imperative declares what action possible by me would be good, and presents the practical rule in relation to a will which does not forthwith perform an action simply because it is good, whether because the subject does not always know that it is good, or because, even if it know this, yet its maxims might be opposed to the objective principles of practical reason.

Accordingly the hypothetical imperative only says that the action is good for some purpose, *possible* or *actual*. In the first case it is a *problematical*, in the second an *assertorial* practical principle. The categorical imperative which declares an action to be objectively necessary in itself without reference to any purpose, that is, without any other end, is valid as an *apodictic* (prac-tical) principle.

Whatever is possible only by the power of some rational being may also be conceived as a possible purpose of some will; and therefore the principles of action as regards the means necessary to attain some possible purpose are in fact infinitely numerous. All sciences have a practical part consisting of problems expressing that some end is possible for us, and of imperatives di-recting how it may be attained. These may, therefore, be called in general im-peratives of *skill*. Here there is no question whether the end is rational and good, but only what one must do in order to attain it. The precepts for the physician to make his patient thoroughly healthy, and for a poisoner to ensure certain death, are of equal value in this respect, that each serves to effect its purpose perfectly. Since in early youth it cannot be known what ends are likely to occur to us in the course of life, parents seek to have their children taught a *great many things*, and provide for their *skill* in the use of means for all sorts of arbitrary ends, of none of which can they determine whether it may not perhaps hereafter be an object to their pupil, but which it is at all events *possible* that he might aim at; and this anxiety is so great that they commonly neglect to form and correct their judgment on the value of the things which may be chosen as ends.

There is *one* end, however, which may be assumed to be actually such to all rational beings (so far as imperatives apply to them, viz., as dependent beings), and, therefore, one purpose which they not merely *may* have, but which we may with certainty assume that they all actually *have* by a natural necessity, and this is *happiness*. The hypothetical imperative which expresses the practical necessity of an action as means to the advancement of happiness is *assertorial*. We are not to present it as necessary for an uncertain and merely possible purpose, but for a purpose which we may presuppose with certainty and *a priori* in every man, because it belongs to his being. Now skill in the choice of means to his own greatest well-being may be called *prudence*, in the narrowest sense. And thus the imperative which refers to the choice of means to one's own happiness, that is, the precept of prudence, is still always *hypothetical*; the action is not commanded absolutely, but only as means to another purpose.

Finally, there is an imperative which commands a certain conduct imme-diately, without having as its condition any other purpose to be attained by it. This imperative is *categorical*. It concerns not the matter of the action, or its intended result, but its form and the principle of which it is itself a result;

and what is essentially good in it consists in the mental disposition, let the consequence be what it may. This imperative may be called that of *moral-ity*. . . .

When I conceive a hypothetical imperative, in general I do not know be-forehand what it will contain until I am given the condition. But when I conceive a categorical imperative, I know at once what it contains. For as the imperative contains besides the law only the necessity that the maxims[1] shall conform to this law, while the law contains no conditions restricting it, there remains nothing but the general statement that the maxim of the action should conform to a universal law, and it is this conformity alone that the imperative properly represents as necessary.

There is therefore but one categorical imperative, namely, this: *Act only on that maxim whereby thou canst at the same time will that it should be-come a universal law.*

Now if all imperatives of duty can be deduced from this one imperative as from their principle, then, although it should remain undecided whether what is called duty is not merely a vain notion, yet at least we shall be able to show what we understand by it and what this notion means.

Since the universality of the law according to which effects are produced constitutes what is properly called *nature* in the most general sense (as to form)—that is, the existence of things so far as it is determined by general laws—the imperative of duty may be expressed thus: *Act as if the maxim of thy action were to become by thy will a universal law of nature.*

We will now enumerate a few duties, adopting the usual division of them into duties to ourselves and to others, and into perfect and imperfect duties.

1. A man reduced to despair by a series of misfortunes feels wearied of life, but is still so far in possession of his reason that he can ask himself whether it would not be contrary to his duty to himself to take his own life. Now he inquires whether the maxim of his action could become a universal law of na-ture. His maxim is: From self-love I adopt it as a principle to shorten my life when its longer duration is likely to bring more evil than satisfaction. It is asked then simply whether this principle founded on self-love can be-come a universal law of nature. Now we see at once that a system of nature of which it should be a law to destroy life by means of the very feeling whose special nature it is to impel to the improvement of life would contradict itself, and therefore could not exist as a system of nature; hence that maxim

---

[1] A "maxim" is a subjective principle of action, and must be distinguished from the *objective principle*, namely, practical law. The former contains the practical rule set by reason according to the conditions of the subject (often its ignorance or its inclinations), so that it is the principle on which the subject *acts*; but the law is the objective principle valid for every rational being, and is the principle on which it *ought to act*—that is an imperative.

cannot possibly exist as a universal law of nature, and consequently would be wholly inconsistent with the supreme principle of all duty.

2. Another finds himself forced by necessity to borrow money. He knows that he will not be able to repay it, but sees also that nothing will be lent to him unless he promises stoutly to repay it in a definite time. He desires to make this promise, but he has still so much conscience as to ask himself: Is it not unlawful and inconsistent with duty to get out of a difficulty in this way? Suppose, however, that he resolves to do so, then the maxim of his action would be expressed thus: When I think myself in want of money, I will borrow money and promise to repay it, although I know that I never can do so. Now this principle of self-love or of one's own advantage may perhaps be consistent with my whole future welfare; but the question now is, Is it right? I change then the suggestion of self-love into a universal law, and state the question thus: How would it be if my maxim were a universal law? Then I see at once that it could never hold as a universal law of nature, but would necessarily contradict itself. For supposing it to be a universal law that every-one when he thinks himself in a difficulty should be able to promise whatever he pleases, with the purpose of not keeping his promise, the promise itself would become impossible, as well as the end that one might have in view in it, since no one would consider that anything was promised to him, but would ridicule all such statements as vain pretenses.

3. A third finds in himself a talent which with the help of some culture might make him a useful man in many respects. But he finds himself in comfortable circumstances and prefers to indulge in pleasure rather than to take pains in enlarging and improving his happy natural capacities. He asks, however, whether his maxim of neglect of his natural gifts, besides agreeing with his inclination to indulgence, agrees also with what is called duty. He sees then that a system of nature could indeed subsist with such a universal law, although men (like the South Sea islanders) should let their talents rest and resolve to devote their lives merely to idleness, amusement, and propaga-tion of their species—in a word, to enjoyment; but he cannot possibly *will* that this should be a universal law of nature, or be implanted in us as such by a natural instinct. For, as a rational being, he necessarily wills that his faculties be developed, since they serve him, and have been given him, for all sorts of possible purposes.

4. A fourth, who is in prosperity, while he sees that others have to contend with great wretchedness and that he could help them, thinks: What concern is it of mine? Let everyone be as happy as Heaven pleases, or as he can make himself; I will take nothing from him nor even envy him, only I do not wish to contribute anything to his welfare or to his assistance in distress! Now no doubt, if such a mode of thinking were a universal law, the human race

might very well subsist, and doubtless even better than in a state in which everyone talks of sympathy and good-will, or even takes care occasionally to put it into practice, but, on the other side, also cheats when he can, betrays the rights of men, or otherwise violates them. But although it is possible that a universal law of nature might exist in accordance with that maxim, it is impossible to *will* that such a principle should have the universal validity of a law of nature. For a will which resolved this would contradict itself, inasmuch as many cases might occur in which one would have need of the love and sympathy of others, and in which, by such a law of nature, sprung from his own will, he would deprive himself of all hope of the aid he desires.

These are a few of the many actual duties, or at least what we regard as such, which obviously fall into two classes on the one principle that we have laid down. We must be *able to will* that a maxim of our action should be a universal law. This is the canon of the moral appreciation of the action generally. Some actions are of such a character that their maxim cannot without contradiction be even *conceived* as a universal law of nature, far from it being possible that we should *will* that it *should* be so. In others, this intrinsic impossibility is not found, but still it is impossible to *will* that their maxim should be raised to the universality of a law of nature, since such a will would contradict itself. It is easily seen that the former violate strict or rigorous (inflexible) duty; the latter only laxer (meritorious) duty. Thus it has been completely shown by these examples how all duties depend as regards the nature of the obligation (not the object of the action) on the same principle.

If now we attend to ourselves on occasion of any transgression of duty, we shall find that we in fact do not will that our maxim should be a universal law, for that is impossible for us; on the contrary, we will that the opposite should remain a universal law, only we assume the liberty of making an *exception* in our own favor or (just for this time only) in favor of our inclination. Consequently, if we considered all cases from one and the same point of view, namely, that of reason, we should find a contradiction in our own will, namely, that a certain principle should be objectively necessary as a universal law, and yet subjectively should not be universal, but admit of exceptions. As, however, we at one moment regard our action from the point of view of a will wholly conformed to reason, and then again look at the same action from the point of view of a will affected by inclination, there is not really any contradiction, but an antagonism of inclination to the precept of reason, whereby the universality of the principle is changed into a mere generality, so that the practical principle of reason shall meet the maxim half way. Now, although this cannot be justified in our own impartial judgment, yet it proves that we do really recognize the validity of the categorical imperative and (with all respect for it) only allow ourselves a few exceptions which we think unimportant and forced from us.

We have thus established at least this much—that if duty is a conception which is to have any import and real legislative authority for our actions, it can only be expressed in categorical, and not at all in hypothetical, imperatives. We have also, which is of great importance, exhibited clearly and definitely for every practical application the content of the categorical imperative, which must contain the principle of all duty if there is such a thing at all. We have not yet, however, advanced so far as to prove a priori that there actually is such an imperative, that there is a practical law which commands absolutely of itself and without any other impulse, and that the following of this law is duty.

With the view of attaining to this it is of extreme importance to remember that we must not allow ourselves to think of deducing the reality of this principle from the *particular attributes of human nature*. For duty is to be a practical, unconditional necessity of action; it must therefore hold for all rational beings (to whom an imperative can apply at all), and *for this reason only* be also a law for all human wills. On the contrary, whatever is deduced from the particular natural characteristics of humanity, from certain feelings and propensions, nay, even, if possible, from any particular tendency proper to human reason, and which need not necessarily hold for the will of every rational being—this may indeed supply us with a maxim but not with a law; with a subjective principle on which we may have a propension and inclination to act, but not with an objective principle on which we should be *enjoined* to act, even though all our propensions, inclinations, and natural dispositions were opposed to it. In fact, the sublimity and intrinsic dignity of the command in duty are so much the more evident, the less the subjective impulses favor it and the more they oppose it, without being able in the slightest degree to weaken the obligation of the law or to diminish its validity.

Here then we see philosophy brought to a critical position, since it has to be firmly fixed, notwithstanding that it has nothing to support it in heaven or earth. Here it must show its purity as absolute director of its own laws, not the herald of those which are whispered to it by an implanted sense or who knows what tutelary nature. Although these may be better than nothing, yet they can never afford principles dictated by reason, which must have their source wholly a priori and thence their commanding authority, expecting everything from the supremacy of the law and the due respect for it, nothing from inclination, or else condemning the man to self-contempt and inward abhorrence.

Thus every empirical element is not only quite incapable of being an aid to the principle of morality, but is even highly prejudicial to the purity of morals; for the proper and inestimable worth of an absolutely good will consists just in this that the principle of action is free from all influence of contingent grounds, which alone experience can furnish. We cannot too much or too often repeat our warning against this lax and even mean habit of thought which seeks for its principle among empirical motives and laws; for human reason in its weariness is glad to rest on this pillow, and in a dream of sweet illusions (in which, instead of Juno, it embraces a cloud) it substitutes for morality a bastard patched up from limbs of various derivation, which looks like anything one chooses to see in it; only not like virtue to one who has once beheld her in her true form.[2]

The question then is this: Is it a necessary law *for all rational beings* that they should always judge of their actions by maxims of which they can themselves will that they should serve as universal laws? If it is so, then it must be connected (altogether *a priori*) with the very conception of the will of a rational being generally. . . .

The will is conceived as a faculty of determining oneself to action *in accordance with the conception of certain laws*. And such a faculty can be found only in rational beings. Now that which serves the will as the objective ground of its self-determination is the *end*, and if this is assigned by reason alone, it must hold for all rational beings. On the other hand, that which merely contains the ground of possibility of the action of which the effect is the end, this is called the *means*. The subjective ground of the desire is the *spring*, the objective ground of the volition is the *motive*; hence the distinction between subjective ends which rest on springs, and objective ends which depend on motives valid for every rational being. Practical principles are *formal* when they abstract from all subjective ends; they are *material* when they assume these, and therefore particular, springs of action. The ends which a rational being proposes to himself at pleasure as *effects* of his actions (material ends) are all only relative, for it is only their relation to the particular desires of the subject that gives them their worth, which therefore cannot furnish principles universal and necessary for all rational beings and for every volition, that is to say, practical laws. Hence all these relative ends can give rise only to hypothetical imperatives.

Supposing, however, that there were something *whose existence* has *in itself* an absolute worth, something which, being *an end in itself*, could be a source of definite laws, then in this and this alone would lie the source of a possible categorical imperative, that is, a practical law.

Now I say: man and generally any rational being *exists* as an end in himself, *not merely as a means* to be arbitrarily used by this or that will, but in all his actions, whether they concern himself or other rational beings, must

[2] To behold virtue in her proper form is nothing else but to contemplate morality stripped of all admixture of sensible things and of every spurious ornament of reward or self-love. How much she then eclipses everything else that appears charming to the affections, every one may readily perceive with the least exertion of his reason, if it be not wholly spoiled for abstraction.

be always regarded at the same time as an end. All objects of the inclinations have only a conditional worth; for if the inclinations and the wants founded on them did not exist, then their object would be without value. But the inclinations themselves, being sources of want, are so far from having an absolute worth for which they should be desired that, on the contrary, it must be the universal wish of every rational being to be wholly free from them. Thus the worth of any object which is *to be acquired* by our action is always conditional. Beings whose existence depends not on our will but on nature's, have nevertheless, if they are not rational beings, only a relative value as means, and are therefore called *things*; rational beings, on the contrary, are called *persons*, because their very nature points them out as ends in themselves, that is, as something which must not be used merely as means, and so far therefore restricts freedom of action (and is an object of respect). These, therefore, are not merely subjective ends whose existence has a worth *for us* as an effect of our action, but *objective ends*, that is, things whose existence is an end in itself—an end, moreover, for which no other can be substituted, which they should subserve *merely* as means, for otherwise nothing whatever would possess *absolute worth*; but if all worth were conditioned and therefore contingent, then there would be no supreme practical principle of reason whatever.

If then there is a supreme practical principle or, in respect of the human will, a categorical imperative, it must be one which, being drawn from the conception of that which is necessarily an end for everyone because it is *an end in itself*, constitutes an *objective* principle of will, and can therefore serve as a universal practical law. The foundation of this principle is: *rational nature exists as an end in itself*. Man necessarily conceives his own existence as being so; so far then this is a *subjective* principle of human actions. But every other rational being regards its existence similarly, just on the same rational principle that holds for me; so that it is at the same time an objective principle from which as a supreme practical law all laws of the will must be capable of being deduced. Accordingly the practical imperative will be as follows: *So act as to treat humanity, whether in thine own person or in that of any other, in every case as an end withal, never as means only*. We will now inquire whether this can be practically carried out.

To abide by the previous examples:

*First*, under the head of necessary duty to oneself: He who contemplates suicide should ask himself whether his action can be consistent with the idea of humanity *as an end in itself*. If he destroys himself in order to escape from painful circumstances, he uses a person merely as *a mean* to maintain a tolerable condition up to the end of life. But a man is not a thing, that is to say, something which can be used merely as means, but must in all his actions be always considered as an end in himself. I cannot, therefore, dispose in any way of a man in my own person so as to mutilate him, to damage or kill him. (It belongs to ethics proper to define this principle more precisely, so as to avoid all misunderstanding, for example, as to the amputation of the limbs in order to preserve myself; as to exposing my life to danger with a view to preserve it, etc. This question is therefore omitted here.)

*Secondly,* as regards necessary duties, or those of strict obligation, towards others: He who is thinking of making a lying promise to others will see at once that he would be using another man *merely as a mean,* without the latter containing at the same time the end in himself. For he whom I propose by such a promise to use for my own purposes cannot possibly assent to my mode of acting towards him, and therefore cannot himself contain the end of this action. This violation of the principle of humanity in other men is more obvious if we take in examples of attacks on the freedom and property of others. For then it is clear that he who transgresses the rights of men intends to use the person of others merely as means, without considering that as rational beings they ought always to be esteemed also as ends, that is, as beings who must be capable of containing in themselves the end of the very same action.

*Thirdly,* as regards contingent (meritorious) duties to oneself: It is not enough that the action does not violate humanity in our own person as an end in itself, it must also *harmonize with it.* Now there are in humanity capacities of greater perfection which belong to the end that nature has in view in regard to humanity in ourselves as the subject; to neglect these might perhaps be consistent with the *maintenance* of humanity as an end in itself, but not with the *advancement* of this end.

*Fourthly,* as regards meritorious duties towards others: The natural end which all men have is their own happiness. Now humanity might indeed subsist although no one should contribute anything to the happiness of others, provided he did not intentionally withdraw anything from it; but after all, this would only harmonize negatively, not positively, with *humanity as an end in itself,* if everyone does not also endeavor, as far as in him lies, to forward the ends of others. For the ends of any subject which is an end in himself ought as far as possible to be *my* ends also, if that conception is to have its *full* effect with me.

This principle that humanity and generally every rational nature is *an end in itself* (which is the supreme limiting condition of every man's freedom of action), is not borrowed from experience, *first,* because it is universal, applying as it does to all rational beings whatever, and experience is not capable of determining anything about them; *secondly,* because it does not present humanity as an end to men (subjectively), that is, as an object which men do of themselves actually adopt as an end; but as an objective end which must as a law constitute the supreme limiting condition of all our subjective ends, let them be what we will; it must therefore spring from pure reason. In fact the objective principle of all practical legislation lies (according to the first principle) in *the rule* and its form of universality which makes it capable of being a law (say, for example, a law of nature); but the *subjective* principle is in the *end*; now by the second principle, the subject of all ends is each rational being inasmuch as it is an end in itself. Hence follows the third practical principle of the will, which is the ultimate condition of its harmony with the universal practical reason, viz., the idea of *the will of every rational being as a universally legislative will*.

On this principle all maxims are rejected which are inconsistent with the will being itself universal legislator. Thus the will is not subject to the law, but so subject that it must be regarded *as itself giving the law*, and on this ground only subject to the law (of which it can regard itself as the author).

In the previous imperatives, namely, that based on the conception of the conformity of actions to general laws, as in a *physical system of nature*, and that based on the universal *prerogative* of rational beings as *ends* in themselves—these imperatives just because they were conceived as categorical excluded from any share in their authority all admixture of any interest as a spring of action; they were, however, only *assumed* to be categorical, because such an assumption was necessary to explain the conception of duty. But we could not prove independently that there are practical propositions which command categorically, nor can it be proved in this section; one thing, however, could be done, namely, to indicate in the imperative itself, by some determinate expression, that in the case of volition from duty all interest is renounced, which is the specific criterion of categorical as distinguished from hypothetical imperatives. This is done in the present (third) formula of the principle, namely, in the idea of the will of every rational being as a *universally legislating will*.

For although a will *which is subject to laws* may be attached to this law by means of an interest, yet a will which is itself a supreme lawgiver, so far as it is such, cannot possibly depend on any interest, since a will so dependent would itself still need another law restricting the interest of its self-love by the condition that it should be valid as universal law.

Thus the *principle* that every human will is *a will which in all its maxims gives universal laws*,[3] provided it be otherwise justified, would be very *well adapted* to be the categorical imperative, in this respect, namely, that just

---

[3] I may be excused from adducing examples to elucidate this principle, as those which have already been used to elucidate the categorical imperative and its formula would all serve for the like purpose here.

because of the idea of universal legislation it is *not based on any interest,* and therefore it alone among all possible imperatives can be *unconditional.* Or still better, converting the proposition, if there is a categorical imperative (that is, a law for the will of every rational being), it can only command that everything be done from maxims of one's will regarded as a will which could at the same time will that it should itself give universal laws, for in that case only the practical principle and the imperative which it obeys are unconditional, since they cannot be based on any interest.

Looking back now on all previous attempts to discover the principle of morality, we need not wonder why they all failed. It was seen that man was bound to laws by duty, but it was not observed that the laws to which he is subject are *only those of his own giving,* though at the same time they are *universal,* and that he is only bound to act in conformity with his own will —a will, however, which is designed by nature to give universal laws. For when one has conceived man only as subject to a law (no matter what), then this law required some interest, either by way of attraction or constraint, since it did not originate as a law from *his own will,* but this will was according to a law obliged by *something else* to act in a certain manner. Now by this necessary consequence all the labor spent in finding a supreme principle of *duty* was irrevocably lost. For men never elicited duty, but only a necessity of acting from a certain interest. Whether this interest was private or otherwise, in any case the imperative must be conditional, and could not by any means be capable of being a moral command. I will therefore call this the principle of *Autonomy* of the will, in contrast with every other which I accordingly reckon as *Heteronomy.*

The conception of every rational being as one which must consider itself as giving in all the maxims of its will universal laws, so as to judge itself and its actions from this point of view—this conception leads to another which depends on it and is very fruitful, namely, that of a *kingdom of ends.*

By a "kingdom" I understand the union of different rational beings in a system by common laws. Now since it is by laws that ends are determined as regards their universal validity, hence, if we abstract from the personal differences of rational beings, and likewise from all the content of their private ends, we shall be able to conceive all ends combined in a systematic whole (including both rational beings as ends in themselves, and also the special ends which each may propose to himself), that is to say, we can conceive a kingdom of ends, which on the preceding principles is possible.

For all rational beings come under the *law* that each of them must treat itself and all others *never merely as means,* but in every case *at the same time as ends in themselves.* Hence results a systematic union of rational beings by common objective laws, that is, a kingdom which may be called a kingdom of ends, since what these laws have in view is just the relation of these beings to one another as ends and means. It is certainly only an ideal.

A rational being belongs as a *member* to the kingdom of ends when, although giving universal laws in it, he is also himself subject to these laws. He belongs to it *as sovereign* when, while giving laws, he is not subject to the will of any other.

A rational being must always regard himself as giving laws either as member or as sovereign in a kingdom of ends which is rendered possible by the freedom of will. He cannot, however, maintain the latter position merely by the maxims of his will, but only in case he is a completely independent being without wants and with unrestricted power adequate to his will.

Morality consists then in the reference of all action to the legislation which alone can render a kingdom of ends possible. This legislation must be capable of existing in every rational being, and of emanating from his will, so that the principle of this will is never to act on any maxim which could not without contradition be also a universal law, and accordingly always so to act *that the will could at the same time regard itself as giving in its maxims universal laws.* If now the maxims of rational beings are not by their own nature coincident with this objective principle, then the necessity of acting on it is called practical necessitation that is, *duty.* Duty does not apply to the sovereign in the kingdom of ends, but it does to every member of it and to all in the same degree.

The practical necessity of acting on this principle, that is, duty, does not rest at all on feelings, impulses, or inclinations, but solely on the relation of rational beings to one another, a relation in which the will of a rational being must always be regarded as *legislative,* since otherwise it could not be conceived as *an end in itself.* Reason then refers every maxim of the will, regarding it as legislating universally, to every other will and also to every action towards oneself; and this not on account of any other practical motive or any future advantage, but from the idea of the *dignity* of a rational being, obeying no law but that which he himself also gives.

In the kingdom of ends everything has either *value* or *dignity.* Whatever has a value can be replaced by something else which is *equivalent;* whatever, on the other hand, is above all value, and therefore admits of no equivalent, has a dignity.

Whatever has reference to the general inclinations and wants of mankind has a *market value;* whatever, without presupposing a want, corresponds to a certain taste, that is, to a satisfaction in the mere purposeless play of our faculties, has a *fancy value;* but that which constitutes the condition under which alone anything can be an end in itself, this has not merely a relative worth, that is, value, but an intrinsic worth, that is, *dignity.*

Now morality is the condition under which alone a rational being can be an end in himself, since by this alone it is possible that he should be a legislating member in the kingdom of ends. Thus morality, and humanity as capable of it, is that which alone has dignity. Skill and diligence in labor have a market value; wit, lively imagination, and humor have fancy value; on the other hand, fidelity to promises, benevolence from principle (not from instinct), have an intrinsic worth. Neither nature nor art contains anything which in default of these it could put in their place, for their worth consists not in the effects which spring from them, not in the use and advantage which they secure, but in the disposition of mind, that is, the maxims of the will which are ready to manifest themselves in such actions, even though they should not have the desired effect. These actions also need no recommendation from any subjective taste or sentiment, that they may be looked on with immediate favor and satisfaction; they need no immediate propension or feeling for them; they exhibit the will that performs them as an object of an immediate respect, and nothing but reason is required to *impose* them on the will; not to *flatter* it into them, which, in the case of duties, would be a contradiction. This estimation therefore shows that the worth of such a disposition is dignity, and places it infinitely above all value, with which it cannot for a moment be brought into comparison or competition without as it were violating its sanctity.

What then is it which justifies virtue or the morally good disposition, in making such lofty claims? It is nothing less than the privilege it secures to the rational being of participating in the giving of universal laws, by which it qualifies him to be a member of a possible kingdom of ends, a privilege to which he was already destined by his own nature as being an end in himself, and on that account legislating in the kingdom of ends; free as regards all laws of physical nature, and obeying those only which he himself gives, and by which his maxims can belong to a system of universal law to which at the same time he submits himself. For nothing has any worth except what the law assigns it. Now the legislation itself which assigns the worth of everything must for that very reason possess dignity, that is, an unconditional incomparable worth; and the word *respect* alone supplies a becoming expression for the esteem which a rational being must have for it. *Autonomy* then is the basis of the dignity of human and of every rational nature. . . .

### The Autonomy of the Will as the Supreme Principle of Morality

Autonomy of the will is that property of it by which it is a law to itself (independently on any property of the objects of volition). The principle of autonomy then is: Always so to choose that the same volition shall comprehend the maxims of our choice as a universal law. . . . That the principle of autonomy in question is the sole principle of morals can be readily shown by mere analysis of the conceptions of morality. For by this analysis we find that its principle must be a categorical imperative, and that what this commands is neither more nor less than this very autonomy.

### Heteronomy of the Will as the Source of All Spurious Principles of Morality

If the will seeks the law which is to determine it *anywhere else* than in the fitness of its maxims to be universal laws of its own dictation, consequently if it goes out of itself and seeks this law in the character of any of its objects, there always results *heteronomy*. The will in that case does not give itself the law, but it is given by the object through its relation to the will. This relation, whether it rests on inclination or on conceptions of reason, only admits of hypothetical imperatives: I ought to do something *because I wish for something else*. On the contrary, the moral, and therefore categorical, imperative says: I ought to do so and so, even though I should not wish for anything else. For example, the former says: I ought not to lie if I would retain my reputation; the latter says: I ought not to lie although it should not bring me the least discredit. The latter therefore must so far abstract from all objects that they shall have no *influence* on the will, in order that practical reason (will) may not be restricted to administering an interest not belonging to it, but may simply show its own commanding authority as the supreme legislation. Thus, for example, I ought to endeavor to promote the happiness of others, not as if its realization involved any concern of mine (whether by immediate inclination or by any satisfaction indirectly gained through reason), but simply because a maxim which excludes it cannot be comprehended as a universal law in one and the same volition.

### Classification Of All Principles of Morality Which Can Be Founded on the Conception of Heteronomy

Here as elsewhere human reason in its pure use, so long as it was not critically examined, has first tried all possible wrong ways before it succeeded in finding the one true way.

All principles which can be taken from this point of view are either *empirical* or *rational*. The *former*, drawn from the principle of *happiness*, are built on physical or moral feelings; the *latter*, drawn from the principle of *perfection*, are built either on the rational conception of perfection as a possible effect, or on that of an independent perfection (the will of God) as the determining cause of our will.

*Empirical principles* are wholly incapable of serving as a foundation for moral laws. For the universality with which these should hold for all rational beings without distinction, the unconditional practical necessity which is thereby imposed on them is lost when their foundation is taken from the *particular constitution of human nature* or the accidental circumstances in which it is placed. The principle of *private happiness*, however, is the most objectionable, not merely because it is false, and experience contradicts the supposition that prosperity is always proportioned to good conduct, nor yet merely because it contributes nothing to the establishment of morality— since it is quite a different thing to make a prosperous man and a good man, or to make one prudent and sharp-sighted for his own interests, and to make him virtuous—but because the springs it provides for morality are such as rather undermine it and destroy its sublimity, since they put the motives to virtue and to vice in the same class, and only teach us to make a better calculation, the specific difference between virtue and vice being entirely extinguished. On the other hand, as to moral feeling, this supposed special sense, the appeal to it is indeed superficial when those who cannot *think* believe that *feeling* will help them out, even in what concerns general laws; and besides, feelings which naturally differ infinitely in degree cannot furnish a uniform standard of good and evil, nor has anyone a right to form judgments for others by his own feelings; nevertheless this moral feeling is nearer to morality and its dignity in this respect that it pays virtue the honor of ascribing to her *immediately* the satisfaction and esteem we have for her, and does not, as it were, tell her to her face that we are not attached to her by her beauty but by profit.

Among the *rational* principles of morality, the ontological conception of *perfection*, notwithstanding its defects, is better than the theological conception which derives morality from a Divine absolutely perfect will. The former is, no doubt, empty and indefinite, and consequently useless for finding in the boundless field of possible reality the greatest amount suitable for us; moreover, in attempting to distinguish specifically the reality of which we are now speaking from every other, it inevitably tends to turn in a circle and cannot avoid tacitly presupposing the morality which it is to explain; it is nevertheless preferable to the theological view, first, because we have no intuition of the Divine perfection, and can only deduce it from our own conceptions the most important of which is that of morality, and our explanation would thus be involved in a gross circle; and, in the next place, if we avoid this, the only notion of the Divine will remaining to us is a conception made up of the attributes of desire of glory and dominion, combined with the awful conceptions of might and vengeance, and any system of morals erected on this foundation would be directly opposed to morality.

However, if I had to choose between the notion of the moral sense and that of perfection in general (two systems which at least do not weaken morality, although they are totally incapable of serving as its foundation), then I should decide for the latter, because it at least withdraws the decision of the question from the sensibility and brings it to the court of pure reason; and although even here it decides nothing, it at all events preserves the indefinite idea (of a will good in itself) free from corruption, until it shall be more precisely defined.

For the rest I think I may be excused here from a detailed refutation of all these doctrines; that would only be superfluous labor, since it is so easy, and is probably so well seen even by those whose office requires them to decide for one of those theories (because their hearers would not tolerate suspension of judgment). But what interests us more here is to know that the prime foundation of morality laid down by all these principles is nothing but heteronomy of the will, and for this reason they must necessarily miss their aim.

In every case where an object of the will has to be supposed, in order that the rule may be prescribed which is to determine the will, there the rule is simply heteronomy; the imperative is conditional, namely, *if* or *because* one wishes for this object, one should act so and so; hence it can never command morally, that is, categorically. Whether the object determines the will by means of inclination, as in the principle of private happiness, or by means of reason directed to objects of our possible volition generally, as in the principle of perfection, in either case the will never determines itself *immediately* by the conception of the action, but only by the influence which the foreseen effect of the action has on the will; *I ought to do something, on this account, because I wish for something else*; and here there must be yet another law assumed in me as its subject, by which I necessarily will this other thing, and this law again requires an imperative to restrict this maxim. For the influence which the conception of an object within the reach of our faculties can exercise on the will of the subject in consequence of its natural properties, depends on the nature of the subject, either the sensibility (inclination and taste) or the understanding and reason, the employment of which is by the peculiar constitution of their nature attended with satisfaction. It follows that the law would be, properly speaking, given by nature, and as such it must be known and proved by experience, and would consequently be contingent, and therefore incapable of being an apodictic practical rule, such as the moral rule must be. Not only so, but it is *inevitably only heteronomy*; the will does not give itself the law, but it is given by a foreign impulse by means of a particular natural constitution of the subject adapted to receive it. An absolutely good will, then, the principle of which must be a categorical imperative, will be indeterminate as regards all objects, and will contain merely the *form of volition* generally, and that as autonomy, that is to say, the capability of the maxims of every good will to make themselves a universal law, is itself the only law which the will of every rational being imposes on itself, without needing to assume any spring or interest as a foundation.

# HASTINGS RASHDALL

HASTINGS RASHDALL (1858–1924) taught at
Oxford University. An Anglican clergyman,
as well as a teacher of philosophy, he wrote
extensively upon ethical and religious subjects. His major works include: *The Theory
of Good and Evil* (1907), *Philosophy and
Religion* (1910), *Is Conscience an Emotion?*
(1914), *Conscience and Christ* (1916), *The
Idea of Atonement in Christian Theology*
(1919), and *Ideas and Ideals* (1928).

## A Critique of the Categorical Imperative*

Two positions (1) that the rightness of actions is perceived immediately
by the Reason, (2) that this rightness ought to be and is capable of becoming
a motive to the Will, are embodied by Kant in the two famous phrases, the
categorical imperative and the autonomy of the will. Duty is a categorical
imperative because when a thing is seen to be right, we feel commanded to do
it categorically, absolutely, as a means to no end beyond itself. If duty meant
merely "Do this if you want to be happy, or to be perfect, or to go to heaven,"
it would be merely a hypothetical imperative: its obligation would depend
on our happening to desire the end to which we saw the action in question to
be a means. As it is, we feel that the rightness of doing what we see to be our
duty is in no way dependent on the presence or absence of any desire or inclination towards what is commanded. It is true that the action cannot be
done unless there is an impulse to do what is right or reasonable on our part,
but such a desire may be created by the Reason which recognizes the rightness: we desire to do the act commanded (in so far as we do desire it) because it is commanded; we do not judge that we are commanded to do the
act simply because we chance to desire it. When then we do a thing because
it is right, the will is autonomous: it is a "law to itself." Though the man
feels commanded to do the act whether he likes it or not, it is nevertheless
the man himself—his own Reason, the highest part of his nature—which
issues the command or makes the law. Hence in the highest sense he is most
free when most completely the slave of duty. . . .

### II

. . . In Kant's own view these positions are associated with two other doctrines which require further examination. In the first place he assumed that

* From *The Theory of Good and Evil*, by Hastings Rashdall, Book I, Chap. 5. Copyright, 1907, Clarendon Press. Used by permission.

out of this bare idea of a categorical imperative, without any appeal to experience, he could extract a moral criterion, i.e., that he could ascertain what is the actual content of the Moral Law, what in detail it is right to do. Secondly, he assumed that, so far as an act is not determined by pure respect for the Moral Law, it possesses no moral value whatever. Let us examine each of these positions in turn. . . .

The rules of action which the categorical imperative is supposed to give us are the following:—

(1) "So act as if the law of thine action were to become by thy will law universal."

(2) "Regard humanity whether in thine own person or in that of any one else always as an end and never as a means only."

(3) "Act as a member of a kingdom of ends."

Let us examine the first of these rules—"Act as if the law of thy action were to become by thy will law universal." Now it is quite true that it does follow from the very idea of there being something which it is right to do irrespectively of inclination that this course must, in the same circumstances, be binding upon every one else. And therefore in a sense it is true that no action can be really a moral rule the principle of which could not be universalized. It is good practical advice to urge that when we have to pronounce upon the morality of a proposed act we should ask ourselves whether it represents a principle which we should think it rational to will as a universal rule of conduct. But this is by itself a merely negative test. . . .

The Kantian maxim, properly interpreted, thus occupies in Ethics the same position which the law of contradiction holds in Logic. The law of contradiction is a negative test of truth: it tells us that two judgements which contradict one another cannot both be true, but as to which judgements in particular are true, it will give us no information: only, when I know that judgement A is true, it will tell me that judgement B, being inconsistent therewith, cannot also be true. In the same way the Kantian rule tells us that a genuine ultimate rule of conduct must not only be logically consistent with itself, but also be such as that all its prescriptions shall be consistent with all other ethical rules. The supreme ethical precept must consist of an harmonious and self-consistent system of precepts. It need hardly be said that this by itself is a most important negative test of ethical truth. It gives us the principle upon which alone inference or reasoning (as distinct from immediate judgements of Reason) is possible in Ethics. The fact that something is a part of the true ethical rule supplies, if we assume this principle to be self-evident, a demonstrative proof that some precept inconsistent with it cannot be a part of it. But as to what rule of action in particular is reasonable, it gives us no information whatever. . . .

How . . . did Kant attempt to extract out of the bare form of the Moral Law a knowledge of the particular actions which are right or wrong?

It is impossible to maintain that Kant gives a clear and consistent meaning to his own dictum. Sometimes the irrationality of willing the universal adoption of the immoral course appears to turn simply upon the fact that the social consequences to which the adoption of such a will would lead are consequences which no rational man could regard as good. We cannot will universal promise-breaking because in that case no promises would be made, and at times the irrationality of willing such a consequence seems to turn upon its injurious social effects. Still more clearly when Kant pronounces that we cannot rationally will the non-development of our faculties, the irrationality of such a course is made to depend simply upon the fact that the rational man actually regards this non-development as bad and their development as good. Here the appeal to consequences which can only be known by experience is scarcely disguised: the *a priori* judgement relates simply to the goodness or badness of the end. But Kant was able to conceal from himself the necessity of this appeal to experience, because in certain carefully selected instances he was able to point to the appearance of *internal* contradition in the reverse of the accepted rule.[1] We cannot rationally will that men shall break their promises, because in that case no promises would be made; and we cannot rationally will something to be done which will make it impossible to observe the very rule which we will. In a society in which there were no promises, it would no longer be possible to observe our proposed rule of universal promise-breaking; if no promises are made, none can be broken. Now even here it is evident that Kant falls back upon his experience of human nature to tell him what will be the consequences of his act: but still he might maintain that, given this much experience, the contradiction is self-evident. Yet it is easy to show that absence of contradiction, in this sense, would be a very irrational test of conduct. Kant himself appears to concede that there would be no internal contradiction in willing that all men should leave their faculties undeveloped. Nor would there be any internal contradiction in adopting as our rule of action the promotion of universal misery, or at least of the maximum of misery which should be consistent with the continued survival of the human race. That is, indeed, according to some Pessimists, precisely the end which is actually realized in the world as we know it.

And, just as we hold many acts to be wrong which involve no internal contradiction, so there are many things which we pronounce right in spite of such contradiction. Kant tells us that we cannot rationally will universal promise-breaking, because the universal adoption of such a rule would lead

---

[1] It is true that even in the selected cases the contradiction is not really internal. It is the actual structure of human society which makes the suggested rule unworkable.

to a state of things in which the rule "Break your promises" could no longer be observed. We must not commit suicide, because if every one did so, there would soon be nobody left to practise the virtue of suicide. Then are we, it may be asked, to deny that Philanthropy is a duty because the universal practice of a reasonable Philanthropy would lead to a state of things in which there would be no poor upon whom to practise that virtue? Shall we refuse to bless the peacemaker, because if every one shared his disposition, there would be no quarrels to adjust? And then, again, how unreasonable is the alternative with which we are presented—either to will universal suicide and universal lying, or to forbid each of these practices in any circumstances whatever! As reasonably might we pronounce Kant's own celibacy a crime because universal celibacy would rapidly extinguish the human race and (consequently) the practice of celibacy. . . .

The fact is that Kant appears to have confused two distinct senses of the term "categorical." When he sets forth that it is of the essence of every moral law to be categorical, he means that it must admit of no exception due to the subjective disinclination of the individual for the course of action which it prescribes. We must not say, "I admit Temperance or Veracity to be right in a general way: only I personally happen to have such a rooted antipathy to Temperance or Veracity, or whatever it be, that I must regard myself as an exception to the general rule." To talk in that way no doubt destroys the very nature of a Moral Law. It is an essential characteristic of the Moral Law that whatever is right for me must be right for every man in precisely the same circumstances. But when Kant tries to make out this mere unconditionality of a rule an absolute test of its reasonableness, he has to assume that the categorical character of an imperative excludes the possibility of an exception based not on the mere subjective disinclination of the individual, but on the nature of the case. He does not see that the rule "Do this except in such and such circumstances" is just as "categorical" and just as little "hypothetical" as the rule "Do this under all circumstances whatever," so long as the exceptions are recognized as no less universal in their application, no less based upon the reason and nature of things, than the original rule. Kant in fact confuses the inclusion of an exception *in* a moral rule with the admission of an exception *to* a moral rule. He does not recognize that the difference between a rule with an exception and a grammatically categorical rule is often a purely verbal one. The precept "Do no murder" admits of no exceptions, because "murder" means "killing except in such and such circumstances." The rule "Thou shalt not kill" has exceptions. So the rule "Lie not" could be represented as equally "categorical" if there were as clear a usage in favour of the proposition that a legitimate untruth is no lie, as there is in favour of the proposition that in certain circumstances killing is no murder. We are obliged sometimes to express a moral rule in the form of a general command with an exception simply because the enumeration of the circumstances to which the rule is inapplicable is shorter and more convenient than an exhaustive enumeration of all the cases to which it is applicable. And it is clear that every rule, however general, implies some set of circumstances in which alone it is capable of being applied. . . .

## III

That duty should be done for duty's sake we have seen to be really implied in the very notion of there being such a thing as duty. But it does not follow that the desire to do one's duty must always be the sole and exclusive motive of right conduct, or that conduct not consciously inspired by respect for the Moral Law as such must possess no moral value at all. Yet such was the assumption of Kant himself. To Kant the most unselfish devotion to wife or child, the most ardent patriotism, the most comprehensive philanthropy, possessed no more moral value than the purest avarice or the most unmitigated selfishness. Unless the man loves, or rather behaves as though he loved (since love, he holds, cannot be commanded) wife, or country, or humanity simply from an actual, conscious respect for the Moral Law, his conduct is worthless—not necessarily wrong (for it is not a crime to promote one's own happiness when duty does not forbid), but entirely without moral value. The will that wills from pure love of the brethren is morally on a level with the will that wills from pure love of self. It is of no more value than the behaviour of an animal. Such is the revolting and inhuman Stoicism to which Kant's ideal logically leads. It is, as Schopenhauer puts it, the "apotheosis of lovelessness, the exact opposite, as it is, of the Christian doctrine of Morals." In well-known lines the poet Schiller makes the disciple of Kant complain:

Gladly, I serve my friends, but alas I do it with pleasure.
Hence I am plagued with the doubt that I am not a virtuous person:

in reply to which the answer given is:

Sure, your only resource is to try to despise them entirely,
And then with aversion to do what your duty enjoins you.

. . . It would be a violent perversion of psychological fact to represent that every man who works hard and resists temptations to self-indulgence from love for his wife and children, or from a zeal for his profession, is inspired by pure respect for the abstract Moral Law; it would be a perversion of moral fact (attested in the only way in which moral fact can be attested, by the evidence of consciousness) to say that such conduct is morally worthless. To do so would involve the denial of moral value not only to much of the normally good conduct of average civilized men, and to all the more elementary morality of children or savages (to whom the idea of a Moral Law or an abstract "duty" can hardly be said to have occurred), but also to some of the very noblest acts of generous but one-sided and imperfect characters. . . .

Even in highly developed moral natures, and in some of the highest actions of such natures, it is often impossible to discover the conscious presence in any high degree of respect for the abstract idea of duty or the Moral Law as such. The philanthropist is carried away by an enthusiasm of humanity which does not stop to ask whether to relieve suffering or to fight against oppression is or is not contained in the categorical imperative of Reason. And such zeal for the things contained in the law we certainly pronounce morally good, however little conscious reference there may be to the law which contains them.

## IV

And from this point of view the thought may occur to us: "if good conduct implies only desire for objects which Reason can recognize as good, why do we need the 'sense of duty' or the categorical imperative at all?" May we not say with Aristotle that a man is not really good unless he likes the things that another may recognize as constituting his duty, or even go beyond Aristotle (who did insist that in developed Morality there should be a conscious recognition that the things desired were good), and say "It is nobler to be so fired by the thought of tyranny and injustice and suffering, so to feel others' wrongs as though they were one's own, that the question never arises at all whether it is a duty to fight against them . . . ? Would it not now show a positive defect in the man's character if he should decline to make a sacrifice which the good of his family demanded till he had calmly reflected that it was a dutiful or a beautiful thing for him to do? Is it not better to be socially useful because one loves one's neighbours as oneself than to regard them with indifference, and yet to feed or serve them only because it is one's duty?" . . .

Kant's categorical imperative has been justly (in some of its aspects) ridiculed by Schopenhauer as a mere survival from the lowest form of the "servile" theological Morality which he professed to have abandoned. "Whether he calls his fetich categorical imperative or Fitziputzli," makes no difference. It was the survival of the drill-sergeant Theology of eighteenth-century Prussia with the drill-sergeant turned into an abstraction. In depersonalizing his imperative and cutting it adrift from its connexion with the real world as a whole, life as a whole, good as a whole, he reduced it to something arbitrary, abstract, almost inhuman. . . .

## VI

It may be desirable to add a word about the second of the three moral criteria put forward by Kant—the rule "Use humanity whether in thine own person or in that of any other always as an end, never as a means only." It is the principle less frequently insisted on in Kant's own writings, and its relation to the other is not very precisely determined. He uses it chiefly to prove the immorality of suicide and of sexual transgression. There can be no question of the deep moral significance of the principle, but it is too vague to be really of any use as a moral criterion without knowledge of a kind which cannot be extracted out of the formula itself. . . . I am using a porter's body as a means when I employ him to carry trunks for me, and there is nothing immoral in my doing so. I am not using him *only* as a means, if I pay him for his work and treat him as a moral being no less entitled to a share in all the true goods of life than myself. Kant never said anything so absurd (though he is constantly cited as doing so) as that we should never use humanity as a means, but only that we should never use it as a means without using it also as an end, and it is impossible (apart from some conception of a concrete end or good of human life) to show that sexual immorality might not be equally compatible with a like recognition of others' claims. We should only have to insist on just and considerate treatment of those who have been called the "priestesses of humanity." The one kind of exchange of services is, on Kant's premises, exactly on a level with the other. Kant's real feeling was no doubt that the conduct in question was inconsistent with a true ideal of the relations between man and woman, but it was impossible for him to prove that inconsistency so long as he narrowed his conception of the ideal human life down to the performance of social duty on the one hand and the indiscriminate enjoyment of pleasure on the other. It is not the treating of humanity as a means that strikes us as wrong (for that might quite well be compatible with recognizing it also as an end), but the treating of humanity as a means *in this particular way*, as a means to such and such a kind of sensual pleasure, to such and such an end in which Reason can find no value. It is only because we have judged already that such treatment is a degradation of humanity that we pronounce it to be using humanity "only as a means."

Once again, we see the impossibility of reducing moral judgements to a merely intellectual, non-moral principle; of getting a criterion out of mere formal conceptions, which take no account of the content or intended consequences on which depends all the morality or the immorality of our actions. Mere universality or freedom of contradiction is no test of goodness or badness. The judgement of value cannot be reduced to any other sort of judgement—a judgement of formal consistency or a judgement as to the relation between ends and means, which takes no account of the character of those ends. It is only in estimating the value of an end that the moral Reason really comes into play. Abstract the form of the law from the matter of it, and there is nothing left on which a judgement of value can be passed. . . .

## VII

It has generally been recognized that the best expression of Kant's fundamental ethical principle is to be found in his third rule—"Act as a member of a kingdom of ends": that is to say "Act in such a way as to treat thyself and every other human being as of equal intrinsic value; behave as a member of a society in which each regards the good of each other as of equal value with its own, and is so treated by the rest," in which each is both end and means, in which each realizes his own good in promoting that of others. That such an ideal of human Society must, as far as it goes, be approved by the moral consciousness, follows from what has been already said: but, considered as a guide to the details of conduct, it suffers from the same fatal ambiguity as the preceding formulae. There is no sufficient definition or explanation of this good of others which we are to promote. We have still got nothing but a "form" without any content. . . .

In truth there run through the whole of Kant's ethical teaching two inconsistent and irreconcilable lines of thought—one of which is the basis (though only the basis) of all sound ethical theory; while the other has proved the fruitful parent of every extravagance, superstition, and absurdity by which the scientific study of Ethics has been, and still is, impeded. Every formula of Kant's may be interpreted, and at times appears to be interpreted by himself, in each of these opposite ways. "Duty is a categorical imperative." That may mean "there is a right course of action which is intrinsically right and reasonable for every man whether he likes it or not," and that is simply an analysis of what duty means to any one to whom it means anything at all. Or it may mean "there are certain acts which we recognize as being right to do without thinking of the ends (social or otherwise) which they will tend to realize," than which no better definition could be given of the irrational in conduct. "Duty for duty's sake" may mean that "we should pursue the good or intrinsically valuable end just because it is good," or it may mean that we should act without reference to an end at all. "Act on a principle fit for law universal" may mean "Pursue the ends which Reason pronounces to be intrinsically valuable for others no less than for thyself," or it may mean "Make the avoidance of internal inconsistency the criterion of thy conduct." "Treat humanity as an end and never merely as means" may mean "Regard the true Well-being of every man as possessing an intrinsic worth," or it may mean "Regard it as beneath thy dignity to be of use to the society in which thou livest, and indulge in phantastic scruples about things which do no real harm to thyself or anybody else." The "kingdom of ends" represents simply a combination of the two last maxims, and is liable to the same charge of ambiguity; though of all the formulae employed by Kant it is the one which lends itself most readily to the more rational interpretation.

## VIII

One more way of expressing our criticism upon the Kantian system shall be attempted, because it will supply a convenient opportunity of giving a definite answer to an ethical question of fundamental importance—the question which is the logically prior conception, the idea of "good" or the idea of "right." Kant never thoroughly made up his mind about this question. He always started with the idea of "right"; and all his difficulties arose from the attempt to give a meaning to, and to find a content for, this idea of "right" without appealing to the idea of "good." In our view the idea of "good" or "value" is logically the primary conception, though psychologically the idea of "right" may often in modern men be the more early developed. That action is right which tends to bring about the good. . . .

Kant generally ends by coming round to this view—that the right or rational act is the act which wills the good. Unfortunately he did not see that with that admission his attempt to avoid the appeal to experience completely breaks down. It is possible, though it is irrational, to will particular acts without attending to the consequences which experience shows likely to result from them; it is impossible to pronounce that something is good until one knows what it is. No experience will tell us what is good unless we include in our idea of "experience" an unavowed judgement of value; but without experience of what a thing is it is impossible to say whether it is good or not. It is obvious that this necessity of experience for sound ethical judgements goes a long way to explain the actual divergences of moral codes. When the Caliph Omar (if the story be not a myth) ordered the Alexandrian library to be burned, it is probable that he knew very imperfectly what the Alexandrian library or any other library really was. I do not deny that there might be fanatics who knowing a good deal about the contents of these books would still have ordered them to be burnt; but it is probable that a more extensive acquaintance with their contents would have modified the Caliph's judgement. The consistent Kantian, i.e., a disciple of Kant in his most logical but least rational movements, ought to be able to say whether they should be burned without knowing what sort of books they were or even that they were books at all.

Our moral judgements are ultimately judgements of Value. The fundamental idea in Morality is the idea of Value, in which the idea of "ought" is implicitly contained. The advantage involved in the use of the term "value" lies in its freedom from many of the exaggerations and mystifications which have sometimes created a prejudice against the term "ought," even in minds which have no prejudice against the reality which it signifies. The idea of "good" and the idea of "right" are, as it seems to me, correlative terms. It is implied in the idea of "good" that it ought to be promoted; the idea of "right" is meaningless apart from a "good" which right actions tend to promote.

## THE CATEGORICAL IMPERATIVE—SUGGESTED READINGS

Broad, C. D., *Five Types of Ethical Theory*, New York, Harcourt, Brace, 1930, Chap. 5. (exposition and criticism)

Dewey, J., *German Philosophy and Politics*, New York, Holt, 1915, Lectures I and II. (criticism)

Field, G. C., *Moral Theory*, 2nd ed., London, Methuen, 1932, Part I. (exposition and criticism)

Körner, S., *Kant*, Baltimore, Penguin Books, 1955, Chap. 6. (exposition and criticism)

Paton, H. J., *The Categorical Imperative*, Chicago, University of Chicago Press, 1948. (sympathetic exposition)

Ross, W. D., *Kant's Ethical Theory*, Oxford, Clarendon Press, 1954. (exposition and criticism)

# B. AN ACT IS RIGHT IF IT PRODUCES GOOD RESULTS

## 1. PLEASURE

Up to this point, the ethical theories discussed have been deontological theories: they have sought to discover the distinguishing mark of a right action in its conformity to some formal moral criterion, disregarding the results of the action. We turn now to consider representatives of teleological ethics, who hold that the rightness of an action depends upon its consequences; an act is right only if it produces, or tends to produce, good results.

It will be recalled that the key problem for teleological ethical theories is to determine what is good. Perhaps the most influential answer to this problem is provided by *hedonism*: the doctrine that the good is pleasure. For those who hold this view, actions are right insofar as they promote pleasure and diminish pain.

One of the most striking contrasts in all of ethical theory is that which exists between the viewpoint of Immanuel Kant and that of the hedonists. For Kant, an act may be right though it does no good or even does harm in its consequences; for the hedonists, good consequences are the only considerations that are ethically relevant. For Kant, if an act is done to achieve pleasure, it loses all its moral character; for the hedonists, pleasure is the proper end of action.

In the selections to follow, BENTHAM lays down the principles of hedonistic ethics. It is his view that an act is to be evaluated only as to the *amount* of pleasure it creates; he remarked on one occasion that if they brought equal pleasures, "pushpin [a child's game] is as good as poetry." Bentham proposes a "calculus" as an aid to determine the amount of pleasure an act will produce; this calculus is to inform men whether, and to what extent, any act is right. MILL agrees with Bentham that the good is pleasure; he defends hedonism against attacks. In contrast to Bentham, however, Mill urges that it is important to evaluate not only the *quantity* but also the *quality* of the pleasures which any act brings. There are "higher" and "lower" pleasures: it is "better to be Socrates dissatisfied than a fool satisfied." EWING criticizes all forms of hedonism, citing situations in which, he says, none of us would be willing to follow hedonistic principles.

162

# JEREMY BENTHAM

JEREMY BENTHAM (1748–1832) was a leading figure in founding the modern utilitarian
movement in ethics. He has been influential
not only for his ethical views but also for
the legal and political reforms which he advocated. His major works include: A *Frag-
ment on Government* (1776), *Defence of
Usury* (1787), *An Introduction to the Principles of Morals and Legislation* (1789),
*Theory of Legislation* (1802), and *Deontol-
ogy* (1834).

## An Introduction to the Principles of Morals and Legislation*

### Chapter I

### Of the Principle of Utility

I.  Nature has placed mankind under the governance of two sovereign
masters, *pain* and *pleasure*. It is for them alone to point out what we ought to
do, as well as to determine what we shall do. On the one hand the standard
of right and wrong, on the other the chain of causes and effects, are fastened
to their throne. They govern us in all we do, in all we say, in all we think;
every effort we can make to throw off our subjection, will serve but to
demonstrate and confirm it. In words a man may pretend to abjure their
empire: but in reality he will remain subject to it all the while. The *principle
of utility*[1] recognizes the subjection, and assumes it for the foundation of that

* From *An Introduction to the Principles of Morals and Legislation*, by Jeremy Bentham, Chaps. 1, 2, 4, and 10 (1789).

[1] To this denomination has of late been added, or substituted, the *greatest happiness or
greatest felicity* principle: this for shortness, instead of saying at length *that principle*
which states the greatest happiness of all those whose interest is in question, as being the
right and proper, and only right and proper and universally desirable, end of human action:
of human action in every situation, and in particular in that of a functionary or set of
functionaries exercising the powers of government. The word *utility* does not so clearly
point to the ideas of *pleasure* and *pain* as the words *happiness* and *felicity* do: nor does
it lead us to the consideration of the *number*, of the interests affected; to the *number*,
as being the circumstance, which contributes, in the largest proportion, to the formation
of the standard here in question; the *standard of right and wrong*, by which alone the
propriety of human conduct, in every situation, can with propriety be tried. This want of
a sufficiently manifest connexion between the ideas of *happiness* and *pleasure* on the one
hand, and the idea of *utility* on the other, I have every now and then found operating, and
with but too much efficiency, as a bar to the acceptance, that might otherwise have been
given, to this principle.

system, the object of which is to rear the fabric of felicity by the hands of reason and of law. Systems which attempt to question it, deal in sounds instead of sense, in caprice instead of reason, in darkness instead of light.

But enough of metaphor and declamation: it is not by such means that moral science is to be improved.

II.   The principle of utility is the foundation of the present work; it will be proper therefore at the outset to give an explicit and determinate account of what is meant by it. By the principle of utility is meant that principle which approves or disapproves of every action whatsoever, according to the tendency which it appears to have to augment or diminish the happiness of the party whose interest is in question; or, what is the same thing in other words, to promote or to oppose that happiness. I say of every action whatsoever; and therefore not only of every action of a private individual, but of every measure of government.

III.   By utility is meant that property in any object, whereby it tends to produce benefit, advantage, pleasure, good, or happiness, (all this in the present case comes to the same thing) or (what comes again to the same thing) to prevent the happening of mischief, pain, evil, or unhappiness to the party whose interest is considered: if that party be the community in general, then the happiness of the community: if a particular individual, then the happiness of that individual.

IV.   The interest of the community is one of the most general expressions that can occur in the phraseology of morals: no wonder that the meaning of it is often lost. When it has a meaning, it is this. The community is a fictitious *body*, composed of the individual persons who are considered as constituting as it were its *members*. The interest of the community then is, what?—the sum of the interests of the several members who compose it.

V.   It is in vain to talk of the interest of the community, without understanding what is the interest of the individual.[2] A thing is said to promote the interest, or to be *for* the interest, of an individual, when it tends to add to the sum total of his pleasures: or, what comes to the same thing, to diminish the sum total of his pains.

VI.   An action then may be said to be conformable to the principle of utility, or, for shortness' sake, to utility, (meaning with respect to the community at large) when the tendency it has to augment the happiness of the community is greater than any it has to diminish it.

VII.   A measure of government (which is but a particular kind of action, performed by a particular person or persons) may be said to be conformable to or dictated by the principle of utility, when in like manner the

---

[2] Interest is one of those words, which not having any superior *genus,* cannot in the ordinary way be defined.

tendency which it has to augment the happiness of the community is greater than any which it has to diminish it.

VIII. When an action, or in particular a measure of government, is supposed by a man to be conformable to the principle of utility, it may be convenient, for the purposes of discourse, to imagine a kind of law or dictate, called a law or dictate of utility: and to speak of the action in question, as being conformable to such law or dictate.

IX. A man may be said to be a partizan of the principle of utility, when the approbation or disapprobation he annexes to any action, or to any measure, is determined by and proportioned to the tendency which he conceives it to have to augment or to diminish the happiness of the community: or in other words, to its conformity or unconformity to the laws or dictates of utility.

X. Of an action that is conformable to the principle of utility, one may always say either that it is one that ought to be done, or at least that it is not one that ought not to be done. One may say also, that it is right it should be done; at least that it is not wrong it should be done: that it is a right action; at least that it is not a wrong action. When thus interpreted, the words *ought*, and *right* and *wrong*, and others of that stamp, have a meaning: when otherwise, they have none.

XI. Has the rectitude of this principle been ever formally contested? It should seem that it had, by those who have not known what they have been meaning. Is it susceptible of any direct proof? It should seem not, for that which is used to prove everything else, cannot itself be proved; a chain of proofs must have their commencement somewhere. To give such proof is as impossible as it is needless.

XII. Not that there is or ever has been that human creature breathing, however stupid or perverse, who has not on many, perhaps on most occasions of his life, deferred to it. By the natural constitution of the human frame, on most occasions of their lives men in general embrace this principle, without thinking of it; if not for the ordering of their own actions, yet for the trying of their own actions, as well as of those of other men. There have been, at the same time, not many, perhaps, even of the most intelligent, who have been disposed to embrace it purely and without reserve. There are even few who have not taken some occasion or other to quarrel with it, either on account of their not understanding always how to apply it, or on account of some prejudice or other which they were afraid to examine into, or could not bear to part with. For such is the stuff that man is made of: in principle and in practice, in a right track and in a wrong one, the rarest of all human qualities is consistency.

XIII. When a man attempts to combat the principle of utility, it is with reason drawn, without his being aware of it, from that very principle itself.[3] His arguments, if they prove anything, prove not that the principle is *wrong*, but that, according to the applications he supposes to be made of it, it is *misapplied*. Is it possible for a man to move the earth? Yes; but he must first find out another earth to stand upon.

XIV. To disapprove the propriety of it by arguments is impossible; but, from the causes that have been mentioned, or from some confused or partial view of it, a man may happen to be disposed not to relish it. Where this is the case, if he thinks the settling of his opinions on such a subject worth the trouble, let him take the following steps, and at length, perhaps, he may come to reconcile himself to it.

1. Let him settle with himself, whether he would wish to discard this principle altogether; if so, let him consider what it is that all his reasonings (in matters of politics especially) can amount to?

2. If he would, let him settle with himself, whether he would judge and act without any principle, or whether there is any other he would judge and act by?

3. If there be, let him examine and satisfy himself whether the principle he thinks he has found is really any separate intelligible principle; or whether it be not a mere principle in words, a kind of phrase, which at bottom expresses neither more nor less than the mere averment of his own unfounded sentiments; that is, what in another person he might be apt to call caprice?

4. If he is inclined to think that his own approbation or disapprobation, annexed to the idea of an act, without any regard to its consequences, is a sufficient foundation for him to judge and act upon, let him ask himself whether his sentiment is to be a standard of right and wrong, with respect to every other man, or whether every man's sentiment has the same privilege of being a standard to itself?

5. In the first case, let him ask himself whether his principle is not despotical, and hostile to all the rest of the human race?

6. In the second case, whether it is not anarchical, and whether at this rate there are not as many different standards of right and wrong as there are men? and whether even to the same man, the same thing, which is right today, may not (without the least change in its nature) be wrong tomorrow? and whether the same thing is not right and wrong in the same place at the same time? and in either case, whether all argument is not at an end? and whether, when two men have said, "I like this," and "I don't like it," they can (upon such principle) have anything more to say?

7. If he should have said to himself, No: for that the sentiment which

---

[3] "The principle of utility, (I have heard it said) is a dangerous principle: it is dangerous on certain occasions to consult it." This is as much as to say, what? that it is not consonant to utility, to consult utility: in short, that it is *not* consulting it, to consult it.

he proposes as a standard must be grounded on reflection, let him say on what particulars the reflection is to turn? if on particulars having relation to the utility of the act, then let him say whether this is not deserting his own principle, and borrowing assistance from that very one in opposition to which he sets it up: or if not on those particulars, on what other particulars?

8. If he should be for compounding the matter, and adopting his own principle in part, and the principle of utility in part, let him say how far he will adopt it?

9. When he has settled with himself where he will stop, then let him ask himself how he justifies to himself the adopting it so far? and why he will not adopt it any farther?

10. Admitting any other principle than the principle of utility to be a right principle, a principle that it is right for a man to pursue; admitting (what is not true) that the word *right* can have a meaning without reference to utility, let him say whether there is any such thing as a *motive* that a man can have to pursue the dictates of it: if there is, let him say what that motive is, and how it is to be distinguished from those which enforce the dictates of utility: if not, then lastly let him say what it is this other principle can be good for?

## Chapter II

### Of Principles Adverse to That of Utility

I.  If the principle of utility be a right principle to be governed by, and that in all cases, it follows from what has been just observed, that whatever principle differs from it in any case must necessarily be a wrong one. To prove any other principle, therefore, to be a wrong one, there needs no more than just to show it to be what it is, a principle of which the dictates are in some point or other different from those of the principle of utility: to state it is to confute it.

II.  A principle may be different from that of utility in two ways: 1. By being constantly opposed to it: this is the case with a principle which may be termed the principle of *asceticism*.[4] 2. By being sometimes opposed to it, and

---

[4] Ascetic is a term that has been sometimes applied to Monks. It comes from a Greek word which signifies *exercise*. The practice by which Monks sought to distinguish themselves from other men were called their Exercises. These exercises consisted in so many contrivances they had for tormenting themselves. By this they thought to ingratiate themselves with the Deity. For the Deity, said they, is a Being of infinite benevolence: now a Being of the most ordinary benevolence is pleased to see others make themselves as happy as they can: therefore to make ourselves as unhappy as we can is the way to please the Deity. If any body asked them, what motive they could find for doing all this? Oh! said they, you are not to imagine that we are punishing ourselves for nothing: we know very well what we are about. You are to know, that for every grain of pain it costs us now, we

sometimes not, as it may happen: this is the case with another, which may be termed the principle of *sympathy* and *antipathy*.

III. By the principle of asceticism I mean that principle, which, like the principle of utility, approves or disapproves of any action, according to the tendency which it appears to have to augment or diminish the happiness of the party whose interest is in question; but in an inverse manner: approving of actions in as far as they tend to diminish his happiness; disapproving of them in as far as they tend to augment it. . . .

IX. The principle of asceticism seems originally to have been the reverie of certain hasty speculators, who having perceived, or fancied, that certain pleasures, when reaped in certain circumstances, have, at the long run, been attended with pains more than equivalent to them, took occasion to quarrel with everything that offered itself under the name of pleasure. Having then got thus far, and having forgot the point which they set out from, they pushed on, and went so much further as to think it meritorious to fall in love with pain. Even this, we see, is at bottom but the principle of utility misapplied.

X. The principle of utility is capable of being consistently pursued; and it is but tautology to say, that the more consistently it is pursued, the better it must ever be for humankind. The principle of asceticism never was, or ever can be, consistently pursued by any living creature. Let but one tenth part of the inhabitants of this earth pursue it consistently, and in a day's time they will have turned it into a hell.

XI. Among principles adverse to that of utility, that which at this day seems to have most influence in matters of government, is what may be called the principle of sympathy and antipathy. By the principle of sympathy and antipathy, I mean that principle which approves or disapproves of certain actions, not on account of their tending to augment the happiness, nor yet on account of their tending to diminish the happiness of the party whose interest is in question, but merely because a man finds himself disposed to approve or disapprove of them: holding up that approbation or disapprobation as a sufficient reason for itself, and disclaiming the necessity of looking out for any extrinsic ground. Thus far in the general department of morals; and in the particular department of politics, measuring out the quantum (as well as determining the ground) of punishment, by the degree of the disapprobation.

---

are to have a hundred grains of pleasure by and by. The case is, that God loves to see us torment ourselves at present: indeed he has as good as told us so. But this is done only to try us, in order just to see how we should behave: which it is plain he could not know, without making the experiment. Now then, from the satisfaction it gives him to see us make ourselves as unhappy as we can make ourselves in this present life, we have a sure proof of the satisfaction it will give him to see us as happy as he can make us in a life to come.

XII.   It is manifest, that this is rather a principle in name than in reality; it is not a positive principle of itself, so much as a term employed to signify the negation of all principle. What one expects to find in a principle is something that points out some external consideration, as a means of warranting and guiding the internal sentiments of approbation and disapprobation; this expectation is but ill fulfilled by a proposition, which does neither more nor less than hold up each of those sentiments as a ground and standard for itself.

XIII.   In looking over the catalogue of human actions (says a partisan of this principle) in order to determine which of them are to be marked with the seal of disapprobation, you need but to take counsel of your own feelings: whatever you find in yourself a propensity to condemn, is wrong for that very reason. For the same reason it is also meet for punishment: what proportion it is adverse to utility, or whether it be adverse to utility at all, is a matter that makes no difference. In that same *proportion* also is it meet for punishment; if you hate much, punish much; if you hate little, punish little; punish as you hate. If you hate not at all, punish not at all; the fine feelings of the soul are not to be overborne and tyrannized by the harsh and rugged dictates of political utility.

XIV.   The various systems that have been formed concerning the standard of right and wrong, may all be reduced to the principle of sympathy and antipathy. One account may serve for all of them. They consist all of them in so many contrivances for avoiding the obligation of appealing to any external standard, and for prevailing upon the reader to accept of the author's sentiment or opinion as a reason for itself. The phrases different, but the principle the same.[5]

[5] It is curious enough to observe the variety of inventions men have hit upon, and the variety of phrases they have brought forward, in order to conceal from the world, and, if possible, from themselves, this very general and therefore very pardonable self-sufficiency.

1. One man says, he has a thing made on purpose to tell him what is right and what is wrong; and that it is called a *moral sense*: and then he goes to work at his ease, and says, such a thing is right, and such a thing is wrong—why? "because my moral sense tells me it is."

2. Another man comes and alters the phrase: leaving out *moral* and putting in *common*, in the room of it. He then tells you, that his common sense teaches him what is right and wrong, as surely as the other's moral sense did: meaning by common sense, a sense of some kind or other, which, he says, is possessed by all mankind: the sense of those, whose sense is not the same as the author's, being struck out of the account as not worth taking. This contrivance does better than the other; for a moral sense, being a new thing, a man may feel about him a good while without being able to find it out: but common sense is as old as the creation; and there is no man but would be ashamed to be thought not to have as much of it as his neighbours. It has another great advantage: by appearing to share power, it lessens envy: for when a man gets up upon this ground, in order to anathematize those who differ from him, it is not by a *sic volo sic jubeo*, but by a *velitis jubeatis*.

3. Another man comes, and says, that as to a moral sense indeed, he cannot find that he has any such thing: that however he has an *understanding*, which will do quite as well. This understanding, he says, is the standard of right and wrong: it tells him so and so. All

XV. It is manifest, that the dictates of this principle will frequently coincide with those of utility, though perhaps without intending any such thing. Probably more frequently than not: and hence it is that the business of penal justice is carried on upon that tolerable sort of footing upon which we see it carried on in common at this day. For what more natural or more general ground of hatred to a practice can there be, than the mischievousness of such practice? What all men are exposed to suffer by, all men will be disposed to hate. It is far yet, however, from being a constant ground: for when a man suffers, it is not always that he knows what it is he suffers by. A man may suffer grievously, for instance, by a new tax, without being able to trace up the cause of his sufferings to the injustice of some neighbour, who has eluded the payment of an old one.

XVI. The principle of sympathy and antipathy is most apt to err on the side of severity. It is for applying punishment in many cases which deserve none: in many cases which deserve some, it is for applying more than they deserve. There is no incident imaginable, be it ever so trivial, and so remote from mischief, from which this principle may not extract a ground of punishment. Any difference in taste: any difference in opinion: upon one

---

good and wise men understand as he does: if other men's understandings differ in any point from his, so much the worse for them: it is a sure sign they are either defective or corrupt.

4. Another man says, that there is an eternal and immutable Rule of Right: that that rule of right dictates so and so: and then he begins giving you his sentiments upon anything that comes uppermost: and these sentiments (you are to take for granted) are so many branches of the eternal rule of right.

5. Another man, or perhaps the same man (it's no matter) says, that there are certain practices conformable, and others repugnant to the Fitness of Things; and then he tells you, at his leisure, what practices are conformable and what repugnant: just as he happens to like a practice or dislike it.

6. A great multitude of people are continually talking of the Law of Nature; and then they go on giving you their sentiments about what is right and what is wrong: and these sentiments, you are to understand, are so many chapters and sections of the Law of Nature.

7. Instead of the phrase, Law of Nature, you have sometimes, Law of Reason, Right Reason, Natural Justice, Natural Equity, Good Order. Any of them will do equally well. This latter is most used in politics. The last three are much more tolerable than the others, because they do not very explicitly claim to be anything more than phrases; they insist but feebly upon the being looked upon as so many positive standards of themselves, and seem content to be taken, upon occasion, for phrases expressive of the conformity of the thing in question to the proper standard, whatever that may be. On most occasions, however, it will be better to say *utility*: *utility* is clearer, as referring more explicitly to pain and pleasure.

8. We have one philosopher, who says, there is no harm in anything in the world but in telling a lie: and that if, for example, you were to murder your own father, this would only be a particular way of saying, he was not your father. Of course, when this philosopher sees anything that he does not like, he says, it is a particular way of telling a lie. It is saying, that the act ought to be done, or may be done, when, *in truth*, it ought not to be done.

9. The fairest and openest of them all is that sort of man who speaks out, and says, I am of the number of the Elect: now God himself takes care to inform the Elect what is right: and that with so good effect, that let them strive ever so, they cannot help not

subject as well as upon another. No disagreement so trifling which perseverance and altercation will not render serious. Each becomes in the other's
eyes an enemy, and, if laws permit, a criminal. This is one of the circumstances by which the human race is distinguished (not much indeed to its
advantage) from the brute creation.

XVII.   It is not, however, by any means unexampled for this principle to
err on the side of lenity. A near and perceptible mischief moves antipathy.
A remote and imperceptible mischief, though not less real, has no effect. . . .

XVIII.   It may be wondered, perhaps, that in all this while no mention
has been made of the *theological* principle; meaning that principle which
professes to recur for the standard of right and wrong to the will of God.
But the case is, this is not in fact a distinct principle. It is never anything
more or less than one or other of the three before-mentioned principles
presenting itself under another shape. The *will* of God here meant cannot be
his revealed will, as contained in the sacred writings: for that is a system
which nobody ever thinks of recurring to at this time of day, for the details
of political administration: and even before it can be applied to the details of private conduct, it is universally allowed, by the most eminent divines

---

only knowing it but practising it. If therefore a man wants to know what is right and what
is wrong, he has nothing to do but to come to me.

It is upon the principle of antipathy that such and such acts are often reprobated on the
score of their being *unnatural*: the practice of exposing children, established among the
Greeks and Romans, was an unnatural practice. Unnatural, when it means any thing,
means unfrequent: and there it means something; although nothing to the present purpose.
But here it means no such thing: for the frequency of such acts is perhaps the great complaint. It therefore means nothing; nothing, I mean, which there is in the act itself. All it
can serve to express is, the disposition of the person who is talking of it: the disposition he
is in to be angry at the thoughts of it. Does it merit his anger? Very likely it may: but
whether it does or no is a question, which to be answered rightly, can only be answered
upon the principle of utility.

Unnatural, is as good a word as moral sense, or common sense; and would be as good
a foundation for a system. Such an act is unnatural; that is, repugnant to nature: for I do
not like to practise it: and, consequently, do not practise it. It is therefore repugnant to
what ought to be the nature of everybody else.

This mischief common to all these ways of thinking and arguing (which, in truth, as we
have seen, are but one and the same method, couched in different forms of words) is their
serving as a cloke, and pretence, and aliment, to despotism: if not a despotism in practice,
a despotism however in disposition: which is but too apt, when pretence and power offer, to
show itself in practice. The consequence is, that with intentions very commonly of the
purest kind, a man becomes a torment either to himself or his fellow-creatures. If he be
of the melancholy cast, he sits in silent grief, bewailing their blindness and depravity:
if of the irascible, he declaims with fury and virulence against all who differ from him;
blowing up the coals of fanaticism, and branding with the charge of corruption and insincerity, every man who does not think, or profess to think, as he does.

If such a man happens to possess the advantages of style, his book may do a considerable
deal of mischief before the nothingness of it is understood.

These principles, if such they can be called, it is more frequent to see applied to morals
than to politics: but their influence extends itself to both. In politics, as well as morals,
a man will be at least equally glad of a pretence for deciding any question in the manner

of all persuasions, to stand in need of pretty ample interpretations; else to what use are the works of those divines? And for the guidance of these interpretations, it is also allowed, that some other standard must be assumed. The will then which is meant on this occasion, is that which may be called the *presumptive* will: that is to say, that which is presumed to be his will on account of the conformity of its dictates to those of some other principle. What then may be this other principle? it must be one or other of the three mentioned above; for there cannot, as we have seen, be any more. It is plain, therefore, that, setting revelation out of the question, no light can ever be thrown upon the standard of right and wrong, by anything that can be said upon the question, what is God's will. We may be perfectly sure, indeed, that whatever is right is conformable to the will of God; but so far is that from answering the purpose of showing us what is right, that it

---

that best pleases him, without the trouble of inquiry. If a man is an infallible judge of what is right and wrong in the actions of private individuals, why not in the measures to be observed by public men in the direction of those actions? accordingly (not to mention other chimeras) I have more than once known the pretended law of nature set up in legislative debates, in opposition to arguments derived from the principle of utility.

"But is it never, then, from any other considerations than those of utility, that we derive our notions of right and wrong?" I do not know: I do not care. Whether a moral sentiment can be originally conceived from any other source than a view of utility, is one question: whether upon examination and reflection it can, in point of fact, be actually persisted in and justified on any other ground, by a person reflecting within himself, is another: whether in point of right it can properly be justified on any other ground, by a person addressing himself to the community, is a third. The two first are questions of speculation: it matters not, comparatively speaking, how they are decided. The last is a question of practice: the decision of it is of as much importance as that of any can be.

"I feel in myself," (say you) "a disposition to approve of such or such an action in a moral view: but this is not owing to any notions I have of its being a useful one to the community. I do not pretend to know whether it be an useful one or not: it may be, for aught I know, a mischievous one." "But is it then," (say I) "a mischievous one? examine; and if you can make yourself sensible that it is so, then, if duty means any thing, that is, moral duty, it is your *duty* at least to abstain from it: and more than that, if it is what lies in your power, and can be done without too great a sacrifice, to endeavour to prevent it. It is not your cherishing the notion of it in your bosom, and giving it the name of virtue, that will excuse you."

"I feel in myself," (say you again) "a disposition to detest such or such an action in a moral view; but this is not owing to any notions I have of its being a mischievous one to the community. I do not pretend to know whether it be a mischievous one or not: it may be not a mischievous one: it may be, for aught I know, an useful one."—"May it indeed," (say I) "an useful one? but let me tell you then, that unless duty, and right and wrong, be just what you please to make them, if it really be not a mischievous one, and any body has a mind to do it, it is no duty of yours, but, on the contrary, it would be very wrong in you, to take upon you to prevent him: detest it within yourself as much as you please; that may be a very good reason (unless it be also a useful one) for your not doing it yourself: but if you go about, by word or deed, to do any thing to hinder him, or make him suffer for it, it is you, and not he, that have done wrong: it is not your setting yourself to blame his conduct, or branding it with the name of vice, that will make him culpable, or you blameless. Therefore, if you can make yourself content that he shall be of one mind, and you of another, about that matter, and so continue, it is well: but if nothing will serve you, but that you and he must needs be of the same mind, I'll tell you what you have to do: it is for you to get the better of your antipathy, not for him to truckle to it."

is necessary to know first whether a thing is right, in order to know from thence whether it be conformable to the will of God.[6]

XIX. There are two things which are very apt to be confounded, but which it imports us carefully to distinguish:—the motive or cause, which, by operating on the mind of an individual, is productive of any act, and the ground or reason which warrants a legislator, or other bystander, in regarding that act with an eye of approbation. When the act happens, in the particular instance in question, to be productive of effects which we approve of, much more if we happen to observe that the same motive may frequently be productive, in other instances, of the like effects, we are apt to transfer our approbation to the motive itself, and to assume, as the just ground for the approbation we bestow on the act, the circumstance of its originating from that motive. It is in this way that the sentiment of antipathy has often been considered as a just ground of action. Antipathy, for instance, in such or such a case, is the cause of an action which is attended with good effects; but this does not make it a right ground of action in that case, any more than in any other. Still farther. Not only the effects are good, but the agent sees beforehand that they will be so. This may make the action indeed a perfectly right action: but it does not make antipathy a right ground for action. For the same sentiment of antipathy, if implicity deferred to, may be, and very frequently is, productive of the very worst effects. Antipathy, therefore, can never be a right ground of action. No more, therefore, can resentment, which, as will be seen more particularly hereafter, is but a modification of antipathy. The only right ground of action, that can possibly subsist, is, after all, the consideration of utility, which, if it is a right principle of action, and of approbation, in any one case, is so in every other. Other principles in abundance, that is, other motives, may be the reasons why such and such an act *has* been done, that is, the reasons or causes of its being done; but it is this alone that can be the reason why it might or ought to have been done. Antipathy or resentment requires always to be regulated, to prevent

---

[6] The principle of theology refers every thing to God's pleasure. But what is God's pleasure? God does not, he confessedly does not now, either speak or write to us. How then are we to know what is his pleasure? By observing what is our own pleasure, and pronouncing it to be his. Accordingly, what is called the pleasure of God, is and must necessarily be (revelation apart) neither more nor less than the good pleasure of the person, whoever he be, who is pronouncing what he believes, or pretends, to be God's pleasure. How know you it to be God's pleasure that such or such an act should be abstained from? whence come you even to suppose as much? "Because the engaging in it would, I imagine, be prejudical upon the whole to the happiness of mankind;" says the partizan of the principle of utility: "Because the commission of it is attended with a gross and sensual, or at least with a trifling and transient satisfaction;" says the partizan of the principle of asceticism: "Because I detest the thoughts of it; and I cannot, neither ought I to be called upon to tell why;" says he who proceeds upon the principle of antipathy. In the words of one or other of these must that person necessarily answer (revelation apart) who professes to take for his standard the will of God.

its doing mischief: to be regulated by what? always by the principle of utility. The principle of utility neither requires nor admits of any other regulator than itself.

## Chapter IV

### *Value of a Lot of Pleasure or Pain, How to Be Measured*

I.   Pleasures then, and the avoidance of pains, are the *ends* which the legislator has in view: it behoves him therefore to understand their *value*. Pleasures and pains are the *instruments* he has to work with: it behoves him therefore to understand their force, which is again, in other words, their value.

II.   To a person considered *by himself*, the value of a pleasure or pain considered *by itself*, will be greater or less, according to the four following circumstances.[7]

1. Its *intensity*.                    3. Its *certainty* or *uncertainty*.
2. Its *duration*.                    4. Its *propinquity* or *remoteness*.

III.   These are the circumstances which are to be considered in estimating a pleasure or a pain considered each of them by itself. But when the value of any pleasure or pain is considered for the purpose of estimating the tendency of any *act* by which it is produced, there are two other circumstances to be taken into the account; these are,

5. Its *fecundity*, or the chance it has of being followed by sensations of the *same* kind: that is, pleasures, if it be a pleasure: pains, if it be a pain.

6. Its *purity*, or the chance it has of *not* being followed by sensations of the *opposite* kind: that is, pains, if it be a pleasure: pleasures, if it be a pain.

These two last, however, are in strictness scarcely to be deemed properties of the pleasures or the pain itself; they are not, therefore, in strictness to be taken into the account of the value of that pleasure or that pain. They are in strictness to be deemed properties only of the act, or other event, by which such pleasure or pain has been produced; and accordingly are only

---

[7] These circumstances have since been denominated *elements* or *dimensions* of *value* in a pleasure or a pain.

Not long after the publication of the first edition, the following memoriter verses were framed, in the view of lodging more effectually, in the memory, these points, on which the whole fabric of morals and legislation may be seen to rest:

> Intense, long, certain, speedy, fruitful, pure—
> Such marks in *pleasures* and in *pains* endure.
> Such pleasures seek, if *private* be thy end:
> If it be *public*, wide let them *extend*.
> Such *pains* avoid, whichever be thy view:
> If pains *must* come, let them *extend* to few.

to be taken into the account of the tendency of such act or such event.

IV.   To a *number* of persons, with reference to each of whom the value of a pleasure or a pain is considered, it will be greater or less, according to seven circumstances: to wit, the six preceding ones; *viz.*

1. Its *intensity*.
2. Its *duration*.
3. Its *cerainty* or *uncertainty*.
4. Its *propinquity* or *remoteness*.
5. Its *fecundity*.
6. Its *purity*.

And one other; to wit:

7. Its *extent*; that is, the number of persons to whom it *extends*; or, (in other words) who are affected by it.

V.   To take an exact account then of the general tendency of any act, by which the interests of a community are affected, proceed as follows. Begin with any one person of those whose interests seem most immediately to be affected by it: and take an account,

1. Of the value of each distinguishable *pleasure* which appears to be produced by it in the *first* instance.

2. Of the value of each *pain* which appears to be produced by it in the *first* instance.

3. Of the value of each pleasure which appears to be produced by it *after* the first. This constitutes the *fecundity* of the first *pleasure* and the *impurity* of the first *pain*.

4. Of the value of each *pain* which appears to be produced by it after the first. This constitutes the *fecundity* of the first *pain*, and the *impurity* of the first pleasure.

5. Sum up all the values of all the *pleasures* on the one side, and those of all the pains on the other. The balance, if it be on the side of pleasure, will give the *good* tendency of the act upon the whole, with respect to the interests of that *individual* person; if on the side of pain, the *bad* tendency of it upon the whole.

6. Take an account of the *number* of persons whose interests appear to be concerned; and repeat the above process with respect to each. *Sum up* the numbers expressive of the degrees of *good* tendency, which the act has, with respect to each individual, in regard to whom the tendency of it is *good* upon the whole: do this again with respect to each individual, in regard to whom the tendency of it is *bad* upon the whole. Take the *balance*; which, if on the side of *pleasure*, will give the general *good tendency* of the act, with respect to the total number of community of individuals concerned; if on the side of pain the general *evil tendency*, with respect to the same community.

VI.   It is not to be expected that this process should be strictly pursued previously to every moral judgment, or to every legislative or judicial operation. It may, however, be always kept in view: and as near as the process actually pursued on these occasions approaches to it, so near will such process approach to the character of an exact one.

VII. The same process is alike applicable to pleasure and pain in whatever shape they appear: and by whatever denomination they are distinguished: to pleasure, whether it be called *good* (which is properly the cause or instrument of pleasure), or *profit* (which is distant pleasure, or the cause or instrument of distant pleasure), or *convenience*, or *advantage*, *benefit*, *emolument*, *happiness*, and so forth: to pain, whether it be called *evil* (which corresponds to *good*), or *mischief*, or *inconvenience*, or *disadvantage*, or *loss*, or *unhappiness*, and so forth.

VIII. Nor is this a novel and unwarranted, any more than it is a useless theory. In all this there is nothing but what the practice of mankind, wheresoever they have a clear view of their own interest, is perfectly conformable to. An article of property, an estate in land, for instance, is valuable, on what account? On account of the pleasures of all kinds which it enables a man to produce, and what comes to the same thing, the pains of all kinds which it enables him to avert. But the value of such an article of property is universally understood to rise or fall according to the length or shortness of the time which a man has in it: the certainty or uncertainty of its coming into possession: and the nearness or remoteness of the time at which, if at all, it is to come into possession. As to the *intensity* of the pleasures which a man may derive from it, this is never thought of, because it depends upon the use which each particular person may come to make of it; which cannot be estimated till the particular pleasures he may come to derive from it, or the particular pains he may come to exclude by means of it, are brought to view. For the same reason, neither does he think of the *fecundity* or *purity* of those pleasures. . . .

## Chapter X

### Motives

#### § 2. No Motives Either Constantly Good, or Constantly Bad

IX. In all this chain of motives, the principle or original link seems to be the last internal motive in prospect; it is to this that all the other motives in prospect owe their materiality; and the immediately acting motive its existence. This motive in prospect, we see, is always some pleasure, or some pain; some pleasure, which the act in question is expected to be a means of continuing or producing: some pain which it is expected to be a means of discontinuing or preventing. A motive is substantially nothing more than pleasure or pain, operating in a certain manner.

X. Now, pleasure is in *itself* a good: nay, even setting aside immunity from pain, the only good: pain is in itself an evil; and, indeed, without exception, the only evil; or else the words good and evil have no meaning. And this is alike true of every sort of pain, and of every sort of pleasure. It follows, therefore, immediately and incontestably, that *there is no such thing as any sort of motive that is in itself a bad one.*[8]

XI. It is common, however, to speak of actions as proceeding from *good* or *bad* motives: in which case the motives meant are such as are internal. The expression is far from being an accurate one; and as it is apt to occur in the consideration of almost every kind of offence, it will be requisite to settle the precise meaning of it, and observe how far it quadrates with the truth of things.

XII. With respect to goodness and badness, as it is with everything else that is not itself either pain or pleasure, so is it with motives. If they are good or bad, it is only on account of their effects: good, on account of their tendency to produce pleasure, or avert pain: bad, on account of their tendency to produce pain, or avert pleasure. Now the case is, that from one and the same motive, and from every kind of motive, may proceed actions that are good, others that are bad, and others that are indifferent. . . .

XXIX. It appears then that there is no such thing as any sort of motive which is a bad one in itself: nor, consequently, any such thing as a sort of motive, which in itself is exclusively a good one. And as to their effects, it appears too that these are sometimes bad, at other times either indifferent or good: and this appears to be the case with every sort of motive. *If any sort of motive then is either good or bad on the score of its effects, this is the case only on individual occasions, and with individual motives;* and this is the case with one sort of motive as well as with another. *If any sort of motive then can, in consideration of its effects, be termed with any propriety a bad one,* it can only be with reference to the balance of all the effects it may have had of both kinds within a given period, that is, of its most usual tendency.

XXX. What then? (it will be said) are not lust, cruelty, avarice, bad motives? Is there so much as any one individual occasion, in which motives like these can be otherwise than bad? No, certainly: and yet the proposition, that there is no one *sort* of motive but what will on many occasions be a good one, is nevertheless true. The fact is, that these are names which, if properly applied, are never applied but in the cases where the motives they

---

[8] Let a man's motive be ill-will; call it even malice, envy, cruelty; it is still a kind of pleasure that is his motive: the pleasure he takes at the thought of the pain which he sees, or expects to see, his adversary undergo. Now even this wretched pleasure, taken by itself, is good: it may be faint; it may be short: it must at any rate be impure: yet while it lasts, and before any bad consequences arrive. it is good as any other that is not more intense.

signify happen to be bad. The names of these motives, considered apart from their effects, are sexual desire, displeasure, and pecuniary interest. To sexual desire, when the effects of it are looked upon as bad, is given the name of lust. Now lust is always a bad motive. Why? Because if the case be such, that the effects of the motive are not bad, it does not go, or at least ought not to go, by the name of lust. The case is, then, that when I say, "Lust is a bad motive," it is a proposition that merely concerns the import of the word lust; and which would be false if transferred to the other word used for the same motive, sexual desire. Hence we see the emptiness of all those rhapsodies of common-place morality, which consist in the taking of such names as lust, cruelty, and avarice, and branding them with marks of reprobation: applied to the *thing*, they are false; applied to the *name*, they are true indeed, but nugatory. Would you do a real service to mankind, show them the cases in which sexual desire *merits* the name of lust; displeasure, that of cruelty; and pecuniary interest, that of avarice.

# JOHN STUART MILL

JOHN STUART MILL (1806–73) was a major British philosopher of his period. As an empiricist in the theory of knowledge and as a leader of the utilitarian movement in ethics, he wrote extensively upon problems of scientific method, epistemology, ethics, and social philosophy. His major works include: A *System of Logic* (1843), *Principles of Political Economy* (1848), *On Liberty* (1859), *Considerations on Representative Government* (1861), and *Utilitarianism* (1863).

## Utilitarianism*

### Chapter I

### General Remarks

There are few circumstances among those which make up the present condition of human knowledge more unlike what might have been expected, or more significant of the backward state in which speculation on the most important subjects still lingers, than the little progress which has been

* From *Utilitarianism*, by J. S. Mill, Chaps. 1–4 (1863).

made in the decision of the controversy respecting the criterion of right and wrong. From the dawn of philosophy, the question concerning the *summum bonum*, or, what is the same thing, concerning the foundation of morality, has been accounted the main problem in speculative thought, has occupied the most gifted intellects and divided them into sects and schools, carrying on a vigorous warfare against one another. And after more than two thousand years the same discussions continue, philosophers are still ranged under the same contending banners, and neither thinkers nor mankind at large seem nearer to being unanimous on the subject than when the youth Socrates listened to the old Protagoras, and asserted (if Plato's dialogue be grounded on a real conversation) the theory of utilitarianism against the popular morality of the so-called sophist.

It is true that similar confusion and uncertainty and, in some cases, similar discordance exist respecting the first principles of all the sciences, not excepting that which is deemed the most certain of them—mathematics, without much impairing, generally indeed without impairing at all, the trustworthiness of the conclusions of those sciences. An apparent anomaly, the explanation of which is that the detailed doctrines of a science are not usually deduced from, nor depend for their evidence upon, what are called its first principles. Were it not so, there would be no science more precarious, or whose conclusions were more insufficiently made out, than algebra, which derives none of its certainty from what are commonly taught to learners as its elements, since these, as laid down by some of its most eminent teachers, are as full of fictions as English law, and of mysteries as theology. The truths which are ultimately accepted as the first principles of a science are really the last results of metaphysical analysis, practised on the elementary notions with which the science is conversant; and their relation to the science is not that of foundations to an edifice, but of roots to a tree, which may perform their office equally well though they be never dug down to and exposed to light. But though in science the particular truth precede the general theory, the contrary might be expected to be the case with a practical art, such as morals or legislation. All action is for the sake of some end, and rules of action, it seems natural to suppose, must take their whole character and color from the end to which they are subservient. When we engage in a pursuit, a clear and precise conception of what we are pursuing would seem to be the first thing we need, instead of the last we are to look forward to. A test of right and wrong must be the means, one would think, of ascertaining what is right or wrong, and not a consequence of having already ascertained it.

The difficulty is not avoided by having recourse to the popular theory of a natural faculty, a sense or instinct, informing us of right and wrong.

For—besides that the existence of such a moral instinct is itself one of the matters in dispute—those believers in it who have any pretensions to philosophy have been obliged to abandon the idea that it discerns what is right or wrong in the particular case in hand, as our other senses discern the sight or sound actually present. Our moral faculty, according to all those of its interpreters who are entitled to the name of thinkers, supplies us only with the general principles of moral judgments; it is a branch of our reason, not of our sensitive faculty; and must be looked to for the abstract doctrines of morality, not for perception of it in the concrete. The intuitive, no less than what may be termed the inductive, school of ethics insists on the necessity of general laws. They both agree that the morality of an individual action is not a question of direct perception, but of the application of a law to an individual case. They recognize also, to a great extent, the same moral laws, but differ as to their evidence and the source from which they derive their authority. According to the one opinion, the principles of morals are evident *a priori*, requiring nothing to command assent except that the meaning of the terms be understood. According to the other doctrine, right and wrong, as well as truth and falsehood, are questions of observation and experience. But both hold equally that morality must be deduced from principles; and the intuitive school affirm as strongly as the inductive that there is a science of morals. Yet they seldom attempt to make out a list of the *a priori* principles which are to serve as the premises of the science; still more rarely do they make any effort to reduce those various principles to one first principle, or common ground of obligation. They either assume the ordinary precepts of morals as of *a priori* authority, or they lay down as the common groundwork of those maxims, some generality much less obviously authoritative than the maxims themselves, and which has never succeeded in gaining popular acceptance. Yet to support their pretensions there ought either to be some one fundamental principle or law at the root of all morality, or, if there be several, there should be a determinate order of precedence among them; and the one principle, or the rule for deciding between the various principles when they conflict, ought to be self-evident.

To inquire how far the bad effects of this deficiency have been mitigated in practice, or to what extent the moral beliefs of mankind have been vitiated or made uncertain by the absence of any distinct recognition of an ultimate standard, would imply a complete survey and criticism of past and present ethical doctrine. It would, however, be easy to show that whatever steadiness or consistency these moral beliefs have attained has been mainly due to the tacit influence of a standard not recognized. Although the non-existence of an acknowledged first principle has made ethics not so much a guide as a consecration of men's actual sentiments, still, as men's sentiments, both in favor and of aversion, are greatly influenced by what they suppose to be the effect of things upon their happiness, the principle of utility, or, as Bentham latterly called it, the greatest happiness principle, has had a large share in forming the moral doctrines even of those who most scornfully reject its authority. Nor is there any school of thought which refuses to admit that the influence of actions on happiness is a most material and even predominant consideration in many of the details, of morals, however unwilling to acknowledge it as the fundamental principle of morality and the source of moral obligation. I might go much further and say that to all those *a priori* moralists who deem it necessary to argue at all, utilitarian arguments are indispensable. It is not my present purpose to criticize these thinkers; but I cannot help referring, for illustration, to a systematic treatise by one of the most illustrious of them, the *Metaphysics of Ethics* by Kant. This remarkable man, whose system of thought will long remain one of the landmarks in the history of philosophical speculation, does, in the treatise in question, lay down a universal first principle as the origin and ground of moral obligation; it is this: "So act that the rule on which thou actest would admit of being adopted as a law by all rational beings." But when he begins to deduce from this precept any of the actual duties of morality, he fails, almost grotesquely, to show that there would be any contradiction, any logical (not to say physical) impossibility, in the adoption by all rational beings of the most outrageously immoral rules of conduct. All he knows is that the *consequences* of their universal adoption would be such as no one would choose to incur.

On the present occasion, I shall, without further discussion of the other theories, attempt to contribute something towards the understanding and appreciation of the "utilitarian" or "happiness" theory, and towards such proof as it is susceptible of. It is evident that this cannot be proof in the ordinary and popular meaning of the term. Questions of ultimate ends are not amenable to direct proof. Whatever can be proved to be good must be so by being shown to be a means to something admitted to be good without proof. The medical art is proved to be good by its conducing to health; but how is it possible to prove that health is good? The art of music is good, for the reason, among others, that it produces pleasure; but what proof is it possible to give that pleasure is good? If, then, it is asserted that there is a comprehensive formula, including all things which are in themselves good, and that whatever else is good is not so as an end but as a means, the formula may be accepted or rejected, but is not a subject of what is commonly understood by proof. We are not, however, to infer that its acceptance or rejection must depend on blind impulse, or arbitrary choice. There is a larger meaning of the word "proof," in which this question is as amenable to it as any other of the disputed questions of philosophy. The subject is within the cognizance of the rational faculty; and neither does that faculty deal with it solely in the way of intuition. Considerations may be presented capable of determining the intellect either to give or withhold its assent to the doctrine; and this is equivalent to proof.

We shall examine presently of what nature are these considerations; in what manner they apply to the case, and what rational grounds, therefore, can be given for accepting or rejecting the utilitarian formula. But it is a preliminary condition of rational acceptance or rejection that the formula should be correctly understood. I believe that the very imperfect notion ordinarily formed of its meaning is the chief obstacle which impedes its reception, and that, could it be cleared even from only the grosser misconceptions the question would be greatly simplified and a large proportion of its difficulties removed. Before, therefore, I attempt to enter into the philosophical grounds which can be given for assenting to the utilitarian standard, I shall offer some illustrations of the doctrine itself, with the view of showing more clearly what it is, distinguishing it from what it is not, and disposing of such of the practical objections to it as either originate in, or are closely connected with, mistaken interpretation of its meaning. Having thus prepared the ground, I shall afterwards endeavor to throw such light as I can call upon the question considered as one of philosophical theory.

## Chapter II

### What Utilitarianism Is

A passing remark is all that needs be given to the ignorant blunder of supposing that those who stand up for utility as the test of right and wrong use the term in that restricted and merely colloquial sense in which utility is opposed to pleasure. An apology is due to the philosophical opponents of utilitarianism, for even the momentary appearance of confounding them with anyone capable of so absurd a misconception; which is the more extraordinary, inasmuch as the contrary accusation, of referring everything to pleasure, and that, too, in its grossest form, is another of the common charges against utilitarianism: and, as has been pointedly remarked by an able writer, the same sort of persons, and often the very same persons, denounce the theory "as impracticably dry when the word 'utility' precedes the word 'pleasure,' and as too practicably voluptuous when the word 'pleasure' precedes the word 'utility'." Those who know anything about the matter are aware that every writer, from Epicurus to Bentham, who maintained the theory of utility, meant by it, not something to be contradistinguished from pleasure, but pleasure itself, together with exemption from pain; and instead of opposing the useful to the agreeable or the ornamental, have always declared that the useful means these, among other things. Yet the common herd, including the herd of writers, not only in newspapers and periodicals, but in books of weight and pretension, are perpetually falling into this shallow mistake. Having caught up the word "utilitarian," while knowing nothing whatever about it but its sound, they habitually express by it the rejection or the neglect of pleasure in some of its forms: of beauty, of ornament, or of amusement. Nor is the term thus ignorantly misapplied solely in disparagement, but occasionally in compliment, as though it implied superiority to frivolity and the mere pleasures of the moment. And this perverted use is the only one in which the word is popularly known, and the one from which the new generation are acquiring their sole notion of its meaning. Those who introduced the word, but who had for many years discontinued it as a distinctive appellation, may well feel themselves called upon to resume it if by doing so they can hope to contribute anything towards rescuing it from this utter degradation.[1]

The creed which accepts as the foundation of morals "utility" or the "greatest happiness principle" holds that actions are right in proportion as they tend to promote happiness, wrong as they tend to produce the reverse of happiness. By happiness is intended pleasure, and the absence of pain; by unhappiness, pain, and the privation of pleasure. To give a clear view of the moral standard set up by the theory, much more requires to be said; in particular, what things it includes in the ideas of pain and pleasure; and to what extent this is left an open question. But these supplementary explanations do not affect the theory of life on which this theory of morality is grounded—namely, that pleasure and freedom from pain are the only things desirable as ends; and that all desirable things (which are as numerous in the utilitarian as in any other scheme) are desirable either for the pleasure inherent in themselves, or as means to the promotion of pleasure and the prevention of pain.

Now such a theory of life excites in many minds, and among them in some of the most estimable in feeling and purpose, inveterate dislike. To suppose that life has (as they express it) no higher end than pleasure—no better and nobler object of desire and pursuit—they designate as utterly mean and groveling; as a doctrine worthy only of swine, to whom the followers of Epicurus were, at a very early period, contemptuously likened; and modern

---

[1] The author of this essay has reason for believing himself to be the first person who brought the word "utilitarian" into use. He did not invent it, but adopted it from a passing expression in Mr. Galt's *Annals of the Parish*. After using it as a designation for several years, he and others abandoned it from a growing dislike to anything resembling a badge or watchword of sectarian distinction. But as a name for one single opinion, not a set of opinions—to denote the recognition of utility as a standard, not any particular way of applying it—the term supplies a want in the language, and offers, in many cases, a convenient mode of avoiding tiresome circumlocution.

holders of the doctrine are occasionally made the subject of equally polite comparisons by its German, French, and English assailants.

When thus attacked, the Epicureans have always answered that it is not they, but their accusers, who represent human nature in a degrading light, since the accusation supposes human beings to be capable of no pleasures except those of which swine are capable. If this supposition were true, the charge could not be gainsaid, but would then be no longer an imputation; for if the sources of pleasure were precisely the same to human beings and to swine, the rule of life which is good enough for the one would be good enough for the other. The comparison of the Epicurean life to that of beasts is felt as degrading, precisely because a beast's pleasures do not satisfy a human being's conceptions of happiness. Human beings have faculties more elevated than the animal appetites and, when once made conscious of them, do not regard anything as happiness which does not include their gratification. I do not, indeed, consider the Epicureans to have been by any means faultless in drawing out their scheme of consequences from the utilitarian principle. To do this in any sufficient manner, many Stoic, as well as Christian, elements require to be included. But there is no known Epicurean theory of life which does not assign to the pleasures of the intellect, of the feelings and imagination, and of the moral sentiments, a much higher value of pleasures than to those of mere sensation. It must be admitted, however, that utilitarian writers in general have placed the superiority of mental over bodily pleasures chiefly in the greater permanency, safety, uncostliness, etc., of the former— that is, in their circumstantial advantages rather than in their intrinsic nature. And on all these points utilitarians have fully proved their case; but they might have taken the other and, as it may be called, higher ground with entire consistency. It is quite compatible with the principle of utility to recognize the fact that some kinds of pleasure are more desirable and more valuable than others. It would be absurd that, while, in estimating all other things, quality is considered as well as quantity, the estimation of pleasures should be supposed to depend on quantity alone.

If I am asked what I mean by difference of quality in pleasures, or what makes one pleasure more valuable than another, merely as a pleasure, except its being greater in amount, there is but one possible answer. Of two pleasures, if there be one to which all or almost all who have experience of both give a decided preference, irrespective of a feeling of moral obligation to prefer it, that is the more desirable pleasure. If one of the two is, by those who are competently acquainted with both, placed so far above the other that they prefer it, even though knowing it to be attended with a greater amount of discontent, and would not resign it for any quantity of the other pleasure which their nature is capable of, we are justified in ascribing to the preferred enjoyment a superiority in quality so far outweighing quantity as to render it, in comparison, of small account.

Now it is an unquestionable fact that those who are equally acquainted with and equally capable of appreciating and enjoying both, do give a most marked preference to the manner of existence which employs their higher faculties. Few human creatures would consent to be changed into any of the lower animals for a promise of the fullest allowance of a beast's pleasures; no intelligent human being would consent to be a fool, no instructed person would be an ignoramus, no person of feeling and conscience would be selfish and base, even though they should be persuaded that the fool, the dunce, or the rascal is better satisfied with his lot than they are with theirs. They would not resign what they possess more than he for the most complete satisfaction of all the desires which they have in common with him. If they ever fancy they would, it is only in cases of unhappiness so extreme that to escape from it they would exchange their lot for almost any other, however undesirable in their own eyes. A being of higher faculties requires more to make him happy, is capable probably of more acute suffering, and certainly accessible to it at more points, than one of an inferior type; but in spite of these liabilities, he can never really wish to sink into what he feels to be a lower grade of existence. We may give what explanation we please of this unwillingness; we may attribute it to pride, a name which is given indiscriminately to some of the most and to some of the least estimable feelings of which mankind are capable: we may refer it to the love of liberty and personal independence, an appeal to which was with the Stoics one of the most effective means for the inculcation of it; to the love of power or to the love of excitement, both of which do really enter into and contribute to it; but its most appropriate appellation is a sense of dignity, which all human beings possess in one form or other, and in some, though by no means in exact, proportion to their higher faculties, and which is so essential a part of the happiness of those in whom it is strong that nothing which conflicts with it could be otherwise than momentarily an object of desire to them. Whoever supposes that this preference takes place at a sacrifice of happiness—that the superior being, in anything like equal circumstances, is not happier than the inferior—confounds the two very different ideas of happiness and content. It is indisputable that the being whose capacities of enjoyment are low has the greatest chance of having them fully satisfied; and a highly endowed being will always feel that any happiness which he can look for, as the world is constituted, is imperfect. But he can learn to bear its imperfections, if they are at all bearable; and they will not make him envy the being who is indeed unconscious of the imperfections, but only because he feels not at all the good which those imperfections qualify. It is better to be a human being dissatisfied than a pig satisfied; better to be Socrates dissatisfied than a fool satisfied. And if the fool, or the pig, are of a different opinion, it is because they only know their own side of the question. The other party to the comparison knows both sides.

It may be objected that many who are capable of the higher pleasures occasionally, under the influence of temptation, postpone them to the lower. But this is quite compatible with a full appreciation of the intrinsic superiority of the higher. Men often, from infirmity of character, make their election for the nearer good, though they know it to be the less valuable; and this no less when the choice is between two bodily pleasures than when it is between bodily and mental. They pursue sensual indulgences to the injury of health, though perfectly aware that health is the greater good. It may be further objected that many who begin with youthful enthusiasm for everything noble, as they advance in years, sink into indolence and selfishness. But I do not believe that those who undergo this very common change voluntarily choose the lower description of pleasures in preference to the higher. I believe that, before they devote themselves exclusively to the one, they have already become incapable of the other. Capacity for the nobler feelings is in most natures a very tender plant, easily killed, not only by hostile influences, but by mere want of sustenance; and in the majority of young persons it speedily dies away if the occupations to which their position in life has devoted them, and the society into which it has thrown them, are not favorable to keeping that higher capacity in exercise. Men lose their high aspirations as they lose their intellectual tastes, because they have not time or opportunity for indulging them; and they addict themselves to inferior pleasures, not because they deliberately prefer them, but because they are either the only ones to which they have access, or the only ones which they are any longer capable of enjoying. It may be questioned whether any one who has remained equally susceptible to both classes of pleasures, ever knowingly and calmly preferred the lower, though many, in all ages, have broken down in an ineffectual attempt to combine both.

From this verdict of the only competent judges, I apprehend there can be no appeal. On a question which is the best worth having of two pleasures, or which of two modes of existence is the most grateful to the feelings, apart from its moral attributes and from its consequences, the judgment of those who are qualified by knowledge of both, or, if they differ, that of the majority of them, must be admitted as final. And there needs be the less hesitation to accept this judgment respecting the quality of pleasures, since there is no other tribunal to be referred to even on the question of quantity. What means are there of determining which is the acutest of two pains, or the intensest of two pleasurable sensations, except the general suffrage of those who are familiar with both? Neither pains nor pleasures are homogeneous, and pain is always heterogeneous with pleasure. What is there to decide whether a particular pleasure is worth purchasing at the cost of a particular pain, except the feelings and judgment of the experienced? When, therefore, those feelings and judgment declare the pleasures derived from the higher faculties to be preferable *in kind*, apart from the question of intensity, to those of which the animal nature, disjoined from the higher faculties, is susceptible, they are entitled on this subject to the same regard.

I have dwelt on this point, as being a necessary part of a perfectly just conception of utility or happiness considered as the directive rule of human conduct. But it is by no means an indispensable condition to the acceptance of the utilitarian standard; for that standard is not the agent's own greatest happiness, but the greatest amount of happiness altogether; and if it may possibly be doubted whether a noble character is always the happier for its nobleness, there can be no doubt that it makes other people happier, and that the world in general is immensely a gainer by it. Utilitarianism, therefore, could only attain its end by the general cultivation of nobleness of character, even if each individual were only benefited by the nobleness of others, and his own, so far as happiness is concerned, were a sheer deduction from the benefit. But the bare enunciation of such an absurdity as this last renders refutation superfluous.

According to the greatest happiness principle, as above explained, the ultimate end, with reference to and for the sake of which all other things are desirable—whether we are considering our own good or that of other people—is an existence exempt as far as possible from pain, and as rich as possible in enjoyments, both in point of quantity and quality; the test of quality and the rule for measuring it against quantity being the preference felt by those who, in their opportunities of experience, to which must be added their habits of self-consciousness and self-observation, are best furnished with the means of comparison. This, being, according to the utilitarian opinion, the end of human action, is necessarily also the standard of morality, which may accordingly be defined "the rules and precepts for human conduct," by the observance of which an existence such as has been described might be, to the greatest extent possible, secured to all mankind; and not to them only, but, so far as the nature of things admits, to the whole sentient creation.

Against this doctrine, however, arises another class of objectors who say that happiness, in any form, cannot be the rational purpose of human life and action; because, in the first place, it is unattainable; and they contemptuously ask, What right hast thou to be happy?—a question which Mr. Carlyle clenches by the addition, What right, a short time ago, hadst thou even *to be?* Next they say that men can do *without* happiness; that all noble human beings have felt this, and could not have become noble but by learning the lesson of *Entsagen*, or renunciation; which lesson, thoroughly learnt and submitted to, they affirm to be the beginning and necessary condition of all virtue.

The first of these objections would go to the root of the matter were it well founded; for if no happiness is to be had at all by human beings, the attainment of it cannot be the end of morality or of any rational conduct. Though, even in that case, something might still be said for the utilitarian theory, since utility includes not solely the pursuit of happiness, but the prevention or mitigation of unhappiness; and if the former aim be chimerical, there will be all the greater scope and more imperative need for the latter, so long at least as mankind think fit to live, and do not take refuge in the simultaneous act of suicide recommended under certain conditions by Novalis. When, however, it is thus positively asserted to be impossible that human life should be happy, the assertion, if not something like a verbal quibble, is at least an exaggeration. If by happiness be meant a continuity of highly pleasurable excitement, it is evident enough that this is impossible. A state of exalted pleasure lasts only moments or in some cases, and with some intermissions, hours or days, and is the occasional brilliant flash of enjoyment, not its permanent and steady flame. Of this the philosophers who have taught that happiness is the end of life were as fully aware as those who taunt them. The happiness which they meant was not a life of rapture; but moments of such, in an existence made up of few and transitory pains, many and various pleasures, with a decided predominance of the active over the passive, and having as the foundation of the whole not to expect more from life than it is capable of bestowing. A life thus composed, to those who have been fortunate enough to obtain it, has always appeared worthy of the name of happiness. And such an existence is even now the lot of many, during some considerable portion of their lives. The present wretched education and wretched social arrangements are the only real hindrance to its being attainable by almost all.

The objectors perhaps may doubt whether human beings, if taught to consider happiness as the end of life, would be satisfied with such a moderate share of it. But great numbers of mankind have been satisfied with much less. The main constituents of a satisfied life appear to be two, either of which by itself is often found sufficient for the purpose: tranquility and excitement. With much tranquility, many find that they can be content with very little pleasure; with much excitement, many can reconcile themselves to a considerable quantity of pain. There is assuredly no inherent impossibility of enabling even the mass of mankind to unite both, since the two are so far from being incompatible that they are in natural alliance, the prolongation of either being a preparation for, and exciting a wish for, the other. It is only those in whom indolence amounts to a vice that do not desire excitement after an interval of repose; it is only those in whom the need of excitement is a disease that feel the tranquility which follows excitement dull and insipid, instead of pleasurable in direct proportion to the excitement which preceded it. When people who are tolerably fortunate in their outward lot do not find in life sufficient enjoyment to make it valuable to them, the cause generally is caring for nobody but themselves. To those who have neither public nor private affections, the excitements of life are much curtailed, and in any case dwindle in value as the time approaches when all selfish interests must be terminated by death; while those who leave after them objects of personal affection, and especially those who have also cultivated a fellow-feeling with the collective interests of mankind, retain as lively an interest in life on the eve of death as in the vigor of youth and health. Next to selfishness, the principal cause which makes life unsatisfactory is want of mental cultivation. A cultivated mind—I do not mean that of a philosopher, but any mind to which the fountains of knowledge have been opened, and which has been taught, in any tolerable degree, to exercise its faculties—finds sources of inexhaustible interest in all that surrounds it: in the objects of nature, the achievements of art, the imaginations of poetry, the incidents of history, the ways of mankind, past and present, and their prospects in the future. It is possible, indeed, to become indifferent to all this, and that too without having exhausted a thousandth part of it, but only when one has had from the beginning no moral or human interest in these things, and has sought in them only the gratification of curiosity.

Now there is absolutely no reason in the nature of things why an amount of mental culture sufficient to give an intelligent interest in these objects of contemplation should not be the inheritance of every one born in a civilized country. As little is there an inherent necessity that any human being should be a selfish egotist, devoid of every feeling or care but those which center in his own miserable individuality. Something far superior to this is sufficiently common even now, to give ample earnest of what the human species may be made. Genuine private affections and a sincere interest in the public good are possible, though in unequal degrees, to every rightly brought up human being. In a world in which there is so much to interest, so much to enjoy, and so much also to correct and improve, every one who has this moderate amount of moral and intellectual requisites is capable of an existence which may be called enviable; and unless such a person, through bad laws or subjection to the will of others, is denied the liberty to use the sources of happiness within his reach, he will not fail to find this enviable existence, if he escape the positive evils of life, the great sources of physical and mental suffering—

such as indigence, disease, and the unkindness, worthlessness, or premature loss of objects of affection. The main stress of the problem lies, therefore, in the contest with these calamities from which it is a rare good fortune entirely to escape; which, as things now are, cannot be obviated, and often cannot be in any material degree mitigated. Yet no one whose opinion deserves a moment's consideration can doubt that most of the great positive evils of the world are in themselves removable, and will, if human affairs continue to improve, be in the end reduced within narrow limits. Poverty, in any sense implying suffering, may be completely extinguished by the wisdom of society combined with the good sense and providence of individuals. Even that most intractable of enemies, disease, may be indefinitely reduced in dimensions by good physical and moral education and proper control of noxious influences, while the progress of science holds out a promise for the future of still more direct conquests over this detestable foe. And every advance in that direction relieves us from some, not only of the chances which cut short own own lives, but, what concerns us still more, which deprive us of those in whom our happiness is wrapt up. As for vicissitudes of fortune other disappointments connected with worldly circumstances, these are principally the effect either of gross imprudence, of ill-regulated desires, or of bad or imperfect social institutions. All the grand sources, in short, of human suffering are in a great degree, many of them almost entirely, conquerable by human care and effort; and though their removal is grievously slow—though a long succession of generations will perish in the breach before the conquest is completed, and this world becomes all that, if will and knowledge were not wanting, it might easily be made—yet every mind sufficiently intelligent and generous to bear a part, however small and inconspicuous, in the endeavour will draw a noble enjoyment from the contest itself, which he would not for any bribe in the form of selfish indulgence consent to be without.

And this leads to the true estimation of what is said by the objectors concerning the possibility and the obligation of learning to do without happiness. Unquestionably it is possible to do without happiness; it is done involuntarily by nineteen-twentieths of mankind, even in those parts of our present world which are least deep in barbarism; and it often has to be done voluntarily by the hero or the martyr, for the sake of something which he prizes more than his individual happiness. But this something, what is it, unless the happiness of others or some of the requisites of happiness? It is noble to be capable of resigning entirely one's own portion of happiness, or chances of it; but, after all, this self-sacrifice must be for some end; it is not its own end; and if we are told that its end is not happiness but virtue, which is better than happiness, I ask, would the sacrifice be made if the hero or martyr did not believe that it would earn for others immunity from similar sacrifices?

Would it be made if he thought that his renunciation of happiness for himself would produce no fruit for any of his fellow creatures, but to make their lot like his, and place them also in the condition of persons who have renounced happiness? All honor to those who can abnegate for themselves the personal enjoyment of life when by such renunciation they contribute worthily to increase the amount of happiness in the world; but he who does it or professes to do it for any other purpose is no more deserving of admiration than the ascetic mounted on his pillar. He may be an inspiriting proof of what men *can* do, but assuredly not an example of what they *should.*

Though it is only in a very imperfect state of the world's arrangements that any one can best serve the happiness of others by the absolute sacrifice of his own, yet, so long as the world is in that imperfect state, I fully acknowledge that the readiness to make such a sacrifice is the highest virtue which can be found in man. I will add that in this condition of the world, paradoxical as the assertion may be, the conscious ability to do without happiness gives the best prospect of realizing such happiness as is attainable. For nothing except that consciousness can raise a person above the chances of life, by making him feel that, let fate and fortune do their worst, they have not power to subdue him; which, once felt, frees him from excess of anxiety concerning the evils of life, and enables him, like many a Stoic in the worst times of the Roman Empire, to cultivate in tranquility the sources of satisfaction accessible to him, without concerning himself about the uncertainty of their duration any more than about their inevitable end.

Meanwhile, let utilitarians never cease to claim the morality of self-devotion as a possession which belongs by as good a right to them as either to the Stoic or to the Transcendentalist. The utilitarian morality does recognize in human beings the power of sacrificing their own greatest good for the good of others. It only refuses to admit that the sacrifice is itself a good. A sacrifice which does not increase or tend to increase the sum total of happiness, it considers as wasted. The only self-renunciation which it applauds is devotion to the happiness, or to some of the means of happiness, of others, either of mankind collectively or of individuals within the limits imposed by the collective interests of mankind.

I must again repeat what the assailants of utilitarianism seldom have the justice to acknowledge, that the happiness which forms the utilitarian standard of what is right in conduct is not the agent's own happiness but that of all concerned. As between his own happiness and that of others, utilitarianism requires him to be as strictly impartial as a disinterested and benevolent spectator. In the golden rule of Jesus of Nazareth, we read the complete spirit of the ethics of utility. "To do as you would be done by," and "to love your neighbor as yourself," constitute the ideal perfection of utilitarian morality. As the means of making the nearest approach to this ideal, utility would enjoin, first, that laws and social arrangements should place the happiness or (as, speaking practically, it may be called) the interest of every individual as nearly as possible in harmony with the interest of the whole; and, secondly, that education and opinion, which have so vast a power over human character, should so use that power as to establish in the mind of every individual an indissoluble association between his own happiness and the good of the whole, especially between his own happiness and the practice of such modes of conduct, negative and positive, as regard for the universal happiness prescribes; so that not only he may be unable to conceive the possibility of happiness to himself, consistently with conduct opposed to the general good, but also that a direct impulse to promote the general good may be in every individual one of the habitual motives of action, and the sentiments connected therewith may fill a large and prominent place in every human being's sentient existence. If the impugners of the utilitarian morality represented it to their own minds in this its true character, I know not what recommendation possessed by any other morality they could possibly affirm to be wanting to it; what more beautiful or more exalted developments of human nature any other ethical system can be supposed to foster, or what springs of action, not accessible to the utilitarian, such systems rely on for giving effect to their mandates.

The objectors to utilitarianism cannot always be charged with representing it in a discreditable light. On the contrary, those among them who entertain anything like a just idea of its disinterested character sometimes find fault with its standard as being too high for humanity. They say it is exacting too much to require that people shall always act from the inducement of promoting the general interests of society. But this is to mistake the very meaning of a standard of morals, and confound the business of ethics to tell us what are our duties, or by what test we may know them; but no system of ethics requires that the sole motive of all we do shall be a feeling of duty; on the contrary, ninety-nine hundreths of all our actions are done from other motives, and rightly so done if the rule of duty does not condemn them. It is the more unjust to utilitarianism that this particular misapprehension should be made a ground of objection to it, inasmuch as utilitarian moralists have gone beyond almost all others in affirming that the motive has nothing to do with the morality of the action, though much with the worth of the agent. He who saves a fellow creature from drowning does what is morally right, whether his motive be duty or the hope of being paid for his trouble; he who betrays the friend that trusts him is guilty of a crime, even if his object be to serve another friend to whom he is under greater obligations. But to speak only of actions done from the motive of duty, and in direct obedience to principle: it is a misapprehension of the utilitarian mode of thought to conceive it as implying that people should fix their minds upon so wide a generality as the world, or society at large. The great majority of good actions are intended not for the benefit of the world, but for that of individuals, of which the good of the world is made up; and the thoughts of the most virtuous man need not on these occasions travel beyond the particular persons concerned, except so far as is necessary to assure himself that in benefiting them he is not violating the rights, that is, the legitimate and authorized expectations, of any one else. The multiplication of happiness is, according to the utilitarian ethics, the object of virtue: the occasions on which any person (except one in a thousand) has it in his power to do this on an extended scale, in other words, to be a public benefactor, are but exceptional; and on these occasions alone is he called on to consider public utility; in every other case, private utility, the interest or happiness of some few persons, is all he has to attend to. Those alone the influence of whose actions extends to society in general need concern themselves habitually about so large an object. In the case of abstinences indeed—of things which people forbear to do from moral considerations, though the consequences in the particular case might be beneficial—it would be unworthy of an intelligent agent not to be consciously aware that the action is of a class which, if practiced generally, would be generally injurious, and that this is the ground of the obligation to abstain from it. The amount of regard for the public interest implied in this recognition is no greater than is demanded by every system of morals, for they all enjoin to abstain from whatever is manifestly pernicious to society.

The same considerations dispose of another reproach against the doctrine of utility, founded on a still grosser misconception of the purpose of a standard of morality, and of the very meaning of the words "right" and "wrong." It is often affirmed that utilitarianism renders men cold and unsympathizing; that it chills their moral feelings towards individuals; that it makes them regard only the dry and hard consideration of the consequences of actions, not taking into their moral estimate the qualities from which those actions emanate. If the assertion means that they do not allow their judgment respecting the rightness or wrongness of an action to be influenced by their opinion of the qualities of the person who does it, this is a complaint not against utilitarianism, but against any standard of morality at all; for certainly no known ethical standard decides an action to be good or bad because it is done by a good or a bad man, still less because done by an amiable, a brave, or a benevolent man, or the contrary. These considerations are relevant, not to the estimation of actions, but of persons; and there is nothing in the utilitarian theory inconsistent with the fact that there are other things which interest us in persons besides the rightness and wrongness of their actions. The Stoics, indeed, with the parodoxical misuse of language which was part of their system, and by which they strove to raise themselves above all concern about anything but virtue, were fond of saying that he who has that has everything; that he, and only he, is rich, is beautiful, is a king. But no claim of this description is made for the virtuous man by the utilitarian doctrine. Utilitarians are quite aware that there are other desirable possessions and qualities besides virtue, and are perfectly willing to allow to all of them their full worth. They are also aware that a right action does not necessarily indicate a virtuous character, and that actions which are blamable often proceed from qualities entitled to praise. When this is apparent in any particular case, it modifies their estimation, not certainly of the act, but of the agent. I grant that they are, notwithstanding, of opinion that in the long run the best proof of a good character is good actions; and resolutely refuse to consider any mental disposition as good of which the predominant tendency is to produce bad conduct. This makes them unpopular with many people; but it is an unpopularity which they must share with every one who regards the distinction between right and wrong in a serious light; and the reproach is not one which a conscientious utilitarian need be anxious to repel.

If no more be meant by the objection than that many utilitarians look on the morality of actions, as measured by the utilitarian standards, with too exclusive a regard, and do not lay sufficient stress upon the other beauties of character which go towards making a human being lovable or admirable, this may be admitted. Utilitarians who have cultivated their moral feelings, but not their sympathies, nor their artistic perceptions, do fall into this mistake; and so do all other moralists under the same conditions. What can be said in excuse for other moralists is equally available for them, namely, that, if there is to be any error, it is better that it should be on that side. As a matter of fact, we may affirm that among utilitarians, as among adherents of other systems, there is every imaginable degree of rigidity and of laxity in the application of their standard; some are even puritanically rigorous, while others are as indulgent as can possibly be desired by sinner or by sentimentalist. But on the whole, a doctrine which brings prominently forward the interest that mankind have in the repression and prevention of conduct which violates the moral law, is likely to be inferior to no other in turning the sanctions of opinion against such violations. It is true, the question, "What does violate the moral law?" is one on which those who recognize different standards of morality are likely now and then to differ. But difference of opinion on moral questions was not first introduced into the world by utilitarianism, while that doctrine does supply, if not always an easy, at all events a tangible and intelligible, mode of deciding such differences.

It may not be superfluous to notice a few more of the common misapprehensions of utilitarian ethics, even those which are so obvious and gross that it might appear impossible for any person of candor and intelligence to fall into them; since persons, even of considerable mental endowment, often give themselves so little trouble to understand the bearings of any opinion against which they entertain a prejudice, and men are in general so little conscious of this voluntary ignorance as a defect, that the vulgarest misunderstandings of ethical doctrines are continually met with in the deliberate writings of persons of the greatest pretensions both to high principle and to philosophy. We not uncommonly hear the doctrine of utility inveighed against as a *godless* doctrine. If it be necessary to say anything at all against so mere an assumption, we may say that the question depends upon what idea we have formed of the moral character of the Deity. If it be a true belief that God desires, above all things, the happiness of his creatures, and that this was his purpose in their creation, utility is not only not a godless doctrine, but more profoundly religious than any other. If it be meant that utilitarianism does not recognize the revealed will of God as the supreme law of morals, I answer that a utilitarian who believes in the perfect goodness and wisdom of God necessarily believes that whatever God has thought fit to reveal on the subject of morals must fulfil the requirements of utility in a supreme degree. But others besides utilitarians have been of opinion that the Christian revelation was intended, and is fitted, to inform the hearts and minds of mankind with a spirit which should enable them to find for themselves what is right, and incline them to do it when found, rather than to tell them, except in a very general way, what it is; and that we need a doctrine of ethics, carefully followed out, to *interpret* to us the will of God. Whether this opinion is correct or not, it is superfluous here to discuss; since whatever aid religion, either natural or revealed, can afford to ethical investigation, is as open to the utilitarian moralist as to any other. He can use it as the testimony of God to the usefulness or hurtfulness of any given course of action, by as good a right as others can use it for the indication of a transcendental law, having no connection with usefulness or with happiness.

Again, utility is often summarily stigmatized as an immoral doctrine by giving it the name of "expediency," and taking advantage of the popular use of that term to contrast it with principle. But the expedient, in the sense in which it is opposed to the right, generally means that which is expedient for the particular interest of the agent himself; as when a minister sacrifices the interests of his country to keep himself in place. When it means anything better than this, it means that which is expedient for some immediate object, some temporary purpose, but which violates a rule whose observance is expedient in a much higher degree. The expedient, in this sense, instead of being the same thing with the useful, is a branch of the hurtful. Thus it would often be expedient, for the purpose of getting over some momentary embarrassment, or attaining some object immediately useful to ourselves or others, to tell a lie. But inasmuch as the cultivation in ourselves of a sensitive feeling on the subject of veracity is one of the most useful, and the enfeeblement of that feeling one of the most hurtful, things to which our conduct can be instrumental; and inasmuch as any, even unintentional, deviation from truth does that much towards weakening the trustworthiness of human assertion, which is not only the principal support of all present social well-being but the insufficiency of which does more than any one thing that can be named to keep back civilization, virtue, everything on which human happiness on the largest scale depends—we feel that the violation, for a present advantage, of a rule of such transcendent expediency is not expedient, and that he who, for the sake of convenience to himself or to some other individual, does what depends on him to deprive mankind of the good, and inflict upon them the evil, involved in the greater or less reliance which they can place in each other's word, acts the part of one of their worst enemies. Yet that even this rule, sacred as it is, admits of possible exceptions is acknowledged by all moralists; the chief of which is when the withholding of some fact (as of information from a malefactor, or of bad news from a person dangerously ill) would save an individual (especially an individual other than oneself) from great and unmerited evil, and when the withholding can only be effected by denial. But in order that the exception may not extend itself beyond the need, and may have the least possible effect in weakening reliance on veracity, it ought to be recognized and, if possible, its limits defined; and, if the principle of utility is good for anything, it must be good for weighing these conflicting utilities against one another, and marking out the region within which one or the other preponderates.

Again, defenders of utility often find themselves called upon to reply to such objections as this—that there is not time, previous to action, for calculating and weighing the effects of any line of conduct on the general happiness. This is exactly as if any one were to say that it is impossible to guide our conduct by Christianity because there is not time, on every occasion on which anything has to be done, to read through the Old and New Testaments. The answer to the objection is that there has been ample time, namely, the whole past duration of the human species. During all that time, mankind have been learning by experience the tendencies of actions; on which experience all the prudence, as well as all the morality, of life are dependent. People talk as if the commencement of this course of experience had hitherto been put off, and as if, at the moment when some man feels tempted to meddle with the property or life of another, he had to begin considering for the first time whether murder and theft are injurious to human happiness. Even then I do not think that he would find the question very puzzling; but, at all events, the matter is now done to his hand. It is truly a whimiscal supposition that, if mankind were agreed in considering utility to be the test of morality, they would remain without any agreement as to what *is* useful, and would take no measures for having their notions on the subject taught to the young, and enforced by law and opinion. There is no difficulty in proving any ethical standard whatever to work ill if we suppose universal idiocy to be conjoined with it; but on any hypothesis short of that, mankind must by this time have acquired positive beliefs as to the effects of some actions on their happiness; and the beliefs which have thus come down are the rules of morality for the multitude, and for the philosopher until he has succeeded in finding better. That philosophers might easily do this, even now, on many subjects; that the received code of ethics is by no means of divine right; and that mankind have still much to learn as to the effects of actions on the general happiness, I admit or rather earnestly maintain. The corollaries from the principle of utility, like the precepts of every practical art, admit of indefinite improvement, and, in a progressive state of the human mind, their improvement is perpetually going on. But to consider the rules of morality as improvable is one thing; to pass over the intermediate generalization entirely and endeavor to test each individual action directly by the first principle is another. It is a strange notion that the acknowledgment of a first principle is inconsistent with the admission of secondary ones. To inform a traveller respecting the place of his ultimate destination is not to forbid the use of landmarks and direction-posts on the way. The proposition that happiness is the end and aim of morality does not mean that no road ought to be laid down to that goal, or that persons going thither should not be advised to take one direction rather than another. Men really ought to leave off talking a kind of nonsense on this subject, which they would neither talk nor listen to on other matters of practical concernment. Nobody argues that the art of navigation is not founded on astronomy because sailors cannot wait to cal· culate the Nautical Almanac. Being rational creatures, they go to sea with it ready calculated; and all rational creatures go out upon the sea of life with their minds made up on the common questions of right and wrong, as well as on many of the far more difficult questions of wise and foolish. And this, as long as foresight is a human quality, it is to be presumed they will continue to do. Whatever we adopt as the fundamental principle of morality, we require subordinate principles to apply it by; the impossibility of doing without them, being common to all systems, can afford no argument against any one in particular; but gravely to argue as if no such secondary principles could be had, and as if mankind had remained till now, and always must remain, without drawing any general conclusions from the experience of human life, is as high a pitch, I think, as absurdity has ever reached in philosophical controversy.

The remainder of the stock arguments against utilitarianism mostly consist in laying to its charge the common infirmities of human nature, and the general difficulties which embarrass conscientious persons in shaping their course through life. We are told that a utilitarian will be apt to make his own particular case an exception to moral rules, and, when under temptation, will see a utility in the breach of a rule, greater than he will see in its observance. But is utility the only creed which is able to furnish us with excuses for evil doing, and means of cheating our own conscience? They are afforded in abundance by all doctrines which recognize as a fact in morals the existence of conflicting considerations, which all doctrines do that have been believed by sane persons. It is not the fault of any creed, but of the complicated nature of human affairs, that rules of conduct cannot be so framed as to require no exceptions, and that hardly any kind of action can safely be laid down as either always obligatory or always condemnable. There is no ethical creed which does not temper the rigidity of its laws by giving a certain latitude, under the moral responsibility of the agent, for accommodation to peculiarities of circumstances; and under every creed, at the opening thus made, self-deception and dishonest casuistry get in. There exists no moral system under which there do not arise unequivocal cases of conflicting obligation. These are the real difficulties, the knotty points both in the theory of ethics and in the conscientious guidance of personal conduct. They are overcome practically, with greater or with less success, according to the intellect and virtue of the individual; but it can hardly be pretended that anyone will be the less qualified for dealing with them, from possessing an ultimate standard to which conflicting rights and duties can be referred. If utility is the ultimate source of moral obligations, utility may be invoked to decide between them when their demands are incompatible. Though the application of the standard may be difficult, it is better than none at all; while in other systems the moral laws all claiming independent authority, there is no common umpire entitled to interfere between them; their claims to precedence one over another rest on little better than sophistry, and, unless determined, as they generally are, by the unacknowledged influence of consideration of utility, afford a free scope for the action of personal desires and partialities. We must remember that only in these cases of conflict between secondary principles is it requisite that first principles should be appealed to. There is no case of moral obligation in which some secondary principle is not involved; and if only one, there can seldom be any real doubt which one it is, in the mind of any person by whom the principle itself is recognized.

## Chapter III

### Of the Ultimate Sanction of the Principle of Utility

The question is often asked, and properly so, in regard to any supposed moral standard—What is its sanction? what are the motives to obey? or more specifically, what is the source of its obligation? whence does it derive its binding force? It is a necessary part of moral philosophy to provide the answer to this question, which, though frequently assuming the shape of an objection to the utilitarian morality, as if it had some special applicability to that above others, really arises in regard to all standards. It arises, in fact, whenever a person is called on to *adopt* a standard, or refer morality to any basis on which he has not been accustomed to rest it. For the customary morality, that which education and opinion have consecrated is the only one which presents itself to the mind with the feeling of being *in itself* obligatory; and when a person is asked to believe that this morality *derives* its obligation from some general principle round which custom has not thrown the same halo, the assertion is to him a paradox; the supposed corollaries seem to have a more binding force than the original theorem; the superstructure seems to stand better without than with what is represented as its foundation. He says to himself, I feel that I am bound not to rob or murder, betray or deceive; but why am I bound to promote the general happiness? If my own happiness lies in something else, why may I not give that the preference?

If the view adopted by the utilitarian philosophy of the nature of the moral sense be correct, this difficulty will always present itself until the influences which form moral character have taken the same hold of the principle which they have taken of some of the consequences—until, by the improvement of education, the feeling of unity with our fellow creatures shall be (what it cannot be denied that Christ intended it to be) as deeply rooted in our character, and to our own consciousness as completely a part of our nature, as the horror of crime is in an ordinarily well brought up young person. In the meantime, however, the difficulty has no peculiar application to the doctrine of utility, but is inherent in every attempt to analyze morality and reduce it to principles; which, unless the principle is already in men's minds invested with as much sacredness as any of its applications, always seems to divest them of a part of their sanctity.

The principle of utility either has, or there is no reason why it might not have, all the sanctions which belong to any other system of morals. Those sanctions are either external or internal. Of the external sanctions it is not necessary to speak at any length. They are the hope of favor and the fear of displeasure from our fellow creatures or from the Ruler of the universe.

along with whatever we may have of sympathy or affection for them, or of love and awe of Him, inclining us to do His will independently of selfish consequences. There is evidently no reason why all these motives for observance should not attach themselves to the utilitarian morality as completely and as powerfully as to any other. Indeed, those of them which refer to our fellow creatures are sure to do so, in proportion to the amount of general intelligence; for whether there be any other ground of moral obligation than the general happiness or not, men do desire happiness; and however imperfect may be their own practice, they desire and commend all conduct in others towards themselves by which they think their happiness is promoted. With regard to the religious motive, if men believe, as most profess to do, in the goodness of God, those who think that conduciveness to the general happiness is the essence or even only the criterion of good must necessarily believe that it is also that which God approves. The whole force therefore of external reward and punishment, whether physical or moral, and whether proceeding from God or from our fellow men, together with all that the capacities of human nature admit of disinterested devotion to either, become available to enforce the utilitarian morality, in proportion as that morality is recognized; and the more powerfully, the more the appliances of education and general cultivation are bent to the purpose.

So far as to external sanctions. The internal sanction of duty, whatever our standard of duty may be, is one and the same—a feeling in our own mind; a pain, more or less intense, attendant on violation of duty, which in properly cultivated moral natures rises, in the more serious cases, into shrinking from it as an impossibility. This feeling, when disinterested and connecting itself with the pure idea of duty, and not with some particular form of it, or with any of the merely accessory circumstances, is the essence of conscience; though in that complex phenomenon as it actually exists, the simple fact is in general all encrusted over with collateral associations derived from sympathy, from love, and still more from fear; from all the forms of religious feeling; from the recollections of childhood and of all our past life; from self-esteem, desire of the esteem of others, and occasionally even self-abasement. This extreme complication is, I apprehend, the origin of the sort of mystical character which, by a tendency of the human mind of which there are many other examples, is apt to be attributed to the idea of moral obligation, and which leads people to believe that the idea cannot possibly attach itself to any other objects than those which, by a supposed mysterious law, are found in our present experience to excite it. Its binding force, however, consists in the existence of a mass of feeling which must be broken through in order to do what violates our standard of right, and which, if we do nevertheless violate that standard, will probably have to be encountered afterwards in the form of remorse. Whatever theory we have of the nature or origin of conscience, this is what essentially constitutes it.

The ultimate sanction, therefore, of all morality (external motives apart) being a subjective feeling in our own minds, I see nothing embarrassing to those whose standard is utility in the question, What is the sanction of that particular standard? We may answer, the same as of all other moral standards —the conscientious feelings of mankind. Undoubtedly this sanction has no binding efficacy on those who do not possess the feelings it appeals to; but neither will these persons be more obedient to any other moral principle than to the utilitarian one. On them morality of any kind has no hold but through the external sanctions. Meanwhile the feelings exist, a fact in human nature, the reality of which, and the great power with which they are capable of acting on those in whom they have been duly cultivated, are proved by experience. No reason has ever been shown why they may not be cultivated to as great intensity in connection with the utilitarian, as with any other rule of morals.

There is, I am aware, a disposition to believe that a person who sees in moral obligation a transcendental fact, an objective reality belonging to the province of "things in themselves," is likely to be more obedient to it than one who believes it to be entirely subjective, having its seat in human consciousness only. But whatever a person's opinion may be on this point of ontology, the force he is really urged by is his own subjective feeling, and is exactly measured by its strength. No one's belief that duty is an objective reality is stronger than the belief that God is so; yet the belief in God, apart from the expectation of actual reward and punishment, only operates on conduct through, and in proportion to, the subjective religious feeling. The sanction, so far as it is disinterested, is always in the mind itself; and the notion, therefore, of the transcendental moralists must be that this sanction will not exist *in* the mind unless it is believed to have its root out of the mind; and that if a person is able to say to himself, "This which is restraining me and which is called my conscience is only a feeling in my own mind," he may possibly draw the conclusion that when the feeling ceases the obligation ceases, and that if he find the feeling inconvenient, he may disregard it and endeavor to get rid of it. But is this danger confined to the utilitarian morality? Does the belief that moral obligation has its seat outside the mind make the feeling of it too strong to be got rid of? The fact is so far otherwise that all moralists admit and lament the ease with which, in the generality of minds, conscience can be silenced or stifled. The question, "Need I obey my conscience?" is quite as often put to themselves by persons who never heard of the principle of utility, as by its adherents. Those whose conscientious feelings are so weak as to allow of their asking this question, if they answer it affirmatively, will not do so because they believe in the transcendental theory, but because of the external sanctions.

It is not necessary, for the present purpose, to decide whether the feeling of duty is innate or implanted. Assuming it to be innate, it is an open question to what objects it naturally attaches itself; for the philosophic supporters of that theory are now agreed that the intuitive perception is of principles of morality and not of the details. If there be anything innate in the matter, I see no reason why the feeling which is innate should not be that of regard to the pleasures and pains of others. If there is any principle of morals which is intuitively obligatory, I should say it must be that. If so, the intuitive ethics would coincide with the utilitarian, and there would be no further quarrel between them. Even as it is, the intuitive moralists, though they believe that there are other intuitive moral obligations, do already believe this to be one; for they unanimously hold that a large *portion* of morality turns upon the consideration due to the interests of our fellow creatures. Therefore, if the belief in the transcendental origin of moral obligation gives any additional efficacy to the internal sanction, it appears to me that the utilitarian principle has already the benefit of it.

On the other hand, if, as is my own belief, the moral feelings are not innate but acquired, they are not for that reason the less natural. It is natural to man to speak, to reason, to build cities, to cultivate the ground, though these are acquired faculties. The moral feelings are not indeed a part of our nature, in the sense of being in any perceptible degree present in all of us; but this, unhappily, is a fact admitted by those who believe the most strenuously in their transcendental origin. Like the other acquired capacities above referred to, the moral faculty, if not a part of our nature, is a natural outgrowth from it; capable, like them, in a certain, small degree, of springing up spontaneously; and susceptible of being brought by cultivation to a high degree of development. Unhappily it is also susceptible, by a sufficient use of the external sanctions and of the force of early impressions, of being cultivated in almost any direction, so that there is hardly anything so absurd or so mischievous that it may not, by means of these influences, be made to act on the human mind with all the authority of conscience. To doubt that the same potency might be given by the same means to the principle of utility, even if it had no foundation in human nature, would be flying in the face of all experience.

But moral associations which are wholly of artificial creation, when intellectual culture goes on, yield by degrees to the dissolving force of analysis; and if the feeling of duty, when associated with utility, would appear equally arbitrary; if there were no leading department of our nature, no powerful class of sentiments, with which that association would harmonize, which would make us feel it congenial and incline us not only to foster it in others (for which we have abundant interested motives), but also to cherish it in ourselves—if there were not, in short, a natural basis of sentiment for utilitarian morality, it might well happen that this association also, even after it had been implanted by education, might be analyzed away.

But there *is* this basis of powerful natural sentiment; and this it is which, when once the general happiness is recognized as the ethical standard, will constitute the strength of the utilitarian morality. This firm foundation is that of the social feelings of mankind; the desire to be in unity with our fellow creatures, which is already a powerful principle in human nature, and happily one of those which tend to become stronger, even without express inculcation, from the influences of advancing civilization. The social state is at once so natural, so necessary, and so habitual to man, that, except in some unusual circumstances or by an effort of voluntary abstraction, he never conceives himself otherwise than as a member of a body; and this association is riveted more and more, as mankind are further removed from the state of savage independence. Any condition, therefore, which is essential to a state of society, becomes more and more an inseparable part of every person's conception of the state of things which he is born into, and which is the destiny of a human being. Now society between human beings, except in the relation of master and slave, is manifestly impossible on any other footing than that the interests of all are to be consulted. Society between equals can only exist on the understanding that the interests of all are to be regarded equally. And since in all states of civilization, every person, except an absolute monarch, has equals, everyone is obliged to live on these terms with somebody; and in every age some advance is made towards a state in which it will be impossible to live permanently on other terms with anybody. In this way people grow up unable to conceive as possible to them a state of total disregard of other people's interests. They are under a necessity of conceiving themselves as at least abstaining from all the grosser injuries, and (if only for their own protection) living in a state of constant protest against them. They are also familiar with the fact of co-operating with others, and proposing to themselves a collective, not an individual, interest as the aim (at least for the time being) of their actions. So long as they are co-operating, their ends are identified with those of others; there is at least a temporary feeling that the interests of others are their own interests. Not only does all strengthening of social ties, and all healthy growth of society, give to each individual a stronger personal interest in practically consulting the welfare of others, it also leads him to identify his *feelings* more and more with their good, or at least with an even greater degree of practical consideration for it. He comes, as though instinctively, to be conscious of himself as a being who *of course* pays regard to others. The good of others becomes to him a thing naturally and necessarily to be attended to, like any of the physical conditions of our existence. Now, whatever amount of this feeling a person has, he is urged by the strongest motive both of interest and of sympathy to demonstrate it, and to the utmost of his power encourage it in others; and even if he has none of it himself, he is as greatly interested as any one else that others should have it. Consequently the smallest germs of the feeling are laid hold of and nourished by the contagion of sympathy and the influences of education; and a complete web of corroborative association is woven round it, by the powerful agency of the external sanctions. This mode of conceiving ourselves and human life, as civilization goes on, is felt to be more and more natural. Every step in political improvement renders it more so, by removing the sources of opposition of interest and levelling those inequalities of legal privilege between individuals or classes, owing to which there are large portions of mankind whose happiness it is still practicable to disregard. In an improving state of the human mind, the influences are constantly on the increase which tend to generate in each individual a feeling of unity with all the rest; which, if perfect, would make him never think of, or desire, any beneficial condition for himself, in the benefits of which they are not included. If we now suppose this feeling of unity to be taught as a religion, and the whole force of education, of institutions, and of opinion, directed, as it once was in the case of religion, to make every person grow up from infancy surrounded on all sides both by the profession and the practice of it, I think that no one who can realize this conception will feel any misgiving about the sufficiency of the ultimate sanction for the happiness morality. To any ethical student who finds the realization difficult, I recommend, as a means of facilitating it, the second of M. Comte's two principal works, the *Traité de politique positive*. I entertain the strongest objections to the system of politics and morals set forth in that treatise; but I think it has superabundantly shown the possibility of giving to the service of humanity, even without the aid of belief in a Providence, both the psychological power and the social efficacy of a religion, making it take hold of human life, and color all thought, feeling, and action, in a manner of which the greatest ascendancy ever exercised by any religion may be but a type and foretaste; and of which the danger is, not that it should be insufficient, but that it should be so excessive as to interfere unduly with human freedom and individuality.

Neither is it necessary to the feeling which constitutes the binding force of the utilitarian morality on those who recognize it, to wait for those social influences which would make its obligation felt by mankind at large. In the comparatively early state of human advancement in which we now live, a person cannot, indeed, feel that entireness of sympathy with all others, which would make any real discordance in the general direction of their conduct in life impossible, but already a person in whom the social feeling is at all developed cannot bring himself to think of the rest of his fellow creatures as struggling rivals with him for the means of happiness, whom he must desire to see defeated in their object in order that he may succeed in his. The deeply rooted conception which every individual even now has of himself as a social being tends to make him feel it one of his natural wants that there should be harmony between his feelings and aims and those of his fellow creatures. If differences of opinion and of mental culture make it impossible for him to share many of their actual feelings—perhaps make him denounce and defy those feelings—he still needs to be conscious that his real aim and theirs do not conflict; that he is not opposing himself to what they really wish for, namely, their own good, but is, on the contrary, promoting it. This feeling in most individuals is much inferior in strength to their selfish feelings, and is often wanting altogether. But to those who have it, it possesses all the characters of a natural feeling. It does not present itself to their minds as a superstition of education, or a law despotically imposed by the power of society, but as an attribute which it would not be well for them to be without. This conviction is the ultimate sanction of the greatest happiness morality. This it is which makes any mind of well-developed feelings work with, and not against, the outward motives to care for others, afforded by what I have called the external sanctions; and, when those sanctions are wanting, or act in an opposite direction, constitutes in itself a powerful internal binding force, in proportion to the sensitiveness and thoughtfulness of the character; since few but those whose mind is a moral blank could bear to lay out their course of life on the plan of paying no regard to others except so far as their own private interest compels.

## Chapter IV

### Of What Sort of Proof the Principle of Utility is Susceptible

It has already been remarked that questions of ultimate ends do not admit of proof, in the ordinary acceptation of the term. To be incapable of proof by reasoning is common to all first principles, to the first premises of our knowledge, as well as to those of our conduct. But the former, being matters of fact, may be the subject of a direct appeal to the faculties which judge of fact—namely, our senses and our internal consciousness. Can an appeal be made to the same faculties on questions of practical ends? Or by what other faculty is cognizance taken of them?

Questions about ends are, in other words, questions what things are desirable. The utilitarian doctrine is that happiness is desirable, and the only thing desirable, as an end; all other things being only desirable as means to that end. What ought to be required of this doctrine, what conditions is it requisite that the doctrine should fulfill—to make good its claim to be believed?

The only proof capable of being given that an object is visible is that people actually see it. The only proof that a sound is audible is that people hear it; and so of the other sources of our experience. In like manner, I apprehend, the sole evidence it is possible to produce that anything is desirable is that people do actually desire it. If the end which the utilitarian doctrine proposes to itself were not, in theory and in practice, acknowledged to be an end, nothing could ever convince any person that it was so. No reason can be given why the general happiness is desirable, except that each person, so far as he believes it to be attainable, desires his own happiness. This, however, being a fact, we have not only all the proof which the case admits of, but all which it is possible to require, that happiness is a good; that each person's happiness is a good to that person, and the general happiness, therefore, a good to the aggregate of all persons. Happiness has made out its title as *one* of the ends of conduct, and consequently one of the criteria of morality.

But it has not, by this alone, proved itself to be the sole criterion. To do that, it would seem, by the same rule, necessary to show, not only that people desire happiness, but that they never desire anything else. Now it is palpable that they do desire things which, in common language, are decidedly distinguished from happiness. They desire, for example, virtue and the absence of vice, no less really than pleasure and the absence of pain. The desire of virtue is not as universal, but it is as authentic a fact as the desire of happiness. And hence the opponents of the utilitarian standard deem that they have a right to infer that there are other ends of human action besides happiness, and that happiness is not the standard of approbation and disapprobation.

But does the utilitarian doctrine deny that people desire virtue, or maintain that virtue is not a thing to be desired? The very reverse. It maintains not only that virtue is to be desired, but that it is to be desired disinterestedly, for itself. Whatever may be the opinion of utilitarian moralists as to the original conditions by which virtue is made virtue, however they may believe (as they do) that actions and dispositions are only virtuous because they promote another end than virtue, yet this being granted, and it having been decided, from considerations of this description, what *is* virtuous, they not only place virtue at the very head of the things which are good as means to the ultimate end, but they also recognize as a psychological fact the possibility of its being, to the individual, a good in itself, without looking to any end beyond it; and hold that the mind is not in a right state, not in a state conformable to utility, not in the state most conducive to the general happiness, unless it does love virtue in this manner—as a thing desirable in itself, even although, in the individual instance, it should not produce those other desirable consequences which it tends to produce, and on account of which it is held to be virtue. This opinion is not, in the smallest degree, a departure from the happiness principle. The ingredients of happiness are very various, and each of them is desirable in itself, and not merely when considered as swelling an aggregate. The principle of utility does not mean that any given pleasure, as music, for instance, or any given exemption from pain, as for example health, is to be looked upon as means to a collective something termed happiness, and to be desired on that account. They are desired and desirable in and for themselves; besides being means, they are a part of the end. Virtue, according to the utilitarian doctrine, is not naturally and originally part of the end, but it is capable of becoming so; and in those who love it disinterestedly it has become so, and is desired and cherished, not as a means to happiness, but as a part of their happiness.

To illustrate this further, we may remember that virtue is not the only thing originally a means, and which if it were not a means to anything else would be and remain indifferent, but which by association with what it is a means to comes to be desired for itself, and that too with the utmost intensity. What, for example, shall we say of the love of money? There is nothing originally more desirable about money than about any heap of glittering pebbles. Its worth is solely that of the things which it will buy; the desires for other things than itself, which it is a means of gratifying. Yet the love of money is not only one of the strongest moving forces of human life, but money is, in many cases, desired in and for itself; the desire to possess it is often stronger than the desire to use it, and goes on increasing when all the desires which point to ends beyond it, to be compassed by it, are falling off. It may, then, be said truly that money is desired not for the sake of an end, but as part of the end. From being a means to happiness, it has come to be itself a principal ingredient of the individual's conception of happiness. The same may be said of the majority of the great objects of human life: power, for example, or fame, except that to each of these there is a certain amount of immediate pleasure annexed, which has at least the semblance of being naturally inherent in them—a thing which cannot be said of money. Still, however, the strongest natural attraction, both of power and of fame, is the immense aid they give to the attainment of our other wishes; and it is the strong association thus generated between them and all our objects of desire which gives to the direct desire of them the intensity it often assumes, so as in some characters to surpass in strength all other desires. In these cases the means have become a part of the end, and a more important part of it than any of the things which they are means to. What was once desired as an instrument for the attainment of happiness has come to be desired for its own sake. In being desired for its own sake it is, however, desired as *part* of happiness. The person is made, or thinks he would be made, happy by its mere possession; and is made unhappy by failure to obtain it. The desire of it is not a different thing from the desire of happiness any more than the love of music or the desire of health. They are included in happiness. They are some of the elements of which the desire of happiness is made up. Happiness is not an abstract idea but a concrete whole; and these are some of its parts. And the utilitarian standard sanctions and approves their being so. Life would be a poor thing, very ill provided with sources of happiness, if there were not this provision of nature by which things originally indifferent, but conducive to, or otherwise associated with, the satisfaction of our primitive desires, become in themselves sources of pleasure more valuable than the primitive pleasures, both in permanency, in the space of human existence that they are capable of covering, and even in intensity.

Virtue, according to the utilitarian conception, is a good of this description. There was no original desire of it, or motive to it, save its conduciveness to pleasure, and especially to protection from pain. But through the association thus formed it may be felt a good in itself, and desired as such with as great intensity as any other good; and with this difference between it and the love of money, of power, or of fame, that all of these may, and often do, render the individual noxious to the other members of the society to which he belongs, whereas there is nothing which makes him so much a blessing to them as the cultivation of the disinterested love of virtue. And consequently, the utilitarian standard, while it tolerates and approves those other acquired desires, up to the point beyond which they would be more injurious to the general happiness than promotive of it, enjoins and requires the cultivation of the love of virtue up to the greatest strength possible, as being above all things important to the general happiness.

It results from the preceding considerations that there is in reality nothing desired except happiness. Whatever is desired otherwise than as a means to some end beyond itself, and ultimately to happiness, is desired as itself a part of happiness, and is not desired for itself until it has become so. Those who desire virtue for its own sake desire it either because the consciousness of it is a pleasure, or because the consciousness of being without it is a pain, or for both reasons united; as in truth the pleasure and pain seldom exist separately, but almost always together—the same person feeling pleasure in the degree of virtue attained, and pain in not having attained more. If one of these gave him no pleasure, and the other no pain, he would not love or desire virtue, or would desire it only for the other benefits which it might produce to himself or to persons whom he cared for.

We have now, then, an answer to the question, of what sort of proof the principle of utility is susceptible. If the opinion which I have now stated is psychologically true—if human nature is so constituted as to desire nothing which is not either a part of happiness or a means of happiness, we can have no other proof, and we require no other, that these are the only things desirable. If so, happiness is the sole end of human action, and the promotion of it the test by which to judge of all human conduct; from whence it necessarily follows that it must be the criterion of morality, since a part is included in the whole.

And now to decide whether this is really so, whether mankind do desire nothing for itself but that which is a pleasure to them, or of which the absence is a pain, we have evidently arrived at a question of fact and experience, dependent, like all similar questions, upon evidence. It can only be determined by practised self-consciousness and self-observation, assisted by observation of others. I believe that these sources of evidence, impartially consulted, will declare that desiring a thing and finding it pleasant, aversion to it and thinking of it as painful, are phenomena entirely inseparable or rather two parts of the same phenomenon; in strictness of language, two different modes of naming the same psychological fact; that to think of an object as desirable (unless for the sake of its consequences) and to think of it as pleasant are one and the same thing; and that to desire anything except in proportion as the idea of it is pleasant, is a physical and metaphysical impossibility.

So obvious does this appear to me that I expect it will hardly be disputed; and the objection made will be, not that desire can possibly be directed to anything ultimately except pleasure and exemption from pain, but that the will is a different thing from desire; that a person of confirmed virtue or any other person whose purposes are fixed carries out his purposes without any thought of the pleasure he has in contemplating them or expects to derive from their fulfilment, and persists in acting on them, even though these pleasures are much diminished by changes in his character or decay of his passive sensibilities, or are outweighed by the pains which the pursuit of the purposes may bring upon him. All this I fully admit and have stated it elsewhere as positively and emphatically as anyone. Will, the active phenomenon, is a different thing from desire, the state of passive sensibility, and, though originally an offshoot from it, may in time take root and detach itself from the parent stock, so much so that in the case of an habitual purpose, instead of willing the thing because we desire it, we often desire it only because we will it. This, however, is but an instance of that familiar fact, the power of habit, and is nowise confined to the case of virtuous actions. Many indifferent things which men originally did from a motive of some sort, they continue to do from habit. Sometimes this is done unconsciously; the consciousness coming only after the action; at other times with conscious volition, but volition which has become habitual and is put in operation by the force of habit, in opposition perhaps to the deliberate preference, as often happens with those who have contracted habits of vicious or hurtful indulgence. Third and last comes the case in which the habitual act of will in the individual instance is not in contradiction to the general intention prevailing at other times, but in fulfilment of it; as in the case of the person of confirmed virtue and of all who pursue deliberately and consistently any determinate end. The distinction between will and desire thus understood is an authentic and highly important psychological fact; but the fact consists solely in this—that will, like all other parts of our constitution, is amenable to habit, and that we may will from habit what we no longer desire for itself, or desire only because we will it. It is not the less true that will, in the beginning, is entirely produced by desire; including in that term the repelling influence of pain as well as the attractive one of pleasure. Let us take into consideration no longer the person who has a confirmed will to do right, but him in whom that virtuous will is still feeble, conquerable by temptation, and not to be fully relied on; by what means can it be strengthened? How can the will to be virtuous, where it does not exist in sufficient force, be implanted or awakened? Only by making the person *desire* virtue— by making him think of it in a pleasurable light, or of its absence in a painful one. It is by associating the doing right with pleasure, or the doing wrong with pain, or by eliciting and impressing and bringing home to the person's experience the pleasure naturally involved in the one or the pain in the other, that it is possible to call forth that will to be virtuous which, when confirmed, acts without any thought of either pleasure or pain. Will is the child of desire, and passes out of the dominion of its parent only to come under that of habit. That which is the result of habit affords no presumption of being intrinsically good; and there would be no reason for wishing that the purpose of virtue should become independent of pleasure and pain were it not that the influence of the pleasurable and painful associations which prompt to virtue is not sufficiently to be depended on for unerring constancy of action until it has acquired the support of habit. Both in feeling and in conduct, habit is the only thing which imparts certainty; and it is because of the importance to others of being able to rely absolutely on one's feelings and conduct, and to oneself of being able to rely on one's own, that the will to do right ought to be cultivated into this habitual independence. In other words, this state of the will is a means to good, not intrinsically a good; and does not contradict the doctrine that nothing is a good to human beings but in so far as it is either itself pleasurable or a means of attaining pleasure or averting pain.

But if this doctrine be true, the principle of utility is proved. Whether it is so or not, must now be left to the consideration of the thoughtful reader.

# A. C. EWING

ALFRED CYRIL EWING (1899–    ) teaches at
Cambridge University. A leading representative of intuitionism in ethics, he has also written extensively upon problems in metaphysics
and social philosophy. His major works include: *The Morality of Punishment* (1929),
*Idealism: A Critical Survey* (1934), *The
Individual, The State, and World Government* (1947), *The Definition of Good*
(1947), *The Fundamental Questions of
Philosophy* (1951), and *Ethics* (1953).

## Ethics*

### Chapter II

#### Selfishness and Unselfishness

One of the first questions that presents itself in Ethics is—Why ought
I to sacrifice myself for the sake of somebody else? If it is shown to me that
some action will have bad consequences for myself, this gives an obvious
reason why I should not do it, but it is often felt that it is not so obvious why
I should not do what is to my own interest because it has bad consequences
for others. Yet every system of ethics has prescribed duties to others as well
as to oneself, and no good man is uninfluenced by the prospect of his proposed
actions producing bad effects on other men. Confronted with this situation
one is tempted to reply by trying to show that the fulfilment of his duties
to others is really to the agent's own interests in the long run, either in this
life or in another. And some philosophers who ought to have known better,
thinking that this can be done, have actually taken the view that ultimately
we cannot be under an obligation to pursue anything but our own greatest
happiness and that our duties towards others are to be commended solely as
efficient, though indirect, means of attaining this happiness. That view is
known as egoistic hedonism. "Hedonism" is derived from a Greek word meaning pleasure, and stands for the ethical doctrine that pleasure is the only
good, no distinction being ordinarily made by hedonists between "pleasure"
and "happiness"; "egoistic" brings out the point that the ultimate aim is
*one's own* pleasure. To be fair to the theory we must realize that "pleasure"
is intended to cover all satisfactions, not only the mundane pleasures of good

dinners and amusements, but the joy of the most selfless and spiritualized love, the unselfish satisfaction of the righteous in furthering the general good, and the delight of the religious mystic in communion with God. Nor does the theory maintain that we should always aim directly at our own pleasure: on the contrary it maintains that we can get pleasure for ourselves best by aiming directly at other things than our own pleasure, particularly the happiness of other men, only it maintains that the sole reason why we ought to aim at the other things is because they are the best means to our own pleasure, not because we are under any obligation to pursue them for their own sake.

The first inclination of most unsophisticated people is to reject egoistic hedonism as blatantly immoral, but even if this turn out to be our final conclusion we must first examine the theory more carefully. And we may feel surprised when we find that such a theory has been held by a number of people of excellent character distinguished for what would normally be described as unselfish devotion to others. This does not indeed prove that the theory is not really in conflict with the most fundamental principles of any tolerable ethics, for a man's practice is often inconsistent with his theory, but it prevents us from dismissing it as mere wickedness or sophistry. And in fact the behaviour that such a theory, consistently carried out, would require of us is not usually by any means so different as one would at first sight expect from the behaviour normally approved ethically. It can easily be shown that under most circumstances the more obvious forms of wrongdoing simply do not pay in happiness even from a completely selfish point of view. Most wicked acts are also highly imprudent, though it is very difficult to get the people who do them to realize this till it is too late. Our happiness is dependent very largely on our relations with other men, and they will be alienated if we are thoroughly unscrupulous and selfish. Happiness also depends very largely on our mind being at peace with itself, and vicious conduct has a very strong tendency to destroy that internal peace. It is a mistake to think of the good as if it were a limited store not capable of increase so that I must inevitably have less if others have more. This is not true even of material wealth, since the common stock may be greatly increased by effort and ingenuity so that there is more to distribute, and since in a commercial exchange both parties commonly benefit. Still less is it true of happiness, which does not depend chiefly on material goods (though a minimum of the latter is necessary). If I acquire more money, it may (though it need not) mean that somebody else will be poorer; but if I gain in happiness through forming more satisfactory relations with others, increasing my ability to appreciate, or becoming more contented with my lot, it will not have the slightest tendency to make anybody else less happy, but rather the reverse. And one of the chief sources of happiness is the consciousness that one is performing a useful function in life and contributing to the welfare of others. The egoist need not deny that we have what are normally called unselfish desires, i.e., desires for the good of others, but he will insist that we gain in happiness ourselves through indulging these desires even more than through indulging the desires which are purely selfish. Bentham, the best known British advocate of the theory I am discussing, was also a great philanthropist, and he was asked whether he was not inconsistent in being so. He replied to the effect that he was not inconsistent, because people took their pleasure in different ways, and he happened to be so constituted that he took his pleasure in philanthrophy, whereas another man might, say, take it in drink.

I think, however, that this argument is often pushed too far. It is by no means possible to show that a man always gains in happiness in proportion to what would generally be regarded as his goodness. Society may punish men for doing wrong, but it can only take cognizance of a small proportion of wrong acts, and suppose society itself is corrupt and punishes people for doing right? It is by no means clear that a good man was at all likely to be happier in Nazi Germany than a bad. Again, in all civilizations of which we know it has been held that it was sometimes a man's duty to risk gravely and even sacrifice his health and life. That is a strange way of acquiring the greatest pleasure possible for the agent! It is not legitimate for the hedonistic egoist to reply that the man will be rewarded in a future life, for even if we grant this we must admit that the only reason for thinking that the action will be rewarded is that we already think it right and admirable, and we cannot, therefore, without committing a vicious circle also hold that the reward makes it right. If our only duty is to pursue our own greatest pleasure, why should we be rewarded for sacrificing our pleasure on this earth to others? *Prima facie* we should be punished. It has often been said that we shall be rendered unhappy by pangs of conscience if we do not sacrifice ourselves for the greater good of others, but we may make a similar reply to this point. Why should we suffer from pangs of conscience if we do not first recognize the action as wrong? And, whilst it may be true of some few people that, if they thought they had saved their own lives by neglecting their duty, they would feel so unhappy about it as to outweigh any pleasure in life, we cannot possibly maintain that this is true of everybody. Surely a man is not excused from the duty to help others because he is so constituted that he can escape the uneasiness about not having helped them by thinking of other things. People's sensitiveness in this matter varies enormously; and when an egoist dwells on the joy of serving others it is difficult to see what he could say if somebody met him with the retort—It is all very well for you, but tastes differ and I am so constituted that I enjoy the selfish pleasures much better than the unselfish.

It seems to me indeed that some of the worst acts ever done could be justified if egoistic hedonism were true. In Ibsen's play, *The Pretenders*, there is a well-known scene in which the villain lying on his death-bed has an opportunity of avenging himself on an enemy by giving rise to a misapprehension about the succession to the throne, knowing that if he does so he will gratuitously cause a civil war in which thousands will be slain. The situation in the play is complicated by the fear of punishment hereafter, but we have seen this to be irrelevant unless the proposed action can be seen to be wrong independently of the punishment, and in any case we may suppose the man thus tempted to be an atheist. Now if the sole criterion of the rightness or wrongness of an action is its conduciveness to one's own pleasure, I think one would have to say that the act of revenge was right because it would make the last few moments of his life happier than they would otherwise have been. It is true that he would have been likely to be a happier man on the whole if he had not indulged his vindictive desires to such an appalling extent in the past as he must have done to make such an act even a serious temptation, but it is too late for him to alter this now. We could not say to him—Control your vindictive desires now and your character will be improved so that you will be capable of greater pleasure in the future, for he would reply—I have no future. For the egoistic hedonist to make oneself miserable for the good of another man should be positively wicked in the only sense in which anything could be wicked at all.

But, even if the egoistic hedonist could show that his view was compatible with the ordinary canons of morality as regards the external nature of actions, he would still not have justified his position. For it is not only the external act, but the motive which counts in ethics, and the motive he suggests is one which we must regard as essentially unethical. Suppose a man admitted that he only refrains from stealing for fear of being sent to prison, or from ill-treating his children because he has been promised a sum of money if he does not ill-treat them, and we believed him, should we regard him as morally worthy? Not at all, we should condemn him as much or almost as much as if he had been guilty of theft and cruelty, for we should not recognize his motive as a proper one at all. And if so, why should we regard his conduct as any more moral if he refrains from wrong acts in general merely because he is bribed by the prospect of happiness or deterred by the fear of unhappiness whether in this life or in another, even if the happiness or unhappiness is not viewed as coming in such crude ways and as further removed in time? The best we could say is that he shows prudence and far-sightedness, not that he is good. The occasions when we feel markedly under a moral obligation are just *not* the occasions when we are exercised about our own happiness, but the occasions on which we feel an obligation to somebody else that strikes us as such quite independently of whether obedience to it is or is not conducive to our happiness. If a man sacrifices his own happiness needlessly without apparently harming others, the natural word that springs to the lips of the observer in speaking of him is "foolish"; if he sacrifices the happiness of another to further his own apparent happiness, the natural word is not "foolish" but "bad" (in the moral sense of that word). I do not deny that some egoistic hedonists were good men, but I do say that they had a wrong theory of the motives which determined and ought to determine their conduct.

In making these criticisms I have argued from what I called "common-sense ethics," namely, I have appealed to what we cannot help believing in particular ethical situations when we try to look reasonably at the question what one ought to do or approve of doing. If anybody says that all our ethical beliefs are illusions, I must admit that I cannot refute him, only prevent him from refuting me by meeting his arguments, but this completely sceptical position about ethics is one which we may indeed defend in a philosophical argument but not seriously hold in daily life. I note that the people who are most sceptical about the truth of ethical judgements commonly show a righteous moral indignation about at least ethical intolerance, and insist very strongly that we "ought" to seek and accept the truth. And I find it extremely difficult to believe that even the most pronounced ethical sceptic would not be convinced that my actions were bad if he saw me, e.g., wantonly torturing a little child. . . . We must go on the assumption . . . that the ordinary moral judgments which we on reflection cannot help making are the main clue to what is right in Ethics, subject to the test of coherence, and we shall have to ask about each rival theory whether it gives a coherent account of these. I have no hesitation in making the above assumption, and if we do not make it we shall have no Ethics at all, because we shall have no ethical data to organize. Of course this rejection of sheer ethical scepticism is compatible with very much disagreement as to what we do exactly when we make ethical judgements and as to many of the ethical judgements we are called on to make.

However, even complete ethical scepticism should certainly not lead to egoistic hedonism. For even the egoistic hedonist makes some ethical assumptions of a positive kind: he assumes at least that his own pleasure is good in itself, and his pain bad. That this is so he does not and cannot prove. It must therefore be something he sees to be true without proof. And it does seem an obvious enough truth. But in admitting it he has already accepted some ethical convictions without proof just because he sees them to be true, which is what philosophers usually mean by "intuition." Now, if he accepts any at all because he sees them intuitively, ought he not, at least in the absence of positive arguments against them, to accept all those which after careful reflection seem to him intuitively obvious in a like degree? And is it not plain that it is intuitively at least as obvious that it is wrong to do things which hurt others needlessly as that it is wrong unnecessarily to hurt oneself? There are other ethical intuitions incompatible with egoistic hedonism which might be cited, but this one is sufficient. If it is wrong to do things which hurt others for our own amusement, and we see it to be wrong just because it does hurt them, egoistic hedonism is false. For according to egoistic hedonism the only reason why anything is wrong is because it is not conducive to the agent's greatest pleasure. Even if in fact it is the case that it is never conducive to my own greatest pleasure to hurt others, it should be plain that this is not the main reason why it is wrong. If we can see clearly that our own pleasure is good, we can see just as clearly that the fact that an action needlessly and intentionally hurts another is quite sufficient to make it wrong, whether it also hurts me or not. So if we are to be consistent, we must accept both intuitions or neither, unless there are positive arguments which show one to be false, and I do not see what these could possibly be. As a matter of fact it may be doubted whether any important philosophers accept the doctrine of egoistic hedonism to-day, but very many have done so in the past, and it is a view which naturally suggests itself to very many people when they start to think about Ethics, so it is important to settle accounts with it before we move on. . . .

## Chapter III

### The Pursuit of the General Happiness

If pleasure or happiness is the only thing good-in-itself—and it is certainly the only thing about the *intrinsic* goodness of which there is anything like universal agreement—it seems irrational to hold that it makes any difference to its goodness who enjoys the happiness. And it seems reasonable to hold that it is our duty to produce as much good as possible and that it is wrong to neglect any opportunities to do so. From these assumptions we get a form of hedonism which differs from the egoistic form and seems to approach much more closely to what we ordinarily believe about ethical matters. The theory is most commonly known by the name of *Utilitarianism*. It is also sometimes called *Universalistic Hedonism*, "universalistic" because it considers everybody's good, and "hedonism" because it holds pleasure to be the only good. It maintains that our sole duty is to produce as much pleasure as possible, counting for this purpose a diminution of pain as equivalent to an increase in pleasure, and holds that in doing so we should count every man's pleasure as of equal worth to that of any other man. (It makes no distinction, any more than does egoistic hedonism, between happiness and pleasure, happiness being regarded as continued pleasure.) It thus agrees with egoistic hedonism as to what is good, but not as to what are the ultimate principles of ethical action. Both theories hold that pleasure is the only good, but while egoistic hedonism thinks we are under no obligation to further the happiness of anybody else except as a means to our own, the theory I am now going to discuss maintains that we are under a direct obligation to pursue happiness as such, to whomever the happiness belongs. The theory is now held by very few moral philosophers, but it was extremely important in the nineteenth and in a less fully thought-out form in the eighteenth century, and is no doubt approximately the working theory of vast numbers of people to-day in so far as they can be said to have an ethical theory at all. Its most important exponents in this country were John Stuart Mill and Sidgwick.

Now it is quite obvious that the amount of happiness or pain produced by our actions should be at least one of the chief criteria for deciding which actions we ought to perform. There are vast numbers of actions which are wrong for no other reason than that they tend to produce pain or unhappiness in other people, and if it can be shown that an act will lead to suffering, this is, usually at least, quite a sufficient reason why we ought not to perform it. Further, a utilitarian can deal with most of the relatively rare cases where it is right to inflict pain by contending that the infliction of pain now is necessary to avoid greater pain in the future or as a means to a gain in happiness which is worth the cost. We must remember, as with egoistic hedonism, that under "pleasure" are meant to be comprised all satisfactions and joys and not only the relatively "lower" ones to which the term pleasure is most commonly applied in ordinary speech. We must further realize that the utilitarian is not bound to suppose that in practice we ought always to settle what we are to do by a direct calculation of the amount of pleasure likely to be produced. He usually insists on the contrary that there are certain rules of behaviour such as those against lying and stealing whose violation human experience has adequately shown to be productive of unhappiness, and that in consequence we do not need to calculate afresh each time the amount of happiness or unhappiness likely to be produced before deciding to obey one of these laws. The ultimate ground for their validity lies in the general happiness, but we need not go back to this ultimate ground each time, any more than we need before applying an established mathematical law go back each time to the axioms on which it is based. Nor can utilitarianism possibly be dismissed as selfish, for it bids us treat the happiness or pain of any other man as no less important than our own. And utilitarianism has the great attraction of being a relatively simple theory and one in close relation to verifiable empirical facts. For an Ethics which admits only one good will obviously be simpler to apply than one which admits several that may on occasion conflict, and pleasure and pain are after all feelings the occurrence of which we can easily verify in a straightforward empirical way. All this does not however prove it to be the true theory.

As compared to common-sense morality a consistent utilitarianism would be in some respects stricter and in others less strict. Ordinarily we consider that we are much more under an obligation to some people than to others. We admit indeed that we are under some obligation to help anyone in need, but we feel a very much stronger obligation to promote the happiness of our own family, as is shown by the general attitude to appeals for charity. It is clear that the money spent by a man in order to provide his son with a university education could save the lives of many people who were perishing of hunger in a famine, yet most people would rather blame than praise a man who should deprive his son of a university education on this account. Further, while the obligation to contribute something to charity if one can afford it is generally recognized, only a very small minority of people have felt it their duty to curtail their comforts and luxuries very seriously on that account, and still less the comforts and luxuries of those dependent on them. Yet there can hardly be any doubt that, even if we allow for any indirect evil effects which might accrue, in most cases money given to any even tolerably well managed charity will do much more good by relieving the suffering of those in distress than would be done by using the same money to increase the pleasure of a person who is at all tolerably comfortable by enabling him to have a more pleasant house, better furniture, more tobacco, more holiday travel, etc. This does not, however, straightway prove the utilitarian wrong. He may reply that all but the very poor ought to give much more money to charity than on the average they do, and in view of the very small proportion of the national income that is spent on this and the vast amount of suffering in the world which calls for help, it seems to me plain that he is so far right. But, even if we grant this, it still seems plain to me, and I am sure would seem so to almost everybody else that, if a man were to deprive his wife and children against their will of all comforts and purchasable pleasures, leaving them only bare necessaries, on the ground that he could use the money thus saved to preserve several families from a greater pain or loss of happiness than he inflicted on his own by giving it to a charitable organization he would be acting wrongly not rightly. Again, suppose he obtained the money to give to the charity by stealing it from a man very much richer than himself. He might argue that the victim of his theft would lose little in happiness by being a few pounds worse off, while the people to whom he gave the money would be saved from great misery. Even if he kept the money himself, he might indeed argue that, being much poorer, he would gain more in happiness from it than the other man lost. These reflections seem to disclose a sharp conflict between utilitarianism and even enlightened common-sense morality. According to the former there is an equal obligation to further the happiness of everybody, according to the latter we have special obligations to some people much stronger than those we have to others; according to the former what produces most happiness is always right, according to the latter it is wrong to produce happiness by stealing and lying.

The utilitarian however will contend that the conflict is not a real but only an apparent one. He will argue that, if we take a more far-sighted view, we can see that greater happiness is produced by recognizing and insisting on special obligations. Family life is a great source of happiness, and family life as we know it would be impossible if we did not look on ourselves as having much stronger obligations to members of our family than to perfect strangers. And, if we admitted the principle that the poor were ethically entitled to steal from the rich, the result would be a social confusion which would be far worse than the present system. But it seems to me that what the utilitarian has done here is to point out that a whole class of acts or system of recognized obligations produces good results in the way of happiness, not that each particular act does so. We may admit that it would be a bad thing if the poorer generally and indiscriminately tried to steal from the richer, but does it necessarily follow from this that to do so in any one instance is wrong? A poor man who is prepared to cheat a richer may say—It would be a bad thing if everybody acted like me, but why should not I do so, when it is certain that my action will not result in everybody acting like me? It seems only possible to answer such a question adequately if we say that it is *unfair* to profit by the rules governing society and yet refuse yourself to obey them. But if we appeal to fairness, we are introducing another consideration besides happiness. It may therefore be doubted whether we can give an adequate account of our obligations without abandoning utilitarianism and admitting that there are other obligations which we should not ignore even in order to produce greater happiness and that it is bad to acquire happiness by unfair means whether for ourselves or others. It is indeed difficult to maintain that it cannot under any circumstances be right to lie, etc., on utilitarian grounds, e.g., to save life, but it seems to me pretty clear that utilitarian principles, logically carried out, would result in far more cheating, lying and unfair action than any good man would tolerate. This is not of course the same thing as saying that utilitarians are more likely to cheat and lie than other people, but only that if they carried out their theory consistently they would be so.

We may add that utilitarianism is far from being so simple a theory to apply as has been claimed by its advocates. How are we going to measure against each other quite different kinds of pleasure and say how many times more pleasure seeing *Hamlet* will give a particular man than will a good dinner? And it becomes still more complicated when we introduce different agents who cannot be expected all to take the same amount of enjoyment in the same pleasures. Yet such calculations are necessary if we are to apply the utilitarian criterion consistently to all practical questions. Similar difficulties will no doubt arise with any ethical theory that takes account of consequences, as we surely must, but at least this shows that utilitarianism has less cause than might be thought to pride itself on its simplicity. It is about as difficult to estimate the relative pleasantness of different pleasures as it would be on a non-hedonistic view to estimate their relative goodness.

It is however very hard to give any conclusive disproof of utilitarianism by considering the kind of actions to which it would logically lead. For suppose I argue that utilitarianism is a mistaken theory because, if carried out consistently, it would require me in a given situation to do something which is wrong. Now in any actual instance of a kind that could provide a ground for dispute the effects will be very complicated and uncertain, so that will always leave a loophole for the utilitarian to argue that I am wrong in my views as to their bearing on general happiness and that the act which seems right to common sense is really after all on a long view that most productive of happiness. And even if there are some instances where this is very unplausible (as indeed I think there are), he may reply by amending common-sense ethics here and saying that the act we ordinarily think right in this case is not really so. We are not bound to and indeed cannot accept the common-sense view (where there is one) about every action. The utilitarian view could only be shaken by a very considerable series of such instances. As I have suggested already, I think that it can be shaken by citing a series of instances of cheating and lying where what a good man could not help regarding as a "dirty trick" seemed to add to the general happiness, but it is easier to attack utilitarianism by considering its bearing not on the question what we ought to do but rather on the question what is good in itself.

Now the answer of utilitarianism to this question is very simple. The only thing good in itself, it maintains, is pleasure. But there are all kinds of pleasures, and it is very difficult to regard them as all of equal value. To take an instance given by G. E. Moore, a man who is watching a Shakespearian tragedy with full understanding and aesthetic appreciation at its highest pitch may be enjoying no more pleasure quantitatively than a drunkard who is amusing himself by smashing crockery, yet it is surely obvious that the former's pleasure is worth more than the latter's. But, if it is, there must be other factors besides pleasure on which the goodness of an experience depends, since the pleasure is *ex hypothesi* not greater in the former case than it is in the latter but only qualitatively better. Mill tried indeed to reconcile his utilitarianism with the admission that a lesser pleasure might rationally be preferred to a greater on the ground of the superior quality of the former, but it is generally, and I think rightly, agreed among philosophers that he failed to escape inconsistency. To say that pleasure is the only good and yet admit that a lesser pleasure may be preferable to a greater is like saying that money is the only thing which counts and then adding that money earned by public work is better than the same amount of money earned by business. If pleasure is the only good, the more pleasure always the better.

In order to decide whether one pleasure can be qualitatively better than another let us consider the following instances. Let us suppose that you were offered 50 more years, each equal in quantity of pleasure to the most pleasant year you have ever spent, but that the pleasure was to be derived entirely from eating, drinking, playing childish games and lying in the sun. Imagine this proposed life shorn of every element of intelligence above that of an imbecile, of all aesthetic experience, of all love of other men. Now suppose that you were offered as an alternative 49 years of equal pleasure, but that in this case the pleasure was no longer to be derived exclusively from these sources but also from the exercise of intelligence, of love, and of a developed capacity to appreciate the best in art and literature, and suppose also that the effect of the two alternative lives on the general happiness would be equal, the superior advantages for other men that one would expect to accrue from the second life being neutralized and only just neutralized by some evil influence that would intervene if you chose the second and not if you chose the first. Can we doubt that it would be better to choose the second? Yet, if utilitarianism were true, it would certainly be better to choose the first since you would thereby obtain a year's more pleasure. The utilitarian may reply that you would soon get bored by the first life and not enjoy it, but suppose some drug or conditioning process were invented that would prevent you getting bored so that you really got the pleasure promised? It is not inconceivable that a drug might be invented which had these properties. To take a slightly less fanciful illustration, I think Huxley's *Brave New World* is a good refutation of hedonism because it shows us an imaginary state of society which is hedonistically most satisfactory and yet ethically revolting.

Suppose again two communities in which an equal amount of pleasure was enjoyed and an equal amount of pain suffered. But suppose that in one community the citizens were selfish, unjust and capable only of pleasures which did not involve considerable intelligence, aesthetic appreciation, goodness or love, and that in the other community they derived their pleasures chiefly from those sources which I have just excluded from the first. Surely it is plain that the state of the second community would be much better than the state of the first. Yet, if utilitarianism were true, the two states should be equal in value. Two objections may be made against this example. First, it may be objected that the qualities possessed by the members of the second community would of their inherent nature necessarily lead to a greater happiness than any possessed by the first. But we can meet this by supposing the second community to be much less advantageously situated than the first as regards wealth, health and external circumstances. These factors might quite conceivably counteract the advantages in respect of happiness which would otherwise accrue to them from their superior character. Secondly, it may be objected that we cannot measure happiness as exactly as these examples presuppose. To this we may reply by substituting "approximately equal" or "equal as far as we can tell" for "exactly equal." If we are not able to compare experiences in respect of pleasure, utilitarianism cannot be applied at all; and if we can compare them, there is a good sense in saying that two lives or two communities are "equal in happiness as far as we can tell," meaning that we have no reason to think either happier than the other. That is all that is needed for my illustrations, and this negative condition certainly may be fulfilled.

Thirdly, let us suppose a man revelling in the infliction of tortures on his enemy. Of course this will be very painful for his victim and may have other less direct detrimental consequences in the future for the general welfare, but we are not now asking whether this state of affairs is conducive to the general good, we are asking about its value or disvalue in itself. Let us just consider the state of mind of the man inflicting the suffering. He is enjoying himself, yet can we say that his state of mind is good in itself? Surely it is on the contrary very bad indeed, and the more so the greater the pleasure. As a matter of fact his state of mind would still be very bad if he were not really inflicting the pain but only thought he was, like a witch-doctor who believed he could make his enemy suffer by roasting his effigy over a slow fire, yet in this case his victim would suffer no pain at all. But, if utilitarianism were true, the state should be good in itself because pleasurable, however deplorable its effects. Still less could it be the case on the utilitarian view that the state was made worse, not better, by increasing the pleasure.

Let us now take other instances which show up the defects of the utilitarian theory. Suppose a shipwreck in which two men are left clinging to a raft unable to support more than one. Let us call them A and B. Now suppose A to be a person whose life is of much less value to society or other individuals than that of B. Under these circumstances we should hold it a very meritorious act of A to surrender his place to B, but we should hold it the reverse of meritorious on the part of B to push off A. Yet the effect of the two acts would be almost the same: by either the life of A is sacrificed and that of B preserved. The only important difference in the effects seems to be that in the second case B will, if he is fundamentally good, be troubled by remorse, and if he is not so troubled, will probably deteriorate in character still further as the result of his action. But this cannot possibly be cited as a reason for the different estimate of the two actions, since unless it is already admitted that the second act is wrong there is no point in the remorse. Of course the utilitarian may argue that we are mistaken in thinking the second act wrong, if B is entitled to be certain that his life is really more important, and that the only reason why we think it wrong is because it would be a dangerous principle in general to allow a man to be judge whether his life was or was not more useful than that of another man. But the very most the utilitarian could maintain with the least show of plausibility would be that the action of B was excusable or not blameworthy, he could not possibly maintain that it was positively admirable, yet we should all admit that the action of A which had practically the same effects was not just excusable but positively admirable. Utilitarianism cannot account for this difference. The latter cannot be explained by effects on happiness but only by something intrinsically good in the nature of the one action. It is not a matter of pleasurable feelings—A probably did not enjoy drowning—but of something quite different from pleasure.

Finally, utilitarianism may be condemned as irreconcilable with the dictates of justice. The principle of utilitarianism tells us only to produce as much happiness as possible, thus implying that the way in which it is distributed does not matter. But justice requires that of two distributions which produce equal happiness we ought to prefer the fairer to the less fair, and that we ought to do this even if slightly less happiness is yielded by the former than by the latter. To take an extreme instance, suppose we could slightly increase the collective happiness of ten men by taking away all happiness from one of them, would it be right to do so? It is perhaps arguable that it would if the difference in happiness of the nine was very large, but not if it was very slight. And if the happiness of the nine were purchased by the actual torture of the one, the injustice of it would seem to poison the happiness and render it worse than valueless even if they were callous enough to enjoy it. Yet on the utilitarian view any distribution of good, however unfair, ought to be preferred to any other, however just, if it would yield *the slightest* additional happiness. Again, ought an innocent man to be punished, if it would on the balance cause less pain with an equal deterrent effect to punish him than it would to punish the guilty? In view of these difficulties it is not surprising that to-day very few philosophers could be found to accept utilitarianism.

## PLEASURE—SUGGESTED READINGS

Blake, R. M., "Why Not Hedonism? A Protest," *International Journal of Ethics*, XXXVII (1926–27), pp. 1–18. (proponent)

Carritt, E. F., *Ethical and Political Thinking*, Oxford, Clarendon Press, 1947, Chaps. 4 and 8. (critic)

Epicurus, *Epicurus: The Extant Remains*, trans. by C. Bailey, Oxford, Clarendon Press, 1926. (proponent)

Moore, G. E., *Principia Ethica*, Cambridge, Eng., Cambridge University Press, 1903, Chap. 3. (critic)

Pratt, J. B., *Reason in the Art of Living*, New York, Macmillan, 1949, Chaps. 10–12 and Chap. 13, pp. 135–8. (critic)

Sidgwick, H., *The Methods of Ethics*, 6th ed., New York, Macmillan, 1901. (proponent)

## 2. SELF-REALIZATION

As we have seen, the key problem for teleological ethical theory is to determine what is good. A second answer to this problem is provided by a group of thinkers who identify the good for man with his self-realization. These philosophers deny that the achievement of pleasure alone constitutes the proper end of human conduct. For them, man's good must be construed more broadly: it is to be found in the balanced fulfillment of the various capacities present within his nature.

But what are the capacities of human nature? And how are we to tell which capacities are most worth developing as man proceeds in the organization of his life? In answering these questions, different theories have been proposed concerning the nature of man's self-realization. The most influential of these theories have been of two types.

For one group of self-realizationists, man is distinguished from other creatures by his possession of reason. Without denying the importance of satisfying the appetitive and emotional sides of man's nature, these philosophers maintain that his highest fulfillment consists in the realization of his distinctive rationality.

According to the second group, the ideal of reason suffers from too narrow a conception of human selfhood; they maintain that self-realization requires an individual progressively to identify his goals with those of the larger communities of which he is a part. For these philosophers, there are stages in the development of human personality: at first, an individual is concerned only with achieving his own particular satisfactions; gradually, his purposes widen to include those of his family, his nation, and all mankind; ultimately, his loyalties find their highest and most inclusive object in the purposes being realized within the universe as a whole. Consequently, for man to realize himself, he must organize his activities in the service of these ever-wider ends.

In the following readings, ARISTOTLE presents a classic statement of the first type of self-realization theory. WRIGHT'S views are representative of the second group of self-realizationists. RASHDALL critically examines various forms of the assertion that self-realization is the end of life and gives his reasons for rejecting them.

ARISTOTLE

ARISTOTLE (384-322 B. C.), one of the greatest figures in the history of philosophy, was associated with Plato at the Academy in Athens
for nearly twenty years. Upon the death of
Plato, Aristotle left Athens and did not return
for approximately twelve years. During this
period, he spent three years as tutor of Alexander (later Alexander the Great), continued
his studies, and travelled. Upon his return to
Athens, he founded his own school, the
Lyceum, and devoted his time to an impressive program of investigation and writing
which encompassed all the learning of his
period. His major works include: *Organon* (a
collection of logical treatises), *Physics, Metaphysics, De Anima* (a psychological treatise),
*Nicomachean Ethics, Eudemian Ethics, Poli-
tics,* and *Poetics.*

## The Nicomachean Ethics*

### Book I

1. Every art and every inquiry, and similarly every action and pursuit, is
thought to aim at some good; and for this reason the good has rightly been
declared to be that at which all things aim. But a certain difference is found
among ends; some are activities, others are products apart from the activities
that produce them. Where there are ends apart from the actions, it is the
nature of the products to be better than the activities. Now, as there are many
actions, arts, and sciences, their ends also are many; the end of the medical
art is health, that of shipbuilding a vessel, that of strategy victory, that of
economics wealth. But where such arts fall under a single capacity—as bridle-
making and the other arts concerned with the equipment of horses fall under
the art of riding, and this and every military action under strategy, in the
same way other arts fall under yet others—in all of these the ends of the master
arts are to be preferred to all the subordinate ends; for it is for the sake of
the former that the latter are pursued. It makes no difference whether the
activities themselves are the ends of the actions, or something else apart from
the activities, as in the case of the sciences just mentioned.

2. If, then, there is some end of the things we do, which we desire for its
own sake (everything else being desired for the sake of this), and if we do
not choose everything for the sake of something else (for at that rate the

* From *The Nicomachean Ethics* of Aristotle, Books I, II, and X. Translated by W. D.
Ross. Copyright, 1925, Clarendon Press. Used by permission.

process would go on to infinity, so that our desire would be empty and vain), clearly this must be the good and the chief good. Will not the knowledge of it, then, have a great influence on life? Shall we not, like archers who have a mark to aim at, be more likely to hit upon what is right? If so, we must try, in outline at least to determine what it is. . . .

3. Our discussion will be adequate if it has as much clearness as the subject-matter admits of, for precision is not to be sought for alike in all discussions, any more than in all the products of the crafts. Now fine and just actions . . . admit of much variety and fluctuation of opinion, so that they may be thought to exist only by convention, and not by nature. And goods also give rise to similar fluctuation because they bring harm to many people; for before now men have been undone by reason of their wealth, and others by reason of their courage. We must be content, then, in speaking of such subjects and with such premises to indicate the truth roughly and in outline, and in speaking about things which are only for the most part true and with premisses of the same kind to reach conclusions that are no better. In the same spirit, therefore, should each type of statement be *received*; for it is the mark of an educated man to look for precision in each class of things just so far as the nature of the subject admits; it is evidently equally foolish to accept probable reasoning from a mathematician and to demand from a rhetorician scientific proofs.

Now each man judges well the things he knows, and of these he is a good judge. And so the man who has been educated in a subject is a good judge of that subject, and the man who has received an all-round education is a good judge in general. Hence a young man is not a proper hearer of lectures on political science; for he is inexperienced in the actions that occur in life, but its discussions start from these and are about these; and, further, since he tends to follow his passions, his study will be vain and unprofitable, because the end aimed at is not knowledge but action. And it makes no difference whether he is young in years or youthful in character; the defect does not depend on time, but on his living, and pursuing each successive object, as passion directs. For to such persons, as to the incontinent, knowledge brings no profit; but to those who desire and act in accordance with a rational principle knowledge about such matters will be of great benefit.

These remarks about the student, the sort of treatment to be expected, and the purpose of the inquiry, may be taken as our preface.

4. Let us resume our inquiry and state, in view of the fact that all knowledge and every pursuit aims at some good, . . . what is the highest of all goods achievable by action. Verbally there is very general agreement; for both the general run of men and people of superior refinement say that it is happiness, and identify living well and doing well with being happy; but with regard

to what happiness is they differ, and the many do not give the same account as the wise. For the former think it is some plain and obvious thing, like pleasure, wealth, or honour; they differ, however, from one another—and often even the same man identifies it with different things, with health when he is ill, with wealth when he is poor; but, conscious of their ignorance, they admire those who proclaim some great ideal that is above their comprehension. Now some thought that apart from these many goods there is another which is self-subsistent and causes the goodness of all these as well. To examine all the opinions that have been held were perhaps somewhat fruitless; enough to examine those that are most prevalent or that seem to be arguable. . . .

5. . . . To judge from the lives that men lead, most men, and men of the most vulgar type, seem (not without some ground) to identify the good, or happiness, with pleasure; which is the reason why they love the life of enjoyment. For there are, we may say, three prominent types of life—that just mentioned, the political, and thirdly the contemplative life. Now the mass of mankind are evidently quite slavish in their tastes, preferring a life suitable to beasts, but they get some ground for their view from the fact that many of those in high places share the tastes of Sardanapallus. A consideration of the prominent types of life shows that people of superior refinement and of active disposition identify happiness with honour; for this is, roughly speaking, the end of the political life. But it seems too superficial to be what we are looking for, since it is thought to depend on those who bestow honour rather than on him who receives it, but the good we divine to be something proper to a man and not easily taken from him. Further, men seem to pursue honour in order that they may be assured of their goodness; at least it is by men of practical wisdom that they seek to be honoured, and among those who know them, and on the ground of their virtue; clearly, then, according to them, at any rate, virtue is better. And perhaps one might even suppose this to be, rather than honour, the end of the political life. But even this appears somewhat incomplete; for possession of virtue seems actually compatible with being asleep, or with lifelong inactivity, and, further, with the greatest sufferings and misfortunes; but a man who was living so no one would call happy, unless he were maintaining a thesis at all costs. But enough of this; for the subject has been sufficiently treated even in the current discussions. Third comes the contemplative life, which we shall consider later.

The life of money-making is one undertaken under compulsion, and wealth is evidently not the good we are seeking; for it is merely useful and for the sake of something else. And so one might rather take the aforenamed objects to be ends; for they are loved for themselves. But it is evident that not even these are ends; yet many arguments have been thrown away in support of them. . . .

7. Let us again return to the good we are seeking, and ask what it can be. It seems different in different actions and arts; it is different in medicine, in strategy, and in the other arts likewise. What then is the good of each? Surely that for whose sake everything else is done. In medicine this is health, in strategy victory, in architecture a house, in any other sphere something else, and in every action and pursuit the end; for it is for the sake of this that all men do whatever else they do. Therefore, if there is an end for all that we do, this will be the good achievable by action, and if there are more than one, these will be the goods achievable by action.

So the argument has by a different course reached the same point; but we must try to state this even more clearly. Since there are evidently more than one end, and we choose some of these (e. g., wealth, flutes, and in general instruments) for the sake of something else, clearly not all ends are final ends; but the chief good is evidently something final. Therefore, if there is only one final end, this will be what we are seeking, and if there are more than one, the most final of these will be what we are seeking. Now we call that which is in itself worthy of pursuit more final than that which is worthy of pursuit for the sake of something else, and that which is never desirable for the sake of something else more final than the things that are desirable both in themselves and for the sake of that other thing, and therefore we call final without qualification that which is always desirable in itself and never for the sake of something else.

Now such a thing happiness, above all else, is held to be; for this we choose always for itself and never for the sake of something else, but honour, pleasure, reason, and every virtue we choose indeed for themselves (for if nothing resulted from them we should still choose each of them), but we choose them also for the sake of happiness, judging that by means of them we shall be happy. Happiness, on the other hand, no one chooses for the sake of these, nor, in general, for anything other than itself.

From the point of view of self-sufficiency the same result seems to follow; for the final good is thought to be self-sufficient. Now by self-sufficient we do not mean that which is sufficient for a man by himself, for one who lives a solitary life, but also for parents, children, wife, and in general for his friends and fellow citizens, since man is born for citizenship. But some limit must be set to this; for if we extend our requirements to ancestors and descendants and friends' friends we are in for an infinite series. . . . The self-sufficient we now define as that which when isolated makes life desirable and lacking in nothing; and such we think happiness to be; and further we think it most desirable of all things, without being counted as one good thing among

others—if it were so counted it would clearly be made desirable by the addition of even the least of goods; for that which is added becomes an excess
of goods, and of goods the greater is always more desirable. Happiness, then,
is something final and self-sufficient, and is the end of action.

Presumably, however, to say that happiness is the chief good seems a platitude, and a clearer account of what it is is still desired. This might perhaps be
given, if we could first ascertain the function of man. For just as for a flute-
player, a sculptor, or any artist, and, in general, for all things that have a
function or activity, the good and the 'well' is thought to reside in the function, so would it seem to be for man, if he has a function. Have the carpenter,
then, and the tanner certain functions or activities, and has man none? Is he
born without a function? Or as eye, hand, foot, and in general each of the
parts evidently has a function, may one lay it down that man similarly has a
function apart from all these? What then can this be? Life seems to be common even to plants, but we are seeking what is peculiar to man. Let us exclude, therefore, the life of nutrition and growth. Next there would be a life
perception, but *it* also seems to be common even to the horse, the ox, and
every animal. There remains, then, an active life of the element that has a
rational principle; of this, one part has such a principle in the sense of being
obedient to one, the other in the sense of possessing one and exercising
thought. And, as 'life of the rational element' also has two meanings, we
must state that life in the sense of activity is what we mean; for this seems
to be the more proper sense of the term. Now if the function of man is an
activity of soul which follows or implies a rational principle, and if we say
'a so-and-so' and 'a good so-and-so' have a function which is the same in
kind, e.g., a lyre-player and a good lyre-player, and so without qualification
in all cases, eminence in respect of goodness being added to the name of
the function (for the function of a lyre-player is to play the lyre, and that of
a good lyre-player is to do so well): if this is the case, [and we state the
function of man to be a certain kind of life, and this to be an activity or
actions of the soul implying a rational principle, and the function of a good
man to be the good and noble performance of these, and if any action is well
performed when it is performed in accordance with the appropriate excellence: if this is the case,] human good turns out to be activity of soul in
accordance with virtue, and if there are more than one virtue, in accordance
with the best and most complete.

But we must add 'in a complete life.' For one swallow does not make
a summer, nor does one day; and so too one day, or a short time, does not
make a man blessed and happy. . . .

13. Since happiness is an activity of soul in accordance with perfect
virtue, we must consider the nature of virtue. . . .

Some things are said about it, adequately enough, even in the discussion outside our school, and we must use these; e.g., that one element in the soul is irrational and one has a rational principle. Whether these are separated as the parts of the body or of anything divisible are, or are distinct by definition but by nature inseparable, like convex and concave in the circumference of a circle, does not affect the present question.

Of the irrational element one division seems to be widely distributed, and vegetative in its nature, I mean that which causes nutrition and growth; for it is this kind of power of the soul that one must assign to all nurslings and to embryos, and this same power to full-grown creatures; this is more reasonable than to assign some different power to them. Now the excellence of this seems to be common to all species and not specifically human; for this part of faculty seems to function most in sleep, while goodness and badness are least manifest in sleep (whence comes the saying that the happy are no better off than the wretched for half their lives; and this happens naturally enough, since sleep is an inactivity of the soul in that respect in which it is called good or bad), unless perhaps to a small extent some of the movements actually penetrate to the soul, and in this respect the dreams of good men are better than those of ordinary people. Enough of this subject, however; let us leave the nutritive faculty alone, since it has by its nature no share in human excellence.

There seems to be also another irrational element in the soul—one which in a sense, however, shares in a rational principle. For we praise the rational principle of the continent man and of the incontinent, and the part of their soul that has such a principle, since it urges them aright and towards the best objects; but there is found in them also another element naturally opposed to the rational principle, which fights against and resists that principle. For exactly as paralysed limbs when we intend to move them to the right turn on the contrary to the left, so is it with the soul; the impulses of incontinent people move in contrary directions. But while in the body we see that which moves astray, in the soul we do not. No doubt, however, we must nonetheless suppose that in the soul too there is something contrary to the rational principle, resisting and opposing it. In what sense it is distinct from the other elements does not concern us. Now even this seems to have a share in a rational principle, as we said; at any rate in the continent man it obeys the rational principle—and presumably in the temperate and brave man it is still more obedient; for in him it speaks, on all matters, with the same voice as the rational principle.

Therefore the irrational element also appears to be twofold. For the vegetative element in no way shares in a rational principle, but the appetitive, and in general the desiring element in a sense shares in it, in so far as it listens to and obeys it; this is the sense in which we speak of 'taking account' of one's father or one's friends, not that in which we speak of 'accounting' for a mathematical property. That the irrational element is in some sense persuaded by a rational principle is indicated also by the giving of advice and by all reproof and exhortation. And if this element also must be said to have a rational principle, that which has a rational principle (as well as that which has not) will be twofold, one subdivision having it in the strict sense and in itself, and the other having a tendency to obey as one does one's father.

Virtue too is distinguished into kinds in accordance with this difference; for we say that some of the virtues are intellectual and others moral, philosophic wisdom and understanding and practical wisdom being intellectual, liberality and temperance moral. For in speaking about a man's character we do not say that he is wise or has understanding but that he is good-tempered or temperate; yet we praise the wise man also with respect to his state of mind; and of states of mind we call those which merit praise virtues.

## Book II

1. Virtue, then, being of two kinds, intellectual and moral, intellectual virtue in the main owes both its birth and its growth to teaching (for which reason it requires experience and time), while moral virtue comes about as a result of habit, whence also its name *ethike* is one that is formed by a slight variation from the word *ethos* (habit). From this it is also plain that none of the moral virtues arises in us by nature; for nothing that exists by nature can form a habit contrary to its nature. For instance the stone which by nature moves downwards cannot be habituated to move upwards, not even if one tries to train it by throwing it up ten thousand times; nor can fire be habituated to move downwards, nor can anything else that by nature behaves in one way be trained to behave in another. Neither by nature, then, nor contrary to nature do the virtues arise in us; rather we are adapted by nature to receive them, and are made perfect by habit.

Again, of all the things that come to us by nature we first acquire the potentiality and later exhibit the activity (this is plain in the case of the senses; for it was not by often seeing or often hearing that we got these senses, but on the contrary we had them before we used them, and did not come to have them by using them); but the virtues we get by first exercising them, as also happens in the case of the arts as well. For the things we have to learn before we can do them, we learn by doing them, e.g., men become builders by building and lyre-players by playing the lyre; so too we become just by doing just acts, temperate by doing temperate acts, brave by doing brave acts. . . .

Again, it is from the same causes and by the same means that every virtue is both produced and destroyed, and similarly every art; for it is from playing the lyre that both good and bad lyre-players are produced. And the corresponding statement is true of builders and of all the rest; men will be good or bad builders as a result of building well or badly. For if this were not so, there would have been no need of a teacher, but all men would have been born good or bad at their craft. This, then, is the case with the virtues also; by doing the acts that we do in our transactions with other men we become just or unjust, and by doing the acts that we do in the presence of danger, and being habituated to feel fear or confidence, we become brave or cowardly. The same is true of appetites and feelings of anger; some men become temperate and good-tempered, others self-indulgent and irascible, by behaving in one way or the other in the appropriate circumstances. Thus, in one word, states of character arise out of like activities. This is why the activities we exhibit must be of a certain kind; it is because the states of character correspond to the differences between these. It makes no small difference, then, whether we form habits of one kind or of another from our very youth; it makes a very great difference, or rather *all* the difference. . . .

5.  Next we must consider what virtue is. Since things that are found in the soul are of three kinds—passions, faculties, states of character—virtue must be one of these. By passions I mean appetite, anger, fear, confidence, envy, joy, friendly feeling, hatred, longing, emulation, pity, and in general the feelings that are accompanied by pleasure or pain; by faculties the things in virtue of which we are said to be capable of feeling these, e.g., of becoming angry or being pained or feeling pity; by states of character the things in virtue of which we stand well or badly with reference to the passions, e.g., with reference to anger we stand badly if we feel it violently or too weakly, and well if we feel it moderately; and similarly with reference to the other passions.

Now neither the virtues nor the vices are *passions*, because we are not called good or bad on the ground of our passions, but are so called on the ground of our virtues and our vices, and because we are neither praised nor blamed for our passions (for the man who feels fear or anger is not praised, nor is the man who simply feels anger blamed, but the man who feels it in a certain way), but for our virtues and our vices we are praised or blamed.

Again, we feel anger and fear without choice, but the virtues are modes of choice or involve choice. Further, in respect of the passions we are said to be moved, but in respect of the virtues and the vices we are said not to be moved but to be disposed in a particular way.

For these reasons also they are not *faculties*; for we are neither called good nor bad, nor praised nor blamed, for the simple capacity of feeling the passions; again, we have the faculties of nature, but we are not made good or bad by nature; we have spoken of this before.

If, then, the virtues are neither passions nor faculties, all that remains is that they should be *states of character*.

Thus we have stated what virtue is in respect of its genus.

6. We must, however, not only describe virtue as a state of character, but also say what sort of state it is. We may remark, then, that every virtue or excellence both brings into good condition the thing of which it is the excellence and makes the work of that thing be done well; e.g., the excellence of the eye makes both the eye and its work good; for it is by the excellence of the eye that we see well. Similarly the excellence of the horse makes a horse both good in itself and good at running and at carrying its rider and at awaiting the attack of the enemy. Therefore, if this is true in every case, the virtue of man also will be the state of character which makes a man good and which makes him do his own work well.

How this is to happen . . . will be made plain . . . by the following consideration of the specific nature of virtue. In everything that is continuous and divisible it is possible to take more, less, or an equal amount, and that either in terms of the thing itself or relatively to us; and the equal is an intermediate between excess and defect. By the intermediate in the object I mean that which is equidistant from each of the extremes, which is one and the same for all men; by the intermediate relatively to us that which is neither too much nor too little—and this is not one, nor the same for all. For instance, if ten is many and two is few, six is the intermediate, taken in terms of the object; for it exceeds and is exceeded by an equal amount; this is intermediate according to arithmetical proportion. But the intermediate relatively to us is not to be taken so; if ten pounds are too much for a particular person to eat and two too little, it does not follow that the trainer will order six pounds; for this also is perhaps too much for the person who is to take it, or too little—too little for Milo,* too much for the beginner in athletic exercises. The same is true of running and wrestling. Thus a master of any art avoids excess and defect, but seeks the intermediate and chooses this—the intermediate not in the object but relatively to us.

If it is thus, then, that every art does its work well—by looking to the intermediate and judging its works by this standard (so that we often say of good works of art that it is not possible either to take away or to add anything, implying that excess and defect destroy the goodness of works of art, while the mean preserves it; and good artists, as we say, look to this in their work), and if, further, virtue is more exact and better than any art, as nature also is, then virtue must have the quality of aiming at the intermediate. I

* A famous wrestler. Translator's footnote.

mean moral virtue; for it is this that is concerned with passions and actions, and in these there is excess, defect, and the intermediate. For instance, both fear and confidence and appetite and anger and pity and in general pleasure and pain may be felt both too much and too little, and in both cases not well; but to feel them at the right times, with reference to the right objects, towards the right people, with the right motive, and in the right way, is what is both intermediate and best, and this is characteristic of virtue. Similarly with regard to actions also there is excess, defect, and the intermediate. Now virtue is concerned with passions and actions, in which excess is a form of failure, and so is defect, while the intermediate is praised and is a form of success; and being praised and being successful are both characteristics of virtue. Therefore virtue is a kind of mean, since, as we have seen, it aims at what is intermediate.

Again, it is possible to fail in many ways (for evil belongs to the class of the unlimited, as the Pythagoreans conjectured, and good to that of the limited), while to succeed is possible only in one way (for which reason also one is easy and the other difficult—to miss the mark easy, to hit it difficult); for these reasons also, then, excess and defect are characteristic of vice, and the mean of virtue;

For men are good in but one way, but bad in many.

Virtue, then, is a state of character concerned with choice, lying in a mean, i.e., the mean relative to us, this being determined by a rational principle, and by that principle by which the man of practical wisdom would determine it. Now it is a mean between two vices, that which depends on excess and that which depends on defect; and again it is a mean because the vices respectively fall short of or exceed what is right in both passions and actions, while virtue both finds and chooses that which is intermediate. Hence in respect of its substance and the definition which states its essence virtue is a mean, with regard to what is best and right and extreme.

But not every action nor every passion admits of a mean; for some have names that already imply badness, e.g., spite, shamelessness, envy, and in the case of actions adultery, theft, murder; for all of these and suchlike things imply by their names that they are themselves bad, and not the excesses or deficiencies of them. It is not possible, then, ever to be right with regard to them; one must always be wrong. Nor does goodness or badness with regard to such things depend on committing adultery with the right woman, at the right time, and in the right way, but simply to do any of them is to go wrong. It would be equally absurd, then, to expect that in unjust, cowardly, and voluptuous action there should be a mean, an excess, and a deficiency; for at that rate there would be a mean of excess and of deficiency, an excess of excess, and a deficiency of deficiency. But as there is no excess and deficiency of temperance and courage because what is intermediate is in a sense an extreme, so too of the actions we have mentioned there is no mean nor any excess and deficiency, but however they are done they are wrong; for in general there is neither a mean of excess and deficiency, nor excess and deficiency of a mean.

7. We must, however, not only make this general statement, but also apply it to the individual facts. For among statements about conduct those which are general apply more widely, but those which are particular are more genuine, since conduct has to do with individual cases, and our statements must harmonize with the facts in these cases. We may take these cases from our table. With regard to feelings of fear and confidence courage is the mean; of the people who exceed, he who exceeds in fearlessness has no name (many of the states have no name), while the man who exceeds in confidence is rash, and he who exceeds in fear and falls short in confidence is a coward. With regard to pleasures and pains—not all of them, and not so much with regard to the pains—the mean is temperance, the excess self-indulgence. Persons deficient with regard to the pleasures are not often found; hence such persons also have received no name. But let us call them 'insensible.'

With regard to giving and taking of money the mean is liberality, the excess and the defect prodigality and meanness. In these actions people exceed and fall short in contrary ways; the prodigal exceeds in spending and falls short in taking, while the mean man exceeds in taking and falls short in spending. . . . With regard to money there are also other dispositions—a mean, magnificence (for the magnificent man differs from the liberal man; the former deals with large sums, the latter with small ones), and excess, tastelessness and vulgarity, and a deficiency, niggardliness. . . .

With regard to honour and dishonour the mean is proper pride, the excess is known as a sort of 'empty vanity,' and the deficiency is undue humility; and as we said liberality was related to magnificence, differing from it by dealing with small sums, so there is a state similarly related to proper pride, being concerned with small honours while that is concerned with great. For it is possible to desire honour as one ought, and more than one ought, and less, and the man who exceeds in his desires is called ambitious, the man who falls short unambitious, while the intermediate person has no name. The dispositions also are nameless, except that that of the ambitious man is called ambition. Hence the people who are at the extremes lay claim to the middle place; and we ourselves sometimes call the intermediate person ambitious and sometimes unambitious, and sometimes praise the ambitious man and sometimes the unambitious. . . .

With regard to anger also there is an excess, a deficiency, and a mean. Although they can scarcely be said to have names, yet since we call the intermediate person good-tempered let us call the mean good temper; of the persons at the extremes let the one who exceeds be called irascible, and his vice irascibility, and the man who falls short an inirascible sort of person, and the deficiency inirascibility.

There are also three other means, which have a certain likeness to one another, but differ from one another: for they are all concerned with intercourse in words and actions, but differ in that one is concerned with truth in this sphere, the other two with pleasantness; and of this one kind is exhibited in giving amusement, the other in all the circumstances of life. We must therefore speak of these two, that we may the better see that in all things the mean is praiseworthy, and the extremes neither praiseworthy nor right, but worthy of blame. Now most of these states also have no names, but we must try, as in the other cases, to invent names ourselves so that we may be clear and easy to follow. With regard to truth, then, the intermediate is a truthful sort of person and the mean may be called truthfulness, while the pretence which exaggerates is boastfulness and the person characterized by it a boaster, and that which understates is mock modesty and the person characterized by it mock-modest. With regard to pleasantness in the giving of amusement the intermediate person is ready-witted and the disposition ready wit, the excess is buffoonery and the person characterized by it a buffoon, while the man who falls short is a sort of boor and his state is boorishness. With regard to the remaining kind of pleasantness, that which is exhibited in life in general, the man who is pleasant in the right way is friendly and the mean is friendliness, while the man who exceeds is an obsequious person if he has no end in view, a flatterer if he is aiming at his own advantage, and the man who falls short and is unpleasant in all circumstances is a quarrelsome and surly sort of person.

There are also means in the passions and concerned with the passions; since shame is not a virtue, and yet praise is extended to the modest man. For even in these matters one man is said to be intermediate, and another to exceed, as for instance the bashful man who is ashamed of everything; while he who falls short or is not ashamed of anything at all is shameless, and the intermediate person is modest. Righteous indignation is a mean between envy and spite, and these states are concerned with the pain and pleasures that are felt at the fortunes of our neighbours; the man who is characterized by righteous indignation is pained at undeserved good fortune, the envious man, going beyond him, is pained at all good fortune, and the spiteful man falls so far short of being pained that he even rejoices. . . .

9. That moral virtue is a mean, then, and in what sense it is so, and

that it is a mean between two vices, the one involving excess, the other deficiency, and that it is such because its character is to aim at what is intermediate in passions and in actions, has been sufficiently stated. Hence also it is no easy task to be good. For in everything it is no easy task to find the middle, e.g., to find the middle of a circle is not for every one but for him who knows; so, too, any one can get angry—that is easy—or give or spend money; but to do this to the right person, to the right extent, at the right time, with the right motive, and in the right way, *that* is not for every one, nor is it easy; wherefore goodness is both rare and laudable and noble. . . .

## Book X

6. . . .What remains is to discuss in outline the nature of happiness, since this is what we state the end of human nature to be. Our discussion will be the more concise if we first sum up what we have said already. We said, then, that it is not a disposition; for if it were it might belong to some one who was asleep throughout his life, living the life of a plant, or, again, to some one who was suffering the greatest misfortunes. If these implications are unacceptable, and we must rather class happiness as an activity, as we have said before, and if some activities are necessary, and desirable for the sake of something else, while others are so in themselves, evidently happiness must be placed among those desirable in themselves, not among those desirable for the sake of something else; for happiness does not lack anything, but is self-sufficient. Now those activities are desirable in themselves from which nothing is sought beyond the activity. And of this nature virtuous actions are thought to be; for to do noble and good deeds is a thing desirable for its own sake.

Pleasant amusements also are thought to be of this nature; we choose them not for the sake of other things; for we are injured rather than benefited by them, since we are led to neglect our bodies and our property. But most of the people who are deemed happy take refuge in such pastimes, which is the reason why those who are ready-witted at them are highly esteemed at the courts of tyrants; they make themselves pleasant companions in the tyrants' favourite pursuits, and that is the sort of man they want. Now these things are thought to be of the nature of happiness because people in despotic positions spend their leisure in them, but perhaps such people prove nothing; for virtue and reason, from which good activities flow, do not depend on despotic position; nor, if these people, who have never tasted pure and generous pleasure, take refuge in the bodily pleasures, should these for that reason be thought more desirable; for boys, too, think the things that are valued among themselves are the best. It is to be expected, then, that, as different things seem valuable to boys and to men, so they should to bad men and to good. Now . . . those things are both valuable and pleasant which are such to the good man; and to each man the activity in accordance with his own disposition is most desirable, and, therefore, to the good man that which is in accordance with virtue. Happiness, therefore, does not lie in amusement; it would, indeed, be strange if the end were amusement, and one were to take trouble and suffer hardship all one's life in order to amuse oneself. For, in a word, everything that we choose we choose for the sake of something else—except happiness, which is an end. Now to exert oneself and work for the sake of amusement seems silly and utterly childish. But to amuse oneself in order that one may exert oneself, as Anacharsis puts it, seems right; for amusement is a sort of relaxation, and we need relaxation because we cannot work continuously. Relaxation, then, is not an end; for it is taken for the sake of activity.

The happy life is thought to be virtuous; now a virtuous life requires exertion, and does not consist in amusement. And we say that serious things are better than laughable things and those connected with amusement, and that the activity of the better of any two things—whether it be two elements of our being or two men—is the more serious; but the activity of the better is *ipso facto* superior and more of the nature of happiness. And any chance person—even a slave—can enjoy the bodily pleasures no less than the best man; but no one assigns to a slave a share in happiness—unless he assigns to him also a share in human life. For happiness does not lie in such occupations, but, as we have said before, in virtuous activities.

7. If happiness is activity in accordance with virtue, it is reasonable that *it* should be in accordance with the highest virtue; and this will be that of the best thing in us. Whether it be reason or something else that is this element which is thought to be our natural ruler and guide and to take thought of things noble and divine, whether it be itself also divine or only the most divine element in us, the activity of this in accordance with its proper virtue will be perfect happiness. That this activity is contemplative we have already said.

Now this would seem to be in agreement with what we said before and with the truth. For, firstly, this activity is the best (since not only is reason the best thing in us, but the objects of reason are the best of knowable objects); and, secondly, it is the most continuous, since we can contemplate truth more continuously than we can *do* anything. And we think happiness has pleasure mingled with it, but the activity of philosophic wisdom is admittedly the pleasantest of virtuous activities; at all events the pursuit of it is thought to offer pleasures marvellous for their purity and their enduringness, and it is to be expected that those who know will pass their time more pleasantly than those who inquire. And the self-sufficiency that

is spoken of must belong most to the contemplative activity. For while a philosopher, as well as a just man or one possessing any other virtue, needs the
necessaries of life, when they are sufficiently equipped with things of that
sort the just man needs people towards whom and with whom he shall act
justly, and the temperate man, the brave man, and each of the others is in
the same case, but the philosopher, even when by himelf, can contemplate
truth, and the better the wiser he is; he can perhaps do so better if he has
fellow-workers, but still he is the most self-sufficient. And this activity alone
would seem to be loved for its own sake; for nothing arises from it apart
from the contemplating, while from practical activities we gain more or less
apart from the action. And happiness is thought to depend on leisure; for
we are busy that we may have leisure, and make war that we may live in
peace. Now the activity of the practical virtues is exhibited in political or
military affairs, but the actions concerned with these seem to be unleisurely.
War-like actions are completely so (for no one chooses to be at war, or
provokes war, for the sake of being at war; any one would seem absolutely
murderous if he were to make enemies of his friends in order to bring about
battle and slaughter); but the action of the statesman is also unleisurely, and
—apart from the political action itself—aims at despotic power and honours,
or at all events happiness, for him and his fellow citizens—a happiness different from political action, and evidently sought as being different. So if among
virtuous actions political and military actions are distinguished by nobility
and greatness, and these are unleisurely and aim at an end and are not desirable for their own sake, but the activity of reason, which is contemplative,
seems both to be superior in serious worth and to aim at no end beyond itself, and to have its pleasure proper to itself (and this augments the activity),
and the self-sufficiency, leisureliness, unweariedness (so far as this is possible
for man), and all the other attributes ascribed to the supremely happy man
are evidently those connected with this activity, it follows that this will be
the complete happiness of man, if it be allowed a complete term of life (for
none of the attributes of happiness is *incomplete*).

But such a life would be too high for man; for it is not in so far as he is
man that he will live so, but in so far as something divine is present in him;
and by so much as this is superior to our composite nature is its activity
superior to that which is the exercise of the other kind of virtue. If reason is
divine, then, in comparison with man, the life according to it is divine in
comparison with human life. But we must not follow those who advise us,
being men, to think of human things, and, being mortal, of mortal things,
but must, so far as we can, make ourselves immortal, and strain every nerve
to live in accordance with the best thing in us; for even if it be small in bulk,
much more does it in power and worth surpass everything. This would seem.

too, to be each man himself, since it is the authoritative and better part of him. It would be strange, then, if he were to choose not the life of his self but that of something else. And what we said before will apply now; that which is proper to each thing is by nature best and most pleasant for each thing; for man, therefore, the life according to reason is best and pleasantest, since reason more than anything else *is* man. This life therefore is also the happiest.

8. But in a secondary degree the life in accordance with the other kind of virtue is happy; for the activities in accordance with this befit our human estate. Just and brave acts, and other virtuous acts, we do in relation to each other, observing our respective duties with regard to contracts and services and all manner of actions and with regard to passions; and all of these seem to be typically human. Some of them seem even to arise from the body, and virtue of character to be in many ways bound up with the passions. Practical wisdom, too, is linked to virtue of character, and this to practical wisdom, since the principles of practical wisdom are in accordance with the moral virtues and rightness in morals is in accordance with practical wisdom. Being connected with the passions also, the moral virtues must belong to our composite nature; and the virtues of our composite nature are human; so, therefore, are the life and the happiness which correspond to these. The excellence of the reason is a thing apart, we must be content to say this much about it, for to describe it precisely is a task greater than our purpose requires. It would seem, however, also to need external equipment but little, or less than moral virtue does. Grant that both need the necessaries, and do so equally, even if the statesman's work is the more concerned with the body and things of that sort; for there will be little difference there; but in what they need for the exercise of their activities there will be much difference. The liberal man will need money for the doing of his liberal deeds, and the just man too will need it for the returning of services (for wishes are hard to discern, and even people who are not just pretend to wish to act justly); and the brave man will need power if he is to accomplish any of the acts that correspond to his virtue, and the temperate man will need opportunity; for how else is either he or any of the others to be recognized? It is debated, too, whether the will or the deed is more essential to virtue, which is assumed to involve both; it is surely clear that its perfection involves both; but for deeds many things are needed, and more, the greater and nobler the deeds are. But the man who is contemplating the truth needs no such thing, at least with a view to the exercise of his activity; indeed they are, one may say, even hindrances, at all events to his contemplation; but in so far as he is a man and lives with a number of people, he chooses to do virtuous acts; he will therefore need such aids to living a human life.

But that perfect happiness is a contemplative activity will appear from the following consideration as well. We assume the gods to be above all other beings blessed and happy; but what sort of actions must we assign to them? Acts of justice? Will not the gods seem absurd if they make contracts and return deposits, and so on? Acts of a brave man, then, confronting dangers and running risks because it is noble to do so? Or liberal acts? To whom will they give? It will be strange if they are really to have money or anything of the kind. And what would their temperate acts be? Is not such praise taste-less, since they have no bad appetites? If we were to run through them all, the circumstances of action would be found trivial and unworthy of gods. Still, every one supposes that they *live* and therefore that they are active; we cannot suppose them to sleep like Endymion. Now if you take away from a living being action, and still more production, what is left but contemplation? Therefore the activity of God, which surpasses all others in blessedness, must be contemplative; and of human activities, therefore, that which is most akin to this must be most of the nature of happiness.

This is indicated, too, by the fact that the other animals have no share in happiness, being completely deprived of such activity. For while the whole life of the gods is blessed, and that of men too in so far as some likeness of such activity belongs to them, none of the other animals is happy, since they in no way share in contemplation. Happiness extends, then, just so far as contemplation does, and those to whom contemplation more fully belongs are more truly happy, not as a mere concomitant but in virtue of the con-templation; for this is in itself precious. Happiness, therefore, must be some form of contemplation.

But, being a man, one will also need external prosperity; for our nature is not self-sufficient for the purpose of contemplation, but our body also must be healthy and must have food and other attention. Still, we must not think that the man who is to be happy will need many things or great things, merely because he cannot be supremely happy without external goods; for self-sufficiency and action do not involve excess, and we can do noble acts without ruling earth and sea; for even with moderate advantages one can act virtuously (this is manifest enough; for private persons are thought to do worthy acts no less than despots—indeed even more); and it is enough that we should have so much as that; for the life of the man who is active in ac-cordance with virtue will be happy. Solon, too, was perhaps sketching well the happy man when he described him as moderately furnished with ex-ternals but as having done (as Solon thought) the noblest acts, and lived tem-perately; for one can with but moderate possessions do what one ought. Anaxagoras also seems to have supposed the happy man not to be rich nor a despot, when he said that he would not be surprised if the happy man were to seem to most people a strange person; for they judge by externals, since these are all they perceive. The opinions of the wise seem, then, to harmonize with our arguments. But while even such things carry some conviction, the truth in practical matters is discerned from the facts of life; for these are the decisive factor. We must therefore survey what we have already said, bringing it to the test of the facts of life, and if it harmonizes with the facts we must accept it, but if it clashes with them we must suppose it to be mere theory. Now he who exercises his reason and cultivates it seems to be both in the best state of mind and most dear to the gods. For if the gods have any care for human affairs, as they are thought to have, it would be reasonable both that they should delight in that which was best and most akin to them (i.e., reason) and that they should reward those who love and honour this most, as caring for the things that are dear to them and acting both rightly and nobly. And that all these attributes belong most of all to the philosopher is manifest. He, therefore, is the dearest to the gods. And he who is that will presumably be also the happiest; so that in this way too the philosopher will more than any other be happy.

# HENRY W. WRIGHT

HENRY WILKES WRIGHT (1878–1959) taught for many years at Lake Forest College, Illinois, and at the University of Manitoba, Canada. An idealist, his major works include: Self-Realization (1913), Faith Justified by Progress (1916), The Moral Standards of Democracy (1925), and The Religious Response (1929).

## The Conditions of Self-Realization in Human Life*

### The Good as Self-Realization

. . . What is the work of an organizing agency? What is meant by organization? Clearly, to organize is to establish a relation of inter-dependence and coöperation among the parts within any whole. This inter-dependence is the most thorough, this coöperation is the closest, that is possible. So thorough is the inter-dependence that every part has its nature altogether

---

* From *Self-Realization*, by Henry W. Wright, Part II, Chaps. 5 and 6. Copyright, 1913, Henry Holt and Company, Inc.; 1940, by Henry W. Wright. Used by permission of Henry Holt and Company, Inc.

constituted by its connection with the other parts of the system, and ceases to exist in independence of it. So close is the coöperation that every part has its life altogether determined by the office it discharges within the system, and ceases to act independently. Organization means, therefore, such a relation within a system that the whole finds expression in every part, and to organize is to establish this relation. Thus it is with the living body which, because such a relation obtains among its parts, is called an *organism*. The members are so related that each has its nature wholly determined by its function within the whole. This is what social organization means, too— such coöperation among the different individuals that each finds expression for his own individuality in the discharge of his specific office in society. To organize a business or industry involves such a distribution and adjustment of its various activities that each department shall work with maximum efficiency in the interest of the whole. Nor is it otherwise in the organization of human conduct through the instrumentality of volition,— to organize is to relate the different activities of the individual so that each may promote most effectively the exercise of all—and organization means that the sum-total of the individual's tendencies and capacities shall find conscious expression in each single act. Now the sum-total of the individual's active tendencies and capacities, *expressed in their conscious unity*, constitute . . . his selfhood or personality. Consequently, the complete organization of conduct, the goal which volition strives to attain, and which is required to satisfy it fully, is identical with complete self-expression—or, in the more familiar phrase, self-realization. Self-realization is therefore the *summum bonum*, the highest human good, which we have been seeking to discover. It is that form of conduct wherein each single act is made contributory to the welfare of the whole self and, conversely, the whole self is given expression in every act. . . .

## 1.  Form and Content in Self-Realization

The Good is now defined as the full realization of the human self. This conception of self-realization is of supreme importance in the science of Ethics. But its establishment does not mark the complete solution of the ethical problem; it only provides a necessary basis for further inquiry. Highly significant as it is, the conception of self-realization as thus far developed is an abstract principle of little value in solving the practical problems of conduct. To be genuinely helpful and illuminating it must be made concrete. We must know something of the actual nature of the human self whose realization is the *summum bonum*—of what capacities it is constituted, through what activities it is expressed. Only through such knowledge can the principle of self-realization furnish guidance and direction to human conduct.

Or, to put the matter in other words, . . . the student of Ethics cannot be content with a principle that is merely formal. He must know the content of the Good as well as its form. What are the activities that go to make up a completely organized life? What are the qualities and characteristics of the self whose nature is completely realized? If mere organization is the Good, will not every life in which the different acts are all strictly subordinated to a ruling purpose—even though, as in the case of the criminal, this purpose is a cruel and sinister one—be morally approved? Suppose a boy is reared in the belief that it is his chief duty to avenge the death of a murdered father. As he grows to manhood such vengeance becomes his ruling purpose—perhaps connecting itself with an ideal of personal honor. In finally gaining his revenge he himself meets death. Is not his life completely organized? Does he not—or does he—fully realize himself? Such an example shows the necessity of going beyond the formal principle of organization and discovering what definite character-istics and capacities are displayed by all normal human beings in the course of their development.

## 2. The Incidental and the Essential in Human Nature

The task now before us is to ascertain what are the fundamental char-acteristics of the human self and to see how these are expressed in the process of self-realization. Now . . . the *content* [of the good] can be determined only by a study of the facts of human nature and human experience. The effects of such a study—especially a first general survey—are discouraging. The facts are many and complicated, and the variations of character between men of different races and ages are apparently endless and certainly bewildering. It seems that all men possess in common only the bare faculties of thought and action, while the many ideas and beliefs which spring from the one, and the varied tendencies and dispositions which pertain to the other, are differ-ent in each individual case. What characteristics have the Norse viking, the mediæval recluse, and the modern man of business in common? To what extent will the course of self-realization for the Kaffir, the Esquimo, and the European be identical? Or even within a modern civilized state, how many activities are shared equally by street-sweeper, stock-broker, and charities-worker?

The activities involved in self-realization must necessarily differ with the time, race, sex, and occupation of the self. In fact, self-realization is bound to have a different meaning for each separate individual; since each possesses certain attributes and abilities peculiar to himself, which enter into his self-realization. Despite this infinite diversity among men there are, nevertheless, certain characteristics which are essential to human nature as such. They are consequently possessed by all normal human individuals, and serve to direct the course of self-realization in each. In fact, these essential characteristics determine the activities which all men must put forth as conditions of their self-realization. They may hence be said to prescribe the laws of self-realization, valid universally within the field of human conduct. . . .

What, then, are the essential characteristics of human nature which constitute the universal and necessary conditions of human self-realization?

### 3. Man as a Natural Being

Man is primarily a natural being, a member of the highest of the animal species. He is the outcome of the same natural evolution that has produced the other living forms, and is, therefore, related to them by descent. His genealogy may be traced down through a succession of species to the earliest and simplest forms of life. As a result of this, his natural origin and development, man possesses certain qualities which must be reckoned as fundamental to his character. Most important in their influence upon conduct are the instincts which all men thus possess. These instincts are a part of man's natural inheritance, and hence are shared in common with the lower animals. They are modifications of the nervous system originally developed in our animal ancestors by natural selection because giving an advantage in the struggle for existence. Originating in this way they have been transmitted by physical heredity and made a permanent part of man's physical structure.

### 4. His Native Instincts

Hence the first of the characteristics fundamental to human nature is the possession by all men of a set of natural instincts. These instincts have an important bearing upon man's conduct, since they cause him at first to react involuntarily to certain kinds of objects and then consciously to desire and voluntarily to seek them. It is difficult, if not impossible, to enumerate and classify the various instincts of man. This is not because their existence is in the least doubtful; but in many cases the objects and movements involved in a group of instinctive reactions are so related that it seems an arbitrary matter whether we attribute the whole group to one instinct or divide it among several. Are the instincts, so-called, of defense, combat, and rivalry three separate instincts, or just varied manifestations of one instinct? Who shall decide? Still it is possible to make a rough catalogue of the more important human instincts, which will be sufficient to our needs; since, for ethical purposes, we do not require a complete classification of every variety of instinctive reaction in man. For purposes of the present discussion, then, man's instinctive reactions may be divided into three classes, in accordance with the nature of the object upon which they are directed, whether it be the individual himself, an inanimate object, or another living individual. Under the first head comes the instinct of self-preservation, which causes man to seek his own health and pleasure, and equally to avoid conditions of harm and pain. Under the second head we may note the instincts of food, drink, shelter, and acquisition. Thirdly, come the social instincts, among which are those of sex and parenthood, of speech and sympathy, of resentment and emulation. We may add as another to these three classes, certain instincts whose object may be either an inanimate thing or another living individual —that is, the instincts of imitation, curiosity, beauty, and play.

Originating as conditions of survival with the lower forms of life, these instincts serve—through the actions they prompt—to maintain the existence of the human organism in the natural world. Thus they relate man as individual to the objects of nature, giving value to material things according as these minister to human needs. The world of the human individual is consequently not a world of objects that merely exist as facts, but a world of objects which appeal as possible ends of action because supplying food, shelter, clothing, amusement, etc. In the same way man's native instincts relate him to other members of his own species. Other individuals acquire interest for him because furnishing companionship, arousing resentment, or appealing to sexual or parental emotions. Through his various natural instincts, therefore, man is set in certain definite relationships to objects of the material world and to other men as natural individuals.

## 5. Man as a Conscious Self

But man is more than a natural individual: he is a conscious self. As a self or person, he is not a material thing with boundaries to separate it from other things in space, he is a spiritual being to whom no such limitations can be assigned. Man's selfhood or personality resides in the conscious unity of his experience. "To have a conception of one's own self," says Hobhouse, "one must be aware of a certain identity running through the mass of past experiences, and inferentially prolonged into the future." Now man's consciousness of the unity of his experience, in which his selfhood consists, depends upon his ability to weave together the facts of his experience into a connected system. He must do more than associate experiences in the order of their occurrence; for this the animals do and yet have no selfhood or personality. He must be able to establish permanent relations among the objects of his consciousness "upon the basis of their affinities and the more remote connections that follow therefrom." Now this work of the organization of experience, which is the condition of conscious selfhood, proceeds ultimately from volition, the spiritual force in man which builds out of the materials of animal life a self-conscious personality. We already know how volition in its first and simplest form begins this work. In discovering the means which must be used to attain the end of desire the individual is made aware of relationships among objects that are permanent and necessary. Imitation and language are, as we have noted, also important factors in the development of the self. The social character of selfhood is therefore marked from the first; since self-development in its earliest stages is dependent upon the influence of other selves and the possibility of communicating with them.

With the appearance of volition, then, in the third or fourth year of human life, the growth of the self begins and it continues through childhood. But full self-consciousness does not arise until the power of free thought and imagination is developed in the later period of adolescence. This power enables the individual to deal with his experience in its larger masses and more comprehensive relationships. He may behold himself as a physical being, a denizen of a planet in a great solar system and an insignificant atom in a vast universe of suns and stars, or in his social nature as one among the many millions of souls now existing in the world. He may view his present in its connection with the past which is fading in memory, and with the long future which stretches out before, filled with unknown posssibilities. In such consciousness of self the existence of other selves is necessarily implied. The very relationships by which the experience of the self is organized are assumed to hold for other selves as well. The real universe in which the self finds its home is assumed to exist for other selves also. In fact, consciousness of self-existence involves constant appeal to the existence of others. From his nature as such, the self-conscious person must identify himself with, and yet at the same time distinguish himself from, other persons. He must recognize that all have the same world, yet each occupies therein his own point of view.

### 6. His Spiritual Capacities

As a conscious self man has certain spiritual capacities the possession of which may rank as the second of the fundamental characteristics of human nature. And as his natural instincts serve to sustain and strengthen his physical existence, so his spiritual capacities maintain and enrich his conscious personality. These capacities are all expressions of the basal activity of volition which, through its work of organization, builds up the unity of selfhood. But in the discharge of its office volition manifests itself in three highly specialized forms which it is permissible to distinguish as different capacities. These spiritual capacities in man are: first, the *Intellectual*, the power of thought, the ability to acquire knowledge; second, the *Technical*, the ablity to contrive, to construct, to invent what is serviceable; third, the *Æsthetic*, the ability to perceive and enjoy what is beautiful. Now the effect of the operation of all three of these capacities is to extend and to enrich the unity of the self. The *intellectual* capacity does this by introducing within the unity of self-consciousness the objects and fixed connections of the real universe. The scientist, with his telescope or microscope, is continually enriching human experience by bringing into it new facts. In a like manner also does every individual enlarge the content of his own personality, who by serious thought discovers a new factor or hidden cause within the ken of his own experience. The *technical* capacity of man extends the unity of his own selfhood by subjecting the agencies of the environment, natural and social, to the ends of intelligence. This the inventor does when he devises a machine by which the forces of nature are compelled to fulfil the purposes of man; the educator, too, when he devises a new method for communicating knowledge—for teaching spelling or arithmetic or grammar. The same ability is exercised by all individuals who, through skill and contrivance, adapt external surroundings to the uses of their own personal intelligence. The *æsthetic* capacity in its way also enriches the content of the unitary self; through exercise of the imagination and perceptive faculties such form and arrangement are given to experiences of color and sound as to create in them new suggestions of meaning, and thus to provide the agent with new sources of satisfaction. This ability is of course displayed primarily in the work of the artist; but in a less degree by all those who enjoy beauty in any of its forms.

Since these activities spring from the nature of the self and all contribute to its extension and development, we should expect that the objects which they seek to realize would be ideal or spiritual. Such is indeed the case; the objects of the three spiritual capacities mentioned are ideal in character and possess none of the limitations of material things. Of course any object which becomes an end of action is of necessity *ideal*. This is just as true of the material object which instinct causes us to desire as it is of the best considered purpose or most comprehensive ideal. But the material object which becomes an end of natural desire is particular in character and limited in time and place; hence it cannot be pursued by all men, but only by a few individuals. Through the power of intelligence, generalizing upon experiences of achievement by race and individual, however, objects of much greater range are furnished as ends for volition in its three-fold capacity—objects extending in their scope to all places and all times and being possible of pursuit by all individuals. In this way simple curiosity about a particular object becomes a wish to know about a whole class of objects, then a number of classes of objects, and at last develops into the craving for knowledge of all possible objects—i.e., for Truth. Interest in the steps which must be taken to secure a particular object grows into a desire to discover the best means or methods for attaining all objects of the same sort: agencies and methods are standardized, technique is developed, and finally Power or

Efficiency is adopted as an end to be sought by all individuals. Liking for a special object which, when seen or heard, gives a peculiar kind of delight develops into an interest in all objects which produce æsthetic pleasure, in their relation to one another, and the conditions of their existence; out of this interest grows the yearning to produce in every sphere the conditions necessary to this species of enjoyment and thus realize Beauty universally.

Truth, Power, and Beauty, the three ideals sought by man as a spiritual being, are therefore ideal in the sense of being *universal,* and thus having a scope and comprehensiveness that natural objects do not possess. In proof of this, compare the ideal of Truth, the object sought in all intellectual activity, with the object of a natural instinct—say, food. Food is material, hence is perishable in character and strictly limited in amount, so that what one individual gains the rest must necessarily lose. Truth, on the contrary, being ideal, survives even the limits of man's natural lifetime, enduring and increasing as the successive generations of men are born and die. It is not restricted in quantity; it cannot be "cornered" by any individual. Rather does the individual, in the measure of his success in obtaining it, increase the possessions of all the rest; for truth requires for its pursuit and discovery the coöperation of many individuals in a community of intelligence. Nor is it otherwise with Power or Efficiency, the end sought in technical activity. The engineer who designs a new type of bridge, and the agricultural expert who devises an improved method of farming are not seeking material things with their narrow limits—combinations of stone and steel, bushels of grain, or tons of hay. Instead their object is ideal—the control of the forces of nature by the power of intelligence. The same may be said of efforts made in the social and political spheres to devise methods and instruments whereby the aims of intelligence may be attained in commerce and government. The purposes which direct these undertakings, because intelligent are universal, and hence the object of the inventor or engineer, the master of industry or the statesman, when attained, is of benefit to all humanity. Thus the originator of the suspension bridge and steam engine pursued and attained ideal objects which, as such, had permanence and universality; for the inventions survived the natural life of the inventor and became the common possession of humanity. Likewise Beauty, which we in our æsthetic capacity seek to create and enjoy, is identical with no block of chiseled marble or piece of painted canvas which can be bought and sold. It is ideal, consisting of the pleasant harmony of imaginative faculties induced by certain aspects of nature and works of art. In seeking it, then, we seek, not a particular object which can be possessed by but one individual, we seek an ideal quality which resides in this object for all persons of cultivated imagination, and thus may be seized on and enjoyed by them all.

Each of the three "spiritual" activities of man has its distinctive end. These three ends constitute the three ruling ideals of self-conscious personality, Truth, Power, and Beauty. In a sense they are coördinate and independent ideals, each having its own distinctive sphere and rightfully demanding supremacy within it. Sometimes, however, the ideal of Goodness is given equal standing with these three or with the first and last, Truth and Beauty. Herein a serious mistake is made; for the ideal of Goodness represents the demands of the agency of volition, of which intellectual, æsthetic, and technical activities are but subordinate expressions. Ultimately, then, the three ideals we have been discussing must all be measured in terms of goodness, and all are subject to the requirements which the complete satisfaction of the power of will imposes on human conduct. By true ideas we mean, in last analysis, ideas that can be realized as ends of action, by efficient agencies or methods the ones that will produce the desired results, and by beautiful presentations those in which the ends of intelligence are immediately apprehended. Thus do intellectual, technical, and æsthetic activities contribute to the satisfaction of volition in its work of organizing and enriching personal life.

## 7. Necessary Stages in Self-Realization

Two characteristics, we find, must be regarded as fundamental to the human self. They are consequences of the fact that man is at once a natural being and a conscious self. The first is the possession by him of a number of natural instincts which relate him to the material objects of his environment and to other individuals of the human species. The second is the development in the human self of certain spiritual capacities which serve to relate it both to other selves and to universal reality. These conditions, fundamental to human nature, determine the course of self-realization for all men. They prescribe what activities must have place in the conduct of every human individual who would realize himself. Hence we are now prepared to learn of the *content* of self-realization, as well as the *form*, to ask what course self-realization must take in human beings thus characterized.

It will be convenient to recognize in advance three leading aspects of self-realization in man, which are consequent upon the above-noted relations in which he stands, as natural being, and conscious self.

Full Self-realization, or the complete organization of human conduct, requires the realization of:

(1) *The Individual Self*. Through such adjustment of the activities in man that all are made means to the promotion of individual interest.

(2) *The Social Self*. Through such adjustment of the interest of the

human individual to the interests of others that his activity is made a means to the furtherance of social welfare.

(3) *The Universal Self.* Through the adjustment of human welfare to the Universal Purpose.

Thus an outline is furnished which may be regarded as provisional until it is filled in and verified in subsequent discussion. Let us now ascertain in further detail what activities are essential to self-realization under the conditions set by the nature of man. Or, since self-realization is achieved by voluntary action, through the pursuit of what succession of ends the self is fully realized.

## 8. (a) The Individual Self

Self-realization within the individual sphere means that the total interest of the individual shall be realized by all of his acts. Now, as we know, the human individual possesses both natural instincts and spiritual capacites. In virtue of these characteristics of his nature, certain objects appeal to him and prompt him to act. In order that his conduct shall express *himself*, it is first necessary that the objects of instinct become the ends of conscious desire. When this is accomplished, he seeks in each succeeding act for the thing which he at the moment desires—be it food, play, companionship, or what-not. But the total interest of the individual is not attained in this way; for these desires often conflict, and to satisfy one to-day may prevent the satisfaction of another to-morrow, or even for days to come. Self-organization, then, requires such adjustment and correlation of these varied and opposing desires that each may receive a measure of fulfilment consistent with the due and proportionate satisfaction of those remaining. This adjustment is not merely a compromise, however, in which all the desires are treated as independent units and thus admitted to have equal rights. Certain desires are given a preference, but—consistent with the principle of Self-realization—upon one ground only, that is, their *greater comprehensiveness*. The measure of fulfilment which self-realization permits to one of the particular desires or purposes of the self is determined entirely by the comprehensiveness of the object concerned, the degree to which it includes other objects sought-for, and hence is expressive of the whole self. As illustrative of difference in this regard, compare the objects of two natural instincts; for example those of food and of resentment or anger. The first is much more comprehensive than the second. Upon the obtainment of a sufficient quantity of the proper food depends the effective exercise of the most of the other activities of the human individual. The other desire has a very narrow range—since the attainment of its object, retaliation, in any but the most restricted form and unusual circumstances, acts as a hindrance to the attainment of other objects desired.

Of all the objects which man seeks through natural instinct, the most comprehensive is *self-preservation*. This instinct leads the individual to desire those pleasant conscious states which are indicative of physical well-being, and equally to shun that consciousness of pain which signifies bodily disorder. Generalizing upon particular experiences of pleasure and pain, he is further led to form the purpose to secure in life the greatest enjoyment, or, in other words, gain the maximum of pleasure. Now pleasure, in the sense of agreeable consciousness, is the most comprehensive of the objects which man is led by instinct to pursue, and therefore the purpose to pursue it deserves to be made supreme over all other desires and purposes having a like source. For the greatest amount of pleasure in the case of the human individual is generally an accompaniment of the highest degree of health, security, and comfort in natural existence. And, since all other instincts which man possesses have been developed to maintain and promote his natural existence, the different objects which they cause him to desire—wealth, amusement, reputation, etc.—fall into subjection as means to the inclusive end of *Pleasure*, or natural well-being. Thus Pleasure emerges as the first of the ends which, in the process of self-realization, represent the whole self in contrast to any of its parts; and we make due recognition of the truth contained in the Hedonistic conception of the Good.

We have already seen, however, that the ideal objects of man's spiritual capacities—Truth, Power, and Beauty—are larger and more comprehensive, not merely than any particular thing which he naturally desires, but even than his natural existence and well-being itself. Self-organization in the individual life requires, therefore, that the end lately made supreme over all natural desires and purposes now be subordinated as a means to the realization of these spiritual capacities. The individual, that is, must make his natural well-being and pleasure a means to the exercise of his intellectual, technical, and æsthetic activities. The ends of these higher activities of the human self taken together may be expressed by the world *Culture*. Culture thus appears as the ideal which transcends all other ends in the conduct of the individual, because representing his largest interest and embracing all lesser goods. To its attainment, the natural existence and well-being of the individual must be made subordinate, including of course such lesser purposes as those to gain wealth, amusement, fame, etc. These have now to be realigned and made instrumental, not to the gaining of Pleasure, but to the attainment of Culture. In thus making Culture supreme among the ends pursued by the individual we provide for the truth in Rationalism, which finds man's Good in spiritual activity rather than natural pleasure. The ideal of Culture on which we dwell, as representing the highest interest of the self as individual, is practically identical with the Highest Good as conceived by Plato and Aristotle.

According to Plato Justice, the supreme and all-inclusive virtue, consists in a strict division of labor and harmonious coöperation between the three principles in the nature of man—it being understood that it is the function of reason to control. Aristotle, in his doctrine of the Mean, would allow to each desire that measure of gratification consistent with the realization of the Supreme End which is the fulfilment of all man's capacities under the direction of reason.

## 9. (b) The Social Self

Man is related as a natural being to other members of the human species, and, as a conscious self, to other selves in a community of intelligence. Self-realization requires that his interest as individual be adjusted to the interests of others in society.

The human individual becomes aware of the existence of others as soon as he becomes conscious of existing himself. One of his leading instincts, moreover,—that of sympathy,—makes him desirous of increasing others' pleasure and lessening their pain. The formation of a general purpose to promote the happiness or well-being of others usually waits upon the development of a definite self-interest in the individual himself. At first the sympathetic impulse is correlated with other natural tendencies of the individual and made a means to the promotion of his own interest, and it is only after a comparatively clear consciousness of self and self-interest arises that there comes also a recognition of the interest of others. This conception of another's interest becomes fuller and more adequate as the development of self-interest proceeds, growing from the idea of another's comfort and happiness merely, to the cultivation of his higher personal capacities. The impulse of sympathy, attaching to such an idea of another's good, makes it attractive as an end of action. Thus a well-defined aim to seek the interests of other individuals appears and exists along with the ideal of self-interest. These varied interests often conflict, so that it seems possible to gain one's own ends as an individual only by thwarting the ambitions of others, and, conversely, others' good can often be realized only at the expense of one's private ambition. Self-organization makes necessary the adjustment of these warring interests. As always, it insists that the less inclusive shall be subordinated to the more inclusive end. Consequently the realization of the self requires the adoption of the ideal of Altruism on the part of the individual—the determination to seek the interests of others with whom he comes into contact as well as his own. This means that he shall surrender his own desire—or partial interest—when it is opposed to the total well-being of another. In cases where *ego* and *alter* seem to have equal interests at stake, Self-realization enforces the doctrine of self-sacrifice, since allowance must be made for the influence of a strong and persistent tendency to over-estimate the interest of self and under-estimate that of others, due to the fact that one's own interest is keenly felt, while that of others is only thought or imagined. There are limits, to be sure, to the extent of self-sacrifice which self-realization requires. It would not, for instance, require the individual to sacrifice his own well-being to the passing whim of another. For here the interest of the self is the more comprehensive end.

Self-realization in the social sphere is not completed when the individual adjusts his own interest to the interests of others of his acquaintance. For the selfhood of which man is conscious is a universal principle present in all human beings and uniting them in a community of intelligence and personality. For full self-realization, therefore, it is not sufficient that man pursue his own highest interest as an individual, or that of other individuals with whom he comes into contact; he must go further and seek the good of human personality, of conscious selfhood, whenever and wherever found. Thus a new end appears, more comprehensive than *Altruism*, which may be called *Humanitarianism*. It means the development of humanity—the full, free, harmonious exercise of all the capacities of human personality. To this ideal, Self-organization requires that the individual subordinate his own interest and the interests of all other particular individuals. The conflict at this point between culture and humanitarianism—between the interest of the individual or a privileged group or class of individuals and the welfare of humanity—while less obvious—may be as acute and persistent as that between egoism and altruism. It cannot be doubted, however, that the fullest expression of the self is found in pursuit of the more comprehensive end, and the highest culture can mean nothing less than the fullest self-development. The artist or the scientist may regard it as a hindrance to be obliged to recognize a social responsibility in their specialized activities. Yet the very capacities, intellectual and æsthetic, which they are exercising are implicitly universal, involving the union of many persons in a common knowledge and appreciation. Can one of these spiritual capacities of man be exercised most effectively, then, unless it contribute to the highest personal development of humanity?

## 10. (c) The Universal Self

Finally, man is related through his spiritual capacities to Universal Reality. His thought discovers the necessary connections of things and shows how all natural objects are part of an inter-related system. Through constructive activity he learns how the objects and forces of nature are adapted as means to the purposes of intelligence. Through his æsthetic faculty he feels the order and harmony of nature. Self-realization in its third and culminating phase requires the adjustment of human interests to this all-comprehensive Reality. Now it is plain that the character of this adjustment will vary in accordance with the degree of development which self-interest has undergone—whether it is still mainly individual or has been broadened to include the welfare of humanity. But since in all cases of incomplete development the adjustment is only provisional we may safely neglect them and consider only the interest of the self when thoroughly socialized. The question is, therefore, that of the adjustment of human welfare to the Real Universe. It must not be thought, however, that here we go outside the boundaries of the self and inquire concerning its relation to an external reality. On the contrary, just because the real universe is a necessary factor in self-consciousness, it must be reckoned with in the process of self-realization. The problem of the relation of man to the universe is of course the problem of religion, and, as such, is an essential aspect of self-realization.

The difficulty of the adjustment in question is that the ultimate character of the All-encompassing Reality is unknown. It cannot be directly observed or logically demonstrated. Hence man can only speculate, and such adjustment as he is able to effect will rest upon an assumption. But speculation upon this subject need not be without rational grounds. In fact, it is man's own moral development that is most illuminating at this point. For, in the process of self-realization, natural objects are sacrificed to spiritual activities because the latter *prove to be more comprehensive.* Is it not reasonable to assume, therefore, that Universal Reality, which is by nature all-comprehensive, is spiritual—that it is the expression of a Universal Self within which all our human interests may be included and harmonized? Of course the existence of such a Universal or Divine self is in last analysis a matter of faith rather than knowledge; but we have seen that faith is called for along the whole course of moral development. The very existence of the self is rooted in an act of will, and each step forward in its realization is a venture, the abandonment of one good which, although restricted, is assured, for the sake of another which, although it promises a larger satisfaction, is uncertain and largely unknown. Religious belief is simply the last of these acts of faith, the final venture, in which man commits his welfare into the hands of the Universe, believing that since Spirit is Universal no natural agency, in life or in death, can lessen or destroy the reality which has been attained by a conscious self.

Man thus subordinates his interest to the Universal or Divine Purpose, adopting the latter, so far as it can be known, as his own good. To describe in detail the character and conditions of this adjustment is the task of religion rather than of Ethics. It involves, for the ordinary man, not a number of specific activities in addition to those prescribed by individual and social duty, but rather, a personal attitude—of resignation to the divine will, and trust in the divine wisdom. The end now pursued is of all the most compre-hensive—the realization of the Universal Purpose, the Cause of Universal Progress.

———

Thus we see that with human nature characterized as it is, the process of self-realization for man is definite in its direction and specific in its requirements. In its three aspects it involves the attainment of a progression of ends, each of which includes and supersedes the one before, until the supreme and all-comprehensive ideal is reached.

In tabulation these ends appear in the following order:

*Self-Realization*

*Agency*—Organizing Activity of Volition.
*Material*—Natural Instincts and Spiritual Capacities of Man.

| *Aspects* | *Ends* |
|---|---|
| Individual . . . . . . . . . . | { Pleasure / Culture |
| Social . . . . . . . . . | { Altruism / Humanitarianism |
| Universal . . . . . . . . . | Universal Progress |

# HASTINGS RASHDALL

HASTINGS RASHDALL (1858–1924) taught at Oxford University. An Anglican clergyman, as well as a teacher of philosophy, he wrote extensively upon ethical and religious subjects. His major works include: *The Theory of Good and Evil* (1907), *Philosophy and Religion* (1910), *Is Conscience an Emotion?* (1914), *Conscience and Christ* (1916), *The Idea of Atonement in Christian Theology* (1919), and *Ideas and Ideals* (1928).

## A Critique of Self-Realization*

We are met by a doctrine very fashionable in philosophical circles which finds the key to all ethical problems in that comfortable word "self-realiza-tion;" . . . I shall here . . . confine myself to the purely ethical aspect of this fascinating formula—"Self-realization is the end of life."

* From *The Theory of Good and Evil*, by Hastings Rashdall, Book II, Chap. 3. Copyright, 1907, Clarendon Press. Used by permission.

In order to subject the doctrine to any profitable criticism, it seems necessary to attempt the by no means easy task of distinguishing the various
possible senses in which this watchword seems to be used by its devotees. The
formula would probably have proved less attractive, had these various senses
been distinguished by those to whom it presents itself as a "short and easy
way" out of all ethical perplexities.

1. Firstly, then, we may suppose that the upholder of self-realization means
exactly what he says. If he does, it seems easy to show that what he is committing himself to is mere self-contradictory nonsense. To realize means to
make real. You cannot make real what is real already, and the self must certainly be regarded as real before we are invited to set about realizing it. Nor
is the task to which we are invited rendered easier when we are assured that
the self, which is to become something that it was not, is out of time, and
consequently (one might have supposed) insusceptible of change.

2. But of course it will be said that what is actually meant by self-
realization is the realization of some potentiality or capacity of the self
which is at present unrealized. In this sense no doubt it is true enough that
Morality must consist in some kind of self-realization. But to say so is to say
something "generally admitted indeed but obscure" . . . as Aristotle would
have put it. In this sense the formula gives us just no information at all.
For whatever you do or abstain from doing, if you only sit still or go to sleep,
you must still be realizing some one of your capacities: since nobody can
by any possibility do anything which he was not first capable of doing.
Morality is self-realization beyond a doubt, but then so is immorality. The
precious formula leaves out the whole differentia of Morality; and it is a
differentia presumably which we are in search of when we ask, "What is
Morality?" and are solemnly told, "It is doing or being something which you
are capable of doing or being."

3. It may be maintained that Morality is the realization of *all* the capacities of human nature. But this is impossible, since one capacity can only be
realized by the non-realization or sacrifice of some other capacity. There can
be no self-realization without self-sacrifice. The good man and the bad alike
realize one element or capacity of their nature, and sacrifice another. The
whole question is which capacity is to be realized and which is to be sacrificed. And as to this our formula gives us just no information.

4. Or more vaguely self-realization may be interpreted to mean an equal,
all-round development of one's whole nature—physical, intellectual, emotional. To such a view I should object that, interpreted strictly and literally,
it is just as impracticable as the last. It is impossible for the most gifted
person to become a first-rate Musician without much less completely realizing any capacity he has of becoming a first-rate Painter. It is impossible to

become really learned in one subject without remaining ignorant of many others: impossible to develop one's athletic capacities to the full without starving and stunting the intellect, impossible (as a simple matter of Physiology) to carry to its highest point the cultivation of one's intellectual faculties without some sacrifice of physical efficiency. There is a similar collision between the demands of intellectual cultivation and those of practical work. . . . Up to a certain point it is no doubt desirable that a man should endeavour to develop different sides of his nature: but that point is soon reached. Beyond that point there must come the inevitable sacrifice —of body to mind or of mind to body, of learning or speculative insight to practical efficiency, or of practical efficiency to learning or insight.

It is the same within the intellectual sphere itself. There too the law of sacrifice prevails. Up to a certain point no doubt the man who is a mere specialist will be a bad specialist, but that point is soon reached. Charles Darwin found that the cultivation of reasoning power and observation had extinguished his once keen imagination and aesthetic sensibility. And yet who would wish—whether in the interests of the world or in the interests of what was best worthy of development in Charles Darwin's own nature— that his work should have been spoiled in order that one of the three hours which was the maximum working day his health allowed should have been absorbed by politics or philanthropy? Who would decide that the origin of species should have been undiscovered, in order that the man who might have discovered it should retain the power of enjoying Wordsworth? This notion of an equal, all-round, "harmonious" development is thus a sheer impossibility, excluded by the very constitution of human nature, and incompatible with the welfare of human society. And, in so far as some approximation to such an ideal of life is possible, it involves a very apotheosis of mediocrity, ineffectiveness, dilettantism.

And there is a more formidable objection to come. If the ideal of self-realization is to be logically carried out, it must involve the cultivation of a man's capacity for what vulgar prejudice calls immorality as well as of his capacity for Morality. It is quite arbitrary to exclude certain kinds of activity as "bad," because what we are in search of was some definition of the good in conduct, and we were told that it was the development of all his capacities. . . .

5. One possible interpretation of our formula remains. Self-realization may mean the realization of a man's highest capacities by the sacrifice of the lower. No doubt, in a sense every school of Moral Philosophy which allows of the distinction between a "higher" and a "lower" at all would admit that Morality does mean the sacrifice of the lower to the higher—though it might be objected that this ideal, taken literally, is too ascetic: the lower capacities of

human nature have a certain value; they ought to be realized to a certain extent—to be subordinated, not "sacrificed," except in so far as their realization is inconsistent with that of the higher. But then there is nothing of all this in the word "self-realization." And even with the gloss that "self-realization" means realization of the "true" or "higher" self, it tells us just nothing at all about the question what this true self-realization is. In fact the formula which is presented to us as the key to the ethical problem of the end of life, turns out on examination to mean merely "The end of life is the end of life." No doubt it has been said that every attempt to define Morality must have the appearance of moving in a circle. In a sense that may be the case. The moral cannot be defined in terms of the non-moral. But then that is just what our formula attempts to do, and that is just the source of its futility.

## SELF-REALIZATION—SUGGESTED READINGS

Bradley, F. H., *Ethical Studies*, 2nd ed., Oxford, Clarendon Press, 1927, esp. Essays II, V, and VII. (proponent)

Green, T. H., *Prolegomena to Ethics*, Oxford, Clarendon Press, 1883. (proponent)

Hill, T. E., *Ethics in Theory and Practice*, New York, Crowell, 1956, Chaps. 8 and 9. (critic)

Plato, *The Republic*. (proponent)

Pratt, J. B., *Reason in the Art of Living*, New York, Macmillan, 1949, Chap. 9. (critic)

Taylor, A. E., "Self-Realization—A Criticism," *International Journal of Ethics*, VI (1895–96), pp. 356–71. (critic)

## 3. FULFILLMENT OF INTEREST

A third type of teleological ethical theory maintains that what is good for man is essentially grounded in human interests, or desires. According to this theory, man does not desire objects because he perceives them to be good; rather, objects become good by being desired. Thus, if there were only one man in the world, whatever he desired would be good. Men *confer* value upon objects by taking an *interest* in them.

But there are many men in the world, not just one, and it is often the case that one man cannot fulfill his interests without depriving another of what he desires. What then is good when interests and desires conflict? Those who hold the theory under consideration answer that the good is the harmonious fulfillment of as many human interests as possible. Actions are to be judged right insofar as they promote this ideal and wrong insofar as they interfere with its attainment. As William James puts it, the aim of morality must be "to satisfy at all times as many demands as we can."

Those who maintain that desire creates what is good, assert that every desire, taken alone, makes a claim to recognition, and that the denial of any such claim is, in itself, bad. Accordingly, the task of morality is to seek new ways to satisfy an ever-wider range of claims; the need is to discover means for the practical resolution and adjustment of desires which now seem incompatible. Thus James calls for *invention* of ways to reconcile conflicting demands, and Perry seeks to describe and recommend what he terms "the method of reflective agreement" as a means of integrating interests without destroying them.

In the readings to follow, JAMES discusses the meaning of such basic ethical concepts as "good," "ill," "obligation," and describes the ultimate moral standard he accepts. PERRY not only offers his views concerning the nature of value and of morality but also discusses how conflicts of interests may be resolved and how the proposed moral standard may be proved. THOMAS examines Perry's views and offers arguments against them. His criticisms may be extended both to James' position and to the general thesis which asserts that what is good depends upon what is desired.

# WILLIAM
# JAMES

WILLIAM JAMES (1842–1910), one of
America's foremost philosophers, taught at
Harvard University. An important psychologist, as well as a philosopher, he founded
the first American experimental laboratory
for psychology in 1876. In philosophy, he
was one of the leading pragmatists and
sought through his writings to show how
the principles of this school might be applied
in the solution of traditional philosophical
problems. His major works include: *The Principles of Psychology* (1890), *The Will to
Believe and Other Essays in Popular Philosophy* (1897), *The Varieties of Religious Experience* (1902), *Pragmatism* (1907), *A
Pluralistic Universe* (1909), and *Essays in
Radical Empiricism* (1912).

## *The Moral Philosopher and the Moral Life**

What [do] we mean by the words "obligation," "good," and "ill"?

First of all, it appears that such words can have no application or relevancy
in a world in which no sentient life exists. Imagine an absolutely material
world, containing only physical and chemical facts, and existing from eternity
without a God, without even an interested spectator: would there be any
sense in saying of that world that one of its states is better than another?
Or if there were two such worlds possible, would there be any rhyme or reason
in calling one good and the other bad—good or bad positively, I mean, and
apart from the fact that one might relate itself better than the other to the
philosopher's private interests? But we must leave these private interests
out of the account, for the philosopher is a mental fact, and we are asking
whether goods and evils and obligations exist in physical facts *per se.* Surely
there is no *status* for good and evil to exist in, in a purely insentient world.
How can one physical fact, considered simply as a physical fact, be "better"
than another? Betterness is not a physical relation. In its mere material
capacity, a thing can no more be good or bad than it can be pleasant or
painful. Good for what? Good for the production of another physical fact,
do you say? But what in a purely physical universe demands the production
of that other fact? Physical facts simply *are* or are *not*; and neither when

* From "The Moral Philosopher and the Moral Life," by William James, an address
to the Yale Philosophical Club, published in *International Journal of Ethics*, I (1891).

present or absent, can they be supposed to make demands. If they do, they can only do so by having desires; and then they have ceased to be purely physical facts, and have become facts of conscious sensibility. Goodness, badness, and obligation must be *realized* somewhere in order really to exist; and the first step in ethical philosophy is to see that no merely inorganic "nature of things" can realize them. Neither moral relations nor the moral law can swing *in vacuo*. Their only habitat can be a mind which feels them; and no world composed of merely physical facts can possibly be a world to which ethical propositions apply.

The moment one sentient being, however, is made a part of the universe, there is a chance for goods and evils really to exist. Moral relations now have their *status*, in that being's consciousness. So far as he feels anything to be good, he *makes* it good. It *is* good, for him; and being good for him, is absolutely good, for he is the sole creator of values in that universe, and outside of his opinion things have no moral character at all.

In such a universe as that it would of course be absurd to raise the question of whether the solitary thinker's judgments of good and ill are true or not. Truth supposes a standard outside of the thinker to which he must conform; but here the thinker is a sort of divinity, subject to no higher judge. Let us call the supposed universe which he inhabits a *moral solitude*. In such a moral solitude it is clear that there can be no outward obligation, and that the only trouble the god-like thinker is liable to have will be over the consistency of his own several ideals with one another. Some of these will no doubt be more pungent and appealing than the rest, their goodness will have a profounder, more penetrating taste; they will return to haunt him with more obstinate regrets if violated. So the thinker will have to order his life with them as its chief determinants, or else remain inwardly discordant and unhappy. Into whatever equilibrium he may settle, though, and however he may straighten out his system, it will be a right system; for beyond the facts of his own subjectivity there is nothing moral in the world.

If now we introduce a second thinker with his likes and dislikes into the universe, the ethical situation becomes much more complex, and several possibilities are immediately seen to obtain.

One of these is that the thinkers may ignore each other's attitude about good and evil together, and each continue to indulge his own preferences, indifferent to what the other may feel or do. In such a case we have a world with twice as much of the ethical quality in it as our moral solitude, only it is without ethical unity. The same object is good or bad there, according as you measure it by the view which this one or that one of the thinkers takes. Nor can you find any possible ground in such a world for saying that one thinker's opinion is more correct than the other's, or that either has the truer moral sense. Such a world, in short, is not a moral universe but a moral dualism. Not only is there no single point of view within it from which the values of things can be unequivocally judged, but there is not even a demand for such a point of view, since the two thinkers are supposed to be indifferent to each other's thoughts and acts. Multiply the thinkers into a pluralism, and we find realized for us in the ethical sphere something like that world which the antique sceptics conceived of—in which individual minds are the measures of all things, and in which no one "objective" truth, but only a multitude of "subjective" opinions, can be found.

But this is the kind of world with which the philosopher, so long as he holds to the hope of a philosophy, will not put up. Among the various ideals represented, there must be, he thinks, some which have the more truth or authority; and to these the others *ought* to yield, so that system and sub-ordination may reign. Here in the word "ought" the notion of *obligation* comes emphatically into view, and the next thing in order must be to make its meaning clear.

Since the outcome of the discussion so far has been to show us that nothing can be good or right except so far as some consciousness feels it to be good or thinks it to be right, we perceive on the very threshold that the real superiority and authority which are postulated by the philosopher to reside in some of the opinions, and the really inferior character which he supposes must belong to others, cannot be explained by any abstract moral "nature of things" existing antecedently to the concrete thinkers themselves with their ideals. Like the positive attributes good and bad, the comparative ones better and worse must be *realized* in order to be real. If one ideal judgment be objectively better than another, that betterness must be made flesh by being lodged concretely in some one's actual perception. It cannot float in the atmosphere, for it is not a sort of meteorological phenomenon, like the aurora borealis or the zodiacal light. Its *esse* is *percipi*, like the *esse* of the ideals themselves between which it obtains. The philosopher, therefore, who seeks to know which ideal ought to have supreme weight and which one ought to be subordinated, must trace the *ought* itself to the *de facto* constitution of some existing consciousness, behind which, as one of the data of the universe, he as a purely ethical philosopher is unable to go. This consciousness must make the one ideal right by feeling it to be right, the other wrong by feeling it to be wrong. But now what particular consciousness in the universe *can* enjoy this prerogative of obliging others to conform to a rule which it lays down?

If one of the thinkers were obviously divine, while all the rest were human, there would probably be no practical dispute about the matter. The divine thought would be the model, to which the others should conform. But still the theoretic question would remain, What is the ground of the obligation, even here?

In our first essays at answering this question, there is an inevitable tendency to slip into an assumption which ordinary men follow when they are disputing with one another about questions of good and bad. They imagine an abstract moral order in which the objective truth resides; and each tries to prove that this pre-existing order is more accurately reflected in his own ideas than in those of his adversary. It is because one disputant is backed by this overarching abstract order that we think the other should submit. Even so, when it is a question no longer of two finite thinkers, but of God and ourselves—we follow our usual habit, and imagine a sort of *de jure* relation, which antedates and overarches the mere facts, and would make it right that we should conform our thoughts to God's thoughts, even though he made no claim to that effect, and though we preferred *de facto* to go on thinking for ourselves.

But the moment we take a steady look at the question, *we see not only that without a claim actually made by some concrete person there can be no obligation, but that there is some obligation wherever there is a claim.* Claim and obligation are, in fact, coextensive terms; they cover each other exactly. Our ordinary attitude of regarding ourselves as subject to an overarching system of moral relations, true "in themselves," is therefore either an out-and-out superstition, or else it must be treated as a merely provisional abstraction from that real Thinker in whose actual demand upon us to think as he does our obligation must be ultimately based. In a theistic-ethical philosophy that thinker in question is, of course, the Deity to whom the existence of the universe is due.

I know well how hard it is for those who are accustomed to what I have called the superstitious view, to realize that every *de facto* claim creates in so far forth an obligation. We inveterately think that something which we call the "validity" of the claim is what gives to it its obligatory character, and that this validity is something outside of the claim's mere existence as a matter of fact. It rains down upon the claim, we think, from some sublime dimension of being, which the moral law inhabits, much as upon the steel of the compass-needle the influence of the Pole rains down from out of the starry heavens. But again, how can such an inorganic abstract character of imperativeness, additional to the imperativeness which is in the concrete claim itself, *exist?* Take any demand, however slight, which any creature, however weak, may make. Ought it not, for its own sole sake, to be satisfied? If not, prove why not. The only possible kind of proof you could adduce would be the exhibition of another creature who should make a demand that ran the other way. The only possible reason there can be why any phenomenon ought to exist is that such a phenomenon actually is desired. Any desire is imperative to the extent of its amount; it *makes* itself valid by the fact that it exists at all. Some desires, truly enough, are small desires; they are put forward by insignificant persons, and we customarily make light of the obligations which they bring. But the fact that such personal demands as these impose small obligations does not keep the largest obligations from being personal demands.

If we must talk impersonally, to be sure we can say that "the universe" requires, exacts, or makes obligatory such or such an action, whenever it expresses itself through the desires of such or such a creature. But it is better not to talk about the universe in this personified way, unless we believe in a universal or divine consciousness which actually exists. If there be such a consciousness, then its demands carry the most of obligation simply because they are the greatest in amount. But it is even then not *abstractly* right that we should respect them. It is only *concretely* right—or right after the fact, and by virtue of the fact, that they are actually made. Suppose we do not respect them, as seems largely to be the case in this queer world. That ought not to be, we say; that is wrong. But in what way is this fact of wrongness made more acceptable or intelligible when we imagine it to consist rather in the laceration of an *a priori* ideal order than in the disappointment of a living personal God? Do we, perhaps, think that we cover God and protect him and make his impotence over us less ultimate, when we back him up with this *a priori* blanket from which he may draw some warmth of further appeal? But the only force of appeal to *us*, which either a living God or an abstract ideal order can wield, is found in the "everlasting ruby vaults" of our own human hearts, as they happen to beat responsive and not irresponsive to the claim. So far as they do feel it when made by a living consciousness, it is life answering to life. A claim thus livingly acknowledged is acknowledged with a solidity and fulness which no thought of an "ideal" backing can render more complete; while if, on the other hand, the heart's response is withheld, the stubborn phenomenon is there of an impotence in the claims which the universe embodies, which no talk about an eternal nature of things can gloze over or dispel. An ineffective *a priori* order is as impotent a thing as an ineffective God; and in the eye of philosophy, it is as hard a thing to explain.

We may now consider that . . . we have learned what the words "good," "bad," and "obligation" severally mean. They mean no absolute natures, independent of personal support. They are objects of feeling and desire, which have no foothold or anchorage in Being, apart from the existence of actually living minds.

Wherever such minds exist, with judgments of good and ill, and demands upon one another, there is an ethical world in its essential features. Were all other things, gods and men and starry heavens, blotted out from this universe, and were there left but one rock with two loving souls upon it, that rock would have as thoroughly moral a constitution as any possible world which the eternities and immensities could harbor. It would be a tragic constitution, because the rock's inhabitants would die. But while they lived, there would be real good things and real bad things in the universe; there would be obligations, claims, and expectations; obediences, refusals, and disappointments; compunctions and longings for harmony to come again, and inward peace of conscience when it was restored; there would, in short, be a moral life, whose active energy would have no limit but the intensity of interest in each other with which the hero and heroine might be endowed.

We, on this terrestrial globe, so far as the visible facts go, are just like the inhabitants of such a rock. Whether a God exist, or whether no God exist, in yon blue heaven above us bent, we form at any rate an ethical republic here below. And the first reflection which this leads to is that ethics have as genuine and real a foothold in a universe where the highest consciousness is human, as in a universe where there is a God as well. "The religion of humanity" affords a basis for ethics as well as theism does. . . .

———

The last fundamental question in Ethics [is] the *casuistic* question.* Here we are, in a world where the existence of a divine thinker has been and perhaps always will be doubted by some of the lookers-on, and where, in spite of the presence of a large number of ideals in which human beings agree, there are a mass of others about which no general consensus obtains. It is hardly necessary to present a literary picture of this, for the facts are too well known. The wars of the flesh and the spirit in each man, the concupiscences of different individuals pursuing the same unshareable material or social prizes, the ideals which contrast so according to races, circumstances, temperaments, philosophical beliefs, etc.—all form a maze of apparently inextricable confusion with no obvious Ariadne's thread to lead one out. Yet the philosopher, just because he is a philosopher, adds his own peculiar ideal to the confusion (with which if he were willing to be a sceptic he would be passably content), and insists that over all these individual opinions there is a *system of truth* which he can discover if he only takes sufficient pains.

We stand ourselves at present in the place of that philosopher, and must

* In an omitted earlier section of this essay, James offers the following definition: "the casuistic question asks what is the *measure* of the various goods and ills which men recognize, so that the philosopher may settle the true order of human obligations." Editors' footnote.

not fail to realize all the features that the situation comports. In the first place we will not be sceptics; we hold to it that there is a truth to be ascertained. But in the second place we have just gained the insight that that truth cannot be a self-proclaiming set of laws, or an abstract "moral reason," but can only exist in act, or in the shape of an opinion held by some thinkers really to be found. There is, however, no visible thinker invested with authority. Shall we then simply proclaim our own ideals as the lawgiving ones? No; for if we are true philosophers we must throw our own spontaneous ideals, even the dearest, impartially in with that total mass of ideals which are fairly to be judged. But how then can we as philosophers ever find a test; how avoid complete moral scepticism on the one hand, and on the other escape bringing a wayward personal standard of our own along with us, on which we simply pin our faith?

The dilemma is a hard one, nor does it grow a bit more easy as we revolve it in our minds. The entire undertaking of the philosopher obliges him to seek an impartial test. That test, however, must be incarnated in the demand of some actually existent person; and how can he pick out the person save by an act in which his own sympathies and prepossessions are implied?

One method indeed presents itself, and has as a matter of history been taken by the more serious ethical schools. If the heap of things demanded proved on inspection less chaotic than at first they seemed, if they furnished their own relative test and measure, then the casuistic problem would be solved. If it were found that all goods *quâ* goods contained a common essence, then the amount of this essence involved in any one good would show its rank in the scale of goodness, and order could be quickly made; for this essence would be *the* good upon which all thinkers were agreed, the relatively objective and universal good that the philosopher seeks. Even his own private ideals would be measured by their share of it, and find their rightful place among the rest.

Various essences of good have thus been found and proposed as bases of the ethical system. Thus, to be a mean between two extremes; to be recognized by a special intuitive faculty; to make the agent happy for the moment; to make others as well as him happy in the long run; to add to his perfection or dignity; to harm no one; to follow from reason or flow from universal law; to be in accordance with the will of God; to promote the survival of the human species on this planet—are so many tests, each of which has been maintained by somebody to constitute the essence of all good things or actions so far as they are good.

No one of the measures that have been actually proposed has, however, given general satisfaction. Some are obviously not universally present in all cases—e.g., the character of harming no one, or that of following a universal law; for the best course is often cruel; and many acts are reckoned good on the sole condition that they be exceptions, and serve not as examples of a universal law. Other characters, such as following the will of God, are unascertainable and vague. Others again, like survival, are quite indeterminate in their consequences, and leave us in the lurch where we most need their help: a philosopher of the Sioux Nation, for example, will be certain to use the survival-criterion in a very different way from ourselves. The best, on the whole, of these marks and measures of goodness seems to be the capacity to bring happiness. But in order not to break down fatally, this test must be taken to cover innumerable acts and impulses that never *aim* at happiness; so that, after all, in seeking for a universal principle we inevitably are carried onward to the *most* universal principle—that *the essence of good is simply to satisfy demand.* The demand may be for anything under the sun. There is really no more ground for supposing that all our demands can be accounted for by one universal underlying kind of motive than there is ground for supposing that all physical phenomena are cases of a single law. The elementary forces in ethics are probably as plural as those of physics are. The various ideals have no common character apart from the fact that they are ideals. No single abstract principle can be so used as to yield to the philosopher anything like a scientifically accurate and genuinely useful casuistic scale.

A look at another peculiarity of the ethical universe, as we find it, will still further show us the philosopher's perplexities. As a purely theoretic problem, namely, the casuistic question would hardly ever come up at all. If the ethical philosopher were only asking after the best *imaginable* system of goods he would indeed have an easy task; for all demands as such are *prima facie* respectable, and the best simply imaginary world would be one in which *every* demand was gratified as soon as made. Such a world would, however, have to have a physical constitution entirely different from that of the one which we inhabit. It would need not only a space, but a time, of *n*-dimensions, to include all the acts and experiences incompatible with one another here below, which would then go on in conjunction—such as spending our money, yet growing rich; taking our holiday, yet getting ahead with our work; shooting and fishing, yet doing no hurt to the beasts; gaining no end of experience, yet keeping our youthful freshness of heart; and the like. There can be no question that such a system of things, however brought about, would be the absolutely ideal system; and that if a philosopher could create universes *a priori*, and provide all the mechanical conditions, that is the sort of universe which he should unhesitatingly create.

But this world of ours is made on an entirely different pattern, and the casuistic question here is most tragically practical. The actually possible in this world is vastly narrower than all that is demanded; and there is always a *pinch* between the ideal and the actual which can only be got through by leaving part of the ideal behind. There is hardly a good which we can imagine except as competing for the possession of the same bit of space and time with some other imagined good. Every end of desire that presents itself appears exclusive of some other end of desire. Shall a man drink and smoke, *or* keep his nerves in condition?—he cannot do both. Shall he follow his fancy for Amelia, *or* for Henrietta?—both cannot be the choice of his heart. Shall he have the dear old Republican party, *or* a spirit of unsophistication in public affairs?—he cannot have both, etc. So that the ethical philosopher's demand for the right scale of subordination in ideals is the fruit of an altogether practical need. Some part of the ideal must be butchered, and he needs to know which part. It is a tragic situation, and no mere speculative conundrum, with which he has to deal.

Now *we* are blinded to the real difficulty of the philosopher's task by the fact that we are born into a society whose ideals are largely ordered already. If we follow the ideal which is conventionally highest, the others which we butcher either die and do not return to haunt us; or if they come back and accuse us of murder, every one applauds us for turning to them a deaf ear. In other words, our environment encourages us not to be philosophers but partisans. The philosopher, however, cannot, so long as he clings to his own ideal of objectivity, rule out any ideal from being heard. He is confident, and rightly confident, that the simple taking counsel of his own intuitive preferences would be certain to end in a mutilation of the fulness of the truth. The poet Heine is said to have written "Bunsen" in the place of "*Gott*" in his copy of that author's work entitled *God in History*, so as to make it read "Bunsen in der Geschichte." Now, with no disrespect to the good and learned Baron, is it not safe to say that any single philosopher, however wide his sympathies, must be just such a *Bunsen in der Geschichte* of the moral world, so soon as he attempts to put his own ideas of order into that howling mob of desires, each struggling to get breathing-room for the ideal to which it clings? The very best of men must not only be insensible, but be ludicrously and peculiarly insensible, to many goods. As a militant, fighting free-handed that the goods to which he *is* sensible may not be submerged and lost from out of life, the philosopher, like every other human being, is in a natural position. But think of Zeno and of Epicurus, think of Calvin and of Paley, think of Kant and Schopenhauer, of Herbert Spencer and John Henry Newman, no longer as one-sided champions of special ideals, but as schoolmasters deciding what all must think—and what more grotesque topic could a satirist wish for on which to exercise his pen? The fabled attempt of Mrs. Partington to arrest the rising tide of the North Atlantic with her broom was a reasonable spectacle compared with their effort to substitute the content of their clean-shaven systems for that exuberant mass of goods with which all human nature is in travail, and groaning to bring to the light of day. Think, furthermore, of such individual moralists, no longer as mere schoolmasters, but as pontiffs armed with the temporal power, and having authority in every concrete case of conflict to order which good shall be butchered and which shall be suffered to survive—and the notion really turns one pale. All one's slumbering revolutionary instincts waken at the thought of any single moralists wielding such powers of life and death. Better chaos forever than an order based on any closet-philosopher's rule, even though he were the most enlightened possible member of his tribe. No! if the philosopher is to keep his judicial position, he must never become one of the parties to the fray.

What can he do, then, it will now be asked, except to fall back on scepticism and give up the notion of being a philosopher at all?

But do we not already see a perfectly definite path of escape which is open to him just because he is a philosopher, and not the champion of one particular ideal? Since everything which is demanded is by that fact a good, must not the guiding principle for ethical philosophy (since all demands conjointly cannot be satisfied in this poor world) be simply to satisfy at all times *as many demands as we can?* That act must be the best act, accordingly, which makes for the *best whole*, in the sense of awakening the least sum of dissatisfactions. In the casuistic scale, therefore, those ideals must be written highest which *prevail at the least cost*, or by whose realization the least possible number of other ideals are destroyed. Since victory and defeat there must be, the victory to be philosophically prayed for is that of the more inclusive side—of the side which even in the hour of triumph will to some degree do justice to the ideals in which the vanquished party's interests lay. The course of history is nothing but the story of men's struggles from generation to generation to find the more and more inclusive order. *Invent some manner* of realizing your own ideals which will also satisfy the alien demands—that and that only is the path of peace! Following this path, society has shaken itself into one sort of relative equilibrium after another by a series of social discoveries quite analogous to those of science. Polyandry and polygamy and slavery, private warfare and liberty to kill, judicial torture and arbitrary royal power have slowly succumbed to actually aroused complaints; and though some one's ideals are unquestionably the worse off for each improvement, yet a vastly greater total number of them find shelter in our civilized society than in the older savage ways. So far then, and up to date, the casuistic scale is made for the philosopher already far better than he can ever make it for himself. An experiment of the most searching kind has proved that the laws and usages of the land are what yield the maximum of satisfaction to the thinkers taken all together. The presumption in cases of conflict must always be in favor of the conventionally recognized good. The philosopher must be a conservative, and in the construction of his casuistic scale must put the things most in accordance with the customs of the community on top.

And yet if he be a true philosopher he must see that there is nothing final in any actually given equilibrium of human ideals, but that, as our present laws and customs have fought and conquered other past ones, so they will in their turn be overthrown by any newly discovered order which will hush up the complaints that they still give rise to, without producing others louder still. "Rules are made for man, not man for rules"—that one sentence is enough to immortalize Green's *Prolegomena to Ethics*. And although a man always risks much when he breaks away from established rules and strives to realize a larger ideal whole than they permit, yet the philosopher must allow that it is at all times open to any one to make the experiment, provided he fear not to stake his life and character upon the throw. The pinch is always here. Pent in under every system of moral rules are innumerable persons whom it weighs upon, and goods which it represses; and these are always rumbling and grumbling in the background, and ready for any issue by which they may get free. See the abuses which the institution of private property covers, so that even today it is shamelessly asserted among us that one of the prime functions of the national government is to help the adroiter citizens to grow rich. See the unnamed and unnamable sorrows which the tyranny, on the whole so beneficent, of the marriage-institution brings to so many, both of the married and the unwed. See the wholesale loss of opportunity under our *régime* of so-called equality and industrialism, with the drummer and the counter-jumper in the saddle, for so many faculties and graces which could flourish in the feudal world. See our kindliness for the humble and the outcast, how it wars with that stern weeding-out which until now has been the condition of every perfection in the breed. See everywhere the struggle and the squeeze; and everlastingly the problem how to make them less. The anarchists, nihilists, and free-lovers; the free-silverites, socialists, and single-tax men; the free-traders and civil-service reformers; the prohibitionists and anti-vivisectionists; the radical Darwinians with their idea of the suppression of the weak—these and all the conservative sentiments of society arrayed against them, are simply deciding through actual experiment by what sort of conduct the maximum amount of good can be gained and kept in this world. These experiments are to be judged, not *a priori*, but by actual finding, after the fact of their making, how much more outcry or how much appeasement comes about. What closet-solutions can possibly anticipate the result of trials made on such a scale? Or what can any superficial theorist's judgment be worth, in a world where every one of hundreds of ideals has its special champion already provided in the shape of some genius expressly born to feel it, and to fight to death in its behalf? The pure philosopher can only follow the windings of the spectacle, confident that the line of least resistance will always be towards the richer and the more inclusive arrangement, and that by one tack after another some approach to the kingdom of heaven is incessantly made.

———

All this amounts to saying that, so far as the casuistic question goes, ethical science is just like physical science, and instead of being deducible all at once from abstract principles, must simply bide its time, and be ready to revise its conclusions from day to day. The presumption of course, in both sciences, always is that the vulgarly accepted opinions are true, and the right casuistic order that which public opinion believes in; and surely it would be folly quite as great, in most of us, to strike out independently and to aim at originality in ethics as in physics. Every now and then, however, some one is born with the right to be original, and his revolutionary thought or action may bear prosperous fruit. He may replace old "laws of nature" by better ones; he may, by breaking old moral rules in a certain place, bring in a total condition of things more ideal than would have followed had the rules been kept.

On the whole, then, we must conclude that no philosophy of ethics is possible in the old-fashioned absolute sense of the term. Everywhere the ethical philosopher must wait on facts. The thinkers who create the ideals come he knows not whence, their sensibilities are evolved he knows not how; and the question as to which of two conflicting ideals will give the best universe then and there, can be answered by him only through the aid of the experience of other men. . . . In point of fact, there are no absolute evils, and no non-moral goods; and the *highest* ethical life—however few may be called to bear its burdens—consists at all times in the breaking of rules which have grown too narrow for the actual case. There is but one unconditional commandment, which is that we should seek incessantly, with fear and trembling, so to vote and to act as to bring about the very largest total universe of good which we can see. Abstract rules indeed can help; but they help the less in proportion as our intuitions are more piercing, and our vocation is the stronger for the moral life. For every real dilemma is in literal strictness a unique situation; and the exact combination of ideals realized and ideals disappointed which each decision creates is always a universe without a precedent, and for which no adequate previous rule exists. The philosopher, then, *quâ* philosopher, is no better able to determine the best universe in the concrete emergency than other men. He sees, indeed, somewhat better than most men what the question always is—not a question of this good or that good simply taken, but of the two total universes with which these goods respectively belong. He knows that he must vote always for the richer universe, for the good which seems most organizable, most fit to enter into complex combinations, most apt to be a member of a more inclusive whole. But which particular universe this is he cannot know for certain in advance; he only knows that if he makes a bad mistake the cries of the wounded will soon inform him of the fact. In all this the philosopher is just like the rest of us non-philosophers, so far as we are just and sympathetic instinctively, and so far as we are open to the voice of complaint. His function is in fact indistinguishable from that of the best kind of statesman at the present day. His books upon ethics, therefore, so far as they truly touch the moral life, must more and more ally themselves with a literature which is confessedly tentative and suggestive rather than dogmatic—I mean with novels and dramas of the deeper sort, with sermons, with books on statecraft and philanthropy and social and economical reform. Treated in this way ethical treatises may be voluminous and luminous as well; but they never can be *final*, except in their abstractest and vaguest features; and they must more and more abandon the old-fashioned, clear-cut, and would-be "scientific" form.

# RALPH BARTON PERRY

RALPH BARTON PERRY (1876–1957) taught at Harvard University. He wrote extensively upon problems in the theory of knowledge, ethics, and social philosophy. In 1936, he received the Pulitzer Prize for *The Thought and Character of William James*, a biography of his teacher and colleague. Among his other major works are: *The Moral Economy* (1909), *General Theory of Value* (1926), *Puritanism and Democracy* (1944), and *Realms of Value* (1954).

## General Theory of Value*

### Value as Any Object of Any Interest

§ 49. *Exposition and Illustration.* It is characteristic of living mind to be *for* some things and *against* others. This polarity is not reducible to that be-

---

* From *General Theory of Value*, by Ralph Barton Perry, Chap. 5. Copyright, 1926, by the President and Fellows of Harvard College; 1954, by Ralph Barton Perry. Used by permission of the Harvard University Press.

tween 'yes' and 'no' in the logical or in the purely cognitive sense, because one can say 'yes' with reluctance or be glad to say 'no.' To be 'for' or 'against' is to view with favor or disfavor; it is a bias of the subject toward or away from. It implies . . . a tendency to create or conserve, or an opposite tendency to prevent or destroy. This duality appears in many forms, such as liking and disliking, desire and aversion, will and refusal, or seeking and avoiding. It is to this all-pervasive characteristic of the motor-affective life, this *state, act, attitude or disposition of favor or disfavor*, to which we propose to give the name of '*interest*.'

This, then, we take to be the original source and constant feature of all value. That which is an object of interest is *eo ipso* invested with value. Any object, whatever it be, acquires value when any interest, whatever it be, is taken in it; just as anything whatsoever becomes a target when anyone whosoever aims at it. In other words, Aristotle was fundamentally mistaken when he said, that a thing's "apparent good" makes it an object of appetite, so its real good makes it the object of "rational desire." By the same token Spinoza was fundamentally correct when he said that

in no case do we strive for, wish for, long for, or desire anything because we deem it to be good, but on the other hand we deem a thing to be good, because we strive for it, wish for it, long for it, or desire it.[1]

The view may otherwise be formulated in the equation: $x$ is valuable $=$ interest is taken in $x$. Value is thus a specific relation into which things possessing any ontological status whatsoever, whether real or imaginary, may enter with interested subjects.

This is value *simpliciter*,—value in the elementary, primordial and generic sense. It follows that any variation of interest or of its object will determine a variety of value; that any derivative of interest or its object will determine value in a derived sense; and that any condition of interest or its object will determine a conditional value. In short, interest being constitutive of value in the basic sense, theory of value will take this as its point of departure and centre of reference; and will classify and systematize values in terms of the different forms which interests and their objects may be found to assume.

This view has rarely found a perfectly clear and consistent expression. It is, however, essentially conveyed in an early work of Mr. George Santayana:

Apart from ourselves, and our human bias, we can see in such a mechanical world no element of value whatever. On removing consciousness, we have removed the possibility of worth. But it is not only in the absence of all conscious-

---

[1] *Ethics*, Part III, Prop. IX, Note, trans. by R. H. M. Elwes, 1901. It is, of course, possible to desire a thing because it is good, where its goodness consists in its being desired by other subjects, or by some other interest of the same subject. But *in the last analysis* good springs from desire and not desire from good.

ness that value would be removed from the world; by a less violent abstraction from the totality of human experience, we might conceive beings of a purely intellectual cast, minds in which the transformations of nature were mirrored without any emotion. . . . No event would be repulsive, no situation terrible. . . . In this case, as completely as if consciousness were absent altogether, all value and excellence would be gone. . . . Values spring from the immediate and inexplicable reaction of vital impulse, and from the irrational part of our nature. . . . The ideal of rationality is itself as arbitrary, as much dependent on the needs of a finite organization, as any other ideal.[2]

A more recent statement, and one more explicitly in accord with the view here proposed, is the following:

Anything is properly said to have value in case, and only in case, it is the object of the affective motor response which we call being *interested* in, positively or negatively. . . . The being liked, or disliked, of the object is its value. And since the being liked or disliked, is being the object of a motor-affective attitude in a subject, some sort of a subject is always requisite to there being value at all—not necessarily a *judging* subject, but a subject capable of at least motor-affective response. For the cat the cream has value, or better and more simply, the cat values the cream, or the warmth, or having her back scratched, quite regardless of her probable inability to conceive cream or to make judgments concerning warmth.[3]

§ 50. *Approximations and Misconceptions.* It may appear surprising that a doctrine so familiar, if not banal, as that just stated, should have received so little authoritative support. Rarity is the last thing that would have been expected of it, either by its advocates who regard it as sound common-sense, or by its opponents who regard it as vulgar error. It is none the less a fact that this doctrine has rarely been explicitly avowed by philosophers. The reasons for this fact are extremely illuminating. . . .

All of these reasons are traceable to an imperfect conception of the prob-lem itself. Theory of value in the contemporary sense has asked a new ques-tion, to which none of the traditional philosophical doctrines is precisely relevant. It may, perhaps, be fair to say that this question has been *tacitly* asked and answered; but it is evident that a tacit answer cannot be quoted. This new question is the question, *In what consists value in the generic sense?* It is because neither philosophy nor common-sense has ordinarily been ex-plicitly and unambiguously concerned with this question that so few explicit and unambiguous answers to it can be found. Most theories of value are in-tended not as answers to this question, but as answers to some one or more of the following questions: What is uniquely valuable? What is superlatively

[2] *The Sense of Beauty*, 1899, pp. 17–19. Cf. also William James: "*The essence of good is to satisfy demand*" (*Will to Believe*, etc., 1898, p. 201).

[3] D. W. Prall, A *Study in the Theory of Value*, Univ. of California Publications in Philosophy, Vol. 3, No. 2, 1921, pp. 215, 227. The present writer is in essential agreement with the whole of this admirable monograph.

valuable? What is reflectively or consciously valuable? The history of thought abounds in opinions which identify value with interest, but in nearly all cases these opinions are formulated in terms of one of these questions, and cannot, therefore, be cited as generic definitions of value in the sense here proposed.

# Realms of Value*

## The Meaning of Morality

### III

Morality is man's endeavor to harmonize conflicting interests: to prevent conflict when it threatens, to remove conflict when it occurs, and to advance from the negative harmony of non-conflict to the positive harmony of coöperation. Morality is the solution of the problem created by conflict—conflict among the interests of the same or of different persons. The solution of the personal problem lies in the substitution for a condition of warring and mutually destructive impulses a condition in which each impulse, being assigned a limited place, may be innocent and contributory. For the weakness of inner discord it substitutes the strength of a unified life in which the several interests of an individual make common cause together. The same description applies to the morality of a social group, all along the line from the domestic family to the family of nations.

Such a moralization of life takes place, insofar as it does take place, through organization—personal and social. This crucial idea of organization must not be conceived loosely, or identified with organism. In organism, as in a work of art, the part serves the whole; in moral organization the whole serves the parts, or the whole only for the sake of the parts. The parts are interests, and they are organized in order that they, the constituent interests themselves, may be saved and fulfilled.

When interests are thus organized there emerges an interest of the totality, or moral interest, whose superiority lies in its being greater than any of its parts—greater by the principle of inclusiveness. It is authorized to speak for all of the component interests when its voice is their joint voice. The height of any claim in the moral scale is proportional to the breadth of its representation. What suits all of a person's interest is exalted above what merely suits a fraction; what suits everybody is exalted above what merely suits somebody.

Certain philosophies and religions of the past have conceived the world as originally a moral order, that is, as *constitutionally* harmonious, all desires and wills being so fitted to one another that each acting for itself is at the same time harmless or helpful to the rest. Such a guarantee of cosmic harmony has been an article of faith in Christian theism, as exemplified in the terrestrial and celestial paradises. In the thought of the eighteenth century this was represented in terms of an idyllic "state of nature." In Kant it was a "kingdom of ends" ruled by the moral imperative. After Kant it assumed another form in the idealistic doctrine of an "absolute spirit." Still later it found expression in the Spencerian doctrine of a "perfectly adjusted society," conceived as the end product of natural evolution.

But Christian theism and the eighteenth century doctrine of nature both found it necessary to acknowledge an unfortunate lapse or "fall," from which men must be redeemed through salvation or through civil institutions. The Kantian kingdom of ends was assigned to a "noumenal" world beyond the reach of knowledge, and affirmed by an act of faith. The idealistic philosophy found it necessary to acknowledge the disharmony of the phenomenal world and to transpose the realization of harmony to a supersensible realm. And science has long since abandoned the idea that harmony is a predetermined outcome of the evolutionary process. Whether as recovery from a fall, or as a bridge from the temporal to the eternal, or as a conscious control of natural forces, it is now recognized as necessary to invoke the human will in order that harmony shall be *made out of* disharmony. Harmony thus becomes an ideal future good; a goal the attainment of which is conditioned by plasticity of circumstance, fidelity of purpose, efficiency of control, and growth of enlightenment.

Morality conceived as the harmonization of interests for the sake of the interests harmonized can be described as a cult of freedom. It does not force interests into a procrustean bed, but gives interests space and air in which to be more abundantly themselves. Its purpose is to provide room. And ideally the benefits of morality are extended to all interests. Hence moral progress takes the double form, of liberalizing the existing organization, and of extending it to interests hitherto excluded. Both of these principles have important applications to the "dynamics" of morality, or to the moral force in human history. The extension of moral organization is made possible by increase of contact and interaction, which, however, then multiplies the possibilities of conflict. Hence the peculiar destiny of man, whose ascent is rendered possible by the same conditions which make possible his fall. There can be no development of a unified personality or society without the risk of inner tensions; no neighborhood, nation, or society of all mankind, without the risk of war.

Morality as progressive achievement requires the integration of interests. They cannot be simply added together. If they are to compose a harmonious will that represents them all, they must be brought into line. At the same time, if such a will is truly to embrace them, which is the ground of its higher claim, they must themselves accept the realignment. Morality is an integration of interests, in which they are rendered harmonious without losing their identity. The procedure by which this is effected is the method of *reflective agreement*, appearing in the personal will, and in the social will.

## IV

Interests are integrated by reflection. In the creation of the personal will there occurs a thinking over, in which the several interests of the same person are reviewed, and invited to present their claims. Reflection overcomes the effects of forgetfulness and disassociation. It corrects the perspectives of time and immediacy, anticipating the interests of tomorrow, and giving consideration to the interests which at the moment are cold or remote. It brings to light the causal relations between one interest and another. From reflection there emerge decisions which fulfill, in some measure, the purpose of harmony: plans, schedules, quotas, substitutions, and other arrangements by which the several interests avoid collision and achieve mutual reinforcement.

The personal will which emerges from reflection is not, as has sometimes been held, merely the strongest among existing interests, prevailing after a struggle of opposing forces. It is not a mere survivor, other contestants having been eliminated. It does not intervene on one side or the other, but takes a line down the middle, analogous to the resultant or vector in a field of forces. It makes its own choices, and sets its own precedents. Its accumulated decisions, having become permanent dispositions, form a character, or unwritten personal constitution.

The achievement of such a personal will cannot be indefinitely postponed. The exigencies of life are imperative, and have to be met with whatever personal will can be achieved. There is always a dateline for action. Any given personal will is thus inevitably premature, provisional, and subject to improvement. But insofar as it is enlightened and circumspect this personal will is considered as finally justified, except insofar as it neglects the similar personal wills of others. Within the domain of its included interests it is a moral ultimate. The several interests which it embraces have no moral cause for complaint insofar as they have been given the opportunity of contributing to the purpose to which they are subordinated.

The relation of the personal will to the person's several interests is primarily one of government, overruling, or dominance. It serves as a check or censor called into play when any of the particular interests tends to exceed bounds.

Like a sentinel it challenges each passing interest and requires it to show its credentials.

The similarity between the personal and social forms of the moral will must not be allowed to obscure their profound difference. It is true that as the personal will emerges from reflection so the social will emerges from communication and discussion. In both cases the emergent will represents a totality of interests, and achieves by organization a substitution of harmony for conflict. The difference lies in the fact that whereas the personal will is composed of sub-personal interests, the social will is composed of persons.

But while the social moral will is a will of persons, society is not a person. Excluding fictitious persons, corporate persons, legal persons, and every metaphorical or figurative use of the term, the only real person is that being which is capable of reflecting, choosing, relating means to ends, making decisions, and subordinating particular interests to an overruling purpose. It follows that there can be no moral will on the social level except as composed of several personal wills which are peculiarly modified and interrelated.

The ramifications of this fact pervade the whole domain of morality and moral institutions. It is echoed in all of those doctrines which exalt the person as an end in himself. It gives meaning to fraternity as the acknowledgment of person by fellow-persons. It gives to the individual man that "dignity" of which we hear so much. It provides for that unique role of the person as thinker, judge, and chooser, which lies at the basis of all representative institutions, and determines the moral priority of individuals to society.

## V

The creation of a social moral will out of personal wills depends on benevolence, that is, one person's positive interest in another person's interest. To be benevolent here means not that I treat you well so far as it happens to suit my existing interests to do so; my concern for your interests is an independent interest. Taking your desires and aversions, your hopes and fears, your pleasures and pains, in short, the interests by which you are actually moved, I act as though these interests were my own. Though I cannot, strictly speaking, *feel* your interests, I can acknowledge them, wish them well, and allow for them in addition to the interests which are already embraced within me. When you are at the same time benevolently disposed to my interests, we then have the same problem of reconciling the same interests, except that my original interests form the content of your benevolence and your original interests the content of mine.

In this pooling of interests I am ordinarily concerned that your benevolence shall actually embrace my original interests; and you are similarly concerned to accent yours. Each of us assumes that the other can safely be trusted to look out for his own. Assuming that each will be biased in favor of his own interests, the bias of each will tend to correct the bias of the other. Each will be the special pleader of his own interests, and his insistence on them will reinforce the other's weaker benevolence.

There will be a further difference. Your interests are best and most immediately served by you, and mine by me. I can for the most part serve you best by letting you serve yourself. The greater part of my benevolence, therefore, will take a permissive form. I will sometimes help you, but more often will abstain from hurting you; or will so follow my own inclinations as to make it possible for you also to follow yours; or accept your inclinations as setting a limit to mine.

No will is here introduced over and above the wills of the two persons, but since the two wills now represent the same interests, they will have achieved a community of end and a coöperative relation of means. In each person the new socialized purpose will have become dominant over his original interests. Neither will have become the mere means to the other since the common end is now each person's governing end. Each can speak with equal authority for that end, and may legitimately use the pronouns 'we' and 'our' in behalf of both. Each, speaking for the common end, can approve or disapprove the other's conduct without arrogance or impertinence.

The social form of the moral will is an agreement of personal wills of which independent benevolence is the essential condition. There are many other factors which conduce to such agreement, and which in their totality make up the method or art of agreement. The first prerequisite of agreement is a desire to agree, rather than to "get the better" of the other party. To induce this attitude it is necessary that both parties should be conscious of the wastefulness of conflict, and the gains, even if they be selfish gains, of peace. The Quaker idea of achieving unanimity, or a "sense of the meeting," which leaves no slumbering grievances and seeds of fresh dispute, is precisely the moral norm which is here defined. The further Quaker idea of periods of silence may or may not be taken to imply a religious doctrine of "inner light"; it may be taken to mean only that an interval of meditation will serve to cool the temper of acrimony.

Agreement is often promoted by shifting the emphasis from points of disagreement to matters in which there is already agreement. This area of agreement may be found either in subsidiary matters or in a common ideal goal. In either case there is created a mood of agreement which is favorable to further agreement. Since interests embrace a factor of cognitive mediation it is always possible to find occasions for cognitive agreement. There are always questions of fact and logic which can be made the focus of discussion. But though this conduces to an agreement of wills, it does not suffice. For practical or moral agreement it is necessary that each person should be *moved* as the other is moved, so as to achieve a harmony of purpose and action.

In the personal will it is sufficient that all of the person's interests shall be represented, whatever they be. Some of his interests may be benevolent, and no doubt will be, human nature and the circumstances of life being what they are; but benevolence is no more essential to the personal will than is hunger or an interest in collecting postage stamps. The social will, on the other hand, *must* be benevolent. Thus the social will is subjected to a double requirement, personality *and* benevolence.

When there is a social will among several persons the conduct which it prescribes will coincide with that which is prescribed by the personal will of each, but that will be only because benevolence has already been introduced into the personal will. This is a very different matter from the coincidence which *may* occur when the requirements of the personal will with or without benevolence, and the social will embracing benevolence, are applied independently. In the latter case the coincidence is accidental, that is, it cannot be deduced from either set of requirements taken separately. If it should occur invariably, it would be a happy miracle of the sort which is credited by the exponents of laissez faire—an echo of the optimistic theism of the seventeenth and eighteenth centuries. Whenever an act dictated by the social will happens to be dictated also by the personal will, this coincidence will serve to give it a double support. Either principle may be invoked to augment the justification afforded by the other.

## VII

Morality may be illustrated by the actual complexities of social life arranged in spheres of expanding inclusiveness. In the more intimate family or local circle there are several persons within the range of familiar acquaintance, each with interests of his own. Through communication and benevolence each adopts as his own the interest of father, mother, son, daughter, brother, sister, friend, neighbor; integrates them, speaks for the family or local group as a whole, and himself accepts this voice as authoritative over his original interests.

When representatives of capital and labor sit around a table and engage in what is called "collective bargaining," and insofar as this is a *moral* transaction which achieves a "right" solution of the problem of conflict, the process is similar except that the interests are represented, instead of being immediately present "in person." Each representative enters the conference as the advocate of one of the conflicting economic interests, and he is expected to advocate it. But he is also expected to take the view of the opposing advocate. He must listen to him, be impressed, concede his point, acknowledge his claims. In proportion as there is this exchange of interests, both parties tend to be actuated by both interests. Their two attitudes tend to converge and to approximate that of a third party, such as "the representative of the public," the judge, or the arbitrator, whose role it is to be equally considerate of both interests, and the partisan advocate of neither.

The procedures that are proper to collective bargaining are those which enable each finally to decide for all. The first step is the desire for agreement. Other proper procedures would include the discovery and amplification of the facts relevant to any of the interests represented; the invention of methods by which interests at present conflicting can both be fulfilled; the recognition of partial agreements already existing and of the commitments which these imply. Actually, other factors come in play—stubbornness, a war of nerves, the relative strength of war chests, endurance, threats, lung power, scowling eyebrows, appeals to the galleries. Undoubtedly the decision is forced and premature, and may have some day to be reopened. But when we speak of a solution of industrial problems which is better than brute force, or say that capital and labor should be partners rather than enemies, or praise the participants as more or less "fair," or judge the outcome to be more or less "just," it is this ideal solution that is appealed to as a standard. Each party makes a personal decision in the light of the interests represented by both, and the decisions tend to agree.

A political will differs from more limited collective wills only in its complexity and in the comparatively long chain of intermediate steps which it requires. It is achieved by discussion, taken as an interchange of personal interests, and of the collective interests of classes or groups. The ruler is the guardian not only of his individual interests and the interests of his group, but also, through benevolence, of the interests of all fellow-nationals. Whether it be the private citizen or the public official in whom this multiplicity of interests is assembled and harmonized, the ultimate decisions are made by a person. The political will is a political form of personal will, repeated among the members. When all agree, each can speak for the rest, and the authority for all; but the voice which speaks is a personal voice, and the agreement must be a personal acceptance. This is the moral core of politics, and the germ of political democracy.

In the judicial process the presiding judge, and the law which he applies and interprets, are supposed to represent both the defendant and the plaintiff. But it is deemed important that each litigant should plead his own case, directly or through an attorney who has identified himself with his client's case. When the decision is left to a judge he must be disinterested not only in the sense of excluding his own personal interest, but in the sense of taking account of all the interests at stake. When the decision is left to a jury it is assumed that this will afford the best guarantee that the interests at stake are sympathetically understood and have reached a unanimous agreement.

What reciprocal and sympathetic acquaintance achieves in the narrower circles of home and neighborhood, what collective bargaining achieves in the reconciliation of economic groups, what popular discussion, campaigning, and elections achieve in the civil polity, what pleading, argument, and judicial decision achieve in the field of law, is achieved in the international area by diplomacy, negotiation, treaty-making, and conference.

In this area one is painfully aware of a mixture of methods. Nations still practice war and power politics. But intermingled with this non-moral heritage from the past there is now an increasing and not wholly unsuccessful attempt to find a moral remedy. This remedy is achieved insofar as nations and peoples "understand one another," that is, benevolently share one another's interests, and seek a harmonizing purpose in which all the interests of mankind are embraced. Insofar as this occurs there can be said to be an international will or a will of mankind; which by virtue of its maximum breadth of representation stands at the summit of the moral hierarchy.

Such a will, like every lesser will, is a will of persons. International will consists of international-mindedness on the part of nations whose national wills consist in turn of the national-mindedness of their subgroups and individual members. It is insofar as each person is directly or indirectly represented that the inclusive requirements of international organization can be said to take precedence of those of any lesser group. Morally speaking international organization is a community of persons, in which because of the identity of their ends millions of men agree upon means; and are thus brought into relations of innocence and mutual aid. Each member of such a universal community of persons would be authorized to say "we" or "our" for all men. There is no other being, unless it be God, that can speak for mankind; no other situation in which this pretension is warranted.

## VIII

Such is the principle of reflective agreement. No claim is here made for the frequency or success of its application. But it means something, it is humanly possible, and it is successfully applied in some measure. If reflective interpersonal agreement be the moral principle, one must be prepared to admit that there is not always a moral solution of a problem of conflict. There is, however, a *way* to such a solution—a *line of effort*. Morality is a *pursuit*, not an infallible recipe. The conflicting parties may not try at all, or they may try and fail. All that moral philosophy can do is to define the moral goal; all that moral prophets can do is to exhort men to aim at the goal; all that moral sages can do is to cite the experience of those who have been successful.

If the conflicting parties do not look for agreement, there is no moral solution; if they do not succeed in reaching agreement, there is no moral solution. In case of unwillingness to agree, or in case of failure to agree, the action of the parties in question must take other grounds—partisanship, egoism, passion, whatever it be.

Morality is like a cultivated field in the midst of the desert. It is a partial and precarious conquest. Ground that is conquered has to be protected against the resurgence of original divisive forces. The moralized life is never immune against *demoralization*. At the same time that morality gains ground in one direction it may lose ground in another. Changes in the natural and historical environment and the development of man himself are perpetually introducing new factors and requiring a moral reorganization to embrace them. In the last analysis all depends on the energy, perseverance, and perpetual vigilance of the human person.

### The Proof of Moral Knowledge

The moral good has been defined as harmonious happiness, or as that organization of interests in which each enjoys the non-interference and support of the others, whether within the personal life or the life of society. This becomes the moral "first principle." It sets the standard by which objects are deemed morally good or bad, and is the premise from which right, duty, and virtue are to be derived. It provides the most general predicate of moral judgment and the basic concept of moral knowledge. How is it to be proved? . . .

### VIII

. . . In the first place, the standard of harmonious happiness is *capable* of being agreed on—both theoreticaly and practically. It satisfies the requirement of cognitive universality and objectivity; that is, it is the same for all knowers who address themselves to the subject. Since the norm of harmonious happiness acknowledges all interests, its affirmation is free from the so-called "personal equation." As the astronomer recognizes all stellar facts regardless of the accidents of the observer's history, and thus overcomes the geocentricism which has led men to affirm that the heavens move about a stationary earth, so the theory of harmonious happiness overcomes that egocentricism which has led moral observers to subordinate all interests to their own, or to those of their neighborhood, class, or nation. It embraces human perspectives within a total system of relationships. It places itself in all points of view, and fits them together. It discovers alien and remote interests, and makes allowance for the ignorance which it cannot wholly dispel. It is impartial. It says, in effect, that since it is interest as such which generates good, and a harmonious relation of interests which constitutes moral good, to him who makes the judgment *his* interest is just one among the rest. Since the principle of harmonious happiness deals with the nature of interest in general, and with its types of relationship, it is applicable to all interests and persons.

But while the theoretical proof of the moral principle is obliged only to satisfy the knower as *knower*, the principle here proposed will tend also to appeal to each knower's will. The good of harmonious happiness, since it embraces all interests, is *to some extent* to everybody's interest, and thereby obtains a breadth of support exceeding that of any other good. Every person, including the person to whom the argument is addressed, has some stake in it.

The extent to which the harmonious happiness of all men will reward any given man will vary widely. In the absence of propinquity, interaction, and communication, and so long as this condition prevails, it may not reward him at all. When this aloofness is diminished, its reward will depend on how his particular personal happiness is constituted. All men, no doubt, have some spark of humanity, and are affected by the happiness or misery of others— but some men more than other men, and some men scarcely at all. The same is true of the extent to which men's means and ends reinforce one another. This varies with men's vocations, all the way from the recluse who is interested in solitude to the man of business whose affairs are complexly intertwined in a network of employers, workers, buyers, sellers, producers, consumers, and bankers, which now extends around the earth.

The norm of harmonious happiness, furthermore, is the only norm which is capable of appealing to all men not only severally but jointly. It is the only norm which promises benefits to each interest *together with* all other interests. It does not rob Peter to pay Paul, but limits Peter in order to pay both Peter and Paul.

Hence the norm of harmonious happiness is doubly universal. It is universal in the theoretical sense: its nature and its implications are objective, and the judgments in which it is employed are equally true for all judges; and being abstracted from particular interests, it is applicable to all human situations. It is also universal in the social sense; its promised benefits accrue to all men, and to all men collectively. It is a norm on which all men can unite and agree—both theoretically and practically.

## IX

Making due allowance for the possibility of error in general, and for the degree of its probability in any particular field of inquiry, it may properly be argued for any theory that it agrees with widespread opinion. Opinion concerning the physical world is trustworthy in proportion as it can be attributed to observation. The relation between the sun and the earth, for example, reflects the observation of the alternation of day and night. This opinion has to be corrected to take account of the place of the observer, and the influence of the religious dogma which made the earth the scene of the drama of salvation. But whether the sun moves about the earth, or the earth about the sun, or the two move relatively to one another, the empirical fact of the periodic rising and setting remains undisturbed. And so with moral opinion. It has to be corrected to take account of non-evidential influences; not only such general influences as also affect physical opinion, but the peculiar pressures which arise from the fact that moral opinion is so closely connected with action as to be of special concern to society. These non-evidential influences being discounted, there remains an "experience of life" which has taught men the consequences of action and the ways to live prosperously together.

Again and again, in all spheres of life, and in all the ages of man, it has been observed that there are certain procedures by which the destructiveness of conflicting interests can be mitigated, and by which they can enjoy the benefits of peace and coöperation. Overlaid as it is by prejudices of many sorts, this lesson has been repeatedly learned, extended to new situations, and transmitted to future generations.

In spite of the marked differences of moral opinion which appear in different social groups and historical epochs there is nevertheless a notable amount of agreement. The disagreement is notable only because there was once an expectation of perfect agreement, and because of the shocked surprise with which the unfamiliar is always greeted. Language provides an analogy. The first stage is the assumption that all people speak the same language; the second stage is the discovery that there are strange, absurd, and unintelligible languages; the third stage is the discovery that all men use language, and that all languages have their common laws and meanings. In the matter of moral opinion the extreme relativists are those who have reached only the second of these stages.

If morality is taken as that organization of life by which conflict is escaped and by which coöperation is achieved, then the moral problem is universal; and it is, after all, not surprising that amidst all historic, ethnic, social, economic, and evolutionary aberrations there should emerge a broad knowledge of the points of the moral compass. This knowledge appears in generally accepted maxims, precepts, and virtues.

The theory here proposed reaffirms the standard virtues of antiquity— courage, temperance, wisdom, and justice. The good of harmonious happiness requires, like any end, a brave will that is not dismayed by obstacles, and effort sustained without complaint through long stretches of time. It requires a moderation of appetites lest in their excessive indulgence they should rob one another. It requires enlightened mediating judgments, that is, a true representation of ends and an intelligent choice of means. It requires a distribution of goods to each interest in accordance with a judgment which represents all interest. Christianity did not reject these virtues, but added faith, hope, and love; and these, also, are endorsed by the present theory. Harmonious happiness is an ideal, and if an ideal is to be pursued there must be a steadfast belief in its attainability by means that lie beyond present knowledge, and a confidence in its actual attainment in the future. The pursuit of the harmonious happiness of all requires a sympathetic concern for one's fellow man—a sensitiveness to their pains or frustrations and an impulse to help.

Other funded moral wisdom falls into line. The most generally accepted of all maxims, the Golden Rule, is justified because the harmonious happiness of all requires that each man shall put himself in the place of other men, and recognize their interests, however cold and remote, as of the same coin with those warm and intimate interests which he calls his own. Veracity signifies the need of communication as the condition of all human intercourse. Honesty is that keeping of agreements which is essential to security and to concerted plans. Selfishness is that preoccupation with the narrower interests of self, family, class, or nation which obstructs the longer and wider vistas demanded by universal happiness.

These maxims and virtues are not invariably accepted. They are sometimes defied and they are frequently ignored. It cannot, however, be said that they are peculiar to Western Europe, or to capitalistic societies, or to Christianity, or to the modern world. They cross all such divisions, and when, as today, life is organized on a wider scale, to include all nations, all dependent and backward groups, and all hitherto unprivileged persons and classes, it is to this body of moral opinion that men appeal. Equally significant is the fact that when men differ as to the specific applications of moral opinion it is to the standard of harmonious happiness that they look for common ground. And it is by this standard that men criticize and justify their major social institutions—conscience itself, polity, law, economy—and by which they define the places in human society that are to be allotted to art, science, education, and religion.

## X

The proof of the moral standard is "empirical" in the full, rather than the limited, sense of that term. In the limited sense, the term 'empirical' is sometimes applied to that part of science which consists of a summary of observations, rather than to that whole in which a conceptual theory is framed in conformity with the requirements of logic and mathematics and then verified by observation. If the theory of morals is to be considered empirical in the full sense, it must be a system of concepts verified by the data of human life.

There is much talk at the present time of a "scientific ethics": an urge to make ethics scientific, and a discussion of whether ethics *can* be scientific. There is no doubt that there can be a science which deals with *conscience*. This is now a recognized part of a scientific sociology, or social psychology, or of a scientific history. There is a certain propriety in giving this inquiry the name of 'ethics,' but if this nomenclature is adopted, then ethics must be distinguished from the science of morals.

The ultimate data of moral science are not men's approbations and disapprobations, but conflicts of interest, and the organizations of interests by which they are rendered non-conflicting and coöperative. The proof of any theory of morality is its adequacy and correctness as a description of these data. It does not attempt, nor can it be expected, to describe man or human life generally. The moral life of man must be human, and it must be living; and a description of it must therefore embrace these sets of facts. But the attention of moral theory is focused on certain selected aspects of man which distinguish him as a "moral" being; and on those aspects of human life which are peculiarly characteristic of his "moral" activity.

It is no disproof of the present doctrine of harmonious happiness to point out that men are not harmoniously happy, or are inharmoniously unhappy. All that needs to be proved is that there is a prolonged and widespread attempt to be harmoniously happy; that men are capable of such an attempt; that they can and do take steps in the direction of harmonious happiness; and that they can and do measure their steps by the standard of harmonious happiness. The fundamental claim for the present view is that it describes a peculiarly widespread, fundamental, and persistent human pursuit for which 'moral' is the most appropriate name.

# GEORGE
# F. THOMAS

GEORGE FINGER THOMAS (1899–     ) is Professor of Religious Thought at Princeton University. A leading Protestant writer in the field of Christian ethics, he edited *The Vitality of the Christian Tradition* (1944) and is the author of *Spirit and Its Freedom* (1939), *Poetry, Religion and the Spiritual Life* (1951), and *Christian Ethics and Moral Philosophy* (1955).

## *The Subjective Theory of R. B. Perry**

Perhaps the most careful statement and defense of the subjective theory of value during the last generation is that of Professor R. B. Perry. According to Perry, value is to be defined as "any object of any interest." "Interest" is a state or attitude which consists in being "for" some things and "against" others, in viewing things with "favor" or "disfavor." Interest, in this sense, "invests" an object with value, and the object "acquires" value when an interest is taken in it. Interest is "constitutive" of value, "confers" value upon the object. In the definition "value is any object of any interest," the emphasis upon the word "any" is meant to affirm that value is not a "*qualified object* of interest" or an "object of *qualified interest*," but *any* object of *any* interest. Thus, Perry's theory is hospitable to interests of all kinds in objects of all kinds.

Since there are no values apart from interests and since there is a diversity of interests among persons, the idea of a scale of values according to which values are ranked as higher or lower becomes meaningless. However, this does not mean that he is not interested in "comparative value." Although values cannot be ranked as higher or lower, they can be compared with one another quantitatively by measuring the amounts of interest involved in them. It is this *comparison of values* which is the basis of Perry's ethical theory. A moral act is one which is conducive to the attainment of the *maximum value* or *fulfillment of interest*. . . .

The "highest good" is the satisfaction or fulfillment of as many interests of as many persons as possible (principle of "inclusiveness") in an harmonious system of interests. . . . This principle implies that *all interests* have a claim to be fulfilled and that *every person's* interests should be included among the interests to be considered.

* From *Christian Ethics and Moral Philosophy*, by George F. Thomas, Chap. 20. Copyright, 1955, by George F. Thomas. Used by permission of Charles Scribner's Sons.

The maximum fulfillment of interests or "highest good" requires an "all-benevolent will" from each person. For the harmony of all interests can be attained only through a "universal love," an "indulgent" love which accepts and supports the interests of every other person. Since this would lead to the greatest happiness, Perry has much in common with the older Utilitarianism.

The main *advantage* of a subjective theory like this over objective theories is that it relates the nature of value more closely to man and his good. Thus, it avoids in a measure the abstractness of the objective theory which reduces moral activity to the realization of values in and for themselves. Moreover, by making the principle of "inclusiveness" the primary standard for the comparison of values, Perry avoids the tendency to self-centeredness in the quest for values. Moral activity is centered upon the fulfillment of the interests of all persons from the motive of "universal love."

Unfortunately, these advantages are purchased at too high a cost, for Perry's theory is vitiated by several fatal errors. The first and most fundamental of these is his *subjective definition of value* as "any object of any interest." The view that value exists exclusively in relation to and by virtue of interest is entirely opposed to men's consciousness of value. In valuing something, they do not think of themselves as bestowing a value upon it but as appreciating and responding to a value which in some sense belongs to it. In experience an object is "given" as beautiful, a moral act is "given" as good. Interest in it presupposes something in it which makes it *appropriate* to be an object of interest. For example, why do men have an interest in truth rather than error unless truth has and error lacks something which makes it worthy of interest? Moreover, higher values like truth are experienced as making claims upon us. If we are to possess them, it must be on their own terms. We must acknowledge truth and goodness where we find them and as we find them; we cannot judge them according to our likes and dislikes but only as they are. . . .

Is it not misleading to speak of an interest as conferring value on "any object" upon which it may momentarily light?

We may illustrate by two examples. In fulfilling their interest in food, men have to learn by experience to discriminate between objects which are right in the sense of healthful and nutritious and those which are not nutritious and may even be harmful. Are we to say that an interest in a certain mushroom or drug is a ground for attributing value to it despite the fact that experience may later prove it to be deadly? Again, the interest in sexual experience often takes forms which, as later experience shows, pervert its true function and even enslave a person. Are they to be regarded as valuable merely because an interest has been taken in them? Both of these examples indicate that a thing or experience may be an object of an interest and yet be without value or even be evil. Perry would doubtless reply that in such cases interest does confer value in the "generic" sense, but that when it is compared with other interests it is found to thwart other and greater values. But a judgment of value is not intended to express merely a tentative, momentary, or unconsidered interest; its purpose is to express the attitude of the self as a whole in the light of its whole experience and reflection. If so, an object of an interest cannot be judged to be valuable unless it fulfills something deeper and more enduring than a present and often fleeting interest. As we cannot say that a passing opinion possesses the value of truth, we cannot say that "any" interest, however casual or superficial, confers value.

The subjective theory of value also inevitably leads to *relativism*. If A is interested in an object but B is not, it is a value for A but not for B. It is impossible to put this view into practice consistently in ethics or politics. For example, if the lack of interest of A, a schoolboy, in knowledge means that it has no value for him, on what ground do his parents and teachers insist that he go to school and study his lessons? Is it not on the ground that truth is a value whether he is interested in it or not? Again, it would seem that, according to Perry's theory, if nation A is interested in justice and liberty for all and B is not, they are values for A but not for B. If so, how can democracy, a form of government which is interested in justice and liberty for all, claim to be the best form of government or even a better form than a tyrannical dictatorship?

Moreover, if values are wholly relative to and dependent upon interest, how can there be any basis of *social unity*? Perry is not disturbed by the danger of social disunity because he believes that if each person in a society has an "all-benevolent will" and is interested in the interests of all the others, the greatest diversity of interests can be permitted without destroying the general harmony. But there is clearly a limit to the diversity of interests which is possible without disrupting a society. For example, it is obvious that the value upon which Perry relies to hold a society together, *i.e.*, benevolence or interest in the interests of others, must be generally if not universally present. But this assumes it to be a value for all, whether they are interested in it or not. Thus, Perry's relativistic tolerance of all interests would be possible only in a society in which all accepted the value of benevolence as an *absolute!*

Finally, there is no adequate basis for *obligation* in Perry's theory. Like the Utilitarians, he seems to think that it is necessary only to define the "highest good" as the maximum fulfillment of interests in an harmonious system and that men with an "all-benevolent will" will seek it. But what is the basis of obligation for those who have no interest in the interests of other persons? If one has no interest in others, why ought he to seek their good? The only possible answer is that it is his *duty* to do so whether he has an interest in doing so or not. This implies that whatever may be thought about nonmoral values like beauty and truth, moral value cannot be either subjective or relative. Indeed, the ethical idealism of Perry's own theory of the "all-benevolent will" is based upon the tacit assumption that *this* value, at least, is objective and absolute.

## FULFILLMENT OF INTEREST—SUGGESTED READINGS

Ewing, A. C., *The Definition of Good*, New York, Macmillan, 1947, Chap. 2, esp. pp. 62–77. (critic)

Parker, D. H., *The Philosophy of Value*, Ann Arbor, Mich., University of Michigan Press, 1957. (proponent)

Perry, R. B., *The Moral Economy*, New York, Scribner's, 1909. (proponent)

Rashdall, H., *Is Conscience an Emotion?*, Boston, Houghton, Mifflin, 1914, Lecture III. (critic)

Tennant, F. R., *Philosophical Theology*, Cambridge, Eng., Cambridge University Press, 1928, Vol. I, Chap. 7. (proponent)

Vivas, E., *The Moral Life and the Ethical Life*, Chicago, University of Chicago Press, 1950, Chaps. 2–4. (critic)

# C. IS THERE A FIXED MORAL STANDARD?

In the preceding readings, some of the major proposals which have been made concerning the nature of a universal moral standard have been explained and supported by a leading proponent of each view. To aid in evaluation, an opponent has also been presented who criticizes each of the proposed standards. A more thoroughgoing criticism of all these views, however, is possible—such a criticism would call into question the validity of the entire search for a fixed moral standard.

It is to be observed that although traditional moralists acknowledge that the circumstances of human life change, they all assume that the ultimate principle of morality is independent of these changes in circumstance. Despite their differences, they find common ground in the belief that the search for a fixed moral standard provides the basic problem for ethical theory.

Against the traditional moralists, there are some philosophers who argue that to establish a fixed moral standard is neither possible nor desirable. They maintain that with the changing circumstances of human life, the ultimate moral values of men both do and ought to change. They also assert that the moral life of man is essentially a creative enterprise for which no fixed rules can be given in advance. For these philosophers, to suppose that there is a single universal moral standard is to deny the changing and creative character of human morality. Accordingly, they contend that not only are the proposals of traditional ethical theories defective, but also that the very problem of traditional ethics must be rejected.

In the following selections, DEWEY first criticizes the aim of traditional moralists; he then gives his own view of the reconstruction of moral conceptions which must take place when the search for a fixed moral standard is abandoned. NIETZSCHE attacks traditional morality as a herd morality which serves the interests of mediocre men; he also asserts that traditional moralists, despite their pretensions of seeking an absolute truth, have served only to codify and record what their particular ages found valuable. He then calls for moral philosophers who will have the creative imagination to propose new values, goods, and ends for men. SARTRE urges that there are no pre-existing moral standards which prescribe for men the ends of life; rather every man must choose for himself what he will become.

# JOHN DEWEY

JOHN DEWEY (1859–1952), one of America's outstanding philosophers, taught for many years both at the University of Chicago and Columbia University. A leading pragmatist, he wrote not only upon topics in all of the major fields of philosophy but he has also been widely influential for his treatment of problems in education, social psychology, and politics. His major works include: *Ethics* (with James H. Tufts, 1908; rev. ed., 1932), *Democracy and Education* (1916), *Reconstruction in Philosophy* (1920; 2nd ed., 1948), *Human Nature and Conduct* (1922), *The Public and Its Problems* (1927), *A Common Faith* (1934), and *The Theory of Valuation* (1939).

## Reconstruction in Moral Conceptions*

The impact of the alteration in methods of scientific thinking upon moral ideas is, in general, obvious. Goods, ends are multiplied. Rules are softened into principles, and principles are modified into methods of understanding. Ethical theory began among the Greeks as an attempt to find a regulation for the conduct of life which should have a rational basis and purpose instead of being derived from custom. But reason as a substitute for custom was under the obligation of supplying objects and laws as fixed as those of custom had been. Ethical theory ever since has been singularly hypnotized by the notion that its business is to discover some final end or good or some ultimate and supreme law. This is the common element among the diversity of theories. Some have held that the end is loyalty or obedience to a higher power or authority; and they have variously found this higher principle in Divine Will, the will of the secular ruler, the maintenance of institutions in which the purpose of superiors is embodied, and the rational consciousness of duty. But they have differed from one another because there was one point in which they were agreed: a single and final source of law. Others have asserted that it is impossible to locate morality in conformity to law-giving power, and that it must be sought in ends that are goods. And some have sought the good in self-realization, some in holiness, some in happiness, some in the greatest possible aggregate of pleasures. And yet these

* From *Reconstruction in Philosophy*, by John Dewey, Chap. 7. Copyright, 1920, Henry Holt and Company, Inc.; 1948, The Beacon Press. Used by permission.

schools have agreed in the assumption that there is a single, fixed and final good. They have been able to dispute with one another only because of their common premise.

The question arises whether the way out of the confusion and conflict is not to go to the root of the matter by questioning this common element. Is not the belief in the single, final and ultimate (whether conceived as good or as authoritative law) an intellectual product of that feudal organization which is disappearing historically and of that belief in a bounded, ordered cosmos, wherein rest is higher than motion, which has disappeared from natural science? It has been repeatedly suggested that the present limit of intellectual reconstruction lies in the fact that it has not as yet been seriously applied in the moral and social disciplines. Would not this further application demand precisely that we advance to a belief in a plurality of changing, moving, individualized goods and ends, and to a belief that principles, criteria, laws are intellectual instruments for analyzing individual or unique situations?

The blunt assertion that every moral situation is a unique situation having its own irreplaceable good may seem not merely blunt but preposterous. For the established tradition teaches that it is precisely the irregularity of special cases which makes necessary the guidance of conduct by universals, and that the essence of the virtuous disposition is willingness to subordinate every particular case to adjudication by a fixed principle. It would then follow that submission of a generic end and law to determination by the concrete situation entails complete confusion and unrestrained licentiousness. Let us, however, follow the pragmatic rule, and in order to discover the meaning of the idea ask for its consequences. Then it surprisingly turns out that the primary significance of the unique and morally ultimate character of the concrete situation is to transfer the weight and burden of morality to intelligence. It does not destroy responsibility; it only locates it. A moral situation is one in which judgment and choice are required antecedently to overt action. The practical meaning of the situation—that is to say the action needed to satisfy it—is not self-evident. It has to be searched for. There are conflicting desires and alternative apparent goods. What is needed is to find the right course of action, the right good. Hence, inquiry is exacted: observation of the detailed makeup of the situation; analysis into its diverse factors; clarification of what is obscure; discounting the more insistent and vivid traits; tracing the consequences of the various modes of action that suggest themselves; regarding the decision reached as hypothetical and tentative until the anticipated or supposed consequences which led to its adoption have been squared with actual consequences. This inquiry is intelligence. Our moral failures go back to some weakness of disposition, some absence of sympathy, some one-sided bias that makes us perform the judgment of the concrete case carelessly or perversely. Wide sympathy, keen sensitiveness, persistence in the face of the disagreeable, balance of interests enabling us to undertake the work of analysis and decision intelligently are the distinctively moral traits—the virtues or moral excellencies.

It is worth noting once more that the underlying issue is, after all, only the same as that which has been already threshed out in physical inquiry. There too it long seemed as if rational assurance and demonstration could be attained only if we began with universal conceptions and subsumed particular cases under them. The men who initiated the methods of inquiry that are now everywhere adopted were denounced in their day (and sincerely) as subverters of truth and foes of science. If they have won in the end, it is because, as has already been pointed out, the method of universals confirmed prejudices and sanctioned ideas that had gained currency irrespective of evidence for them; while placing the initial and final weight upon the individual case, stimulated painstaking inquiry into facts and examination of principles. In the end, loss of eternal truths was more than compensated for in the accession of quotidian facts. The loss of the system of superior and fixed definitions and kinds was more than made up for by the growing system of hypotheses and laws used in classifying facts. After all, then, we are only pleading for the adoption in moral reflection of the logic that has been proved to make for security, stringency and fertility in passing judgments upon physical phenomena. And the reason is the same. The old method in spite of its nominal and esthetic worship of reason discouraged reason, because it hindered the operation of scrupulous and unremitting inquiry.

More definitely, the transfer of the burden of the moral life from following rules or pursuing fixed ends over to the detection of the ills that need remedy in a special case and the formation of plans and methods for dealing with them, eliminates the causes which have kept moral theory controversial, and which have also kept it remote from helpful contact with the exigencies of practice. The theory of fixed ends inevitably leads thought into the bog of disputes that cannot be settled. If there is one *summum bonum*, one supreme end, what is it? To consider this problem is to place ourselves in the midst of controversies that are as acute now as they were two thousand years ago. Suppose we take a seemingly more empirical view, and say that while there is not a single end, there also are not as many as there are specific situations that require amelioration; but there are a number of such natural goods as health, wealth, honor or good name, friendship, esthetic appreciation, learning and such moral goods as justice, temperance, benevolence, etc. What or who is to decide the right of way when these ends conflict with one another, as they are sure to do? Shall we resort to the method that once brought such disrepute upon the whole business of ethics: Casuistry?

Or shall we have recourse to what Bentham well called the *ipse dixit* method: the arbitrary preference of this or that person for this or that end? Or shall we be forced to arrange them all in an order of degrees from the highest good down to the least precious? Again we find ourselves in the middle of unreconciled disputes with no indication of the way out.

Meantime, the special moral perplexities where the aid of intelligence is required go unenlightened. We cannot seek or attain health, wealth, learning, justice or kindness in general. Action is always specific, concrete, individualized, unique. And consequently judgments as to acts to be performed must be similarly specific. To say that a man seeks health or justice is only to say that he seeks to live healthily or justly. These things, like truth, are adverbial. They are modifiers of action in special cases. How to live healthily or justly is a matter which differs with every person. It varies with his past experience, his opportunities, his temperamental and acquired weaknesses and abilities. Not man in general but a particular man suffering from some particular disability aims to live healthily, and consequently health cannot mean for him exactly what it means for any other mortal. Healthy living is not something to be attained by itself apart from other ways of living. A man needs to be healthy *in* his life, not apart from it, and what does life mean except the aggregate of his pursuits and activities? A man who aims at health as a distinct end becomes a valetudinarian, or a fanatic, or a mechanical performer of exercises, or an athlete so one-sided that his pursuit of bodily development injures his heart. When the endeavor to realize a so-called end does not temper and color all other activities, life is portioned out into strips and fractions. Certain acts and times are devoted to getting health, others to cultivating religion, others to seeking learning, to being a good citizen, a devotee of fine art and so on. This is the only logical alternative to subordinating all aims to the accomplishment of one alone—fanaticism. This is out of fashion at present, but who can say how much of distraction and dissipation in life, and how much of its hard and narrow rigidity is the outcome of men's failure to realize that each situation has its own unique end and that the whole personality should be concerned with it? Surely, once more, what a man needs is to live healthily, and this result so affects all the activities of his life that it cannot be set up as a separate and independent good.

Nevertheless the general notions of health, disease, justice, artistic culture are of great importance: Not, however, because this or that case may be brought exhaustively under a single head and its specific traits shut out, but because generalized science provides a man as physician and artist and citizen, with questions to ask, investigations to make, and enables him to understand the meaning of what he sees. Just in the degree in which a physician is an artist in his work he uses his science, no matter how extensive and accurate, to furnish him with tools of inquiry into the individual case, and with methods of forecasting a method of dealing with it. Just in the degree in which, no matter how great his learning, he subordinates the individual case to some classification of diseases and some generic rule of treatment, he sinks to the level of the routine mechanic. His intelligence and his action become rigid, dogmatic, instead of free and flexible.

*Moral* goods and ends exist only when something has to be done. The fact that something has to be done proves that there are deficiencies, evils in the existent situation. This ill is just the specific ill that it is. It never is an exact duplicate of anything else. Consequently the good of the situation has to be discovered, projected and attained on the basis of the exact defect and trouble to be rectified. It cannot intelligently be injected into the situation from without. Yet it is the part of wisdom to compare different cases, to gather together the ills from which humanity suffers, and to generalize the corresponding goods into classes. Health, wealth, industry, temperance, amiability, courtesy, learning, esthetic capacity, initiative, courage, patience, enterprise, thoroughness and a multitude of other generalized ends are acknowledged as goods. But the *value* of this systematization is intellectual or analytic. Classifications *suggest* possible traits to be on the lookout for in studying a particular case; they suggest methods of action to be tried in removing the inferred causes of ill. They are tools of insight; their value is in promoting an individualized response in the individual situation.

Morals is not a catalogue of acts nor a set of rules to be applied like drugstore prescriptions or cook-book recipes. The need in morals is for specific methods of inquiry and of contrivance: Methods of inquiry to locate difficulties and evils; methods of contrivance to form plans to be used as working hypotheses in dealing with them. And the pragmatic import of the logic of individualized situations, each having its own irreplaceable good and principle, is to transfer the attention of theory from preoccupation with general conceptions to the problem of developing effective methods of inquiry.

Two ethical consequences of great moment should be remarked. The belief in fixed values has bred a division of ends into intrinsic and instrumental, of those that are really worth while in themselves and those that are of importance only as means to intrinsic goods. Indeed, it is often thought to be the very beginning of wisdom, of moral discrimination, to make this distinction. Dialectically, the distinction is interesting and seems harmless. But carried into practice it has an import that is tragic. Historically, it has been the source and justification of a hard and fast difference between ideal goods on one side and material goods on the other. At present those who would be liberal conceive intrinsic goods as esthetic in nature rather than as exclusively religious or as intellectually contemplative. But the effect is the same. So-called intrinsic goods, whether religious or esthetic, are divorced from those interests of daily life which because of their constancy and urgency form the preoccupation of the great mass. Aristotle used this distinction to declare that slaves and the working class though they are necessary *for* the state—the commonweal—are not constitutents *of* it. That which is regarded as *merely* instrumental must approach drudgery; it cannot command either intellectual, artistic or moral attention and respect. Anything becomes *unworthy* whenever it is thought of as intrinsically lacking worth. So men of "ideal" interests have chosen for the most part the way of neglect and escape. The urgency and pressure of "lower" ends have been covered up by polite conventions. Or, they have been relegated to a baser class of mortals in order that the few might be free to attend to the goods that are really or intrinsically worth while. This withdrawal, in the name of higher ends, has left, for mankind at large and especially for energetic "practical" people the lower activities in complete command.

No one can possibly estimate how much of the obnoxious materialism and brutality of our economic life is due to the fact that economic ends have been regarded as *merely* instrumental. When they are recognized to be as intrinsic and final in their place as any others, then it will be seen that they are capable of idealization, and that if life is to be worth while, they must acquire ideal and intrinsic value. Esthetic, religious and other "ideal" ends are now thin and meagre or else idle and luxurious because of the separation from "instrumental" or economic ends. Only in connection with the latter can they be woven into the texture of daily life and made substantial and pervasive. The vanity and irresponsibility of values that are merely final and not also in turn means to the enrichment of other occupations of life ought to be obvious. But now the doctrine of "higher" ends gives aid, comfort and support to every socially isolated and socially irresponsible scholar, specialist, esthete and religionist. It protects the vanity and irresponsibility of his calling from observation by others and by himself. The moral deficiency of the calling is transformed into a cause of admiration and gratulation.

The other generic change lies in doing away once for all with the traditional distinction between moral goods, like the virtues, and natural goods like health, economic security, art, science and the like. The point of view under discussion is not the only one which has deplored this rigid distinction and endeavored to abolish it. Some schools have even gone so far as to regard moral excellencies, qualities of character as of value only because they promote natural goods. But the experimental logic when carried into morals makes every quality that is judged to be good according as it contributes to amelioration of existing ills. And in so doing, it enforces the moral meaning of natural science. When all is said and done in criticism of present social deficiencies, one may well wonder whether the root difficulty does not lie in the separation of natural and moral science. When physics, chemistry, biology, medicine, contribute to the detection of concrete human woes and to the development of plans for remedying them and relieving the human estate, they become moral; they become part of the apparatus of moral inquiry of science. The latter then loses its peculiar flavor of the didactic and pedantic; its ultra-moralistic and hortatory tone. It loses its thinness and shrillness as well as its vagueness. It gains agencies that are efficacious. But the gain is not confined to the side of moral science. Natural science loses its divorce from humanity; it becomes itself humanistic in quality. It is something to be pursued not in a technical and specialized way for what is called truth for its own sake, but with the sense of its social bearing, its intellectual indispensableness. It is technical only in the sense that it provides the technique of social and moral engineering.

When the consciousness of science is fully impregnated with the consciousness of human value, the greatest dualism which now weighs humanity down, the split between the material, the mechanical, the scientific and the moral and ideal will be destroyed. Human forces that now waver because of this division will be unified and reinforced. As long as ends are not thought of as individualized according to specific needs and opportunities, the mind will be content with abstractions, and the adequate stimulus to the moral or social use of natural science and historical data will be lacking. But when attention is concentrated upon the diversified concretes, recourse to all intellectual materials needed to clear up the special cases will be imperative. At the same time that morals are made to focus in intelligence, things intellectual are moralized. The vexatious and wasteful conflict between naturalism and humanism is terminated.

These general considerations may be amplified. First: Inquiry, discovery take the same place in morals that they have come to occupy in sciences of nature. Validation, demonstration become experimental, a matter of consequences. Reason, always an honorific term in ethics, becomes actualized in the methods by which the needs and conditions, the obstacles and resources, of situations are scrutinized in detail, and intelligent plans of improvement are worked out. Remote and abstract generalities promote jumping at conclusions, "anticipations of nature." Bad consequences are then deplored as due to natural perversity and untoward fate. But shifting the issue to analysis of a specific situation makes inquiry obligatory and alert observation of consequences imperative. No past decision nor old principle can ever be wholly relied upon to justify a course of action. No amount of pains taken in forming a purpose in a definite case is final; the consequences of its adoption must be carefully noted, and a purpose held only as a working hypothesis until results confirm its rightness. Mistakes are no longer either mere unavoidable accidents to be mourned or moral sins to be expiated and forgiven. They are lessons in wrong methods of using intelligence and instructions as to a better course in the future. They are indications of the need of revision, development, readjustment. Ends grow, standards of judgment are improved. Man is under just as much obligation to develop his most advanced standards and ideals as to use conscientiously those which he already possesses. Moral life is protected from falling into formalism and rigid repetition. It is rendered flexible, vital, growing.

In the second place, every case where moral action is required becomes of equal moral importance and urgency with every other. If the need and deficiencies of a specific situation indicate improvement of health as the end and good, then for that situation health is the ultimate and supreme good. It is no means to something else. It is a final and intrinsic value. The same thing is true of improvement of economic status, of making a living, of attending to business and family demands—all of the things which under the sanction of fixed ends have been rendered of secondary and merely instrumental value, and so relatively base and unimportant. Anything that in a given situation is an end and good at all is of equal worth, rank and dignity with every other good of any other situation, and deserves the same intelligent attention.

We note thirdly the effect in destroying the roots of Phariseeism. We are so accustomed to thinking of this as deliberate hypocrisy that we overlook its intellectual premises. The conception which looks for the end of action within the circumstances of the actual situation will not have the same measure of judgment for all cases. When one factor of the situation is a person of trained mind and large resources, more will be expected than with a person of backward mind and uncultured experience. The absurdity of applying the same standard of moral judgment to savage peoples that is used with civilized will be apparent. No individual or group will be judged by whether they come up to or fall short of some fixed result, but by the direction in which they are moving. The bad man is the man who no matter how good he *has* been is beginning to deteriorate, to grow less good. The good man is the man who no matter how morally unworthy he *has* been is moving to become better. Such a conception makes one severe in judging himself and humane in judging others. It excludes that arrogance which always accompanies judgment based on degree of approximation to fixed ends.

In the fourth place, the process of growth, of improvement and progress, rather than the static outcome and result, becomes the significant thing. Not health as an end fixed once and for all, but the needed improvement in health—a continual process—is the end and good. The end is no longer a terminus or limit to be reached. It is the active process of transforming the existent situation. Not perfection as a final goal, but the ever-enduring process of perfecting, maturing, refining is the aim in living. Honesty, industry, temperance, justice, like health, wealth and learning, are not goods to be possessed as they would be if they expressed fixed ends to be attained. They are directions of change in the quality of experience. Growth itself is the only moral "end."

Although the bearing of this idea upon the problem of evil and the controversy between optimism and pessimism is too vast to be here discussed, it may be worth while to touch upon it superficially. The problem of evil ceases to be a theological and metaphysical one, and is perceived to be the practical problem of reducing, alleviating, as far as may be removing, the evils of life. Philosophy is no longer under obligation to find ingenious methods for proving that evils are only apparent, not real, or to elaborate schemes for explaining them away or, worse yet, for justifying them. It assumes another obligation:—That of contributing in however humble a way to methods that will assist us in discovering the causes of humanity's ills. Pessimism is a paralyzing doctrine. In declaring that the world is evil wholesale, it makes futile all efforts to discover the remediable causes of specific evils and thereby destroys at the root every attempt to make the world better and happier. Wholesale optimism, which has been the consequence of the attempt to explain evil away, is, however, equally an incubus.

After all, the optimism that says that the world is already the best possible of all worlds might be regarded as the most cynical of pessimisms. If this is the best possible, what would a world which was fundamentally bad be like? Meliorism is the belief that the specific conditions which exist at one moment, be they comparatively bad or comparatively good, in any event may be bettered. It encourages intelligence to study the positive means of good and the obstructions to their realization, and to put forth endeavor for the improvement of conditions. It arouses confidence and a reasonable hopefulness as optimism does not. For the latter in declaring that good is already realized in ultimate reality tends to make us gloss over the evils that concretely exist. It becomes too readily the creed of those who live at ease, in comfort, of those who have been successful in obtaining this world's rewards. Too readily optimism makes the men who hold it callous and blind to the sufferings of the less fortunate, or ready to find the cause of troubles of others in their personal viciousness. It thus co-operates with pessimism, in spite of the extreme nominal differences between the two, in benumbing sympathetic insight and intelligent effort in reform. It beckons men away from the world of relativity and change into the calm of the absolute and eternal.

The import of many of these changes in moral attitude focusses in the idea of happiness. Happiness has often been made the object of the moralists' contempt. Yet the most ascetic moralist has usually restored the idea of happiness under some other name, such as bliss. Goodness without happiness, valor and virtue without satisfaction, ends without conscious enjoyment —these things are as intolerable practically as they are self-contradictory in conception. Happiness is not, however, a bare possession; it is not a fixed attainment. Such a happiness is either the unworthy selfishness which moralists have so bitterly condemned, or it is, even if labelled bliss, an insipid tedium, a millennium of ease in relief from all struggle and labor. It could satisfy only the most delicate of molly-coddles. Happiness is found only in success; but success means succeeding, getting forward, moving in advance. It is an active process, not a passive outcome. Accordingly it includes the overcoming of obstacles, the elimination of sources of defect and ill. Esthetic sensitiveness and enjoyment are a large constituent in any worthy happiness. But the esthetic appreciation which is totally separated from renewal of spirit, from re-creation of mind and purification of emotion is a weak and sickly thing, destined to speedy death from starvation. That the renewal and re-creation come unconsciously not by set intention but makes them the more genuine.

Upon the whole, utilitarianism has marked the best in the transition from the classic theory of ends and goods to that which is now possible. It had definite merits. It insisted upon getting away from vague generalities, and down to the specific and concrete. It subordinated law to human achievement instead of subordinating humanity to external law. It taught that institutions are made for man and not man for institutions; it actively promoted all issues of reform. It made moral good natural, humane, in touch with the natural goods of life. It opposed unearthly and other worldly morality. Above all, it acclimatized in human imagination the idea of social welfare as a supreme test. But it was still profoundly affected in fundamental points by old ways of thinking. It never questioned the idea of a fixed, final and supreme end. It only questioned the current notions as to the nature of this end; and then inserted pleasure and the greatest possible aggregate of pleasures in the position of the fixed end.

Such a point of view treats concrete activities and specific interests not as worth while in themselves, or as constituents of happiness, but as mere external means to getting pleasures. The upholders of the old tradition could therefore easily accuse utilitarianism of making not only virtue but art, poetry, religion and the state into mere servile means of attaining sensuous enjoyments. Since pleasure was an outcome, a result valuable on its own account independently of the active processes that achieve it, happiness was a thing to be possessed and held onto. The acquisitive instincts of man were exaggerated at the expense of the creative. Production was of importance not because of the intrinsic worth of invention and reshaping the world, but because its external results feed pleasure. Like every theory that sets up fixed and final aims, in making the end passive and possessive, it made all active operations *mere* tools. Labor was an unavoidable evil to be minimized. Security in possession was the chief thing practically. Material comfort and ease were magnified in contrast with the pains and risk of experimental creation.

These deficiencies, under certain conceivable conditions, might have remained merely theoretical. But the disposition of the times and the interests of those who propagated the utilitarian ideas, endowed them with power for social harm. In spite of the power of the new ideas in attacking old social abuses, there were elements in the teaching which operated or protected to sanction new social abuses. The reforming zeal was shown in criticism of the evils inherited from the class system of feudalism, evils economic, legal and political. But the new economic order of capitalism that was superseding feudalism brought its own social evils with it, and some of these ills utilitarianism tended to cover up or defend. The emphasis upon acquisition and possession of enjoyments took on an untoward color in connection with the contemporary enormous desire for wealth and the enjoyments it makes possible.

If utilitarianism did not actively promote the new economic materialism, it had no means of combating it. Its general spirit of subordinating productive activity to the bare product was indirectly favorable to the cause of an unadorned commercialism. In spite of its interest in a thoroughly social aim, utilitarianism fostered a new class interest, that of the capitalistic property-owning interests, provided only property was obtained through free competition and not by governmental favor. The stress that Bentham put on security tended to consecrate the legal institution of private property provided only certain legal abuses in connection with its acquisition and transfer were abolished. *Beati possidentes*—provided possessions had been obtained in accord with the rules of the competitive game—without, that is, extraneous favors from government. Thus utilitarianism gave intellectual confirmation to all those tendencies which make "business" not a means of social service and an opportunity for personal growth in creative power but a way of accumulating the means of private enjoyments. Utilitarian ethics thus afford a remarkable example of the need of philosophic reconstruction which these lectures have been presenting. Up to a certain point, it reflected the meaning of modern thought and aspirations. But it was still tied down by fundamental ideas of that very order which it thought it had completely left behind: The idea of a fixed and single end lying beyond the diversity of human needs and acts rendered utilitarianism incapable of being an adequate representative of the modern spirit. It has to be reconstructed through emancipation from its inherited elements.

If a few words are added upon the topic of education, it is only for the sake of suggesting that the educative process is all one with the moral process, since the latter is a continuous passage of experience from worse to better. Education has been traditionally thought of as preparation: as learning, acquiring certain things because they will later be useful. The end is remote, and education is getting ready, is a preliminary to something more important to happen later on. Childhood is only a preparation for adult life, and adult life for another life. Always the future, not the present, has been the significant thing in education: Acquisition of knowledge and skill for future use and enjoyment; formation of habits required later in life in business, good citizenship and pursuit of science. Education is thought of also as something needed by some human beings merely because of their dependence upon others. We are born ignorant, unversed, unskilled, immature, and consequently in a state of social dependence. Instruction, training, moral discipline are processes by which the mature, the adult, gradually raise the helpless to the point where they can look out for themselves. The business of childhood is to grow into the independence of adulthood by means of the guidance of those who have already attained it. Thus the process of education as the main business of life ends when the young have arrived at emancipation from social dependence.

These two ideas, generally assumed but rarely explicitly reasoned out, contravene the conception that growing, or the continuous reconstruction of experience, is the only end. If at whatever period we choose to take a person, he is still in process of growth, then education is not, save as a by-product, a preparation for something coming later. Getting from the present the degree and kind of growth there is in it is education. This is a constant function, independent of age. The best thing that can be said about any special process of education, like that of the formal school period, is that it renders its subject capable of further education: more sensitive to conditions of growth and more able to take advantage of them. Acquisition of skill, possession of knowledge, attainment of culture are not ends: they are marks of growth and means to its continuing.

The contrast usually assumed between the period of education as one of social dependence and of maturity as one of social independence does harm. We repeat over and over that man is a social animal, and then confine the significance of this statement to the sphere in which sociality usually seems least evident, politics. The heart of the sociality of man is in education. The idea of education as preparation and of adulthood as a fixed limit of growth are two sides of the same obnoxious untruth. If the moral business of the adult as well as the young is a growing and developing experience, then the instruction that comes from social dependencies and interdependencies are as important for the adult as for the child. Moral independence for the adult means arrest of growth, isolation means induration. We exaggerate the intellectual dependence of childhood so that children are too much kept in leading strings, and then we exaggerate the independence of adult life from intimacy of contacts and communication with others. When the identity of the moral process with the processes of specific growth is realized, the more conscious and formal education of childhood will be seen to be the most economical and efficient means of social advance and reorganization, and it will also be evident that the test of all the institutions of adult life is their effect in furthering continued education. Government, business, art, religion, all social institutions have a meaning, a purpose. That purpose is to set free and to develop the capacities of human individuals without respect to race, sex, class or economic status. And this is all one with saying that the test of their value is the extent to which they educate every individual into the full stature of his possibility. Democracy has many meanings, but if it has a moral meaning, it is found in resolving that the supreme test of all political institutions and industrial arrangements shall be the contribution they make to the all-around growth of every member of society.

# FRIEDRICH NIETZSCHE

FRIEDRICH NIETZSCHE (1844–1900) was born and educated in Germany. After completing his education, he was appointed Professor of Classical Philology at the University of Basel in Switzerland, a position which he held for ten years until ill health forced his retirement. For the remainder of his life, he traveled, studied, and wrote. Writing often in an aphoristic style, he became famous for his biting criticisms of traditional European morality and for the new values which he proposed. His major works include: *Beyond Good and Evil* (1886), *The Genealogy of Morals* (1887), *Thus Spake Zarathustra* (1883–85), and *The Will to Power* (1909–10).

## *The Will to Power**

### I

*Whose will to power is morality?*  The *common factor* of all European history since the time of *Socrates* is the attempt to make the *moral values* dominate all other values, in order that they should not be only the leader and judge of life, but also of: (1) knowledge, (2) Art, (3) political and social aspirations. . . .

What is the meaning of this *will to power on the part of moral values,* which has played such a part in the world's prodigious evolutions?

Answer: Three powers lie concealed behind it: (1) the instinct of the *herd* opposed to the strong and independent; (2) the instinct of all *sufferers* and all *abortions* opposed to the happy and well-constituted; (3) the instinct of the mediocre opposed to the exceptions. . . .

### II

*The tendency of moral evolution.*  Every one's desire is that there should be no other teaching and valuation of things than those by means of which he himself succeeds. Thus the *fundamental tendency* of the *weak* and *mediocre* of all times, has been to *enfeeble the strong and to reduce them to the level of*

---

* From *The Will to Power*, by Friedrich Nietzsche, Sections 274, 345, 280, 276, 279, 285, 870, 390, 957, 1008, 399, and 972. Translated by A. M. Ludovici in *The Complete Works of Nietzsche*, Vols. XIV and XV. Copyright, 1924, The Macmillan Company. Used by permission.

*the weak: their chief weapon in this process* was the *moral principle.* The attitude of the strong towards the weak is branded as evil; the highest states of the strong become bad bywords. . . .

### III

The instinct of the herd values the *juste milieu* and the *average* as the highest and most precious of all things: the spot where the majority is to be found, and the air that it breathes there. In this way it is the opponent of all order of rank; it regards a climb from the level to the heights in the same light as a descent from the majority to the minority. The herd regards the *exception,* whether it be above or beneath its general level, as something which is antagonistic and dangerous to itself. Their trick in dealing with the exceptions above them, the strong, the mighty, the wise, and the fruitful, is to persuade them to become guardians, herdsmen, and watchmen—in fact, to become their *head-servants:* thus they convert a danger into a thing which is useful. In the middle, fear ceases: here a man is alone with nothing; here there is not much room even for misunderstandings; here there is equality; here a man's individual existence is not felt as a reproach, but as the *right* existence; here contentment reigns supreme. Mistrust is active only towards the exceptions; to be an exception is to be a sinner.

### IV

The whole of the morality of Europe is based upon the values *which are useful to the herd:* the sorrow of all higher and exceptional men is explained by the fact that everything which distinguishes them from others reaches their consciousness in the form of a feeling of their own smallness and egregiousness. It is the *virtues* of modern men which are the causes of pessimistic gloominess; the mediocre, like the herd, are not troubled much with questions or with conscience—they are cheerful. (Among the gloomy strong men, Pascal and Schopenhauer are noted examples.)

*The more dangerous a quality seems to the herd, the more completely it is condemned.*

### V

*A criticism of the virtues of the herd.* Inertia is active: (1) In confidence, because mistrust makes suspense, reflection, and observation necessary. (2) In veneration, where the gulf that separates power is great and submission necessary: then, so that fear may cease to exist, everybody tries to love and esteem, while the difference in power is interpreted as a difference of value: and thus the relationship to the powerful *no longer has anything revolting in it.* (3) In the sense of truth. What is truth? Truth is that explanation of things which causes us the smallest amount of mental exertion (apart from this, lying is extremely fatiguing). (4) In sympathy. It is a relief to know one's self on the same level with all, to feel as all feel, and to *accept* a belief which is already current; it is something passive beside the activity which appropriates and continually carries into practice the most individual rights of valuation (the latter process allows of no repose). (5) In impartiality and coolness of judgement: people scout the strain of being moved, and prefer to be detached and "objective." (6) In uprightness: people prefer to obey a law which is to hand rather than to *create* a new one, rather than to command themselves and others; the fear of commanding—it is better to submit than to rebel. (7) In toleration; the fear of exercising a right or of enforcing a judgment.

## VI

My teaching is this, that the herd seeks to maintain and preserve one type of man, and that it defends itself on two sides—that is to say, against those which are decadents from its ranks (criminals, etc.), and against those who rise superior to its dead level. The instincts of the herd tend to a stationary state of society; they merely preserve. They have no creative power. . . .

## VII

*The root of all evil*: that the slave morality of modesty, chastity, selflessness, and absolute obedience should have triumphed. Dominating natures were thus condemned (1) to hypocrisy, (2) to qualms of conscience—creative natures regarded themselves as rebels against God, uncertain and hemmed in by eternal values. . . .

## VIII

My ultimate conclusion is, that the *real* man represents a much higher value than the "desirable" man of any ideal that has ever existed hitherto; that all "desiderata" in regard to mankind have been absurd and dangerous dissipations by means of which a particular kind of man has sought to establish *his* measures of preservation and of growth as a law for all; that every "desideratum" of this kind which has been made to dominate has *reduced* man's worth, his strength, and his trust in the future; that the indigence and mediocre intellectuality of man becomes most apparent, even today, when he reveals a *desire*; that man's ability to fix values has hitherto been developed too inadequately to do justice to the actual, not merely to the "desirable," *worth of man*; that, up to the present, ideals have really been the power which has most slandered man and the world, the poisonous fumes which have hung over reality, and which have *seduced men to yearn for nonentity*. . . .

## IX

The question, and at the same time the task, is approaching with hesitation, terrible as Fate, but nevertheless inevitable: how shall the earth as a whole be ruled? And to what end shall man as a whole—no longer as a people or as a race—be reared and trained?

Legislative moralities are the principal means by which one can form mankind, according to the fancy of a creative and profound will: provided, of course, that such an artistic will of the first order gets the power into its own hands, and can make its creative will prevail over long periods in the form of legislation, religions, and morals. At present, and probably for some time to come, one will seek such colossally creative men, such really great men, as I understand them, in vain: they will be lacking, until, after many disappointments, we are forced to begin to understand why it is they are lacking, and that nothing bars with greater hostility their rise and development, at present and for some time to come, than that which is now called *the* morality in Europe. Just as if there were no other kind of morality, and could be no other kind, than the one we have already characterized as herd-morality. It is this morality which is now striving with all its power to attain to that green-meadow happiness on earth, which consists in security, absence of danger, ease, facilities for livelihood, and, last but not least, "if all goes well," even hopes to dispense with all kinds of shepherds and bellwethers. The two doctrines which it preaches most universally are "equality of rights" and "pity for all sufferers"—and it even regards suffering itself as something which must be got rid of absolutely. That such ideas may be modern leads one to think very poorly of modernity. He, however, who has reflected deeply concerning the question, how and where the plant man has hitherto grown most vigorously, is forced to believe that this has always taken place under the opposite conditions; that to this end the danger of the situation has to increase enormously, his inventive faculty and dissembling powers have to fight their way under long oppression and compulsion, and his will to life has to be increased to the unconditioned will to power, to over-power: he believes that danger, severity, violence, peril in the street and in the heart, inequality of rights, secrecy, stoicism, seductive art, and devilry of every kind —in short, the opposite of all gregarious desiderata—are necessary for the elevation of man. Such a morality with opposite designs, which would rear man upwards instead of to comfort and mediocrity; such a morality, with the intention of producing a ruling caste—the future lords of the earth—must, in order to be taught at all, introduce itself as if it were in some way correlated to the prevailing moral law, and must come forward under the cover of the latter's words and forms. But seeing that, to this end, a host of transitionary and deceptive measures must be discovered, and that the life of a single individual stands for almost nothing in view of the accomplishment of such lengthy tasks and aims, the first thing that must be done is to rear a *new kind* of man in whom the duration of the necessary will and the necessary instincts is guaranteed for many generations. This must be a new kind of ruling species and caste—this ought to be quite as clear as the somewhat lengthy and not easily expressed consequences of this thought. The aim should be to prepare a *transvaluation of values* for a particularly strong kind of man, most highly gifted in intellect and will, and, to this end, slowly and cautiously to liberate in him a whole host of slandered instincts hitherto held in check: whoever meditates about this problem belongs to us, the free spirits. . . .

## X

Any doctrine would be superfluous for which everything is not already prepared in the way of accumulated forces and explosive material. A transvaluation of values can only be accomplished when there is a tension of new needs, and a new set of needy people who feel all old values as painful—although they are not conscious of what is wrong.

## XI

These are the things I demand of you—however badly they may sound in your ears: that you subject moral valuations themselves to criticism. That you should put a stop to your instinctive moral impulse—which in this case demands submission and not criticism—with the question: "why precisely submission?" That this yearning for a "why?"—for a criticism of morality should not only be your present form of morality, but the sublimest of all moralities, and an honour to yourselves and to the age you live in. . . .

## XII

*The lawgivers of the future.* After having tried for a long time in vain to attach a particular meaning to the word "philosopher"—for I found many antagonistic traits—I recognised that we can distinguish between two kinds of philosophers:—

(1) Those who desire to establish any large system of values (logical or moral);

(2) Those who are the *lawgivers* of such valuations.

The former try to seize upon the world of the present or the past, by embodying or abbreviating the multifarious phenomena by means of signs: their object is to make it possible for us to survey, to reflect upon, to comprehend, and to utilise everything that has happened hitherto—they serve the purpose of man by using all past things to the benefit of his future.

The second class, however, are *commanders*; they say: "Thus shall it be!"

They alone determine the "whither" and the "wherefore," and that which will be useful and beneficial to man; they have command over the previous work of scientific men, and all knowledge is to them only a means to their creations. This second kind of philosopher seldom appears; and as a matter of fact their situation and their danger is appalling. How often have they not intentionally blindfolded their eyes in order to shut out the sight of the small strip of ground which separates them from the abyss and from utter destruction. Plato, for instance, when he persuaded himself that "the good," as he wanted it, was not Plato's good, but "the good in itself," the eternal treasure which a certain man of the name of Plato had chanced to find on his way! This same will to blindness prevails in a much coarser form in the case of the founders of religion; their "Thou shalt" must on no account sound to their ears like "I will"—they only dare to pursue their task as if under the command of God; their legislation of values can only be a burden they can bear if they regard it as "revelation," in this way their conscience is not crushed by the responsibility.

As soon as those two comforting expedients—that of Plato and that of Muhammed—have been overthrown, and no thinker can any longer relieve his conscience with the hypothesis "God" or "eternal values," the claim of the lawgiver to determine new values rises to an awfulness which has not yet been experienced. . . .

## Beyond Good and Evil*

### I

I insist upon it that people finally cease confounding philosophical workers, and in general scientific men, with philosophers—that precisely here one should strictly give "each his own," and not give those far too much, these far too little. It may be necessary for the education of the real philosopher that he himself should have once stood upon all those steps upon which his servants, the scientific workers of philosophy, remain standing, and *must* remain standing: he himself must perhaps have been critic, and dogmatist, and historian, and besides, poet, and collector, and traveler, and riddle-reader, and moralist, and seer, and "free spirit," and almost everything, in order to traverse the whole range of human values and estimations, and that he may *be able* with a variety of eyes and consciences to look from a height to any distance, from a depth up to any height, from a nook into any expanse. But

* From *Beyond Good and Evil*, by Friedrich Nietzsche, Sections 211 and 212. Translated by Helen Zimmern in *The Complete Works of Nietzsche*, Vol. XII. Copyright, 1924, The Macmillan Company. Used by permission.

all these are only preliminary conditions for his task; this task itself demands something else—it requires him *to create values*. The philosophical workers, after the excellent pattern of Kant and Hegel, have to fix and formalise some great existing body of valuations—that is to say, former *determinations of value*, creations of value, which have become prevalent, and are for a time called "truths"—whether in the domain of the *logical*, the *political* (moral), or the *artistic*. It is for these investigators to make whatever has happened and been esteemed hitherto, conspicuous, conceivable, intelligible, and manageable, to shorten everything long, even "time" itself, and to *subjugate* the entire past: an immense and wonderful task, in the carrying out of which all refined pride, all tenacious will, can surely find satisfaction. *The real philosophers, however, are commanders and law-givers*; they say: "Thus *shall* it be!" They determine first the Whither and the Why of mankind, and thereby set aside the previous labour of all philosophical workers, and all subjugators of the past—they grasp at the future with a creative hand, and whatever is and was, becomes for them thereby a means, an instrument, and a hammer. Their "knowing" is *creating*, their creating is a law-giving, their will to truth is—*Will to Power*. —Are there at present such philosophers? Have there ever been such philosophers? *Must* there not be such philosophers some day? . . .

## II

It is always more obvious to me that the philosopher, as a man *indispensable* for the morrow and the day after the morrow, has ever found himself, and *has been obliged* to find himself, in contradiction to the day in which he lives; his enemy has always been the ideal of his day. Hitherto all those extraordinary furtherers of humanity whom one calls philosophers—who rarely regarded themselves as lovers of wisdom, but rather as disagreeable fools and dangerous interrogators—have found their mission, their hard, involuntary, imperative mission (in the end however the greatness of their mission), in being the bad conscience of their age. In putting the vivisector's knife to the breast of the very *virtues of their age*, they have betrayed their own secret; it has been for the sake of a *new* greatness of man, a new untrodden path to his aggrandisement. They have always disclosed how much hypocrisy, indolence, self-indulgence, and self-neglect, how much falsehood was concealed under the most venerated types of contemporary morality, how much virtue was *outlived*; they have always said: "We must remove hence to where *you* are least at home." . . .

# JEAN-PAUL SARTRE

JEAN-PAUL SARTRE (1905–      ), a leading French existentialist, was Professor of Philosophy at Lycée Condorcet in Paris from 1935 to 1942. A successful playwright and novelist, as well as a philosopher, Sartre has given up teaching to devote his time to writing. His major works include: *The Wall* (a short story, 1938), *The Emotions: Outline of a Theory* (1939), *Being and Nothingness* (1943), *The Flies* (a play, 1943), *No Exit* (a play, 1945), *The Age of Reason* (a novel, 1945), and *Existentialism and Humanism* (1946).

## Existentialism*

Atheistic existentialism, of which I am a representative, declares . . . that if God does not exist there is at least one being whose existence comes before its essence, a being which exists before it can be defined by any conception of it. That being is man or . . . the human reality. What do we mean by saying that existence precedes essence? We mean that man first of all exists, encounters himself, surges up in the world—and defines himself afterwards. If man as the existentialist sees him is not definable, it is because to begin with he is nothing. He will not be anything until later, and then he will be what he makes of himself. Thus, there is no human nature, because there is no God to have a conception of it. Man simply is. Not that he is simply what he conceives himself to be, but he is what he wills, and as he conceives himself after already existing—as he wills to be after that leap towards existence Man is nothing else but that which he makes of himself. That is the first principle of existentialism. And this is what people call its "subjectivity," using the word as a reproach against us. But what do we mean to say by this, but that man is of a greater dignity than a stone or a table? For we mean to say that man primarily exists—that man is, before all else, something which propels itself towards a future and is aware that it is doing so. Man is, indeed, a project which possesses a subjective life, instead of being a kind of moss, or a fungus or a cauliflower. Before that projection of the self nothing exists; not even in the heaven of intelligence: man will only attain existence when he is what he purposes to be. Not, however, what he may wish to be. For

* From *Existentialism and Humanism*, by Jean-Paul Sartre. Copyright, 1946, Editions Nagel. Translated by Philip Mairet, published, 1948, by Methuen and Company, Ltd. Used by permission of Methuen and Company, Ltd., and Philosophical Library.

what we usually understand by wishing or willing is a conscious decision taken—much more often than not—after we have made ourselves what we are. I may wish to join a party, to write a book or to marry—but in such a case what is usually called my will is probably a manifestation of a prior and more spontaneous decision. If, however, it is true that existence is prior to essence, man is responsible for what he is. Thus, the first effect of existentialism is that it puts every man in possession of himself as he is, and places the entire responsibility for his existence squarely upon his own shoulders. And, when we say that man is responsible for himself, we do not mean that he is responsible only for his own individuality, but that he is responsible for all men. The word "subjectivism" is to be understood in two senses, and our adversaries play upon only one of them. Subjectivism means, on the one hand, the freedom of the individual subject and, on the other, that man cannot pass beyond human subjectivity. It is the latter which is the deeper meaning of existentialism. When we say that man chooses himself, we do mean that every one of us must choose himself; but by that we also mean that in choosing for himself he chooses for all men. For in effect, of all the actions a man may take in order to create himself as he wills to be, there is not one which is not creative, at the same time, of an image of man such as he believes he ought to be. To choose between this or that is at the same time to affirm the value of that which is chosen; for we are unable ever to choose the worse. What we choose is always the better; and nothing can be better for us unless it is better for all. If, moreover, existence precedes essence and we will to exist at the same time as we fashion our image, that image is valid for all and for the entire epoch in which we find ourselves. Our responsibility is thus much greater than we had supposed, for it concerns mankind as a whole. If I am a worker, for instance, I may choose to join a Christian rather than a Communist trade union. And if, by that membership, I choose to signify that resignation is, after all, the attitude that best becomes a man, that man's kingdom is not upon this earth, I do not commit myself alone to that view. Resignation is my will for everyone, and my action is, in consequence, a commitment on behalf of all mankind. Or if, to take a more personal case, I decide to marry and to have children, even though this decision proceeds simply from my situation, from my passion or my desire, I am thereby committing not only myself, but humanity as a whole, to the practice of monogamy. I am thus responsible for myself and for all men, and I am creating a certain image of man as I would have him to be. In fashioning myself I fashion man.

This may enable us to understand what is meant by such terms—perhaps a little grandiloquent—as anguish, abandonment and despair. As you will soon see, it is very simple. First, what do we mean by anguish? The existentialist frankly states that man is in anguish. His meaning is as follows—When a man commits himself to anything, fully realizing that he is not only choosing what he will be, but is thereby at the same time a legislator deciding for the whole of mankind—in such a moment a man cannot escape from the sense of complete and profound responsibility. There are many, indeed, who show no such anxiety. But we affirm that they are merely disguising their anguish or are in flight from it. Certainly, many people think that in what they are doing they commit no one but themselves to anything: and if you ask them, "What would happen if everyone did so?" they shrug their shoulders and reply, "Everyone does not do so." But in truth, one ought always to ask oneself what would happen if everyone did as one is doing; nor can one escape from that disturbing thought except by a kind of self-deception. The man who lies in self-excuse, by saying "Everyone will not do it" must be ill at ease in his conscience, for the act of lying implies the universal value which it denies. By its very disguise his anguish reveals itself. This is the anguish that Kierkegaard called "the anguish of Abraham." You know the story: An angel commanded Abraham to sacrifice his son: and obedience was obligatory, if it really was an angel who had appeared and said, "Thou, Abraham, shalt sacrifice thy son." But anyone in such a case would wonder, first, whether it was indeed an angel and secondly, whether I am really Abraham. Where are the proofs? A certain mad woman who suffered from hallucinations said that people were telephoning to her, and giving her orders. The doctor asked, "But who is it that speaks to you?" She replied: "He says it is God." And what, indeed, could prove to her that it was God? If an angel appears to me, what is the proof that it is an angel; or, if I hear voices, who can prove that they proceed from heaven and not from hell, or from my own subconsciousness or some pathological condition? Who can prove that they are really addressed to me?

Who, then, can prove that I am the proper person to impose, by my own choice, my conception of man upon mankind? I shall never find any proof whatever; there will be no sign to convince me of it. If a voice speaks to me, it is still I myself who must decide whether the voice is or is not that of an angel. If I regard a certain course of action as good, it is only I who choose to say that it is good and not bad. There is nothing to show that I am Abraham: nevertheless I also am obliged at every instant to perform actions which are examples. Everything happens to every man as though the whole human race had its eyes fixed upon what he is doing and regulated its conduct accordingly. So every man ought to say, "Am I really a man who has the right to act in such a manner that humanity regulates itself by what I do." If a man does not say that, he is dissembling his anguish. Clearly, the anguish with which we are concerned here is not one that could lead to quietism or inaction. It is anguish pure and simple, of the kind well known to all those who have borne responsibilities. When, for instance, a military leader takes upon himself the responsibility for an attack and sends a number of men to their death, he chooses to do it and at bottom he alone chooses. No doubt he acts under a higher command, but its orders, which are more general, require interpretation by him and upon that interpretation depends the life of ten, fourteen or twenty men. In making the decision, he cannot but feel a certain anguish. All leaders know that anguish. It does not prevent their acting, on the contrary it is the very condition of their action, for the action presupposes that there is a plurality of possibilities, and in choosing one of these, they realize that it has value only because it is chosen. Now it is anguish of that kind which existentialism describes, and moreover, as we shall see, makes explicit through direct responsibility towards other men who are concerned. Far from being a screen which could separate us from action, it is a condition of action itself.

And when we speak of "abandonment" . . . we only mean to say that God does not exist, and that it is necessary to draw the consequences of his absence right to the end. The existentialist is strongly opposed to a certain type of secular moralism which seeks to suppress God at the least possible expense. Towards 1880, when the French professors endeavored to formulate a secular morality, they said something like this:—God is a useless and costly hypothesis, so we will do without it. However, if we are to have morality, a society and a law-abiding world, it is essential that certain values should be taken seriously; they must have an *à priori* existence ascribed to them. It must be considered obligatory *à priori* to be honest, not to lie, not to beat one's wife, to bring up children and so forth; so we are going to do a little work on this subject, which will enable us to show that these values exist all the same, inscribed in an intelligible heaven although, of course, there is no God. In other words—and this is, I believe, the purport of all that we in France call radicalism—nothing will be changed if God does not exist; we shall rediscover the same norms of honesty, progress and humanity, and we shall have disposed of God as an out-of-date hypothesis which will die away quietly of itself. The existentialist, on the contrary, finds it extremely embarrassing that God does not exist, for there disappears with Him all possibility of finding values in an intelligible heaven. There can no longer be any good *à priori*, since there is no infinite and perfect consciousness to think it. It is nowhere written that "the good" exists, that one must be honest or must not lie, since we are now upon the plane where there are only men. Dostoevsky once wrote "If God did not exist, everything would be permitted"; and that, for existentialism, is the starting point. Everything is indeed permitted if God does not exist, and man is in consequence forlorn, for he cannot find anything to depend upon either within or outside himself. He discovers forthwith, that he is without excuse. For if indeed existence precedes essence, one will never be able to explain one's action by reference to a given and specific human nature; in other words, there is no determinism —man is free, man *is* freedom. Nor, on the other hand, if God does not exist, are we provided with any values or commands that could legitimize our behavior. Thus we have neither behind us, nor before us in a luminous realm of values, any means of justification or excuse. We are left alone, without excuse. That is what I mean when I say that man is condemned to be free. Condemned, because he did not create himself, yet is nevertheless at liberty, and from the moment that he is thrown into this world he is responsible for everything he does. The existentialist does not believe in the power of passion. He will never regard a grand passion as a destructive torrent upon which a man is swept into certain actions as by fate, and which, therefore, is an excuse for them. He thinks that man is responsible for his passion. Neither will an existentialist think that a man can find help through some sign being vouchsafed upon earth for his orientation: for he thinks that the man himself interprets the sign as he chooses. He thinks that every man, without any support or help whatever, is condemned at every instant to invent man. . . .

As an example by which you may the better understand this state of abandonment, I will refer to the case of a pupil of mine, who sought me out in the following circumstances. His father was quarrelling with his mother and was also inclined to be a "collaborator"; his elder brother had been killed in the German offensive of 1940 and this young man, with a sentiment somewhat primitive but generous, burned to avenge him. His mother was living alone with him, deeply afflicted by the semi-treason of his father and by the death of her eldest son, and her one consolation was in this young man. But he, at this moment, had the choice between going to England to join the Free French Forces or of staying near his mother and helping her to live. He fully realized that this woman lived only for him and that his disappearance—or perhaps his death—would plunge her into despair. He also realized that, concretely and in fact, every action he performed on his mother's behalf would be sure of effect in the sense of aiding her to live, whereas anything he did in order to go and fight would be an ambiguous action which might vanish like water into sand and serve no purpose. For instance, to set out for England he would have to wait indefinitely in a Spanish camp on the way through Spain; or, on arriving in England or in Algiers he might be put into an office to fill up forms. Consequently, he found himself confronted by two very different modes of action; the one concrete, immediate, but directed towards only one individual; and the other an action addressed to an end infinitely greater, a national collectivity, but for that very reason ambiguous—and it might be frustrated on the way. At the same time, he was hesitating between two kinds of morality; on the one side the morality of sympathy, of personal devotion and, on the other side, a morality of wider scope but of more debatable validity. He had to choose between those two. What could help him to choose? Could the Christian doctrine? No. Christian doctrine says: Act with charity, love your neighbour, deny yourself for others, choose the way which is hardest, and so forth. But which is the harder road? To whom does one owe the more brotherly love, the patriot or the mother? Which is the more useful aim, the general one of fighting in and for the whole community, or the precise aim of helping one particular person to live? Who can give an answer to that à priori? No one. Nor is it given in any ethical scripture. The Kantian ethic says, Never regard another as a means, but always as an end. Very well; if I remain with my mother, I shall be regarding her as the end and not as a means: but by the same token I am in danger of treating as means those who are fighting on my behalf; and the converse is also true, that if I go to the aid of the combatants I shall be treating them as the end at the risk of treating my mother as a means.

If values are uncertain, if they are still too abstract to determine the particular, concrete case under consideration, nothing remains but to trust in our instincts. That is what this young man tried to do; and when I saw him he said, "In the end, it is feeling that counts; the direction in which it is really pushing me is the one I ought to choose. If I feel that I love my mother enough to sacrifice everything else for her—my will to be avenged, all my longings for action and adventure—then I stay with her. If, on the contrary, I feel that my love for her is not enough, I go." But how does one estimate the strength of a feeling? The value of his feeling for his mother was determined precisely by the fact that he was standing by her. I may say that I love a certain friend enough to sacrifice such or such a sum of money for him, but I cannot prove that unless I have done it. I may say, "I love my mother enough to remain with her," if actually I have remained with her. I can only estimate the strength of this affection if I have performed an action by which it is defined and ratified. But if I then appeal to this affection to justify my action, I find myself drawn into a vicious circle. . . .

In other words, feeling is formed by the deeds that one does; therefore I cannot consult it as a guide to action. And that is to say that I can neither seek within myself for an authentic impulse to action, nor can I expect, from some ethic, formulae that will enable me to act. You may say that the youth did, at least, go to a professor to ask for advice. But if you seek counsel—from a priest, for example—you have selected that priest; and at bottom you already knew, more or less, what he would advise. In other words, to choose an adviser is nevertheless to commit oneself by that choice. If you are a Christian, you will say, Consult a priest; but there are collaborationists, priests who are resisters and priests who wait for the tide to turn: which will you choose? Had this young man chosen a priest of the resistance, or one of the collaboration, he would have decided beforehand the kind of advice he was to receive. Similarly, in coming to me, he knew what advice I should give him, and I had but one reply to make. You are free, therefore choose—that is to say, invent. No rule of general morality can show you what you ought to do: no signs are vouchsafed in this world. . . . That is what "abandonment" implies, that we ourselves decide our being. And with this abandonment goes anguish.

As for "despair," the meaning of this expression is extremely simple. It merely means that we limit ourselves to a reliance upon that which is within our wills, or within the sum of the probabilities which render our action feasible. Whenever one wills anything, there are always these elements of probability. If I am counting upon a visit from a friend, who may be coming by train or by tram, I presuppose that the train will arrive at the appointed time, or that the tram will not be derailed. I remain in the realm of possibilities; but one does not rely upon any possibilities beyond those that are strictly concerned in one's action. Beyond the point at which the possibilities under consideration cease to affect my action, I ought to disinterest myself. For there is no God and no prevenient design, which can adapt the world and all its possibilities to my will. When Descartes said, "Conquer yourself rather than the world," what he meant was, at bottom, the same— that we should act without hope. . . .

To say that it does not matter what you choose is not correct. In one sense choice is possible, but what is not possible is not to choose. I can always choose, but I must know that if I do not choose, that is still a choice. This, although it may appear merely formal, is of great importance as a limit to fantasy and caprice. For, when I confront a real situation—for example, that I am a sexual being, able to have relations with a being of the other sex and able to have children—I am obliged to choose my attitude to it, and in every respect I bear the responsibility of the choice which, in committing myself, also commits the whole of humanity. . . . Man finds himself in an organized situation in which he is himself involved: his choice involves mankind in its entirety, and he cannot avoid choosing. Either he must remain single, or he must marry without having children, or he must marry and have children. In any case, and whichever he may choose, it is impossible for him, in respect of this situation, not to take complete responsibility. Doubtless he chooses without reference to any pre-established values, but it is unjust to tax him with caprice. Rather let us say that the moral choice is comparable to the construction of a work of art.

But here I must at once digress to make it quite clear that we are not propounding an aesthetic morality, for our adversaries are disingenuous enough to reproach us even with that. I mention the work of art only by way of comparison. That being understood, does anyone reproach an artist, when he paints a picture, for not following rules established à priori? Does one ever ask what is the picture that he ought to paint? As everyone knows, there is no pre-defined picture for him to make; the artist applies himself to the composition of a picture, and the picture that ought to be made is precisely that which he will have made. As everyone knows, there are no aesthetic values à priori, but there are values which will appear in due course in the coherence of the picture, in the relation between the will to create and the finished work. No one can tell what the painting of tomorrow will be like; one cannot judge a painting until it is done. What has that to do with morality? We are in the same creative situation. We never speak of a work of art as irresponsible; when we are discussing a canvas by Picasso, we understand very well that the composition became what it is at the time when he was painting it, and that his works are part and parcel of his entire life.

It is the same upon the plane of morality. There is this in common between art and morality, that in both we have to do with creation and invention. We cannot decide à priori what it is that should be done. I think it was made sufficiently clear to you in the case of that student who came to see me, that to whatever ethical system he might appeal, the Kantian or any other, he could find no sort of guidance whatever; he was obliged to invent the law for himself. Certainly we cannot say that this man, in choosing to remain with his mother—that is, in taking sentiment, personal devotion and concrete charity as his moral foundations—would be making an irresponsible choice, nor could we do so if he preferred the sacrifice of going away to England. Man makes himself; he is not found ready-made; he makes himself by the choice of his morality, and he cannot but choose a morality, such is the pressure of circumstances upon him.

## IS THERE A FIXED MORAL STANDARD?
## —SUGGESTED READINGS

Dewey, J., and Tufts, J. H., *Ethics*, rev. ed., New York, Holt, 1932, esp. Part II.

Hook, S., *John Dewey: An Intellectual Portrait*, New York, Day, 1939, Chap. 7. (exposition)

Kaufmann, W. (ed.), *Existentialism from Dostoevsky to Sartre*, New York, Meridian, 1956. (selections from the writings of leading existentialists)

Kaufmann, W., *Nietzsche: Philosopher, Psychologist, Antichrist*, Princeton, Princeton University Press, 1950, esp. Parts III and IV. (exposition)

Mounier, E., *Existentialist Philosophies: An Introduction*, New York, Macmillan, 1949. (exposition)

Nietzsche, F., *The Genealogy of Morals*, 1887.

# III. The Analytic Approach
## to Ethics

UP TO THIS POINT, we have been concerned with discussion *in* ethics, most particularly with proposals purporting to define a universal moral standard. Such has always been the traditonal form of ethical inquiry. In recent years, however, many moral philosophers have become unwilling to take ethical discourse for granted; they have come to believe that before we make statements *in* ethics, we ought first to give consideration to certain important matters *about* ethics (*metaethics*). Their concern has been to clarify the basic concepts of ethics, to determine precisely what it is that we assert when we say something is "good" or "right," to state with precision the extent to which ethical propositions serve to communicate knowledge, to elucidate the rules of usage for ethical discourse, and to formulate what methods, if any, may be appropriate for the resolution of moral controversy. Since all these tasks require the patient analysis of the language and logic of morals, these moral philosophers may be said to adopt an *analytic approach* to ethics.

In what follows, three groups of analytic ethical philosophers are represented. Those who belong to the *intuitionist* school hold that their analyses provide the ground for urging that man possesses genuine knowledge concerning what is good and right. Those who adopt the *emotive theory* use analyses of ethical terms and statements to support the contention that ethical propositions do not convey knowledge but function to express and redirect man's emotions. Members of the third group conclude from their analyses that, although it would be incorrect to assert that ethical propositions function primarily to impart knowledge, there are nevertheless *good reasons* which can be given in support of our moral judgments.

# A. INTUITIONISM

Intuitionists maintain that when the basic questions of ethical theory are clearly formulated, it is obvious that the fundamental propositions of ethics are not susceptible of proof by argument. For them, ethical knowledge is attainable through direct moral insight, or intuition. Thus, G. E. Moore asserts that our apprehension of the quality *goodness* is like our immediate awareness of a color; we simply know directly that the quality in question is, or is not, present.

Intuitionists, therefore, would assert that the expression "x is good" (or "right") is similar in status to the expression "x is yellow." In each case, a person who uses such expressions is asserting that a quality belongs to the thing in question. For the intuitionists, a further parallel between these expressions is to be noted. If one man says that x is yellow and another maintains that x is not yellow, one of the two must be wrong. Similarly, the intuitionists would argue, if one man says that x is good (or right) and another asserts that x is not good (or right), one must be mistaken. For the intuitionists, then, our moral judgments, like our judgments of color, are either true or false; the man who makes a false judgment can only be asked to "look again."

The intuitionists are agreed that it is a fundamental mistake to attempt to define certain of our basic moral concepts. According to Moore, for example, "good" does not *mean* pleasure, or self-realization, or fulfillment of interest; goodness *is* an immediately apprehended quality that is what it is and not any other thing. Thus Moore argues that whenever teleological ethical theories try to define good in any way at all, they necessarily commit what he calls "the naturalistic fallacy."

In the selections to follow, MOORE states his view that goodness is an indefinable quality which men directly apprehend. He then urges that *right* is definable as that which produces the greatest *good*.* Against Moore, ROSS argues that rightness is also an indefinable quality and that Moore commits a fallacy of his own in attempting to define or explain right in terms of good. According to Ross, we can directly apprehend that it is right to perform certain kinds of acts; we do not always need to consider the good which they bring into existence. Ross argues, for example, that we know that it is right to keep our promises, although sometimes keeping our promises may not promote the greatest good.† PRICHARD maintains that the characteristic mistake of moral philosophy has been to suppose that argument can persuade us to do what we ought to do. According to Prichard, no one can prove to us that we ought to do anything; he would agree with Ross that the only basis of man's sense of moral obligation is a direct or intuitive apprehension of his duties.

* Because Moore regards "goodness" as the fundamental moral concept, he may be classified as a teleologist in ethics.

† Because Ross, regards "rightness" as a fundamental moral concept, he may be classified as a deontologist in ethics.

Three criticisms of intuitionism are presented. MACBEATH offers a criticism which is based upon an appeal to facts. If intuitionism were true, he says, then (1) there would be no widespread disagreement between men of different cultures as to what is good or right; and (2) all men would regard their moral judgments as universally valid. In the light of evidence from anthropology, Macbeath urges that we must reject both of these propositions. TOULMIN presents a criticism of intuitionism based upon an analysis of linguistic usage. He maintains that it is a fundamental mistake to suppose that the expression "x is good" (or "right") is similar in status to the expression "x is yellow." NOWELL-SMITH criticizes intuitionism by pointing out what he holds to be a practical consequence of the view: he contends that intuitionism may readily lead to intolerance and to the persecution of one's opponents for their moral beliefs.

# G. E. MOORE

GEORGE EDWARD MOORE (1873–1958) was Professor of Philosophy at Cambridge University; for many years he also served as editor of the British periodical *Mind*. He was a pioneer figure in the development of contemporary analytic philosophy: his great concern was for clarity in formulating both philosophic questions and answers to them. In ethics he espoused an intuitionist interpretation of utilitarianism. His major works include: *Principia Ethica* (1903), *Ethics* (1912), *Philosophical Studies* (1922), and *Some Main Problems of Philosophy* (1953).

## Principia Ethica*

### Preface

It appears to me that in Ethics, as in all other philosophical studies, the difficulties and disagreements, of which its history is full, are mainly due to a very simple cause: namely to the attempt to answer questions, without first discovering precisely *what* question it is which you desire to answer. I do not know how far this source of error would be done away, if philosophers would *try* to discover what question they were asking, before they set about to answer it; for the work of analysis and distinction is often very difficult: we may often fail to make the necessary discovery, even though we make a definite attempt to do so. But I am inclined to think that in many cases a resolute attempt would be sufficient to ensure success; so that, if only this attempt were made, many of the most glaring difficulties and disagreements in philosophy would disappear. At all events, philosophers seem, in general, not to make the attempt; and, whether in consequence of this omission or not, they are constantly endeavouring to prove that 'Yes' or 'No' will answer questions, to which *neither* answer is correct, owing to the fact that what they have before their minds is not one question, but several, to some of which the true answer is 'No,' to others 'Yes.'

I have tried . . . to distinguish clearly two kinds of question, which moral philosophers have always professed to answer, but which, as I have tried to shew, they have almost always confused both with one another and with other questions. These two questions may be expressed, the first in the form: What kind of things ought to exist for their own sakes? the second in the form: What kind of actions ought we to perform? I have tried to shew exactly what it is that we ask about a thing, when we ask whether it ought to exist for its own sake, is good in itself or has intrinsic value; and exactly what it is that we ask about an action, when we ask whether we ought to do it, whether it is a right action or a duty.

But from a clear insight into the nature of these two questions, there appears to me to follow a second most important result: namely, what is the nature of the evidence, by which alone any ethical proposition can be proved or disproved, confirmed or rendered doubtful. Once we recognise the exact meaning of the two questions, I think it also becomes plain exactly what kind of reasons are relevant as arguments for or against any particular answer to them. It becomes plain that, for answers to the *first* question, no relevant evidence whatever can be adduced: from no other truth, except themselves alone, can it be inferred that they are either true or false. We can guard against error only by taking care, that, when we try to answer a question of this kind, we have before our minds that question only, and not some other or others; but that there is great danger of such errors of confusion I have tried to shew, and also what are the chief precautions by the use of which we may guard against them. As for the *second* question, it becomes equally plain, that any answer to it *is* capable of proof or disproof—that, indeed, so many different considerations are relevant to its truth or falsehood, as to make the attainment of probability very difficult, and the attainment of certainty impossible. Nevertheless the *kind* of evidence, which is both necessary and alone relevant to such proof and disproof, is capable of exact definition. Such evidence must contain propositions of two kinds and of two kinds only: it must consist, in the first place, of truths with regard to the results of the action in question—of *causal* truths—but it must *also* contain ethical truths of our first or self-evident class. Many truths of both kinds are necessary to the proof that any action ought to be done; and any other kind of evidence is wholly irrelevant. It follows that, if any ethical philosopher offers for propositions of the first kind any evidence whatever, or if, for propositions of the second kind, he either fails to adduce both causal and ethical truths, or adduces truths that are neither, his reasoning has not the least tendency to establish his conclusions. But not only are his conclusions totally devoid of weight: we have, moreover, reason to suspect him of the error of confusion; since the offering of irrelevant evidence generally indicates that the philosopher who offers it has had before his mind, not the question which he professes to answer, but some other entirely different one. Ethical discussion, hitherto, has perhaps consisted chiefly in reasoning of this totally irrelevant kind. . . .

### Chapter I

5. . . . How 'good' is to be defined, is the most fundamental question in all Ethics. That which is meant by 'good' is, in fact, except its converse 'bad,' the *only* simple object of thought which is peculiar to Ethics. Its definition is, therefore, the most essential point in the definition of Ethics; and moreover a mistake with regard to it entails a far larger number of erroneous ethical judgments than any other. Unless this first question be fully understood, and its true answer clearly recognised, the rest of Ethics is as good as useless from the point of view of systematic knowledge. . . .

6. What, then, is good? How is good to be defined? Now, it may be thought that this is a verbal question. A definition does indeed often mean the expressing of one word's meaning in other words. But this is not the sort of definition I am asking for. Such a definition can never be of ultimate importance in any study except lexicography. If I wanted that kind of definition I should have to consider in the first place how people generally used the word 'good'; but my business is not with its proper usage, as established by custom. I should, indeed, be foolish, if I tried to use it for something which it did not usually denote: if, for instance, I were to announce that, whenever I used the word 'good,' I must be understood to be thinking of that object which is usually denoted by the word 'table.' I shall, therefore, use the word in the sense in which I think it is ordinarily used; but at the same time I am not anxious to discuss whether I am right in thinking that it is so used. My business is solely with that object or idea, which I hold, rightly or wrongly, that the word is generally used to stand for. What I want to discover is the nature of that object or idea, and about this I am extremely anxious to arrive at an agreement.

But, if we understand the question in this sense, my answer to it may seem a very disappointing one. If I am asked 'What is good?' my answer is that good is good, and that is the end of the matter. Or if I am asked 'How is good to be defined?' my answer is that it cannot be defined, and that is all

I have to say about it. But disappointing as these answers may appear, they are of the very last importance. To readers who are familiar with philosophic terminology, I can express their importance by saying that they amount to this: That propositions about the good are all of them synthetic and never analytic; and that is plainly no trivial matter. And the same thing may be expressed more popularly, by saying that, if I am right, then nobody can foist upon us such an axiom as that 'Pleasure is the only good' or that 'The good is the desired' on the pretence that this is 'the very meaning of the word.'

7.   Let us, then, consider this position. My point is that 'good' is a simple notion, just as 'yellow' is a simple notion; that, just as you cannot, by any manner of means, explain to any one who does not already know it, what yellow is, so you cannot explain what good is. Definitions of the kind that I was asking for, definitions which describe the real nature of the object or notion denoted by a word, and which do not merely tell us what the word is used to mean, are only possible when the object or notion in question is something complex. You can give a definition of a horse, because a horse has many different properties and qualities, all of which you can enumerate. But when you have enumerated them all, when you have reduced a horse to his simplest terms, then you can no longer define those terms. They are simply something which you think of or perceive, and to any one who cannot think of or perceive them, you can never, by any definition, make their nature known. It may perhaps be objected to this that we are able to describe to others, objects which they have never seen or thought of. We can, for instance, make a man understand what a chimaera is, although he has never heard of one or seen one. You can tell him that it is an animal with a lioness's head and body, with a goat's head growing from the middle of its back, and with a snake in place of a tail. But here the object which you are describing is a complex object; it is entirely composed of parts, with which we are all perfectly familiar —a snake, a goat, a lioness; and we know, too, the manner in which those parts are to be put together, because we know what is meant by the middle of a lioness's back, and where her tail is wont to grow. And so it is with all objects, not previously known, which we are able to define: they are all complex; all composed of parts, which may themselves, in the first instance, be capable of similar definition, but which must in the end be reducible to simplest parts, which can no longer be defined. But yellow and good, we say, are not complex: they are notions of that simple kind, out of which definitions are composed and with which the power of further defining ceases.

8.   When we say, as Webster says, 'The definition of horse is "A hoofed quadruped of the genus Equus,"' we may, in fact, mean three different things. (1) We may mean merely: 'When I say "horse," you are to understand that I am talking about a hoofed quadruped of the genus Equus.'

This might be called the arbitrary verbal definition: and I do not mean that good is indefinable in that sense. (2) We may mean, as Webster ought to mean: 'When most English people say "horse," they mean a hoofed quadruped of the genus Equus.' This may be called the verbal definition proper, and I do not say that good is indefinable in this sense either; for it is certainly possible to discover how people use a word: otherwise, we could never have known that 'good' may be translated by 'gut' in German and by 'bon' in French. But (3) we may, when we define horse, mean something much more important. We may mean that a certain object, which we all of us know, is composed in a certain manner: that it has four legs, a head, a heart, a liver, etc., etc., all of them arranged in definite relations to one another. It is in this sense that I deny good to be definable. I say that it is not composed of any parts, which we can substitute for it in our minds when we are thinking of it. We might think just as clearly and correctly about a horse, if we thought of all its parts and their arrangement instead of thinking of the whole: we could, I say, think how a horse differed from a donkey just as well, just as truly, in this way, as now we do, only not so easily; but there is nothing whatsoever which we could so substitute for good; and that is what I mean, when I say that good is indefinable.

9. But I am afraid I have still not removed the chief difficulty which may prevent acceptance of the proposition that good is indefinable. I do not mean to say that *the* good, that which is good, is thus indefinable; if I did think so, I should not be writing on Ethics, for my main object is to help towards discovering that definition. It is just because I think there will be less risk of error in our search for a definition of 'the good,' that I am now insisting that *good* is indefinable. I must try to explain the difference between these two. I suppose it may be granted that 'good' is an adjective. Well 'the good,' 'that which is good,' must therefore be the substantive to which the adjective 'good' will apply: it must be the whole of that to which the adjective will apply, and the adjective must *always* truly apply to it. But if it is that to which the adjective will apply, it must be something different from that adjective itself; and the whole of that something different, whatever it is, will be our definition of *the* good. Now it may be that this something will have other adjectives, beside 'good,' that will apply to it. It may be full of pleasure, for example; it may be intelligent: and if these two adjectives are really part of its definition, then it will certainly be true, that pleasure and intelligence are good. And many people appear to think that, if we say 'Pleasure and intelligence are good,' or if we say 'Only pleasure and intelligence are good,' we are defining 'good.' Well, I cannot deny that propositions of this nature may sometimes be called definitions; I do not know well enough how the word is generally used to decide upon this

point. I only wish it to be understood that that is not what I mean when I say there is no possible definition of good, and that I shall not mean this if I use the word again. I do most fully believe that some true proposition of the form 'Intelligence is good and intelligence alone is good' can be found; if none could be found, our definition of *the* good would be impossible. As it is, I believe *the* good to be definable; and yet I still say that good itself is indefinable.

10. 'Good,' then, if we mean by it that quality which we assert to belong to a thing, when we say that the thing is good, is incapable of any definition, in the most important sense of that word. The most important sense of 'definition' is that in which a definition states what are the parts which invariably compose a certain whole; and in this sense 'good' has no definition because it is simple and has no parts. It is one of those innumerable objects of thought which are themselves incapable of definition, because they are the ultimate terms by reference to which whatever *is* capable of definition must be defined. That there must be an indefinite number of such terms is obvious, on reflection; since we cannot define anything except by an analysis, which, when carried as far as it will go, refers us to something, which is simply different from anything else, and which by that ultimate difference explains the peculiarity of the whole which we are defining: for every whole contains some parts which are common to other wholes also. There is, therefore, no intrinsic difficulty in the contention that 'good' denotes a simple and indefinable quality. There are many other instances of such qualities.

Consider yellow, for example. We may try to define it, by describing its physical equivalent; we may state what kind of light-vibrations must stimulate the normal eye, in order that we may perceive it. But a moment's reflection is sufficient to shew that those light-vibrations are not themselves what we mean by yellow. *They* are not what we perceive. Indeed we should never have been able to discover their existence, unless we had first been struck by the patent difference of quality between the different colours. The most we can be entitled to say of those vibrations is that they are what corresponds in space to the yellow which we actually perceive.

Yet a mistake of this simple kind has commonly been made about 'good.' It may be true that all things which are good are *also* something else, just as it is true that all things which are yellow produce a certain kind of vibration in the light. And it is a fact, that Ethics aims at discovering what are those other properties belonging to all things which are good. But far too many philosophers have thought that when they named those other properties they were actually defining good; that these properties, in fact, were simply not 'other,' but absolutely and entirely the same with goodness. This view I propose to call the 'naturalistic fallacy' and of it I shall now endeavour to dispose.

11. Let us consider what it is such philosophers say. And first it is to be noticed that they do not agree among themselves. They not only say that they are right as to what good is, but they endeavour to prove that other people who say that it is something else, are wrong. One, for instance, will affirm that good is pleasure, another, perhaps, that good is that which is desired; and each of these will argue eagerly to prove that the other is wrong. But how is that possible? One of them says that good is nothing but the object of desire, and at the same time tries to prove that it is not pleasure. But from his first assertion, that good just means the object of desire, one of two things must follow as regards his proof:

(1) He may be trying to prove that the object of desire is not pleasure. But, if this be all, where is his Ethics? The position he is maintaining is merely a psychological one. Desire is something which occurs in our minds, and pleasure is something else which so occurs; and our would-be ethical philosopher is merely holding that the latter is not the object of the former. But what has that to do with the question in dispute? His opponent held the ethical proposition that pleasure was the good, and although he should prove a million times over the psychological proposition that pleasure is not the object of desire, he is no nearer proving his opponent to be wrong. The position is like this. One man says a triangle is a circle: another replies 'A triangle is a straight line, and I will prove to you that I am right: *for*' (this is the only argument) 'a straight line is not a circle.' 'That is quite true,' the other may reply; 'but nevertheless a triangle is a circle, and you have said nothing whatever to prove the contrary. What is proved is that one of us is wrong, for we agree that a triangle cannot be both a straight line and a circle: but which is wrong, there can be no earthly means of proving, since you define triangle as straight line and I define it as circle.'—Well, that is one alternative which any naturalistic Ethics has to face; if good is *defined* as something else, it is then impossible either to prove that any other definition is wrong or even to deny such definition.

(2) The other alternative will scarcely be more welcome. It is that the discussion is after all a verbal one. When A says 'Good means pleasant' and B says 'Good means desired,' they may merely wish to assert that most people have used the word for what is pleasant and for what is desired respectively. And this is quite an interesting subject for discussion: only it is not a whit more an ethical discussion than the last was. Nor do I think that any exponent of naturalistic Ethics would be willing to allow that this was all he meant. They are all so anxious to persuade us that what they call the good is what we really ought to do. 'Do, pray, act so, because the word "good" is generally used to denote actions of this nature': such, on this view, would be the substance of their teaching. And in so far as they tell us how we ought to act, their teaching is truly ethical, as they mean it

to be. But how perfectly absurd is the reason they would give for it! 'You are to do this, because most people use a certain word to denote conduct such as this.' 'You are to say the thing which is not, because most people call it lying.' That is an argument just as good!—My dear sirs, what we want to know from you as ethical teachers, is not how people use a word; it is not even, what kind of actions they approve, which the use of this word 'good' may certainly imply: what we want to know is simply what *is* good. We may indeed agree that what most people do think good, is actually so; we shall at all events be glad to know their opinions: but when we say their opinions about what *is* good, we do mean what we say; we do not care whether they call that thing which they mean 'horse' or 'table' or 'chair,' 'gut' or 'bon' or 'ἀγαθός'; we want to know what it is that they so call. When they say 'Pleasure is good,' we cannot believe that they merely mean 'Pleasure is pleasure' and nothing more than that.

12.  Suppose a man says 'I am pleased'; and suppose that is not a lie or a mistake but the truth. Well, if it is true, what does that mean? It means that his mind, a certain definite mind, distinguished by certain definite marks from all others, has at this moment a certain definite feeling called pleasure. 'Pleased' *means* nothing but having pleasure, and though we may be more pleased or less pleased, and even, we may admit for the present, have one or another kind of pleasure; yet in so far as it is pleasure we have, whether there be more or less of it, and whether it be of one kind or another, what we have is one definite thing, absolutely indefinable, some one thing that is the same in all the various degrees and in all the various kinds of it that there may be. We may be able to say how it is related to other things: that, for example, it is in the mind, that it causes desire, that we are conscious of it, etc., etc. We can, I say, describe its relations to other things, but define it we can *not*. And if anybody tried to define pleasure for us as being any other natural object; if anybody were to say, for instance, that pleasure *means* the sensation of red, and were to proceed to deduce from that that pleasure is a colour, we should be entitled to laugh at him and to distrust his future statements about pleasure. Well, that would be the same fallacy which I have called the naturalistic fallacy. That 'pleased' does not mean 'having the sensation of red,' or anything else whatever, does not prevent us from understanding what it does mean. It is enough for us to know that 'pleased' does mean 'having the sensation of pleasure,' and though pleasure is absolutely indefinable, though pleasure is pleasure and nothing else whatever, yet we feel no difficulty in saying that we are pleased. The reason is, of course, that when I say 'I am pleased,' I do *not* mean that 'I' am the same thing as 'having pleasure.' And similarly no difficulty need be found in my saying that 'pleasure is good' and yet not meaning that 'pleasure' is

the same thing as 'good,' that pleasure *means* good, and that good *means* pleasure. If I were to imagine that when I said 'I am pleased,' I meant that I was exactly the same thing as 'pleased,' I should not indeed call that a naturalistic fallacy, although it would be the same fallacy as I have called naturalistic with reference to Ethics. The reason of this is obvious enough. When a man confuses two natural objects with one another, defining the one by the other, if for instance, he confuses himself, who is one natural object, with 'pleased' or with 'pleasure' which are others, then there is no reason to call the fallacy naturalistic. But if he confuses 'good,' which is not in the same sense a natural object, with any natural object whatever, then there is a reason for calling that a naturalistic fallacy; its being made with regard to 'good' marks it as something quite specific, and this specific mistake deserves a name because it is so common. As for the reasons why good is not to be considered a natural object, they may be reserved for discussion in another place. But, for the present, it is sufficient to notice this: Even if it were a natural object, that would not alter the nature of the fallacy nor diminish its importance one whit. All that I have said about it would remain quite equally true: only the name which I have called it would not be so appropriate as I think it is. And I do not care about the name: what I do care about is the fallacy. It does not matter what we call it, provided we recognise it when we meet with it. It is to be met with in almost every book on Ethics; and yet it is not recognised: and that is why it is necessary to multiply illustrations of it, and convenient to give it a name. It is a very simple fallacy indeed. When we say that an orange is yellow, we do not think our statement binds us to hold that 'orange' means nothing else than 'yellow,' or that nothing can be yellow but an orange. Supposing the orange is also sweet! Does that bind us to say that 'sweet' is exactly the same thing as 'yellow,' that 'sweet' must be defined as 'yellow'? And supposing it be recognised that 'yellow' just means 'yellow' and nothing else whatever, does that make it any more difficult to hold that oranges are yellow? Most certainly it does not: on the contrary, it would be absolutely meaningless to say that oranges were yellow, unless yellow did in the end mean just 'yellow' and nothing else whatever—unless it was absolutely indefinable. We should not get any very clear notion about things, which are yellow—we should not get very far with our science, if we were bound to hold that everything which was yellow, *meant* exactly the same thing as yellow. We should find we had to hold that an orange was exactly the same thing as a stool, a piece of paper, a lemon, anything you like. We could prove any number of absurdities; but should we be the nearer to the truth? Why then, should it be different with 'good'? Why, if good is good and indefinable, should I be held to deny that pleasure is good? Is there any difficulty in holding both to be true at once?

On the contrary, there is no meaning in saying that pleasure is good, unless good is something different from pleasure. It is absolutely useless, so far as Ethics is concerned, to prove, as Mr. Spencer tries to do, that increase of pleasure coincides with increase of life, unless good *means* something different from either life or pleasure. He might just as well try to prove that an orange is yellow by shewing that it always is wrapped up in paper.

13. In fact, if it is not the case that 'good' denotes something simple and indefinable, only two alternatives are possible: either it is a complex, a given whole, about the correct analysis of which there may be disagreement; or else it means nothing at all, and there is no such subject as Ethics. In general, however, ethical philosophers have attempted to define good, without recognising what such an attempt must mean. They actually use arguments which involve one or both of the absurdities considered in § 11. We are, therefore, justified in concluding that the attempt to define good is chiefly due to want of clearness as to the possible nature of definition. There are, in fact, only two serious alternatives to be considered, in order to establish the conclusion that 'good' does denote a simple and indefinable notion. It might possibly denote a complex, as 'horse' does; or it might have no meaning at all. Neither of these possibilities has, however, been clearly conceived and seriously maintained, as such, by those who presume to define good; and both may be dismissed by a simple appeal to facts.

(1) The hypothesis that disagreement about the meaning of good is disagreement with regard to the correct analysis of a given whole, may be most plainly seen to be incorrect by consideration of the fact that, whatever definition be offered, it may be always asked, with significance, of the complex so defined, whether it is itself good. To take, for instance, one of the more plausible, because one of the more complicated, of such proposed definitions, it may easily be thought, at first sight, that to be good may mean to be that which we desire to desire. Thus if we apply this definition to a particular instance and say 'When we think that A is good, we are thinking that A is one of the things which we desire to desire,' our proposition may seem quite plausible. But, if we carry the investigation further, and ask ourselves 'Is it good to desire to desire A?' it is apparent, on a little reflection, that this question is itself as intelligible, as the original question 'Is A good?'—that we are, in fact, now asking for exactly the same information about the desire to desire A, for which we formerly asked with regard to A itself. But it is also apparent that the meaning of this second question cannot be correctly analysed into 'Is the desire to desire A one of the things which we desire to desire?': we have not before our minds anything so complicated as the question 'Do we desire to desire to desire to desire A?' Moreover any one can easily convince himself by inspection that the predicate of this proposition—'good'—is

positively different from the notion of 'desiring to desire' which enters into its subject: 'That we should desire to desire A is good' is *not* merely equivalent to 'That A should be good is good.' It may indeed be true that what we desire to desire is always also good; perhaps, even the converse may be true: but it is very doubtful whether this is the case, and the mere fact that we understand very well what is meant by doubting it, shews clearly that we have two different notions before our minds.

(2) And the same consideration is sufficient to dismiss the hypothesis that 'good' has no meaning whatsoever. It is very natural to make the mistake of supposing that what is universally true is of such a nature that its negation would be self-contradictory: the importance which has been assigned to analytic propositions in the history of philosophy shews how easy such a mistake is. And thus it is very easy to conclude that what seems to be a universal ethical principle is in fact an identical proposition; that, if, for example, whatever is called 'good' seems to be pleasant, the proposition 'Pleasure is the good' does not assert a connection between two different notions, but involves only one, that of pleasure, which is easily recognised as a distinct entity. But whoever will attentively consider with himself what is actually before his mind when he asks the question 'Is pleasure (or whatever it may be) after all good?' can easily satisfy himself that he is not merely wondering whether pleasure is pleasant. And if he will try this experiment with each suggested definition in succession, he may become expert enough to recognise that in every case he has before his mind a unique object, with regard to the connection of which with any other object, a distinct question may be asked. Every one does in fact understand the question 'Is this good?' When he thinks of it, his state of mind is different from what it would be, were he asked 'Is this pleasant, or desired, or approved?' It has a distinct meaning for him, even though he may not recognise in what respect it is distinct. Whenever he thinks of 'intrinsic value,' or 'intrinsic worth,' or says that a thing 'ought to exist,' he has before his mind the unique object—the unique property of things—which I mean by 'good.' Everybody is constantly aware of this notion, although he may never become aware at all that it is different from other notions of which he is also aware. But, for correct ethical reasoning, it is extremely important that he should become aware of this fact; and, as soon as the nature of the problem is clearly understood, there should be little difficulty in advancing so far in analysis. . . .

15.   Our first conclusion as to the subject-matter of Ethics is, then, that there is a simple, indefinable, unanalysable object of thought by reference to which it must be defined. By what name we call this unique object is a matter of indifference, so long as we clearly recognise what it is and that it does differ from other objects. The words which are commonly taken as

the signs of ethical judgments all do refer to it; and they are expressions of
ethical judgments solely because they do so refer. . . . But, although all
such judgments do refer to that unique notion which I have called 'good,'
they do not all refer to it in the same way. They may either assert that this
unique property does always attach to the thing in question, or else they may
assert only that the thing in question is *a cause or necessary condition* for
the existence of other things to which this unique property does attach. The
nature of these two species of universal ethical judgments is extremely different; and a great part of the difficulties, which are met with in ordinary
ethical speculation, are due to the failure to distinguish them clearly. Their
difference has, indeed, received expression in ordinary language by the contrast between the terms 'good as means' and 'good in itself,' 'value as a means'
and 'intrinsic value.' But these terms are apt to be applied correctly only in
the more obvious instances; and this seems to be due to the fact that the
distinction between the conceptions which they denote has not been made
a separate object of investigation. This distinction may be briefly pointed out
as follows.

16.   Whenever we judge that a thing is 'good as a means,' we are making
a judgment with regard to its causal relations: we judge *both* that it will
have a particular kind of effect, *and* that that effect will be good in itself.
But to find causal judgments that are universally true is notoriously a matter
of extreme difficulty. The late date at which most of the physical sciences
became exact, and the comparative fewness of the laws which they have
succeeded in establishing even now, are sufficient proofs of this difficulty.
With regard, then, to what are the most frequent objects of ethical judgments, namely actions, it is obvious that we cannot be satisfied that any of
our universal causal judgments are true, even in the sense in which scientific
laws are so. We cannot even discover hypothetical laws of the form 'Exactly
this action will always, under these conditions, produce exactly that effect.'
But for a correct ethical judgment with regard to the effects of certain actions
we require more than this in two respects. (1) We require to know that a
given action will produce a certain effect, *under whatever circumstances it
occurs.* But this is certainly impossible. It is certain that in different circumstances the same action may produce effects which are utterly different in all
respects upon which the value of the effect depends. Hence we can never be
entitled to more than a *generalisation*—to a proposition of the form 'This
result *generally* follows this kind of action'; and even this generalisation will
only be true, if the circumstances under which the action occurs are generally
the same. This is in fact the case, to a great extent, within any one particular
age and state of society. But, when we take other ages into account, in many
most important cases the normal circumstances of a given kind of action will

be so different, that the generalisation which is true for one will not be true for another. With regard then to ethical judgments which assert that a certain kind of action is good as a means to a certain kind of effect, none will be *universally* true; and many, though *generally* true at one period, will be generally false at others. But (2) we require to know not only that *one* good effect will be produced, but that, among all subsequent events affected by the action in question, the balance of good will be greater than if any other possible action had been performed. In other words, to judge that an action is generally a means to good is to judge not only that it generally does *some* good, but that it generally does the greatest good of which the circumstances admit. In this respect ethical judgments about the effects of action involve a difficulty and a complication far greater than that involved in the establishment of scientific laws. For the latter we need only consider a single effect; for the former it is essential to consider not only this, but the effects of that effect, and so on as far as our view into the future can reach. It is, indeed, obvious that our view can never reach far enough for us to be certain that any action will produce the best possible effects. We must be content, if the greatest possible balance of good seems to be produced within a limited period. But it is important to notice that the whole series of effects within a period of considerable length is actually taken account of in our common judgments that an action is good as a means; and that hence this additional complication, which makes ethical generalisations so far more difficult to establish than scientific laws, is one which is involved in actual ethical discussions, and is of practical importance. The commonest rules of conduct involve such considerations as the balancing of future bad health against immediate gains; and even if we can never settle with any certainty how we shall secure the greatest possible total of good, we try at least to assure ourselves that probable future evils will not be greater than the immediate good.

17. There are, then, judgments which state that certain kinds of things have good effects; and such judgments, for the reasons just given, have the important characteristics (1) that they are unlikely to be true, if they state that the kind of thing in question *always* has good effects, and (2) that, even if they only state that it *generally* has good effects, many of them will only be true of certain periods in the world's history. On the other hand there are judgments which state that certain kinds of things are themselves good; and these differ from the last in that, if true at all, they are all of them universally true. It is, therefore, extremely important to distinguish these two kinds of possible judgments. Both may be expressed in the same language: in both cases we commonly say 'Such and such a thing is good.' But in the one case 'good' will mean 'good as means,' i.e., merely that the thing is a means to good—will have good effects: in the other case

it will mean 'good as end'—we shall be judging that the thing itself has the property which, in the first case, we asserted only to belong to its effects. It is plain that these are very different assertions to make about a thing; it is plain that either or both of them may be made, both truly and falsely, about all manner of things; and it is certain that unless we are clear as to which of the two we mean to assert, we shall have a very poor chance of deciding rightly whether our assertion is true or false. It is precisely this clearness as to the meaning of the question asked which has hitherto been almost entirely lacking in ethical speculation. Ethics has always been predominantly concerned with the investigation of a limited class of actions. With regard to these we may ask *both* how far they are good in themselves *and* how far they have a general tendency to produce good results. And the arguments brought forward in ethical discussion have always been of both classes—both such as would prove the conduct in question to be good in itself and such as would prove it to be good as a means. But that these are the only questions which any ethical discussion can have to settle, and that to settle the one is *not* the same thing as to settle the other—these two fundamental facts have in general escaped the notice of ethical philosophers. Ethical questions are commonly asked in an ambiguous form. It is asked 'What is a man's duty under these circumstances?' or 'Is it right to act in this way?' or 'What ought we to aim at securing?' But all these questions are capable of further analysis; a correct answer to any of them involves both judgments of what is good in itself and causal judgments. This is implied even by those who maintain that we have a direct and immediate judgment of absolute rights and duties. Such a judgment can only mean that the course of action in question is *the* best thing to do; that, by acting so, every good that *can* be secured will have been secured. Now we are not concerned with the question whether such a judgment will ever be true. The question is: What does it imply, if it is true? And the only possible answer is that, whether true or false, it implies both a proposition as to the degree of goodness of the action in question, as compared with other things, and a number of causal propositions. For it cannot be denied that the action will have consequences: and to deny that the consequences matter is to make a judgment of their intrinsic value, as compared with the action itself. In asserting that the action is *the* best thing to do, we assert that it together with its consequences presents a greater sum of intrinsic value than any possible alternative. And this condition may be realised by any of the three cases:—(*a*) If the action itself has greater intrinsic value than any alternative, whereas both its consequences and those of the alternatives are absolutely devoid either of intrinsic merit or intrinsic demerit; or (*b*) if, though its consequences are intrinsically bad, the balance of intrinsic value is greater than would be produced by any alternative; or *(c)* if, its consequences being intrinsically good, the degree of value belonging to them and it conjointly is greater than that of any alternative series. In short, to assert that a certain line of conduct is, at a given time, absolutely right or obligatory, is obviously to assert that more good or less evil will exist in the world, if it be adopted, than if anything else be done instead. But this implies a judgment as to the value both of its own consequences and of those of any possible alternative. And that an action will have such and such consequences involves a number of causal judgments. . . .

## Chapter V

88.  . . . What ought we to do?

The answering of this question . . . introduces into Ethics . . . an entirely new question—the question what things are related as *causes* to that which is good in itself; and this question can only be answered by an entirely new method—the method of empirical investigation; by means of which causes are discovered in the other sciences. To ask what kind of actions we ought to perform, or what kind of conduct is right, is to ask what kind of effects such action and conduct will produce. Not a single question in practical Ethics can be answered except by a causal generalisation. All such questions do, indeed, *also* involve an ethical judgment proper—the judgment that certain effects are better, in themselves, than others. But they *do* assert that these better things are effects—are causally connected with the actions in question. Every judgment in practical Ethics may be reduced to the form: This is a cause of that good thing.

89.  That this is the case, that the questions, What is right? what is my duty? what ought I to do? belong exclusively to this . . . branch of ethical enquiry, is the first point to which I wish to call attention. All moral laws, I wish to shew, are merely statements that certain kinds of actions will have good effects. The very opposite of this view has been generally prevalent in Ethics. 'The right' and 'the useful' have been supposed to be at least *capable* of conflicting with one another, and, at all events, to be essentially distinct. It has been characteristic of a certain school of moralists, as of moral common sense, to declare that the end will never justify the means. What I wish first to point out is that 'right' does and can mean nothing but 'cause of a good result,' and is thus identical with 'useful'; whence it follows that the end always will justify the means, and that no action which is not justified by its results can be right. That there may be a true proposition, meant to be conveyed by the assertion 'The end will not justify the means,' I fully admit: but that, in another sense, and a sense far more fundamental for ethical theory, it is utterly false, must first be shewn.

That the assertion 'I am morally bound to perform this action' is identical with the assertion 'This action will produce the greatest possible amount of good in the Universe' has already been briefly shewn in Chap. I. (§ 17); but it is important to insist that this fundamental point is demonstrably certain. This may, perhaps, be best made evident in the following way. It is plain that when we assert that a certain action is our absolute duty, we are asserting that the performance of that action at that time is unique in respect of value. But no dutiful action can possibly have unique value in the sense that it is the sole thing of value in the world; since, in that case, *every* such action would be the *sole* good thing, which is a manifest contradiction. And for the same reason its value cannot be unique in the sense that it has more intrinsic value than anything else in the world; since *every* act of duty would then be the *best* thing in the world, which is also a contradiction. It can, therefore, be unique only in the sense that the whole world will be better, if it be performed, than if any possible alternative were taken. And the question whether this is so cannot possibly depend solely on the question of its own intrinsic value. For any action will also have effects different from those of any other action; and if any of these have intrinsic value, their value is exactly as relevant to the total goodness of the Universe as that of their cause. It is, in fact, evident that, however valuable an action may be in itself, yet, owing to its existence, the sum of good in the Universe may conceivably be made less than if some other action, less valuable in itself, had been performed. But to say that this is the case is to say that it would have been better that the action should not have been done; and this again is obviously equivalent to the statement that it ought not to have been done —that it was not what duty required. 'Fiat iustitia, ruat caelum' can only be justified on the ground that by the doing of justice the Universe gains more than it loses by the falling of the heavens. It is, of course, possible that this is the case: but, at all events, to assert that justice *is* a duty, in spite of such consequences, is to assert that it is the case.

Our 'duty,' therefore, can only be defined as that action, which will cause more good to exist in the Universe than any possible alternative. And what is 'right' or 'morally permissible' only differs from this, as what will *not* cause *less* good than any possible alternative. When, therefore, Ethics presumes to assert that certain ways of acting are 'duties' it presumes to assert that to act in those ways will always produce the greatest possible sum of good. If we are told that to 'do no murder' is a duty, we are told that the action, whatever it may be, which is called murder, will under no circumstances cause so much good to exist in the Universe as its avoidance.

# W. D. ROSS

SIR WILLIAM DAVID ROSS (1877–     ) served Oxford University as Professor of Philosophy and as Provost of Oriel College. Equally well known as a leading intuitionist in ethical theory and as a scholar with broad interests in the history of philosophy, his major works include: *Aristotle* (1923), *The Right and the Good* (1930), *Foundations of Ethics* (1939), *Plato's Theory of Ideas* (1951), and *Kant's Ethical Theory* (1954).

## The Right and the Good*

### Chapter I

### The Meaning of 'Right'

. . . Are we to hold that 'right' can be defined in the sense of being reduced to elements simpler than itself? At first sight it might appear that egoism and utilitarianism are attempts to define 'right'—to define it as 'productive of the greatest possible pleasure to the agent' or as 'productive of the greatest possible pleasure to mankind'; and I think these theories have often been so understood by some of those who accept them. But the leaders of the school are not unanimous in so understanding their theory. Bentham seems to understand it so. He says that 'when thus interpreted' (i.e., as meaning 'comformable to the principle of utility'), 'the words *ought* and right . . . and others of that stamp, have a meaning; when otherwise, they have none.' And elsewhere he says 'admitting (what is not true) that the word *right* can have a meaning without reference to utility.' Yet, as Sidgwick points out, 'when Bentham explains (*Principles of Morals and Legislation*, Chap. I, § 1, note) that his fundamental principle "states the greatest happiness of all those whose interest is in question as being the right and proper end of human action," we cannot understand him really to *mean* by the word "right" "conducive to the general happiness"; for the proposition that it is conducive to general happiness to take general happiness as an end of action, though not exactly a tautology, can hardly serve as the fundamental principle of a moral system.' Bentham has evidently not made up his mind clearly whether he thinks that 'right' *means* 'productive of the general happiness,' *or* that being productive of the general happiness is what makes right acts right; and would very likely have thought the difference unimportant. Mill does

* From *The Right and the Good,* by W. D. Ross, Chaps. 1 and 2. Copyright, 1930, Clarendon Press. Used by permission.

not so far as I know discuss the question whether right is definable. He states his creed in the form 'actions are right in proportion as they tend to promote happiness,' where the claim that is made is not that this is what 'right' means, but that this is the other characteristic in virtue of which actions that are right are right. . . .

The most deliberate claim that 'right' is definable as 'productive of so and so' is made by Prof. G. E. Moore, who claims in *Principia Ethica* that 'right' means 'productive of the greatest possible good.' Now it has often been pointed out against hedonism, and by no one more clearly than by Professor Moore, that the claim that 'good' just means 'pleasant' cannot seriously be maintained; that while it may or may not be true that the only things that are good are pleasant, the statement that the good is just the pleasant is a synthetic, not an analytic proposition; that the words 'good' and 'pleasant' stand for distinct qualities, even if the things that possess the one are precisely the things that possess the other. If this were not so, it would not be intelligible that the proposition 'the good is just the pleasant' should have been maintained on the one hand, and denied on the other, with so much fervour; for we do not fight for or against analytic propositions; we take them for granted. Must not the same claim be made about the statement 'being right means being an act productive of the greatest good producible in the circumstances'? Is it not plain on reflection that this is not what we *mean* by right, even if it be a true statement about what *is* right? It seems clear for instance that when an ordinary man says it is right to fulfil promises he is not in the least thinking of the total consequences of such an act, about which he knows and cares little or nothing. 'Ideal utilitarianism'[1] is, it would appear, plausible only when it is understood not as an analysis or definition of the notion of 'right' but as a statement that all acts that are right, and only these, possess the further characteristic of being productive of the best possible consequences, and are right because they possess this other characteristic.

If I am not mistaken, Professor Moore has moved to this position, from the position that 'right' is *analysable* into 'productive of the greatest possible good.' In *Principia Ethica* the latter position is adopted: e.g., 'This use of "right," as denoting what is good as a means, whether or not it is also good as an end, is indeed the use to which I shall confine the word.' 'To assert that a certain line of conduct is, at a given time, absolutely right or obligatory, is obviously to assert that more good or less evil will exist in the world, if it be adopted, than if anything else be done instead.'[2] 'To ask

---

[1] I use this as a well-known way of referring to Professor Moore's view. 'Agathistic utilitarianism' would indicate more distinctly the difference between it and hedonistic utilitarianism.

[2] P. 25 [p. 341 this volume].

what kind of actions one ought to perform, or what kind of conduct is right, is to ask what kind of effects such action and conduct will produce . . . What I wish first to point out is that "right" does and can mean nothing but "cause of a good result," and is thus always identical with "useful" . . . That the assertion "I am morally bound to perform this action" is identical with the assertion "this action will produce the greatest possible amount of good in the Universe" has already been briefly shewn . . . ; but it is important to insist that this fundamental point is demonstrably certain. . . . Our "duty," therefore, can only be defined as that action, which will cause more good to exist in the Universe than any possible alternative. And what is "right" or "morally permissible" only differs from this, as what will *not* cause *less* good than any possible alternative.'[3]

In his later book, *Ethics*, Professor Moore seems to have to adopt the other position, though perhaps not quite unequivocally. On page 8 he names as one of the 'more fundamental questions' of ethics the question 'what, after all, is it that we mean to say of an action when we say that it is right or ought to be done?' Here it is still suggested that 'right' is perhaps analysable or definable. But to this question *Ethics* nowhere distinctly offers an answer, and on page 9 we find, 'Can we discover any single reason, applicable to all right actions equally, which is, in every case, *the* reason why an action is right, when it is right?' This is the question which Professor Moore in fact sets himself to answer. But the *reason* for an action's being right is evidently not the same thing as its *rightness*, and Professor Moore seems already to have passed to the view that productivity of maximum good is not the definition of 'right' but another characteristic which underlies and accounts for the rightness of right acts. Again, he describes hedonistic utilitarianism as asking, 'can we discover any characteristic, over and above the mere fact that they *are* right, which belongs to absolutely *all* voluntary actions which are right, and which at the same time does not belong to any except those which are right?' This is the question which he describes hedonism as essentially answering, and since his own view differs from hedonism not in logical form but just by the substitution of 'good' for 'pleasure,' his theory also seems to be essentially an answer to this question, i.e., not to the question what is rightness but to the question what is the universal accompaniment and, as he is careful to add, the necessitating ground of rightness. Again, he describes hedonistic utilitarianism as giving us 'a criterion, or test, or standard by which we could discern with regard to any action whether it is right or wrong.' And similarly, I suppose, he regards his own theory as offering a different criterion of rightness. But obviously a criterion of rightness is not rightness itself. And, most plainly of all, he says, 'It is

[3] Pp. 146-8 [pp. 341-2 this volume].

indeed quite plain, I think, that the meaning of the two words' ('duty' and 'expediency,' the latter being equivalent to 'tendency to produce the maximum good') 'is *not* the same; for, if it were, then it would be a mere tautology to say that it is always our duty to do what will have the best possible consequences.' If we contrast this with *Principia Ethica*, page 169, 'if I ask whether an action is *really* my duty or *really* expedient, the predicate of which I question the applicability to the action in question is precisely the same,' we see how much Professor Moore has changed his position, and changed it in the direction in which, as I have been urging, it must be changed if it is to be made plausible. And if it is clear that 'right' does not mean 'productive of the greatest possible good,' it is *a fortiori* clear that it does not *mean* 'productive of the greatest possible pleasure, for the agent or for mankind,' but that productivity of the greatest possible pleasure for the agent or for mankind is at most the ground of the rightness of acts, rightness itself being admitted to be a distinct characteristic, and one which utilitarianism does not claim to define.

But there are theories other than utilitarianism which claim to define 'right.' It would be tedious to try to refute all such theories. With regard to many of them it seems to be enough to ask one's readers whether it is not clear to them on reflection that the proposed definition of 'right' bears in fact no resemblance to what they mean by 'right.' . . .

Any one who is satisfied that neither the subjective theories of the meaning of 'right,' nor what is far the most attractive of the attempts to reduce it to simpler objective elements, is correct, will probably be prepared to agree that 'right' is an irreducible notion.

Nor is this result impugned by inquiries into the historical development of our present moral notions from an earlier state of things in which 'what is right' was hardly disentangled from 'what the tribe ordains.' The point is that we can now see clearly that 'right' does not mean 'ordained by any given society.' And it may be doubted whether even primitive men thought that it did. Their thoughts about what in particular was right were to a large extent limited by the customs and sanctions of their race and age. But this is not the same as to say that they thought that 'right' just meant 'what my race and age ordains.' Moral progress has been possible just because there have been men in all ages who have seen the difference and have practised, or at least preached, a morality in some respects higher than that of their race and age. And even the supporters of the lower morality held, we may suspect, that their laws and customs were in accordance with a 'right' other than themselves. 'It is the custom' has been accompanied by 'the custom is right,' or 'the custom is ordained by some one who has the right to command.' And if human consciousness is continuous, by descent, with a lower consciousness which had no notion of the right at all, that need not make us doubt that the notion is an ultimate and irreducible one, or that the rightness (*prima facie*)—of certain types of act is self-evident; for the nature of the self-evident is not to be evident to every mind however undeveloped, but to be apprehended directly by minds which have reached a certain degree of maturity, and for minds to reach the necessary degree of maturity the development that takes place from generation to generation is as much needed as that which takes place from infancy to adult life. . . .

## Chapter II

### What Makes Right Acts Right?

The real point at issue between hedonism and utilitarianism on the one hand and their opponents on the other is not whether 'right' means 'productive of so and so'; for it cannot with any plausibility be maintained that it does. The point at issue is that to which we now pass, *viz.*, whether there is any general character which makes right acts right, and if so, what it is. Among the main historical attempts to state a single characteristic of all right actions which is the foundation of their rightness are those made by egoism and utilitarianism. But I do not propose to discuss these, not because the subject is unimportant, but because it has been dealt with so often and so well already, and because there has come to be so much agreement among moral philosophers that neither of these theories is satisfactory. A much more attractive theory has been put forward by Professor Moore: that what makes actions right is that they are productive of more *good* than could have been produced by any other action open to the agent.

This theory is in fact the culmination of all the attempts to base rightness on productivity of some sort of result. The first form this attempt takes is the attempt to base rightness on conduciveness to the advantage or pleasure of the agent. This theory comes to grief over the fact, which stares us in the face, that a great part of duty consists in an observance of the rights and a furtherance of the interests of others, whatever the cost to ourselves may be. Plato and others may be right in holding that a regard for the rights of others never in the long run involves a loss of happiness for the agent, that 'the just life profits a man.' But this, even if true, is irrelevant to the rightness of the act. As soon as a man does an action *because* he thinks he will promote his own interests thereby, he is acting not from a sense of its rightness but from self-interest.

To the egoistic theory hedonistic utilitarianism supplies a much-needed amendment. It points out correctly that the fact that a certain pleasure will be enjoyed by the agent is no reason why he *ought* to bring it into being rather than an equal or greater pleasure to be enjoyed by another, though, human nature being what it is, it makes it not unlikely that he *will* try to bring it into being. But hedonistic utilitarianism in its turn needs a correction. On reflection it seems clear that pleasure is not the only thing in life that we think good in itself, that for instance we think the possession of a good character, or an intelligent understanding of the world, as good or better. A great advance is made by the substitution of 'productive of the greatest good' for 'productive of the greatest pleasure.'

Not only is this theory more attractive than hedonistic utilitarianism, but its logical relation to that theory is such that the latter could not be true unless *it* were true, while it might be true though hedonistic utilitarianism were not. It is in fact one of the logical bases of hedonistic utilitarianism. For the view that what produces the maximum pleasure is right has for its bases the views (1) that what produces the maximum good is right, and (2) that pleasure is the only thing good in itself. If they were not assuming that what produces the maximum *good* is right, the utilitarians' attempt to show that pleasure is the only thing good in itself, which is in fact the point they take most pains to establish, would have been quite irrelevant to their attempt to prove that only what produces the maximum *pleasure* is right. If, therefore, it can be shown that productivity of the maximum good is not what makes all right actions right, we shall *a fortiori* have refuted hedonistic utilitarianism.

When a plain man fulfils a promise because he thinks he ought to do so, it seems clear that he does so with no thought of its total consequences, still less with any opinion that these are likely to be the best possible. He thinks in fact much more of the past than of the future. What makes him think it right to act in a certain way is the fact that he has promised to do so—that and, usually, nothing more. That his act will produce the best possible consequences is not his reason for calling it right. What lends colour to the theory we are examining, then, is not the actions (which form probably a great majority of our actions) in which some such reflection as 'I have promised' is the only reason we give ourselves for thinking a certain action right, but the exceptional cases in which the consequences of fulfilling a promise (for instance) would be so disastrous to others that we judge it right not to do so. It must of course be admitted that such cases exist. If I have promised to meet a friend at a particular time for some trivial purpose, I should certainly think myself justified in breaking my engagement if by doing so I could prevent a serious accident or bring relief to the victims of one. And the supporters of the view we are examining hold that my thinking so is due to my thinking that I shall bring more good into existence by the one action than by the other. A different account may, however, be given of the matter, an account which will, I believe, show itself to be the true one. It may be said that besides the duty of fulfilling promises I have and recognize a duty of relieving distress, and that when I think it right to do the latter at the cost of not doing the former, it is not because I think I shall produce more good thereby but because I think it the duty which is in the circumstances more of a duty. This account surely corresponds much more closely with what we really think in such a situation. If, so far as I can see, I could bring equal amounts of good into being by fulfilling my promise and by helping some one to whom I had made no promise, I should not hesitate to regard the former as my duty. Yet on the view that what is right is right because it is productive of the most good I should not so regard it.

There are two theories, each in its way simple, that offer a solution of such cases of conscience. One is the view of Kant, that there are certain duties of perfect obligation, such as those of fulfilling promises, of paying debts, of telling the truth, which admit of no exception whatever in favour of duties of imperfect obligation, such as that of relieving distress. The other is the view of, for instance, Professor Moore and Dr. Rashdall, that there is only the duty of producing good, and that all 'conflicts of duties' should be resolved by asking 'by which action will most good be produced?' But it is more important that our theory fit the facts than that it be simple, and the account we have given above corresponds (it seems to me) better than either of the simpler theories with what we really think, *viz.*, that normally promise-keeping, for example, should come before benevolence, but that when and only when the good to be produced by the benevolent act is very great and the promise comparatively trivial, the act of benevolence becomes our duty.

In fact the theory of 'ideal utilitarianism,' if I may for brevity refer so to the theory of Professor Moore, seems to simplify unduly our relations to our fellows. It says, in effect, that the only morally significant relation in which my neighbours stand to me is that of being possible beneficiaries by my action. They do stand in this relation to me, and this relation is morally significant. But they may also stand to me in the relation of promisee to promiser, of creditor to debtor, of wife to husband, of child to parent, of friend to friend, of fellow countryman to fellow countryman, and the like; and each of these relations is the foundation of a *prima facie* duty, which is more or less incumbent on me according to the circumstances of the case. When I am in a situation, as perhaps I always am, in which more than one of these *prima facie* duties is incumbent on me, what I have to do is to study the situation as fully as I can until I form the considered opinion (it is never more) that in the circumstances one of them is more incumbent than any other; then I am bound to think that to do this *prima facie* duty is my duty *sans phrase* in the situation.

I suggest '*prima facie* duty' or 'conditional duty' as a brief way of referring to the characteristic (quite distinct from that of being a duty proper) which an act has, in virtue of being of a certain kind (e.g., the keeping of a promise), of being an act which would be a duty proper if it were not at the same time of another kind which is morally significant. Whether an act is a duty proper or actual duty depends on *all* the morally significant kinds it is an instance of. . . .

There is nothing arbitrary about these *prima facie* duties. Each rests on a definite circumstance which cannot seriously be held to be without moral significance. Of *prima facie* duties I suggest, without claiming completeness or finality for it, the following division.[4]

(1) Some duties rest on previous acts of my own. These duties seem to include two kinds, (*a*) those resting on a promise or what may fairly be called an implicit promise, such, as the implicit undertaking not to tell lies which seems to be implied in the act of entering into conversation (at any rate by civilized men), or of writing books that purport to be history and not fiction. These may be called the duties of fidelity. (*b*) Those resting on a previous wrongful act. These may be called the duties of reparation. (2) Some rest on previous acts of other men, i.e., services done by them to me. These may be loosely described as the duties of gratitude. (3) Some rest on the fact or possibility of a distribution of pleasure or happiness (or of the means thereto) which is not in accordance with the merit of the persons concerned; in such cases there arises a duty to upset or prevent such a distribution. These are the duties of justice. (4) Some rest on the mere fact that there are other beings in the world whose condition we can make better in respect of virtue, or of intelligence, or of pleasure. These are the duties of beneficence. (5) Some rest on the fact that we can improve our own condition in respect of virtue or of intelligence. These are the duties of self-improvement. (6) I think that we should distinguish from (4) the duties that may be summed up under the title of 'not injuring

---

[4] I should make it plain at this stage that I am *assuming* the correctness of some of our main convictions as to *prima facie* duties, or, more strictly, am claiming that we *know* them to be true. To me it seems as self-evident as anything could be, that to make a promise, for instance, is to create a moral claim on us in someone else. Many readers will perhaps say that they do *not* know this to be true. If so, I certainly cannot prove it to them; I can only ask them to reflect again, in the hope that they will ultimately agree that they also know it to be true. The main moral convictions of the plain man seem to me to be, not opinions which it is for philosophy to prove or disprove, but knowledge from the start; and in my own case I seem to find little difficulty in distinguishing these essential convictions from other moral convictions which I also have, which are merely fallible opinions based on an imperfect study of the working for good or evil of certain institutions or types of action.

others.' No doubt to injure others is incidentally to fail to do them good; but it seems to me clear that non-maleficence is apprehended as a duty distinct from that of beneficence, and as a duty of a more stringent character. It will be noticed that this alone among the types of duty has been stated in a negative way. An attempt might no doubt be made to state this duty, like the others, in a positive way. It might be said that it is really the duty to prevent ourselves from acting either from an inclination to harm others or from an inclination to seek our own pleasure, in doing which we should incidentally harm them. But on reflection it seems clear that the primary duty here is the duty not to harm others, this being a duty whether or not we have an inclination that if followed would lead to our harming them; and that when we have such an inclination the primary duty not to harm others gives rise to a consequential duty to resist the inclination. The recognition of this duty of non-maleficence is the first step on the way to the recognition of the duty of maleficence; and that accounts for the prominence of the commands 'thou shalt not kill,' 'thou shalt not commit adultery,' 'thou shalt not steal,' 'thou shalt not bear false witness,' in so early a code as the Decalogue. But even when we have come to recognize the duty of beneficence, it appears to me that the duty of non-maleficence is recognized as a distinct one, and as *prima facie* more binding. We should not in general consider it justifiable to kill one person in order to keep another alive, or to steal from one in order to give alms to another.

The essential defect of the 'ideal utilitarian' theory is that it ignores, or at least does not do full justice to, to the highly personal character of duty. If the only duty is to produce the maximum of good, the question who is to have the good—whether it is myself, or my benefactor, or a person to whom I have made a promise to confer that good on him, or a mere fellow man to whom I stand in no such special relation—should make no difference to my having a duty to produce that good. But we are all in fact sure that it makes a vast difference. . . .

It is necessary to say something by way of clearing up the relation between *prima facie* duties and the actual or absolute duty to do one particular act in particular circumstances. If, as almost all moralists except Kant are agreed, and as most plain men think, it is sometimes right to tell a lie or to break a promise, it must be maintained that there is a difference between *prima facie* duty and actual or absolute duty. When we think ourselves justified in breaking, and indeed morally obliged to break, a promise in order to relieve some one's distress, we do not for a moment cease to recognize a *prima facie* duty to keep our promise, and this leads us to feel, not indeed shame or repentance, but certainly compunction, for behaving as we do; we recognize, further, that it is our duty to make up somehow to the promisee for the breaking of the promise. We have to distinguish from the characteristic of being our duty that of tending to be our duty. Any act that we do contains various elements in virtue of which it falls under various categories. In virtue of being the breaking of a promise, for instance, it tends to be wrong; in virtue of being an instance of relieving distress it tends to be right. Tendency to be one's duty may be called a parti-resultant attribute, i.e., one which belongs to an act in virtue of some one component in its nature. *Being* one's duty is a toti-resultant attribute, one which belongs to an act in virtue of its whole nature and of nothing less than this. . . .

Another instance of the same distinction may be found in the operation of natural laws. *Qua* subject to the force of gravitation towards some other body, each body tends to move in a particular direction with a particular velocity; but its actual movement depends on *all* the forces to which it is subject. It is only by recognizing this distinction that we can preserve the absoluteness of laws of nature, and only by recognizing a corresponding distinction that we can preserve the absoluteness of the general principles of morality. But an important difference between the two cases must be pointed out. When we say that in virtue of gravitation a body tends to move in a certain way, we are referring to a causal influence actually exercised on it by another body or other bodies. When we say that in virtue of being deliberately untrue a certain remark tends to be wrong, we are referring to no causal relation, to no relation that involves succession in time, but to such a relation as connects the various attributes of a mathematical figure. And if the word 'tendency' is thought to suggest too much a causal relation, it is better to talk of certain types of act as being *prima facie* right or wrong (or of different persons as having different and possibly conflicting claims upon us), than of their tending to be right or wrong.

Something should be said of the relation between our apprehension of the *prima facie* rightness of certain types of act and our mental attitude towards particular acts. It is proper to use the word 'apprehension' in the former case and not in the latter. That an act, *qua* fulfilling a promise, or *qua* effecting a just distribution of good, or *qua* returning services rendered, or *qua* promoting the good of others, or *qua* promoting the virtue or insight of the agent, is *prima facie* right, is self-evident; not in the sense that it is evident from the beginning of our lives, or as soon as we attend to the proposition for the first time, but in the sense that when we have reached sufficient mental maturity and have given sufficient attention to the proposition it is evident without any need of proof, or of evidence beyond itself. It is self-evident just as a mathematical axiom, or the validity of a form of inference, is evident. The moral order expressed in these propositions is just as much part of the fundamental nature of the universe (and, we may add, of any possible universe in which there were moral agents at all) as is the spatial or numerical structure expressed in the axioms of geometry or arithmetic. In our confidence that these propositions are true there is involved the same trust in our reason that is involved in our confidence in mathematics; and we should have no justification for trusting it in the latter sphere and distrusting it in the former. In both cases we are dealing with propositions that cannot be proved, but that just as certainly need no proof. . . .

Our judgements about our actual duty in concrete situations have none of the certainty that attaches to our recognition of the general principles of duty. A statement is certain, i.e., is an expression of knowledge, only in one or other of two cases: when it is either self-evident, or a valid conclusion from self-evident premises. And our judgements about our particular duties have neither of these characters. (1) They are not self-evident. Where a possible act is seen to have two characteristics, in virtue of one of which it is *prima facie* right, and in virtue of the other *prima facie* wrong, we are (I think) well aware that we are not certain whether we ought or ought not to do it; that whether we do it or not, we are taking a moral risk. We come in the long run, after consideration, to think one duty more pressing than the other, but we do not feel certain that it is so. And though we do not always recognize that a possible act has two such characteristics, and though there *may* be cases in which it has not, we are never certain that any particular possible act has not, and therefore never certain that it is right, nor certain that it is wrong. For, to go no further in the analysis, it is enough to point out that any particular act will in all probability in the course of time contribute to the bringing about of good or of evil for many human beings, and thus have a *prima facie* rightness or wrongness of which we know nothing. (2) Again, our judgements about our particular duties are not logical conclusions from self-evident premises. The only possible premises would be the general principles stating their *prima facie* rightness or wrongness *qua* having the different characteristics they do have; and even if we could (as we cannot) apprehend the extent to which an act will tend on the one hand, for example, to bring about advantages for our benefactors, and on the other hand to bring about disadvantages for fellow men who are not our benefactors, there is no principle by which we can draw the conclusion that it is on the whole right or on the whole wrong. In this respect the judgement as to the rightness of a particular act is just like the judgement as to the beauty of a particular natural object or work of art. A poem is, for instance, in respect of certain qualities beautiful and in respect of certain others not beautiful; and our judgement as to the degree of beauty it possesses on the whole is never reached by logical rea-

soning from the apprehension of its particular beauties or particular defects. Both in this and in the moral case we have more or less probable
opinions which are not logically justified conclusions from the general
principles that are recognized as self-evident. . . .

Supposing it to be agreed, as I think on reflection it must, that no
one *means* by 'right' just 'productive of the best possible consequences,'
or 'optimific,' the attributes 'right' and 'optimific' might stand in either
of two kinds of relation to each other. (1) They might be so related that
we could apprehend *a priori*, either immediately or deductively, that any
act that is optimific is right and any act that is right is optimific, as we
can apprehend that any triangle that is equilateral is equiangular and
*vice versa*. Professor Moore's view is, I think, that the coexistensiveness
of 'right' and 'optimific' is apprehended immediately. He rejects the possibility of any proof of it. Or (2) the two attributes might be such that
the question whether they are invariably connected had to be answered
by means of an inductive inquiry. Now at first sight it might seem as if
the constant connexion of the two attributes could be immediately apprehended. It might seem absurd to suggest that it could be right for any
one to do an act which would produce consequences less good than those
which would be produced by some other act in his power. Yet a little
thought will convince us that this is not absurd. The type of case in which
it is easier to see that this is so is, perhaps, that in which one has made a
promise. In such a case we all think that *prima facie* it is our duty to fulfil
the promise irrespective of the precise goodness of the total consequences.
And though we do not think it is necessarily our actual or absolute duty
to do so, we are far from thinking that any, even the slightest, gain in the
value of the total consequences will necessarily justify us in doing something else instead. Suppose, to simplify the case by abstraction, that the
fulfilment of a promise to A would produce 1,000 units of good for him,
but that by doing some other act I could produce 1,001 units of good for B,
to whom I have made no promise, the other consequences of the two acts
being of equal value; should we really think it self-evident that it was our
duty to do the second act and not the first? I think not. We should, I fancy,
hold that only a much greater disparity of value between the total consequences would justify us in failing to discharge our *prima facie* duty to A.
After all, a promise is a promise, and is not to be treated so lightly as the
theory we are examining would imply. What, exactly, a promise is, is not
so easy to determine, but we are surely agreed that it constitutes a serious
moral limitation to our freedom of action. To produce the 1,001 units of
good for B rather than fulfil our promise to A would be to take, not perhaps
our duty as philanthropists too seriously, but certainly our duty as makers of
promises too lightly.

Or consider another phase of the same problem. If I have promised to confer on A a particular benefit containing 1,000 units of good, is it self-evident that if by doing some different act I could produce 1,001 units of good for A himself (the other consequences of the two acts being supposed equal in value), it would be right for me to do so? Again, I think not. Apart from my general *prima facie* duty to do A what good I can, I have another *prima facie* duty to do him the particular service I have promised to do him, and this is not to be set aside in consequence of a disparity of good of the order of 1,001 to 1,000, though a much greater disparity might justify me in so doing.

Or again, suppose that A is a very good and B a very bad man, should I then, even when I have made no promise, think it self-evidently right to produce 1,001 units of good for B rather than 1,000 for A? Surely not. I should be sensible of a *prima facie* duty of justice, i.e., of producing a distribution of goods in proportion to merit, which is not outweighed by such a slight disparity in the total goods to be produced.

Such instances—and they might easily be added to—make it clear that there is no self-evident connexion between the attributes 'right' and 'optimific.' The theory we are examining has a certain attractiveness when applied to our decision that a particular act is our duty (though I have tried to show that it does not agree with our actual moral judgements even here). But it is not even possible when applied to our recognition of *prima facie* duty. For if it were self-evident that the right coincides with the optimific, it should be self-evident that what is *prima facie* right is *prima facie* optimific. But whereas we are certain that keeping a promise is *prima facie* right, we are not certain that it is *prima facie* optimific (though we are perhaps certain that it is *prima facie* bonific). Our certainty that it is *prima facie* right depends not on its consequences but on its being the fulfilment of a promise. The theory we are examining involves too much difference between the evident ground of our conviction about *prima facie* duty and the alleged ground of our conviction about actual duty.

The coextensiveness of the right and the optimific is, then, not self-evident. And I can see no way of proving it deductively; nor, so far as I know, has any one tried to do so. There remains the question whether it can be established inductively. Such an inquiry, to be conclusive, would have to be very thorough and extensive. We should have to take a large variety of the acts which we, to the best of our ability, judge to be right. We should have to trace as far as possible their consequences, not only for the persons directly affected but also for those indirectly affected, and to these no limit can be set. To make our inquiry thoroughly conclusive, we should have to do what we cannot do, *viz.*, trace these consequences into an unending future. And even to make it reasonably conclusive, we should have to trace them far into the future. It is clear that the most we could possibly say is that a large variety of typical acts that are judged right appear, so far as we can trace their consequences, to produce more good than any other acts possible to the agents in the circumstances. And such a result falls far short of proving the constant connexion of the two attributes. But it is surely clear that no inductive inquiry justifying even this result has ever been carried through. The advocates of utilitarian systems have been so much persuaded either of the identity or of the self-evident connexion of the attributes 'right' and 'optimific' (or 'felicific') that they have not attempted even such an inductive inquiry as is possible. And in view of the enormous complexity of the task and the inevitable inconclusiveness of the result, it is worth no one's while to make the attempt. What, after all, would be gained by it? If, as I have tried to show, for an act to be right and to be optimific are not the same thing, and an act's being optimific is not even the ground of its being right, then if we could ask ourselves (though the question is really unmeaning) which we ought to do, right acts because they are right or optimific acts because they are optimific, our answer must be 'the former.' If they are optimific as well as right, that is interesting but not morally important; if not, we still ought to do them (which is only another way of saying that they *are* the right acts), and the question whether they are optimific has no importance for moral theory.

There is one direction in which a fairly serious attempt has been made to show the connexion of the attributes 'right' and 'optimific.' One of the most evident facts of our moral consciousness is the sense which we have of the sanctity of promises, a sense which does not, on the face of it, involve the thought that one will be bringing more good into existence by fulfilling the promise than by breaking it. It is plain, I think, that in our normal thought we consider that the fact that we have made a promise is in itself sufficient to create a duty of keeping it, the sense of duty resting on remembrance of the past promise and not on thoughts of the future consequences of its fulfilment. Utilitarianism tries to show that this is not so, that the sanctity of promises rests on the good consequences of the fulfilment of them and the bad consequences of their nonfulfilment. It does so in this way: it points out that when you break a promise you not only fail to confer a certain advantage on your promisee but you diminish his confidence, and indirectly the confidence of others, in the fulfilment of promises. You thus strike a blow at one of the devices that have been found most useful in the relations between man and man—the device on which, for example, the whole system of commercial credit rests—and you tend to bring about a state of things wherein each man, being entirely unable to rely on the keeping of promises by others, will have to do everything for himself, to the enormous impoverishment of human well-being.

To put the matter otherwise, utilitarians say that when a promise ought to be kept it is because the total good to be produced by keeping it is greater than the total good to be produced by breaking it, the former including as its main element the maintenance and strengthening of general mutual confidence, and the latter being greatly diminished by a weakening of this confidence. They say, in fact, that the case I put some pages back never arises —the case in which by fulfilling a promise shall bring into being 1,000 units of good for my promisee, and by breaking it 1,001 units of good for some one else, the other effects of the two acts being of equal value. The other effects, they say, never are of equal value. By keeping my promise I am helping to strengthen the system of mutual confidence; by breaking it I am helping to weaken this; so that really the first act produces $1,000+x$ units of good, and the second $1,001-y$ units, and the difference between $+x$ and $-y$ is enough to outweigh the slight superiority in the *immediate* effects of the second act. In answer to this it may be pointed out that there must be *some* amount of good that exceeds the difference between $+x$ and $-y$ (i.e. exceeds $x+y$); say, $x+y+z$. Let us suppose the *immediate* good effects of the second act to be assessed not at 1,001 but at $1,000+x+y+z$. Then its *net* good effects are $1,000+x+z$, i.e., greater than those of the fulfilment of the promise; and the utilitarian is bound to say forthwith that the promise should be broken. Now, we may ask whether that is really the way we think about promises? Do we really think that the production of the slightest balance of good, no matter who will enjoy it, by the breach of a promise frees us from the obligation to keep our promise? We need not doubt that a system by which promises are made and kept is one that has great advantages for the general well-being. But that is not the whole truth. To make a promise is not merely to adapt an ingenious device for promoting the general well-being; it is to put oneself in a new relation to one person in particular, a relation which creates a specifically new *prima facie* duty to him, not reducible to the duty of promoting the general well-being of society. By all means let us try to foresee the net good effects of keeping one's promise and the net good effects of breaking it, but even if we assess the first at $1,000+x$ and the second at $1,000+x+z$, the question still remains whether it is not our duty to fulfil the promise. It may be suspected, too, that the effect of a single keeping or breaking of a promise in strengthening or weakening the fabric of mutual confidence is greatly exaggerated by the theory we are examining. And if we suppose two men dying together alone, do we think that the duty of one to fulfil before he dies a promise he has made to the other would be extinguished by the fact that neither act would have any effect on the general confidence? Any one who holds this may be suspected of not having reflected on what a promise is.

I conclude that the attributes 'right' and 'optimific' are not identical, and that we do not know either by intuition, by deduction, or by induction that they coincide in their application, still less that the latter is the foundation of the former. It must be added, however, that if we are ever under no special obligation such as that of fidelity to a promisee or of gratitude to a benefactor, we ought to do what will produce most good; and that even when we are under a special obligation the tendency of acts to promote general good is one of the main factors in determining whether they are right.

In what has preceded, a good deal of use has been made of 'what we really think' about moral questions; a certain theory has been rejected because it does not agree with what we really think. It might be said that this is in principle wrong; that we should not be content to expound what our present moral consciousness tells us but should aim at a criticism of our existing moral consciousness in the light of theory. Now I do not doubt that the moral consciousness of men has in detail undergone a good deal of modification as regards the things we think right, at the hands of moral theory. But if we are told, for instance, that we should give up our view that there is a special obligatoriness attaching to the keeping of promises because it is self-evident that the only duty is to produce as much good as possible, we have to ask ourselves whether we really, when we reflect, *are* convinced that this is self-evident, and whether we really *can* get rid of our view that promise-keeping has a bindingness independent of productiveness of maximum good. In my own experience I find that I cannot, in spite of a very genuine attempt to do so; and I venture to think that most people will find the same, and that just because they cannot lose the sense of special obligation, they cannot accept as self-evident, or even as true, the theory which would require them to do so. In fact it seems, on reflection, self-evident that a promise, simply as such, is something that *prima facie* ought to be kept, and it does *not*, on reflection, seem self-evident that production of maximum good is the only thing that makes an act obligatory. And to ask us to give up at the bidding of a theory our actual apprehension of what is right and what is wrong seems like asking people to repudiate their actual experience of beauty, at the bidding of a theory which says 'only that which satisfies such and such conditions can be beautiful.' If what I have called our actual apprehension is (as I would maintain that it is) truly an apprehension, i.e., an instance of knowledge, the request is nothing less than absurd.

I would maintain, in fact, that what we are apt to describe as 'what we think' about moral questions contains a considerable amount that we do not think but know, and that this forms the standard by reference to which the truth of any moral theory has to be tested, instead of having itself to be tested by reference to any theory. I hope that I have in what precedes indicated what in my view these elements of knowledge are that are involved in our ordinary moral consciousness.

It would be a mistake to found a natural science on 'what we really think,' i.e., on what reasonably thoughtful and well-educated people think about the subjects of the science before they have studied them scientifically. For such opinions are interpretations, and often misinterpretations, of sense-experience; and the man of science must appeal from these to sense-experience itself, which furnishes his real data. In ethics no such appeal is possible. We have no more direct way of access to the facts about rightness and good-ness and about what things are right or good, than by thinking about them; the moral convictions of thoughtful and well-educated people are the data of ethics just as sense-perceptions are the data of a natural science. Just as some of the latter have to be rejected as illusory, so have some of the former; but as the latter are rejected only when they are in conflict with other more accurate sense-perceptions, the former are rejected only when they are in conflict with other convictions which stand better the test of reflection. The existing body of moral convictions of the best people is the cumulative product of the moral reflection of many generations, which has developed an extremely delicate power of appreciation of moral distinctions; and this the theorist cannot afford to treat with anything other than the greatest respect. The verdicts of the moral consciousness of the best people are the foundation on which he must build; though he must first compare them with one an-other and eliminate any contradictions they may contain.

It is worth while to try to state more definitely the nature of the acts that are right. We may try to state first what (if anything) is the universal nature of *all* acts that are right. It is obvious that any of the acts that we do has countless effects, directly or indirectly, on countless people, and the probability is that any act, however right it be, will have adverse effects (though these may be very trivial) on some innocent people. Similarly, any wrong act will probably have beneficial effects on some deserving people. Every act therefore, viewed in some aspects, will be *prima facie* right, and viewed in others, *prima facie* wrong, and right acts can be distinguished from wrong acts only as being those which, of all those possible for the agent in the circumstances, have the greatest balance of *prima facie* right-ness, in those respects in which they are *prima facie* right, over their *prima facie* wrongness, in those respects in which they are *prima facie* wrong—*prima facie* rightness and wrongness being understood in the sense previously explained. For the estimation of the comparative stringency of these *prima facie* obligations no general rules can, so far as I can see, be laid down. We can only say that a great deal of stringency belongs to the duties of 'perfect obligation'—the duties of keeping our promises, of repairing wrongs we have done, and of returning the equivalent of services we have received. For the rest, ἐν τῇ αἰσθήσει ἡ κρίσις. ["The decision rests with perception," *Nicomachean Ethics* 1109b, 1126b]. This sense of our particular duty in particular circumstances, preceded and informed by the fullest reflection we can bestow on the act in all its bearings, is highly fallible, but it is the only guide we have to our duty.

# H. A. PRICHARD

HAROLD ARTHUR PRICHARD (1871–1947) taught at Oxford University. A leading intuitionist, his major works include: *Kant's Theory of Knowledge* (1909), *Duty and Interest* (1928), *Moral Obligation* (1949), and *Knowledge and Perception* (1950).

## Does Moral Philosophy Rest on a Mistake?*

Probably to most students of Moral Philosophy there comes a time when they feel a vague sense of dissatisfaction with the whole subject. And the sense of dissatisfaction tends to grow rather than to diminish. It is not so much that the positions, and still more the arguments, of particular thinkers seem unconvincing, though this is true. It is rather that the aim of the subject becomes increasingly obscure. 'What,' it is asked, 'are we really going to learn by Moral Philosophy?' 'What are books on Moral Philosophy really trying to show, and when their aim is clear, why are they so unconvincing and artificial?' And again: 'Why is it so difficult to substitute anything better?' Personally, I have been led by growing dissatisfaction of this kind to wonder whether the reason may not be that the subject, at any rate as usually understood, consists in the attempt to answer an improper question. And in this article I shall venture to contend that the existence of the whole subject, as usually understood, rests on a mistake, and on a mistake parallel to that on which rests, as I think, the subject usually called the Theory of Knowledge.

If we reflect on our own mental history or on the history of the subject, we feel no doubt about the nature of the demand which originates the subject. Any one who, stimulated by education, has come to feel the

* "Does Moral Philosophy Rest on a Mistake?" by H. A. Prichard, *Mind*, XXI (1912). Used by the kind permission of the editor of *Mind*.

force of the various obligations in life, at some time or other comes to feel the irksomeness of carrying them out, and to recognize the sacrifice of interest involved; and, if thoughtful, he inevitably puts to himself the question: 'Is there really a reason why I should act in the ways in which hitherto I have thought I ought to act? May I not have been all the time under an illusion in so thinking? Should not I really be justified in simply trying to have a good time?' Yet, like Glaucon, feeling that somehow he ought after all to act in these ways, he asks for a *proof* that this feeling is justified. In other words, he asks '*Why* should I do these things?', and his and other people's moral philosophizing is an attempt to supply the answer, i.e., to supply by a process of reflection a proof of the truth of what he and they have prior to reflection believed immediately or without proof. This frame of mind seems to present a close parallel to the frame of mind which originates the Theory of Knowledge. Just as the recognition that the doing of our duty often vitally interferes with the satisfaction of our inclinations leads us to wonder whether we really ought to do what we usually call our duty, so the recognition that we and others are liable to mistakes in knowledge generally leads us, as it did Descartes, to wonder whether hitherto we may not have been always mistaken. And just as we try to find a proof, based on the general consideration of action and of human life, that we ought to act in the ways usually called moral, so we, like Descartes, propose by a process of reflection on our thinking to find a test of knowledge, i.e., a principle by applying which we can show that a certain condition of mind was really knowledge, a condition which *ex hypothesi* existed independently of the process of reflection.

Now, how has the moral question been answered? So far as I can see, the answers all fall, and fall from the necessities of the case, into one of two species. *Either* they state that we ought to do so and so, because, as we see when we fully apprehend the facts, doing so will be for our good, i.e., really, as I would rather say, for our advantage, or better still, for our happiness; *or* they state that we ought to do so and so, because something realized either in or by the action is good. In other words, the reason 'why' is stated in terms either of the agent's happiness or of the goodness of something involved in the action.

To see the prevalence of the former species of answer, we have only to consider the history of Moral Philosophy. To take obvious instances, Plato, Butler, Hutcheson, Paley, Mill, each in his own way seeks at bottom to convince the individual that he ought to act in so-called moral ways by showing that to do so will really be for his happiness. Plato is perhaps the most significant instance, because of all philosophers he is the one to whom we are least willing to ascribe a mistake on such matters, and a mistake on his part would be evidence of the deep-rootedness of the tendency to make it. To show that Plato really justifies morality by its profitableness, it is only necessary to point out (1) that the very formulation of the thesis to be met, *viz.*, that justice is ἀλλότριον ἀγαθόν [someone else's advantage], implies that any refutation must consist in showing that justice is οἰκεῖον ἀγαθόν, i.e., really, as the context shows, one's own advantage, and (2) that the term λνσιτελεῖν [to be to someone's advantage] supplies the key not only to the problem but also to its solution.

The tendency to justify acting on moral rules in this way is natural. For if, as often happens, we put to ourselves the question 'Why should we do so and so?' we are satisfied by being convinced either that the doing so will lead to something which we want (e.g., that taking certain medicine will heal our disease), or that the doing so itself, as we see when we appreciate its nature, is something that we want or should like, e.g., playing golf. The formulation of the question implies a state of unwillingness or indifference towards the action, and we are brought into a condition of willingness by the answer. And this process seems to be precisely what we desire when we ask, e.g., 'Why should we keep our engagements to our own loss?'; for it is just the fact that the keeping of our engagements runs counter to the satisfaction of our desires which produced the question.

The answer is, of course, not an answer, for it fails to convince us that we ought to keep our engagements; even if successful on its own lines, it only makes us *want* to keep them. And Kant was really only pointing out this fact when he distinguished hypothetical and categorical imperatives, even though he obscured the nature of the fact by wrongly describing his so-called 'hypothetical imperatives' as imperatives. But if this answer be no answer, what other can be offered? Only, it seems, an answer which bases the obligation to do something on the *goodness* either of something to which the act leads or of the act itself. Suppose, when wondering whether we really ought to act in the ways usually called moral, we are told as a means of resolving our doubt that those acts are right which produce happiness. We at once ask: 'Whose happiness?' If we are told 'Our own happiness,' then, though we shall lose our hesitation to act in these ways, we shall not recover our sense that we ought to do so. But how can this result be avoided? Apparently, only by being told one of two things; *either* that anyone's happiness is a thing good in itself, and that *therefore* we ought to do whatever will produce it, *or* that working for happiness is itself good, and that the intrinsic goodness of such an action is the reason why we ought to do it. The advantage of this appeal to the goodness of something consists in the fact that it avoids reference to desire, and, instead, refers to something impersonal and objective. In this way it seems possible to avoid the resolution of obligation into inclination. But just for this reason it is of the essence of the answer, that to be effective it must neither include nor involve the view that the apprehension of the goodness of anything necessarily arouses the desire for it. Otherwise the answer resolves itself into a form of the former answer by substituting desire or inclination for the sense of obligation, and in this way it loses what seems its special advantage.

Now it seems to me that both forms of this answer break down, though each for a different reason.

Consider the first form. It is what may be called Utilitarianism in the generic sense, in which what is good is not limited to pleasure. It takes its stand upon the distinction between something which is not itself an action, but which can be produced by an action, and the action which will produce it, and contends that if something which is not an action is good, then we *ought* to undertake the action which will, directly or indirectly, originate it.

But this argument, if it is to restore the sense of obligation to act, must presuppose an intermediate link, *viz.*, the further thesis that what is good ought to be. The necessity of this link is obvious. An 'ought,' if it is to be derived at all, can only be derived from another 'ought.' Moreover, this link tacitly presupposes another, *viz.*, that the apprehension that something good which is not an action ought to be involves just the feeling of imperativeness or obligation which is to be aroused by the thought of the action which will originate it. Otherwise the argument will not lead us to feel the obligation to produce it by the action. And, surely, both this link and its implication are false.[1] The word 'ought' refers to actions and to actions alone. The proper language is never 'So and so ought to be,' but 'I ought to do so and so.' Even if we are sometimes moved to say that the world or something in it is not what it ought to be, what we really mean is that God or some human being has not made something what he ought to have made it. And it is merely stating another side of this fact to urge that we can only feel the imperativeness upon us of something which is in our power; for it is actions and actions alone which, directly at least, are in our power.

Perhaps, however, the best way to see the failure of this view is to see its failure to correspond to our actual moral convictions. Suppose we ask ourselves whether our sense that we ought to pay our debts or to tell the truth arises from our recognition that in doing so we should be originating something good, e.g., material comfort in A or true belief in B, i.e., suppose we ask ourselves whether it is this aspect of the action which leads to our recognition that we ought to do it. We at once and without hesitation answer 'No.' Again, if we take as our illustration our sense that we ought

---

[1] When we speak of anything, e.g., of some emotion or of some quality of a human being, as good, we never dream in our ordinary consciousness of going on to say that therefore it ought to be.

to act justly as between two parties, we have, if possible, even less hesitation in giving a similar answer; for the balance of resulting good may be,
and often is, not on the side of justice.

At best it can only be maintained that there is this element of truth in
the Utilitarian view, that unless we recognized that something which an
act will originate is good, we should not recognize that we ought to do the
action. Unless we thought knowledge a good thing, it may be urged, we
should not think that we ought to tell the truth; unless we thought pain a
bad thing, we should not think the infliction of it, without special reason,
wrong. But this is not to imply that the badness of error is the reason why
it is wrong to lie, or the badness of pain the reason why we ought not to
inflict it without special cause.[2]

It is, I think, just because this form of the view is so plainly at variance
with our moral consciousness that we are driven to adopt the other form
of the view, viz., that the act is good in itself and that its intrinsic goodness
is the reason why it ought to be done. It is this form which has always made
the most serious appeal; for the goodness of the act itself seems more closely
related to the obligation to do it than that of its mere consequences or results, and therefore, if obligation is to be based on the goodness of something, it would seem that this goodness should be that of the act itself.
Moreover, the view gains plausibility from the fact that moral actions are
most conspicuously those to which the term 'intrinsically good' is applicable.

Nevertheless this view, though perhaps less superficial, is equally untenable. For it leads to precisely the dilemma which faces everyone who
tries to solve the problem raised by Kant's theory of the good will. To see
this, we need only consider the nature of the acts to which we apply the
term 'intrinsically good.'

There is, of course, no doubt that we approve and even admire certain
actions, and also that we should describe them as good, and as good in
themselves. But it is, I think, equally unquestionable that our approval and
our use of the term 'good' is always in respect of the motive and refers to
actions which have been actually done and of which we think we know the
motive. Further, the actions of which we approve and which we should
describe as intrinsically good are of two and only two kinds. They are
either actions in which the agent did what he did because he thought he
ought to do it, or actions of which the motive was a desire prompted by
some good emotion, such as gratitude, affection, family feeling, or public
spirit, the most prominent of such desires in books on Moral Philosophy

[2] It may be noted that if the badness of pain were the reason why we ought not to
inflict pain on another, it would equally be a reason why we ought not to inflict pain
on ourselves; yet, though we should allow the wanton infliction of pain on ourselves
to be foolish, we should not think of describing it as wrong.

being that ascribed to what is vaguely called benevolence. For the sake of simplicity I omit the case of actions done partly from some such desire and partly from a sense of duty; for even if all good actions are done from a combination of these motives, the argument will not be affected. The dilemma is this. If the motive in respect of which we think an action good is the sense of obligation, then so far from the sense that we ought to do it being derived from our apprehension of its goodness, our apprehension of its goodness will presuppose the sense that we ought to do it. In other words, in this case the recognition that the act is good will plainly *presuppose* the recognition that the act is right, whereas the view under consideration is that the recognition of the goodness of the act *gives rise* to the recognition of its rightness. On the other hand, if the motive in respect of which we think an action good is some intrinsically good desire, such as the desire to help a friend, the recognition of the goodness of the act will equally fail to give rise to the sense of obligation to do it. For we cannot feel that we ought to do that the doing of which is *ex hypothesi* prompted solely by the desire to do it.

The fallacy underlying the view is that while to base the rightness of an act upon its intrinsic goodness implies that the goodness in question is that of the motive, in reality the rightness or wrongness of an act has nothing to do with any question of motives at all. For, as any instance will show, the rightness of an action concerns an action not in the fuller sense of the term in which we include the motive in the action, but in the narrower and commoner sense in which we distinguish an action from its motive and mean by an action merely the conscious origination of something, an origination which on different occasions or in different people may be prompted by different motives. The question 'Ought I to pay my bills?' really means simply 'Ought I to bring about my tradesmen's possession of what by my previous acts I explictly or implicitly promised them?' There is, and can be, no question of whether I ought to pay my debts from a particular motive. No doubt we know that if we pay our bills we shall pay them with a motive, but in considering whether we ought to pay them we inevitably think of the act in abstraction from the motive. Even if we knew what our motive would be if we did the act, we should not be any nearer an answer to the question.

Moreover, if we eventually pay our bills from fear of the county court, we shall still have done *what* we ought, even though we shall not have done it *as* we ought. The attempt to bring in the motive involves a mistake similar to that involved in supposing that we can will to will. To feel that I ought to pay my bills is to be *moved towards* paying them. But what I can be moved towards must always be an action and not an action in which I am moved in a particular way, i.e., an action from a particular motive; otherwise I should be moved towards being moved, which is impossible. Yet the view under consideration involves this impossibility, for it really resolves the sense that I ought to do so and so, into the sense that I ought to be moved to do it in a particular way.[3]

So far my contentions have been mainly negative, but they form, I think, a useful, if not a necessary, introduction to what I take to be the truth. This I will now endeavour to state, first formulating what, as I think, is the real nature of our apprehension or appreciation of moral obligations, and then applying the result to elucidate the question of the existence of Moral Philosophy.

The sense of obligation to do, or of the rightness of, an action of a particular kind is absolutely underivative or immediate. The rightness of an action consists in its being the origination of something of a certain kind A in a situation of a certain kind, a situation consisting in a certain relation B of the agent to others or to his own nature. To appreciate its rightness two preliminaries may be necessary. We may have to follow out the consequences of the proposed action more fully than we have hitherto done, in order to realize that in the action we should originate A. Thus we may not appreciate the wrongness of telling a certain story until we realize that we should thereby be hurting the feelings of one of our audience. Again, we may have to take into account the relation B involved in the situation, which we had hitherto failed to notice. For instance, we may not appreciate the obligation to give X a present, until we remember that he has done us an act of kindness. But, given that by a process which is, of course, merely a process of general and not of moral thinking we come to recognize that the proposed act is one by which we shall originate A in a relation B, then we appreciate the obligation immediately or directly, the appreciation being an activity of *moral* thinking. We recognize, for instance, that this performance of a service to X, who has done us a service, just in virtue of its being the performance of a service to one who has rendered a service to the would-be agent, ought to be done by us. This apprehension is immediate, in precisely the sense in which a mathematical apprehension is immediate, e.g., the apprehension that this three-sided figure, in virtue of its being three-sided, must have three angles. Both apprehensions are immediate in the sense that in both insight into the nature of the subject directly leads us to recognize its possession of the predicate; and it is only stating this fact from the other side to say that in both cases the fact apprehended is self-evident.

The plausibility of the view that obligations are not self-evident but

---

[3] It is of course not denied here that an action done from a particular motive may be *good*; it is only denied that the *rightness* of an action depends on its being done with a particular motive.

need proof lie in the fact that an act which is referred to as an obligation may be incompletely stated, what I have called the preliminaries to appreciating the obligation being incomplete. If, e.g., we refer to the act of repaying X by a present merely as giving X a present, it appears, and indeed is, necessary to give a reason. In other words, wherever a moral act is regarded in this incomplete way the question 'Why should I do it?' is perfectly legitimate. This fact suggests, but suggests wrongly, that even if the nature of the act is completely stated, it is still necessary to give a reason, or, in other words, to supply a proof.

The relations involved in obligations of various kinds are, of course, very different. The relation in certain cases is a relation to others due to a past act of theirs or ours. The obligation to repay a benefit involves a relation due to a past act of the benefactor. The obligation to pay a bill involves a relation due to a past act of ours in which we have either said or implied that we would make a certain return for something which we have asked for and received. On the other hand, the obligation to speak the truth implies no such definite act; it involves a relation consisting in the fact that others are trusting us to speak the truth, a relation the apprehension of which gives rise to the sense that communication of the truth is something owing by us to them. Again, the obligation not to hurt the feelings of another involves no special relation of us to that other, i.e., no relation other than that involved in our both being men, and men in one and the same world. Moreover, it seems that the relation involved in an obligation need not be a relation to another at all. Thus we should admit that there is an obligation to overcome our natural timidity or greediness, and that this involves no relations to others. Still there is a relation involved, viz., a relation to our own disposition. It is simply because we can and because others cannot directly modify our disposition that it is our business to improve it, and that it is not theirs, or, at least, not theirs to the same extent.

The negative side of all this is, of course, that we do not come to appreciate an obligation by an argument, i.e., by a process of nonmoral thinking, and that, in particular, we do not do so by an argument of which a premiss is the ethical but not moral activity of appreciating the goodness either of the act or of a consequence of the act; i.e., that our sense of the rightness of an act is not a conclusion from our appreciation of the goodness either of it or of anything else.

It will probably be urged that on this view our various obligations form, like Aristotle's categories, an unrelated chaos in which it is impossible to acquiesce. For, according to it, the obligation to repay a benefit, or to pay a debt, or to keep a promise, presupposes a previous act of another; whereas the obligation to speak the truth or not to harm another does not; and,

again, the obligation to remove our timidity involves no relations to others
at all. Yet, at any rate, an effective *argumentum ad hominem* is at hand
in the fact that the various qualities which we recognize as good are equally
unrelated; e.g., courage, humility, and interest in knowledge. If, as is plainly
the case, ἀγαθά [goods] differ ᾗ ἀγαθά [qua goods], why should not obligations
equally differ *qua* their obligatoriness? Moreover, if this were not so there
could in the end be only one obligation, which is palpably contrary to fact.[4]

Certain observations will help to make the view clearer.

In the first place, it may seem that the view, being—as it is—avowedly
put forward in opposition to the view that what is right is derived from
what is good, must itself involve the opposite of this, *viz.*, the Kantian position that what is good is based upon what is right, i.e., that an act, if it be
good, is good because it is right. But this is not so. For, on the view put forward, the rightness of a right action lies solely in the origination in which
the act consists, whereas the intrinsic goodness of an action lies solely
in its motive; and this implies that a morally good action is morally good not
simply because it is a right action but because it is a right action done
because it is right, i.e., from a sense of obligation. And this implication, it
may be remarked incidentally, seems plainly true.

In the second place, the view involves that when, or rather so far as, we
act from a sense of obligation, we have no purpose or end. By a 'purpose'
or 'end' we really mean something the existence of which we desire, and
desire of the existence of which leads us to act. Usually our purpose is something which the act will originate, as when we turn round in order to look at
a picture. But it may be the action itself, i.e., the origination of something,
as when we hit a golf-ball into a hole or kill someone out of revenge.[5] Now

---

[4] Two other objections may be anticipated: (1) that obligations cannot be self-evident,
since many actions regarded as obligations by some are not so regarded by others, and (2)
that if obligations are self-evident, the problem of how we ought to act in the presence of
conflicting obligations is insoluble.

To the first I should reply:

(*a*) That the appreciation of an obligation is, of course, only possible for a developed moral being, and that different degrees of development are possible.

(*b*) That the failure to recognize some particular obligations is usually due to the
fact that, owing to a lack of thoughtfulness, what I have called the preliminaries to this
recognition are incomplete.

(*c*) That the view put forward is consistent with the admission that, owing to a
lack of thoughtfulness, even the best men are blind to many of their obligations, and
that in the end our obligations are seen to be co-extensive with almost the whole of our life.

To the second objection I should reply that obligation admits of degrees, and that
where obligations conflict, the decision of what we ought to do turns not on the question 'Which of the alternative courses of action will originate the greater good?' but on the
question 'Which is the greater obligation?'

[5] It is no objection to urge that an action cannot be its own purpose, since the purpose of something cannot be the thing itself. For, speaking strictly, the purpose is not
the *action's* purpose but *our* purpose, and there is no contradiction in holding that our
purpose in acting may be the action.

if by a purpose we mean something the existence of which we desire and desire for which leads us to act, then plainly, so far as we act from a sense of obligation, we have no purpose, consisting either in the action or in anything which it will produce. This is so obvious that it scarcely seems worth pointing out. But I do so for two reasons. (1) If we fail to scrutinize the meaning of the terms 'end' and 'purpose,' we are apt to assume uncritically that all deliberate action, i.e., action proper, must have a purpose; we than become puzzled both when we look for the purpose of an action done from a sense of obligation, and also when we try to apply to such an action the distinction of means and end, the truth all the time being that since there is no end, there is no means either. (2) The attempt to base the sense of obligation on the recognition of the goodness of something is really an attempt to find a purpose in a moral action in the shape of something good which, as good, we want. And the expectation that the goodness of something underlies an obligation disappears as soon as we cease to look for a purpose.

The thesis, however, that, so far as we act from a sense of obligation, we have no purpose must not be misunderstood. It must not be taken either to mean or to imply that so far as we so act we have no *motive*. No doubt in ordinary speech the words 'motive' and 'purpose' are usually treated as correlatives, 'motive' standing for the desire which induces us to act, and 'purpose' standing for the object of this desire. But this is only because, when we are looking for the motive of the action, say, of some crime, we are usually presupposing that the act in question is prompted by a desire and not by the sense of obligation. At bottom, however, we mean by a motive what moves us to act; a sense of obligation does sometimes move us to act; and in our ordinary consciousness we should not hesitate to allow that the action we were considering might have had as its motive a sense of obligation. Desire and the sense of obligation are coordinate forms or species of motive.

In the third place, if the view put forward be right, we must sharply distinguish morality and virtue as independent, though related, species of goodness, neither being an aspect of something of which the other is an aspect, nor again a form of species of the other, nor again something deducible from the other; and we must at the same time allow that it is possible to do the same act either virtuously or morally or in both ways at once. And surely this is true. An act, to be virtuous, must, as Aristotle saw, be done willingly or with pleasure; as such it is just not done from a sense of obligation but from some desire which is intrinsically good, as arising from some intrinsically good emotion. Thus, in an act of generosity the motive is the desire to help another arising from sympathy with that other; in an act which is courageous and no more, i.e., in an act which is not at the same time an act of public spirit or family affection or the like, we prevent ourselves from being dominated by a feeling of terror, desiring to do so from a sense of shame at being terrified. The goodness of such an act is different from the goodness of an act to which we apply the term moral in the strict and narrow sense, viz., an act done from a sense of obligation. Its goodness lies in the intrinsic goodness of the emotion and of the consequent desire under which we act, the goodness of this motive being different from the goodness of the moral motive proper, viz., the sense of duty or obligation. Nevertheless, at any rate in certain cases, an act can be done either virtuously or morally or in both ways at once. It is possible to repay a benefit either from desire to repay it, or from the feeling that we ought to do so, or from both motives combined. A doctor may tend his patients either from a desire arising out of interest in his patients or in the exercise of skill, or from a sense of duty, or from a desire and a sense of duty combined. Further, although we recognize that in each case the act possesses an intrinsic goodness, we regard that action as the best in which both motives are combined; in other words, we regard as the really best man the man in whom virtue and morality are united.

It may be objected that the distinction between the two kinds of motive is untenable, on the ground that the *desire* to repay a benefit, for example, is only the manifestation of that which manifests itself as the *sense of obligation* to repay whenever we think of something in the action which is other than the repayment and which we should not like, such as the loss or pain involved. Yet the distinction can, I think, easily be shown to be tenable. For, in the analogous case of revenge, the desire to return the injury and the sense that we ought not to do so, leading, as they do, in opposite directions, are plainly distinct; and the obviousness of the distinction here seems to remove any difficulty in admitting the existence of a parallel distinction between the desire to return a benefit and the sense that we ought to return it.[6]

Further, the view implies that an obligation can no more be based on or derived from a virtue than a virtue can be derived from an obligation, in which latter case a virtue would consist in carrying out an obligation. And the implication is surely true and important. Take the case of courage. It is untrue to urge that, since courage is a virtue, we ought to act courageously. It is and must be untrue, because, as we see in the end, to feel an obligation

---

[6] This sharp distinction of virtue and morality as co-ordinate and independent forms of goodness will explain a fact which otherwise it is difficult to account for. If we turn from books on Moral Philosophy to any vivid account of human life and action such as we find in Shakespeare, nothing strikes us more than the comparative remoteness of the discussions of Moral Philosophy from the facts of actual life. Is not this largely because, while Moral Philosophy has, quite rightly, concentrated its attention on the fact of obligation, in the case of many of those whom we admire most and whose lives are of the greatest interest, the sense of obligation, though it may be an important, is not a dominating factor in their lives?

to act courageously would involve a contradiction. For, as I have urged before, we can only feel an obligation to *act*; we cannot feel an obligation to *act from a certain desire*, in this case the desire to conquer one's feelings of terror arising from the sense of shame which they arouse. Moreover, if the sense of obligation to act in a particular way leads to an action, the action will be an action done from a sense of obligation, and therefore not, if the above analysis of virtue be right, an act of courage.

The mistake of supposing that there can be an obligation to act courageously seems to arise from two causes. In the first place, there is often an obligation to do that which involves the conquering or controlling of our fear in the doing of it, e.g., the obligation to walk along the side of a precipice to fetch a doctor for a member of our family. Here the acting on the obligation is externally, though only externally, the same as an act of courage proper. In the second place there is an obligation to acquire courage, i.e., to do such things as will enable us afterwards to act courageously, and this may be mistaken for an obligation to act courageously. The same considerations can, of course, be applied, *mutatis mutandis,* to the other virtues.

The fact, if it be a fact, that virtue is no basis for morality will explain what otherwise it is difficult to account for, *viz.,* the extreme sense of dissatisfaction produced by a close reading of Aristotle's *Ethics.* Why is the *Ethics* so disappointing? Not, I think, because it really answers two radically different questions as if they were one: (1) 'What is the happy life?' (2) 'What is the virtuous life?' It is, rather, because Aristotle does not do what we as moral philosophers want him to do, *viz.,* to convince us that we really ought to do what in our non-reflective consciousness we have hitherto believed we ought to do, or if not, to tell us what, if any, are the other things which we really ought to do, and to prove to us that he is right. Now, if what I have just been contending is true, a systematic account of the virtuous character cannot possibly satisfy this demand. At best it can only make clear to us the details of one of our obligations, *viz.,* the obligation to make ourselves better men; but the achievement of this does not help us to discover what we ought to do in life as a whole, and why; to think that it did would be to think that our only business in life was self-improvement. Hence it is not surprising that Aristotle's account of the good man strikes us as almost wholly of academic value, with little relation to our real demand, which is formulated in Plato's words: οὐ γὰρ περὶ τοῦ ἐπιτυχόντος ὁ λόγος, ἀλλὰ περὶ τοῦ ὅντινα τρόπον χρὴ ζῆν. ["For no light matter is at stake, nothing less than the rule of human life." *Republic,* Bk. I, 352].

I am not, of course, *criticizing* Aristotle for failing to satisfy this demand, except so far as here and there he leads us to think that he intends to satisfy it. For my main contention is that the demand cannot be satisfied, and cannot be satisfied because it is illegitimate. Thus we are brought to the question: 'Is there really such a thing as Moral Philosophy, and, if there is, in what sense?'

We should first consider the parallel case—as it appears to be—of the Theory of Knowledge. As I urged before, at some time or other in the history of all of us, if we are thoughtful, the frequency of our own and of others' mistakes is bound to lead to the reflection that possibly we and others have *always* been mistaken in consequence of some radical defect of our faculties. In consequence, certain things which previously we should have said without hesitation that we *knew*, as e.g., that $4 \times 7 = 28$, become subject to doubt; we become able only to say that we thought we knew these things. We inevitably go on to look for some general procedure by which we can ascertain that a given condition of mind is really one of knowledge. And this involves the search for a criterion of knowledge, i.e., for a principle by applying which we can settle that a given state of mind is really knowledge. The search for this criterion and the application of it, when found, is what is called the Theory of Knowledge. The search implies that instead of its being the fact that the knowledge that A is B is obtained directly by consideration of the nature of A and B, the knowledge that A is B, in the full or complete sense, can only be obtained by first knowing that A is B, and then knowing that we knew it by applying a criterion, such as Descartes's principle that what we clearly and distinctly conceive is true.

Now it is easy to show that the doubt whether A is B, based on this speculative or general ground, could, if genuine, never be set at rest. For if, in order really to know that A is B, we must first know that we knew it, then really, to know that we knew it, we must first know that we knew that we knew it. But—what is more important—it is also easy to show that this doubt is not a genuine doubt but rests on a confusion the exposure of which removes the doubt. For when we *say* we doubt whether our previous condition was one of knowledge, what we *mean*, if we mean anything at all, is that we doubt whether our previous *belief* was *true*, a belief which we should express as the *thinking* that A is B. For in order to doubt whether our previous condition was one of knowledge, we have to think of it not as knowledge but as only belief, and our only question can be 'Was this belief true?' But as soon as we see that we are thinking of our previous condition as only one of belief, we see that what we are now doubting is not what we first *said* we were doubting, *viz.*, whether a previous condition of knowledge was really knowledge. Hence, to remove the doubt, it is only necessary to appreciate the real nature of our consciousness in apprehending, e.g., that $7 \times 4 = 28$, and thereby see that it was no mere condition of believing but a condition of knowing, and then to notice that in our subsequent doubt what we are really doubting is not whether this consciousness was really knowledge, but whether a consciousness of another kind, *viz.*, a belief that $7 \times 4 = 28$, was true. We thereby see that though a doubt based on speculative grounds is possible, it is not a doubt concerning what we believed the doubt concerned, and that a doubt concerning this latter is impossible.

Two results follow. In the first place, if, as is usually the case, we mean by the 'Theory of Knowledge' the knowledge which supplies the answer to the question 'Is what we have hitherto thought knowledge really knowledge?,' there is and can be no such thing, and the supposition that there can is simply due to a confusion. There can be no answer to an illegitimate question, except that the question is illegitimate. Nevertheless the question is one which we continue to put until we realize the inevitable immediacy of knowledge. And it is positive knowledge that knowledge is immediate and neither can be, nor needs to be, improved or vindicated by the further knowledge that it was knowledge. This positive knowledge sets at rest the inevitable doubt, and, so far as by the 'Theory of Knowledge' is meant this knowledge, then even though this knowledge be the knowledge that there is no Theory of Knowledge in the former sense, to that extent the Theory of Knowledge exists.

In the second place, suppose we come genuinely to doubt whether, e.g., $7 \times 4 = 28$ owing to a genuine doubt whether we were right in believing yesterday that $7 \times 4 = 28$, a doubt which can in fact only arise if we have lost our hold of, i.e., no longer remember, the real nature of our consciousness of yesterday, and so think of it as consisting in believing. Plainly, the only remedy is to do the sum again. Or, to put the matter generally, if we do come to doubt whether it is true that A is B, as we once thought, the remedy lies not in any process of reflection but in such a reconsideration of the nature of A and B as leads to the knowledge that A is B.

With these considerations in mind, consider the parallel which, as it seems to me, is presented—though with certain differences—by Moral Philosophy. The sense that we ought to do certain things arises in our unreflective consciousness, being an activity of moral thinking occasioned by the various situations in which we find ourselves. At this stage our attitude to these obligations is one of unquestioning confidence. But inevitably the appreciation of the degree to which the execution of these obligations is contrary to our interest raises the doubt whether after all these obligations are really obligatory, i.e., whether our sense that we ought not to do certain things is not illusion. We then want to have it *proved* to us that we ought to do so, i.e., to be convinced of this by a process which, as an argument, is different in kind from our original and unreflective appreciation of it. This demand is, as I have argued, illegitimate.

Hence, in the first place, if, as is almost universally the case, by **Moral**

Philosophy is meant the knowledge which would satisfy this demand, there is no such knowledge, and all attempts to attain it are doomed to failure because they rest on a mistake, the mistake of supposing the possibility of proving what can only be apprehended directly by an act of moral thinking. Nevertheless the demand, though illegitimate, is inevitable until we have carried the process of reflection far enough to realize the self-evidence of our obligations, i.e., the immediacy of our apprehension of them. This realization of their self-evidence is positive knowledge, and so far, and so far only, as the term Moral Philosophy is confined to this knowledge and to the knowledge of the parallel immediacy of the apprehension of the goodness of the various virtues and of good dispositions generally, is there such a thing as Moral Philosophy. But since this knowledge may allay doubts which often affect the whole conduct of life, it is, though not extensive, important and even vitally important.

In the second place, suppose we come genuinely to doubt whether we ought, for example, to pay our debts, owing to a genuine doubt whether our previous conviction that we ought to do so is true, a doubt which can, in fact, only arise if we fail to remember the real nature of what we now call our past conviction. The only remedy lies in actually getting into a situation which occasions the obligation, or—if our imagination be strong enough— in imagining ourselves in that situation, and then letting our moral capacities of thinking do their work. Or, to put the matter generally, if we do doubt whether there is really an obligation to originate A in a situation B, the remedy lies not in any process of general thinking, but in getting face to face with a particular instance of the situation B, and then directly appreciating the obligation to originate A in that situation.

# ALEXANDER MACBEATH

ALEXANDER MACBEATH (1888–    ) taught for many years at The Queen's University, Belfast, and is now Head of the Department of Moral Philosophy at Edinburgh University. Concerned especially with the relationship of work in social anthropology to problems in ethics and religion, his major works include: *The Relationship of Primitive Morality and Religion* (1949) and *Experiments in Living* (1952).

## Anthropology and Ethics*

Some ethical theorists tell us that we can see or know that certain moral rules are right with the same certainty with which we see that two and two are four, or that the three angles of a triangle are together equal to two right angles. We do not, they contend, merely believe these propositions. We know that they are true. Similarly, they tell us, we immediately apprehend as self-evident truths the rightness of certain moral rules or the obligatoriness of certain acts or sorts of acts. Other ethical theorists tell us that we immediately apprehend or perceive by inspection that certain sorts of things or states of affairs are intrinsically good, in the same direct way in which we perceive that a rose is red or a primrose yellow; and that those actions are right which produce or promote, or are intended to produce or promote, such things.

According to these views, if a person does not immediately see that the rules in question are right or the ends good, the only advice that can be given to him is to look again and try to remove the obstacles and prejudices which prevent him from seeing; just as the only advice that can be given to the schoolboy who says that he does not see that the three angles of a triangle are together equal to two right angles is to look again, to follow the argument more carefully and with more concentrated attention. If he still does not see, there is nothing that can be done for him, except hope that providence will open his eyes. So if, after due attention, a person still fails to see the rightness of so-called self-evident moral rules or the goodness of so-called intrinsic goods, he must be regarded as in some way deficient in moral sense or moral reason.

Now I entirely agree that, if the obligatoriness of certain sorts of acts is genuinely self-evident, the proposed method of procedure is the only one open to us. I agree also that the ultimate principle on which the moral agent proceeds in his judgements, that is, the moral criterion, must be of this kind —self-authenticating, unmediated, containing its evidence within itself—so that a person has only to grasp its nature to recognise its self-evidence. If, therefore, we were completely satisfied that the judgements in question had the self-evidence claimed for them by some theorists, we should have no alternative to accepting them as true, even if we were thereby forced to conclude that the moral consciousness of those who think otherwise is constituted in a different way from our own. Such a conclusion would in effect mean that the judgements of those who differ from us on this question are not expressions of the moral consciousness at all. For it is difficult to see any difference between a moral consciousness which operates on a different principle from ours and one which is not moral at all.

But . . . it is by no means easy to be sure that in any given judgement we have an authentic deliverance of the moral consciousness, i.e., a deliverance uninfluenced by conditions which are peculiar to the agent who makes the judgement or to his people. And there are at least three reasons for doubting the claim that it is an authentic deliverance of the moral consciousness that the rightness of certain rules or the obligatoriness of certain sorts of acts is self-evident. (1) This character is claimed for the acts and rules in question when they are considered by themselves in isolation. But they never do occur in isolation; and it is difficult to be sure that the context in which they normally occur has nothing to do with their obligatoriness appearing to be self-evident. (2) . . . These acts are never described with the precision and freedom from ambiguity which are essential to the terms of a proposition which is to be recognised as self-evident. (3) We find little agreement, even among the most careful thinkers who claim that there are self-evident moral judgements, as to which moral judgements have this character. What seemed self-evident to Sidgwick is not accepted as such by Moore; and what Moore regards as self-evident is not accepted as even true by Ross. In view of these doubts, it is desirable to consider such judgements in different contexts, and especially in different cultural conditions, to discover whether they retain their apparent self-evidence in all contexts. If we find that they are not regarded as true by all men everywhere—let alone as self-evidently true—we should hesitate to accept their self-evidence as an authentic deliverance of the moral consciousness; for any judgement which is really self-evident should be recognised as such by all who have the capacity to grasp it and have paid sufficient attention to it. Accordingly, those who claim that certain moral rules are self-evident tend to minimise the differences between the moral judgements of different peoples, and attribute the failure of primitive peoples to recognise certain rules as self-evident either to their not having the capacity to grasp the terms involved in them or to their not having sufficiently attended to them.[1] If the evidence compels us to reject this explanation, the only alternatives[2] open to us are either to reject their claim to self-evidence or to deny that the primitive moral consciousness functions according to the same principle as ours; and the latter alternative amounts, as I have said, to a denial that primitive peoples are moral beings at all, in the sense in which we use the term.

Accordingly, in our attempts to test the adequacy of ethical theories which rely on what I shall call the method of isolation, that is the method which assumes that we can pass final moral judgements on acts or sorts of acts or ends or states of affairs in isolation from their context, the evidence about the moralities of primitive peoples is relevant in at least three ways. (1) It shows that some of the judgements which are regarded as self-evident by contemporary moralists are not even regarded as true by some primitive peoples. (2) It enables us to decide whether we can accept as adequate the explanation offered by contemporary moralists as to why some primitive peoples reject what are claimed to be self-evident moral judgements. . . . (3) It shows that some primitive peoples have moral rules of their own, which appear to them obviously right, but some of which are different from, and inconsistent with, those accepted by contemporary moralists. . . .

I think the most fundamental difference between the views of anthropologists dealing with primitives and most recent and contemporary ethical theorists is to be found in the difference between the answers which they respectively give to the question: What is the simplest unit of conduct which has to be taken into consideration in passing a considered moral judgement, or in trying to understand the moral judgement of another? As I pointed out earlier, a moral judgement is a final or ultimate judgement, one from which there is no appeal to a higher court or a wider context. What, then, is the simplest entity, which is sufficiently self-contained to warrant a final judgement of rightness or goodness—a judgement which is not liable to require alteration or modification in the light of any further facts or factors?

Recent ethical theorists tend to regard the units in question as relatively simple. They tend to use what I have called the method of isolation. They regard isolated, or at least isolable, elements in the moral life or moral ideal as capable of sustaining such a judgement. Thus it is held that the obliga-

---

[1] More often they simply ignore the moral judgements of other times and places, and the problem which the differences between the moral judgements of different peoples present for their theories.

[2] That is, on the assumption which is shared by the theories under consideration, that moral judgements are really statements, and are therefore true or false.

toriness of certain moral rules can be recognised as self-evident, when the rules are considered by themselves apart from any context. The judgement that certain sorts of acts are right is regarded as final or ultimate, in the sense that it does not need any reason or justification beyond itself. It is true that the obligatoriness of such acts is no longer regarded as absolute but as prima facie, i.e., they are actually obligatory unless they conflict with more urgent obligations; but the judgement that they have this obligatoriness is infallible or self-justifying without reference to any context. Again, certain ends or states of affairs or experiences are regarded as intrinsically good, by which is meant that they would be good even if they existed quite alone, even if there were nothing else in the universe. We find this view in a variety of forms—not only in the Ideal Utilitarianism of Moore, or combined with Intuitionism as by Ross, but also in some theories of the self-realisation type. Urban, e.g., gives a list of values which, when considered by themselves, can, he thinks, be arranged on a scale which has universal validity.

We are not here concerned with the details of these views but only with the method of isolation by which they try to get rules, ends or values which have by themselves an absolute or self-evident claim that they should be obeyed, pursued or realised. It is worth pointing out, however, that, even if we could get such atomic absolutes the task of the moral agent would not be so easy as it might at first sight appear. For an act is not normally just an instance of one rule or just the pursuit of one end or just the realisation of one value. It may also be the violation of another rule, the neglect of another end or the denial of another value. And the real problem of the moral agent, in trying to discover what he ought to do, is to discover which rule is the more urgent, which intrinsic good or sum of intrinsic goods is the greater, which act will realise the higher value. The theories in question suggest no principle by which the moral agent can make his choice. They counsel him merely to do his best and trust his fallible judgement. But until some principle is forthcoming on which he can make this, his most crucial choice, the principles 'obey the most urgent rule,' 'produce the greatest amount of intrinsic good,' or 'realise the higher value' are of little practical use to the moral agent.

What concerns us, however, is whether such atomic absolutes, which contain the grounds of their rightness or goodness within themselves, can in fact be found. The unanimous and oft-repeated view of recent and contemporary social anthropologists is that, among primitives, at least, they cannot. They hold in effect that the results of any attempt to apply the method of isolation to the moral judgements of primitives are not only valueless but misleading. Indeed, . . . their main criticism of the earlier anthropologists is just that they used the method of isolation, and tried to understand primitive actions and customs and value-judgements without taking account of the cultural context which alone renders them intelligible. According to their view, what we find among primitives is not rules whose obligatoriness is self-evident when they are considered in isolation, but rules which are the conditions of the working of certain interrelated institutions; not acts which have intrinsic goods as consequences, but acts which are good in their context; not a scale of values whose relative order can be decided in abstraction, but a system of values embodied in a way of life which determines their order of preference at any given moment. . . .

This of course does not mean that it is not legitimate, and even necessary, to distinguish the different elements in a way of life and to consider them separately. What it does mean is that we cannot appreciate the way in which they appear to the person who lives the life and passes judgements of value on them, unless we look at them in their context. Nor does it mean that the ways of life of most, or indeed perhaps of any, peoples are the consistent expression of one principle. Their degree of coherence varies from people to people, and the unity of the resulting patterns generally takes the form of functional interdependence between the parts, rather than the expression of a rationally coherent plan of life. Similar variations are to be found in the extent to which different individuals, even in the same community, enter into the spirit of their way of life and appreciate its pattern as a whole. But whatever be the degree of integration of the pattern and to whatever extent individuals appreciate it as a whole, the anthropological evidence suggests that their conception of it provides the operative ideal which determines their duties and obligations, that what appears to them right and good is conditioned by it, and that, therefore, however immediate and intuitive their judgement may seem, they are not unconditional or self-justifying, but at least partly dependent on, and conditioned by, the background of the way of life of the people concerned. In the discussion of moral questions this background is normally taken for granted; and as long as it is common to all the individuals concerned in the discussion, the neglect of it, and of the way in which it conditions their judgements, need occasion no difficulty. But when we consider the differences between the value-judgements of different peoples, and especially of primitives and ourselves, the relevance of the different ways of life which they presuppose becomes clear. We find that they are all conditioned by the context in relation to which they are made. The only judgement which is strictly unconditional and self-justifying is that passed on a way of life as a whole. . . .

Those who proceed by the method of isolation contend that certain moral rules are self-evident, unmediated, containing the grounds of their rightness within themselves. Now rules which have this character should be recognised as such by all who have the capacity to grasp the concepts involved in them and have sufficiently attended to them. And if such rules are recognised at all, they should be recognised as being strictly universal. For their rightness is independent of any context and, therefore, holds in every context. Their rightness is independent of, and additional to, the goodness of any state of affairs to which their observance leads, or of which it may be a condition. That certain moral rules have this self-evidence and strict universality and independent rightness is the claim of the intuitionists. What we have to consider is how far this claim is consistent with the facts about primitive morality.

In considering this question we have to ask: (1) How far do primitives recognise as binding the same rules as we do, in particular those which intuitionists claim to be self-evident? And (2) so far as they do recognise them, how far do they regard them as self-evident or self-authenticating? . . .

Let me try to sum up . . . the attitude of primitive peoples to their moral rules: (1) Few, if any, primitive people regard their moral rules as universal in the sense that they apply to all men. Some of them do not regard all their moral rules as applicable to all even of those to whom some of them are applicable. (2) While many moral rules abstractly stated may appear to be common to the codes of many peoples, the interpretations which different peoples put on the terms used in them, and the exceptions to them which they regard as right, are so different that the rules in question, in any sense in which they can be said to be common to most peoples, lack the precision and freedom from ambiguity necessary to any rules which are to be apprehended as self-evident. (3) Many people fail to recognise as right at all some of the rules regarded by contemporary intuitionists as prima facie obligations. (4) The rules which primitives do recognise as binding they do not regard as self-authenticating or unmediated, but as deriving their authority from the form of life whose conditions they are. And (5) some primitives regard as obviously right some rules which we do not recognise as right at all and which are indeed inconsistent with some of those which we do regard as binding obligations.

If these conclusions are well founded, they seem to show that most of the moral rules, for which self-evidence has been claimed, are not really self-evident in the sense that they are recognised as such by all who understand them and have attended to them. And if we accept the view, as I think we must, that a satisfactory ethical theory must be consistent with the moral judgements of all men everywhere, this means that intuitionism cannot in any of its forms be regarded as a satisfactory ethical theory.

# STEPHEN E. TOULMIN

STEPHEN EDELSTON TOULMIN (1922–    )
is Professor of Philosophy at the University of
Leeds, England. Writing from the viewpoint
of contemporary analytic philosophy, his
major works include: *An Examination of the
Place of Reason in Ethics* (1950), *The
Philosophy of Science* (1953), and *The Uses
of Argument* (1958).

## *The Objective Approach**

Let us begin by considering one of the oldest and most familiar doctrines of philosophical ethics, the doctrine that, in saying that anything is
good or right, we are mentioning a *property* which it has, the property of
goodness or rightness. This doctrine I shall call, for short, the 'objective'
doctrine (for although the question, 'Is goodness objective?', may not be the
most important one involved, it is one to which its supporters have traditionally paid great attention). . . .

### *Is Goodness a Directly-Perceived Property?*

. . . Suppose . . . that someone says to me, not 'Cochineal is red,' but a
sentence which on the face of it is very similar, 'Meekness is good.' . . .

What if someone else comes along and says 'Meekness is bad'? What will
the first man say then? Will he put the disagreement down to a linguistic
difference?

No! The natural reaction will be for him to say, 'Well, he's wrong,' or 'I
may be mistaken, but I must say I like it myself,' or 'He may think it's bad
but it's really good,' or 'Of course, it depends upon the circumstances.' In
exceptional cases he may say, 'He's pulling your leg—he doesn't really mean
it,' or 'Don't take any notice of him—he's notoriously insensitive over matters
of ethics' (with implications of deliberate deception or natural defect). But
the one thing I shall not expect him to say is, 'He doesn't understand plain
English': and this, if goodness *were* a property, is just what he should say.

If I am confident that both men are candid and in full possession of their
faculties, and that they employ the same language, dialect and usage (i.e., if
all the sources of disagreement over simple qualities are removed), there will

be no point in my asking whether they agree or disagree about the colour of a pillar-box: there is no room for disagreement. If, in addition, I know that they have counted together the sides of a given polygon, it will be as pointless to ask whether they agree about its 259-sidedness. But, though I know all this, it will still not be silly to wonder, for example, whether they will agree that meekness is good, or that such-and-such is the right decision. Even if there is neither deception nor defect on either side, even if both parties are fully informed about the case and both mean the same by 'good' and 'right,' it still makes sense to inquire whether their moral judgements are in fact the same. . . .

### Goodness not a Directly-Perceived Property

If we consider the contexts in which we normally use ethical concepts, we shall find that to treat them as properties ('non-natural' or otherwise) leads to paradoxical results.

Suppose that I am talking to a philosopher (who accepts the objective doctrine) about a mutual friend, a man noted for his high moral character, for his kindness, incorruptibility, thoughtfulness, sobriety, modesty, understanding, public spirit, and wide interests; and who, when asked why he has done any particular act, always gives what we should consider good reasons, referring (for example) to the needs of others, the importance of fair dealing or the welfare of his family or community.

'Surely,' I may say, 'if ever a man knew what goodness was, he does!'

'I imagine that he does,' the philosopher will say.

'And yet,' I may reply, 'I have asked him whether, when making up his mind what to do, he is conscious of observing any "non-natural property," any "fittingness," in the action he decides on, and he says that he isn't. He says that he does what he does because there's a good reason for doing it, and that he isn't interested in any additional, "non-natural properties" of his actions.'

To be consistent, the philosopher will have to answer, 'If that is the case, he may know *what things are good*, he may know *what it is to be good*, but he cannot know *what goodness is*.'

'But this is absurd,' I shall retort. 'Not know what goodness is? Is such a man to be classed with a kleptomaniac, a poor sneak-thief who doesn't know what goodness is? Is he to be put on the same level as a young delinquent, whose wretched home and irregular upbringing have sent him into the world with no knowledge of what goodness is? How laughable!' . . .

If I am told that someone does not know what goodness is, I shall expect him to break his promises, to lie, steal or cheat, and in so doing I shall be recognising what we do in fact mean by 'goodness' and by 'He does not know what goodness is.' A philosopher who, out of fidelity to a theory, is driven into saying that a thoroughly virtuous and upright man does not know what goodness is, is assuredly up the garden path. He may think that, in telling us this, he is giving up factual information about the virtuous man, but he is doing nothing of the sort. If he were doing that, his remark would—philosophically—be trivial; as if he had said, 'One can be upright and virtuous and yet never have read the Bible.' The point of what he says is otherwise: he wants to deny something which is merely a piece of idiomatic usage— that 'to be virtuous and upright and to give good reasons for one's actions' *is* 'to know what goodness is'—and to demand instead that the phrase 'know-what-goodness-is' shall be reserved for 'intuitive insight' (or something) into the 'non-natural properties' of actions.

Now this is to misrepresent our concept of 'goodness,' and to burke the problem with which we began. As long as we take it literally, there is something seriously at fault with the objective approach, and it is not at all likely to elucidate for us the place of reason in ethics.

### The Sources of the Objective Doctrine

At the same time, we can hardly be satisfied to leave the objective approach in this state. Those who have adopted it have evidently felt very strongly that 'goodness' was a property of some kind or other—in spite of the fact that, in the ordinary sense of the word, it is no such thing—and, being men of the highest intelligence, they would hardly have done so without some reason. Before leaving the subject, therefore, we are bound to inquire why anyone should have felt that goodness *must* be a property, and have trusted this feeling in the face of serious (and comparatively obvious) objections.

One explanation, which will occur to any student of psychology, is that this is an instance of the phenomenon of 'projection'; that is to say, that the philosopher, seeking some outside authority or standard to support and justify his own moral decisions and judgements, creates one himself, by treating the abstract noun 'goodness' as the name of a property possessed by the objects of his judgements. Now this may be valuable as a psychological account, but it does not reveal any logical reason for the plausibility of the objective doctrine. At the best, it only points to a predisposing factor, which makes certain philosophers particularly liable to fall for some kinds of deceptive argument rather than others. What we want to find is the faulty argument itself . . . which lends so much colour to the objective doctrine and explains the popularity of the objective approach.

We have already remarked upon one of the factors which may play a part —the superficial but far-reaching resemblance between the forms of words we use when talking of values and when talking of properties. The statement 'Meekness is good' is on the face of it a statement of the same form as

'Cochineal is red,' and this similarity is apparent also in the comparative and superlative forms. 'Meekness is better than truculence' may be compared with 'Diamond is harder than carborundum,' 'Meekness is the best of personal qualities' with 'Diamond is the hardest of materials.' 'This decision was immoral' may be paralleled by 'This hope was vain'; 'Would it be right?' by 'Would it be successful?'; 'Henry VII was the first of the Tudors' by 'Henry VII was the worst of the Tudors.'

These facts are suggestive, but they are not enough by themselves to explain the plausibility of the objective doctrine, as we shall see if we remember that the same forms are used with words for 'subjective relations'—'pleasant,' 'amazing,' 'incredible'—concepts from which the supporters of the objective doctrine are very much concerned to distinguish goodness and rightness. However, when an additional factor is borne in mind, a more adequate reconstruction of the argument can be given.

Consider under what circumstances disagreements amount to contradictions. Suppose that I ask two people, in turn, 'Which of the boys in this class is the tallest?', 'Which summer sport is the most enjoyable?' and 'Which of these courses of action is the right one?'—questions about a 'property,' a 'subjective relation' and a 'value' respectively—and suppose that in each case they disagree, one saying, 'N,' and the other, 'No, not N, but M.' In which cases do they contradict one another?

In the first case, the disagreement between them is certainly a contradiction, and it can be resolved by measuring the heights of the boys and seeing which is in fact the tallest. In the second, there is no contradiction, since the two people may very well enjoy different sports. In the ethical case, there is again a contradiction—or so the unsophisticated would say. (I realise that some philosophers, *after* thinking about this, have ended by saying that 'This is right' and 'This is not right' do not contradict one another. Still, the unsophisticated would regard that as paradoxical, and they have this very material fact on their side—that, if I ask which of two courses of action is the right one, there is usually no question of my doing both . . .)

It is these facts about contradiction—this similarity between properties and values and this dissimilarity between values and subjective relations—which the supporter of the objective doctrine wishes to emphasise. In addition, he has an idea that values must be classed either as properties or as subjective relations. The fatal conclusion follows at once.

But though it follows in the philosopher's mind, why does it not follow logically? Let us examine the argument more closely. Suppose that one man says 'O is X' and the other says 'O *is not* X.' If 'X' is a word for a property, say 'red,' we may say that one man is attributing to the object the property of redness, and that the other is withholding it; or, that one is attributing the predicate 'red' to the object, and that the other is withholding it—in the case of simple qualities, these statements are equivalent and unexceptionable. We may also say that one is attributing to the object the very same predicate that the other is withholding from it; and we may go on to say that, since they are contradicting each other, there must be something in common to both and neutral between them, about which they are disagreeing. What is this neutral thing in common to them? Why, clearly, the property of redness!

Now let 'X' be 'right'; we may again say that, since there is a real contradiction, one must be attributing to the object the very same predicate that the other is withholding, and we may go on as before to conclude that there is something neutral in common to them, which one attributes to the object, but which the other withholds. What is this neutral thing in common to them? . . . The model provided by 'red' is so compelling that the impulse to say 'The property of rightness' is almost irresistible.

However, as so often, the 'logical conclusion' is the most illogical thing in the world. 'Rightness' is not a property; and when I asked the two people which course of action was the right one I was not asking them about a property—what I wanted to know was whether there was any reason for choosing one course of action rather than another; and, provided that they are arguing about the reasons for my doing different things, we are perfectly justified in talking of a genuine contradiction between 'N is right' and 'No, not N, but M.' The idea (which the philosopher takes for granted) that, if one man attributes the predicate 'X' to anything and another withholds it, they cannot be contradicting one another unless 'X' stands at least for a *property*, is a fallacy. All that two people need (and all that they have) to contradict one another about in the case of ethical predicates are the *reasons* for doing this rather than that or the other. . . .

This reconstruction explains why those philosophers who are attracted to the objective approach pay so little attention to what we regard as the central question—the place of reason in ethics. In adopting the objective approach (so as to 'preserve the possibility of contradiction' in ethics) they say, in effect: 'Reasons are not enough. Ethical predicates must correspond to ethical properties, and "knowing-what-goodness-is" means recognising the presence of such a property.' The objective doctrine is, therefore, not just unhelpful to us: it is a positive hindrance, diverting on to arguments about a purely imaginary 'property' the attention which should be paid to the question of ethical reasoning.

# P. H. NOWELL-SMITH

PATRICK   HORACE   NOWELL-SMITH   (1914–
) is Professor of Philosophy at the University of Leicester, England. Applying the
methods of linguistic analysis to ethical problems, he has published a number of articles
in recent philosophical journals. His major
published work is *Ethics* (1954).

## *The Reconciliation of Conflicts**

For the extreme intuitionist there is no problem about reconciling the conflicting moral insights of different people. If I clearly apprehend the truth I may grieve at your inability to see it; but I cannot be troubled by any anxiety that I may have failed to see it myself. But if once this possibility is admitted, if I can wonder whether what I took to be a genuine intuition might not have been a spurious one, the problem becomes serious. How does the appeal to intuition help us to settle radical differences that cannot be attributed to disagreement about the non-moral facts of the case?

Let us see first of all how a subjectivist would describe such disagreement. If I disagree with you about the rightness of an action or the goodness of a person or the morality of some general line of conduct, my arguments, he would say, must be of one of two kinds.

(a) I might try to convince you that you were mistaken about some non-moral fact. For example you thought it wrong of me to have refused money to that blind beggar, and the dispute ceases when I point out that I happen to know him to be a fraud. There was never any *moral* dispute between us, since we both wished to advocate charity towards genuine beggars, not frauds.

(b) I might try to convince you that my moral judgement follows from or is a special case of some more general moral judgement which I know that you accept. For example you might approve of giving money to beggars be-cause it relieves distress—and we both approve of relieving distress. If I convinced you that your sort of charity creates more distress than it alleviates, which is a question of empirical *fact*, then you must withdraw your censure and the dispute ceases.

Both these forms of argument presuppose that there is some common moral ground between us, if only we can find it. Many disputes, say the sub-

---

jectivists, turn out to be disputes about the facts or about the validity of deductions made from those facts and our common ethical premises. But, they say, a point may be reached when there is no disagreement of a factual or logical kind; and yet a *moral* disagreement remains. You approve of one thing and I approve of another. And when this point is reached it is tauto- logical to say that the dispute cannot be settled by *rational* argument. We must either agree to differ or resort to flattery, cajolery, bribery, or other non- rational methods of persuasion. Or I must use force or submit to your using force on me.

Now this is not a palatable conclusion, especially when it is erroneously believed to lead to the doctrine that Might is Right.[1] And one of the most important claims that has been made for 'objective values' is that they enable us to escape from it. We do not think it necessary to resort to force where logical, mathematical, or empirical truths are concerned. And if moral truths can be apprehended in the same sort of way, if there are criteria that anyone can use to discover them, it ought to be possible to settle moral disputes without recourse to force, by rational argument.

But does the notion of objective values in fact help us to reconcile con- flicts without recourse to force? Clearly it cannot. For I will claim this status for the values that I intuit, and you will claim it for yours. If the empirical analogy is used, it will make sense for me to say that my view is 'true' and yours 'mistaken,' terms which the subjectivist must deny himself; but we are no nearer a solution of the conflict, which still remains exactly what it was before, a conflict between the moral facts that I claim to descry and those that you claim to descry. If I do not recognize the truth of your state- ments of objective moral fact, you can do nothing to convince me by argu- ment but are, like the subjectivist, thrown back on force or acquiescence. Wars are not fought over logical or empirical issues, just because men do in the end agree about what they see to be the case or 'see' to be logically valid. But wars are fought over moral issues, and the only difference between the subjectivist and the objectivist is that to the former this fact is not surprising.

Theoretically the objective theory cannot help us to reconcile conflicts, since it conceals a difficulty endemic in all theories involving 'intuition.' In- tuitions of objective properties are either infallible or they are not. If they are fallible, the mere *existence* of an objective property or value is no guar-

---

[1] The conclusion that Might is Right does not in fact follow from the subjective thesis, though it is surprising how often it has been thought to do so. Subjectivism is a theory about the nature of moral judgements. To put it crudely, it is the theory that they are expressions of a man's personal attitudes, his approvals and disapprovals. It does not imply the theory that most men approve of trampling on their neighbours; nor need the sub- jectivist himself approve of this.

antee that anyone has apprehended it properly. However convinced you may be that you are right, it is still open to me to deny the genuineness of your intuition. If, on the other hand, intuitions are infallible, then disputes cannot be genuine. If I disagree with you, you must charge me either with insincerity or with moral blindness. And that this account of the matter is false is shown by the fact that we do often allow others to be sincere when their moral views differ from our own.

And in practice the objectivist is, as we should expect, in a far worse position for solving moral conflicts. He necessarily attributes his opponent's denial of truth to wilful perversity; and, holding as he does that in spite of his denials his opponent must really see the truth all the time, he realizes that what his opponent needs is not argument but castigation. For arguments cannot convince a man who already sees the light. The objective theory, so far from minimizing the use of force to settle moral conflicts, can be, and constantly has been used to justify it. It is no accident that religious persecutions are the monopoly of objective theorists.

The theory underlying persecution is admirably explained by Samuel Clarke. "These things are so notoriously plain and self-evident, that nothing but the extremest stupidity of mind, corruption of manners or perversity of spirit can possibly make any man entertain the least doubt concerning them. For a man endued with Reason to deny the truth of these things, is the very same thing, as if a man who has the use of his sight should, at the same time that he beholds the sun, deny that there is any such thing as light in the world; or as if a man that understands geometry or arithmetic, should deny the most obvious and known proportions of lines or numbers, and *perversely* contend that the whole is not equal to all its parts. . . . And 'tis as *absurd* and *blameworthy* to mistake negligently plain right and wrong . . . as it would be absurd and ridiculous for a man in arithmetical matters ignorantly to believe that twice two is not equal to four or wilfully and obstinately to contend, *against his own clear knowledge*, that the whole is not equal to all its parts."[2]

If the analogy between moral knowledge and sight or mathematics is as close as Clarke makes out those who disagree with us on a moral issue must be insincere. It is force, not argument that they need. It is hardly necessary to add that this theory has had the most tragic consequences in international affairs. To suppose that people whose professed moral principles differ from ours do not really hold them is to invite disaster.

[2] *On Natural Religion.* Selby-Bigge: *British Moralists*, Vol. II, pp. 6 and 13 (my italics).

## INTUITIONISM—SUGGESTED READINGS

Edwards, P., *The Logic of Moral Discourse*, Glencoe, Ill., Free Press, 1955, esp. Chap. 4. (critic)

Ewing, A. C., *The Definition of Good*, New York, Macmillan, 1947. (proponent)

Moore, G. E., *Ethics*, London, Oxford University Press, 1912. (proponent)

Rice, P. B., *On the Knowledge of Good and Evil*, New York, Random House, 1955, Chap. 2. (critic)

Ross, W. D., *Foundations of Ethics*, Oxford, Clarendon Press, 1939. (proponent)

Strawson, P. F., "Ethical Intuitionism," *Philosophy*, XXIV (1949), pp. 23–33. (critic)

# B. THE EMOTIVE THEORY

According to those who hold the emotive theory in ethics, we best come to understand the bases for our moral beliefs by inquiring upon what grounds a belief of any kind may be said to be true. The emotivists assert that statements may be true only in two ways: they may be true by definition, or they may be true as a matter of fact. For example, "all spinsters are unmarried" is true by definition, while "all spinsters are unhappy" may or may not be true in fact. Emotivists hold that we may determine the truth of all statements either by referring to the meaning of the words we use (if the statement is true by definition) or by employing scientific methods of inquiry (if it is true in fact).

How then are we to regard ethical statements, statements containing words such as "ought" and "should," statements such as "all spinsters ought to marry"? Such statements are neither true by definition, nor, say the emotivists, are they true as a matter of fact—they cannot be verified by scientific methods. Therefore, the emotivist holds, ethical statements are neither true nor false; they are not statements which impart *knowledge.*

What then *is* the purpose of ethical discourse? The emotivists would assert that the expression "x is good" is similar in status to the complex expression "I approve of x, do so also." For emotivists, ethical language does not function to convey knowledge, but to *express* emotional preferences and to *redirect* the preferences of others. Thus, men do not contradict each other when they disagree as to whether x is good; they simply express different attitudes approving or disapproving x, and each attempts to induce the other to adopt his attitude toward x.

HUME, in a passage which seems to anticipate the development of the emotive theory, argues (1) that the ultimate goals of life are necessarily set by the passions, not by reason; and (2) that we cannot correctly reason from premises stating matters of fact to a conclusion containing the word "ought." AYER offers an analysis of ethical statements, and concludes that ethical concepts are "pseudo-concepts" only, which do not state truths but only serve to express feelings. STEVENSON holds that ethical discourse is employed to *influence* other men, to make them come to share the speaker's attitudes of approval or disapproval. BLANSHARD rejects the emotive theory of ethics because, he says, if it were true, there could be no objective basis for rational argument as to what is good or right. The emotive theory, Blanshard maintains, would reduce moral arguments to mere contests of persuasiveness or perhaps to contests of physical force.

# DAVID HUME

DAVID HUME (1711–76), one of the outstanding British empiricists, was born in
Edinburgh and spent most of his life there.
He wrote not only upon philosophical subjects but also became famous as an historian.
His major works include: A *Treatise of
Human Nature* (1739–40), *Essays on Moral
and Political Subjects* (1741–42), *An Enquiry
Concerning the Human Understanding*
(1748), *An Enquiry Concerning the Principles of Morals* (1751), *History of England*
(1754–62), and *Dialogues Concerning Natural Religion* (1779).

## A Treatise of Human Nature*

### Book II, Part III, Section III

### Of the influencing motives of the will

Nothing is more usual in philosophy, and even in common life, than
to talk of the combat of passion and reason, to give the preference to reason,
and to assert that men are only so far virtuous as they conform themselves
to its dictates. Every rational creature, 'tis said, is obliged to regulate his
actions by reason; and if any other motive or principle challenge the direction
of his conduct, he ought to oppose it, 'till it be entirely subdued, or at least
brought to a conformity with that superior principle. On this method of
thinking the greatest part of moral philosophy, ancient and modern, seems to
be founded; nor is there an ampler field, as well for metaphysical arguments,
as popular declamations, than this supposed pre-eminence of reason above
passion. The eternity, invariableness, and divine origin of the former have
been displayed to the best advantage: The blindness, unconstancy and de-
ceitfulness of the latter have been as strongly insisted on. In order to shew
the fallacy of all this philosophy, I shall endeavour to prove *first,* that reason
alone can never be a motive to any action of the will; and *secondly,* that it
can never oppose passion in the direction of the will.

The understanding exerts itself after two different ways, as it judges from
demonstration or probability; as it regards the abstract relations of our ideas,
or those relations of objects, of which experience only gives us information.

---

* From A *Treatise of Human Nature,* by David Hume, Book II, Part 3, and Book III,
Part 1 (1740).

I believe it scarce will be asserted, that the first species of reasoning alone is ever the cause of any action. As its proper province is the world of ideas, and as the will always places us in that of realities, demonstration and volition seem, upon that account, to be totally removed, from each other. Mathematics, indeed, are useful in all mechanical operations, and arithmetic in almost every art and profession: But 'tis not of themselves they have any influence. Mechanics are the art of regulating the motions of bodies *to some designed end or purpose;* and the reason why we employ arithmetic in fixing the proportions of numbers, is only that we may discover the proportions of their influence and operation. A merchant is desirous of knowing the sum total of his accounts with any person: Why? but that he may learn what sum will have the same *effects* in paying his debt, and going to market, as all the particular articles taken together. Abstract or demonstrative reasoning, therefore, never influences any of our actions, but only as it directs our judgment concerning causes and effects; which leads us to the second operation of the understanding.

'Tis obvious, that when we have the prospect of pain or pleasure from any object, we feel a consequent emotion of aversion or propensity, and are carried to avoid or embrace what will give us this uneasiness or satisfaction. 'Tis also obvious, that this emotion rests not here, but making us cast our view on every side, comprehends whatever objects are connected with its original one by the relation of cause and effect. Here then reasoning takes place to discover this relation; and according as our reasoning varies, our actions receive a subsequent variation. But 'tis evident in this case, that the impulse arises not from reason, but is only directed by it. 'Tis from the prospect of pain or pleasure that the aversion or propensity arises towards any object: And these emotions extend themselves to the causes and effects of that object, as they are pointed out to us by reason and experience. It can never in the least concern us to know, that such objects are causes, and such others effects; if both the causes and effects be indifferent to us. Where the objects themselves do not affect us, their connexion can never give them any influence; and 'tis plain, that as reason is nothing but the discovery of this connexion, it cannot be by its means that the objects are able to affect us.

Since reason alone can never produce any action, or give rise to volition, I infer, that the same faculty is as incapable of preventing volition, or of disputing the preference with any passion or emotion. This consequence is necessary. 'Tis impossible reason could have the latter effect of preventing volition, but by giving an impulse in a contrary direction to our passion; and that impulse, had it operated alone, would have been able to produce volition. Nothing can oppose or retard the impulse of passion, but a contrary impulse; and if this contrary impulse ever arises from reason, that latter faculty must have an original influence on the will, and must be able to cause, as well as hinder any act of volition. But if reason has no original influence, 'tis impossible it can withstand any principle, which has such an efficacy, or ever keep the mind in suspence a moment. Thus it appears, that the principle, which opposes our passion, cannot be the same with reason, and is only called so in an improper sense. We speak not strictly and philosophically when we talk of the combat of passion and of reason. Reason is, and ought only to be the slave of the passions, and can never pretend to any other office than to serve and obey them. . . .

Passions can be contrary to reason only so far as they are *accompanied* with some judgment or opinion. According to this principle, which is so obvious and natural, 'tis only in two senses, that any affection can be called unreasonable. First, When a passion, such as hope or fear, grief or joy, despair or security, is founded on the supposition of the existence of objects, which really do not exist. Secondly, When in exerting any passion in action, we chuse means insufficient for the designed end, and deceive ourselves in our judgment of causes and effects. Where a passion is neither founded on false suppositions, nor chuses means insufficient for the end, the understanding can neither justify nor condemn it. 'Tis not contrary to reason to prefer the destruction of the whole world to the scratching of my finger. 'Tis not contrary to reason for me to chuse my total ruin, to prevent the least uneasiness of an *Indian* or person wholly unknown to me. 'Tis as little contrary to reason to prefer even my own acknowledged lesser good to my greater, and have a more ardent affection for the former than the latter. A trivial good may, from certain circumstances, produce a desire superior to what arises from the greatest and most valuable enjoyment; nor is there any thing more extraordinary in this, than in mechanics to see one pound weight raise up a hundred by the advantage of its situation. In short, a passion must be accompanied with some false judgment, in order to its being unreasonable; and even then 'tis not the passion, properly speaking, which is unreasonable, but the judgment. . . .

### Book III, Part I, Section I

#### Moral distinctions not derived from reason

It has been observed, that nothing is ever present to the mind but its perceptions; and that all the actions of seeing, hearing, judging, loving, hating, and thinking, fall under this denomination. The mind can never exert itself in any action, which we may not comprehend under the term of *perception*; and consequently that term is no less applicable to those judgments, by which we distinguish moral good and evil, than to every other operation of the mind. To approve of one character, to condemn another, are only so many different perceptions.

Now as perceptions resolve themselves into two kinds, viz., *impressions* and *ideas*, this distinction gives rise to a question, with which we shall open up our present enquiry concerning morals, *Whether 'tis by means of our ideas or impressions we distinguish betwixt vice and virtue, and pronounce an action blameable or praise-worthy?* This will immediately cut off all loose discourses and declamations, and reduce us to something precise and exact on the present subject.

Those who affirm that virtue is nothing but a conformity to reason; that there are eternal fitnesses and unfitnesses of things, which are the same to every rational being that considers them; that the immutable measures of right and wrong impose an obligation, not only on human creatures, but also on the Deity himself: All these systems concur in the opinion, that morality, like truth, is discerned merely by ideas, and by their juxta-position and comparison. In order, therefore, to judge of these systems, we need only consider, whether it be possible, from reason alone, to distinguish betwixt moral good and evil, or whether there must concur some other principles to enable us to make that distinction.

If morality had naturally no influence on human passions and actions, 'twere in vain to take such pains to inculcate it; and nothing would be more fruitless than that multitude of rules and precepts, with which all moralists abound. Philosophy is commonly divided into *speculative* and *practical*; and as morality is always comprehended under the latter division, 'tis supposed to influence our passions and actions, and to go beyond the calm and indolent judgments of the understanding. And this is confirmed by common experience, which informs us, that men are often governed by their duties, and are deterred from some actions by the opinion of injustice, and impelled to others by that of obligation.

Since morals, therefore, have an influence on the actions and affections, it follows, that they cannot be derived from reason; and that because reason alone, as we have already proved, can never have any such influence. Morals excite passions, and produce or prevent actions. Reason of itself is utterly impotent in this particular. The rules of morality, therefore, are not conclusions of our reason.

No one, I believe, will deny the justness of this inference; nor is there any other means of evading it, than by denying that principle, on which it is founded. As long as it is allowed, that reason has no influence on our passions and actions, 'tis in vain to pretend, that morality is discovered only by a deduction of reason. An active principle can never be founded on an inactive; and if reason be inactive it itself, it must remain so in all its shapes and appearances, whether it exerts itself in natural or moral subjects, whether it considers the powers of external bodies, or the actions of rational beings.

It would be tedious to repeat all the arguments, by which I have proved, that reason is perfectly inert, and can never either prevent or produce any action or affection. 'Twill be easy to recollect what has been said upon that subject. I shall only recall on this occasion one of these arguments, which I shall endeavour to render still more conclusive, and more applicable to the present subject.

Reason is the discovery of truth or falsehood. Truth or falsehood consists in an agreement or disagreement either to the *real* relations of ideas, or to *real* existence and matter of fact. Whatever, therefore, is not susceptible of this agreement or disagreement, is incapable of being true or false, and can never be an object of our reason. Now 'tis evident our passions, volitions, and actions, are not susceptible of any such agreement or disagreement; being original facts and realities, complete in themselves, and implying no reference to other passions, volitions, and actions. 'Tis impossible, therefore, they can be pronounced either true or false, and be either contrary or conformable to reason.

This argument is of double advantage to our present purpose. For it proves *directly*, that actions do not derive their merit from a conformity to reason, nor their blame from a contrariety to it; and it proves the same truth more *indirectly*, by shewing us, that as reason can never immediately prevent or produce any action by contradicting or approving of it, it cannot be the source of moral good and evil, which are found to have that influence. Actions may be laudable or blameable; but they cannot be reasonable or unreasonable: Laudable or blameable, therefore, are not the same with reasonable or unreasonable. The merit and demerit of actions frequently contradict, and sometimes controul our natural propensities. But reason has no such influence. Moral distinctions, therefore, are not the offspring of reason. Reason is wholly inactive, and can never be the source of so active a principle as conscience, or a sense of morals.

But perhaps it may be said, that tho' no will or action can be immediately contradictory to reason, yet we may find such a contradiction in some of the attendants of the action, that is, in its causes or effects. The action may cause a judgment, or may be *obliquely* caused by one, when the judgment concurs with a passion; and by an abusive way of speaking, which philosophy will scarce allow of, the same contrariety may, upon that account, be ascribed to the action. How far this truth or falsehood may be the source of morals, 'twill now be proper to consider.

It has been observed, that reason, in a strict and philosophical sense, can have an influence on our conduct only after two ways: Either when it excites a passion by informing us of the existence of something which is a proper object of it; or when it discovers the connexion of causes and effects, so as to afford us means of exerting any passion. These are the only kinds of judgment, which can accompany our actions, or can be said to produce them in any manner; and it must be allowed, that these judgments may often be false and erroneous. A person may be affected with passion, by supposing a pain or pleasure to lie in an object, which has no tendency to produce either of these sensations, or which produces the contrary to what is imagined. A person may also take false measures for the attaining his end, and may retard, by his foolish conduct, instead of forwarding the execution of any project. These false judgments may be thought to affect the passions and actions, which are connected with them, and may be said to render them unreasonable, in a figurative and improper way of speaking. But tho' this be acknowledged, 'tis easy to observe, that these errors are so far from being the source of all immorality, that they are commonly very innocent, and draw no manner of guilt upon the person who is so unfortunate as to fall into them. They extend not beyond a mistake of *fact*, which moralists have not generally supposed criminal, as being perfectly involuntary. I am more to be lamented than blamed, if I am mistaken with regard to the influence of objects in producing pain or pleasure, or if I know not the proper means of satisfying my desires. No one can ever regard such errors as a defect in my moral character. A fruit, for instance, that is really disagreeable, appears to me at a distance, and thro' mistake I fancy it to be pleasant and delicious. Here is one error. I choose certain means of reaching this fruit, which are not proper for my end. Here is a second error; nor is there any third one, which can ever possibly enter into our reasonings concerning actions. I ask, therefore, if a man, in this situation, and guilty of these two errors, is to be regarded as vicious and criminal, however unavoidable they might have been? Or if it be possible to imagine, that such errors are the sources of all immorality?

And here it may be proper to observe, that if moral distinctions be derived from the truth or falsehood of those judgments, they must take place wherever we form the judgments; nor will there be any difference, whether the question be concerning an apple or a kingdom, or whether the error be avoidable or unavoidable. For as the very essence of morality is supposed to consist in an agreement or disagreement to reason, the other circumstances are entirely arbitrary, and can never either bestow on any action the character of virtuous or vicious, or deprive it of that character. . . .

Thus upon the whole, 'tis impossible, that the distinction betwixt moral good and evil, can be made by reason; since that distinction has an influence upon our actions, of which reason alone is incapable. Reason and judgment may, indeed, be the mediate cause of an action, by prompting, or by directing a passion: But it is not pretended, that a judgment of this kind, either in its truth or falsehood, is attended with virtue or vice. . . .

But to be more particular, and to shew, that those eternal immutable fitnesses and unfitnesses of things cannot be defended by sound philosophy, we may weigh the following considerations.

If the thought and understanding were alone capable of fixing the boundaries of right and wrong, the character of virtuous and vicious either must lie in some relations of objects, or must be a matter of fact, which is discovered by our reasoning. This consequence is evident. As the operations of human understanding divide themselves into two kinds, the comparing of ideas, and the inferring of matter of fact; were virtue discovered by the understanding; it must be an object of one of these operations, nor is there any third operation of the understanding, which can discover it. There has been an opinion very industriously propagated by certain philosophers, that morality is susceptible of demonstration; and tho' no one has ever been able to advance a single step in those demonstrations; yet 'tis taken for granted, that this science may be brought to an equal certainty with geometry or algebra. Upon this supposition, vice and virtue must consist in some relations; since 'tis allowed on all hands, that no matter of fact is capable of being demonstrated. Let us, therefore, begin with examining this hypothesis, and endeavour, if possible, to fix those moral qualities, which have been so long the objects of our fruitless researches. Point out distinctly the relations, which constitute morality or obligation, that we may know wherein they consist, and after what manner we must judge of them.

If you assert, that vice and virtue consist in relations susceptible of certainty and demonstration, you must confine yourself to those *four* relations, which alone admit of that degree of evidence; and in that case you run into absurdities, from which you will never be able to extricate yourself. For as you make the very essence of morality to lie in the relations, and as there is no one of these relations but what is applicable, not only to an irrational, but also to an inanimate object; it follows, that even such objects must be susceptible of merit or demerit. *Resemblance, contrariety, degrees in quality,* and *proportions in quantity and number;* all these relations belong as properly to matter, as to our actions, passions, and volitions. 'Tis unquestionable, therefore, that morality lies not in any of these relations, nor the sense of it in their discovery. . . .

But to make these general reflexions more clear and convincing, we may illustrate them by some particular instances, wherein this character of moral good or evil is the most universally acknowledged. Of all crimes that human creatures are capable of committing, the most horrid and unnatural is ingratitude, especially when it is committed against parents, and appears in the more flagrant instances of wounds and death. This is acknowledged by all mankind, philosophers as well as the people; the question only arises among philosophers, whether the guilt or moral deformity of this action be discovered by demonstrative reasoning, or be felt by an internal sense, and by means of some sentiment, which the reflecting on such an action naturally occasions. This question will soon be decided against the former opinion, if we can shew the same relations in other objects, without the notion of any guilt or iniquity attending them. Reason or science is nothing but the comparing of ideas, and the discovery of their relations; and if the same relations have different characters, it must evidently follow, that those characters are not discovered merely by reason. To put the affair, therefore, to this trial, let us chuse any inanimate object, such as an oak or elm; and let us suppose, that by the dropping of its seed, it produces a sapling below it, which springing up by degrees, at last overtops and destroys the parent tree: I ask, if in this instance there be wanting any relation, which is discoverable in parricide or ingratitude? Is not the one tree the cause of the other's existence; and the latter the cause of the destruction of the former, in the same manner as when a child murders his parent? 'Tis not sufficient to reply, that a choice or will is wanting. For in the case of parricide, a will does not give rise to any *different* relations, but is only the cause from which the action is derived; and consequently produces the *same* relations, that in the oak or elm arise from some other principles. 'Tis a will or choice, that determines a man to kill his parent; and they are the laws of matter and motion, that determine a sapling to destroy the oak, from which it sprung. Here then the same relations have different causes; but still the relations are the same: And as their discovery is not in both cases attended with a notion of immorality, it follows, that that notion does not arise from such a discovery.

But to chuse an instance, still more resembling; I would fain ask any one, why incest in the human species is criminal, and why the very same action, and the same relations in animals have not the smallest moral turpitude and deformity? If it be answered, that this action is innocent in animals, because they have not reason sufficient to discover its turpitude; but that man, being endowed with that faculty, which *ought* to restrain him to his duty, the same action instantly becomes criminal to him; should this be said, I would reply, that this is evidently arguing in a circle. For before reason can perceive this turpitude, the turpitude must exist; and consequently is independent of the decisions of our reason, and is their object more properly than their effect. According to this system, then, every animal, that has sense, and appetite, and will; that is, every animal must be susceptible of all the same virtues and vices, for which we ascribe praise and blame to human creatures. All the difference is, that our superior reason may serve to discover the vice or virtue, and by that means may augment the blame or praise: But still this discovery supposes a separate being in these moral distinctions, and a being, which depends only on the will and appetite, and which, both in thought and reality, may be distinguished from the reason. Animals are susceptible of the same relations, with respect to each other, as the human species, and therefore would also be susceptible of the same morality, if the essence of morality consisted in these relations. Their want of a sufficient degree of reason may hinder them from perceiving the duties and obligations of morality, but can never hinder these duties from existing; since they must antecedently exist, in order to their being perceived. Reason must find them, and can never produce them. This argument deserves to be weighed, as being, in my opinion, entirely decisive.

Nor does this reasoning only prove, that morality consists not in any relations, that are the objects of science; but if examined, will prove with equal certainty, that it consists not in any *matter of fact*, which can be discovered by the understanding. This is the *second* part of our argument; and if it can be made evident, we may conclude, that morality is not an object of reason. But can there be any difficulty in proving, that vice and virtue are not matters of fact, whose existence we can infer by reason? Take any action allowed to be vicious: Wilful murder, for instance. Examine it in all lights, and see if you can find that matter of fact, or real existence, which you call *vice*. In which-ever way you take it, you find only certain passions, motives, volitions and thoughts. There is no other matter of fact in the case. The vice entirely escapes you, as long as you consider the object. You never can find it, till you turn your reflexion into your own breast, and find a sentiment of disapprobation, which arises in you, towards this action. Here is a matter of fact; but 'tis the object of feeling, not of reason. It lies in yourself, not in the object. So that when you pronounce any action or character to be vicious, you mean nothing, but that from the constitution of your nature you have a feeling or sentiment of blame from the contemplation of it. . . .

I cannot forbear adding to these reasonings an observation, which may, perhaps, be found of some importance. In every system of morality, which I have hitherto met with, I have always remarked, that the author proceeds for some time in the ordinary way of reasoning, and establishes the being of a God, or makes observations concerning human affairs; when of a sudden I am surprized to find, that instead of the usual copulations of propositions, *is*, and *is not*, I meet with no proposition that is not connected with an *ought*, or an *ought not*. This change is imperceptible; but is, however, of the last consequence. For as this *ought*, or *ought not*, expresses some new relation or affirmation, 'tis necessary that it should be observed and explained; and at the same time that a reason should be given, for what seems altogether inconceivable, how this new relation can be a deduction from others, which are entirely different from it. But as authors do not commonly use this precaution, I shall presume to recommend it to the readers; and am persuaded, that this small attention would subvert all the vulgar systems of morality, and let us see, that the distinction of vice and virtue is not founded merely on the relations of objects, nor is perceived by reason.

# A. J. AYER

ALFRED JULES AYER (1910–    ) taught at the University of London for a number of years and was recently appointed to a professorship of philosophy at Oxford University. A leading spokesman for the philosophy of logical positivism, his major works include: *Language, Truth and Logic* (1936; 2nd ed., 1946), *The Foundations of Empirical Knowledge* (1940), *Philosophical Essays* (1954), and *The Problem of Knowledge* (1956).

## Critique of Ethics*

It is our business to give an account of "judgements of value" which is both satisfactory in itself and consistent with our general empiricist principles. We shall set ourselves to show that in so far as statements of value are significant, they are ordinary "scientific" statements; and that in so far as they are not scientific, they are not in the literal sense significant, but are simply expressions of emotion which can be neither true nor false. In maintaining this view, we may confine ourselves for the present to the case of ethical statements. . . .

The ordinary system of ethics, as elaborated in the works of ethical philosophers, is very far from being a homogeneous whole. Not only is it apt to contain pieces of metaphysics, and analyses of non-ethical concepts: its actual ethical contents are themselves of very different kinds. We may divide them, indeed, into four main classes. There are, first of all, propositions which express definitions of ethical terms, or judgements about the legitimacy or possibility of certain definitions. Secondly, there are propositions describing the phenomena of moral experience, and their causes. Thirdly, there are exhortations to moral virtue. And, lastly, there are actual

* From *Language, Truth and Logic*, by A. J. Ayer, Chap. 6. Copyright, 1936 and 1946, Victor Gollancz, Ltd. Used by permission of Dover Publications.

ethical judgements. It is unfortunately the case that the distinction between these four classes, plain as it is, is commonly ignored by ethical philosophers; with the result that it is often very difficult to tell from their works what it is that they are seeking to discover or prove.

In fact, it is easy to see that only the first of our four classes, namely that which comprises the propositions relating to the definitions of ethical terms, can be said to constitute ethical philosophy. The propositions which describe the phenomena of moral experience, and their causes, must be assigned to the science of psychology, or sociology. The exhortations to moral virtue are not propositions at all, but ejaculations or commands which are designed to provoke the reader to action of a certain sort. Accordingly, they do not belong to any branch of philosophy or science. As for the expressions of ethical judgements, we have not yet determined how they should be classified. But inasmuch as they are certainly neither definitions nor comments upon definitions, nor quotations, we may say decisively that they do not belong to ethical philosophy. A strictly philosophical treatise on ethics should therefore make no ethical pronouncements. But it should, by giving an analysis of ethical terms, show what is the category to which all such pronouncements belong. And this is what we are now about to do.

A question which is often discussed by ethical philosophers is whether it is possible to find definitions which would reduce all ethical terms to one or two fundamental terms. But this question, though it undeniably belongs to ethical philosophy, is not relevant to our present enquiry. We are not now concerned to discover which term, within the sphere of ethical terms, is to be taken as fundamental; whether, for example, "good" can be defined in terms of "right" or "right" in terms of "good," or both in terms of "value." What we are interested in is the possibility of reducing the whole sphere of ethical terms to non-ethical terms. We are enquiring whether statements of ethical value can be translated into statements of empirical fact.

That they can be so translated is the contention of those ethical philosophers who are commonly called subjectivists, and of those who are known as utilitarians. For the utilitarian defines the rightness of actions, and the goodness of ends, in terms of the pleasure, or happiness, or satisfaction, to which they give rise; the subjectivist, in terms of the feelings of approval which a certain person, or group of people, has towards them. Each of these types of definition makes moral judgements into a sub-class of psychological or sociological judgements; and for this reason they are very attractive to us. For, if either was correct, it would follow that ethical assertions were not generically different from the factual assertions which are ordinarily contrasted with them; and the account which we have already given of empirical hypotheses would apply to them also.

Nevertheless we shall not adopt either a subjectivist or a utilitarian analysis of ethical terms. We reject the subjectivist view that to call an action right, or a thing good, is to say that it is generally approved of, because it is not self-contradictory to assert that some actions which are generally approved of are not right, or that some things which are generally approved of are not good. And we reject the alternative subjectivist view that a man who asserts that a certain action is right, or that a certain thing is good, is saying that he himself approves of it, on the ground that a man who confessed that he sometimes approved of what was bad or wrong would not be contradicting himself. And a similar argument is fatal to utilitarianism. We cannot agree that to call an action right is to say that of all the actions possible in the circumstances it would cause, or be likely to cause, the greatest happiness, or the greatest balance of pleasure over pain, or the greatest balance of satisfied over unsatisfied desire, because we find that it is not self-contradictory to say that it is sometimes wrong to perform the action which would actually or probably cause the greatest happiness, or the greatest balance of pleasure over pain, or of satisfied over unsatisfied desire. And since it is not self-contradictory to say that some pleasant things are not good, or that some bad things are desired, it cannot be the case that the sentence "x is good" is equivalent to "x is pleasant," or to "x is desired." And to every other variant of utilitarianism with which I am acquainted the same objection can be made. And therefore we should, I think, conclude that the validity of ethical judgements is not determined by the felicific tendencies of actions, any more than by the nature of people's feelings; but that it must be regarded as "absolute" or "intrinsic," and not empirically calculable.

If we say this, we are not, of course, denying that it is possible to invent a language in which all ethical symbols are definable in non-ethical terms, or even that it is desirable to invent such a language and adopt it in place of our own; what we are denying is that the suggested reduction of ethical to non-ethical statements is consistent with the conventions of our actual language. That is, we reject utilitarianism and subjectivism, not as proposals to replace our existing ethical notions by new ones, but as analyses of our existing ethical notions. Our contention is simply that, in our language, sentences which contain normative ethical symbols are not equivalent to sentences which express psychological propositions, or indeed empirical propositions of any kind.

It is advisable here to make it plain that it is only normative ethical symbols, and not descriptive ethical symbols, that are held by us to be indefinable in factual terms. There is a danger of confusing these two types of symbols, because they are commonly constituted by signs of the same sensible form. Thus a complex sign of the form "x is wrong" may constitute a sentence which expresses a moral judgement concerning a certain type of conduct, or it may constitute a sentence which states that a certain type of conduct is repugnant to the moral sense of a particular society. In the latter case, the symbol "wrong" is a descriptive ethical symbol, and the sentence in which it occurs expresses an ordinary sociological proposition; in the former case, the symbol "wrong" is a normative ethical symbol, and the sentence in which it occurs does not, we maintain, express an empirical proposition at all. It is only with normative ethics that we are at present concerned; so that whenever ethical symbols are used in the course of this argument without qualification, they are always to be interpreted as symbols of the normative type.

In admitting that normative ethical concepts are irreducible to empirical concepts, we seem to be leaving the way clear for the "absolutist" view of ethics—that is, the view that statements of value are not controlled by observation, as ordinary empirical propositions are, but only by a mysterious "intellectual intuition." A feature of this theory, which is seldom recognized by its advocates, is that it makes statements of value unverifiable. For it is notorious that what seems intuitively certain to one person may seem doubtful, or even false, to another. So that unless it is possible to provide some criterion by which one may decide between conflicting intuitions, a mere appeal to intuition is worthless as a test of a proposition's validity. But in the case of moral judgements, no such criterion can be given. Some moralists claim to settle the matter by saying that they "know" that their own moral judgements are correct. But such an assertion is of purely psychological interest, and has not the slightest tendency to prove the validity of any moral judgement. For dissentient moralists may equally well "know" that their ethical views are correct. And, as far as subjective certainty goes, there will be nothing to choose between them. When such differences of opinion arise in connection with an ordinary empirical proposition, one may attempt to resolve them by referring to, or actually carrying out, some relevant empirical test. But with regard to ethical statements, there is, on the "absolutist" or "intuitionist" theory, no relevant empirical test. We are therefore justified in saying that on this theory ethical statements are held to be unverifiable. They are, of course, also held to be genuine synthetic propositions.

Considering the use which we have made of the principle that a synthetic proposition is significant only if it is empirically verifiable, it is clear that the acceptance of an "absolutist" theory of ethics would undermine the whole of our main argument. And as we have already rejected the "naturalistic" theories which are commonly supposed to provide the only alternative to "absolutism" in ethics, we seem to have reached a difficult position. We shall meet the difficulty by showing that the correct treatment of ethical statements is afforded by a third theory, which is wholly compatible with our radical empiricism.

We begin by admitting that the fundamental ethical concepts are unanalysable, inasmuch as there is no criterion by which one can test the validity of the judgements in which they occur. So far we are in agreement with the absolutists. But, unlike the absolutists, we are able to give an explanation of this fact about ethical concepts. We say that the reason why they are unanalysable is that they are mere pseudo-concepts. The presence of an ethical symbol in a proposition adds nothing to its factual content. Thus if I say to someone, "You acted wrongly in stealing that money," I am not stating anything more than if I had simply said, "You stole that money." In adding that this action is wrong I am not making any further statement about it. I am simply evincing my moral disapproval of it. It is as if I had said, "You stole that money," in a peculiar tone of horror, or written it with the addition of some special exclamation marks. The tone, or the exclamation marks, adds nothing to the literal meaning of the sentence. It merely serves to show that the expression of it is attended by certain feelings in the speaker.

If now I generalise my previous statement and say, "Stealing money is wrong," I produce a sentence which has no factual meaning—that is, expresses no proposition which can be either true or false. It is as if I had written "Stealing money!!"—where the shape and thickness of the exclamation mark show, by a suitable convention, that a special sort of moral disapproval is the feeling which is being expressed. It is clear that there is nothing said here which can be true or false. Another man may disagree with me about the wrongness of stealing, in a sense that he may not have the same feelings about stealing as I have, and he may quarrel with me on account of my moral sentiments. But he cannot, strictly speaking, contradict me. For in saying that a certain type of action is right or wrong, I am not making any factual statement, not even a statement about my own state of mind. I am merely expressing certain moral sentiments. And the man who is ostensibly contradicting me is merely expressing his moral sentiments. So that there is plainly no sense in asking which of us is in the right. For neither of us is asserting a genuine proposition.

What we have just been saying about the symbol "wrong" applies to all normative ethical symbols. Sometimes they occur in sentences which record ordinary empirical facts besides expressing ethical feeling about those facts: sometimes they occur in sentences which simply express ethical feeling about a certain type of action, or situation, without making any statement of fact. But in every case in which one would commonly be said to be making an ethical judgement, the function of the relevant ethical word is purely "emotive." It is used to express feeling about certain objects, but not to make any assertion about them.

It is worth mentioning that ethical terms do not serve only to express feeling. They are calculated also to arouse feeling, and so to stimulate action. Indeed some of them are used in such a way as to give the sentences in which they occur the effect of commands. Thus the sentence "It is your duty to tell the truth" may be regarded both as the expression of a certain sort of ethical feeling about truthfulness and as the expression of the command "Tell the truth." The sentence "You ought to tell the truth" also involves the command "Tell the truth," but here the tone of the command is less emphatic. In the sentence "It is good to tell the truth" the command has become little more than a suggestion. And thus the "meaning" of the word "good," in its ethical usage, is differentiated from that of the word "duty" or the word "ought." In fact we may define the meaning of the various ethical words in terms both of the different feelings they are ordinarily taken to express, and also the different responses which they are calculated to provoke.

We can now see why it is impossible to find a criterion for determining the validity of ethical judgements. It is not because they have an "absolute" validity which is mysteriously independent of ordinary sense-experience, but because they have no objective validity whatsoever. If a sentence makes no statement at all, there is obviously no sense in asking whether what it says is true or false. And we have seen that sentences which simply express moral judgements do not say anything. They are pure expressions of feeling and as such do not come under the category of truth and falsehood. They are unverifiable for the same reason as a cry of pain or a word of command is unverifiable—because they do not express genuine propositions.

Thus, although our theory of ethics might fairly be said to be radically subjectivist, it differs in a very important respect from the orthodox subjectivist theory. For the orthodox subjectivist does not deny, as we do, that the sentences of a moralizer express genuine propositions. All he denies is that they express propositions of a unique non-empirical character. His own view is that they express propositions about the speaker's feelings. If this were so, ethical judgements clearly would be capable of being true or false. They would be true if the speaker had the relevant feelings, and false if he had not. And this is a matter which is, in principle, empirically verifiable. Furthermore they could be significantly contradicted. For if I say, "Tolerance is a virtue," and someone answers, "You don't approve of it," he would, on the ordinary subjectivist theory, be contradicting me. On our theory, he would not be contradicting me, because, in saying that tolerance was a virtue, I should not be making any statement about my own feelings or about anything else. I should simply be evincing my feelings, which is not at all the same thing as saying that I have them.

The distinction between the expression of feeling and the assertion of feeling is complicated by the fact that the assertion that one has a certain feeling often accompanies the expression of that feeling, and is then, indeed, a factor in the expression of that feeling. Thus I may simultaneously express boredom and say that I am bored, and in that case my utterance of the words, "I am bored," is one of the circumstances which make it true to say that I am expressing or evincing boredom. But I can express boredom without actually saying that I am bored. I can express it by my tone and gestures, while making a statement about something wholly unconnected with it, or by an ejaculation, or without uttering any words at all. So that even if the assertion that one has a certain feeling always involves the expression of that feeling, the expression of a feeling assuredly does not always involve the assertion that one has it. And this is the important point to grasp in considering the distinction between our theory and the ordinary subjectivist theory. For whereas the subjectivist holds that ethical statements actually assert the existence of certain feelings, we hold that ethical statements are expressions and excitants of feeling which do not necessarily involve any assertions.

We have already remarked that the main objection to the ordinary subjectivist theory is that the validity of ethical judgements is not determined by the nature of their author's feelings. And this is an objection which our theory escapes. For it does not imply that the existence of any feelings is a necessary and sufficient condition of the validity of an ethical judgement. It implies, on the contrary, that ethical judgements have no validity.

There is, however, a celebrated argument against subjectivist theories which our theory does not escape. It has been pointed out by Moore that if ethical statements were simply statements about the speaker's feelings, it would be impossible to argue about questions of value. To take a typical example: if a man said that thrift was a virtue, and another replied that it was a vice, they would not, on this theory, be disputing with one another. One would be saying that he approved of thrift, and the other that *he* didn't; and there is no reason why both these statements should not be true. Now Moore held it to be obvious that we do dispute about questions of value, and accordingly concluded that the particular form of subjectivism which he was discussing was false.

It is plain that the conclusion that it is impossible to dispute about questions of value follows from our theory also. For as we hold that such

sentences as "Thrift is a virtue" and "Thrift is a vice" do not express propositions at all, we clearly cannot hold that they express incompatible propositions. We must therefore admit that if Moore's argument really refutes
the ordinary subjectivist theory, it also refutes ours. But, in fact, we deny
that it does refute even the ordinary subjectivist theory. For we hold that
one really never does dispute about questions of value.

This may seem, at first sight, to be a very paradoxical assertion. For
we certainly do engage in disputes which are ordinarily regarded as disputes
about questions of value. But, in all such cases, we find, if we consider the
matter closely, that the dispute is not really about a question of value, but
about a question of fact. When someone disagrees with us about the moral
value of a certain action or type of action, we do admittedly resort to argument in order to win him over to our way of thinking. But we do not
attempt to show by our arguments that he has the "wrong" ethical feeling
towards a situation whose nature he has correctly apprehended. What we
attempt to show is that he is mistaken about the facts of the case. We argue
that he has misconceived the agent's motive: or that he has misjudged the
effects of the action, or its probable effects in view of the agent's knowledge; or that he has failed to take into account the special circumstances
in which the agent was placed. Or else we employ more general arguments about the effects which actions of a certain type tend to produce, or
the qualities which are usually manifested in their performance. We do
this in the hope that we have only to get our opponent to agree with us
about the nature of the empirical facts for him to adopt the same moral
attitude towards them as we do. And as the people with whom we argue
have generally received the same moral education as ourselves, and live in
the same social order, our expectation is usually justified. But if our opponent happens to have undergone a different process of moral "conditioning" from ourselves, so that, even when he acknowledges all the facts, he
still disagrees with us about the moral value of the actions under discussion,
then we abandon the attempt to convince him by argument. We say that
it is impossible to argue with him because he has a distorted or undeveloped
moral sense; which signifies merely that he employs a different set of values
from our own. We feel that our own system of values is superior, and therefore speak in such derogatory terms of his. But we cannot bring forward
any arguments to show that our system is superior. For our judgement that
it is so is itself a judgement of value, and accordingly outside the scope of
argument. It is because argument fails us when we come to deal with pure
questions of value, as distinct from questions of fact, that we finally resort
to mere abuse.

In short, we find that argument is possible on moral questions only if some system of values is presupposed. If our opponent concurs with us in expressing moral disapproval of all actions of a given type *t*, then we may get him to condemn a particular action A, by bringing forward arguments to show that A is of type *t*. For the question whether A does or does not belong to that type is a plain question of fact. Given that a man has certain moral principles, we argue that he must, in order to be consistent, react morally to certain things in a certain way. What we do not and cannot argue about is the validity of these moral principles. We merely praise or condemn them in the light of our own feelings.

If anyone doubts the accuracy of this account of moral disputes, let him try to construct even an imaginary argument on a question of value which does not reduce itself to an argument about a question of logic or about an empirical matter of fact. I am confident that he will not succeed in producing a single example. And if that is the case, he must allow that its involving the impossibility of purely ethical arguments is not, as Moore thought, a ground of objection to our theory, but rather a point in favour of it.

Having upheld our theory against the only criticism which appeared to threaten it, we may now use it to define the nature of all ethical enquiries. We find that ethical philosophy consists simply in saying that ethical concepts are pseudo-concepts and therefore unanalysable. The further task of describing the different feelings that the different ethical terms are used to express, and the different reactions that they customarily provoke, is a task for the psychologist. There cannot be such a thing as ethical science, if by ethical science one means the elaboration of a "true" system of morals. For we have seen that, as ethical judgements are mere expressions of feeling, there can be no way of determining the validity of any ethical system, and, indeed, no sense in asking whether any such system is true. All that one may legitimately enquire in this connection is, What are the moral habits of a given person or group of people, and what causes them to have precisely those habits and feelings? And this enquiry falls wholly within the scope of the existing social sciences.

# C. L. STEVENSON

CHARLES LESLIE STEVENSON (1908–    ) is Professor of Philosophy at the University of Michigan. A leading proponent of the emotive theory in ethics, he has published a number of articles in recent philosophical journals. His major published work is *Ethics and Language* (1944).

## The Emotive Meaning of Ethical Terms*

### I

Ethical questions first arise in the form "Is so and so good?" or "Is this alternative better than that?" These questions are difficult partly because we don't quite know what we are seeking. We are asking, "Is there a needle in that haystack?" without even knowing just what a needle is. So the first thing to do is to examine the questions themselves. We must try to make them clearer, either by defining the terms in which they are expressed, or by any other method that is available.

The present paper is concerned wholly with this preliminary step of making ethical questions clear. In order to help answer the question "Is X good?" we must *substitute* for it a question which is free from ambiguity and confusion.

It is obvious that in substituting a clearer question we must not introduce some utterly different kind of question. It won't do (to take an extreme instance of a prevalent fallacy) to substitute for "Is X good?" the question "Is X pink with yellow trimmings?" and then point out how easy the question really is. This would beg the original question, not help answer it. On the other hand, we must not expect the substituted question to be strictly "identical" with the original one. The original question may embody hypostatization, anthropomorphisms, vagueness, and all the other ills to which our ordinary discourse is subject. If our substituted question is to be clearer, it must remove these ills. The questions will be identical only in the sense that a child is identical with the man he later becomes. Hence we must not demand that the substitution strike us, on immediate introspection, as making no change in meaning.

Just how, then, must the substituted question be related to the original?

* "The Emotive Meaning of Ethical Terms," by C. L. Stevenson, *Mind*, XLVI (1937). Used by the kind permission of the author and of the editor of *Mind*.

Let us assume (inaccurately) that it must result from replacing "good" by some set of terms which define it. The question then resolves itself to this: How must the defined meaning of "good" be related to its original meaning?

I answer that it must be *relevant*. A defined meaning will be called "relevant" to the original meaning under these circumstances: Those who have understood the definition must be able to say all that they then want to say by using the term in the defined way. They must never have occasion to use the term in the old, unclear sense. (If a person did have to go on using the word in the old sense, then to this extent his meaning would not be clarified, and the philosophical task would not be completed.) It frequently happens that a word is used so confusedly and ambiguously that we must give it *several* defined meanings, rather than one. In this case only the whole set of defined meanings will be called "relevant," and any one of them will be called "partially relevant." This is not a rigorous treatment of *relevance*, by any means; but it will serve for the present purposes.

Let us now turn to our particular task—that of giving a relevant definition of "good." Let us first examine some of the ways in which others have attempted to do this.

The word "good" has often been defined in terms of *approval*, or similar psychological attitudes. We may take as typical examples: "good" means *desired by me* (Hobbes); and "good" means *approved by most people* (Hume, in effect). It will be convenient to refer to definitions of this sort as "interest theories," following Mr. R. B. Perry, although neither "interest" nor "theory" is used in the most usual way.

Are definitions of this sort relevant?

It is idle to deny their *partial* relevance. The most superficial inquiry will reveal that "good" is exceedingly ambiguous. To maintain that "good" is *never* used in Hobbes's sense, and never in Hume's, is only to manifest an insensitivity to the complexities of language. We must recognize, perhaps, not only these senses, but a variety of similar ones, differing both with regard to the kind of interest in question, and with regard to the people who are said to have the interest.

But this is a minor matter. The essential question is not whether interest theories are *partially* relevant, but whether they are *wholly* relevant. This is the only point of intelligent dispute. Briefly: Granted that some senses of "good" may relevantly be defined in terms of interest, is there some *other* sense which is *not* relevantly so defined? We must give this question careful attention. For it is quite possible that when philosophers (and many others) have found the question "Is X good?" so difficult, they have been grasping for this *other* sense of "good," and not any sense relevantly defined in terms of interest. If we insist on defining "good" in terms of interest, and answer the question when thus interpreted, we may be begging *their* question entirely. Of course this *other* sense of "good" may not exist, or it may be a complete confusion; but that is what we must discover.

Now many have maintained that interest theories are *far* from being completely relevant. They have argued that such theories neglect the very sense of "good" which is most vital. And certainly, their arguments are not without plausibility.

Only . . . what *is* this "vital" sense of "good"? The answers have been so vague, and so beset with difficulties, that one can scarcely determine.

There are certain requirements, however, with which this "vital" sense has been expected to comply—requirements which appeal strongly to our common sense. It will be helpful to summarize these, showing how they exclude the interest theories:

In the first place, we must be able sensibly to *disagree* about whether something is "good." This condition rules out Hobbes's definition. For consider the following argument: "This is good." "That isn't so; it's not good." As translated by Hobbes, this becomes: "I desire this." "That isn't so, for I don't." The speakers are not contradicting one another, and think they are, only because of an elementary confusion in the use of pronouns. The definition, "good" means *desired by my community*, is also excluded, for how could people from different communities disagree?

In the second place, "goodness" must have, so to speak, a magnetism. A person who recognizes X to be "good" must *ipso facto* acquire a stronger tendency to act in its favour than he otherwise would have had. This rules out the Humian type of definition. For according to Hume, to recognize that something is "good" is simply to recognize that the majority approve of it. Clearly, a man may see that the majority approve of X without having, himself, a stronger tendency to favour it. This requirement excludes any attempt to define "good" in terms of the interest of people *other* than the speaker.

In the third place, the "goodness" of anything must not be verifiable solely by use of the scientific method. "Ethics must not be psychology." This restriction rules out all of the traditional interest theories, without exception. It is so sweeping a restriction that we must examine its plausibility. What are the methodological implications of interest theories which are here rejected?

According to Hobbes's definition, a person can prove his ethical judgments, with finality, by showing that he is not making an introspective error about his desires. According to Hume's definition, one may prove ethical judgments (roughly speaking) by taking a vote. *This* use of the empirical method, at any rate, seems highly remote from what we usually accept as proof, and reflects on the complete relevance of the definitions which imply it.

But aren't there more complicated interest theories which are immune from such methodological implications? No, for the same factors appear; they are only put off for a while. Consider, for example, the definition: "X is good" means *most people would approve of X if they knew its nature and consequences.* How, according to this definition, could we prove that a certain X was good? We should first have to find out, empirically, just what X was like, and what its consequences would be. To this extent the empirical method, as required by the definition, seems beyond intelligent objection. But what remains? We should next have to discover whether most people would approve of the sort of thing we had discovered X to be. This couldn't be determined by popular vote—but only because it would be too difficult to explain to the voters, beforehand, what the nature and consequences of X really were. Apart from this, voting would be a pertinent method. We are again reduced to counting noses, as a *perfectly final* appeal.

Now we need not scorn voting entirely. A man who rejected interest theories as irrelevant might readily make the following statement: "If I believed that X would be approved by the majority, when they knew all about it, I should be strongly *led* to say that X was good." But he would continue: "*Need* I say that X was good, under the circumstances? Wouldn't my acceptance of the alleged 'final proof' result simply from my being democratic? What about the more aristocratic people? They would simply say that the approval of most people, even when they knew all about the object of their approval, simply had nothing to do with the goodness of anything, and they would probably add a few remarks about the low state of people's interests." It would indeed seem, from these considerations, that the definition we have been considering has presupposed democratic ideals from the start; it has dressed up democratic propaganda in the guise of a definition.

The omnipotence of the empirical method, as implied by interest theories and others, may be shown unacceptable in a somewhat different way. Mr. G. E. Moore's familiar objection about the open question is chiefly pertinent in this regard. No matter what set of scientifically knowable properties a thing may have (says Moore, in effect), you will find, on careful introspection, that it is an open question to ask whether anything having these properties is *good.* It is difficult to believe that this recurrent question is a totally confused one, or that it seems open only because of the ambiguity of "good." Rather, we must be using some sense of "good" which is not definable, relevantly, in terms of anything scientifically knowable. That is, the scientific method is not sufficient for ethics.

These, then, are the requirements with which the "vital" sense of "good" is expected to comply: (1) goodness must be a topic for intelligent disagreement; (2) it must be "magnetic"; and (3) it must not be discoverable solely through the scientific method.

## II

Let us now turn to my own analysis of ethical judgments. First let me present my position dogmatically, showing to what extent I vary from tradition.

I believe that the three requirements, given alone, are perfectly sensible; that there is some *one* sense of "good" which satisfies all three requirements; and that no traditional interest theory satisfies them all. But this does not imply that "good" must be explained in terms of a Platonic Idea, or of a Categorical Imperative, or of an unique, unanalyzable property. On the contrary, the three requirements can be met by a *kind* of interest theory. *But we must give up a presupposition which all the traditional interest theories have made.*

Traditional interest theories hold that ethical statements are *descriptive* of the existing state of interests—that they simply *give information* about interests. (More accurately, ethical judgments are said to describe what the state of interests is, was, or will be, or to indicate what the state of interests *would* be under specified circumstances.) It is this emphasis on description, on information, which leads to their incomplete relevance. Doubtless there is always *some* element of description in ethical judgments, but this is by no means all. Their major use is not to indicate facts, but to *create an influence*. Instead of merely describing people's interests, they *change* or *intensify* them. They *recommend* an interest in an object, rather than state that the interest already exists.

For instance: When you tell a man that he oughtn't to steal, your object isn't merely to let him know that people disapprove of stealing. You are attempting, rather, to get *him* to disapprove of it. Your ethical judgment has a quasi-imperative force which, operating through suggestion, and intensified by your tone of voice, readily permits you to begin to *influence*, to *modify*, his interests. If in the end you do not succeed in getting *him* to disapprove of stealing, you will feel that you've failed to convince him that stealing is wrong. You will continue to feel this, even though he fully acknowledges that you disapprove of it, and that almost everyone else does. When you point out to him the consequences of his actions—consequences which you suspect he already disapproves of—these *reasons* which support your ethical judgment are simply a means of facilitating your influence. If you think you can change his interests by making vivid to him how others will disapprove of him, you will do so; otherwise not. So the consideration about other people's interest is just an additional means you may employ, in order to move him, and is not a part of the ethical judgment itself. Your ethical judgment doesn't merely describe interests to him, it directs his very interests. The difference between the traditional interest theories and my view is like the difference between describing a desert and irrigating it.

Another example: A munition maker declares that war is a good thing. If he merely meant that he approved of it, he would not have to insist so strongly, nor grow so excited in his argument. People would be quite easily convinced that he approved of it. If he merely meant that most people approved of war, or that most people would approve of it if they knew the consequences, he would have to yield his point if it were proved that this wasn't so. But he wouldn't do this, nor does consistency require it. He is not *describing* the state of people's approval; he is trying to *change* it by his influence. If he found that few people approved of war, he might insist all the more strongly that it was good, for there would be more changing to be done.

This example illustrates how "good" may be used for what most of us would call bad purposes. Such cases are as pertinent as any others. I am not indicating the *good* way of using "good." I am not influencing people, but am describing the way this influence sometimes goes on. If the reader wishes to say that the munition maker's influence is bad—that is, if the reader wishes to awaken people's disapproval of the man, and to make him disapprove of his own actions—I should at another time be willing to join in this undertaking. But this is not the present concern. I am not using ethical terms, but am indicating how they *are* used. The munition maker, in his use of "good," illustrates the persuasive character of the word just as well as does the unselfish man who, eager to encourage in each of us a desire for the happiness of all, contends that the supreme good is peace.

Thus ethical terms are *instruments* used in the complicated interplay and readjustment of human interests. This can be seen plainly from more general observations. People from widely separated communities have different moral attitudes. Why? To a great extent because they have been subject to different social influences. Now clearly this influence doesn't operate through sticks and stones alone; words play a great part. People praise one another, to encourage certain inclinations, and blame one another, to discourage others. Those of forceful personalities issue commands which weaker people, for complicated instinctive reasons, find it difficult to disobey, quite apart from fears of consequences. Further influence is brought to bear by writers and orators. Thus social influence is exerted, to an enormous extent, by means that have nothing to do with physical force or material reward.

The ethical terms facilitate such influence. Being suited for use in *suggestion*, they are a means by which men's attitudes may be led this way or that. The reason, then, that we find a greater similarity in the moral attitudes of one community than in those of different communities is largely this: ethical judgments propagate themselves. One man says "This is good"; this may influence the approval of another person, who then makes the same ethical judgment, which in turn influences another person, and so on. In the end, by a process of mutual influence, people take up more or less the same attitudes. Between people of widely separated communities, of course, the influence is less strong; hence different communities have different attitudes.

These remarks will serve to give a general idea of my point of view. We must now go into more detail. There are several questions which must be answered: How does an ethical sentence acquire its power of influencing people—why is it suited to suggestion? Again, what has this influence to do with the *meaning* of ethical terms? And finally, do these considerations really lead us to a sense of "good" which meets the requirements mentioned in the preceding section?

Let us deal first with the question about *meaning*. This is far from an easy question, so we must enter into a preliminary inquiry about meaning in general. Although a seeming digression, this will prove indispensable.

### III

Broadly speaking, there are two different *purposes* which lead us to use language. On the one hand we use words (as in science) to record, clarify, and communicate *beliefs*. On the other hand we use words to give vent to our feelings (interjections), or to create moods (poetry), or to incite people to actions or attitudes (oratory).

The first use of words I shall call "descriptive"; the second, "dynamic." Note that the distinction depends solely upon the *purpose* of the *speaker*.

When a person says "Hydrogen is the lightest known gas," his purpose *may* be simply to lead the hearer to believe this, or to believe that the speaker believes it. In that case the words are used descriptively. When a person cuts himself and says "Damn," his purpose is not ordinarily to record, clarify, or communicate any belief. The word is used dynamically. The two ways of using words, however, are by no means mutually exclusive. This is obvious from the fact that our purposes are often complex. Thus when one says "I want you to close the door," part of his purpose, ordinarily, is to lead the hearer to believe that he has this want. To that extent the words are used descriptively. But the major part of one's purpose is to lead the hearer to *satisfy* the want. To that extent the words are used dynamically.

It very frequently happens that the same sentence may have a dynamic use on one occasion, and may not have a dynamic use on another; and that it may have different dynamic uses on different occasions. For instance: A man says to a visiting neighbour, "I am loaded down with work." His purpose may be to let the neighbour know how life is going with him. This would *not* be a dynamic use of words. He may make the remark, however, in order to drop a hint. This *would* be dynamic usage (as well as descriptive). Again, he may make the remark to arouse the neighbour's sympathy. This would be a *different* dynamic usage from that of hinting.

Or again, when we say to a man, "Of course you won't make those mistakes any more," we *may* simply be making a prediction. But we are more likely to be using "suggestion," in order to encourage him and hence *keep* him from making mistakes. The first use would be descriptive; the second, mainly dynamic.

From these examples it will be clear that we can't determine whether words are used dynamically or not, merely by reading the dictionary—even assuming that everyone is faithful to dictionary meanings. Indeed, to know whether a person is using a word dynamically, we must note his tone of voice, his gestures, the general circumstances under which he is speaking, and so on.

We must now proceed to an important question: What has the dynamic use of words to do with their *meaning*? One thing is clear—we must not define "meaning" in a way that would make meaning vary with dynamic usage. If we did, we should have no use for the term. All that we could say about such "meaning" would be that it is very complicated, and subject to constant change. So we must certainly distinguish between the dynamic use of words and their meaning.

It doesn't follow, however, that we must define "meaning" in some non-psychological fashion. We must simply restrict the psychological field. Instead of identifying meaning with *all* the psychological causes and effects that attend a word's utterance, we must identify it with those that it has a *tendency* (causal property, dispositional property) to be connected with. The tendency must be a particular kind, moreover. It must exist for all who speak the language; it must be persistent; and must be realizable more or less independently of determinate circumstances attending the word's utterance. There will be further restrictions dealing with the interrelation of words in different contexts. Moreover, we must include, under the psychological responses which the words tend to produce, not only immediately introspectable experiences, but *dispositions* to react in a given way with appropriate stimuli. I hope to go into these matters in a subsequent paper. Suffice it now to say that I think "meaning" may be thus defined in a way to include "propositional" meaning as an important kind. Now a word may *tend* to have causal relations which in fact it sometimes doesn't; and it may sometimes have causal relations which it *doesn't tend* to have. And since the tendency of words which constitutes their meaning must be of a particular kind, and may include, as responses, dispositions to reactions, of which any of *several* immediate experiences may be a sign, then there is nothing surprising in the fact that words have a permanent meaning, in spite of the fact that the immediately introspectable experiences which attend their usage are so highly varied.

When "meaning" is defined in this way, meaning will not include dynamic use. For although words are sometimes accompanied by dynamic purposes, they do not *tend* to be accompanied by them in the way above mentioned. E.g., there is no tendency realizable independently of the determinate circumstances under which the words are uttered.

There will be a kind of meaning, however, in the sense above defined, which has an intimate relation to dynamic usage. I refer to "emotive" meaning (in a sense roughly like that employed by Ogden and Richards). The emotive meaning of a word is a tendency of a word, arising through the history of its usage, to produce (result from) *affective* responses in people. It is the immediate aura of feeling which hovers about a word. Such tendencies to produce affective responses cling to words very tenaciously. It would be difficult, for instance, to express merriment by using the interjection "alas." Because of the persistence of such affective tendencies (among other reasons) it becomes feasible to classify them as "meanings."

Just *what* is the relation between emotive meaning and the dynamic use of words? Let us take an example. Suppose that a man is talking with a group of people which includes Miss Jones, aged 59. He refers to her, without thinking, as an "old maid." Now even if his purposes are perfectly innocent—even if he is using the words purely descriptively—Miss Jones won't think so. She will think he is encouraging the others to have contempt for her, and will draw in her skirts, defensively. The man might have done better if instead of saying "old maid" he had said "elderly spinster." The latter words could have been put to the same descriptive use, and would not so readily have caused suspicions about the dynamic use.

"Old maid" and "elderly spinster" differ, to be sure, only in emotive meaning. From the example it will be clear that certain words, because of their emotive meaning, are suited to a certain kind of dynamic use—so well suited, in fact, that the hearer is likely to be misled when we use them in any other way. The more pronounced a word's emotive meaning is, the less likely people are to use it purely descriptively. Some words are suited to encourage people, some to discourage them, some to quiet them, and so on.

Even in these cases, of course, the dynamic purposes are not to be identified with any sort of meaning; for the emotive meaning accompanies a word much more persistently than do the dynamic purposes. But there is an important contingent relation between emotive meaning and dynamic purpose: the former assists the latter. Hence if we define emotively laden terms in a way that neglects their emotive meaning, we are likely to be confusing. *We lead people to think that the terms defined are used dynamically less often than they are.*

*IV*

Let us now apply these remarks in defining "good." This word may be used morally or non-morally. I shall deal with the non-moral usage almost entirely, but only because it is simpler. The main points of the analysis will apply equally well to either usage.

As a preliminary definition, let us take an inaccurate approximation. It may be more misleading than helpful, but will do to begin with. Roughly, then, the sentence "X is good" means *We like X.* ("We" includes the hearer or hearers.)

At first glance this definition sounds absurd. If used, we should expect to find the following sort of conversation: A. "This is good." B. "But I *don't* like it. What led you to believe that I did?" The unnaturalness of B's reply, judged by ordinary word-usage, would seem to cast doubt on the relevance of my definition.

B's unnaturalness, however, lies simply in this: he is assuming that "We like it" (as would occur implicitly in the use of "good") is being used descriptively. This won't do. When "We like it" is to take the place of "This is good," the former sentence must be used not purely descriptively, but dynamically. More specifically, it must be used to promote a very subtle (and for the non-moral sense in question, a very easily resisted) kind of *suggestion.* To the extent that "we" refers to the hearer, it must have the dynamic use, essential to suggestion, of leading the hearer to *make* true what is said, rather than merely to believe it. And to the extent that "we" refers to the speaker, the sentence must have not only the descriptive use of indicating belief about the speaker's interest, but the quasi-interjectory, dynamic function of giving direct expression to the interest. (This immediate expression of feelings assists in the process of suggestion. It is difficult to disapprove in the face of another's enthusiasm.)

For an example of a case where "We like this" is used in the dynamic way that "This is good" is used, consider the case of a mother who says to her several children, "One thing is certain, *we all like to be neat.*" If she really believed this, she wouldn't bother to say so. But she is not using the words descriptively. She is *encouraging* the children to like neatness. By telling them that they like neatness, she will lead them to *make* her statement true, so to speak. If, instead of saying "We all like to be neat" in this way, she had said "It's a good thing to be neat," the effect would have been approximately the same.

But these remarks are still misleading. Even when "We like it" is used for suggestion, it isn't quite like "This is good." The latter is more subtle. With such a sentence as "This is a good book," for example, it would be practically impossible to use instead "We like this book." When the latter is used, it must be accompanied by so exaggerated an intonation, to prevent its becoming confused with a descriptive statement, that the force of suggestion becomes stronger, and ludicrously more overt, than when "good" is used.

The definition is inadequate, further, in that the definiens has been restricted to dynamic usage. Having said that dynamic usage was different from meaning, I should not have to mention it in giving the *meaning* of "good."

It is in connection with this last point that we must return to emotive meaning. The word "good" has a pleasing emotive meaning which fits it especially for the dynamic use of suggesting favourable interest. But the sentence "We like it" has no such emotive meaning. Hence my definition has neglected emotive meaning entirely. Now to neglect emotive meaning is likely to lead to endless confusions, as we shall presently see; so I have sought to make up for the inadequacy of the definition by letting the restriction about dynamic usage take the place of emotive meaning. What I should do, of course, is to find a definiens whose emotive meaning, like that of "good," simply does *lead* to dynamic usage.

Why didn't I do this? I answer that it isn't possible, if the definition is to afford us increased clarity. No two words, in the first place, have quite the same emotive meaning. The most we can hope for is a rough approximation. But if we seek for such an approximation for "good," we shall find nothing more than synonyms, such as "desirable" or "valuable"; and these are profitless because they do not clear up the connection between "good" and favourable interest. If we reject such synonyms, in favour of non-ethical terms, we shall be highly misleading. For instance: "This is good" has something like the meaning of "I *do* like this; do so as well." But this is certainly not accurate. For the imperative makes an appeal to the conscious efforts of the hearer. Of course he can't like something just by trying. He must be led to like it through suggestion. Hence an ethical sentence differs from an imperative in that it enables one to make changes in a much more subtle, less fully conscious way. Note that the ethical sentence centres the hearer's attention not on his interests, but on the object of interest, and thereby facilitates suggestion. Because of its subtlety, moreover, an ethical sentence readily permits counter-suggestion, and leads to the give and take situation which is so characteristic of arguments about values.

Strictly speaking, then, it is impossible to define "good" in terms of favourable interest if emotive meaning is not to be distorted. Yet it is possible to say that "This is good" is *about* the favourable interest of the speaker and the hearer or hearers, and that it has a pleasing emotive meaning which fits the words for use in suggestion. This is a rough description of meaning, not a definition. But it serves the same clarifying function that a definition ordinarily does; and that, after all, is enough.

A word must be added about the moral use of "good." This differs from the above in that it is about a different kind of interest. Instead of being about what the hearer and speaker *like*, it is about a stronger sort of approval. When a person *likes* something, he is pleased when it prospers, and disappointed when it doesn't. When a person *morally approves* of something, he experiences a rich feeling of security when it prospers, and is indignant, or "shocked" when it doesn't. These are rough and inaccurate examples of the many factors which one would have to mention in distinguishing the two kinds of interest. In the moral usage, as well as in the non-moral, "good" has an emotive meaning which adapts it to suggestion.

And now, are these considerations of any importance? Why do I stress emotive meanings in this fashion? Does the omission of them really lead people into errors? I think, indeed, that the errors resulting from such omissions are enormous. In order to see this, however, we must return to the restrictions, mentioned in section I, with which the "vital" sense of "good" has been expected to comply.

## V

The first restriction, it will be remembered, had to do with disagreement. Now there is clearly some sense in which people disagree on ethical points; but we must not rashly assume that all disagreement is modelled after the sort that occurs in the natural sciences. We must distinguish between "disagreement in belief" (typical of the sciences) and "disagreement in interest." Disagreement in belief occurs when A believes $p$ and B disbelieves it. Disagreement in interest occurs when A has a favourable interest in X, when B has an unfavourable one in it, and when neither is content to let the other's interest remain unchanged.

Let me give an example of disagreement in interest. A. "Let's go to a cinema to-night." B. "I don't want to do that. Let's go to the symphony." A continues to insist on the cinema, B on the symphony. This is disagreement in a perfectly conventional sense. They can't agree on where they want to go, and each is trying to redirect the other's interest. (Note that imperatives are used in the example.)

It is disagreement in *interest* which takes places in ethics. When C says "This is good," and D says "No, it's bad," we have a case of suggestion and counter-suggestion. Each man is trying to redirect the other's interest. There obviously need be no domineering, since each may be willing to give ear to the other's influence; but each is trying to move the other none the less. It is in this sense that they disagree. Those who argue that certain interest theories make no provision for disagreement have been misled, I believe, simply because the traditional theories, in leaving out emotive meaning, give the impression that ethical judgments are used descriptively only; and of course when judgments are used purely descriptively, the only disagreement that can arise is disagreement *in belief*. Such disagreement may be disagreement in belief *about* interests; but this is not the same as disagreement *in* interest. My definition doesn't provide for disagreement in belief about interests, any more than does Hobbes's; but that is no matter, for there is no reason to believe, at least on common-sense grounds, that this kind of disagreement exists. There is only disagreement *in* interest. (We shall see in a moment that disagreement in interest does not remove ethics from sober argument—that this kind of disagreement may often be resolved through empirical means.)

The second restriction, about "magnetism," or the connection between goodness and actions, requires only a word. This rules out *only* those interest theories which do *not* include the interest of the speaker, in defining "good." My account does include the speaker's interest; hence is immune.

The third restriction, about the empirical method, may be met in a way that springs naturally from the above account of disagreement. Let us put the question in this way: When two people disagree over an ethical matter, can they completely resolve the disagreement through empirical considerations, assuming that each applies the empirical method exhaustively, consistently, and without error?

I answer that sometimes they can, and sometimes they cannot; and that at any rate, even when they can, the relation between empirical knowledge and ethical judgments is quite different from the one which traditional interest theories seem to imply.

This can best be seen from an analogy. Let's return to the example where A and B couldn't agree on a cinema or a symphony. The example differed from an ethical argument in that imperatives were used, rather than ethical judgments; but was analogous to the extent that each person was endeavouring to modify the other's interest. Now how would these people argue the case, assuming that they were too intelligent just to shout at one another?

Clearly, they would give "reasons" to support their imperatives. A might say, "But you know, Garbo is at the Bijou." His hope is that B, who admires Garbo, will acquire a desire to go to the cinema when he knows what play will be there. B may counter, "But Toscanini is guest conductor to-night, in an all-Beethoven programme." And so on. Each supports his imperative ("*Let's* do so and so") by reasons which may be empirically established.

To generalize from this: disagreement in interest may be rooted in disagreement in belief. That is to say, people who disagree in interest would often cease to do so if they knew the precise nature and consequences of the object of their interest. To this extent disagreement in interest may be resolved by securing agreement in belief, which in turn may be secured empirically.

This generalization holds for ethics. If A and B, instead of using imperatives, had said, respectively, "It would be *better* to go to the cinema," and "It would be better to go to the symphony," the reasons which they would advance would be roughly the same. They would each give a more thorough account of the object of interest, with the purpose of completing the redirection of interest which was begun by the suggestive force of the ethical sentence. On the whole, of course, the suggestive force of the ethical statement merely exerts enough pressure to start such trains of reasons, since the reasons are much more essential in resolving disagreement in interest than the persuasive effect of the ethical judgment itself.

Thus the empirical method is relevant to ethics simply because our knowledge of the world is a determining factor to our interests. But note that empirical facts are not inductive grounds from which the ethical judgment problematically follows. (This is what traditional interest theories imply.) If someone said "Close the door," and added the reason "We'll catch cold," the latter would scarcely be called an inductive ground of the former. Now imperatives are related to the reasons which support them in the same way that ethical judgments are related to reasons.

Is the empirical method *sufficient* for attaining ethical agreement? Clearly not. For empirical knowledge resolves disagreement in interest only to the extent that such disagreement is rooted in disagreement in belief. Not all disagreement in interest is of this sort. For instance: A is of a sympathetic nature, and B isn't. They are arguing about whether a public dole would be good. Suppose that they discovered all the consequences of the dole. Isn't it possible, even so, that A will say that it's good, and B that it's bad? The disagreement in interest may arise not from limited factual knowledge, but simply from A's sympathy and B's coldness. Or again, suppose, in the above argument, that A was poor and unemployed, and that B was rich. Here again the disagreement might not be due to different factual knowledge. It would be due to the different social positions of the men, together with their predominant self-interest.

When ethical disagreement is not rooted in disagreement in belief, is there *any* method by which it may be settled? If one means by "method" a *rational* method, then there is no method. But in any case there is a "way." Let's consider the above example, again, where disagreement was due to A's sympathy and B's coldness. Must they end by saying, "Well, it's just a matter of our having different temperaments"? Not necessarily. A, for instance, may try to *change* the temperament of his opponent. He may pour out his enthusiasms in such a moving way—present the sufferings of the poor with such appeal —that he will lead his opponent to see life through different eyes. He may build up, by the contagion of his feelings, an influence which will modify B's temperament, and create in him a sympathy for the poor which didn't previously exist. This is often the only way to obtain ethical agreement, if there is any way at all. It is persuasive, not empirical or rational; but that is no reason for neglecting it. There is no reason to scorn it, either, for it is only by such means that our personalities are able to grow, through our contact with others.

The point I wish to stress, however, is simply that the empirical method is instrumental to ethical agreement only to the extent that disagreement in interest is rooted in disagreement in belief. There is little reason to believe that all disagreement is of this sort. Hence the empirical method is not sufficient for ethics. In any case, ethics is not psychology, since psychology doesn't endeavour to *direct* our interests; it discovers facts about the ways in which interests are or can be directed, but that's quite another matter.

To summarize this section: my analysis of ethical judgments meets the three requirements for the "vital" sense of "good" that were mentioned in section I. The traditional interest theories fail to meet these requirements simply because they neglect emotive meaning. This neglect leads them to neglect dynamic usage, and the sort of disagreement that results from such usage, together with the method of resolving the disagreement. I may add that my analysis answers Moore's objection about the open question. Whatever scientifically knowable properties a thing may have, it *is* always open to question whether a thing having these (enumerated) qualities is good. For to ask whether it is good is to ask for *influence*. And whatever I may know about an object, I can still ask, quite pertinently, to be influenced with regard to my interest in it.

## VI

And now, have I really pointed out the "vital" sense of "good"?

I suppose that many will still say "No," claiming that I have simply failed to set down *enough* requirements which this sense must meet, and that my analysis, like all others given in terms of interest, is a way of begging the issue. They will say: "When we ask 'Is X good?' we don't want mere influence, mere advice. We decidedly don't want to be influenced through persuasion, nor are we fully content when the influence is supported by a wide scientific knowledge of X. The answer to our question will, of course, modify our interests. But this is only because an unique sort of *truth* will be revealed to us—a truth which must be apprehended *a priori*. We want our interests to be guided by this truth, and by nothing else. To substitute for such a truth mere emotive meaning and suggestion is to conceal from us the very object of our search."

I can only answer that I do not understand. What is this truth to be *about?* For I recollect no Platonic Idea, nor do I know what to *try* to recollect. I find no indefinable property, nor do I know what to look for. And the "self-evident" deliverances of reason, which so many philosophers have claimed, seem, on examination, to be deliverances of their respective reasons only (if of anyone's) and not of mine.

I strongly suspect, indeed, that any sense of "good" which is expected both to unite itself in synthetic *a priori* fashion with other concepts, and to influence interests as well, is really a great confusion. I extract from this meaning the power of influence alone, which I find the only intelligible part. If the rest is confusion, however, then it certainly deserves more than the shrug of one's shoulders. What I should like to do is to *account* for the confusion —to examine the psychological needs which have given rise to it, and to show how these needs may be satisfied in another way. This is *the* problem, if confusion is to be stopped at its source. But it is an enormous problem, and my reflections on it, which are at present worked out only roughly, must be reserved until some later time.

I may add that if "X is good" is essentially a vehicle for suggestion, it is scarcely a statement which philosophers, any more than many other men, are called upon to make. To the extent that ethics predicates the ethical terms of anything, rather than explains their meaning, it ceases to be a reflective study. Ethical statements are social instruments. They are used in a co-operative enterprise in which we are mutually adjusting ourselves to the interests of others. Philosophers have a part in this, as do all men, but not the major part.

# BRAND
# BLANSHARD

BRAND BLANSHARD (1892–      ) is Professor
of Philosophy at Yale University. A representative of the idealist school of philosophy,
he has published numerous articles in leading
philosophical journals. His major published
work is *The Nature of Thought* (1939).

## The New Subjectivism in Ethics*

By the new subjectivism in ethics I mean the view that when anyone
says "this is right" or "this is good," he is only expressing his own feeling;
he is not asserting anything true or false, because he is not asserting or judging at all; he is really making an exclamation that expresses a favorable
feeling.

This view has recently come into much favor. With variations of detail, it
is being advocated by Russell, Wittgenstein and Ayer in England, and by
Carnap, Stevenson, Feigl, and others, in this country. Why is it that the
theory has come into so rapid a popularity? Is it because moralists of insight
have been making a fresh and searching examination of moral experience and
its expression? No, I think not. A consideration of the names just mentioned
suggests a truer reason. All these names belong, roughly speaking, to a single
school of thought in the theory of knowledge. If the new view has become
popular in ethics, it is because certain persons who were at work in the theory
of knowledge arrived at a new view *there*, and found, on thinking it out, that
it required the new view in ethics; the view comes less from ethical analysis
than from logical positivism.

As positivists, these writers held that every judgment belongs to one or
other of two types. On the one hand, it may be *a priori* or necessary. But then
it is always analytic, i.e., it unpacks in its predicate part or all of its subject.
Can we safely say that $7+5$ make 12? Yes, because 12 is what we mean by
"$7+5$." On the other hand, the judgment may be empirical, and then, if we
are to verify it, we can no longer look to our meanings only; it refers to sense
experience and there we must look for its warrant. Having arrived at this division of judgments, the positivists raised the question where value judgments
fall. The judgment that knowledge is good, for example, did not seem to be

* From "The New Subjectivism in Ethics," by Brand Blanshard, *Philosophy and
Phenomenological Research*, IX (1949). Used by the kind permission of the author and
of the editor of *Philosophy and Phenomenological Research*.

analytic; the value that knowledge might have did not seem to be part of our concept of knowledge. But neither was the statement empirical, for goodness was not a quality like red or squeaky that could be seen or heard. What were they to do, then, with these awkward judgments of value? To find a place for them in their theory of knowledge would require them to revise the theory radically, and yet that theory was what they regarded as their most important discovery. It appeared that the theory could be saved in one way only. If it could be shown that judgments of good and bad were not judgments at all, that they asserted nothing true or false, but merely expressed emotions like "Hurrah" or "Fiddlesticks," then these wayward judgments would cease from troubling and weary heads could be at rest. This is the course the positivists took. They explained value judgments by explaining them away.

Now I do not think their view will do. But before discussing it, I should like to record one vote of thanks to them for the clarity with which they have stated their case. It has been said of John Stuart Mill that he wrote so clearly that he could be found out. This theory has been put so clearly and precisely that it deserves criticism of the same kind, and this I will do my best to supply. The theory claims to show by analysis that when we say, "That is good," we do not mean to assert a character of the subject of which we are thinking. I shall argue that we do mean to do just that.

Let us work through an example, and the simpler and commoner the better. There is perhaps no value statement on which people would more universally agree than the statement that intense pain is bad. Let us take a set of circumstances in which I happen to be interested on the legislative side and in which I think every one of us might naturally make such a statement. We come upon a rabbit that has been caught in one of the brutal traps in common use. There are signs that it has struggled for days to escape and that in a frenzy of hunger, pain, and fear, it has all but eaten off its own leg. The attempt failed: the animal is now dead. As we think of the long and excruciating pain it must have suffered, we are very likely to say: "It was a bad thing that the little animal should suffer so." The positivist tells us that when we say this we are only expressing our present emotion. I hold, on the contrary, that we mean to assert something of the pain itself, namely, that it was bad—bad when and as it occurred.

Consider what follows from the positivist view. On that view, nothing good or bad happened in the case until I came on the scene and made my remark. For what I express in my remark is something going on in me at the time, and that of course did not exist until I did come on the scene. The pain of the rabbit was not itself bad; nothing evil was happening when that pain was being endured; badness, in the only sense in which it is involved at all, waited for its appearance till I came and looked and felt. Now that this is at odds with our meaning may be shown as follows. Let us put to ourselves the hypothesis that we had not come on the scene and that the rabbit never was discovered. Are we prepared to say that in that case nothing bad occurred in the sense in which we said it did? Clearly not. Indeed we should say, on the contrary, that the accident of our later discovery made no difference whatever to the badness of the animal's pain, that it would have been every whit as bad whether a chance passer-by happened later to discover the body and feel repugnance or not. If so, then it is clear that in saying the suffering was bad we are not expressing our feelings only. We are saying that the pain was bad when and as it occurred and before anyone took an attitude toward it.

The first argument is thus an ideal experiment in which we use the method of difference. It removes our present expression and shows that the badness we meant would not be affected by this, whereas on positivist grounds it should be. The second argument applies the method in the reverse way. It ideally removes the past event, and shows that this would render false what we mean to say, whereas on positivist grounds it should not. Let us suppose that the animal did not in fact fall into the trap and did not suffer at all, but that we mistakenly believe it did, and say as before that its suffering was an evil thing. On the positivist theory, everything I sought to express by calling it evil in the first case is still present in the second. In the only sense in which badness is involved at all, whatever was bad in the first case is still present in its entirety, since all that is expressed in either case is a state of feeling, and that feeling is still there. And our question is, is such an implication consistent with what we meant? Clearly it is not. If anyone asked us, after we made the remark that the suffering was a bad thing, whether we should think it relevant to what we said to learn that the incident had never occurred and no pain had been suffered at all, we should say that it made all the difference in the world, that what we were asserting to be bad was precisely the suffering we thought had occurred back there, that if this had not occurred, there was nothing left to be bad, and that our assertion was in that case mistaken. The suggestion that in saying something evil had occurred we were after all making no mistake, because we had never meant anyhow to say anything about the past suffering, seems to me merely frivolous. If we did not mean to say this, why should we be so relieved on finding that the suffering had not occurred? On the theory before us, such relief would be groundless, for in that suffering itself there was nothing bad at all, and hence in its nonoccurrence there would be nothing to be relieved about. The positivist theory would here distort our meaning beyond recognition.

So far as I can see, there is only one way out for the positivist. He holds that goodness and badness lie in feelings of approval or disapproval. And there is a way in which he might hold that badness did in this case precede our own feeling of disapproval without belonging to the pain itself. The pain in itself was neutral; but unfortunately the rabbit, on no grounds at all, took up toward this neutral object an attitude of disapproval, and that made it for the first time, and in the only intelligible sense, bad. This way of escape is theoretically possible, but since it has grave difficulties of its own and has not, so far as I know, been urged by positivists, it is perhaps best not to spend time over it.

I come now to a third argument, which again is very simple. When we come upon the rabbit and make our remark about its suffering being a bad thing, we presumably make it with some feeling; the positivists are plainly right in saying that such remarks do usually express feeling. But suppose that a week later we revert to the incident in thought and make our statement again. And suppose that the circumstances have now so changed that the feeling with which we made the remark in the first place has faded. The pathetic evidence is no longer before us; and we are now so fatigued in body and mind that feeling is, as we say, quite dead. In these circumstances, since what was expressed by the remark when first made is, on the theory before us, simply absent, the remark now expresses nothing. It is as empty as the word "Hurrah" would be when there was no enthusiasm behind it. And this seems to me untrue. When we repeat the remark that such suffering was a bad thing, the feeling with which we made it last week may be at or near the vanishing point, but if we were asked whether we meant to say what we did before, we should certainly answer Yes. We should say that we made our point with feeling the first time and little or no feeling the second time, but that it was the same point we were making. And if we can see that what we meant to say remains the same, while the feeling varies from intensity to near zero, it is not the feeling that we primarily meant to express.

I come now to a fourth consideration. We all believe that toward acts or effects of a certain kind one attitude is fitting and another not; but on the theory before us such a belief would not make sense. Broad and Ross have lately contended that this fitness is one of the main facts of ethics, and I suspect they are right. But that is not exactly my point. My point is this: whether there is such fitness or not, we all assume that there is, and if we do, we express in moral judgments more than the subjectivists say we do. Let me illustrate.

In his novel *The House of the Dead*, Dostoevsky tells of his experiences in a Siberian prison camp. Whatever the unhappy inmates of such camps are like today, Dostoevsky's companions were about as grim a lot as can be imagined. "I have heard stories," he writes, "of the most terrible, the most unnatural actions, of the most monstrous murders, told with the most spontaneous, childishly merry laughter." Most of us would say that in this delight at the killing of others or the causing of suffering there is something very unfitting. If we were asked why we thought so, we should say that these things involve great evil and are wrong, and that to take delight in what is evil or wrong is plainly unfitting. Now on the subjectivist view, this answer is ruled out. For before someone takes up an attitude toward death, suffering, or their infliction, they have no moral quality at all. There is therefore nothing about them to which an attitude of approval or condemnation could be fitting. They are in themselves neutral, and, so far as they get a moral quality, they get it only through being invested with it by the attitude of the onlooker. But if that is true, why is any attitude more fitting than any other? Would applause, for example, be fitting if, apart from the applause, there were nothing good to applaud? Would condemnation be fitting if, independently of the condemnation, there were nothing bad to condemn? In such a case, any attitude would be as fitting or unfitting as any other, which means that the notion of fitness has lost all point.

Indeed we are forced to go much farther. If goodness and badness lie in attitudes only and hence are brought into being by them, those men who greeted death and misery with childishly merry laughter are taking the only sensible line. If there is nothing evil in these things, if they get their moral complexion only from our feeling about them, why shouldn't they be greeted with a cheer? To greet them with repulsion would turn what before was neutral into something bad; it would needlessly bring badness into the world; and even on subjectivist assumptions that does not seem very bright. On the other hand, to greet them with delight would convert what before was neutral into something good; it would bring goodness into the world. If I have murdered a man and wish to remove the stain, the way is clear. It is to cry, "Hurrah for murder."

What is the subjectivist to reply? I can only guess. He may point out that the inflicting of death is *not* really neutral before the onlooker takes his attitude, for the man who inflicted the death no doubt himself took an attitude, and thus the act had a moral quality derived from this. But that makes the case more incredible still, for the man who did the act presumably approved it, and if so it was good in the only sense in which anything is good, and then our conviction that the laughter is unfit is more unaccountable still. It may be replied that the victim, too, had his attitude and that since this was unfavorable, the act was not unqualifiedly good. But the answer is plain. Let the killer be expert at his job; let him despatch his victim instantly before he has time to take an attitude, and then gloat about his perfect crime without ever telling anyone. Then, so far as I can see, his act will be good without any qualification. It would become bad only if someone found out about it and disliked it. And that would be a curiously irrational procedure, since the man's approving of his own killing is in itself just as neutral as the killing that it approves. Why then should anyone dislike it?

It may be replied that we can defend our dislike on this ground that, if the approval of killing were to go unchecked and spread, most men would have to live in insecurity and fear, and these things are undesirable. But surely this reply is not open; these things are not, on the theory, undesirable, for nothing is; in themselves they are neutral. Why then should I disapprove men's living in this state? The answer may come that if other men live in insecurity and fear, I shall in time be infected myself. But even in my own insecurity and fear there is, on the theory before us, nothing bad whatever, and therefore, if I disapprove them, it is without a shadow of ground and with no more fitness in my attitude than if I cordially cheered them. The theory thus conflicts with our judgments of fitness all along the line.

I come now to a fifth and final difficulty with the theory. It makes mistakes about values impossible. There is a whole nest of inter-connected criticisms here, some of which have been made so often that I shall not develop them again, such as that I can never agree or disagree in opinion with anyone else about an ethical matter, and that in these matters I can never be inconsistent with others or with myself. I am not at all content with the sort of analysis which says that the only contradictions in such cases have regard to facts and that contradictions about value are only differences of feeling. I think that if anyone tells me that having a bicuspid out without an anaesthetic is not a bad experience and I say it is a very nasty experience indeed, I am differing with him in opinion, and differing about the degree of badness of the experience. But without pressing this further, let me apply the argument in what is perhaps a fresh direction.

There is an old and merciful distinction that moralists have made for many centuries about conduct—the distinction between what is subjectively and what is objectively right. They have said that in any given situation there is some act which, in view of all the circumstances, would be the best act to do; and this is what would be objectively right. The notion of an objectively right act is the ground of our notion of duty: our duty is always to find and do this act if we can. But of course we often don't find it. We often hit upon and do acts that we think are the right ones, but we are mistaken; and then our act is only subjectively right. Between these two acts the disparity may be continual; Professor Prichard suggested that probably few of us in the course of our lives ever succeed in dong *the* right act.

Now so far as I can see, the new subjectivism would abolish this difference at a stroke. Let us take a case. A boy abuses his small brother. We should commonly say, "That is wrong, but perhaps he doesn't know any better. By reason of bad teaching and a feeble imagination, he may see nothing wrong in what he is doing, and may even be proud of it. If so, his act may be subjectively right, though it is miles away from what is objectively right." What concerns me about the new subjectivism is that it prohibits this distinction. If the boy feels this way about his act, then it is right in the only sense in which anything is right. The notion of an objective right lying beyond what he has discovered, and which he ought to seek and do is meaningless. There might, to be sure, be an act that would more generally arouse favorable feelings in others, but that would not make it right for him unless he thought of it and approved it, which he doesn't. Even if he did think of it, it would not be obligatory for him to feel about it in any particular way, since there is nothing in any act, as we have seen, which would make any feeling more suitable than any other.

Now if there is no such thing as an objectively right act, what becomes of the idea of duty? I have suggested that the idea of duty rests on the idea of such an act, since it is always our duty to find that act and do it if we can. But if whatever we feel approval for at the time is right, what is the point of doubting and searching further? Like the little girl in Boston who was asked if she would like to travel, we can answer, "Why should I travel when I'm already there?" If I am reconciled in feeling to my present act, no act I could discover by reflection could be better, and therefore why reflect or seek at all? Such a view seems to me to break the mainspring of duty, to destroy the motive for self-improvement, and to remove the ground for self-criticism. It may be replied that by further reflection I can find an act that would satisfy my feelings more widely than the present one, and that this is the act I should seek. But this reply means either that such general satisfaction is objectively better, which would contradict the theory, or else that, if at the time I don't feel it better, it isn't better, in which case I have no motive for seeking it. When certain self-righteous persons took an inflexible line with Oliver Cromwell, his very Cromwellian reply was, "Bethink ye, gentlemen, by the bowels of Christ, that ye may be mistaken." It was good advice. I hope nobody will take from me the privilege of finding myself mistaken. I should be sorry to think that the self of thirty years ago was as far along the path as the self of today, merely because he was a smug young jackanapes, or even that the paragon of today has as little room for improvement as would be allowed by his myopic complacency.

One final remark. The great problems of the day are international problems. Has the new subjectivism any bearing upon these problems? I think it has, and a somewhat sinister bearing. I would not suggest, of course, that those who hold the theory are one whit less public-spirited than others; surely there are few who could call themselves citizens of the world with more right (if "rights" have meaning any longer) than Mr. Russell. But Mr.

Russell has confessed himself discontented with his ethical theory, and in view of his breadth of concern, one cannot wonder. For its general acceptance would, so far as one can see, be an international disaster. The assumption behind the old League and the new United Nations was that there is such a thing as right and wrong in the conduct of a nation, a right and wrong that do not depend on how it happens to feel at the time. It is implied, for example, that when Japan invaded Manchuria in 1931 she might be wrong, and that by discussion and argument she might be shown to be wrong. It was implied that when the Nazis invaded Poland they might be wrong, even though German public sentiment overwhelmingly approved it. On the theory before us, it would be meaningless to call these nations mistaken; if they felt approval for what they did, then it was right with as complete a justification as could be supplied for the disapproval felt by the rest of the world. In the present dispute between Russia and our own country over southeast Europe, it is nonsense to speak of the right or rational course for either of us to take; if with all the facts before the two parties, each feels approval for its own course, both attitudes are equally justified or unjustified; neither is mistaken; there is no common reason to which they can take an appeal; there are no principles by which an international court could pronounce on the matter; nor would there be any obligation to obey the pronouncement if it were made. This cuts the ground from under any attempt to establish one's case as right or anyone else's case as wrong. So if our friends the subjectivists still hold their theory after I have applied my little ruler to their knuckles, which of course they will, I have but one request to make of them: Do keep it from Mr. Molotov and Mr. Vishinsky.

## THE EMOTIVE THEORY—SUGGESTED READINGS

Ayer, A. J., *Philosophical Essays*, London, Macmillan, 1954, Chap. 10. (proponent)

Carnap, R., *Philosophy and Logical Syntax*, London, Kegan Paul, Trench, Trubner, 1935 Sections 1, 2, and 4. (proponent)

Carritt, E. F., *Ethical and Political Thinking*, Oxford, Clarendon Press, 1947, Chap. 3, pp. 28–44. (critic)

Joad, C. E. M., A *Critique of Logical Positivism*, Chicago, University of Chicago Press, 1950, Chaps. 8 and 9. (critic)

*Logical Positivism and Ethics*, The Aristotelian Society, Supplementary Volume XXII (1948), Articles by W. H. F. Barnes, R. C. Cross, H. J. Paton, and R. Robinson. (proponents and critics)

Stevenson, C. L., *Ethics and Language*, New Haven, Yale University Press, 1944. (proponent)

# C. THE "GOOD REASONS" APPROACH

A third form of the analytic approach to ethics deserves our consideration although it is of such recent origin that no finally definitive statement or criticism of the view is as yet possible. Within the last twenty years, there has arisen in Great Britain a school of philosophy which holds that a careful analysis of the rules of use for ordinary language offers the best means to deal with traditional philosophic problems. Stuart Hampshire, Stephen Toulmin, and R. M. Hare, all members of this new group of philosophers, have written on ethics: each adopts what may be called the "good reasons" approach to moral philosophy.

Hampshire, Toulmin and Hare reject intuitionism (some of Toulmin's criticisms are given above, p. 381). They also find the emotive theory inadequate, insofar as the theory would seem to imply that moral arguments are mere contests of persuasion or force. Hampshire, Toulmin and Hare maintain that the job of ethical philosophy is not thus to dismiss moral argument; rather, moral philosophers should try to discover the different contexts in which we give reasons for our moral decisions, and what, within each of these contexts, we would regard as good reasons.

In the selections to follow, a passage from ARISTOTLE concerning what has been called the "practical syllogism" is presented first. This brief passage, in suggesting that the conclusion of ethical reasoning can be an action rather than a proposition, has been widely cited with approval by philosophers who adopt the "good reasons" approach. In the second selection, HAMPSHIRE criticizes moral philosophers who assume that because moral judgments cannot logically be deduced from factual judgments, an "unbridgeable gulf" therefore exists between these two kinds of judgments. In the third selection, TOULMIN discusses the different kinds of good reasons which may be given to establish both the rightness of an individual action and the rightness of a social practice or rule. In the final selection, HARE insists that all moral choices are *decisions* of *principle;* he contends that we misunderstand and oversimplify the very nature of ethical reasoning when we neglect either its element of general rule or its element of preference and choice.

# ARISTOTLE

ARISTOTLE (384–322 B.C.), one of the greatest figures in the history of philosophy, was
associated with Plato at the Academy in
Athens for nearly twenty years. Upon the
death of Plato, Aristotle left Athens and did
not return for approximately twelve years.
During this period, he spent three years as
tutor of Alexander (later Alexander the
Great), continued his studies, and traveled.
Upon his return to Athens, he founded his
own school, the Lyceum, and devoted his
time to an impressive program of investigation and writing which encompassed all the
learning of his period. His major works include: *Organon* (a collection of logical
treatises), *Physics, Metaphysics, De Anima*
(a psychological treatise), *Nicomachean
Ethics, Eudemian Ethics, Politics,* and
*Poetics.*

## *The Practical Syllogism**

But how is it that thought [viz., sense, imagination, and thought
proper] is sometimes followed by action, sometimes not; sometimes by movement, sometimes not? What happens seems parallel to the case of thinking
and inferring about the immovable objects of science. There the end is the
truth seen (for, when one conceives the two premises, one at once conceives
and comprehends the conclusion), but here the two premises result in a
conclusion which is an action—for example, one conceives that every man
ought to walk, one is a man oneself: straightway one walks; or that, in this
case, no man should walk, one is a man: straightway one remains at rest.
And one so acts in the two cases provided that there is nothing in the one
case to compel or in the other to prevent. Again, I ought to create a good,
a house is good: straightway I make a house. I need a covering, a coat is a
covering: I need a coat. What I need I ought to make, I need a coat: I make
a coat. And the conclusion I must make a coat is an action. And the action
goes back to the beginning or first step. If there is to be a coat, one must first
have B, and if B then A, so one gets A to begin with. Now that the action
is the conclusion is clear. But the premises of action are of two kinds, of
the good and of the possible.

And as in some cases of speculative inquiry we suppress one premise so

* From *De Motu Animalium* of Aristotle, Chap. 7. Translated by A. S. Farquharson in
*The Works of Aristotle,* Vol. V. Copyright, 1912, Clarendon Press. Used by permission.

here the mind does not stop to consider at all an obvious minor premise; for example if walking is good for man, one does not dwell upon the minor 'I am a man'. And so what we do without reflection, we do quickly. For when a man actualizes himself in relation to his object either by perceiving, or imagining or conceiving it, what he desires he does at once. For the actualizing of desire is a substitute for inquiry or reflection. I want to drink, says appetite; this is drink, says sense or imagination or mind: straightway I drink. In this way living creatures are impelled to move and to act, and desire is the last or immediate cause of movement, and desire arises after perception or after imagination and conception. And things that desire to act now create and now act under the influence of appetite or impulse or of desire or wish.


# STUART HAMPSHIRE

STUART HAMPSHIRE (1914–    ) teaches at Oxford University. Concerned primarily with problems of modern logical theory and the theory of language, he has published a number of articles in recent philosophical journals. He is also the author of *Spinoza* (1951) and editor of *The Age of Reason* (1956).


## *Fallacies in Moral Philosophy**

### I

In 1912 there appeared in *Mind* an article by the late Professor Prichard entitled "Does Moral Philosophy Rest on a Mistake?" I wish to ask the same question about contemporary moral philosophy, but to suggest different reasons for an affirmative answer. Most recent academic discussions of moral philosophy have directly or indirectly reflected the conception of the subject-matter of moral philosophy which is stated or implied in Professor Prichard's article; and this conception of the subject was in turn directly derived from Kant. Kant's influence has been so great, that it is now difficult to realise how revolutionary it was; yet I think that his main thesis, now generally accepted without question by philosophers as the starting-point of moral philosophy, had not been advocated or even seriously entertained, by any philosopher who preceded him. I shall suggest that the *unbridgeable*

* "Fallacies in Moral Philosophy," by Stuart Hampshire, *Mind*, LVIII (1949). Used by the kind permission of the author and of the editor of *Mind*.

separation between moral judgments and factual judgments, which Kant introduced, has had the effect, in association with certain logical assumptions, of leading philosophers away from the primary and proper questions of moral philosophy.[1]

What I shall summarily call the post-Kantian thesis, now so widely accepted without question, is: there is an unbridgeable logical gulf between sentences which express statements of fact and sentences which express judgments of value and particularly moral judgments; this absolute logical independence, ignored or not clearly stated by Aristotle, must be the starting-point of moral philosophy, and constitutes its peculiar problem. Post-Kantian philosophers of different logical persuasions have, of course, given very different accounts of the logic and use of value judgments; but they have generally agreed in regarding the logical independence of moral and empirical beliefs as defining the main problem of ethics.

If one reads the Nichomachean Ethics after reading the works of (for example) Professor G. E. Moore or Sir David Ross or Professor Stevenson, one has the impression of confronting a wholly different subject. The first point of difference can be tentatively expressed by saying that Aristotle is almost entirely concerned to analyse the problems of the moral *agent*, while most contemporary moral philosophers seem to be primarily concerned to analyse the problems of the moral *judge* or critic. Aristotle describes and analyses the processes of thought, or types of argument, which lead up to the *choice* of one course of action, or way of life, in preference to another, while most contemporary philosophers describe the arguments (or lack of arguments) which lead up to the acceptance or rejection of a moral *judgment about actions*. Aristotle's Ethics incidentally mentions the kind of arguments we use as spectators in justifying sentences which express moral praise and blame of actions already performed, while many contemporary moral philosophers scarcely mention any other kind of argument. Aristotle's principal question is—What sort of arguments do we use in practical deliberation about policies and courses of action and in choosing one kind of life in preference to another? What are the characteristic differences between moral and theoretical problems? The question posed by most contemporary moral philosophers seems to be—What do we mean by, and how (if at all) do we establish the truth of, sentences used to express moral judgments about our own or other people's actions?

The difference between these two approaches to the problems of moral philosophy emerges most clearly from the analogy between aesthetics and

---

[1] Hume never denied that our moral judgments are based on arguments about matters of fact; he only showed that these arguments are not logically conclusive or deductive arguments.

ethics to which allusion is made both in Aristotle's Ethics and also in most modern discussions of so-called value judgments (e.g., by Sir David Ross in 'The Right and the Good' and by Professor Ayer in 'Language, Truth and Logic'). For Aristotle (as for Plato) the aesthetic analogy which illuminates the problem of moral philosophy is the analogy between the artist or crafts-man's characteristic procedures in designing and executing his work and the similar, but also different, procedures which we all use in designing and executing practical policies in ordinary life. For contemporary moral philoso-phers, largely preoccupied with elucidating sentences which express moral praise or blame (moral 'judgments' in the sense in which a judge gives judgments), the relevant analogy is between sentences expressing moral praise or condemnation and sentences expressing aesthetic praise or con-demnation. As aesthetics has become the study of the logic and language of aesthetic *criticism*, so moral philosophy has become largely the study of the logic and language of moral criticism.

No one will be inclined to dispute that the processes of thought which are characteristic of the artist or craftsman in conceiving and executing his de-signs, are essentially different from the processes of the critic who passes judgment on the artist's work; it is notorious that the processes involved in, and the gifts and training required for, the actual making of a work of art are different from those which are required for the competent appraisal of the work; the artist's problem is not the critic's problem. An aesthetician may choose—and in fact most modern aestheticians have chosen—to confine himself to an analysis of the characteristic arguments involved in arriving at a judgment about a work of art (theories of a special aesthetic emotion, of objective standards of taste, etc.). Alternatively he may analyse and char-acterise the creative process itself (theories of imagination, the relation of technique to conception, the formation of style, the nature of inspiration, etc.). He may decide that the two inquiries, though certainly distinguishable and separable, are in some respects complementary, or at least that there are some questions contained within the first which cannot be answered without a prior answer to the second. But, however complementary they may be, the first inquiry certainly does not include the second. Those who wish to dis-tinguish more clearly the peculiar characteristics of artistic activity, will learn little or nothing from the typical aestheticians' discussions of the objective and subjective interpretations of critical aesthetic judgments. But it seems now to be generally assumed that to ask whether sentences expressing moral praise or blame are to be classified as true or false statements, or alternatively as mere expressions of feeling, is somehow a substitute for the analysis of the processes of thought by which as moral agents we decide what we ought to do and how we ought to behave. Unless this is the underlying assumption, it is difficult to understand why moral philosophers should concentrate attention primarily on the analysis of ethical terms as they are used in sentences expressing moral praise and blame; for we are not primarily interested in moral criticism, or even self-criticism, except in so far as it is directly or indirectly an aid to the solution of practical problems, to deciding what we ought to do in particular situations or types of situation; we do not normally perplex ourselves deeply in moral appraisal for its own sake, in allotting moral marks to ourselves or to other people. The typical moral problem is not a spectator's problem or a problem of classifying or describing conduct, but a problem of practical choice and decision.

But the aesthetic analogy may be misleading, in that the relation of the value judgments of the art critic to the characteristic problems of the artist or craftsman cannot be assumed to be the same as the relation of the sentences expressing moral praise or blame to the problems of the moral agent.[2] To press the analogy would be question-begging, although the validity of the analogy between the problems of ethics and aesthetics is so often assumed. Leaving aside the analogy, the issue is—Is the answer to the question 'What are the distinguishing characteristics of sentences expressing moral praise or blame?' necessarily the same as the answer to the question 'What are the distinguishing characteristics of moral problems as they present themselves to us as practical agents?'? Unless these two questions are identical, or unless the first includes the second, much of contemporary moral philosophy is concerned with a relatively trivial side-issue, or is at the very least incomplete. My thesis is that the answer to the second question must contain the answer to the first, but that, if one tries to answer the first question without approaching it as part of the second, the answer will tend to be, not only incomplete, but positively misleading; and that the now most widely accepted philosophical interpretations of moral judgments, their logical status and peculiarities, are radically misleading for this reason. They purport to be logical characterisations of moral judgments and of the distinguishing features of moral arguments, but in these characterisations the *primary* use of moral judgments ( = decisions) is largely or even entirely ignored.

---

[2] In so far as we now distinguish between the creative artist and the mere craftsman, a work of art by definition is not the answer to any problem; the artist is only said to have problems when conceived as a craftsman, that is, as having technical problems of devising means towards a given or presumed end. Where there is no problem posed, there can be no question of a right or wrong solution of it. Therefore the critic of poetry cannot be expected to show how the poem should be re-written; he describes, but he does not prescribe or make a practical judgment, as does the critic of conduct or technique. So the aesthetic analogy misleads in at least this respect; the valued critic of art excels in description and classification; he is not the artist's adviser, while moral or technical criticism is necessarily the giving of practical advice.

## II

Suppose (what probably occurs occasionally in most people's experience) one is confronted with a difficult and untrivial situation in which one is in doubt what one ought to do, and then, after full consideration of the issues involved, one arrives at a conclusion. One's conclusion, reached after deliberation, expressed in the sentence 'x is the best thing to do in these circumstances,' is a pure or primary moral judgment (the solution of a practical problem). It is misleading to the point of absurdity to describe this sentence, as used in such a context, as meaningful only in the sense in which an exclamation is meaningful, or as having no literal significance, or as having the function merely of expressing and evoking feeling. It is also misleading to describe it as a statement about the agent's feeling or attitude; for such a description suggests that the judgment would be defended, if attacked, primarily by an appeal to introspection. It is surely misleading to describe the procedure by which such a judgment or decision is established as right as one of comparing degrees of moral emotion towards alternative courses of action. I am supposing (what is normal in such cases) that the agent has reasoned and argued about the alternatives, and am asserting that he would then justify his conclusion, if it were attacked, by reference to these arguments; and a statement about his own moral feelings or attitudes would not be, within the ordinary use of language, either a necessary or sufficient justification. Therefore the characterisation of such judgments as purely, or even largely, reports of feelings or attitudes is at the least incomplete and misleadingly incomplete, because in this characterisation the typical procedures of deliberation on which the judgment is based are suppressed or ignored. It is also paradoxical and misleading to introduce the word 'intuition,' as another group of post-Kantian philosophers have done, in describing the procedure by which such a judgment is arrived at, or by which it is justified and defended; for the force of the word 'intuition' is to suggest that the conclusion is not established by any recognised form of argument, by any ratiocinative process involving a succession of steps which are logically criticisable; the word 'intuition' carries the suggestion that we do not, or even cannot, deliberate and calculate in deciding what we ought to do; but we always can and often actually do deliberate and calculate.

If the procedure of practical deliberation does not conform, either in its intermediate steps or in the form of its conclusions, with any forms of argument acknowledged as respectable in logical text-books, this is a deficiency of the logical text-books. Or rather it is a mistake in the *interpretation* of text-books of logic to assume that they provide, or that they are intended to provide, patterns of all forms of reasoning or arguments which can properly be described as rational argument. Arguments may be, in the ordinary and wider sense, rational, without being included among the types of argument which are ordinarily studied by logicians, since logicians are generally concerned exclusively with the types of argument which are characteristic of the *a priori* and empirical sciences. There are other patterns of argument habitually used outside the sciences, which may be described as more or less rational in the sense that they are more or less strictly governed by recognised (though not necessarily formulated) rules of relevance. If one criticises a sequence of sentences by saying that assertion or denial of the earlier members of the sequence is irrelevant to acceptance or rejection of their successors, then this sequence is being regarded as constituting an argument. Aristotle at least remarks that not all arguments are theoretical arguments, terminating in a conclusion which is intended as a statement, either factual or logically true; there are also practical arguments—he naturally says 'syllogisms'—the form of which is similar in many respects to some types of theoretical argument, but which are also characteristically different in their form; in particular they differ in the form of their conclusion, which is not a theoretical or true-or-false statement, but has the distinctive form of a practical judgment, e.g., 'this is the right action' or 'this is the best thing to do,' or 'this ought to be done.'

Even when sentences containing moral terms are used by spectators (not agents) in contexts in which they seem to be in fact associated with a purely emotional reaction to a decision or action, it is misleadingly incomplete to characterise them as having the logical force only, or largely, of expressions of, or statements about, the speaker's or writer's feelings or attitudes. If a purely critical and apparently emotional moral judgment of this kind is challenged and needs to be defended and justified, it will be justified by the same kind of arguments which one would have used as an agent in practical deliberation. If I am not prepared to produce such practical arguments, pointing to what ought to have been done, I shall admit that I am not making a genuine moral judgment, but merely expressing or reporting my own feelings; and I shall admit that it was misleading to use the form of sentence ordinarily associated with moral judgments, and not with expressions of feeling. Doubtless many sentences containing moral terms are ambiguous, and may be normally used both as expressions of practical judgments and as expressions of feeling; but the important point is that, if challenged about our intentions, we are required to *distinguish* between such uses; and our languages, by providing the distinctive quasi-imperative form of the practical judgment, enable us to distinguish. But moral philosophers, tacitly assuming that moral judgments must be descriptive statements, have represented a moral problem as a critic's or spectator's problem of proper classification and description.

If, following Aristotle, one begins by describing how moral problems differ both from technical and theoretical problems, one will have begun to answer the question about the distinctive nature of moral judgments, even in their purely critical use. But if one begins by separating them from their context in practical deliberation, and considers them as quasi-theoretical[3] expressions of moral praise and condemnation, the resulting characterisation of them must be misleadingly incomplete.

### III

The fact that moral judgments, in spite of the peculiarity of their form as practical judgments, are established by familiar patterns of argument, has been under-emphasised by post-Kantian moral philosophers as a consequence of three connected logical doctrines: (*a*) the doctrine that so-called value judgments cannot be derived from factual judgments: (*b*) the doctrine that, although we deliberate and argue about the facts of moral situations (e.g., about the probable consequences of various possible actions), no further argument is possible when once the facts of the situation have been determined; we are thus left in every case of practical deliberation with (*c*) an ultimate moral judgment, which cannot be replaced by any statement of fact, or by an empirical statement of any kind, and which cannot itself be defended by further argument. From no consideration of facts, or accumulation of factual knowledge, can we ever deduce a moral judgment of the form 'this ought to be done' or 'this is the right action in these circumstances.' Therefore all appeal to the procedure of deliberation is irrelevant to the real problem, which is the analysis or characterisation of these *ultimate* moral judgments.

The fallacy in this position, as I have stated it, emerges in the words 'derive' and 'deduce.' It is only in limiting cases that, in describing the logic of any class of sentences of ordinary discourse, one can reasonably expect to find another class of sentences from which the problem-sentences are logically deducible. Statements about physical things cannot be deduced, or logically derived, from statements about sensations; statements about people's character or dispositions cannot be deduced, or logically derived from, statements about their behaviour; yet in both cases the truth of the first kind of statement is established exclusively by reference to the second kind. In general, one kind of sentence may be established and defended exclusively by reference to another kind, without the first kind being deducible, or logically derivable, from the second. When as philosophers we ask how a particular kind of sen-

---

[3] To pose the problem of ethics as the problem of 'ethical predicates' or 'non-natural characteristics,' is at the outset to suggest that moral judgments are to be interpreted as a peculiar kind of descriptive statement.

tence is to be categorised or described, we are asking ourselves by what sort of arguments it is established and how we justify its use if it is disputed; to explain its logic and meaning is generally to describe and illustrate by examples the kind of sentences which are conventionally accepted as sufficient grounds for its assertion or rejection. So we may properly elucidate moral or practical judgments by saying that they are established and supported by arguments consisting of factual judgments of a particular range, while admitting that they are never strictly deducible, or in this sense logically derivable, from any set of factual judgments.

Certainly no practical judgment is logically deducible from any set of statements of fact; for if practical judgments were so deducible, they would be redundant; we could confine ourselves simply to factual or theoretical judgments; this is in effect what strict Utilitarians, such as Bentham, proposed that we should do. Bentham recommended the removal of distinctively moral terms from the language, so that moral problems would be replaced by technical problems, or problems of applied science. He made this proposal quite self-consciously and deliberately, wishing to introduce a science of morals, in which all moral problems would be experimentally decidable as technical problems. The distinctive form in which moral problems are posed and moral conclusions expressed disappears in his usage, precisely because he makes arguments about matters of fact *logically conclusive* in settling moral problems; and it is precisely to this *replacement* of moral terms that critics of strict Utilitarians have always objected (e.g., Professor G. E. Moore in *Principia Ethica*); they have argued that Utilitarians confuse the reasons on which moral judgments may be based with those judgments themselves; and this confusion arises from supposing that the reasons must be logically conclusive reasons, so that to accept the empirical premises and to deny the moral conclusion is self-contradictory. But it does not follow from the fact that moral or practical judgments are not in their normal use so deducible that they must be described as ultimate, mysterious, and removed from the sphere of rational discussion. All argument is not deduction, and giving reasons in support of a judgment or statement is not necessarily, or even generally, giving logically conclusive reasons.

Once this assumption is removed, it is possible to reconsider, without philosophical prejudice, what is the difference and the relation between ordinary empirical statements and moral judgments as we actually use them when we are arguing with ourselves, or with others, about what we ought to do. It is important to consider examples of practical or moral problems which are neither trivial in themselves nor abstractly described; for it is only by reflecting on our procedure when confronted with what would ordinarily be called a genuine moral problem that the characteristic types of argument can be seen clearly deployed. A simplified variant of the situation presented in a recent novel[4] may serve the purpose. Suppose that I am convinced that if I continue to live, I cannot avoid inflicting great and indefinitely prolonged unhappiness on one or both of two people, and at the same time on myself; by committing suicide without detection I can avoid this accumulation of unhappiness; I therefore decide, after careful deliberation, that the right or best thing to do is to commit suicide. This is a moral judgment of the primary kind. (Having reached this conclusion, I may of course in any particular case fail to act in accordance with it; as Aristotle points out, deciding *that* x is the best thing to do and deciding *to* do x are both distinguishable and separable.) Suppose that in this case the moral judgment, which is the conclusion of my deliberation, is challenged by someone who at the same time agrees with me in my assessment of all the facts of the situation; that is, he agrees with me about the probable consequences of all the possible courses of action, but does not agree with my conclusion that it is right to commit suicide. An argument develops; we each give our reasons for saying that suicide under these circumstances is right or wrong. However the argument may develop in detail, it will generally exhibit the following features. (1) Although it is assumed that my disputant agrees with me about the facts of this particular situation (probable consequences of various actions, etc.), he will in his argument appeal to other facts or beliefs about the world, which are not strictly describable as beliefs about the facts of this particular situation. For instance, we might both recognise as relevant a dispute, partly empirical and partly logical, about whether there is life after death, and whether the Christian dogmas on this subject are true or significant; or we may become involved in a largely historical argument about the social effects of suicide; and it would be recognised as pertinent to produce psychological arguments to the effect that intense unhappiness is often preferred to mere loneliness and *therefore* (and this 'therefore' is not the sign of an entailment) it would be better not to desert the other two people involved. *The point is that it does not follow from the fact that two people are in agreement about the facts of a particular situation, but disagree in their moral judgment, that their disagreement is ultimate and admits of no further rational argument*; hence (2) our disagreement about the moral or practical conclusion, which is not a disagreement about the facts of the particular situation, is nevertheless, a disagreement to which empirical arguments, beliefs about an indefinitely wide range of matters of fact, are recognised to be relevant. If we are deliberating or arguing about whether suicide is right or wrong in these particular circumstances (or in any circumstances), then our psychological, historical and religious beliefs are always taken to be relevant parts of the

[4] *The Heart of the Matter*, by Graham Greene.

argument. By representing so-called value judgments as ultimate and logically divorced from ordinary factual judgments, philosophers have implicitly or explicitly suggested that such sentences as 'suicide is always wrong' or 'suicide is wrong in these circumstances' cannot be defended or refuted by appeals to facts or to the empirical sciences. This paradox is a legacy of Kant's anxiety to underline as strongly as possible the difference between practical problems which are moral problems and those which are purely technical problems. Almost all previous philosophers—and most people without Kantian or other philosophical prejudices—have assumed accumulating knowledge, or changing beliefs arising out of the study of history, psychology, anthropology and other empirical sciences, to be relevant to their moral judgments; to be relevant, not in the sense that the falsity of moral judgments previously accepted as true can be *deduced* from some empirical propositions of history, psychology or any natural science, but in the sense in which (for example) propositions about somebody's conduct are relevant to propositions about his character; that is, previous moral judgments are shown to be groundless, the empirical propositions on which they were based having been contradicted as scientific or historical knowledge increases. The conflicting moral conclusions of a Marxist and a Christian Fundamentalist, or the differences which may arise even between two contemporary and similarly educated liberal unbelievers, will generally (but not always or necessarily) be shown in argument to rest on different empirical or at least corrigible beliefs about the constitution of the universe. Whenever we argue about any moral question which is not trivial, our beliefs and assumptions, however rudimentary and half-formulated, about psychological, sociological and probably theological questions are recognised as relevant, as logically involved in the nature of the dispute.

The result of the supposed argument about my judgment that suicide is the right policy in this particular circumstance might be that I am convinced that my judgment was wrong, and am persuaded that suicide is not the right policy. I might be persuaded to withdraw my original judgment, either because I have been made to recognise a fault in the logic of my previous argument, or because I have been persuaded to abandon admittedly relevant beliefs about matters of fact, or because my attention has been directed to new facts as being relevant to the decision, facts which I had known but the relevance of which I had previously overlooked. To direct attention to further known facts as relevant to a judgment is perhaps the most important effect and function of oral arguments or practical deliberation (e.g., of giving practical advice). It is misleading to speak of 'the facts of a situation' in such a way as to suggest that there must be a closed set of propositions which, once established, precisely determine the situation.[5] The situations in which we must act or abstain from acting, are 'open' in the sense that they cannot be uniquely described and finally circumscribed. Situations do not present themselves with their labels attached to them; if they did, practical problems would be conclusively soluble theoretical problems, the philosopher's dream; but ἐν τῇ αἰσθήσει ἡ κρίσις—the crux is in the labelling, or the decision depends on how we see the situation.

For these reasons the logical divorce between so-called judgments of value and factual judgments is misleading; for arguments about practical conclusions are arguments about facts. Our moral or practical judgments— 'x is the right or best course of action (in these or in all circumstances)'— are corrigible by experience and observation; we feel certain about some, and very doubtful about others.

## IV

Certainly there may (logically) be cases in which we cannot attribute conflicting solutions of practical moral problems to conflicting beliefs about matters of fact; that is, two disputants, in giving their reasons for conflicting moral judgments, may be unable to find among their reasons any empirical proposition which is accepted by one of them and rejected by the other. It is logically possible that A and B should agree entirely e.g., about the effects of capital punishment, and furthermore should find no relevant differences in their general psychological or sociological or other beliefs, and yet disagree as to whether capital punishment should or should not now be abolished. However rare such situations may be (and I believe them to be much more rare than is commonly allowed) such so-called 'ultimate' moral differences may occur. Both A and B, if they can claim to be making a moral judgment and not merely expressing their own feelings about, or attitudes towards, capital punishment, will be able to give the reasons which seem to them sufficient to justify their conclusion; but what is accepted by A as a sufficient reason for a practical conclusion is not accepted by B as a sufficient reason and *vice versa*. They may then argue further to ensure that each does recognise the reason which he is claiming to be sufficient in this case as sufficient in other cases; but, when this consistency of use is once established, the argument must terminate. How is such an 'ultimate' or irresoluble difference about a moral judgment properly described?

[5] The word 'fact,' here as always, is treacherous, involving the old confusion between the actual situation and the description of it; the situation is given, but not 'the facts of the situation'; to state the facts is to analyse and interpret the situation. And just this is the characteristic difficulty of actual practical decisions, which disappears in the text-book cases, where the 'relevant facts' are pre-selected. So the determining arguments are cut out of the text-book, and the gap is filled by 'intuition' or feeling.

Compare this ultimate difference about the practical judgment with a similar ultimate difference about a theoretical judgment: if A and B were to disagree about whether somebody is intelligent, and yet find that they did not disagree about the facts (actual behaviour) or probabilities (how he is likely to behave under hypothetical conditions) on which their judgment is based, they would describe their difference as a difference in the use of the word 'intelligent'; they would say 'you use a different criterion of intelligence, and so do not mean by "intelligent" exactly what I mean.'[6] Similarly when it has been shown that A and B generally apply wholly or largely different tests in deciding whether something ought or ought not to be done, they might properly describe their so-called ultimate difference by saying that they do not both mean the same, or exactly the same, thing when they say that something ought or ought not to be done; and in most such cases of ulti-mate or irresoluble moral differences this is in fact what we do say—that different societies (and even different individuals within the same society) may have more or less different moral terminologies, which are not mutually translatable. But of practical judgments one cannot say that differences which are in principle irresoluble are *simply* terminological misunderstandings and in *no* sense genuine contradictions; for it is the distinguishing characteristic of practical judgments that they have a prescriptive or quasi-imperative force as part of their meaning. There is therefore one sense in which, when A says that capital punishment ought to be abolished and B says that it ought not, they are contradicting each other; their judgments contradict each other in the sense in which two conflicting commands or recommendations may be said to contradict each other. They can only argue about which of their prescriptions is right if they can agree on some common criteria of rightness. A, following the practice of all reforming moralists and many moral philosophers, may try to influence B's actions by giving moral reasons for preferring his own criteria of use to B's use; but in his advocacy of his own use of moral terms, he will be using his moral terms in his own way. The argument might have shown B that his conclusion was wrong in A's sense of 'wrong' or even in his own sense of 'wrong'; but no argument can show that B *must* use the criteria which A uses and so much attach the same meaning (in this sense) to moral terms as A. Between two consistently applied terminologies, whether in theoretical science or in moral decision, ultimately we must simply choose; we can give reasons for our choice, but not reasons for reasons for . . . *ad infinitum.*

[6] 'What do you mean by saying that he is intelligent?' is ordinarily interpreted as the same question as 'what are your reasons for saying or why do you say, that he is intelligent?' Similarly, 'What do you mean by saying that that was a wrong decision?' is the same question as 'Why do you say that that was a wrong decision?' To find the different reasons in different cases is to find the meaning of 'wrong,' although no *one* set of reasons is *the* meaning.

## V

We may find that many people do not deliberate and so can scarcely be said to make moral judgments, but simply act as they have been conditioned to act, and, when challenged, repeat the moral sentences which they have been taught to repeat or merely state or express personal feelings or attitudes. A second, and much smaller class, act generally, and even wholly, on impulse, in the sense that they do not propose practical problems to themselves or choose policies, but simply do whatever they feel inclined to do—and such people are to be distinguished from those who have *decided that* to act on impulse, or to do what one feels inclined to do, is the right policy; for this is to make a moral judgment. But the great majority of people for some part of their lives are thinking about what is the best thing to do, sometimes reaching a conclusion and failing to act on it, sometimes reaching a conclusion which, in the light of corrections of their empirical beliefs or their logic, they later recognise to have been a wrong conclusion, and sometimes reaching a conclusion which they are prepared to defend by argument and acting in accordance with it.

'Thinking what is the best thing to do' describes a procedure which it is unprofitable, if not impossible, to analyse, or find a paraphrase for, in general terms without constant reference to specific cases. Aristotle begins by describing it as calculating means to a vaguely conceived end (happiness or welldoing), the nature of the end being more precisely determined by the means chosen as involved in its realisation. But he progressively qualifies and complicates this schematic account in such a way as to suggest that to make a moral decision is not to choose means to an already decided end, but to choose a policy of means-to-end which is judged right or wrong as a whole. Practical problems are (as Kant emphasised and over-emphasised) sub-divisible into moral and purely technical problems; the choice of the most efficient means to an already determined end is not called a moral choice. It is the defining characteristic of a moral problem, that it requires an unconditional decision, the choice of an action or policy as a whole.

## VI

There is another and related logical fallacy, often implicitly assumed and not explicitly stated, which has led philosophers to describe moral or practical judgments as expressions or reports of feeling or as established by *a priori* intuitions, and to neglect their normal occurrence as the corrigible conclusions of arguments involving the facts of a particular situation and our general beliefs about the world; this is the fallacy of assuming that all literally significant sentences must correspond to something, or describe something. As ordinary empirical statements were said to correspond to facts, so some philosophers have introduced the word 'values' in order that there should be something to which moral (and aesthetic) judgments can be said to correspond; we are said to 'intuit' or to 'apprehend' these values, these words being used to suggest an analogy with sense-perception. Other philosophers, wishing to define the world as the totality of facts, or as the objects of sense and introspection, have inferred that, as moral judgments cannot be said to correspond to anything in the external world, they must either correspond to something in the internal world (i.e., to feelings) or, failing that, that they cannot be admitted to be literally significant. The question 'what do moral judgments correspond to?' or 'what do they describe?' suggests itself particularly to those who are preoccupied with the critical use of these judgments as expressions of retrospective praise or blame; in so far as we relate them to practical deliberations and decisions, we come to recognise them as not descriptions of, but prescriptions for, actions. Practical judgments, no less than theoretical or descriptive statements, are in the natural sense of the words, literally significant, although they do not in the normal sense describe. If I say 'this is (or would have been) the right action in these circumstances,' this judgment can be significantly denied; but, as it is not a descriptive statement or statement of fact, the denial is not normally expressed in the form 'it is *false* that this is the best action in these circumstances'; 'true' and 'false' are more naturally used with theoretical judgments and statements of fact.[7] Of course this distinction between true or false descriptive statements and right or wrong practical judgments is not absolute and clear; many sentences are partly descriptive and are partly expressions of practical judgments. But there is a distinction which emerges clearly in simple cases of pure moral judgments and purely descriptive statements. One *can* describe somebody's behaviour or character without making any moral judgment (i.e., prescription), even if in fact prescriptions and descriptions are often almost inextricably combined.

## VII

There is (I think) a widespread impression that the concentration of academic moral philosophers on the attempt to *define* ethical expressions—'good,' 'right,' 'ought,' etc.—as being the principal problem of moral philosophy has tended to make the subject sterile and unenlightening. One is inclined to say that it does not *matter* whether 'right,' as ordinarily used, is definable in terms of 'good' or not. There is the feeling that the clarifications which one expects from the moral philosopher cannot be answered by verbal definitions or the discovery of paraphrases. And I think this ap-

[7] Although we can speak of believing that this is the right action we cannot speak of evidence that it is right. 'Evidence' is tied to statements which are true or false.

parently philistine impatience with the search of verbal definitions or equivalences has good logical grounds. If we wish to clarify our own or somebody else's use of moral terms, the discovery of verbal equivalences or paraphrases among these terms is not an answer, but, at the most, a preliminary step towards an answer. I can become clear about what somebody means by saying 'this is the right action in these circumstances' only by finding out under what conditions he makes this judgment, and what reasons (and there may be many) he regards as sufficient to justify it. What we want to know, in clarification of differences in our use of moral (or aesthetic) terms, is—What makes me (in the logical, not the causal sense) decide that this is the right action? There is no reason to expect a simple answer in terms of a single formula, e.g., 'it is likely to increase happiness.' But to search only for definitions or verbal equivalences is to assume that there must be a single sufficient reason from which I always and necessarily derive my judgment. This is another expression of the fundamental fallacy of thinking of analysis or clarification of the standard use of words or sentences as necessarily a matter of exhibiting deducibilities or entailments. If I am asked what I mean by saying of someone that he is intelligent, I explain my use of the word by describing specimens of the type of behaviour to which I apply the word; I give some specimens of the types of statements about his behaviour which would be taken as sufficient grounds for asserting or denying that he is intelligent. Similarly, one can only clarify the use of the principal moral (or aesthetic) terms—'good,' 'right,' 'ought,' etc.—by describing specimens of conduct to which they are applied, that is, by quoting the different characteristics of actions which are normally and generally taken to be sufficient grounds for deciding that they are the right actions. The type of analysis which consists in defining, or finding synonyms for the moral terms of a particular language cannot illuminate the nature of moral decisions or practical problems; it is no more than local dictionary-making, or the elimination of redundant terms, which is useful only as a preliminary to the study of typical moral arguments. An informative treatise on ethics— or on the ethics of a particular society or person—would contain an accumulation of examples selected to illustrate the kind of decisions which are said to be right in various circumstances, and the reasons given and the arguments used in concluding that they are right. An uninformative treatise on ethics consists of specimens of moral sentences, separated from actual or imaginable contexts of argument about particular practical problems, and treated as texts for the definition of moral terms; and many academic text-books follow this pattern.

*Summary*—The four logically related fallacies underlying the typical post-Kantian approach to moral philosophy are (*a*) The assimilation of moral or practical judgments to descriptive statements, which is associated with concentration on the use of moral terms in sentences expressing a spectator's praise or blame; (b) the inference from the fact that moral or practical judgment cannot be logically derived from statements of fact that they cannot be based on, or established exclusively by reference to, beliefs about matters of fact; hence theories that moral judgments must be ultimate and irrational, that they are established by intuition or are not literally significant; (c) the assumption that all literally significant sentences must correspond to or describe something; moral decisions do not correspond to or describe anything, but they may, nevertheless, be said to be rational or irrational, right or wrong;[8] (d) the confusion between clarifying the use of ethical terms with discovering definitions of, or verbal equivalences between, these terms; the search for definitions is another expression of the old obsession of philosophers with entailment and deducibility as the only admissible relation between sentences in rational argument. To interpret 'rational argument' so narrowly is, although misleading, not in itself fallacious; but if, on the basis of this arbitrary restriction, moral judgments are relegated to a logical limbo, labelled 'emotive,' the study of the characteristic logic of these sentences, and of the types of argument in which they occur, is obscured and suppressed.

[8] 'I decided that $x$ was the right thing to do' is a descriptive statement, true or false; but '$x$ was the right thing to do' is a practical or moral judgment, right or wrong.

# STEPHEN E. TOULMIN

STEPHEN EDELSTON TOULMIN (1922–    )
is Professor of Philosophy at the University
of Leeds, England. Writing from the viewpoint of contemporary analytic philosophy,
his major works include: *An Examination of
the Place of Reason in Ethics* (1950), *The
Philosophy of Science* (1953), and *The Uses
of Argument* (1958).

## An Examination of the Place of Reason in Ethics*

### Chapter X

### The Function and Development of Ethics

### 10.3 The Development of Ethics. (I)

Historically and psychologically alike, the development of ethics is most conveniently described in two contrasted stages. This division we shall find later reflected in the logic of ethics.

The first and most obvious way of preventing conflicts of interest in a community (whether a tribe or a family) is for all its members to have the same aims, the same interests, the same desires, hopes and fears; in fact the same dispositions. In its early stages, therefore, morality boils down to 'doing the done thing': and this is true, both of the way in which a child learns from its parents, and, in social pre-history, of moral codes. Primitive ethics is 'deontological,' a matter of rigid duties, taboos, customs and commandments. It prevents conflicts of interest by keeping the dispositions of all concerned aligned, and condemns behaviour directed away from the prescribed aims. Further, these aims are not advocated but imposed, the use of ethical language being part of the behaviour adopted by 'those in authority' for enforcing co-operation: so no wonder if ethical utterances are often 'rhetorical.'

Respect for fixed 'social practices' (or 'done things'), though most characteristic of primitive morality, continues throughout the later stages of development, and can be recognised in our own societies. Although 'doing the done thing' may be merely conventionalism, it may equally be anything but that; especially in those situations in which *some* common practice must be adopted and, within limits, it does not matter what.

The Rule of the Road is a good example. By appealing to this practice, the statements, 'It is right to drive on the left in England' and 'You ought to be driving on the left,' may be used to alter the hearer's disposition, so that in the future he drives on the left. (The ethical judgements are here used 'persuasively.') But the same utterances can also be used simply to draw attention to the rule, or to evince the speaker's displeasure.

Now consider two more subtle examples: first, that of the schoolboy who hears that he has been given his cricket colours. His immediate reaction will probably be one of pleasure, and he will cry out, 'Why, that is good news!' But his school-fellows may feel differently about it, especially if they suspect that he has been given them only because the cricket captain is fond of him. Then they will do their best to make him feel that his rejoicing is misplaced, pointing out (for example) that another, better batsman has had to go without colours as a result. If the schoolboy has a tender conscience, accepts the 'principle' that cricket colours should go to the best cricketers, and not just to the captain's favourites, and admits both that he is rather a friend of the captain's, and that the man who has had to go without has the better batting record and more 1st XI matches to his credit; then he may eventually say, 'Well, naturally I was pleased at the time, but I see now that I *ought not really* to have been given them.'

In this example, several of the most characteristic features of ethics are displayed. To start with, an ethical term is used simply to evince pleasure. Next, contrary feelings are aroused in, and evinced by others. These are concerned at the way in which the schoolboy's award has cut across another's interest—in this case, someone's 'natural right' to colours, based on a generally accepted practice. (The conflict between one schoolboy's winning his colours, and the other's failure to obtain them, is a typically ethical one, in that it is only possible for one of them to have them.) Reasons are advanced for the view that the award was not *really good*. The principle is appealed to as authority. Finally, the schoolboy admits the facts, accepts the principle, and agrees that, though the news originally *seemed* good to him, it was not *really* good.

Again, suppose that I am already rich, and then win £10,000 in a lottery. At first, I may excusably rejoice. But now someone may try to persuade me that I *ought not* to be so glad. He may remind me of all the shillings paid by labourers out of their wages, that went to make up my prize; he may point out that I already have as much money as I have any use for; and he may insist that the prize-money would do more good anywhere but in my bank. In the end, I may come to admit that, however pleased I was to win the prize, it was, all in all, not a good thing that I did. Though it *seemed* good to me at first, it was not *really* good. In this case, a number of 'principles' may be appealed to—for instance, the 'principles' that opportunities for satisfying people's needs should not be neglected; that no one should retain more than he needs of anything while others suffer through going without; and that one should not accept anything which has been got by unnecessary suffering.

Appeal to a 'principle' in ethics is like appeal to a 'law' in science: 'principles' and 'laws of nature' may both be thought of as shorthand summaries of experience—as condensed comparisons. If I explain the 'bending' of a stick in water by reference to the laws of optics, my purpose is to relate the present experience to past observations and experiments; the explanation in terms of 'Snell's Law' is then shorthand for, 'If you had put the stick above a bonfire, you'd have expected it to shimmer in the heated air, wouldn't you? And if. . . . And if. . . . So you see, the look of bentness in this case was to be expected.' Likewise, appeal to the 'principle' that you should not accept anything got by unnecessary suffering can be thought of as shorthand for, 'If you found out that your garden was being cultivated by a team of slaves, who were whipped until they produced all the flowers and vegetables you asked for, you wouldn't ask for them any more, would you? And if. . . . And if. . . . So you see, winning £10,000 in this lottery was nothing to be so pleased about.'

Like scientific theories again, all principles are not equally well established; some refer to wider, some to narrower ranges of experience. There is an air of conventionality about the principle that the best cricketers shall be given their colours, which is absent from the principles involved in the second example. The principle that all promises ought to be kept may seem less compelling than the principle that unnecessary suffering ought to be prevented; but, equally, it is less conventional than the rules by which colours are distributed. We shall have to return to these differences in discussing the next stage of development.

### 10.4 The Development of Ethics. (II)

In any particular community, certain principles are current—that is to say, attention is paid to certain types of argument, as appealing to accepted criteria of 'real goodness,' 'real rightness,' 'real obligation,' etc. From these, the members of the community are expected to try and regulate their lives and judgements. And such a set of principles, of 'prima facie obligations,'[1] of 'categorical imperatives,'[2] is what we call the 'moral code' of the community.

At the primitive stage of development, this is something fixed and unalter-

[1] W. D. Ross, *The Right and the Good*, p. 19. [this volume, p. 350.]
[2] Immanuel Kant, *Fundamental Principles of the Metaphysics of Ethics*, tr. Abbott (10th ed., 1926), p. 37 [this volume, p. 137.]

able. There is no room for criticism of the moral code as a whole, as there is of a particular action, expression of pleasure, or ethical judgement. However, the methods used in primitive communities to harmonise the desires and actions of their members are very crude and, although at first they may do their job, something always happens to throw doubt on them. New opportunities emerge. People discover that different principles of the code conflict. As a result of contact with other peoples having different codes, or of changes within the community, they begin to question not only the rightness of particular actions but also the standards laid down in the code. They realise that, as a result of these changes, the present code is causing frustration and suffering which, by making a specific alteration in the practices of the community, could be avoided—and avoided without incurring any comparable evil.

The same situation arises within the family, when the growing child, having learnt to accept appeal to a principle as an argument for and against actions, begins to question the need for some of the principles with which he has been brought up, and to argue that they cause needless annoyance. When this happens, he ceases to accept authority as the sole moral argument, and becomes himself a 'responsible being.'

At this stage, there are two possible reactions: either for those in authority —those who enforce the existing 'code'—to assert its absolute rightness, and to attempt to legislate for every possibility; or for them to agree, first to criticism, and eventually to modification of the code, so as to remove its objectionable features. If the first course is adopted, the continual changes in the circumstances of the community tend only to aggravate the situation: the second course, on the other hand, represents a natural extension of the process by which moral codes themselves grow out of conflicts of interest— i.e., it takes account of the function of ethics.

When it is recognised that the members of a community have the right to criticise the existing practices, and to suggest new ones, a new phase in the development of ethics begins. In this phase, it is the *motives* of actions and the *results* of social practices, rather than 'the letter of the law,' which are emphasised. The 'deontological' code was at first supreme; the 'teleological' criterion now amplifies it, and provides a standard by which to criticise it. This does not mean that morality becomes wholly teleological, as Utilitarianism would suggest. All that happens is that the initially inflexible system of taboos is transformed into a *developing* moral code—a code which, in unambiguous cases, remains mandatory, but whose interpretation in equivocal cases and whose future development are controlled by appeal to the function of ethics; that is, to the general requirement that preventable suffering shall be avoided.

The contrast between the two main phases of development is strikingly reflected in the contrast between the Old and New Testaments. The moral code of the Israelites—a nomadic tribe in a hostile environment—was understandably strict; but, in the more settled atmosphere of Palestine under Roman rule, anomalies arose in this code. Jesus was therefore able to criticise contemporary ethical practices in a spirit to which the Pharisees could hardly take open exception. Whatever form their questions took, they could not get him to say that his teaching was meant to *supersede* the Law and the Prophets: in fact, whenever there was any discussion of the Jewish code, he made it clear that he took it as his starting-point. Instead, it was his aim throughout to get the existing code applied in a more intelligent manner: to point out that the prevention of human suffering is more important than formal respect for obsolete customs. Thus, when challenged in the Temple about the propriety of healing the sick on the Sabbath, he asked, 'Whether is it lawful on the sabbath days to do good or to do evil? to save life or for to destroy it?', and went on to heal the man with a withered hand. Again, in a phrase echoed by Kant[3] he declared, 'Whatsoever ye would that men should do to you, even so do ye to them. This is the law and the Prophets.' He was ready to criticise the existing code, certainly; but only by reference to its function—the function which he expressed, in his own way, as the 'New Commandment,' to love one another.

We can trace the beginnings of this new outlook further back: it is clearly to be seen, breaking through the old, rigid morality, in the more 'advanced' of the Greek tragedies. Contrast, for example, the approaches which different dramatists adopted towards the same traditional stories, and the lessons which they drew from them. Both Sophocles and Euripedes wrote plays, which have survived, using the story of Electra and Orestes as their foundation. Sophocles produced an archaic 'drama of duty.' In his play, the central figures perform their ritual act of vengeance—the murder of their own mother, Clytemnestra—without emotion: 'there is no shrinking back, no question of conscience at all.' Euripides' play is in vivid contrast: it is a psychological 'drama of motive.' After the murder, Orestes and Electra suffer 'a long agony of remorse'; and even the gods, through the mouth of Castor, are made to condemn the act. For Euripides, the blood-feud has lost its absolute authority. For Sophocles, however, old ways held good, and there could be no question of blame.

We can now see how it is that different 'moral principles' have such different degrees of 'conventionality.' To return to the three examples discussed before: the 'duty' to give cricket-colours to the best cricketers, the

---

[3] Cf. *Fundamental Principles of the Metaphysic of Ethics* (tr. Abbott), p. 66: 'Act always on such a maxim as thou canst at the same time will to be a universal law.'

'duty' to keep a promise, and the 'duty' to prevent avoidable suffering. The reason why the first of these appears comparatively conventional, the last comparatively compelling, is clear, when we bear in mind the overall requirement that, wherever we can, we shall prevent suffering from being inflicted upon others. To abolish the custom of giving cricket-colours would have a trivial effect by these standards; to abandon the social practice of promise-keeping might, by the same standards, be expected to have intolerable results; and the third principle cannot be rejected, without completely abandoning the very ideas of 'duty' and of 'ethics.'

## Chapter XI

### The Logic of Moral Reasoning

It is in relation to this background that we have to discuss the logic of ethical reasoning. I do not mean that the validity of our results will depend at all on the truth of any historical and psychological facts that I have quoted: this will not be the case. Such facts will be useful more as illustrating the parts which different kinds of ethical question and statement play in our lives. The only facts, upon which the truth of what we have to say will depend, are those more familiar, unquestionable facts of usage—of the kind that we found obliquely expressed in the 'anthropological law,' 'All communities recognise the absolute value of duty'—namely, facts about the ways in which we do recognise a 'duty,' a 'community' and so on.

Bearing this background in mind, then, what questions shall we expect to find arising in ethical contexts, and how are they to be answered?

### 11.1  Questions about the Rightness of Actions

Consider, first, the simplest and commonest ethical question, 'Is this the right thing to do?' We are taught when young to behave in ways laid down as appropriate to the situations we are in. Sometimes there is a doubt whether or no a proposed action conforms to the moral code. It is to resolve such doubts that we are taught to use the question, 'Is this the right thing to do?', and, provided the code contains a relevant principle, the answer is 'Yes' or 'No,' according as the proposed action does or does not conform. Questions like, 'What is the right thing to do?', 'What ought really to have been done?' and 'Was this the correct decision?' do similar jobs, and can be understood in similar ways.

In consequence, if someone complains, 'That wasn't the thing to do' or 'That was hardly the way of going about things, was it?', his remark may have a genuinely ethical force. And this remains the case, although the only fact at issue is whether the action in question belongs to a class of actions generally approved of in the speaker's community. Some people have been misled by this into arguing that many so-called 'ethical' statements are just disguised statements of fact; that 'what seems to be an ethical judgement is very often a factual classification of an action.' But this is a mistake. What makes us call a judgement 'ethical' is the fact that it is used to harmonise people's actions (rather than to give a recognisable description of a state of affairs, for instance); judgements of the kind concerned are unquestionably 'ethical' by this standard; and the fact that the action belongs to a certain class of actions is not so much the 'disguised meaning of' as the 'reason for' the ethical judgement.

Furthermore, the test for answering questions of this simple kind remains the accepted practice, even though the particular action may have unfortunate results. Suppose that I am driving along a winding, country road, and deliberately keep on the left-hand side going round blind corners. It may happen that a driver going the other way is cutting his corners, so that we collide head-on; but this does not affect the propriety of my driving. My care to keep to the left remains 'right,' my decision not to take any risks on the corners remains 'correct,' in spite of the fact that the consequences, in the event, were unfortunate. Provided that I had no reason to expect such an upset, provided that I was not to know how the other man was behaving—knowledge which would have made a material difference to my decision, and would have taken my situation out of the straight-forward class to which the rule applies—the existence of the Rule of the Road is all that is needed to make my decision 'correct.'

## 11.2 *Reasoning about the Rightness of Actions*

This brings us to questions about one's 'reasons' for a decision or an action.

If the policeman investigating the accident asks the other driver, 'Why were you driving on the right-hand side of the road?', he will have to produce a long story in order to justify himself. If, however, I am asked why I was driving on the *left*, the only answer I can give is that the left-hand side is the one on which one *does* drive in England—that the Rule of the Road *is* to drive on the left.

Again, the schoolboy who gets his colours through favouritism may ask, 'And why shouldn't I have been given them?' If he does so, his schoolfellows will point out that it is the practice (and in fact the whole point of colours) for them to go to the best cricketers; and that there were better cricketers to whom they could have been given. And this will be all the justification needed.

Finally, an example in which the logical structure of this type of 'reasoning' is fully set out: suppose that I say, 'I feel that I ought to take this book and give it back to Jones' (so reporting on my feelings). You may ask me, 'But ought you really to do so?' (turning the question into an ethical one), and it is up to me to produce my 'reasons,' if I have any. To begin with, then, I may reply that I ought to take it back to him, 'because I promised to let him have it back before midday'—so classifying my position as one of type $S_1$. 'But ought you *really?*', you may repeat. If you do, I can relate $S_1$ to a more general $S_2$, explaining, 'I ought to, because I promised to let him have it back.' And if you continue to ask, 'But why ought you really?', I can answer, in succession, 'Because I ought to do whatever I promise him to do' ($S_3$), 'Because I ought to do whatever I promise anyone to do' ($S_4$), and 'Because anyone ought to do whatever he promises anyone else that he will do' or 'Because it was a promise' ($S_5$). Beyond this point, however, the question cannot arise: there is no more general 'reason' to be given beyond one which relates the action in question to an accepted social practice.

## 11.3  Conflicts of Duties

This straightforward method of answering the questions, 'Is this the right thing to do?' and 'Why ought you to do that?', can apply only in situations to which a rule of action is unambiguously appropriate. The most interesting practical questions, however, always arise in those situations in which one set of facts drives us one way, and another pulls us in the opposite direction.

If the muck-heap at the bottom of my garden bursts into flames in midsummer, and someone says, 'There's nothing to be surprised at in that: it's a simple case of spontaneous combustion. Surely you've heard of ricks burning in the same kind of way?', his explanation may satisfy me: the analogy between the burning of muck-heap and the spontaneous combustion of a hayrick is close enough for it to be plausible. But, if it is late January, I may reject the explanation, and protest, 'That's all very well in July or August, but not in midwinter: whoever heard of a hayrick catching fire with snow on the ground?', and, unless he can assure me that it does quite frequently happen, I shall continue to hanker after a different explanation.

In much the same way, the fact that I promised to let Jones have his book back will seem to me reason enough for taking it to him on time—if that is all that there is to it. But, if I have a critically ill relative in the house, who cannot be left, the issue is complicated. The situation is not sufficiently unambiguous for reasoning from the practice of promise-keeping to be conclusive: I may therefore argue, 'That's all very well in the ordinary way, but not when I've got my grandmother to look after: whoever heard of risking someone else's life just to return a borrowed book?' Unless evidence is produced that the risks involved in breaking my promise to Jones are even greater than those attending my grandmother, if she is left alone, I shall conclude that it is my duty to remain with her.

Given two conflicting claims, that is to say, one has to weigh up, as well as one can, the risks involved in ignoring either, and choose 'the lesser of the two evils.' Appeal to a single current principle, though the primary test of the rightness of an action, cannot therefore be relied on as a universal test: where this fails, we are driven back upon our estimate of the probable consequences. And this is the case, not only where there is a conflict of duties, but also, for instance, in circumstances in which, although no matter of principle is involved, some action of ours can nevertheless meet another's need. Here again we naturally and rightly conclude that the action is one that we 'ought' to perform, but we record in our usage the difference between such circumstances and those in which a matter of principle *is* involved: although we should say that we 'ought' to perform the action, we should not usually say that we had a 'moral obligation' to perform it, or even that it was our 'duty.' We here appeal to consequences in the absence of a relevant principle, or 'duty.'

So it comes about that we can, in many cases, justify an individual action by reference to its estimated consequences. Such a reference is no substitute for a principle, where any principle is at issue: but moral reasoning is so complex, and has to cover such a variety of types of situation, that no one logical test (such as 'appeal to an accepted principle') can be expected to meet every case.

### 11.4  Reasoning about the Justice of Social Practices

All these types of question are intelligible by reference to the primitive stage in the development of ethics. As soon as we turn to the second stage, however, there is room for questions of a radically different type.

Recall our analysis of 'explanation.' There I pointed out that, although on most occasions the question, 'Is this really straight?', has a use, situations might be encountered in which the question, in its ordinary sense, simply cannot be asked. These occasions were of two kinds:

(i) those on which the criterion of straightness is itself questioned, within the framework of a particular theory, and

(ii) those on which the criteria of straightness used in alternative theories are found to be different.

The same kinds of situation arise (and, indeed, are more familiar) in ethics. To give an example of the first: so long as one confines oneself to a particular moral code, no more general 'reason' can be given for an action than one which relates it to a practice (or principle) within that code. If an astronomer, who is discussing light-rays in outer space in terms of non-

Euclidean geometry, is asked what reason he has for saying that they are straight, he can only reply, 'Well, they just *are*': in the same way, if I am asked why one ought to keep a particular promise, all that I can say is, 'Well, one just *ought*.' Within the framework of a particular scientific theory, one can ask of most things, 'Is *this* really straight?', but the *criterion* of straightness cannot be questioned: within the framework of a particular moral code, one can ask of most individual actions, 'Is *this* really right?', but the *standards* of rightness cannot be questioned.

As an example of the second type of situation: the question, 'Which is it really right to do—to have only one wife like a Christian, or to have anything up to four like the Mohammedans?', is odd in the same way as the question, 'Is a light-ray going past the sun really straight, as a non-Euclidean theorist declares, or deflected, as a Euclidean theorist says?' If corresponding standards in two moral codes are found to be different, the question, 'Which of these is really right?', cannot arise. Or rather (to put the same thing in another way), if the question *does* arise, it arises in a very different way, serves a different purpose, and requires an answer of a different sort.

What kind of purpose does it serve, and what kind of answer does it require? In science, if I insist on asking of the standard of straightness, 'But is *it* really straight?', I am going outside the framework of that particular scientific theory. To question the standard is to question the theory—to criticise the theory *as a whole*—not to ask for an explanation of the phenomenon ostensibly under discussion (the properties of light-rays in outer space). So again in ethics: if I ask of the behaviour prescribed in any standard of conduct, 'Is *it* really right?', I am going outside the moral code; and my question is a criticism of the practice *as a practice*, not a request for a justification of a particular case of promise-keeping (or whatever it may be).

To question the rightness of a particular action is one thing: to question the justice of a practice *as a practice* is another. It is this second type of question which becomes intelligible when we turn to the second stage of development. If a society has a developing moral code, changes in the economic, social, political or psychological situation may lead people to regard the existing practices as unnecessarily restrictive, or as dangerously lax. If this happens, they may come to ask, for instance, 'Is it right that women should be debarred from smoking in public?', or 'Would it not be better if there were no mixed bathing after dark?', in each case questioning the practice concerned *as a whole*. The answer to be given will (remembering the function of ethics) be reached by estimating the probable consequences

(i) of retaining the present practice, and

(ii) of adopting the suggested alternative.

If, as a matter of fact, there is good reason to suppose that the sole consequences of making the proposed change would be to avoid some existing distresses, then, as a matter of ethics, there is certainly a good reason for making the change. As usual, however, the logically straightforward case is a comparatively uninteresting one: in practice, the interesting problems are those which arise when the happy consequences of the change are not so certain, or when they are likely to be accompanied by new, though perhaps less serious, distresses. And what stake may reasonably be risked for any particular likelihood of gain is something only to be settled with confidence— if then—by appeal to experience.

## 11.5  The Two Kinds of Moral Reasoning

Two cautions are necessary. Although, as a matter of logic, it makes sense to discuss the justice of any social practice, some practices will in fact always remain beyond question. It is inconceivable (for instance) that any practice will ever be suggested, to replace promising and promise-keeping, which would be anything like as effective. Even in the most 'advanced' stages of morality, therefore, promise-keeping will remain right.

Again, the fact that I can discuss the rightness of promise-keeping as a practice, in this way, does not imply that there is any way of calling in question the rightness of keeping individual promises. In arguing that promise-keeping will remain right at all stages, 'because its abolition would lead to suffering,' I am doing something different in important respects from what I am doing, if I say that I ought to take this book back to Jones now, 'because I promised to.' I can justify the latter statement by pointing out that I am in any of the situations $S_1$ to $S_5$.[4] and such reasons will be acceptable in any community which expects promises to be fulfilled. But I cannot further justify it by saying, 'Because one must not inflict avoidable suffering': this kind of reason is appropriate only when discussing whether a social practice should be retained or changed.

The two kinds of moral reasoning which we have encountered are, therefore, distinct. Each provides its own logical criteria—criteria which are appropriate to the criticism of individual actions, or social practices, but not both. It was this distinction between the 'reasons' for an individual action and the 'reasons' for a social practice which Socrates made as he waited for the hemlock: he was ready to die rather than repudiate it—refusing, when given the chance, to escape from the prison and so avoid execution. As an Athenian citizen, he saw that it was his duty (regardless of the actual consequences in his particular case) to respect the verdict and sentence of the court. To have escaped would have been to ignore this duty. By doing so, he would not merely have questioned the justice of the verdict in his case:

4 See § 11.2 above.

he would have renounced the Athenian constitution and moral code as a whole. This he was not prepared to do.

The history of Socrates illustrates the nature of the distinction, and the kind of situation in which it is important: the kind of situation in which it ceases to be of value can be seen from the story of Hampden and the 'ship-money.' It is those principles which we recognise as just which we have to respect most scrupulously: if we are prepared to dispute the justice of a principle, everything is altered. One of the most striking ways of disputing the justice of a principle is, indeed, by refusing to conform on a particular occasion: and such refusals give rise, in law and morality alike, to the notion of a 'test case.'

Over 'test cases,' the distinction between the two sorts of moral reasoning vanishes. In justifying the action concerned, one no longer refers to the current practice: it is the injustice of the accepted code, or the greater justice of some alternative proposal, which is now important. The justification of the action is made 'a matter of principle' and the change in the logical criteria appropriate follows accordingly. In making an action a test case one must, however, take care that one's intentions are clear. If this is not done, the action may be criticised on the wrong level. It may be condemned, either by reference to the very principle it was intended to dispute, or as self-interested, or both; and the question of principle may go against one by default. There is an element of pathos about a test case which goes wrong for this reason; but those men whose protests are carried off successfully are often remembered as heroes.

## 11.6  The Limited Scope of Comparisons between Social Practices

The scope of ethical reasoning is limited as well as defined by the framework of activities in which it plays its part. We have already encountered one limitation: that, in unequivocal cases, once it has been shown that an action is in accordance with an established practice, there is no further room for the question, 'But is this *really* the right thing to do?' The other questions which we have been discussing are, however, limited in similar ways, which we must now turn and consider.

Consider, first, the kinds of circumstance in which we question the rightness of a social practice. If, for example, it is regarded as disgusting for women to smoke in public, and I ask, 'But ought they really to be debarred from doing so?', the nature of my inquiry is clear: I am suggesting that in future, when a lady lights a cigarette, people need not turn away in disapproval, look horrified, or cut her from their acquaintance. The change I propose is quite sufficiently indicated in my question for us to be able to discuss it as it stands, and even reach a decision about it, on its merits.

If, on the other hand, I ask, 'Is it really right to have only one wife, like the Christians, or would it be better to have anything up to four, according to the old Mohammedan practice?', my question is a good deal less intelligible. In the first place, there seems to be a suggestion that we abandon our present practice in favour of an alternative one; but the exact nature of the change proposed is not clear; so how can one begin to estimate its probable consequences? Secondly, it is questionable whether the practices compared can be regarded as 'alternatives' at all. The ramifications, both in Christian and in Muslim societies, of the institution of marriage, its relations to the institutions of property, of parenthood and so on, are so complex that there is no question of simply replacing the one institution by the other. Such different parts does the institution of 'marriage' play in the ways of life of a Christian society and of a Muslim one that we might even feel it hardly right to describe Christian and Muslim marriage as being instances of the 'same' institution at all.

The question, 'Which of these institutions is "right"?', is therefore an unreal one, and there is no conceivable way of answering it—as it stands. The only way of understanding it is to regard it as an even more general question, in a disguised form. As we saw, the question, 'Is this the right thing to do?', when persisted in beyond a certain point, has to be understood as an inquiry about the justice of the social practice of which 'this' is an instance—but an inquiry couched in an inappropriate form: so now the question, 'Is it right for me to marry one wife or four?', has to be transformed, first into, 'Is Christian marriage or Muslim marriage the better pactice?'; and then again into, 'Is the Christian or the Muslim *way of life* the better?'

When someone asks of two superficially similar institutions, from different ways of life, 'Which is the better?', one may have to say that, by themselves, they are not comparable: all that can be compared are the ways of life *as wholes*. And *this* comparison is, if anything, a private one: which is to say, not that it *cannot* be reasoned about, but that, reason as you may, the final decision is personal. There is no magic wand which will turn the English social system into a Muslim one overnight: the only practical use for the question, 'Which way of life is the better?', is in the service of a personal decision—for example, whether to remain here in our society, such as it is, or to go and live as an Arab tribesman in the desert.

In general, then, if one is to *reason* about social practices, the only occasions on which one can discuss the question which of two practices is the better are those on which they are genuine alternatives: when it would be practicable to change from one to the other *within one society*. Given this, the question, 'Which is the better?', has the force of, 'If we changed from one to the other, would the change have happy or unhappy consequences on the whole?' But, if this condition is not satisfied, there is, morally speaking, *no* reasoning about the question, and pretended arguments about the merits of rival systems—personal preferences apart—are of value only as rhetoric.

### 11.7   The Limits to the Analysis of Ethical Concepts

Consider, secondly, the musty old conundrum over which moral philosophers have battled for so long: namely, whether the 'real' analysis of 'X is right' is 'X is an instance of a rule of action (or maxim, or prima facie obligation),' or 'X is the alternative which of all those open to us is likely to have the best results.' If the scope of ethical reasoning is limited by its function, does this question fall within or outside the limits?

To begin with, it must be clear from our discussion that, in talking of the 'analysis' of 'X is right,' philosophers cannot be referring to the 'meaning' of 'X is right.' The 'meaning' of 'X is right' is certainly neither of the alternatives proposed: it is 'X is the thing to do in these circumstances, to encourage others to do in similar circumstances, etc. etc.' To suppose otherwise is to be trapped into the 'naturalistic fallacy'—that is to say, it is to confuse facts and values (the reasons for an ethical judgement, and the judgement itself), by attempting to express the 'meaning' of an *ethical* judgement in *factual* form. The question which the 'analysis' of 'X is right' *can* answer is the question, 'Which kinds of reason are required in order to show that something is right (i.e., the thing to do, to encourage others to do, etc.)—(i) that it is an instance of a rule of action, or (ii) that it is the alternative likely to have the best results?'

The answer, with comparatively little over-simplification, is that it depends upon the nature of the 'thing.' If it is an action which is an unambiguous instance of a maxim generally accepted in the community concerned, it will be right just because it *is* an instance of such a maxim; but, if it is an action over which there is a 'conflict of duties,' or is itself a principle (or social practice) as opposed to a particular action, it will be right or wrong according as its consequences are likely to be good or bad.

When we bear in mind the function of ethics, therefore, we see that the answer to the philosophers' question is, 'Either, depending on the nature of the case.' The question, in other words, falls within the logical limits set by the function of ethics—provided only that you are prepared to accept 'Either' as an answer.

As a matter of history, philosophers have not been so prepared: they have tended to demand an 'unequivocal' answer—'The first' or 'The second,' and not 'Either'—and to assume that either the 'deontological' or the 'teleological' answer must be 'true,' and the other 'false.' But this is to mistake the nature of the problem. Questions presenting a pair of alternants, 'Which is true—A or B?' are of two kinds: those to which the answer can sensibly be 'Either' or 'Neither,' and those to which the only possible answers are 'A' and 'B.' If I report to the police that I have seen a stolen car being driven along the Bath Road, and they ask me, 'In which direction was it going?', the only positive answers I can give are 'Eastwards' and 'Westwards.' I can, of course, say, 'I didn't notice,' but I *cannot* say 'Either' or 'Neither': if it was being driven along the Bath Road at all, it *must* have been going in the one direction or the other. This seems to be the kind of model which philosophers have had before them when attempting to answer their question, 'Which is the analysis of "X is right"—A or B?' In any case, they have certainly overlooked the resemblance of their question to the other, verbally-similar type of question, represented in the extreme case by the algebraic query, 'Which is the correct solution of the equation $x^2 - 5x + 6 = 0$, $x = 2$ or $x = 3$?'—the answer to which is, 'Either, depending on the conditions of the particular problem.'

If we must answer the philosophers' question about the 'analysis' of 'X is right,' it will be along the lines of the algebraic query, rather than along those of the policeman's enquiry. It is, in fact, only as long as one is prepared to accept this kind of answer that the function of ethics leaves one room to ask the question at all. . . .

### 11.9 Is any 'Justification' of Ethics Needed?

In talking about the logic of ethical reasoning in the light of the function of ethics, I have tried to indicate two things:

(i) the different types of question which naturally arise in ethical contexts, and the ways in which they are answered; and

(ii) the limits of ethical reasoning—that is, the kinds of occasion on which questions and considerations of an ethical kind can no longer arise.

So far, however, I have not given an explicit answer to the question from which we set out: namely, 'What is it, in an ethical discussion, that makes a reason a good reason, or an argument a valid argument?'. . .

I have not attempted to give a 'theory of ethics'; I have simply tried to describe the occasions, on which we are in fact prepared to call judgements 'ethical' and decisions 'moral,' and the part which reasoning plays on such occasions. This description has led us to see how, in *particular types* of ethical question and argument, good reasoning is distinguished from bad, and valid argument from invalid—to be specific, by applying to individual judgements the test of principle, and to principles the test of general fecundity.

Now we have to ask, 'Is any further answer needed? Given particular rules applicable to different kinds of ethical judgement and question, have we not all we want? And, if any more were needed, could it not be supplied from an account, more detailed and accurate than has been given, but of the same kind?'

I myself do not feel the need for any *general* answer to the question, 'What makes some ethical reasoning "good" and some ethical arguments "valid"?': answers applicable to particular types of argument are enough. In fact, it seems to me that the demand for any such general answer (however it is to be obtained) must lead one to paradox. . . . For either such a general answer will, in particular cases, be equivalent to the rules which we have found, or it will contradict them. In the first case, it can do one of two things. Either it can distort our account, so that one of the criteria alone seems important; or else it can point out, in a more or less roundabout way, the advantages—indeed, 'the absolute necessity to the existence of society'— of harmonious co-operation. Instead, however, it may contradict our results. What then? What if we try to adopt the new rules for criticising arguments about conduct, which this general answer lays down?

If we do adopt these new criteria, then it will no longer be 'ethical' reasoning, 'moral' considerations, arguments from 'duty' and questions about what we 'ought' to do that we are criticising: it will be questions, arguments and considerations of another kind—in fact, a different mode of reasoning. This can be shown quite quickly. For suppose that, far from radically changing our criteria, all that the new rules do is to select one of them as the *universal* criterion. If the test of principle is chosen, so that we are never to be allowed to question the pronouncements of those who administer the moral code, then it is not 'morality' to which they apply—it is 'authority,' and authority of a kind which may reasonably be expected to develop rapidly into tyranny. And conversely, if the test of principle is itself ruled out in favour of a universal test of consequence (of the estimated effects on others), then we are faced with something which is no more 'morality' than the other—it would now be better described as 'expediency.' But arguments from expediency and arguments from authority are no more 'ethical' than experienced guess-work is 'scientific.' Consequently, even if all we do is to give up one or other of our present logical criteria, we turn ethics into something other than it is. And if this is the case there is no need for us to go on and consider more drastic alterations: they can be ruled out at once.

No doubt those philosophers who search for more general rules will not be satisfied. No doubt they will still feel that they want an explicit and unique answer to our central question. And no doubt they will object that, in all this, I have not even 'justified' our using reason in ethics at all. 'It's all very well your laying down the law about particular types of ethical argument,' they will say; 'but what is the justification for letting *any* reasoning affect how we decide to behave? Why *ought* one to do what is right, anyway?'

They are sufficiently answered by the peculiarity of their own questions. For let us consider what kind of answer they want when they ask, 'Why ought one to do what is right?' There is no room *within* ethics for such a question. Ethical reasoning may be able to show why we ought to do this action as opposed to that, or advocate this social practice as opposed to that, but it is no help where there can be no choice. And their question does not present us with genuine alternatives at all. For, since the notions of 'right' and of 'obligation' originate in the same situations and serve similar purposes, it is a self-contradiction (taking 'right' and 'ought' in their simplest senses) to suggest that we 'ought' to do anything but what is 'right.' This suggestion is as unintelligible as the suggestion that some emerald objects might not be green, and the philosophers' question is on a level with the question, 'Why are all scarlet things red?' We can therefore parry it only with another question—'What else "ought" one to do?'

Similar oddities are displayed by all their questions—as long as we take them literally. Ethics may be able to 'justify' one of a number of courses of action, or one social practice as opposed to another: but it does not extend to the 'justification' of all reasoning about conduct. One course of action can be opposed to another: one social practice can be opposed to another. But to what are we expected to oppose 'ethics-as-a-whole'? There can be no discussion about the proposition, 'Ethics is ethics'; any argument treating 'ethics' as something other than it is must be false; and, if those who call for a 'justification' of ethics want 'the case for morality'; as opposed to 'the case for expediency,' etc., then they are giving philosophy a job which is not its own. To show that you ought to choose certain actions is one thing: to make you *want to do* what you ought to do is another, and not a philosopher's task.

RICHARD MERVYN HARE (1919–      ) teaches
at Oxford University. Concerned principally
with the logic of moral discourse, he has published a number of articles in recent philosophical journals. His major published work
is *The Language of Morals* (1952).

# R. M. HARE

## *Decisions of Principle**

4.1 There are two factors which may be involved in the making of any
decision to do something. Of these, the first may at any rate theoretically be
absent, the second is always present to some degree. They correspond to the
major and minor premisses of the Aristotelian practical syllogism. The major
premiss is a principle of conduct; the minor premiss is a statement, more or
less full, of what we should in fact be doing if we did one or other of the
alternatives open to us. Thus if I decide not to say something, because it is
false, I am acting on a principle, 'Never (or never under certain conditions)
say what is false,' and I must know that this, which I am wondering whether
to say, is false.

Let us take the minor premiss first, since it presents less difficulty. We
plainly cannot decide what to do unless we know at least something about
what we should be doing if we did this or that. For example, suppose that I
am an employer, and am wondering whether or not to sack a clerk who habitually turns up at the office after the hour at which he has undertaken to turn
up. If I sack him I shall be depriving his family of the money on which they
live, perhaps giving my firm a reputation which will lead clerks to avoid it
when other jobs are available, and so on; if I keep him, I shall be causing the
other clerks to do work which otherwise would be done by this clerk; and
the affairs of the office will not be transacted so quickly as they would if all
the clerks were punctual. These would be the sorts of consideration that I
should take into account in making my decision. They would be the effects
on the total situation of the alternative actions, sacking him or not sacking
him. It is the effects which determine what I should be doing; it is between
the two sets of effects that I am deciding. The whole point about a decision is
that it makes a difference to what happens; and this difference is the difference
between the effects of deciding one way, and the effects of deciding the other.

It sometimes seems to be implied by writers on ethics that it is immoral,

---

* From *The Language of Morals*, by R. M. Hare, Chap. 4. Copyright, 1952, Clarendon
Press. Used by permission.

on certain sorts of occasion, to consider the effects of doing something. We ought, it is said, to do our duty no matter what the effects of doing it. As I am using the word 'effects,' this cannot be maintained. I am not making a claim for 'expediency' (in the bad sense) as against 'duty.' Even to do our duty—in so far as it is *doing* something—is effecting certain changes in the total situation. It is quite true that, of the changes that it is possible to effect in the total situation, most people would agree that we ought to consider certain kinds more relevant than others (which than which, it is the purpose of moral principles to tell us). I do not think that the immediacy or remoteness of the effects makes any difference, though their certainty or uncertainty does. The reason why it is considered immoral to fail to right an injustice whose effects will maximize pleasure, is not that in such a choice the effects are considered when they should not have been; it is that certain of the effects —namely, the maximization of pleasure—are given a relevance which they should not have, in view of the prior claim of those other effects which would have consisted in the righting of the injustice.

For reasons which will become apparent when we have examined the logic of value-words, it is most important, in a verbal exposition of an argument about what to do, not to allow value-words in the minor premiss. In setting out the facts of the case, we should be as factual as we can. Those versed in the logic of these words, and therefore forewarned against its pitfalls, may in the interests of brevity neglect this precaution; but for the inexperienced it is very much better to keep value-expressions where they belong, in the major premiss. This will prevent the inadvertent admission of an ambiguous middle term. . . . I do not mean that in discussing the facts of the case we should not admit any words which could possibly have an evaluative meaning; for this, in view of the way in which evaluative meaning pervades our language, would be well-nigh impossible. I only mean that we must be sure that, as we are using the words in the minor premiss, there are definite tests (not themselves involving evaluation) for ascertaining its truth or falsity. In the last paragraph I was using the word 'pleasure' in such a sense, though it is not always so used.

4.2 The relation between the two premisses may perhaps be made clearer by considering an artificial example. Let us suppose that a man has a peculiar kind of clairvoyance such that he can know everything about the effects of all the alternative actions open to him. But let us suppose that he has so far formed for himself, or been taught, no principles of conduct. In deciding between alternative courses of action, such a man would know, fully and exactly, between what he was deciding. We have to ask to what extent, if any, such a man would be handicapped, in coming to a decision, by not having any formed principles. It would seem beyond doubt that he could choose between two courses; it would be strange, even, to call such a choice necessarily arbitrary or ungrounded; for if a man knows to the last detail exactly what he is doing, and what he might otherwise have done, his choice is not arbitrary in the sense in which a choice would be arbitrary if made by the toss of a coin without any consideration of the effects. But suppose that we were to ask such a man 'Why did you choose this set of effects rather than that? Which of the many effects were they that led you to decide the way you did?' His answer to this question might be of two kinds. He might say 'I can't give any reasons; I just felt like deciding that way; another time, faced with the same choice, I might decide differently.' On the other hand, he might say 'It was this and this that made me decide; I was deliberately avoiding such and such effects, and seeking such and such.' If he gave the first of these two answers, we might in a certain sense of that word call his decision arbitrary (though even in that case he had *some* reason for his choice, namely, that he felt that way); but if he gave the second, we should not.

Let us see what is involved in this second type of answer. Although we have assumed that the man has no formed principles, he shows, if he gives the second answer, that he has started to form principles for himself; for to choose effects *because* they are such and such is to begin to act on a principle that such and such effects are to be chosen. We see in this example that in order to act on principle it is not necessary in some sense to have a principle already, before you act; it may be that the decision to act in a certain way, because of something about the effects of acting in that way, *is* to subscribe to a principle of action—though it is not necessarily to adopt it in any permanent sense.

Ordinary men are not so fortunate as the man in our artificial example. They start, indeed, without any knowledge of the future at all; and when they acquire knowledge it is not of this intuitive kind. The kind of knowledge that we have of the future—unless we are clairvoyant—is based upon principles of prediction which we are taught, or form for ourselves. Principles of prediction are one kind of principle of action; for to predict is to act in a certain way. Thus, although there is nothing logically to prevent someone doing entirely without principles, and making all his choices in the arbitrary manner exhibited in the first kind of answer, this never in fact occurs. Moreover, our knowledge of the future is fragmentary and only probable; and therefore in many cases the principles which we are taught or form for ourselves say, not 'Choose this kind of effect rather than that,' but 'You do not know for certain what will be the effects; but do this rather than that, and the effects are most likely to be such as you would have chosen, if you had known them.' It is important to remember, in this connexion, that 'likely' and 'probable' are value-words; in many contexts 'It is probable (or likely) that P' is adequately rendered by 'There is *good* reason (or evidence) for holding that P.'

4.3. We may distinguish, so far, two reasons why we have principles. The first reason applies to anyone, even a man with complete insight into the future, who decides to choose something because it is of a certain character. The second reason applies to us because we do not in fact have complete knowledge of the future, and because such knowledge as we do have involves principles. To these reasons a third must now be added. Without principles, most kinds of teaching are impossible, for what is taught is in most cases a principle. In particular, when we learn *to do* something, what we learn is always a principle. Even to learn or be taught a fact (like the names of the five rivers of the Punjab) is to learn how to answer a question; it is to learn the principle 'When asked "What are the names of the five rivers of the Punjab?" answer "The Jhelum, the Chenab, &c.".' By this I do not of course mean, that to learn to do anything is to learn to recite by rote some universal imperative sentence. This would involve us in a vicious regress; for learning to recite is a kind of learning, and must have its principles; but in that case we should have to learn to recite the principles of reciting. The point is rather this, that to learn to do anything is never to learn to do an individual act; it is always to learn to do acts of a certain kind in a certain kind of situation; and this is to learn a principle. Thus, in learning to drive, I learn, not to change gear *now*, but to change gear when my engine makes a certain kind of noise. If this were not so, instruction would be of no use at all; for if all an instructor could do were to tell us to change gear *now*, he would have to sit beside us for the rest of our lives in order to tell us just when, on each occasion, to change gear.

Thus without principles we could not learn anything whatever from our elders. This would mean that every generation would have to start from scratch and teach itself. But even if each generation were able to teach itself, it could not do so without principles; for self-teaching, like all other teaching, is the teaching of principles. This may be seen by recurring to our artificial example. Let us suppose that our clairvoyant made all his choices on some principle, but always forgot, as soon as he had made the choice, what the principle had been. He would have, accordingly, each time he made a decision, to go over all the effects of the alternative actions. This would be so time-consuming that he would not have the leisure to make many decisions in the course of his life. He would spend his whole time deciding matters like whether to step off with the right or the left foot, and would never reach what we should call the more important decisions. But if he could remember the principles on which he acted, he would be in a much better position; he could *learn* how to act in certain kinds of circumstance; he could learn to single out quickly the relevant aspects of a situation, including the effects of the various possible actions, and so choose quickly, and in many cases habitually. Thus his powers of considered decision would be set free for more momentous decisions. When the cabinet-maker has learnt how to make a dovetail without thinking much about it, he will have time to think about such things as the proportions and aesthetic appearance of the finished product. And it is the same with our conduct in the moral sphere; when the performance of the lesser duties has become a matter of habit, we have time to think about the greater.

There is a limit in practice to the amount that can be taught to someone by someone else. Beyond this point, self-teaching is necessary. The limit is set by the variety of conditions which may be met with in doing whatever is being taught; and this variety is greater in some cases than in others. A sergeant can teach a recruit almost all there is to be known about fixing bayonets on parade, because one occasion of fixing bayonets on parade is much like another; but a driving instructor cannot do more than begin to teach his pupil the art of driving, because the conditions to be met with in driving are so various. In most cases, teaching cannot consist in getting the learner to perform faultlessly a fixed drill. One of the things that has to be included in any but the most elementary kinds of instruction is the opportunity for the learner to make decisions for himself, and in so doing to examine, and even modify to suit particular types of case, the principles which are being taught. The principles that are taught us initially are of a provisional kind. . . . Our training, after the initial stages, consists in taking these principles, and making them less provisional; we do this by using them continually in our own decisions, and sometimes making exceptions to them; some of the exceptions are made because our instructor points out to us that certain cases are instances of classes of exceptions to the principle; and some of the exceptions we decide on for ourselves. This presents no more difficulty than our clairvoyant had in deciding between two sets of effects. If we learn from experiment that to follow a certain principle would have certain effects, whereas to modify it in a certain way would have certain other effects, we adopt whichever form of the principle leads to the effects which we choose to pursue.

We may illustrate this process of modifying principles from the example already used, that of learning to drive. I am told, for instance, always to draw into the side of the road when I stop the car; but later I am told that this does not apply when I stop before turning into a side-road to the off-side —for then I must stop near the middle of the road until it is possible for me to turn. Still later I learn that in this manœuvre it is not necessary to stop at all if it is an uncontrolled junction and I can see that there is no traffic which I should obstruct by turning. When I have picked up all these modifications to the rule, and the similar modifications to all the other rules, and practice them habitually as so modified, then I am said to be a good driver, because my car is always in the right place on the road, travelling at the right speed, and so on. The good driver is, among other things, one whose actions are so exactly governed by principles which have become a habit with him, that he normally does not have to *think* just what to do. But road conditions are exceedingly various, and therefore it is unwise to let all one's driving become a matter of habit. One can never be certain that one's principles of driving are perfect—indeed, one can be very sure that they are not; and therefore the good driver not only drives well from habit, but constantly attends to his driving habits, to see whether they might not be improved; he never stops learning.

It is hardly necessary to point out that principles of driving, like other principles, are normally not inculcated by their verbal repetition, but by example, demonstration, and other practical means. We learn to drive, not by precept, but by being shown how to do particular bits of driving; the precepts are usually only explanatory or mnemonic of what we are being shown. Thereafter, we try to do the particular manœuvres ourselves, and are criticized for failures, commended when we do them well, and so gradually get the hang of the various principles of good driving. For although our instruction is far from being purely verbal, nevertheless what we are being taught are principles. The fact that the derivation of particular acts (or commands to do them) from principles is normally done non-verbally does not show that it is not a logical process, any more than the inference:

> The clock has just struck seven times
> The clock strikes seven times at seven o'clock only
> ∴It is just after seven o'clock

is shown to be non-logical because it is never made explicitly in words.

Drivers often know just what to do in a certain situation without being able to enunciate in words the principle on which they act. This is a very common state of affairs with all kinds of principles. Trappers know just where to set their traps, but often cannot explain just why they have put a trap in a particular place. We all know how to use words to convey our meaning; but if a logician presses us for the exact definition of a word we have used, or the exact rules for its use, we are often at a loss. This does not mean that the setting of traps or the use of words or the driving of cars does not proceed according to principles. One may know how, without being able to say how—though if a skill is to be taught, it is easier if we *can* say how.

We must not think that, if we can decide between one course and another without further thought (it seems self-evident to us, which we should do), this necessarily implies that we have some mysterious intuitive faculty which tells us what to do. A driver does not know when to change gear by intuition; he knows it because he has learnt and not forgotten; what he knows is a principle, though he cannot formulate the principle in words. The same is true of moral decisions which are sometimes called 'intuitive.' We have moral 'intuitions' because we have learnt how to behave, and have different ones according to how we have learnt to behave.

It would be a mistake to say that all that had to be done to a man to make him into a good driver was to tell him, or otherwise inculcate into him, a lot of general principles. This would be to leave out the factor of decision. Very soon after he begins to learn, he will be faced with situations to deal with which the provisional principles so far taught him require modification; and he will then have to decide what to do. He will very soon discover which decisions were right and which wrong, partly because his instructor tells him, and partly because having seen the effects of the decisions he determines in future not to bring about such effects. On no account must we commit the mistake of supposing that decisions and principles occupy two separate spheres and do not meet at any point. All decisions except those, if any, that are completely arbitrary are to some extent decisions of principle. We are always setting precedents for ourselves. It is not a case of the principle settling everything down to a certain point, and decision dealing with everything below that point. Rather, decision and principles interact throughout the whole field. Suppose that we have a principle to act in a certain way in certain circumstances. Suppose then that we find ourselves in circumstances which fall under the principle, but which have certain other peculiar features, not met before, which make us ask 'Is the principle really intended to cover cases like this, or is it incompletely specified —is there here a case belonging to a class which should be treated as exceptional?' Our answer to this question will be a decision, but a decision of principle, as is shown by the use of the value-word 'should.' If we decide that this should be an exception, we thereby modify the principle by laying down an exception to it.

Suppose, for example, that in learning to drive I have been taught always to signal before I slow down or stop, but have not yet been taught what to do when stopping in an emergency; if a child leaps in front of my car, I do not signal, but keep both hands on the steering-wheel; and thereafter I accept the former principle with this exception, that in cases of emergency it is better to steer than to signal. I have, even on the spur of the moment, made a decision of principle. To understand what happens in cases like this is to understand a great deal about the making of value-judgements.

4.4.   I do not wish to seem to be pressing too far my comparison, in respect of the way in which they are learnt, between principles of driving and principles of conduct. It is necessary also to bear in mind some distinctions. In the first place, the expression 'good driver' is itself ambiguous in that it is not immediately clear what standard is being applied. It might be simply a standard of expertness; we might call a person a good driver if he were able to do just what he wanted with his car; we might say 'Although a very good driver, he is most inconsiderate to other road users.' On the other hand, we sometimes expect a good driver to have moral qualities as well; we do not, according to this criterion, call a man a good driver if he drives expertly, but without the slightest heed for the convenience or safety of other people. The line between these two standards of good driving is not easy to draw in practice. There is also a third standard, according to which a driver is said to be good if he conforms to the accepted principles of good driving as laid down, for example, in the *Highway Code*. Since the *Highway Code* is compiled with a definite purpose in view, this standard coincides to a great extent with the second.

Secondly, there are two ways of looking at driving instruction:

(1) We establish at the beginning certain ends, for example the avoidance of collisions, and instruction consists in teaching what practices are conducive to those ends. According to this way of looking at them, the principles of good driving are hypothetical imperatives.

(2) We teach at first simple rules of thumb, and the learner only gradually comes to see what the ends are, at which the instruction is aimed.

It must not be thought that either (1) or (2) by itself gives a complete account of our procedure. Which method we adopt depends to a great extent on the maturity and intelligence of the learner. In teaching African soldiers to drive, we might incline more to the second method; if I had to teach my two-year-old son to drive, I should have to adopt the same methods as I now adopt for teaching him to refrain from interfering with the controls when I am driving myself. With a highly intelligent learner, on the other hand, we may adopt a method which has more of (1) in it than of (2).

It must not be thought, however, that method (2) is ever entirely without a place even in the case of the most rational of learners. It may be that the desirability of avoiding collisions is at once understood and accepted even by comparatively stupid learners; but there are a great many more ends than this which a good driver has to aim at. He has to avoid causing many kinds of avoidable inconvenience both to himself and to others; he has to learn not to do things which result in damage to his vehicle, and so on. It is of no use to establish at the beginning a general end, 'the avoidance of avoidable inconvenience'; for 'inconvenience' is a value-word, and until he has had experience of driving, the learner will not know what sorts of situation are to count as avoidable inconvenience. The general end or principle is vacuous until by our detailed instruction we have given it content. Therefore it is always necessary to start, to some extent, by teaching our learner *what* to do, and leaving it for him to find out later *why*. We may therefore say that although moral principles, which are normally taught us when we are immature, are taught largely by method (2), and principles of driving preponderantly by method (1), there is not an absolute division between the two sorts of principle in this respect. What I have just said about first learning *what* to do, and about the initial vacuity of the general end, is borrowed from Aristotle. The one fundamental distinction between principles of driving and principles of conduct is that the latter are, in Aristotle's term, 'architectonic' of the former; for the ends of good driving (safety, the avoidance of inconvenience to others, the preservation of property, and so on) are justified ultimately, if justification is sought, by appeal to moral considerations.

It would be folly, however, to say that there is only one way of learning a skill or any other body of principles, or of justifying a particular decision made in the practice of it. There are many ways, and I have tried to make the above account sufficiently general to cover all of them. It is sometimes said by writers on morals that we have to justify an act by reference to its effects, and that we tell which effects are to be sought, which avoided, by reference to some principle. Such a theory is that of the utilitarians, who bid us look at the effects, and examine these in the light of the principle of utility, to see which effects would maximize pleasure. Sometimes, on the other hand, it is said (as by Mr. Toulmin)[1] that an act is justified directly by reference to the principles which it observes, and these principles in their turn by reference to the effects of always observing them. Sometimes it is said that we should observe principles and ignore the effects—though for the reasons given above 'effects' cannot be here intended in the sense in which I have been using it. What is wrong with these theories is not what they say, but their assumption that they are telling us the only way to justify actions, or decide what actions to do. We do, indeed, justify and decide on actions in all these ways; for example, sometimes, if I asked why we did A, we say, 'Because it was a case falling under principle P,' and if asked to justify P in turn, we go into the effects of observing it and of not observing it. But sometimes, when asked the same question 'Why did you do A?' we say 'Because if I hadn't, E would have happened,' and if asked what was wrong about E happening, we appeal to some principle.

The truth is that, if asked to justify as completely as possible any decision, we have to bring in both effects—to give content to the decision—and principles, and the effects in general of observing those principles, and so on,

[1] *Reason in Ethics*, pp. 144 ff. [this volume pp. 456 ff.]

until we have satisfied our inquirer. Thus a complete justification of a decision would consist of a complete account of its effects, together with a complete account of the principles which it observed, and the effects of observing those principles—for, of course, it is the effects (what obeying them in fact consists in) which give content to the principles too. Thus, if pressed to justify a decision completely, we have to give a complete specification of the way of life of which it is a part. This complete specification it is impossible in practice to give; the nearest attempts are those given by the great religions, especially those which can point to historical persons who carried out the way of life in practice. Suppose, however, that we can give it. If the inquirer still goes on asking 'But why *should* I live like that?' then there is no further answer to give him, because we have already, *ex hypothesi*, said everything that could be included in this further answer. We can only ask him to make up his own mind which way he ought to live; for in the end everything rests upon such a decision of principle. He has to decide whether to accept that way of life or not; if he accepts it, then we can proceed to justify the decisions that are based upon it; if he does not accept it, then let him accept some other, and try to live by it. The sting is in the last clause. To describe such ultimate decisions as arbitrary, because *ex hypothesi* everything which could be used to justify them has already been included in the decision, would be like saying that a complete description of the universe was utterly unfounded, because no further fact could be called upon in corroboration of it. This is not how we use the words 'arbitrary' and 'unfounded.' Far from being arbitrary, such a decision would be the most well-founded of decisions, because it would be based upon a consideration of everything upon which it could possibly be founded.

It will be noticed how, in talking of decisions of principle, I have inevitably started talking value-language. Thus we decide that the principle *should* be modified, or that it is *better* to steer than to signal. . . . To make a value-judgement is to make a decision of principle. To ask whether I ought to do A in these circumstances is (to borrow Kantian language with a small though important modification) to ask whether or not I will that doing A in such circumstances should become a universal law. It may seem a far cry from Kant to Professor Stevenson; but the same question could be put in other words by asking 'What attitude shall I adopt and recommend towards doing A in such circumstances?'; for 'attitude,' if it means anything, means a principle of action. Unfortunately Stevenson, unlike Kant, devotes very little space to the examination of this first-person question; had he paid due attention to it, and avoided the dangers of the word 'persuasive,' he might have reached a position not unlike that of Kant.

4.5. As Kant points out in the important passage on the Autonomy of the Will, . . . we have to make our own decisions of principle. Other people cannot make them for us unless we have first decided to take their advice or obey their orders. There is an interesting analogy here with the position of the scientist, who also has to rely on his own observations. It might be said that there is a difference here between decisions and observations, to the detriment of the former, in that an observation, once made, is public property, whereas decisions have to be made by the agent himself on each occasion. But the difference is only apparent. A scientist would not have become a scientist unless he had convinced himself that the observations of other scientists were in general reliable. He did this by making some observations of his own. When we learnt elementary chemistry at school, we had some theoretical periods and some practical. In the theoretical periods we studied books; in the practical periods we made experiments, and found, if we were lucky, that the results tallied with what the books said. This showed us that what the books said was not all nonsense; so that even if, by reason of disturbing factors ignored by us, our experiments came out wrong, we were inclined to trust the books and acknowledge that we had made a mistake. We were confirmed in this assumption by the fact that we often discover later what the mistake had been. If our observations, however carefully we did them, were always at variance with the textbooks, we should not be tempted to make science our profession. Thus the confidence of the scientist in other people's observations is ultimately based, among other things, on his own observations and his own judgements about what is reliable. He has in the end to rely on himself.

The case of the moral agent is not dissimilar. When in our early days we are given our elementary moral instruction, there are some things that we are told, and some things that we do. If, when we did as we were told, the total effects of our so doing, when they happened, were always such as we would not have chosen, had we known, then we should seek better advice, or, if prevented from so doing, either work out our own salvation or become moral defectives. If we are in general given what we subsequently come to see to have been good advice, we decide in general to follow the advice and adopt the principles of those who have given us this good advice in the past. This is what happens to any child who is well brought up. Just as the scientist does not try to rewrite all that is in the textbooks, but takes that for granted and sticks to his own particular researches, so this fortunate child will take over bodily the principles of his elders and adapt them in detail, by his own decisions, to suit his own circumstances from time to time. This is how in a well-ordered society morality remains stable, and at the same time gets adapted to changing circumstances.

4.6.   There are, however, many ways in which this happy state of affairs can deteriorate. Let us consider a process that seems to occur quite often in history; it occurred in Greece during the fifth and fourth centuries, and it has occurred in our own time. Suppose that the people of a certain generation—I will call it the first generation—have got very settled principles, inherited from their fathers. Suppose that they have become so settled as to be second nature, so that generally speaking people act on the principles without thinking, and their power of making considered decisions of principle becomes atrophied. They act always by the book, and come to no harm, because the state of the world in their time remains much the same as that for which the principles were thought out. But their sons, the second generation, as they grow up, find that conditions have changed (e.g., through a protracted war or an industrial revolution), and that the principles in which they have been brought up are no longer adequate. Since, in their education, much stress has been laid on observing principles, and very little on making the decisions on which these principles are ultimately based, their morality has no roots, and becomes completely unstable. Books on 'The Whole Duty of Man' are no longer written or read. Often, when they do what it says in such books, they subsequently find cause to regret their decisions; and there are too many cases of this kind for any confidence in the old principles, as a body, to remain. No doubt there are among these old principles certain very general ones, which will remain acceptable unless human nature and the state of the world undergo a most fundamental change; but the second generation, not having been brought up to make decisions of principle, but to do what it says in the book, will not, most of them, be able to make those crucial decisions which would determine which principles to keep, which to modify, and which to abandon. Some people, the Polemarchuses of the second generation, will have been so steeped in the old principles that they just follow them come what may; and these will on the whole be more fortunate than the others, for it is better to have some principles, even if they sometimes lead to decisions which we regret, than to be morally adrift. The bulk of the second generation, and still more perhaps of the third, will not know which of the principles to keep and which to reject; and so they will come more and more to live from day to day—not a bad thing, because it trains their powers of decision, but it is an unpleasant and dangerous state to be in. A few among them, the rebels, will shout from the housetops that some or all of the old moral principles are worthless; some of these rebels will advocate new principles of their own; some will have nothing to offer. Though they increase the confusion, these rebels perform the useful function of making people decide between their rival principles; and if they not only advocate new principles, but sincerely try to live by them, they are conducting a moral experiment which may be of the utmost value to man (in which case they go down in history as great moral teachers), or may, on the other hand, prove disastrous both to them and to their disciples.

It may take several generations for this disease to play itself out. Morality regains its vigour when ordinary people have learnt afresh to decide for themselves what principles to live by, and more especially what principles to teach their children. Since the world, though subject to vast material changes, changes only very slowly in matters that are fundamental from the moral point of view, the principles which win the acceptance of the mass of people are not likely to differ enormously from those which their fathers came to distrust. The moral principles of Aristotle resemble those of Aeschylus more than they differ from them, and we ourselves shall perhaps come back to something recognizably like the morality of our grandfathers. But there will be some changes; some of the principles advocated by the rebels will have been adopted. That is how morality progresses—or retrogresses. The process is, as we shall see, reflected by very subtle changes in the uses of value-words; the impossibility of translating Aristotle's catalogue of virtues into modern English may serve as an example, and the disappearance without trace of the word 'righteous' may serve as another.

4.7. The question 'How shall I bring up my children?' which we have mentioned, is one to the logic of which, since ancient times, few philosophers have given much attention. A child's moral upbringing has an effect upon him which will remain largely untouched by anything that happens to him thereafter. If he has had a stable upbringing, whether on good principles or on bad ones, it will be extremely difficult for him to abandon those principles in later life—difficult but not impossible. They will have for him the force of an objective moral law; and his behaviour will seem to give much evidence in support of intuitionist ethical theories, provided that it is not compared with the behaviour of those who stick just as firmly to quite different principles. But nevertheless, unless our education has been so thorough as to transform us into automata, we can come to doubt or even reject these principles; that is what makes human beings, whose moral systems change, different from ants, whose moral system does not. Therefore, even if for me the question 'What shall I do in such and such a situation?' is almost invariably answered without ambiguity by the moral intuition which my up-bringing has given me, I may, if I ask myself 'How shall I bring up my children?' pause before giving an answer. It is here that the most fundamental moral decisions of all arise; and it is here, if only moral philosophers would pay attention to them, that the most characteristic uses of moral words are to be found. Shall I bring up my children *exactly* as I was brought up, so that they have the same intuitions about morals as I have? Or have circumstances altered, so that the moral character of the father will not provide a suitable equipment for the children? Perhaps I shall try to bring them up like their father, and shall fail; perhaps their new environment will be too strong for me, and they will come to repudiate my principles. Or I may have become so bewildered by the strange new world that, although I still act from force of habit on the principles that I have learnt, I simply do not know what principles to impart to my children, if, indeed, one in my condition can impart any settled principles at all. On all these questions, I have to make up my mind; only the most hide-bound father will try to bring up his children, without thinking, in exactly the way that he himself was brought up; and even he will usually fail disastrously.

Many of the dark places of ethics become clearer when we consider this dilemma in which parents are liable to find themselves. We have already noticed that, although principles have in the end to rest upon decisions of principle, decisions as such cannot be taught; only principles can be taught. It is the powerlessness of the parent to make for his son those many decisions of principle which the son during his future career will make, that gives moral language its characteristic shape. The only instrument which the parent possesses is moral education—the teaching of principles by example and precept, backed up by chastisement and other more up-to-date psychological methods. Shall he use these means, and to what extent? Certain generations of parents have had no doubts about this question. They have used them to the full; and the result has been to turn their children into good intuitionists, able to cling to the rails, but bad at steering round corners. At other times parents—and who shall blame them?—suffer from lack of confidence; they are not sure enough what they themselves think, to be ready to impart to their children a stable way of life. The children of such a generation are likely to grow up opportunists, well able to make individual decisions, but without the settled body of principles which is the most priceless heritage that any generation can leave to its successors. For, though principles are in the end built upon decisions of principle, the building is the work of many generations, and the man who has to start from the beginning is to be pitied; he will not be likely, unless he is a genius, to achieve many conclusions of importance, any more than the average boy, turned loose without instruction upon a desert island, or even in a laboratory, would be likely to make any of the major scientific discoveries.

The dilemma between these two extreme courses in education is plainly a false one. Why it is a false one is apparent, if we recall what was said earlier about the dynamic relation between decisions and principles. It is very like learning to drive. It would be foolish, in teaching someone to drive, to try to inculcate into him such fixed and comprehensive principles that he would never have to make an independent decision. It would be equally foolish to go to the other extreme and leave it to him to find his own way of driving. What we do, if we are sensible, is to give him a solid basis of principles, but at the same time ample opportunity of making the decisions upon which these principles are based, and by which they are modified, improved, adapted to changed circumstances, or even abandoned if they become entirely unsuited to a new environment. To teach only the principles, without giving the opportunity of subjecting them to the learner's own decisions of principle, is like teaching science exclusively from the textbooks without entering the laboratory. On the other hand, to abandon one's child or one's driving-pupil to his own self-expression is like putting a boy into a laboratory and saying 'Get on with it.' The boy may enjoy himself or kill himself, but will probably not learn much science.

The moral words, of which we may take 'ought' as an example, reflect in their logical behaviour this double nature of moral instruction—as well they may, for it is in moral instruction that they are most typically used. The sentences in which they appear are normally the expression of decisions of principle—and it is easy to let the decisions get separated, in our discussion of the subject, from the principles. This is the source of the controversy between the 'objectivists,' as intuitionists sometimes call themselves, and the 'subjectivists,' as they often call their opponents. The former lay stress on the fixed principles that are handed down by the father, the latter on the new decisions which have to be made by the son. The objectivist says 'Of course you know what you ought to do; look at what your conscience tells you, and if in doubt go by the consciences of the vast majority of men.' He is able to say this, because our consciences are the product of the principles which our early training has indelibly planted in us, and in one society these principles do not differ much from one person to another. The subjectivist, on the other hand, says 'But surely, when it comes to the point—when I have listened to what other people say, and given due weight to my own intuitions, the legacy of my up-bringing—I have in the end to decide for myself what I ought to do. To deny this is to be a conventionalist; for both common moral notions and my own intuitions are the legacy of tradition, and—apart from the fact that there are so many different traditions in the world—traditions cannot be started without someone doing what I now feel called upon to do, decide. If I refuse to make my own decisions, I am, in merely copying my fathers, showing myself a lesser man than they; for whereas they must have initiated, I shall be merely accepting.' This plea of the subjectivist is quite justified. It is the plea of the adolescent who wants to be adult. To become morally adult is to reconcile these two apparently conflicting positions by learning to make decisions of principle; it is to learn to use 'ought'-sentences in the realization that they can only be verified by reference to a standard or set of principles which we have by our own decision accepted and made our own. This is what our present generation is so painfully trying to do.


## THE "GOOD REASONS" APPROACH—SUGGESTED READINGS

Baier, K., *The Moral Point of View*, Ithaca, N. Y., Cornell University Press, 1958. (proponent)

Falk, W. D., "Goading and Guiding," *Mind*, LXII (1953), pp. 145–71. (proponent)

Hall, E. W., "Practical Reason(s) and the Deadlock in Ethics," *Mind*, LXIV (1955), pp. 319–32. (summary and criticism)

Rice, P. B., *On the Knowledge of Good and Evil*, New York, Random House, 1955, Chap. 4. (summary and criticism)

Urmson, J. O., "On Grading," *Mind*, LIX (1950), pp. 145–69. (proponent)

White, M., *Toward Reunion in Philosophy*, Cambridge, Mass., Harvard University Press, 1956, Chap. 13. (summary and criticism)